The Economist

DESK COMPANION

The Economist

DESK COMPANION

How to measure, convert, calculate and define practically anything

A Henry Holt Reference Book
HENRY HOLT AND COMPANY
NEW YORK

A Henry Holt Reference Book
First published in the United States in 1992 by Henry Holt and Company, Inc., 115 West 18th Street, New York, New York 10011.
Originally published in Great Britain in 1992 by Century Business, an imprint of Random Century Limited, in association with The Economist Books Ltd.

Library of Congress Catalog Card Number: 92-53161

ISBN 0-8050-2380-1

Henry Holt Reference Books are available at special discounts for bulk purchases for sales promotions, premiums, fund-raising, or educational use. Special editions or book excerpts can also be created to specification.

For details contact: Special Sales Director, Henry Holt and Company, Inc., 115 West 18th Street, New York, New York 10011.

First American Edition—1992

Printed in the United Kingdom
10 9 8 7 6 5 4 3 2 1

Editor Penny Butler
Sub-Editor Penny Williams
Editorial Assistant Eleanor Martlew
Production Assistant Christine Campbell
Design Jonathan Newdick

Editorial Director Stephen Brough
Art Director Douglas Wilson
Production Manager Charles James

CONTENTS

INTRODUCTION

The Economist Desk Companion has been developed from the internationally renowned **World Measurement Guide**. The material has been fully revised, updated and extended to incorporate both the existing unique set of data and international changes in measurement systems, the most outstanding of which is the changeover to the metric system, based on SI, which is more or less international. Of course local measurements in local areas still prevail even in the industrialised countries of the UK and the USA, but by the year 2000 the metric system will be current everywhere.

The contents list gives a clear view of the exhaustive range of information the book contains. Using that and the detailed index should enable you to look up anything you want to.

The book is in four parts.

Part I is an introduction describing the three major world measurement systems: metric (SI), British and American.

Part II gives a subject-by-subject listing of definitions, special measurements, formulae and calculations for the various subject areas, in alphabetical order.

Part III contains 175 pages of conversion tables providing instant answers to complicated sums such as net present value for a variety of assumptions, pounds-force per square inch into kilograms-force per square centimetre.

In Part IV are to be found abbreviations, rough conversions and a valuable body of weights and measures used historically and in the countries of the world apart from the UK and USA, as well as a small section on the historic measures of the UK.

Acknowledgements and sources

The publishers wish to thank the following individuals and organisations for their valuable contributions to this book.

Weights and measures
National Physical Laboratory
National Weights and Measures Laboratory
United States Information Service, London
World Almanac: A Book of Facts, 1992

Agriculture, fishing and forestry
The Biscuit, Cake, Chocolate & Confectionery Alliance
British Wool Marketing Board
British Wool Textile Council
Commonwealth Development Corporation
Commonwealth Secretariat
Czarnikow
The Economist Intelligence Unit
Food and Agriculture Organization (FAO)
FAO, *Trade Yearbook*
Forestry Commission
Fresh Produce Desk Book, Lockwood Press Ltd, 1991
AW Gordon
P Harrison
Herring Buyers' Association
International Tobacco Growers' Association
International Sugar Organization
International Wool Secretariat
Meat and Livestock Commission
Milk Marketing Board
Ministry of Agriculture, Fishing and Forestry (MAFF)
Oil World, Hamburg
Overseas Development Association (ODA)
Shellfish Association of Great Britain
Skin, Hide and Leather Traders Association
J Strak
Tea Council Ltd
The Textile Institute
Tobacco Advisory Council
Tobacco Journal International
White Fish Authority

Chemicals, industrial
The Economist Intelligence Unit
AW Gordon
Royal Society of Chemistry
A Taylor

Chemistry
Professor Mills
National Physical Laboratory
P Williams

Computers
J Worsfold

Construction
Brick Development Association
British Cement Association
British Ready Mixed Concrete Association
JJ Butler
Chartered Institution of Building Services Engineers
Everett, A, *Materials*, BT Batsford, 1978
Institute of Hydrology
Paintmakers Association of Great Britain Ltd
Pilkington Glass Limited
R Stutely

Country codes and currencies
Deutsches Institut für Normung e.V. (DIN)
International Organisation for Standardisation (ISO)

Economics
R Stutely

Electronics
Electronics Weekly
L Lindo

Energy
Martin Quinlan
AEA Technology
British Coal Corporation
British Gas plc
Petroleum Industry Association Limited
Institute of Petroleum
British Nuclear Fuels plc

Engineering
Advanced Manufacturing Technology Research Institute
British Industrial Fasteners Association
Imperial College (IC) Consultants Ltd
Tinsley Wire (Sheffield) Ltd

Finance
R Stutely

Food and drink
The Brewers' Society
P Lewis
Report of the Panel of Dietary Reference Values of the Committee on Medical Aspects of Food Policy, *Dietary Reference Values for Energy and Nutrients for the UK*
Webster's International Publishers

Health
Institute of Virology, Oxford
S Kingman
Ministry of Health
World Health Organisation, *Diseases*, 1990

Iron and steel
International Iron and Steel Institute, *World Steel in Figures 1991*
Dr A Nicolson

Light, optics and photography
Imperial College (IC) Consultants Ltd

Mathematics and statistics
Richard Stutely

Minerals and alloys
British Steel Technical Swinden Laboratories
Imperial College (IC) Consultants Ltd

Paper, packaging and printing
Arjo Wiggins Research and Development Ltd
Pira International

Sound and music
Imperial College (IC) Consultants Ltd

Textiles
R Anson
British Footwear Association
The Economist Intelligence Unit
P Harrison
The Textile Institute

Transport
AMTRAK
The Chartered Institute of Transport
International Maritime Organisation
Lev Sychrava Associates
Maxwell Stamp plc
E Scully

Weapons
International Institute for Strategic Studies (IISS)

PART I

SYSTEMS OF MEASUREMENT

Metric system

The system outlined here is the modern form of the metric system, referred to as the International System of Units (Système International d'Unités, or SI), as agreed at the General Conference on Weights and Measures (Conférence Générale des Poids et Mesures – CGPM) which meets in Paris at regular intervals. The general form of this system was agreed in 1960, being designed to replace other forms of the metric system, such as the CGS system based on the centimetre, gram and second, and the MKS system based on the metre, kilogram and second.

Units or names not forming part of the main system of SI units, or recommended in that system for limited use, are marked in this section with an asterisk* (eg, hectometre*).

Definitions of SI base units

Length: metre (m) is the length of the path travelled by light in vacuum during a time interval of 1/299 792 458 of a second.

Mass: kilogram (kg) is equal to the mass of the international prototype of the kilogram, which is in the custody of the Bureau International des Poids et Mesures (BIPM) at Sèvres, near Paris, France. This is a unit of mass and not of weight or force; it is approximately the same as the mass of 1 cubic decimetre (litre) of water at maximum density (4°C).

Time: second (s) is the duration of 9 192 631 770 periods of the radiation corresponding to the transition between the two hyperfine levels of the ground state of the caesium 133 atom. Thus the SI unit is defined in terms of the length of time for a certain frequency of vibration of a caesium 133 atom; the number of periods was chosen to define a second approximately the same as the "ephemeris" second which is the fraction 1/86 400 of an average day for the tropical year 1900 of about $365\frac{1}{4}$ days. **See pages 132–133.**

Electric current: ampere (A) is that constant current which, if maintained in two straight parallel conductors of infinite length, of negligible circular cross-section, and placed 1 metre apart in vacuum, would produce between these conductors a force equal to 2×10^{-7} newton per metre of length.

Thermodynamic temperature: kelvin (K) is the fraction 1/273.16 of the thermodynamic temperature of the triple point of water. The triple point of water is the point where water, ice and water vapour are in equilibrium; it is 273.16 K.

Amount of substance: mole (mol) is the amount of substance of a system which contains as many elementary entities as there are atoms in 0.012 kilogram of carbon 12. The realisation of the mole is the determination of the Avogadro constant.

When the mole is used, the elementary entities must be specified and may be atoms, molecules, ions, electrons, other particles, or specified groups of such particles.

Luminous intensity: candela (cd) is the luminous intensity, in a given direction, of a source which emits monochromatic radiation of frequency 540×10^{12} hertz and that has a radiant intensity in that direction of 1/683 watt per steradian.

Outline of the main International System of Units (SI)

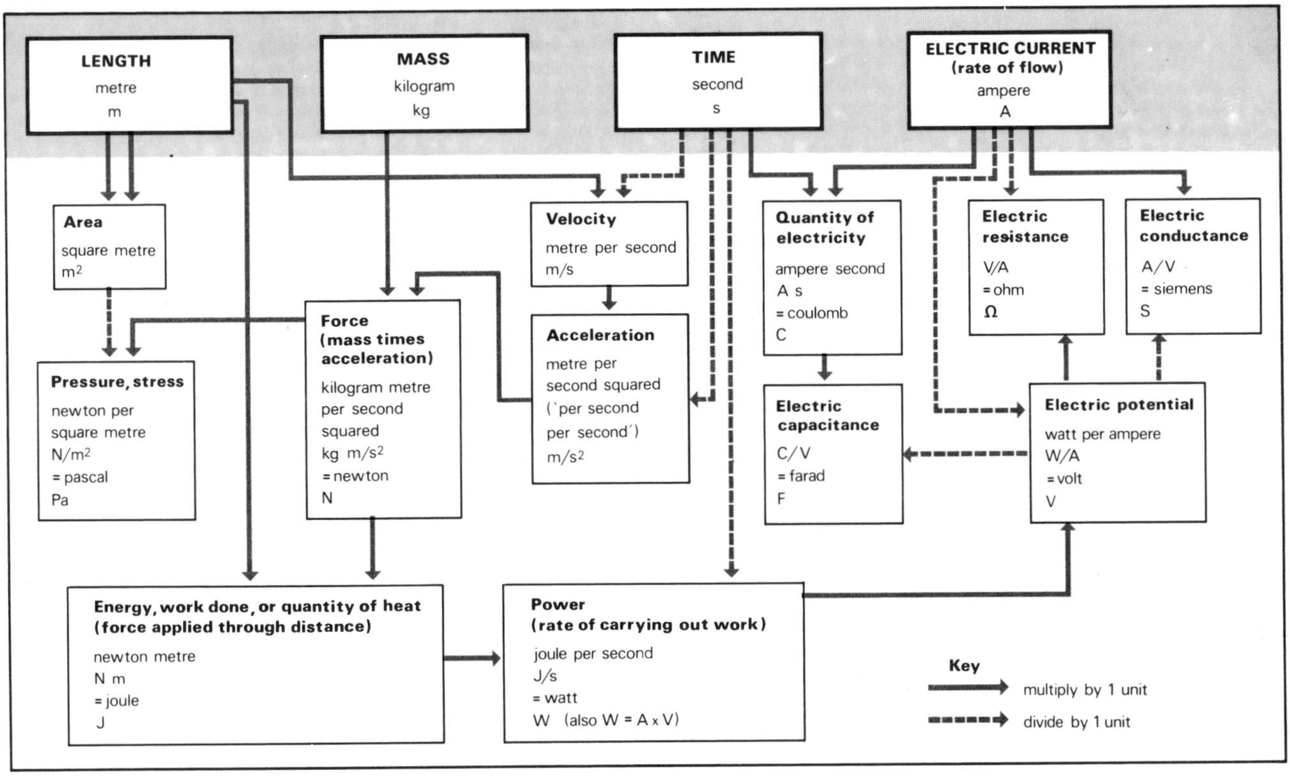

Definitions of SI supplementary units

In order to maintain the internal coherence of the International System based on only seven base units, the International Committee for Weights and Measures (Comité Internationale des Poids et Mesures – CIPM) specified that the supplementary units radian and steradian are dimensionless derived units. This implies that the quantities plane angle and solid angle are considered as dimensionless derived quantities.

Plane angle: radian (rad) is the plane angle between two radii of a circle which cut off on the circumference an arc equal in length to the radius.

Solid angle: steradian (sr) is the solid angle which, having its vertex in the centre of a sphere, cuts off an area of the surface of the sphere equal to that of a square with sides of length equal to the radius of the sphere.

Multiples and submultiples

The multiples and submultiples of the base and other units are shown for various types of measure. These are formed by applying established prefixes, which are the same whichever unit is used; eg, milligram (mg), millimetre (mm), kilowatt (kW), megawatt (MW).

Only one multiplying prefix is applied at one time to a given unit. Thus 1 thousandth of a milligram is not referred to as a millimilligram but as a microgram (μg). There are a few cases where, in attaching a prefix to the name of a unit, a contraction of the prefix name is made for convenience in pronunciation; eg, megohm, microhm and hectare. Unit names take a plural "s" when associated with numbers greater than 1, eg, 1.5 metres; the names hertz, lux and siemens are, however, the same in the plural. Symbols are not altered in the plural form; eg, 1.5m.

The names and values of prefixes in use are given below; also indicated are the equivalent powers to base 10 of the multiplying factors which can be used to relate any multiple or submultiple to the main unit; eg, 1 mm = 10^{-3} m and 1 MN = 10^{6} N. The general use of prefixes representing 10 raised to a power which is a multiple of ± 3 is recommended in SI; eg, millimetre (10^{-3} m), metre (m) and kilometre (10^{3} m). Other prefixes, notably centi, deci, deka and hecto can be used where others are inconvenient. Myria, as a prefix symbol, is not an SI multiple, but is included for reference.

Prefix name	Prefix symbol	Factor by which the unit is multiplied		Description
yocto	y	10^{-24}	0.000 000 000 000 000 000 000 001	
zepto	z	10^{-21}	0.000 000 000 000 000 000 001	
atto	a	10^{-18}	0.000 000 000 000 000 001	one UK trillionth; US quintillionth
femto	f	10^{-15}	0.000 000 000 000 001	one UK billiardth, US quadrillionth
pico	p	10^{-12}	0.000 000 000 001	one UK billionth; US trillionth
nano	n	10^{-9}	0.000 000 001	one UK milliardth; US billionth
micro	μ	10^{-6}	0.000 001	one millionth
milli	m	10^{-3}	0.001	one thousandth
centi	c	10^{-2}	0.01	one hundredth
deci	d	10^{-1}	0.1	one tenth
deca (or deka)	da[a]	10^{1}	10	ten
hecto	h	10^{2}	100	one hundred
kilo	k	10^{3}	1 000	one thousand
myria*	my*	10^{4}	10 000	ten thousand
mega	M	10^{6}	1 000 000	one million
giga	G	10^{9}	1 000 000 000	one thousand million; UK milliard; US billion
tera	T	10^{12}	1 000 000 000 000	one million million; UK billion[b], US trillion
peta	P	10^{15}	1 000 000 000 000 000	one UK billiard; US quadrillion
exa	E	10^{18}	1 000 000 000 000 000 000	one UK trillion; US quintillion
zetta	Z	10^{21}	1 000 000 000 000 000 000 000	
yotta	Y	10^{24}	1 000 000 000 000 000 000 000 000	

[a] Sometimes dk is used (eg in Germany). [b] The definition of 1 billion as 1 thousand million is now common in the UK.

Length

1 000 picometres (pm)	= 1 nanometre (nm)
10 ångström (Å)*	= 1 nanometre
1 000 nanometres	= 1 micrometre (μm), or micron (μ)*
	= 1 millimetre (mm)
1 000 micrometres	= 1 centimetre (cm)
10 millimetres	= 1 decimetre (dm)
100 millimetres	= 1 decimetre
10 centimetres	= 1 metre
1 000 millimetres	= 1 metre
100 centimetres	= 1 metre
10 decimetres	= 1 hectometre (hm)*
100 metres	= 1 kilometre (km)
1 000 metres	= 1 kilometre
10 hectometres*	= 1 megametre (Mm)
1 000 kilometres	

Nautical

1 852 metres	= 1 international nautical mile (n mile)

Area

100 square millimetres = 1 square centimetre (cm^2)
(mm^2)
100 square centimetres = 1 square decimetre (dm^2)

1 000 000 square millimetres	= 1 square metre (m^2)
10 000 square centimetres	= 1 square metre
100 square decimetres	= 1 square metre
100 square metres	= 1 are (a)
10 ares	= 1 dekare or decare (daa)
10 000 square metres	= 1 square hectometre (hm^2)*
	= 1 hectare (ha)
100 ares	= 1 hectare
10 dekares (or decares)	= 1 hectare
1 000 000 square metres	= 1 square kilometre (km^2)
100 square hectometres*	= 1 square kilometre
100 hectares	= 1 square kilometre

Volume and capacity

1 000 cubic millimetres (mm^3)	= 1 cubic centimetre (cm^3 or cc*)
1 000 cubic centimetres	= 1 cubic decimetre (dm^3)
1 000 cubic decimetres	= 1 cubic metre (m^3)
1 000 cubic metres	= 1 cubic dekametre (dam^3)*
1 000 cubic dekametres*	= 1 cubic hectometre (hm^3)*
1 000 cubic hectometres*	= 1 cubic kilometre (km^3)

The litre is defined for general use with SI units as 1 litre = 1 cubic decimetre.

The symbol L for litre was adopted officially as an option to l in 1979.

1 microlitre (µl)	= 1 lambda*
1 000 microlitres	= 1 millilitre (ml)
1 millilitre	= 1 cubic centimetre
10 millilitres	= 1 centilitre (cl)
10 centilitres	= 1 decilitre (dl)
1 000 millilitres	= 1 litre (l or L)
100 centilitres	= 1 litre
100 litres	= 1 hectolitre (hl)
1 000 litres	= 1 kilolitre (kl)*
	= 1 cubic metre
10 hectolitres	= 1 cubic metre

Time

1 000 nanoseconds (ns)	= 1 microsecond (µs)
1 000 microseconds	= 1 millisecond
1 000 milliseconds	= 1 second
1 000 seconds	= 1 kilosecond (ks)

Frequency

Definition: hertz (Hz) is the number of repetitions of a regular occurrence in 1 second.

1 000 hertz (Hz)	= 1 kilohertz (kHz)
1 000 kilohertz	= 1 megahertz (MHz)
1 000 megahertz	= 1 gigahertz (GHz)
1 000 gigahertz	= 1 terahertz (THz)
	= 1 fresnel*
1 000 terahertz	= 1 petahertz (PHz)
1 000 petahertz	= 1 exahertz (EHz)

Velocity

3.6 kilometres per hour (km/h)	= 1 metre per second (m/s)
3 600 kilometres per hour	= 1 kilometre per second (km/s)

Nautical

1 international nautical mile per hour = 1 international knot (kn)

Acceleration

Definition: international standard gravity value (g_n) is 9.806 65 metres per second squared.

1 galileo (Gal or gal*)*	= 1 centimetre per second squared (cm/s^2)*
100 centimetres per second squared*	= 1 metre per second squared (m/s^2)

Mass (weight)

The kilogram is the unit of mass in the International System; weight has a specialised meaning in metrology which is that the weight of a body is the product of its mass and the acceleration due to gravity. In SI units this would be a force (kg m/s^2) which is measured in newtons. Where there is no ambiguity, it is common practice to use the term weight as meaning mass under the force of the earth's gravity, measured by comparing one body with another which is a standard of mass. Where there may be ambiguity, m (for mass) and f (for force) are sometimes added to the symbol: eg, kgm (kilogram mass), kgf (kilogram force).

1 000 nanograms (ng)	= 1 microgram (µg or mcg*)[a]
1 000 micrograms	= 1 milligram (mg)
200 milligrams	= 1 metric carat (CM)[b]
1 000 milligrams	= 1 gram (g)
5 metric carats	= 1 gram
25 grams	= 1 mounce*[c]
100 grams	= 1 hectogram (hg)*
0.980 665 kilograms	= 1 glug*
1 000 000 milligrams	= 1 kilogram (kg)
1 000 grams	= 1 kilogram
9.806 65 kilograms	= 1 metric technical unit of mass[d]
100 kilograms	= 1 quintal (q)*
1 000 000 grams	= 1 megagram (Mg)
1 000 kilograms	= 1 megagram
10 quintals*	= 1 megagram
	= 1 tonne (t)
	= 1 metric ton
	= 1 millier*

[a] Or gamma (γ)*. [b] CM is the UK abbreviation; abbreviations vary by country (eg, for Germany it is Kt). [c] Or metric ounce. [d] Metric technical unit of mass is the mass that acquires an acceleration of 1 metre per second squared under the influence of a 1 kilogram force (see also **Acceleration** above). Also called the metric slug or hyl and shown as kgm (kilogram mass).

Density and concentration

1 gram per cubic metre (g/m^3)	= 1 milligram per cubic decimetre (mg/dm^3)
1 000 milligrams per cubic decimetre	= 1 gram per cubic decimetre (g/dm^3)
	= 1 gram per litre (g/l)
	= 1 kilogram per cubic metre (kg/m^3)
1 000 kilograms per cubic metre	= 1 tonne per cubic metre (t/m^3)
	= 1 kilogram per cubic decimetre (kg/dm^3)

= 1 kilogram per litre (kg/l)
= 1 gram per cubic centimetre (g/cm^3)
= 1 gram per millilitre (g/ml)

Force

Definitions

1. newton (N) is that force which, applied to a mass of 1 kilogram, gives it an acceleration of 1 metre per second squared.
2. kilogram-force (kgf)*, also called kilopond (kp)*, is that force which, applied to a mass of 1 kilogram, gives it the standard gravitational acceleration ("free fall") of 9.806 65 metres per second squared.
3. dyne (dyn)* is that force which, applied to a mass of 1 gram, gives it an acceleration of 1 centimetre per second squared $= 10^{-5}$ N.

10 micronewtons (μN)	= 1 dyne (dyn)*
1 000 micronewtons	= 1 millinewton (mN)
9.806 65 millinewtons	= 1 pond (p)*
10 millinewtons (mN)	= 1 centinewton (cN)
10 000 dynes*	= 1 crinal*
100 000 dynes*	= 1 newton
1 000 millinewtons (mN)	= 1 newton
9.806 65 newtons	= 1 kilogram-force (kgf)*
	= 1 kilopond (kp)*
1 000 newtons	= 1 kilonewton (kN)
	= 1 sthène or sten (sn)*
1 000 kilonewtons	= 1 meganewton (MN)

Pressure and stress

Definition: pascal (Pa) is the pressure produced by a force of 1 newton applied, uniformly distributed, over an area of 1 square metre.

1 000 micropascals (μPa)	= 1 millipascal (mPa)
100 millipascals	= 1 dyne per square centimetre (dyn/cm^2)*
	= 1 barye*
	= 1 microbar (μbar)
1 000 millipascals	= 1 pascal (Pa)
10 microbars	= 1 pascal
	= 1 newton per square metre (N/m^2)
9.806 65 pascals	= 1 millimetre of water, conventional (mm H_2O)*
1 000 microbars	= 1 millibar (mbar or mb*)
100 pascals	= 1 millibar
	= 1 vac*
9.806 65 × 13.595 1 = 133.322 (approx.) pascals	= 1 millimetre of mercury, conventional (mm Hg)*
	= 1 torr (approx.)*
1 000 pascals	= 1 kilopascal (kPa)
10 millibars	= 1 kilopascal
	= 1 sthène per square metre (sn/m^2)*
	= 1 pièze (pz)*
9 806.65 pascals	= 1 metre of water, conventional (m H_2O)*
98 065.5 pascals	= 1 technical atmosphere (at)*
	= 1 kilogram-force per square centimetre (kgf/cm^2)*
	= 0.980 665 bar (bar or b*)
100 000 pascals	= 1 bar
1 000 millibars	= 1 bar
	= 1 hectopièze (hpz)
101 325 pascals	= 1 standard atmosphere (atm)*
760 torrs*	= 1 standard atmosphere*
	= 1.013 25 bars
1 000 000 pascals	= 1 megapascal (MPa)
1 000 kilopascals	= 1 megapascal
10 bars	= 1 megapascal
	= 1 newton per square millimetre (N/mm^2)
100 bars	= 1 hectobar (hbar)
1 000 bars	= 1 kilobar (kbar)
1 000 megapascals	= 1 gigapascal (GPa)

Viscosity

Dynamic (or absolute)

1 centipoise (cP)	= 1 millipascal second (mPa s)
100 centipoises	= 1 poise (P)*
	= 1 dyne second per square centimetre (dyn s/cm^2)*
	= 100 millipascal seconds
1 000 millipascal seconds	= 1 pascal second (Pa s)
	= 1 newton second per square metre (N s/m^2)
	= 1 000 centipoises
	= 10 poises

Kinematic

1 centistokes (cSt)	= 1 square millimetre per second (mm^2/s)
100 centistokes	= 1 stokes (St)*
	= 1 square centimetre per second (cm^2/s)*
10 000 stokes*	= 1 square metre per second (m^2/s)

Energy, work and quantity of heat

Definitions

1. joule (J) is the work done when the point of application of a force of 1 newton is displaced through a distance of 1 metre in the direction of the force.
2. erg is 1 dyn acting through a distance of 1 centimetre $= 10^{-7}$ J.

10 000 ergs*	= 1 millijoule (mJ)
10 000 000 ergs*	= 1 joule
1 000 millijoules	= 1 joule
1 000 joules	= 1 kilojoule (kJ)
1 000 kilojoules	= 1 megajoule (MJ)
3.6 megajoules	= 1 kilowatt hour (kWh)
1 000 megajoules	= 1 gigajoule (GJ)
1 000 gigajoules	= 1 terajoule (TJ)

Power

Definitions

1. watt (W) is the power which in 1 second gives rise to energy of 1 joule.
2. metric horsepower (ch, CV, cv, PS or pk): the power which

raises 75 kilograms against the force of gravity through a distance of 1 metre per second
= 75 × 9.806 65 joules per second = 735.498 75 watts.

1 000 microwatts (μw)	= 1 milliwatt (mW)
1 000 milliwatts	= 1 watt
1 000 watts	= 1 kilowatt (kW)
1 000 kilowatts	= 1 megawatt (MW)
1 000 000 kilowatts	= 1 gigawatt (GW)
1 000 megawatts	= 1 gigawatt
1 000 gigawatts	= 1 terawatt (TW)

Temperature

Definition: the unit "degree Celsius" is equal to the unit "kelvin". The zero of the Celsius scale is the temperature of the ice point, which is 273.15 K (0.01 below the triple point of water); ie, degrees Celsius (°C) = K − 273.15.

Electricity and magnetism

1 000 picoamperes (pA)	= 1 nanoampere (nA)
1 000 nanoamperes	= 1 microampere (μA)
1 000 microamperes	= 1 milliampere (mA)
1 000 milliamperes	= 1 ampere
1 000 amperes	= 1 kiloampere (kA)

Definitions of other (derived) SI units

1. coulomb (C) is the quantity of electricity carried in 1 second by a current of 1 ampere

1 000 picocoulombs (pC)	= 1 nanocoulomb (nC)
1 000 nanocoulombs	= 1 microcoulomb (μC)
1 000 microcoulombs	= 1 millicoulomb (mC)
1 000 millicoulombs	= 1 coulomb
1 000 coulombs	= 1 kilocoulomb (kC)
1 000 kilocoulombs	= 1 megacoulomb (MC)

2. volt (V) is the difference of electric potential between two points of a conducting wire carrying a constant current of 1 ampere, when the power dissipated between these points is equal to 1 watt.

1 000 microvolts (μV)	= 1 millivolt (mV)
1 000 millivolts	= 1 volt
1 000 volts	= 1 kilovolt (kV)
1 000 kilovolts	= 1 megavolt (MV)

3. ohm (Ω) is the electric resistance between two points of a conductor when a constant potential difference of 1 volt, applied to these points, produces in the conductor a current of 1 ampere, the conductor not being the seat of any electromotive force.

1 000 microhm (μΩ)	= 1 milliohm (mΩ)
1 000 milliohm	= 1 ohm
1 000 ohms	= 1 kilohm (kΩ)
1 000 kilohms	= 1 megohm (MΩ)
1 000 megohms	= 1 gigohm (GΩ)

4. siemens (S) is 1 ampere per volt, being the unit of electric conductance; this unit has also been known as the reciprocal ohm (ohm^{-1}) or mho.

1 000 microsiemens (μS)	= 1 millisiemens (mS)
1 000 millisiemens	= 1 siemens
1 000 siemens	= 1 kilosiemens (kS)

5. farad (F) is the capacitance of a capacitor between the plates of which there appears a difference of electric potential of 1 volt when it is charged by a quantity of electricity of 1 coulomb.

1 puff*	= 1 picofarad (pF)
1 000 000 picofarads	= 1 microfarad (μF)
1 000 000 microfarads	= 1 farad

6. weber (Wb) is the magnetic flux which, linking a circuit of 1 turn, would produce in it an electromotive force of 1 volt if it were reduced to zero at a uniform rate in 1 second.

7. henry (H) is the inductance of a closed circuit in which an electromotive force of 1 volt is produced when the electric current in the circuit varies uniformly at the rate of 1 ampere per second.

1 000 picohenrys (pH)	= 1 nanohenry (nH)
1 000 nanohenrys	= 1 microhenry (μH)
1 000 microhenrys	= 1 millihenry (mH)
1 000 millihenrys	= 1 henry

8. tesla (T) is the flux density in vacuum produced by a magnetic field of strength 1 ampere per metre; this is the unit of magnetic flux density and equals 1 weber per square metre.

1 000 nanoteslas (nT)	= 1 microtesla (μT)
1 000 microteslas	= 1 millitesla (mT)
1 000 milliteslas	= 1 tesla

Luminous flux

Definitions

1. lumen (lm) is the luminous flux emitted within unit solid angle of 1 steradian by a point source having a uniform luminous intensity of 1 candela.
2. lux (lx) is an illuminance of 1 lumen per square metre.

Radiation

Definition for radioactivity: becquerel (Bq) is 1 reciprocal second, being the unit of activity of a radionuclide. The activity is the number of radioactive disintegrations occurring per unit of time in a given quantity of the radionuclide.

1 000 becquerels	= 1 kilobecquerel (kBq)
1 000 kilobecquerels	= 1 megabecquerel (MBq)
1 000 megabecquerels	= 1 gigabecquerel (GBq)

Definition for absorbed dose: gray (Gy) = 1 joule per kilogram, being the unit of absorbed dose in the field of ionising radiation. The absorbed dose is the mean energy imparted by ionising radiation to matter, per unit of mass of irradiated material, at the place of interest.

See also Health, pages 102–103.

United Kingdom

The imperial system was established as such in 1824. The imperial gallon was defined as the only legal gallon, replacing the different ale and wine gallons. Although the troy pound was defined as the imperial standard under the 1824 act, in 1855 the avoirdupois pound became the imperial standard. In 1878 the troy pound was abolished, although the troy ounce remained in use.

The imperial system was, until the late 1960s, the main system of measurement used in the British Commonwealth and South Africa; virtually every country using the imperial system began a changeover to the metric system beginning in the late 1960s and 1970s.

In the UK the change is taking place gradually. The 1963 Weights and Measures Act established units of both the imperial and metric systems as "UK primary standards", and the base units of the yard and pound were defined in terms of the metre and kilogram. The gallon was defined in terms of the cubic decimetre (litre) in 1976.

In the list below, units which are not officially authorised following the changes to the metric system, or which are generally obsolescent, are marked with an asterisk* (eg, rod*). A substantial number of UK units have not been officially authorised for UK use since 1980, including square inch, square mile, cubic foot, grain, stone, hundredweight, ton and horsepower. The following units are expected to cease to be authorised from January 1st 1995:

- inch, foot, yard, mile;
- square foot, square yard, acre;
- fluid ounce, gill, pint, quart, gallon;
- troy ounce, ounce (avoirdupois), pound.

Retention is allowed until December 31st 1999 for:

- fathom for marine navigation;
- fluid ounce and pint for beer, cider, water, lemonades and fruit juices in returnable containers;
- ounce (avoirdupois) and pound for goods sold loose from bulk;
- therm for gas supply;

and without time limit for:

- inch, foot, yard, mile for road traffic signs and related distance and speed measurements;
- pint for dispensing of draught beer and cider, and milk in returnable containers;
- acre for land registration;
- troy ounce for transactions in precious metals.

Relationships are exact except where noted as approximate.

See pages 258–261 for Historical UK measures.

Length

Base unit definition. 1 yard = 0.914 4 metre.

1 000 000 micro-inches (μin)	= 1 inch (in)
1 000 milli-inches[a]	= 1 inch
4 inches	= 1 hand*[b]
7.92 inches	= 1 link (lk)*
12 inches	= 1 foot (ft)
3 feet	= 1 yard (yd)
25 links*	= 1 rod*
5.5 yards	= 1 rod*, pole* or perch*
100 links*	= 1 chain (ch)*[b,c]
66 feet	= 1 chain*[b]
22 yards	= 1 chain*[b]
4 rods*	= 1 chain*[b]
100 feet	= 1 engineer's chain*[b,d]
220 yards	= 1 furlong*[b]
10 chains*	= 1 furlong*[b]
5 280 feet	= 1 mile (mi)
1 760 yards	= 1 mile
80 chains*	= 1 mile
8 furlongs*	= 1 mile
3 miles	= 1 league*
Nautical	
6 feet	= 1 fathom
100 fathoms (approx.)	= 1 cable length*[e]
6 080 feet	= 1 nautical mile*
	= the length of 1 minute of the meridian through Greenwich, that is 1/60th of the degree of latitude
6 087 feet	= 1 telegraph nautical mile*
10 cable lengths*	= 1 nautical mile*

[a]A milli-inch is sometimes called a mil* or a thou*. [b]In general, not lawful for UK trade since 1978. [c]Also called a Gunter's or surveyor's chain. [d]Also called a Ramden's chain. [e]An alternative, less usual, value was 120 fathoms.

Area

Base unit definition. 1 square yard is a superficial area equal to that of a square each side of which measures 1 yard.

1 circular mil	= area of a circle of diameter 0.001 inch ($=\pi/4 \times 0.000\,001$ square inch)
144 square inches*	= 1 square foot (ft^2)
9 square feet	= 1 square yard (yd^2)
30.25 square yards	= 1 square rod*, pole* or perch*
484 square yards	= 1 square chain (ch^2)*
1 210 square yards	= 1 rood*
4 840 square yards	= 1 acre (ac)
160 square rods*	= 1 acre
640 acres	= 1 square mile*

Volume

Base unit definition. 1 cubic yard is a volume equal to that of a cube each edge of which measures 1 yard.

1 728 cubic inches*	= 1 cubic foot (ft^3)*
46 656 cubic inches*	= 1 cubic yard (yd^3)*
27 cubic feet*	= 1 cubic yard*
Nautical	
100 cubic feet*	= 1 register ton (shipping)

Capacity

Base unit definition (1976). 1 gallon = 4.546 09 cubic decimetres (exactly).

1 gallon (1963) = 1.000 000 41 gallon (1976)
1 gallon (1976) = 0.999 999 59 gallon (1963)

60 minims	= 1 fluid drachm (fl drm)
8 fluid drachms*	= 1 fluid ounce (fl oz)
5 fluid ounces	= 1 gill
20 fluid ounces	= 1 pint (pt)
4 gills	= 1 pint
40 fluid ounces	= 1 quart (qt)
2 pints	= 1 quart
160 fluid ounces	= 1 gallon (gal)
8 pints	= 1 gallon
4 quarts	= 1 gallon
2 gallons	= 1 peck*
4 pecks*	= 1 bushel (bu)*
8 gallons	= 1 bushel*
64 gallons	= 1 quarter (qr)*
8 bushels*	= 1 quarter*

Velocity

1 mile per hour (mph) = 88 feet per minute (ft/min)
= $1\frac{7}{15}$ feet per second (ft/s)

Weight (mass)

Definition. 1 grain = 64.798 91 milligrams (the grain is the same whether avoirdupois or troy weight).

Avoirdupois

Base unit definition. 1 pound = 0.453 592 37 kilogram.

437.5 grains (gr)*	= 1 ounce (oz)
16 drams (dr)*	= 1 ounce
7 000 grains*	= 1 pound (lb)
256 drams*	= 1 pound
16 ounces	= 1 pound
14 pounds	= 1 stone*
2 stones*	= 1 quarter (qr)*
9.806 65/0.3048 pounds = 32.174 (approx.) pounds	= 1 slug (technical unit of mass)
100 pounds	= 1 cental (ctl)*
112 pounds	= 1 hundredweight (cwt)*
4 quarters*	= 1 hundredweight*
35 840 ounces	= 1 ton*
2 240 pounds	= 1 ton* (or long ton)
20 hundredweights*	= 1 ton*
1 ton	= 1.102 short tons
0.984 tons	= 1 metric tonne

Troy. For weighing gold, silver, jewels, etc; sometimes called fine instead of troy.

480 grains*	= 1 ounce (oz tr)
24 grains*	= 1 pennyweight (dwt tr)*
20 pennyweights*	= 1 ounce
5 760 grains*	= 1 pound*
12 ounces	= 1 pound*

Force

Definitions

1. Poundal is that force which applied to a mass of 1 pound, gives it an acceleration of 1 foot per second per second.
2. Pound-force is that force which, applied to a mass of 1 pound, gives it the standard gravitational acceleration of 9.806 65 metres (approximately 32.174 048 feet) per second per second.

32.174 (approx.) poundals (pdl)*	= 1 pound-force (lbf)*
16 ounces-force (ozf)*	= 1 pound-force*
2 240 pounds-force*	= 1 ton-force (tonf)*

Power

Definition. Horsepower is the power needed to raise 550 pounds through a height of 1 foot in 1 second.

550 foot pounds-force per second (ft lbf/s)* = 1 horsepower (hp)*

Quantity of heat

Definition. 1 British thermal unit = 2.326 × 0.453 592 37 kilojoules or approximately 1.055 056 kilojoules as defined internationally in 1956; the UK definition is "the heat needed to raise the temperature of 1 pound of water through 1 degree Fahrenheit at or near 39.1 degrees Fahrenheit".

100 000 British thermal units (Btu)* = 1 therm

The therm was officially abolished in 1992.

Heat flow

288 000 British thermal units per day (Btu/d)*	= 1 ton of refrigeration
12 000 British thermal units per hour (Btu/h)	= 1 ton of refrigeration

United States of America

Two systems of measurement exist in the USA: the US Customary System and the International System (SI). Customary units were inherited from the UK imperial system but there are many differences. SI units are being used to an increasing extent and have been predominant in science and the pharmaceutical industry for many years. Since the automotive industry became largely metric the use of SI units has risen rapidly throughout manufacturing industry.

The 1988 Trade Act calls for the federal government to adopt metric specifications by December 31st 1992.

In this section US spelling is used for meter, liter, etc.

See summary table (pages 160–163) for full details of conversions for US and metric (SI) measures.

US CUSTOMARY WEIGHTS AND MEASURES

Linear measure

12 inches (in)	= 1 foot (ft)
3 feet	= 1 yard (yd)
5.5 yards	= 1 rod (rd), pole or perch
40 rods	= 1 furlong (fur)
8 furlongs	= 1 statute mile (mi) = 1 760 yards
3 miles	= 1 league
6 076.12 feet	= 1 international nautical mile

There is a difference between the "international" and the "survey" foot. The survey foot is still used for geodetic surveys within the USA.

1 international foot	= 0.999 998 survey foot (exactly)
1 survey foot	= 1 200/3 937 meter (exactly)
1 international foot	= 12 × 0.025 4 meter (exactly)

Liquid measure

When necessary to distinguish liquid from dry measures the word "liquid" or "liq" should be used in combination with the name of the liquid unit.

4 gills	= 1 pint (pt) = 28.875 cubic inches
2 pints	= 1 quart (qt) = 57.75 cubic inches
4 quarts	= 1 gallon (gall) = 231 cubic inches

Area measure

144 square inches	= 1 square foot (ft^2)
9 square feet	= 1 square yard (yd^2)
30.25 square yards	= 1 square rod (rd^2)
140 square rods	= 1 acre
640 acres	= 1 square mile (mi^2)
1 mile square	= 1 section (of land)
6 miles square	= 1 township = 36 sections

Cubic measure

1 cubic foot (ft^3)	= 1.728 cubic inches (in^3)
27 cubic feet	= 1 cubic yard (yd^3)

Gunter's or surveyor's chain measure

7.92 inches (in)	= 1 link
100 links	= 1 chain (ch) = 4 rods = 66 feet
80 chains	= 1 survey mile = 320 rods = 5 280 feet

Troy weight

24 grains	= 1 pennyweight (dwt)
20 pennyweights	= 1 ounce troy (oz t)
12 ounces troy	= 1 pound troy (lb t)

Dry measure

To distinguish dry from liquid measures the word "dry" should be used in combination with the name of the dry unit.

2 pints (pt)	= 1 quart (qt) = 67.2006 cubic inches
8 quarts	= 1 peck (pk) = 537.605 cubic inches
4 pecks	= 1 bushel (bu) = 2 150.42 cubic inches

Avoirdupois weight

When necessary to distinguish avoirdupois from troy measures the abbreviation "avdp" should be used in combination with the name of the avoirdupois unit. (The grain is the same in both.)

27.34 grains	= 1 dram (dr)
16 drams	= 1 ounce (oz)
16 ounces	= 1 pound (lb)
100 pounds	= 1 hundredweight (cwt)
20 hundredweights	= 1 ton = 2 000 pounds

Please note that when the terms hundredweight and ton are used unmodified they are understood to mean the 100 lb hundredweight and 2 000 lb ton respectively. They may be designated "net" or "short" when necessary to distinguish them from the "gross" or "long" measure.

The following values apply to "gross" or "long" measure:

112 pounds	= 1 gross or long hundredweight
20 gross or long hundredweights	= 1 gross or long ton = 2 240 pounds

See also United Kingdom, pages 18–19.

TABLE OF EQUIVALENTS

Equivalents involving decimals are rounded off to the third decimal place; exact equivalents are marked *.

Length

1 cable's length	= 219 meters
	= 720* survey feet
	= 120* fathoms
1 chain (Gunter's or surveyor's)	= 20.117 meters
1 chain (engineer's)	= 30.48* meters
	= 100 feet
1 degree (geographical)	= 111.123 kilometers
	= 69.047 miles
of latitude	= 68.708 miles at equator
	= 69.403 miles at poles
of longitude	= 69.171 miles at equator
1 fathom	= 1.828 8* meters
	= 6* survey feet
1 foot	= 0.304 8* meter
1 furlong	= 201.168 meters
	= 10* surveyor's chains
1 inch	= 2.54* centimeters

1 league	=4.828 kilometers
	=3* survey miles
1 link (Gunter's or surveyor's)	=0.201 meter
1 link (engineer's)	=0.305 meter
	=1 foot
1 mile (statute or land)	=1.609 kilometers
1 international nautical mile	=1.852 kilometers
	=1.151 survey miles
1 rod, pole or perch	=5.029 meters
1 yard	=0.914 4* meter

Area or surface

1 acre	=0.405 hectare
1 are (a)	=119.599 square yards
	=0.025 acre
1 bolt (cloth measure)	
length	=100 yards (on modern looms)
width	=42 inches (cotton)
	=60 inches (wool)
1 square foot	=929.030 square centimeters
1 square inch	=6.451 6* square centimeters
1 square mile	=258.999 hectares
1 square rod, pole or perch	=25.293 square meters
1 square yard	=0.836 square meter

Capacity or volume

There are a variety of barrels, eg: federal taxes on fermented liquors are based on a 31 gallon barrel; many state laws define a barrel for liquids as 31.5 gallons; federal law recognises a 40 gallon barrel for proof spirits; a 42 gallon barrel is used for crude oil or petroleum products for statistical purposes.

1 barrel (bbl): liquid	=31–42 gallons
1 barrel: fruit, vegetables, other dry commodities (excl. dry cranberries)	=7 056 cubic inches
	=105 dry quarts
	=3.281 bushels, struck measure
1 barrel: cranberries	=5 826 cubic inches
	=86.703 dry quarts
	=2.709 bushels, struck measure
1 board foot (lumber measure)	=1 foot square board 1 inch thick
1 bushel (struck measure)	=35.239 liters
	=2 150.42* cubic inches
1 bushel (heaped)	=1.278 bushels (struck measure)
1 cord (cd) firewood	=128* cubic feet
1 cubic foot	=28.317 cubic decimeters
	=7.481 gallons
1 cubic inch	=16.387 cubic centimeters
	=0.554 fluid ounce
	=4.433 fluid drams
1 cubic yard	=0.765 cubic meter
1 gallon	=3.785 liters
	=231* cubic inches
	=128* fluid ounces
1 gill	=0.118 liter
	=7.219 cubic inches
	=4* fluid ounces
1 ounce (liquid)	=29.573 milliliters
	=1.805 cubic inches
1 peck	=8.810 liters
1 pint (dry)	=0.551 liter
	=33.600 cubic inches
1 pint (liquid)	=0.473 liter
1 quart (dry)	=1.101 liters
1 quart (liquid)	=0.946 liter

Weight or mass

1 assay ton[a] (AT)	=29.167 grams
1 bale (cotton measure)	=500 pounds
1 carat (c)	=200* milligrams
	=3.086 grains
1 dram (avdp)	=1.772 grams
1 grain	=64.799 milligrams
1 hundredweight (gross or long)[b]	=50.802 kilograms
1 hundredweight (net or short)	=45.359 kilograms
1 ounce (avdp)	=28.350 grams
	=0.911 troy ounce
1 ounce (troy)	=31.103 grams
	=1.097 avdp ounces
1 pennyweight	=1.555 grams
1 pound (avdp)	=453.592 37* grams
	=1.215 troy pounds
1 pound (troy)	=373.242 grams
	=0.823 avdp pound
1 ton (gross or long)[b]	=1.016 tonnes
	=1.12 net tons
1 ton (net or short)	=0.907 tonne
	=9.893 gross ton

[a]Used in assaying. It bears the same relation to the milligram as 1 net ton bears to 1 troy ounce.
[b]Limited commercial use in the USA, usually in restricted industrial fields.

PART II

AN A–Z OF DEFINITIONS, TERMS AND SPECIAL MEASUREMENTS

Accountancy

RATIOS

Working capital

Working capital ratio is current assets/current liabilities, where current assets = stock + debtors + cash at bank and in hand + quoted investments, etc; current liabilities = creditors + overdraft at bank + taxation + dividends, etc.

The ratio varies according to type of trade and conditions; a ratio of 1–3 is usual with a ratio above 2 being generally good.

Liquidity ratio is liquid (quick) assets/current liabilities, where liquid assets = debtors + cash at bank and in hand + quoted investments (ie, assets which can be realised within a month or so, which may not apply to all investments); current liabilities are those which may need to be repaid within the same short period, which may not necessarily include a bank overdraft where it is likely to be renewed. The liquidity ratio is sometimes referred to as the acid test; a ratio under 1 suggests a possibly difficult situation, while too high a ratio may mean that assets are not being usefully employed.

Turnover of working capital is sales/average working capital. The ratio varies according to type of trade; generally a low ratio can mean poor use of resources, while too high a ratio can mean overtrading.

Turnover of stock is sales/average stock, or (where cost of sales is known) cost of sales/average stock.

The cost of sales turnover figure is to be preferred as both figures are then on the same valuation basis. This ratio can be expressed as a number of times per year, or time taken for stock to be turned over once = (52/number of times) weeks. A low turnover of stock can be a sign of stocks which are difficult to move, and is usually a sign of adverse conditions.

Turnover of debtors is credit sales/average debtors. This indicates efficiency in collecting accounts. An average credit period of about one month is usual, but varies according to credit stringency conditions in the economy.

A commonly used measure of performance is days' sales outstanding (DSO) calculated by: total debtors/(annual turnover/365). A lower DSO indicates a more efficient debt recovery cycle.

Effective credit period given (in days) is (average debtors/sales) × 365.

Effective credit period taken (in days) is (average creditors/purchases) × 365. If the credit period taken is greater than the credit period given then there is a positive cash flow impact.

Turnover of creditors is purchases/average creditors. Average payment period is best maintained in line with turnover of debtors.

Sales

Export ratio is exports as a percentage of sales.

Sales per employee are sales/average number of employees.

Assets

Ratios of assets can vary according to the measure of assets used.

Total assets are current assets + fixed assets + other assets, where fixed assets = property + plant and machinery + motor vehicles, etc, and other assets = long-term investments + goodwill, etc.

Net assets (net worth) are total assets – total liabilities, and share capital + reserves.

Turnover of net assets is sales/average net assets. As for turnover of working capital, a low ratio can mean poor use of resources.

Assets per employee are assets/average number of employees. This indicates the amount of investment backing for employees.

Profits

Gross profit is sales – direct cost of sales.

Profit margin is (profit/sales) × 100 = profits as a percentage of sales; usually profits before tax.

Profit per employee is profit before tax/average number of employees.

Profitability is (profit/total assets) × 100 = profits as a percentage of total assets.

Return on capital is (profit/net assets) × 100 = profits as a percentage of net assets (net worth or capital employed).

Two other commonly used terms are return on capital employed (ROCE) and return on investment (ROI).

All ratios are best compared with those for companies in similar industries, and also compared over time. In addition growth rates for each item (eg, sales, profits, etc) can be obtained by calculating the percentage change over various periods and using the tables to obtain the growth rate per annum. Growth rates then provide comparability as between periods of varying lengths.

See tables on pages 208–215.

INVESTMENT APPRAISAL

Appraisal for investment usually means considering the rates of return for various projects and selecting the one with the best return. Methods of appraisal for investment depend first on the estimation of the net cash flow from an investment, where all taxes, subsidies, grants, etc, have been allowed for in estimating the cash flow. Methods differ according to the way in which the flows of cash over time are related to the initial investment.

Rate of return is the total of the estimated cash flows over the

Year	Cash flow	Year	Cash flow
1	10.0	2	11.0
3	12.1	7	17.7
4	13.3	8	19.5
5	14.6	9	21.4
6	16.1	10	23.6
		TOTAL	159.3

life of the investment divided by the number of years' life, and expressed as a percentage of the investment. Where a unit of 100 is invested the following net cash flows accrue over 10 years.

The crude rate of return is the total of those flows (159.3) divided by 10. This average of 15.93 is 15.93% as a percentage of the 100 units originally invested.

Pay back is the number of years after which the original investment would have been recouped. In the above example, this would be after year 8, when a cumulative amount of 114.3 would have been received net.

Discounted cash flow

The above two methods make no allowance for the time factor in the cash flows; as any sum could be earning interest in an alternative investment, it is more realistic to discount the cash flows to be received in future years by an expected rate of interest.

The discount factor, giving the present value of any future amount allowing for the rate of interest concerned, is the reciprocal of the figure in the accumulation tables.

Tables for the amount accumulated by 1 unit at different rates of interest and for different periods are included on pages 216–219.

The following table shows the effect of discounting the cash flows in the above example at interest rates of 5% and 10%; this follows the convention of regarding the first year as not subject to discounting, so that year 2 is discounted at the rate for 1 year as shown in the discount factor table. Further, the convention of regarding all receipts and payments as taking place on one day of each year is adopted.

Period	Net cash flow	Interest at 5% Discount factor	Present value	Interest at 10% Discount factor	Present value
1	10.0	1.000 0	10.0	1.000 0	10.0
2	11.0	0.952 4	10.5	0.909 1	10.0
3	12.1	0.907 0	11.0	0.826 4	10.0
4	13.3	0.863 8	11.5	0.751 3	10.0
5	14.6	0.822 7	12.0	0.683 0	10.0
6	16.1	0.783 5	12.6	0.620 9	10.0
7	17.7	0.746 2	13.2	0.564 5	10.0
8	19.5	0.710 7	13.9	0.513 2	10.0
9	21.4	0.676 8	14.5	0.466 5	10.0
10	23.6	0.644 6	15.2	0.424 1	10.0

The total cash flow at present value is 124.4 discounted at 5%, and 100 discounted at 10%, compared with the crude total flow of 159.3. Assuming an interest rate of 5% the investment of 100 units will give a profit of 24.4, and assuming an interest rate of 10%, the investment of 100 gives a return of exactly 100, so it yields no profit at that rate of interest (this is because the net cash flows used in the example are the same as the amount accumulated from 10 at 10% per annum).

See table on page 218.

Where the present value of the flow of cash, discounted at a certain rate, exactly equals the initial amount of investment, that rate is sometimes called the DCF solution rate, since it is the rate of return given by the investment made. In the above example, 10% is the DCF solution rate. DCF solution rates are usually calculated by interpolation from rates which are approximately known.

Where the investment is spread over more than one period, allowance is made for discounting the investment payments. In the following table the effect of spreading a 100 unit investment over three periods is illustrated, discounting taking place at the DCF solution rate which differs accordingly.

Period	Investment in 1 period Net cash flow	Present value	Investment in 3 periods Net cash flow	Present value
Investment				
1	100	100	25	25.0
2			50	37.8
3			25	14.3
Returns				
1	20	20.0	20	20.0
2	20	16.6	20	15.1
3	20	13.8	20	11.5
4	20	11.5	20	8.7
5	20	9.6	20	6.6
6	20	8.0	20	5.0
7	20	6.6	20	3.8
8	20	5.5	20	2.8
9	20	4.6	20	2.2
10	20	3.8	20	1.6

The total discounted amount or present value is 100 for the one period investment example, with a DCF solution rate of 20.3%; for the example with investment over three periods, the total discounted amount is 77.2 units (since investment flows are also discounted) with a DCF solution rate of 32.2%. The higher rate is obtained because the investment does not need to be made immediately, but the returns are nevertheless the same.

Agriculture, fishing and forestry

In the process of change to the metric system most countries adopt the nearest equivalent in metric terms for the same basic unit; eg, a 100 lb unit = 45.359 kg, which may become a 45 kg or 50 kg unit in the metric system. Many capacity units shown here with weight equivalents in rounded imperial units are changing to rounded metric units.

The special units shown in this section are usually capacity measures for which the weight contained varies according to the density of the product concerned; eg, hectolitre.

Extraction and equivalent rates are in general averages and vary from year to year.

CEREALS OTHER THAN RICE

Breadgrains. Usually defined as wheat and rye.

Foddergrains or coarse grains. Barley, oats, maize, sorghum and millet.

Corn. The term is often used locally to describe the main cereal crop of the district; eg, in England it may refer to wheat, in Scotland and Ireland to oats; it now means wheat, barley, oats, rye and maize. British corn means any such produce of the UK, Channel Islands or Isle of Man. Throughout the USA, Canada and South America corn specifically refers to maize.

Yield. For wheat, half the crop is grain and half straw; for rye, one-third is grain and two-thirds straw.

UK measures

The agriculture industry in the UK in general uses the metric system.

See Historical UK measures, page 260, for old units.

Measures in other countries

International corn bushel = 27.216 kg = 60 lb

Most countries now use metric measures. The units listed in the following table may be used instead of or as well as metric units in the countries indicated.

Commodity	Unit	Country	kg	lb
Barley	ardab/ardeb	Egypt	120	264.555
		Sudan	144	317.466
	bag/muid	South Africa, Zimbabwe	68.039	150
		Zambia	70	154.32
	bolsa	Uruguay	50	110
	bushel	Australia, New Zealand	22.680	50
		Canada, USA	21.772	48
	fanega	Ecuador	113	249.122
		Spain	33.2	73.194
	hectolitre	Finland, Netherlands, Norway	65	143.3
	kilé/kileh	Turkey	26	57
	koku	Japan	108.75[a]	239.754[a]
			138.75[b]	305.892[b]
	last	Netherlands	1 950	4 299
	suk	South Korea	99[a]	281.258[a]
Corn	bushel	Canada, USA	25.401	56
Maize	ardab/ardeb	Egypt	140	308.647
		Sudan	151	332.898
	bag/muid	South Africa, Zimbabwe	90.718	200
		Zambia	90	198.4
	bushel	Australia, Canada, New Zealand, USA	25.401	56
	fanega	Costa Rica	348.36	768
		Spain	40	88.185
	koku	Japan	131.25	289.358
Millet	ardab/ardeb	Egypt	140	308.647
		South Africa, Zimbabwe	90.718	200
	bushel	Australia	27.216	60
		New Zealand	15.876	35
		USA	22.680	50
Mixed grains	bushel	Canada	20.412	45
Oats	bag/muid	South Africa, Zimbabwe	68.039	150
		Zambia	70[c]	154.32[c]
	bushel	Australia, New Zealand	18.144	40
		Canada	15.422	34
		USA	14.515	32
	fanega	Spain	25	55.116
	hectolitre	Finland, Netherlands	50	110.231
		Norway	51	112.436
	kilé/kileh	Turkey	24	53
	koku	Japan	78.75	173.615
	korn tonde	Denmark	70	154.324
	last	Netherlands	1 500	3 306.9
	suk	South Korea	78	171.961
Rye	ardab/ardeb	Sudan	162	357.149
	bag/muid	South Africa, Zimbabwe	90.718	200
		Zambia	90	198.4
	bushel	Australia	27.216	60
		Canada, New Zealand, USA	25.401	56
	hectolitre	Finland, Norway	72	158.733
		Netherlands	70	154.324
	kilé/kileh	Cyprus	27.216	60
		Turkey	28	62
	koku	Japan	141.5	311.954
	last	Netherlands	2 100	4 629.7
	suk	South Korea	124	273.373
Sorghum	ardab/ardeb	Egypt	140	308.647
		Sudan	146	321.875
	bag/muid	South Africa, Zimbabwe	90.718	200
	bushel	Australia	27.216	60
		USA	25.401	56
Wheat	ardab/ardeb	Egypt	150	330.693
		Sudan	162	357.149
	bag/muid	South Africa, Zimbabwe	90.718	200
		Zambia	90	198.4
	basket	Myanmar	32.659	72

Commodity	Unit	Country	kg	lb
	bolsa	Uruguay	66–71	145–157
	bushel	Generally applicable	27.216	60
	chombol	Lebanon	150	330.693
	fanega	Ecuador	113	249.122
		Morocco	44	97.003
		Spain	43.240	95.328
	hectolitre	Finland	79	174.165
		Morocco, Norway	77	169.756
		Netherlands	75	165.347
	kilá	Egypt	12.5	27.558
	kilé/kileh	Cyprus	26.671	58.8
		Turkey	30	66
	koku	Japan	137.25	302.584
	korn tonde	Denmark	107.5	237
	last	Netherlands	2 250	4 960.4
	modd	Malta	222.260	490
	mudd/med	Lebanon	18–20	40–44
	suk	South Korea	138	304.238

[a]Common. [b]Naked. [c]Uncrushed.

Wheat flour

Conversion factor (general). Wheat is converted to wheat flour at an extraction rate of 72%.

US measure. 1 barrel = 196 lb = 88.904 kg

See Historical UK measures, page 260, for old UK units.

RICE

Harvested rice is known as paddy, rough, raw or unhusked. When the husk is removed it is called brown or cargo rice. Rice which is subsequently put through a milling process is known as milled, cleaned, polished or white rice.

Milled rice is further classified according to the proportion of broken rice, colour, chalkiness, degree of damage, foreign matters and moisture content.

Measures

Many countries still use the traditional measures as listed below. However, most countries use kilograms and metric tonnes for milled rice. An exception is the USA, where hundredweights (cwt) and pounds (lb) are still in use.

Unit	Type of rice	Country	kg	lb
ardab/ardeb	paddy	Egypt	120	264.555
	milled		100	220.462
bag/sack	paddy	Brazil	50	110.2
	paddy	Ghana	76.204	168
	milled		108.862	240
	paddy	Malawi	72.575	160
	milled		90.718	200
	paddy	South Africa	68.039	150
	milled		72.575	160
	paddy	Surinam	70	154.324
	milled		100	220.462
	paddy	Taiwan	118	260.145
	milled		100	220.462
	paddy	Zambia	68	149.914
bandu	paddy	Malaysia/Sabah	24.192	53.333
basket	paddy	Myanmar	20.865	46
	milled		34.019	75
bushel	paddy	Australia	19.051	42
	paddy	Sri Lanka	20.865	46
	milled		29.03	64
	paddy	USA	20.412	45
catty	milled	Taiwan	0.60	1.323
cavan	paddy	Philippines	44	97.003
	milled		56	123.459
chupak	milled	Brunei	0.9	2
dariba	paddy	Egypt	945	2 083.368
gantang	paddy	Brunei, Malaysia	2.42	5.333
	milled		3.629	8
katang	paddy	Cambodia	6	13.228
	milled		7.5	16.535
koku	paddy	Japan	101.25	223.218
	milled		146.25	322.426
kwien	paddy	Thailand	1 010	2 226.667
	milled		1 380	3 042.379
pocket	milled	Swaziland	45.359	100
		Zambia	45	99.208
suk	paddy	South Korea	100	220.462
	milled		144	317.466
tao	paddy	Cambodia	12	26.455
	milled		15	33.069
thang	paddy	Cambodia	24	52.911
	milled		30	66.139

Extraction rates

FAO general	66.7
USA	71.5
Malaysia	65.0

FRUIT AND VEGETABLES

Fruit and vegetables are sold in the retail trade by pack weight, mostly in metric units of kilograms or grams. However, some countries still use imperial pounds or ounces and others use local measures. Some produce is sold by count, ie, numbers of fruit, or by bunch.

See also UK and US measures for variations, pages 18–21; and Historical UK measures, pages 260–261, for old UK units.

UK regulations

Fruit and vegetables are sold by weight, count and bunch, and are subject to weights and measures control. All produce must be marked with the selling price when prepacked and a unit price when loose.

See also Food and drink, pages 91–92.

Prepacked. All fruit and vegetables, except soft fruit and mushrooms, countable and bunched produce, must be sold by net weight and the package marked with an indication of net weight.

Soft fruit and mushrooms may also be sold by gross weight with permitted container weights, and the quantity made known to the buyer by marking the goods, weighing in their presence, stating the weight on a notice or verbally. Countable produce may also be sold by number and the container marked with an indication of the number. Bunched produce may also be sold by the bunch.

Potatoes must be sold by net weight and prepacked in any of the following sizes: 500 g, 1 kg, 1.5 kg, 2 kg, 2.5 kg or multiples of 2.5 kg; 8 oz, 12 oz, 1 lb, 1.5 lb or multiples of 1 lb. They need not be made up in these pack sizes where the net weight of each potato is not less than 175 g and the pack is more than 25 kg.

Not prepacked. All fruit and vegetables must be sold by net weight or gross weight within the permitted container weights.

Countable produce may be sold by number and bunched produce by the bunch.

Measures

The table below lists produce and countries in which metric units are not used, and those in which metric units are used together with other systems.

Commodity	Unit	Country
Apricots	lb	Cyprus, USA
Artichokes, Jerusalem	lb	UK
Asparagus	lb	Ireland, Malaysia, New Zealand, Peru, UK, USA, Zambia, Zimbabwe
Aubergines	lb	Cyprus, Gambia, Jamaica, Jordan
Avocados	lb	Jamaica
Bananas	lb	All countries
Beans	lb	Cyprus, Kenya, Nigeria, UK
Beetroot	lb	UK
Brussels sprouts	lb	Italy, UK
Cabbages	lb	UK
Calabrese	lb	Jersey
Capsicums	lb	Cyprus, UK
Carrots	lb	UK, USA
Cauliflowers	ct[a]	Belgium, France, Italy, Jersey, Netherlands, Spain, UK
Celery	ct	Netherlands, UK
	ct, kg	France, Israel, Italy, Spain, USA
Cherries	carton	New Zealand
	lb	Argentina, Cyprus, Iran, UK, USA
Chinese leaves	ct	UK
	lb	USA
Courgettes	lb	Cyprus, Jamaica, Jersey, UK
Cranberries	punnet, bag, g	USA
Cucumbers	ct	Guernsey, Netherlands, UK
	ct, kg	Spain
	ct, lb	Canaries
Dates	oz	Algeria, Iraq, Tunisia
Figs	ct	Cyprus, France
	6 × 1 lb punnet	Peru
Gooseberries	lb	UK
Grapes	lb	Yugoslavia
	lb, kg	Cyprus
Grapefruit	ct	Israel
	ct, kg	Egypt, USA
Leeks	kg, 10 × 1 kg bunch	Netherlands
	lb	UK
Lemons	ct, kg	USA
Lettuce	ct	All countries[b]
Limes	ct	Israel
	lb	USA
Marrows	ct	UK
Melons	ct	Antigua, Netherlands, Portugal
	ct, kg	Colombia, Kenya
	ct, lb	Cyprus
Mushrooms	lb	Ireland, UK
Nectarines	ct, lb	USA
	kg, punnet	Spain
Onions	lb	France
Oranges	ct	Zimbabwe
	ct, kg	Egypt, Greece, USA
Parsley	4 kg/20 bunches	France
	lb	Jersey, UK
Parsnips	lb	UK
Peaches	basket of 10 kg	Italy
	ct	Turkey
	ct, kg	New Zealand
	ct, lb	USA
	kg, punnet	Spain
Pears	kg, tray	France
	lb	Italy, UK
Peas	lb	UK
Pineapples	ct	Kenya
Plums	lb	Romania, UK, USA
Radishes	15–30 bunches	Netherlands
	oz	USA
Raspberries	oz	UK, USA
Rhubarb	lb	UK
Soft citrus	ct[c]	Israel
	ct, kg	Cyprus, Spain, USA
Spinach	kg, bunch	Cyprus, UK
	lb	UK
Spring onions	bunch	All countries
Strawberries	lb	Peru
	oz	USA
	oz, lb	UK
Swedes	lb	UK
Sweetcorn	ct	France, Spain, Zambia, Zimbabwe
	ct, oz	UK
Tomatoes	lb	Jersey, UK
Turnips	lb	France, UK
Watercress	lb	UK

[a]Count. [b]USA uses kg. [c]Some fruit only.

Old measures in selected countries

The following table shows wholesale measures used in countries other than the UK. Some of these may now be obsolete.

For old UK units see Historical UK measures, pages 260–261.

Fruit	Unit	Country	kg	lb
Apples	box	USA	19.504	43
	bushel	Australia	19.051	42
		Canada	20.412	45
		New Zealand	18.144	40
		USA	21.772	48
	count: 100	Brazil	10	22
Apricots	bushel	Australia	21.772	48
		New Zealand	19.051	42
	lug	USA	10.9–11.3	24–25
Bananas[a]	bunch/stem	Belize, Dominican Rep.	22.680	50
		Brazil	10–12	22–26
		Colombia	25	55
		Costa Rica	36.287	80
		Ecuador	33	72.8
		Fiji	16.329	36
		Guatemala	32.205	71
		Mexico	20	44.1
		Nicaragua	15.876	35
		Panama	36	79.4
		Paraguay, Venezuela	17	37.5
	bushel	Australia	25.401	56
	case	Fiji	32.659	72
	count: 100	Puerto Rico	15	33
Beans, dry	bushel	Canada, USA	27.216	60
	hectolitre	Portugal	76	167.551
	suk	South Korea	144	317.466
Broad beans	ardab/ardeb	Egypt: whole	155	341.716
		split	144	317.466
Cherries	bushel	Australia	21.772	48
		Canada	22.680	50
		New Zealand	19.051	42
	lug	USA	8.2–9.1	18–20
Chickpeas	ardab/ardeb	Egypt	150	330.693
	hectolitre	Portugal	77	169.756
Cranberries	carton	USA	10.886	24
Grapefruit	box	USA	29–38.6	64–85
	bushel/case	Australia	19.051	42
	case	Jamaica	34.019	75
	count: 100	Surinam	50	110.2
		Turkey	25	50.1
Grapes	lug	USA	10–10.4	22–23
Lemons	box	USA	34.473	76
	bushel	Australia	21.772	48
	case	Israel[b]	15–16	33–35
	count: 100	Cyprus	12.5	27.6
Lentils	ardab/ardeb	Egypt: whole	160	352.740
		split	148	326.284
Oranges	box/case	Israel	15–21	33–46
		Jamaica, Trinidad	36.287	80
		USA	34.4–40.8	76–90
	bushel	Australia	21.772	48
	count: 100	Brazil	20	44
Peaches	bushel	Australia	20.412	45
		USA	21.772	48
Pears	bushel	Australia	20.412	45
		Canada	22.680	50
	carton	USA	16.3–21.8	36–48
	count: 100	Brazil	14	30.865
Peas, dry	ardab/ardeb	Egypt	160	352.740
	bushel	Canada, USA	27.216	60
Pineapples	bushel	Australia	19.051	42
	count: 100	Brazil	230	507.1
Plums	bushel	Australia	26.308	58
		New Zealand	19.051	42
	carton/lug	USA	12.7	28
Potatoes	bushel	Canada, USA	27.216	60

[a]Traded in stems, bunches or cases of different size and weight, according to the different varieties grown. [b]Exports.

SUGAR

Measures

The sugar industry uses both metric and imperial measures.

Weight of 1 bag (or sack) of raw sugar

Country	kg	lb
Brazil	132.3	60
Colombia	110.2	50
Cuba: 250 libras[a]	253.6	115.0
325 libras[a]	329.6	149.5
Dominican Republic	250–260	113–118
Philippines	140	63.5

[a]Spanish pound.

Extraction rates

Units of refined sugar per 100 units of raw sugar

FAO	92
Australia	96.5
Canada	93
Jamaica	92.3
Mexico	94.3
USA	93.46

Units of raw sugar per 100 units of sugar beet

France	14.09
UK	14.30

Units of raw sugar per 100 units of sugar cane

Australia	15.30
Jamaica	10.60
Mexico	11.00
Philippines	12.00

Conversion factors

The factor used to convert refined sugar to raw sugar is 1.087 for all countries.

The International Sugar Organization uses the formula (2P – 100)/92, where P is the degree of polarisation as tested by polariscope, to convert sugar to its raw sugar standard (96° polarisation) which is used for all its sugar statistics.

However, it should be emphasised that this is not a technical conversion ratio (which depends on the efficiency of the refinery and many other factors) but simply a theoretical conversion based on the structure of the sugar molecule which the organisation uses in order to be able to express all its statistics in the same units.

COCOA

The word cocoa is an English corruption of "cacao". There are very approximately 400 cocoa beans to the pound, or 900 per kilo.

Measures

The unit most generally used is the bag or sack of 60 kg (132.277 lb). Other measures used nationally include the following.

Country	Measure	Weight (kg)
Brazil	arroba	15
Ghana, Nigeria	bag	62.5
Cameroon, Ivory Coast	sac	65
Ghana	load	30

Conversion factors

1 tonne of beans = 800 kg of cocoa liquor or paste
= 400 kg of cocoa butter
= 400 kg of cocoa cake and powder

The 1986 International Cocoa Agreement gives the following factors for the bean equivalent of cocoa products (ie, products made exclusively from cocoa beans such as cocoa paste/liquor, cocoa butter, unsweetened cocoa powder, cocoa cake and cocoa nibs).

Cocoa butter = 1.33
Cocoa cake and powder = 1.18
Cocoa paste/liquor and nibs = 1.25

COFFEE

The two types of coffee generally consumed are arabica and robusta; of which arabica is widely regarded as the superior.

Measures

Most official statistics refer to green (ie, unroasted) coffee, and the most commonly used unit is a bag of 60 kg (132.277 lb). In some Latin American countries a bag of 69 kg is used.

1 metric quintal = 1.67 bags (of 60 kg)
1 tonne = 16.67 bags (of 60 kg)

Processing

Primary processing. There are two ways of converting the fresh fruit (known as cherry) to green bean. Dry processing, which gives a "hard" or "unwashed" green bean, begins with sun-drying the cherry, followed by decortication, polishing and grading. Wet processing, which gives a "washed", "soft" or "mild" coffee, begins with soaking the cherry in water to remove the pulp and drying the resulting "parchment" (a white parchment-like integument enclosing a pair of beans) followed by decortication, polishing and grading.

Secondary processing. The bulk of green coffee is simply roast and ground; some is then converted to soluble coffee before final consumption, by spray or freeze drying.

Conversion factors

The following conversion factors are those used by the International Coffee Organisation (ICO), the intergovernmental body which administers the International Coffee Agreement and which monitors international trade in coffee. In practice, ratios vary.

1 tonne of fresh cherry = 333 kg of dry cherry
= 420 kg of parchment
= 166 kg of green bean
1 tonne of dry cherry = 500 kg of green bean
1 tonne of parchment = 800 kg of green bean
1 tonne of green bean = 840 kg of roast coffee
= 385 kg of soluble coffee

TEA

Tea is made from the plant *Camellia sinensis*. There are two main types of tea, produced from the same plant: green tea is unfermented, while black tea undergoes full fermentation. There are other types, including oolong tea, which is partially fermented.

Measures

Metric measures are used internationally, although imperial units (pounds) may be used locally. The following table lists some special measures by country.

Country	Unit	kg	Country	Unit	kg
Bangladesh	package	47.2	Japan	kin	0.6
China	chest	35–58	Kenya	chest	55–56
India	chest	45–58	Malawi	sack	56–60
Indonesia	chest	55	Sri Lanka	sack	48–55

There is an additional measure, the break. This is a specified number of chests or sacks from one estate. The average break is 40–60 sacks or chests, on a pallet.

Herbal teas are made from other plants and herbs, such as camomile, peppermint, rose hip.

OILSEEDS AND OILS

Measures

Commodity	Unit	Country	kg	lb
Coconuts	number	–	–	–
Copra	candy	Sri Lanka	254.012	560
Cottonseed	ardab/ardeb	Egypt	120	264.555
	bushel[a]	USA	14.515	32
Groundnuts[b]	ardab/ardeb	Egypt	75	165.35
Virginia	bushel	USA	7.711	17
Runners			9.525	21
Spanish			11.340	25
Linseed	ardab/ardeb	Egypt	122	268.964
	bushel	Australia, Canada, USA	25.401	56
Rapeseed	bushel	USA	22.7/27.2	50/60
	koku	Japan	120	264.555
Sesame seed	ardab/ardeb	Egypt	120	264.555
	bushel	Sri Lanka	22.680	50
		USA	20.865	46
	koku	Japan	114	251.327
Soyabeans	bushel	Canada, USA	27.216	60
	koku	Japan	129	284.396
	suk	South Korea	135	297.624

[a]Average. [b]Unshelled.

Conversion factors

Coconuts. Numbers of coconuts are converted to weight on the average basis of 1 000 nuts = 1 tonne (unless official conversion factors are available).

Groundnuts. Nuts-in-the-shell are converted to shelled equivalent using a conversion factor of 70%.

Oils: volume to weight

Average US rates

	1 litre weighs kg[a]	lb	1 US gallon weighs kg	lb
Castor oil	0.96	2.1	3.6	8.0
Cottonseed oil	0.92	2.0	3.5	7.7
Groundseed oil	0.92	2.0	3.5	7.7
Linseed oil	0.92	2.0	3.5	7.7
Olive oil	0.91	2.0	3.5	7.6
Palm oil	0.92	2.0	3.5	7.7
Soyabean oil	0.92	2.0	3.5	7.7

[a]Figures are approximately the same as relative density.

Oils: extraction rates

Extraction rates for oilseeds can vary greatly; the percentage rates given in the table below are average.

Average oil equivalent of 100 units of oilseed

Castor seed	45	Linseed	33	Rapeseed	38
Copra	62	Mustard seed	23	Safflower seed	30
Cottonseed	15	Niger seed	35	Sesame seed	43
Groundnuts:		Oiticica seed	45	Soyabeans	18
shelled	40	Olives	15	Sunflower seed	40
unshelled	28	Palm kernels	44	Tung nuts	16
Hempseed	24	Perilla seed	37	Others	30
Kapok seed	18	Poppy seed	41		

EGGS

EC egg grades

The following grades apply to Class A quality eggs.

Grade	g	Grade	g
0	75	4	55–60
1	70	5	50–55
2	65–70	6	45–50
3	60–75	7	under 45

Measures

Measures for eggs-in-the-shell are by number or by weight, and sometimes both. Appropriate conversion factors may be used to convert numbers into weight.

UK
1 great or long hundred = 120 eggs
1 case or box = 360 eggs

Conversion factors. Of a 60 g egg, about 8 g is shell, 15 g is yolk, 37 g is white.

100 units of shell eggs make 80 units of frozen eggs
100 units of shell eggs make 24 units of dried eggs

USA
1 case = 360 eggs = 47 lb
1 average egg = 59 g
100 units of eggs make 26 units of dried whole eggs

FAO numbers and weights

	Eggs per tonne	Grams per egg		Eggs per tonne	Grams per egg
Africa			**Asia**		
Ethiopia	25 000	40	Cyprus, Israel	17 600	57
Kenya, Malawi,			Turkey	18 800	53
South Africa,			Other	20 000	50
Zambia,			**Europe, Western**		
Zimbabwe	17 600	57	Denmark	16 667	60
Other	20 000	50	Other	17 600	57
America, N.			**Europe, Eastern**		
Greenland	16 667	60	Bulgaria	17 840	56
Other	17 600	57	Former Soviet		
America, S.	17 600	57	Union, Other	18 000	55
			Oceania	17 600	57

MILK AND MILK PRODUCTS

Milk measures

UK
1 litre = 2.27 lb = 1.03 kg
1 gallon = 10.32 lb = 4.68 kg
1 million gallons = 4 600 tons = 4 681 tonnes

USA
1 US gallon = 8.6 lb = 3.9 kg

The weight of a litre or gallon of milk varies according to the density, which is determined by the fat content. For the UK, 1 litre of milk with butterfat content of 3.7% weighs 1.029 7 kg, 1.029 7 being the density. The base butterfat level of milk in the UK is 3.98%. The UN uses a relative density of 1.031 for milk.

See Historical UK measures, page 261, for old units.

Conversion rates

UK

	England, Wales	Scotland	Northern Ireland
Litres of milk for 1 tonne of product[a]			
Milk	971	971	971
Condensed milk: full cream	2 289	2 595	. . .
skimmed	4 215	. . .	. . .
Milk powder: full cream	8 054	8 054	8 054
skimmed	10 680	10 800	10 772
whey	16 644	16 644	16 644
Cream[a]			
with fat content of: 12%		2 983	
18%		4 481	
23%		5 787	
35%		8 815	
48%		12 215	
55%		13 998	
Butter			
Summer	21 279	21 950	22 170
Winter			21 395
Cheese			
Cheddar	9 825	10 000	10 181
Litres of skimmed milk			
Casein			
Edible	36 690	36 690	36 690
Industrial: May–Nov	36 690	36 690	36 690
Dec–Apr	39 820	39 820	39 820

[a]Assumes milk of 3.9% fat content.

USA. Units of milk (average) required for 1 unit of each product are as follows.

Butter	21.7	Cream, sweetened	10.8
Cheese, cheddar	8.7	Dry milk, whole	7.2
Condensed milk, whole	2.3	Evaporated milk, whole	2.1

MEAT

Measures

UK and US meat producers, such as farmers and abattoirs, use metric measures. Retailers, however, particularly in the UK, largely use the imperial system although the food industry is scheduled to become completely metric by the end of 1994.

See also Food and drink, page 91, and pages 260–261 for old units.

Live weight. Weight of animal on the hoof.

Carcass, dead or slaughter weight. Weight of carcass when killed, ie, live weight less the weight of hide, feet, head, blood, offal, etc.

Livestock units

Livestock are sometimes computed in terms of livestock units, the average live or carcass weight of animals.

Average relationships for live weight as used by the FAO are shown in the following table.

From 1 unit of: / To:	Camels	Buffalo, horses, mules	Cattle, asses	Pigs	Sheep, goats
Camels	1.0	1.1	1.4	5.5	11
Buffalo, horses, mules	0.9	1.0	1.25	5.0	10
Cattle, asses	0.7	0.8	1.0	4.0	8
Pigs	0.2	0.2	0.25	1.0	2
Sheep, goats	0.1	0.1	0.125	0.5	1

Live weight to carcass weight

The following table shows the approximate units of carcass weight per 100 units of live weight.

	Beef, veal	Pork	Mutton, lamb	Horse meat	Poultry
Africa	52	70	50	52	70
America, North	57	60	50	51	89
America, South	55	67	48	64	75
Asia: Middle East	48	74	49	. . .	70
Other	50	58	57	48	75
Europe	53	73	48	51	72
Oceania	55	70	49	50	75
World average	55	66	51	51	82

NATURAL FIBRES: FROM ANIMALS

Alpaca

The staple length is 150–300 mm (6–12 inches) and the quality is finer than llama.

Angora

The hairs from the Angora rabbit can be up to 130 mm (5 inches) long, averaging about 60 mm (2.5 inches) and one rabbit will yield about 0.25–1 kg (0.5–2 lb) of hair a year.

Camel

The undercoat hairs are 25–130 mm (1–5 inches) long; the coarse overcoat is 130–300 mm (5–12 inches) long; a camel yields about 2–4.5 kg (5–10 lb) of hair a year.

Cashmere

The undercoat hairs from the Cashmere goat are 38–90 mm (1.5–3.5 inches) in length and very soft; the outercoat is 50–130 mm (2–5 inches) and is much coarser. Each animal yields about 100 g (4 oz) of fibre a year.

Hides and skins

Hides and skins are produced dry, wet-salted or washed.

Measures

The industry in the EC member countries uses the metric system. The rest of the world uses imperial measures and some countries still use local measures. The table shows the conversion factors for the pesada, still used in Argentina.

	libra[a]	kg	lb
1 pesada of:			
dry hides	35	16.1	35.45
salted hides	60	27.6	60.77
washed sheepskins	30	13.8	30.38

[a]Spanish pound.

Average weight per piece (wet-salted)

	kg	lb
Cattle hides[a]	12–25	26–55
Calfskins	5	11
Sheepskins	2	4
Goatskins	1.75	3.86

[a]Varies according to country of origin.

See Historical UK units, page 261, for old units.

Llama

The staple length is 250–300 mm (10–12 inches); hair is coarse.

Mohair

Mohair comes from the Angora goat. The staple length is 100–250 mm (4–10 inches); the Bradford quality grouping is 28s to 50s. Clean yield is about 80% greasy weight.

Silk

The silk worm produces a continuous filament of two threads stuck together, which is woven into a cocoon. There may be up to 4 000 metres of silk in a cocoon, but only about 600–900 metres can be reeled off into the continuous filament known as "nett silk". The tough outer husk and the soft inner portions can be combed and spun into "spun silk", consisting of fibres.

Conversion factors
Raw silk equivalent = 25% of actual weight of cocoons
Reeled silk = 17% of actual weight of cocoons

Wool

Greasy. Raw wool shorn from the sheep's back; 25% up to a maximum of 70% can consist of dirt and other impurities. Average weight of fleece per sheep is 4.5–5.5 kg.

Back or rough washed wool. Wool which has been washed on the sheep before clipping; it has a clean wool content of about 80%.

Scoured. Wool that has been clipped and then washed, and has a clean wool content of around 95%. Weight of scoured wool is roughly 60% of weight of greasy wool.

Slipe, pulled or skin wool. Wool from dead sheep skins which have been rough washed; the clean wool content is about 80%

Actual weight. Used in trade returns and includes all forms (greasy, scoured, backwashed and pulled) with no regard to the clean content.

Clean content. A statistical term representing the weight of the wool if it could be completely clean and free from moisture. Average world conversion factor from greasy to clean basis is 0.60.

Measures

The metric system is used in the wool trade. The following table shows bale sizes in various countries.

Country	Type of wool	Bale size (kg)
Argentina	average	420
Australia	greasy	175
New Zealand	greasy	163
South Africa	scoured	140
	greasy	143
UK	greasy	230

See Historical UK measures, page 261, for old UK units.

Quality. The term is used in a very special sense in the wool trade. It embraces such properties as fineness, length, crimp, colour, handle, uniformity, style, etc, in other words, the sum total of the fibre's physical characteristics. In one context "quality" implies "fitness for purpose", in another it implies a statement of the type and origin of the raw wool.

At the beginning of this century "quality" in the UK was related to the yarn counts to which the wool would spin. For example, 64s quality meant that the wool would spin to 64s worsted count, that is 64 × 560 yards of yarn per pound of fibre. This definition no longer applies; there are few, if any, 64s wools capable of spinning to 64s yarn count under modern processing conditions. The reasons are as follows.

- The interpretation of wool quality has deteriorated over the years.
- The invention of short process drawing and high draft spinning on to large packages has necessitated the use of thicker yarn counts.
- The multiplicity of spinning machines available; eg, a top that will spin to 32s worsted count on a large package ring frame might well spin commercially to 48s count on a small package cap frame.
- A 64s wool with an average micron diameter of 22.5 and a mean fibre length of 65 mm will spin to finer counts than a wool of similar diameter but with a mean fibre length of 50 mm.

Thus the word "quality" in the wool trade has a rather vague connotation. There is no agreed uniformity between individual firms in the same geographical area. Despite intense competition one manufacturer will always claim that its 60s quality is as good as another's 64s.

There are three main quality groups for wool generally used, the top two being for apparel; the following division is based on Bradford quality counts.

Wool	Microns	Yarn count
Merino	23 and finer	60s and up
Crossbred	36–25	46s–58s
Carpet	38 and coarser	Up to 44s

Bradford quality groups are based on the fineness of wool; the 100s level was originally determined as the level for the finest wool that could be spun. The table below shows some approximate relationships for different types of wool classification. There used to be no general international standard classification, but in recent years fibre diameter measurement in terms of microns (micrometres) has been used to an increasing extent and is now almost universally accepted. The comparisons below, supplied by the Commonwealth Secretariat, show micron groupings alongside the principal quality group systems they have now largely replaced.

See also Textiles, page 144.

Quality classification of wool

Fibre diameter in micrometres (microns)	UK Bradford quality groups	USA Boston quality groups	France	Germany	Argentina
Merino					
19–21	70–64s	64s	105	AA–A	Fine supra
21	64s	64–60s	Prime merino	A	Merina
21–23	64–60s	60s	Prime croisée	A–B	Merina prima
23	60s	60–58s	Prime croisée I	B	Prima
Crossbred					
Fine					
23–25	60–58s	58s fine	Croisée I	B–CI	Prima–Cruza I
25	58s fine	58–56s	Croisée I–II	CI	Cruza (fina) I
25–28	58–56s	56s	Croisée II	CI–CII	Cruza (fina) I–II
28	56s fine	56–50s	Croisée II–III	CII	Cruza (fina) II
Medium					
28–31	56–52s	50s fine	Croisée III	CII–DI	Cruza (mediana) II–III
31	52s	50–48s	Croisée III–IV	DI	Cruza (mediana) III
33–34	50–48s	48–46s	Croisée IV	DI–DII	Cruza (mediana) III–IV
Coarse					
33–34	50–48s	48–46s	Croisée IV–V	DII	Cruza (gruesa) IV
34–36	48–46s	46–44s	Croisée V	DII–E	Cruza (gruesa) V
36	46s	44s	Croisée V–VI	E	Cruza (gruesa) VI

Clean yields of wool. The figures in the following table are average estimates made by the Commonwealth Secretariat of the clean yield conversion factors for the chief types of wool entering international trade.

Country of origin	Overall clip 1989–90	Exports 1989–90
Australasia		
Australia		
Greasy shorn	66	67½
Scoured/carbonised	93	93
Slipe/pulled skin	80	80
New Zealand		
Greasy shorn	75	77
Scoured/carbonised	95	95
Slipe/pulled skin	81	81
South Africa		
Greasy shorn	59½	61½
Lesotho & Transkei, greasy shorn	41½	43
Karakul, greasy shorn	64½	66
Scoured/carbonised	92	92
South America		
Argentina		
Greasy shorn	60	61
Scoured/carbonised	95	95
Slipe/pulled skin	80	80
Chile		
Greasy shorn	58	60
Uruguay		
Greasy shorn	68	69
Scoured/carbonised	98	98
UK		
Greasy shorn	67	68
Fleece (washed)	77	77
Slipe/pulled skin	80	80
Scoured/carbonised	95	95

NATURAL FIBRES: FROM PLANTS

Coir

The source of the fibre is coconut husks; it is removed after allowing the fruit to "ret" (ie, to soak until the fibre becomes free). 1 000 coconuts provide about 130 kg (290 lb) of mattress fibre and 136 kg (300 lb) of better quality bristle fibre.

Cotton

Unginned, raw or seed cotton comes straight from the plant. After it has been processed the seeds are separated from the lint (seed hairs) by a gin, and the fibre which is produced is called ginned cotton or cotton lint.

In addition to cotton lint, the cotton plant produces cotton linters, which are short white lengths of fuzz of almost pure cellulose. This clings to the cotton seed and is extracted and used separately from the cotton lint.

To convert unginned cotton to ginned or lint the overall conversion factor generally used is one-third. An average conversion in the USA is 1 lb ginned = 3.26 lb unginned, including trash; the rate varies widely.

Staple length of cotton is usually about $\frac{5}{8}$–2 in (approximately 15–50 mm) and can be classified according to the length of the filaments as:

	in	mm
Short staple	Under $\frac{7}{8}$	Under 22.2
Medium staple	$\frac{7}{8}$–$1\frac{1}{8}$	22.2–28.6
Long staple	$1\frac{1}{8}$–$1\frac{5}{16}$	28.6–33.3
Extra-long staple	Over $1\frac{5}{16}$	Over 33.3

Longer staple types produce the finest cottons. Sea Island cotton has a staple length over 2 in (50 mm).

Cotton fibre has a diameter of about 10–20 micrometres (microns), and a relative density of about 1.5. Cellulose content is 88–96%.

Measures

In general the imperial system is still used in the cotton trade. A running bale is an actual bale, ie, a bale of any weight. A standard bale is 500 lb gross (226.8 kg) or 478 lb net (216.8 kg).

Country	Unit	lb	kg
USA	bale (gross[a])	500	226.796
	bale (net)	480	217.724
Bangladesh,	bale,	392	177.808
India, Pakistan	candy	784	355.616
Brazil	bale	396.8	180
Egypt	bale	730	331.122
Venezuela	paca (bale)	110–441	50–200

[a]Including sack.

Flax

After harvesting, flax is retted to remove the fibre from the stalks and the resultant straw is then dried and scutched (beaten to remove bark, etc, from fibres). The yield of scutched flax is 5–15% of straw weight or 2–5% of green weight; short broken fibres are referred to as tow. Flaxseed ("linseed") is the source of linseed oil; other flax varieties are used for linen fibre.

UK bale = 203.209 kg = 448 lb

Hemp

The term hemp describes fibres obtained from the hemp plant (*Cannabis sativa L.*). Hemp-type fibres may be divided into soft and hard.

Soft: examples are true hemp (see above) and sunn (or Indian hemp).

Hard: examples are sisal, manila (or abaca), henequen, Mauritius hemp, phormium (or New Zealand flax or hemp) and maguey.

Measures

Country	Unit	kg	lb
Mexico	paca (bale)[a] of henequen	184	405.7
New Zealand	bale of phormium	181.437	400
Philippines	bale of manila	126	278
UK	stone	14.515	32

[a] Average.

Jute

After harvesting, the fibre is removed from the stalk by retting; dry fibre yield from green weight of plant is 5–7%.

Measures

Country	unit	kg	lb
Bangladesh	bale	181.437	400
Brazil	bale	200	440.9
India	bale	180	396.8

Kenaf (mesta)

This fibre is similar to jute but of lower quality. Finest qualities of kenaf are equivalent to medium quality jute, while average qualities are used in a mixture with jute.

Marine rope

Trawl warps. Standard coil lengths are: 200 m, 400 m, 600 m, 800 m.

Trawl marks are at 50 m and 20 m for inshore fishing.

RUBBER

Almost all natural rubber (in chemical terms, natural cis-polyisoprene) begins with raw latex tapped from the bark of the rubber tree, *Hevea Brasiliensis*. Unless it is to be sold as liquid latex, this is then processed into solid natural rubber. Coagulation (usually with formic acid) is followed by rolling into sheets or comminution, then by drying and baling.

For latex to be sold as such, the raw latex is concentrated (typically to a dry rubber content of 60%) in a centrifuge before the addition of preservatives.

See also Chemicals, industrial, page 45.

Measures

Solid rubber is sold in "bareback" bales (wrapped in sheets of rubber) of 34 kg (75 lb), or in smaller bales wrapped in plastic sheeting, and in a variety of grades.

For the traditional "Green Book" grades, of which No. 1 Ribbed Smoked Sheet (RSS 1) is the best known, rubber is graded mainly by physical appearance. Performance criteria are used for the technically specified grades of natural rubber.

TOBACCO

There are five main types of tobacco produced for commercial use: Burley (air-cured); other light air-cured; oriental; dark leaf (which can be air-, sun-, or fire-cured).

The green weight basis (or farm sales weight or wet weight) represents the weight at which tobacco is sold by the grower after curing, and is about 20% of the weight before curing.

On purchase from the grower the tobacco is dried and consequently, for flue-cured tobacco, the dry weight of leaf is about 90% of the green weight. After curing and drying (and usually a certain amount of stemming and stripping) the tobacco may be stored in this condition for several years. Flue-cured tobacco loses about 11.3%, and air-cured about 13.6%, of sales weight.

Before the tobacco undergoes final manufacture it has to be thoroughly stemmed or stripped (having the mid-rib of the leaf removed). The dry weight after stemming forms 70–80% of the dry weight of the unstemmed leaf.

1 000 average sized cigarettes contain aproximately 1 kg (2.205 lb) of tobacco; 100 contain 100 g (3.5 oz). 1 000 cigarillos or cigars contain approximately 1.1–8.4 kg (2.5–18.6 lb) of tobacco depending on size. An average rate for 1 000 cigars is 4.5 kg (10 lb).

Measures

Hogshead. A wooden barrel taking a number of different sizes, used to transport, store and age tobacco, particularly Virginia, Kentucky, Maryland and Burley. The practice, which originated in the USA, was extended to cover Virginia and Burley varieties from all over the world. However, hogsheads are now being increasingly replaced by corrugated cartons or containers weighing 200 kg or bales weighing 100 kg. This is especially true where overseas shipment is concerned because of the bulk involved and because of containerisation and the mechanisation of warehouses and ports; certain countries with trade restrictions still require them, however. Hogsheads are preferred for transport in the USA because they can hold larger amounts of tobacco and therefore make handling easier.

The following table shows packaging units used for leaf tobacco in various countries.

Tobacco	Packaging	Weight (kg)
Brazil: Bahia	jute bales	70–80
flue-cured	jute bales	100
	cardboard cartons	200
Bulgaria	jute bales	18–30
China	hogsheads/bales	220, 225, 250
Colombia	serones/jute	65
Cuba: Havana	flax serones, banana leaves	50–100
Dominican Republic	rush mats	72–75
Germany	jute	100–150
Greece	jute bales	28–30, 100
	tonga bales	18–30
Hungary	jute bales	100–180
India	jute bales	100
	cardboard cartons	200
Indonesia: Sumatra	rush mats	75
Vorstenlanden	rush mats	80
other	rush mats	90–100

Tobacco	Packaging	Weight (kg)
Italy: Burley, flue-cured	hogsheads, cardboard cartons	200
oriental	bales	20
Mexico	serones	80–100
Netherlands	jute	100
Paraguay	jute bales	100
Philippines: flue-cured,		
Burley	cardboard cartons	200
cigar tobacco	jute bales	115
Turkey	jute bales (tonga)	52–55
USA: Seedleaf	boxes	150–200
Maryland	hogsheads	270–360
Burley	hogsheads	400–450
	cardboard cartons	200–250
Virginia	hogsheads	400–500
	cardboard cartons	200–250
Kentucky	hogsheads	600–800
Yugoslavia	jute bales	20–100

FISHING

The main fishing terms used by the FAO are as follows.

Gross removal (total live weight of fish caught or killed) less pre-catch losses (including losses through gear lost)
= gross catch (total live weight of fish caught) less discarded catch (undersized or undesirable fish discarded)
= retained catch (total live weight of fish retained) less net utilisation and other (consumption by crew, bait, dumped, etc)
= nominal catch (live weight equivalent of landings) less losses due to dressing, etc (dumped heads, etc)
= landings (net weight of gutted, filleted, etc fish products as landed).

Catch usually means nominal catch; the term catch is more suitable for use in the case of whales and seals, where original data are in terms of numbers. The term production is more suitable than nominal catch for primary production of seaweeds, guano, seabirds' eggs, pearls, shells, sponges, etc.

Measures

Pelagic, ie, herring and mackerel. The metric system is used for these species. 1 box = 25 kg; 100 kg = 1 unit; 10 units = 1 tonne. Boxes of 40 kg are also sold.

Demersal, ie, white fish, etc. The imperial system is used for these species. Average box = 7 stones. Smaller sizes of 0.5, 1 and 2 stones are sometimes used.

The larger fish processers may buy in metric containers.

Shellfish. In general the metric system is used but some imperial and local measures are used in certain ports. For example, shrimps may be sold by the gallon and cockles by the peck (see below) or bushel. 1 bag of cockles or mussels in shell = 8 stones (51 kg).

Old UK measures. Some of these measures are still used in certain ports.

Barrel. For Scottish herring (discontinued 1963) = 121 l. 1 barrel contained 700–1 100 Scotch cured herring and weighed about 320 lb (145 kg). For whale oil = 375 lb (170 kg). 1 continental barrel = 100 kg.
Basket. Contents of a basket of herring = approx. 44 kg. Formerly 1 basket = $\frac{1}{4}$ cran (42.6 l).
Box. A box of kippers contained 24 average pairs and weighed about 14 lb (6.33 kg). For herring 1 box = $\frac{1}{4}$ or $\frac{1}{6}$ cran.
Bushel. For sprats = 56 lb (25.5 kg).
Cran. Before 1975 herring not sold by weight were sold by the cran, a measure of volume; unlawful for trade since 1980.
1 cran = 37.5 gal (170.5 l). Contents varied according to season and ground, in the range 700–2 500 fish weighing 25–30 stones (160–190 kg).
Draft. For eels = 21 lb (9.5 kg).
Kit. 63.5 kg. Formerly 1 kit = 10 stones; 16 kits = 1 UK ton.
Last. 100 long hundreds.
Long hundred. 132 fresh herrings or 120 mackerel.
Margarine. 66 lb (30 kg) fresh herrings or 14 lb (6.33 kg) kippers.
Peck. For shrimps = 10–14 lb (4.5–6.33 kg).
Tub. 3 pecks or 6 gal (27 l).
Warp. 4 herrings or mackerel.
Wash. 4 gal (18 l) of oysters.

Densities and stowage rates

The following are average rates.

	Density		Stowage rate	
	kg/m^3	lb/ft^3	m^3/tonne	ft^3/ton
Whole fresh herring in bulk	930	58.2	38.5	1.1
Whole fresh mackerel in bulk	800	50.0	45	1.3
Whole fresh sprats in bulk	850	53.2	42	1.2
Whole fresh capelin in bulk	1 000	62.5	36	1.0
Whole fresh cod in bulk, gutted	920	57.5	39	1.1
Crushed block ice	640	40	56	1.6

Conversions

The UN uses a multiplying factor of 0.66 to convert quantities from a wet salted to a dried salted basis.

The FAO uses a wide range of conversion factors for converting between landings (of fish in various stages) and nominal catch (live weight of the fish). Examples of conversion factors are as follows.

Atlantic cod (fresh, chilled, iced)

Multiplying factors to convert from landings to live weight equivalent

Gutted, tail on	Head on	Head off	Fillets, skin on	
Belgium	1.18	1.64	Poland (Baltic Sea)	2.56
Canada	1.20	1.38		
Denmark	1.18	1.60		
England & Wales	1.20	1.50		
Greenland	1.22	1.52		
Poland (Baltic Sea)	1.17	1.68		

The table below shows multiplying factors for converting from landed weight of whole fish to weight of fish product. Whole fish are taken as landed gutted with heads on, except for the ollowing which are normally landed whole ungutted: herring, prat, mackerel, pilchard, redfish, salmon and dogfish.

roduct	Multiplying factor	Product	Multiplying factor
Vet fillets with skin		**Smoked fish**	
od	0.47	Kipper	0.65–0.70
laddock: large	0.47	Red herring	0.60–0.80
lake	0.55		
laice	0.52	**Edible portion in general**	
edfish	0.35	Salmon	0.64
Vhite fish in general	0.47	Sea trout	0.63
lerring in general	0.53	Brown trout	0.68
		Lobster	0.44
Vet steaks		Norway lobster	0.20–0.27
almon	0.60–0.65	Prawn	0.40
lalibut	0.70–0.75	Oyster	0.11–0.17
		Mussel	0.08–0.20

lassification

A 3-alpha identifier system is used by the FAO for identifying ish; some main codes are as follows.

LK Alaska Pollack
OD Atlantic cod
AD Haddock
ER Atlantic
AP Japanese pilchard (sardine)
EM Lemon sole
AC Atlantic mackerel
NEP Norway lobster (nephrops)
PIL European pilchard (sardine)
PLE European plaice
POK Saithe (pollock)
RED Atlantic redfishes
SCA Sea scallop
MUS Blue mussel
SKJ Skipjack tuna
SPR Sprat

Major fishing areas for statistical purposes

The chart outlines the main fishing areas as used by the FAO; the key to the numbers in the chart is as follows.

Inland waters
01 Africa
02 America, North and Central
03 America, South
04 Asia
05 Europe
06 Oceania
07 Former Soviet Union
08 Antarctica

Marine areas

Atlantic ocean and adjacent seas
18 Arctic sea
21 Atlantic, North-West
27 Atlantic, North-East
31 Atlantic, Western Central
34 Atlantic, Eastern Central
37 Mediterranean and Black Sea
41 Atlantic, South-West
47 Atlantic, South-East
48 Atlantic, Antarctic

Indian ocean and adjacent seas
51 Indian ocean, Western
57 Indian ocean, Eastern
58 Indian ocean, Antarctic

Pacific ocean and adjacent seas
61 Pacific, North-West
67 Pacific, North-East
71 Pacific, Western Central
77 Pacific, Eastern Central
81 Pacific, South-West
87 Pacific, South-East
88 Pacific, Antarctic

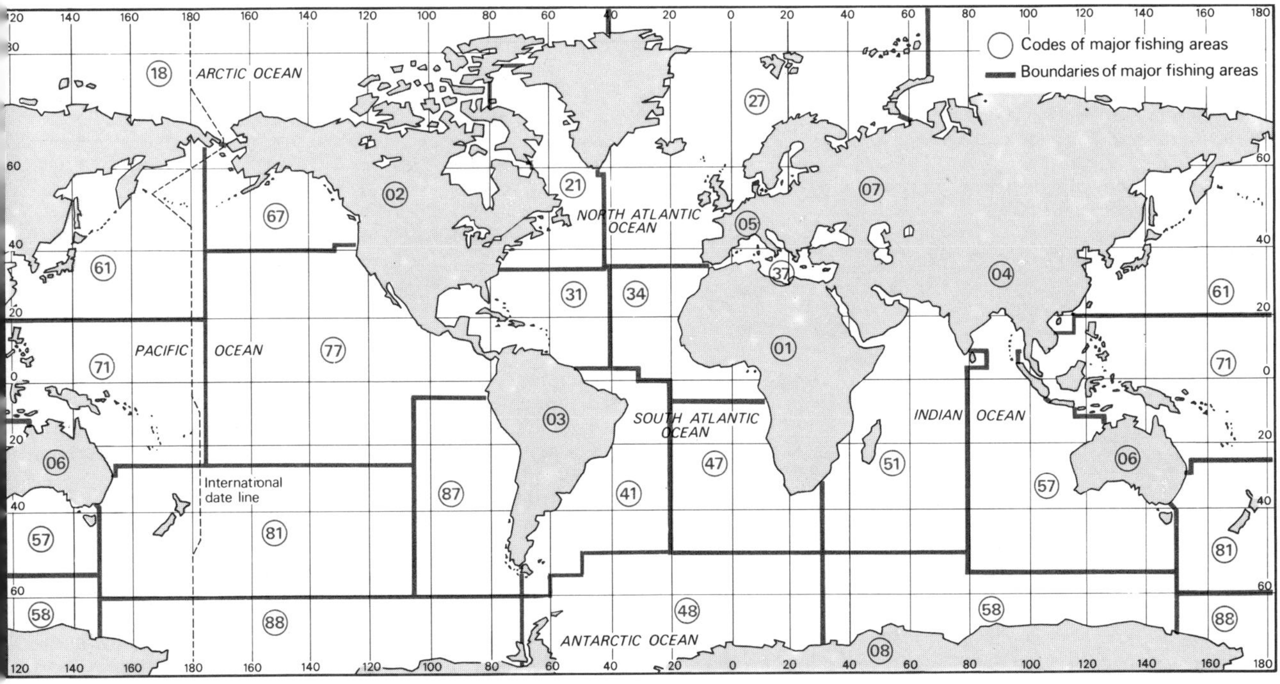

FORESTRY

Definitions

Coniferous (softwoods). All woods derived from trees classified botanically as gymnosperms; eg pine, spruce, larch, etc. The term softwood is used in some countries to include woods which are physically soft, even though some of them may be taken from broadleaved trees.

Non-coniferous (hardwoods). All woods derived from trees classified botanically as angiosperms; eg oak, beech, maple, ebony. Most of this group are physically hard. This category also includes broadleaved species such as the poplar which are physically soft and in some countries are grouped as softwoods.

Measures

Although many countries now use metric units, the units listed below are still used extensively, eg in the USA (board feet) and India (hoppus feet). Piled measures are stacked wood, with air between different pieces of wood. Board foot, foot board measure (fbm), board measure, or super foot = a unit of lumber measuring 1 foot long, 1 foot wide and 1 inch thick or its equivalent = $\frac{1}{12}$ cubic foot.

Cunit = 100 cubic feet = 283.16 cubic metres
Cord = 128 piled cubic feet = 8 cord feet = 3.625 piled cubic metres
Fathom = 216 piled cubic feet = 6.116 piled cubic metres
Hoppus foot = cylinder 1 foot long, with circumference (girth) of 4 feet (quarter-girth of 1 foot)
Load = 40 cubic feet of roundwood
= 50 cubic feet of sawnwood (= 1 ton of 50 cubic feet)
Stack = 180 cubic feet of roundwood
Standard: St Petersburg (Petrograd) = 165 piled cubic feet
Göteborg = 180 piled cubic feet
English = 270 piled cubic feet
Stère (st) = Raummeter (Rm) = Festmeter (Fm) = wisse = 1 piled cubic metre = 35.315 piled cubic feet

See detailed conversions below, and between hoppus feet and cubic metres on page 194.

Volume conversions

Solid volume

From / To	Cubic metres	Cubic feet	Hoppus feet	1 000 board feet	Standards (Petrograd)
	multiply by				
Cubic metres	1	35.3	27.7	0.424	0.214
Cubic feet	0.028	1	0.785	0.012	0.006
Hoppus feet	0.036	1.273	1	0.015	0.008
1 000 board feet	2.36	83.3	65.4	1	0.505
Standards (Petrograd)	4.67	165	129.6	1.98	1
Loads: roundwood	1.13	40	31.4	0.48	0.242
sawnwood	1.42	50	39.27	0.6	0.303
Cords	3.62	128	100.53	1.54	0.776
Fathoms	6.12	216	169.65	2.59	1.309

For conversion from piled to true solid volume also apply the percentages indicated below in the range 65–75%; eg, a fathom of pitprops, converting from piled to solid volume without bark, is, in terms of hoppus feet, 70% of 169.65 = 119 hoppus feet (in practice usually taken as 120 hoppus feet).

Recovery (saleable timber). For sawmilling the usable product can be as high as 60% of underbark volume for coniferous, and 75% for broadleaved. For the pulp and board industries it is virtually 100%. Conversion of the product to roundwood equivalent underbark is therefore obtained by multiplying by 1.67, 1.33 and 1.00 respectively for sawn softwood, sawn hardwood and pulp or board. Bark constitutes on average 12.5%, so conversion to overbark volume requires a further multiplier of 1.14.

Conversion from piled volume overbark to solid volume underbark is usually in the range 1.33–1.43, except broadleaved, which is about 1.55 because of irregularity.

Densities

The average weight at shipment of different types of wood given below are those used by the FAO.

		lb/ft³	kg/m³	Relative density tonnes/m³	m³/tonne
Saw logs:	coniferous	44	700	0.70	1.43
	broadleaved	46–50	730–800	0.73–0.80	1.25–1.37
Pulpwood:	coniferous	41	650	0.65	1.54
	broadleaved	47	750	0.75	1.33
	general	42	675	0.68	1.48
Pitprops:	coniferous	44	700	0.70	1.43
	broadleaved	50	800	0.80	1.25
	general	45	725	0.73	1.38
Other industrial wood:					
	coniferous	44	700	0.70	1.43
	broadleaved	50	800	0.80	1.25
	general	47	750	0.75	1.33
Fuelwood:	coniferous	39	625	0.63	1.60
	broadleaved	47	750	0.75	1.33
	general	45	725	0.73	1.38
Sawnwood:	coniferous	34	550	0.55	1.82
	broadleaved	44	700	0.70	1.42
Sleepers		49	780	0.78	1.28
Plywood		41	650	0.65	1.54
Veneer sheets		47	750	0.75	1.33

The weight (mass) of timber can be obtained from the volume table (**page 196**) by multiplying the number of cubic metres by the value of kilograms or tonnes per cubic metre shown above.

For cut timber, weight (mass) can be obtained for various sizes by using the steel tables on pages 228–229, in conjunction with a multiplier to allow for different densities; some calculated multipliers are given on page 106.

Bark

The following table gives some estimates of the percentage amount of bark on roundwood (adapted from tables of the UK Forestry Commission).

nder bark p iameter nm)	Bark as % (approximate) of underbark volume (percentages applying for lengths of 2–8 m)				
	Norway spruce	Sitka spruce	Douglas fir	Scots pine	European larch
00	10.0	13.5	16.5	16.5	25.0
50	10.0	11.0	14.0	14.0	22.0
00	9.5	10.0	13.0	14.0	20.5
50	9.0	9.0	13.0	15.5	20.0
00	8.5	8.5	13.5	17.5	20.5
50	8.0	8.0	13.5	19.5	21.0
00	7.5	7.5	14.0	21.5	21.5
00	6.5	7.0	14.5	23.5	22.5
00	6.0	7.0	15.0	25.0	23.5
00	6.0	6.5	15.0	26.0	24.5
00	6.0	6.5	15.5	27.0	25.0

ote. The above percentages are for converting from underbark volume overbark volume, by adding the percentages specified to underbark olume. For example, the percentage reversal of 10 is 9.1; so, for orway spruce with a top-diameter underbark of 100–150 mm, the ercentage to be subtracted from overbark volume to obtain underbark olume is 9.1% or approximately 9%.

he percentages to be subtracted from overbark volume to btain underbark volume can be obtained by using the ercentage reversals table on page 165.

Top diameter refers to the end of timber with the smallest iameter; the other measure normally used is mid-diameter, hich is approximately equal to the average diameter for any ngth of timber.

Chemicals, industrial

UK chemical industries had changed to the metric system by 1973. Measures of special interest are included below.

FERTILISERS

Primary nutrients

There are three main nutrients in fertiliser.

1. Nitrogen (N), taken up by plants in nitrate (NO_3) or ammonium (NH_4) form.
2. Phosphorus (P), usually in the form of P_2O_5 (phosphate), where the weight of P is converted to P_2O_5 by multiplying by 2.29, and conversely P_2O_5 is converted to P by multiplying by 0.44.
3. Potassium (K), usually in the form of K_2O (potash), where the weight of K is converted to K_2O by multiplying by 1.2, and conversely K_2O is converted to K by multiplying by 0.83.

Soil

Classification of soils, in terms of the diameter of solid particles, is shown in the following table.

Type of soil	mm
Gravel & stones	over 2
Sand	0.06–2
Silt	0.002–0.06
Clay	under 0.002

Classification in terms of nutrient content is made by means of soil analysis indexes, which classify in terms of milligrams of each element per litre of air-dried, ground soil. The indexes are shown in the following table.

Index	Phosphorus (P) Mg/l	Potassium (K) mg/l	Magnesium (Mg) mg/l	Nitrate (N) mg/l
0	0–9	0–60	0–25	0–25
1	10–15	61–120	26–50	26–50
2	16–25	121–240	51–100	51–100
3	26–45	241–400	101–175	101–150
4	46–70	401–600	176–250	151–250
5	71–100	601–900	251–350	251–350
6	101–140	901–1 500	351–600	over 350
7	141–200	1 501–2 400	601–1 000	
8	201–280	2 401–3 600	1 001–1 500	
9	over 280	over 3 600	over 1 500	

Analysis of the soil by various methods gives a measure of the index for each element, and recommendations as to amounts of fertiliser are usually made in relation to the index level of any soil. For example, at soil P or K index 2 or above, economic responses in the UK of cereals, grasses and legumes to additional P or K are rare, and it is only necessary to maintain existing nutrient levels for those crops.

The amount of nitrogen used will be based on expected yield. It is also related to the level of output; eg, whether the crop is grazed or used for silage.

It is not possible in general to determine the N index by testing, and the estimate is usually based on past crops; eg, a last crop of peas or potatoes will have left an N index of 1.

An index is also used to express the concentration of soluble salts in the soil; this is the measure of conductivity, expressed in units of microsiemens. The index is shown in the following table.

Index	Conductivity	Index	Conductivity	Index	Conductivity
0	1 900–2 200	4	2 710–2 800	8	3 710–4 000
1	2 210–2 400	5	2 810–3 000	9	4 010 and over
2	2 410–2 600	6	3 010–3 300		
3	2 610–2 700	7	3 310–3 700		

Additional amounts of fertiliser required are usually expressed in the metric system as kilograms per hectare, litres per hectare, or grams per litre; eg, UK recommendations for barley grown on light soils at index 0 would be 125 kg/ha N, 75 kg/ha P_2O_5 and 75 kg/ha K_2O.

Relationships between metric and other units are as follows.

1 kilogram per hectare (kg/ha)	= 0.008 hundredweight per acre (cwt/acre)
1 hundredweight per acre (cwt/acre)	= 125.535 kilograms per hectare (kg/ha)
1 litre per hectare (l/ha)	= 0.106 9 US gallon per acre (US gal/acre)
1 US gallon per acre (US gal/acre)	= 9.354 litres per hectare (l/ha)

Soil reaction

This is measured by pH (hydrogen ion concentration), which denotes the acidity and alkalinity of a substance. A pH of 7 means a neutral substance, 0–7 that it is acidic, and 7–14 that it is alkaline.

Normal UK agricultural soil has a value for pH of 4–8. Adding lime reduces acidity (increases pH).

The following table indicates for some crops the soil pH levels for the UK below which crop growth is affected on mineral soils, and so the danger level at which lime must be applied.

Crop	pH	Crop	pH
Arable		**Fruit**	
Barley	5.9	Apples	5.6
Beet, sugar	5.9	Pears	5.3
Maize	5.5	Plums	5.6
Oats	5.3	Strawberries	5.1
Oilseed rape	5.6		
Potatoes	4.9	**Grasses and clovers**	
Swedes	5.4	Clover, red	5.9
Wheat	5.5	Clover, wild white	4.7
		Lucerne	6.2
Flowers		Rye grass	4.7
Begonias	5.3	Timothy	5.3
Carnations	6.0		
Daffodils	6.1	**Vegetables**	
Hydrangeas (pink)	5.9	Asparagus	5.9
Hydrangeas (blue)	4.1	Cabbages	5.4
Lavender	6.1	Carrots	5.7
Roses, hybrid tea	5.6	Cauliflowers	5.6
Tulips	5.9	Cucumbers	5.5

rop	pH	Crop	pH
ettuce	6.1	Rhubarb	5.4
lint	6.6	Spinach	5.8
nions	5.7	Tomatoes (outdoor)	5.1
arsnips	5.4		
eas	5.9	Turnips	5.1

esponse to fertilisers

unit of plant nutrients (N–P–K) produces very roughly 10 nits of basic food. 1 tonne of basic food provides pproximately 5 000 (21 kilojoules) per day for 1 year.

UBRICATING OIL

'iscosity

he most important property of lubricating oil, viscosity is a ieasure of its ability to flow; low viscosity oil is thin and flows eely, and high viscosity oil is thick and flows slowly. Dynamic r absolute viscosity, η, is measured in units of pascal seconds Pa s). Since flow is also related to the density of a liquid, inematic viscoscity, ν, is also used as a measure, being lynamic viscosity divided by density, $\nu = \eta/\varrho$; kinematic iscosity is measured in square millimetres per second mm²/s). Two older non-SI units are also used: the poise, P (and entipoise, cP) for dynamic viscosity, where 1 cP = 1 mPa s; and he stokes, St, (and centistokes, cSt) for kinematic viscosity, vhere 1 cSt = 1 mm^2/s.

'iscosity values

ubricating oils have viscosities in the range 10–1 000 entistokes at 37.8°C (100°F); by comparison water has a iscosity of about 1 centistoke.

:entipoises = centistokes × density (at the relevant emperature)

Viscosity varies with temperature; this is indicated in the ollowing table for water.

emperature C	Viscosity cP
0	1.79
20	1.00
00	0.28

hus viscosity falls as temperature rises. Conversely fluidity ises with temperature; this is measured by the rhe:

rhe = 1/poise or "reciprocal" poise.

ensity

he density of lubricating oil is, in general, as follows.

C	°F	kg/l
-18	0	0.9
99	210	0.825

Other measures

There is a range of other measures for viscosity, which are not directly related to the SI units.

SAE. The Society of Automotive Engineers in the USA developed a system which grades oils. Multi-grade oils combine low viscosity of 10W grades for easy low-temperature starting (fluidity is comparatively high), with the high viscosity of the 30–50 grades for better load capacity in bearings (viscosity remains relatively high) at normal engine running temperature. The effect of temperature can be seen from the following table, which gives SAE grades for engine oils.

SAE viscosity grade	Viscosity[a] (cP) at temperature (°C) max	Borderline pumping temperature[b] (°C) max	Viscosity[c] (cSt) at 100°C min	max
0W	3 250 at −30	−35	3.8	–
5W	3 500 at −25	−30	3.8	–
10W	3 500 at −20	−25	4.1	–
15W	3 500 at −15	−20	5.6	–
20W	4 500 at −10	−15	5.6	–
25W	6 000 at −5	−10	9.3	–
20	–	–	5.6	<9.3
30	–	–	5.6	<12.5
40	–	–	12.5	<16.3
50	–	–	16.3	<21.9
60	–	–	21.9	<26.1

[a]This method covers the laboratory determination of apparent viscosity of engine oils between −40 and 0°C and at high shear rates using the cold cranking simulator. [b]Kinematic viscosity. [c]Some engine manufacturers also recommend limits on viscosity measured at 150°C and $10^6 s^{-1}$.

Saybolt. This system is based on the time taken for the flow of liquid from one vessel to another. The Saybolt Universal Second (SUS) is the time in seconds for 60 ml of oil to flow out of the cup in a Saybolt viscometer through a carefully specified opening. This measure is only very roughly related to centistokes; approximately, for the values in the SAE table, SUS is equal to cSt multiplied by 4.5–7.5. Saybolt Furol Seconds are used for viscous oils. Very roughly: 1 Saybolt Furol Second = 10 Saybolt Universal Seconds.

Redwood. This is a UK system based on the time for a flow as in the case of Saybolt. Relatively mobile oils are measured in a number of seconds Redwood I, and more viscous oils in seconds Redwood II; a larger orifice speeds up the time of flow by about 10. Very roughly, 1 second Redwood II = 10 seconds Redwood I. This measure is again only roughly related to centistokes: approximately, for the values in the SAE table, sec Red I is equal to cSt multiplied by 4–7; very roughly sec Red I is 87.5–90% of SUS.

Engler. This system, used in Germany, Italy and some other European countries, is based on the ratio of the time for flow of oil to the time for an equal volume of distilled water at the same temperature. Results are given in terms of the Engler degree (°E). Very approximately, for the values in the SAE table, °E is equal to 13–18% of cSt. Very roughly, °E is 2.8–3.2% of SUS and 3.0–3.7% of sec Red I.

PETROCHEMICALS

Crude petroleum is predominantly a complex mixture of chemical compounds called hydrocarbons; so called because they are composed largely of the two elements hydrogen and carbon.

Since crude oil is a mixture it has no fixed boiling point, but it has a boiling or distillation range which may start as low as 20°C and end above 400°C; generally a low boiling point is associated with a low number of carbon atoms in the molecule. Distillation makes use of the difference in volatility or boiling point of different components or fractions in the mixture. The main fractions into which crude oil can be separated by distillation are shown in the table below.

	Boiling-point range °C	Carbon atoms in the molecule
Light distillates		
Petroleum gases	below 0	1–4
Gasoline (petrols)	0–65	5–6
Naphtha	65–170	6–10
Kerosene (paraffin)	170–250	10–14
Middle distillates		
Gas oil	250–340	14–19
Residue		
Lubricating oil, wax feedstocks	340–500	19–35
Bitumen feedstocks	over 500	over 35

Simplest of the structures is one where four hydrogen atoms are joined to a single carbon atom; this is the gas methane (CH_4). Other basic structures are ethylene (C_2H_4) and benzene (C_6H_6).

Plastics and resins

UN production estimates refer to the production of plastic materials and artificial resins (excluding synthetic rubber, man-made fibres, etc) obtained by chemical transformation of natural organic substances or by chemical synthesis. These are classified in three groups.

Condensation including polycondensation and polyaddition products, formed by reaction between several molecules of the same or of different chemical constitution, in which the structural units are normally linked together by functional groups (eg, aminoplasts, alkyd resins, epoxy resins, silicones).

Polymerisation including copolymerisation, obtained by the union of monomers with multiple-carbon carbon bonds or molecules of different chemical constitution (eg, polyethylene, polystyrene, polyvinyl derivatives).

Other processes including regenerated cellulose, hardened proteins, natural resins modified by fusion, artificial resins, chemical derivatives of natural rubber, and other high polymers, artificial resins and artificial plastic materials (including alginic acid and linoxyn).

Synthetic fibres

Polyamides (eg, nylon)
Polyamide microfibre (eg, Tactel)
Polyesters
Polyacrylics
Polypropylene
Polyurethanes (eg, Lycra)

Detergents

These are synthetic soaps made from organic chemicals largely derived from petroleum. The basic ingredients of any detergent are the same – ie, surfactants, builders and organic additives. Surfactants (surface active agents) have properties that include cleaning, foaming, wetting, emulsifying, solubilising and dispersing. Widely used surfactants include linear alkyl benzene (LAB), linear alkyl benzene sulphonates (LAS), ethoxylates and alkoxylates. Builders include phosphates (eg, sodium tripolyphosphate–STPP), zeolites, nitrilo-triacetate (NTA) and sodium silicate which augment the effects of the surfactants (eg, removing hardness ions from the wash). Other additives include optical brighteners and bleaches.

Pesticides and fertilisers

DDT is a chlorinated hydrocarbon (dichloro-diphenyl-trichloroethane). Ammonia and sulphur are derived from oil and natural gas; ammonia is a basic source of nitrogen for fertilisers.

Solvents for paints, cosmetics and pharmaceuticals

Chemical solvents usually contain oxygen and chlorine as well as hydrogen and carbon. Ethylene oxide and ethyl alcohol (C_2H_5OH) are among the basic materials used.

Boiling points of the main alcohols

	°C
Methyl alcohol (or methanol)	65 (low boiling)
Ethyl alcohol (or ethanol)	78 (low boiling)
Isopropyl alcohol	82 (low boiling)
Secondary butyl alcohol	100 (low boiling)
Isobutyl alcohol	107 (medium boiling)
Normal butyl alcohol	118 (medium boiling)
Methyl isobutyl carbitol	132 (medium boiling)

Base chemicals

Lower olefins (ethylene, propylene, butylene)
Aromatics (benzene, toluene, xylene)
Higher olefins (C_6–C_{18})
Other base chemicals include methane, acetylene, methanol, ammonia.

Industrial chemicals

Hydrocarbon solvents (eg, white spirits)
Chemical (oxygenated) solvents (eg, isopropyl alcohol, acetone)
Phenol

:thylene glycol (eg, anti-freeze)
:thylene oxide
:pichlorohydrin
)iphenylol propane
-ligher olefins (C_6–C_{16})
;ynthetic detergent intermediates (alcohols, alkylates)
'lasticiser alcohols
)rganic acids

RUBBER

'or natural rubber see Agriculture, fishing and forestry, page 37.

Synthetic rubber is a family of petroleum-derived polymers nost of which mimic the properties of natural rubber.)riginally developed in wartime Germany as a substitute for natural rubber, synthetic rubber is now more widely used than natural rubber and has become more specialised in its applications. Like natural rubber, synthetic rubber's qualities are enhanced by "vulcanising" (heating in combination with sulphur and other chemicals). This converts it from a thermoplastic material into a substance with rubbery properties. Rubber's definitional property is elasticity: rubber has "memory" which enables it to return to its original shape after deformation. Other properties are hardness and plasticity, tests for which are detailed below.

Rubber hardness

The hardness of a rubber is its resistance to indentation and is related to other forms of deformation. It is measured by penetration of a rigid indenter applied with force. Measurement is usually made in terms of the following.

Shore durometer A which has a pointer pressed under certain conditions of pressure into a rubber sample; the scale measures from 0° for soft to 100° for absolutely hard (maximum indentation = 0°, zero indentation = 100°).

Shore durometer D which has a truncated cone indenter, measured also on a scale of 0–100°.

Wallace hardness meter which reads in terms of international rubber hardness degrees (IRHD).

International rubber hardness degrees measure hardness, as with the Shore scales, from 0° to 100°. The scale is based on a logarithmic progression, with conditions that $\log_{10}M$ at the midpoint of the curve of the progression is 0.364, and the maximum slope is equal to 57 IRHD per 1 increase in $\log_{10}M$, where M = meganewtons per square metre (MN/m^2).

Different methods of testing are related through the amount of differential indentation (usually in 0.01 mm) to IRHD. Shore A readings are usually within ±1° of IRHD, except below about 30° where they are rather lower; for synthetic rubber, correspondence may be less close.

Examples of rubber hardness

Rubber	Shore A (approx IRHD)
Natural	20–100
Sytrene butadiene	35–90
Butyl	40–70
Hard	65–95

Rubber viscosity

Viscosity (plasticity) is usually measured in terms of Mooney viscosity. This measures the drag ("torque") when a rotor is revolved at 2 rpm within a rubber sample under specified conditions; a specific temperature is maintained, usually 100°C. The scale runs from 0 to 200, with 0 meaning maximum viscosity (zero force applied) and 200 zero viscosity (maximum force applied); the basic torque applied is 8.31 N m when forces of 100 N are applied to the rotor.

SULPHURIC ACID

Sulphuric acid (H_2SO_4) is one of the most important industrial chemicals. It is used in the manufacture of a wide variety of materials including: fertilisers, detergents, paints, rayon, plastics, explosives and pesticides. It is also used in oil refining and car batteries.

Chemistry

UNITS AND DIMENSIONS

In science today quantities are generally quoted in units of the International System (SI). The most important SI units are given in the table. The first six are SI base units; the others are derived units related to the base units as indicated. There are many derived units; the list given is only a brief selection.

For more information on SI units see pages 13–17.

Quantity name	Symbol	SI unit Name	Symbol	Relation
Length	l	metre	m	
Mass	m	kilogram	kg	
Time	t	second	s	
Electric current	I	ampere	A	
Thermodynamic temperature	T	kelvin	K	
Amount of substance	n	mole	mol	
Area	A	metre^2	m^2	
Velocity	v	metre per second	m/s	
Force	F	newton	N	N = kg m/s^2
Pressure	p	pascal	Pa	Pa = N/m^2
Energy	E	joule	J	J = kg m^2/s^2
Electric charge	Q	coulomb	C	C = A s
Electric potential	E, U	volt	V	V = J/C
Power	P	watt	W	W = J/s

Some non-SI units are still in everyday use, but in a scientific context only a few remain. The most commonly used are listed in the following table.

Quantity	Name of unit	Symbol	Definition
Length	ångstrom	Å	Å = 10^{-10} m
	inch	in	in = 2.54 cm
	mile	mi	mi = 1 609.344 m
Time	minute	min	min = 60 s
	hour	h	h = 3 600 s
	day	d	d = 86 400 s
Mass	unified atomic mass unit	u	u = m(C-12)/12 = 1.660 540 × 10^{-27} kg
	ounce (avoirdupois)	oz	oz = 28.349 5 g
	ounce (troy)	oz(troy)	oz = 31.103 5 g
	pound	lb	lb = 453.59 g
Area	are	a	a = 100 m^2
	hectare	ha	ha = 10^4 m^2
Temperature	degree Celsius	°C	t/°C = T/K − 273.15
	degree Fahrenheit	°F	t/°F = (9/5)t/°C + 32
Pressure	bar	bar	bar = 10^5 Pa
	standard atmosphere	atm	atm = 1.016 32 × 10^5 Pa
Volume	litre	L, l	L = dm^3 = 10^3 cm^3

FUNDAMENTAL DATA ON THE STRUCTURE OF MATTER

All matter is built from atoms. Atoms are small: 1 g of material may contain more than 10^{23} atoms. Molecules are built from atoms, where the number of atoms in a molecule may vary from 2 (as in nitrogen, N_2, and oxygen, O_2, in the atmosphere) or 3 (as in water H_2O) to more than 1 000 (as in a molecule of a polymer such as polythene), or more than 100 000 000 in the organic molecule DNA). An atom consists of a small central positively charged nucleus surrounded by a cloud of negatively charged electrons; more than 99.9% of the mass of an atom is in the nucleus. The nucleus is itself composed of approximately equal numbers of protons and neutrons.

Each proton carries a unit positive charge, each neutron is neutral, and each electron carries a unit negative charge, where the unit of charge is called the elementary charge, denoted e, equal to about 1.602 2 × 10^{-19} coulomb. The number of electrons in an atom is always equal to the number of protons in the nucleus, so that atoms are electrically neutral. The mass of a proton is approximately equal to the mass of a neutron and is about 1.673 × 10^{-27} kg; the mass of an electron, denoted m_e, is about 9.109 5 × 10^{-31} kg, smaller by a factor of about 1 830.

Atoms are typically 1–5 Å in diameter (0.1–0.5 nm). The nucleus and the electrons from which atoms are built are smaller than this by a factor of around 10^4, so that there is a lot of empty space between the particles. In a molecule, atoms are held together by chemical bonds, the distance between the centres of atoms being similar to their diameter. The separation between molecules in a liquid or solid is greater than the spacing of atoms in a molecule by a factor of about 2 or 3, but in a gas the separation between molecules is greater by a factor of around 1 000, which accounts for the much lower density of gases.

Elementary atomic particles are held together by various forces. The exchange forces binding together the protons and neutrons in a nucleus are very strong, so that non-radioactive atomic nuclei can only be broken apart by bombardment, as in an atomic reactor, an atomic explosion, or accelerator. The electromagnetic forces that bind the electrons to the nucleus in an atom, and the forces that bind atoms together to form molecules, are much weaker by a factor of around 100: they are the forces associated with chemical bonding, which can be broken in a chemical reaction, such as burning. Finally the forces that hold molecules together to form a liquid or a solid are weaker still by a factor of around 20: they are associated with intermolecular attraction, and they are broken when a liquid evaporates or when a solid melts or sublimes. Synthetic polymers and similar materials derive their strength from the fact that they are composed of long and sometimes cross-linked molecules.

Chemical amount or amount of substance. The quantity of material in a sample may be measured by its mass, or by its volume, but chemists often measure quantities by a third method: by counting the molecules. Because the number of molecules in a typical sample is so large, the chemical amount or amount of substance is measured in moles (symbol mol) where 1 mole contains a large but fixed number of molecules specified by the Avogadro constant. The definition of this number is as follows: 1 mole (of any substance) contains as many atoms or molecules (the entity must be specified) as there are atoms in 12 g of carbon-12.

In general the chemical amount or amount of substance, denoted n, is obtained by dividing the number of entities N by the Avogadro constant N_A, $n = N/N_A$. The value of the Avogadro constant is approximately $N_A = 6.022\,137 \times 10^{-23}$ mol.

The elements

Over 100 different types of atom exist; these are called the elements. Elements are characterised by their atomic number which is equal to the number of protons in the nucleus or the number of surrounding electrons. The names, symbols, and atomic numbers of the elements are listed in the table. Most atoms also occur as two or more different isotopic species, characterised by different numbers of neutrons and hence by slightly different atomic masses (although the chemical properties of different isotopes of the same atom remain the same). The sum of the number of protons and the number of neutrons is called the mass number. For example, carbon (C) has an atomic number 6, and it occurs in nature as carbon-12 (6 protons and 6 neutrons) with an abundance 98.9%, and carbon-13 (6 protons and 7 neutrons) with an abundance 1.1%; the numbers 12 and 13 are the mass numbers of the two isotopes.

Some isotopic species are unstable, in the sense that the nucleus spontaneously breaks up to form a new nucleus (or nuclei) of different species, usually with the release of (a possibly large amount of) energy, in a nuclear reaction. This is called radioactive decay. It is always characterised by a half life, equal to the time in which half of a given sample will decay. For example, there exists a third isotope of carbon, carbon-14, which is radioactive with a half life of 5 730 years (this is used in carbon dating). Half lives vary from minutes to thousands of years. For uranium-238 it is 4.47×10^9 years, and for uranium-235 it is 7.04×10^8 years; for radium-226 it is 1 600 years, and for lead-214 it is 26.8 minutes. Nuclear reactions can also be induced to occur rapidly by irradiating the sample with neutrons, as occurs in a reactor or in an atomic explosion.

Most radioactive elements (or isotopes of elements) occur high in the periodic table. Elements with an atomic number above 92, uranium, are known as transuranic elements; they have no stable isotopic species, and are all radioactive.

A nuclide is an atomic species of a single atomic number and a single mass number.

Atomic weights

The mass of 1 mole of any element is known as its molar mass. The ratio of the molar mass to $\frac{1}{12} \times$ (the molar mass of carbon-12) is known as the relative molar mass or atomic weight. (The atomic weight is also equal to the ratio of the atomic mass to the unified atomic mass unit u; $u = m(\text{C-12})/12$.) Since the molar mass of carbon-12 is by definition equal to 12 g/mol exactly, the atomic weight (which is dimensionless) is always equal to the numerical value of the average molar mass (of all naturally occurring isotopic species) in g/mol, or the numerical value of the average atomic mass (of all naturally occurring isotopic species) in u. The atomic weights of the elements are usually quoted as a weighted mean over all naturally occurring isotopic species according to their natural abundances. The following table lists the symbols, atomic numbers, names and average molar masses (or atomic weights) of the elements.

The elements

Name	Symbol	Atomic number	Atomic weight; or molar mass/g mol^{-1}
Actinium	Ac	89	(227)
Aluminium	Al	13	26.981 39
Americium	Am	95	(243)
Antimony (Stibium)	Sb	51	121.75
Argon	Ar	18	39.948
Arsenic	As	33	74.921 59
Astatine	At	85	(210)
Barium	Ba	56	137.327
Berkelium	Bk	97	(247)
Beryllium	Be	4	9.012 182
Bismuth	Bi	83	208.980 37
Boron	B	5	10.811
Bromine	Br	35	79.904
Cadmium	Cd	48	112.411
Caesium	Cs	55	132.905 43
Calcium	Ca	20	40.078
Californium	Cf	98	(251)
Carbon	C	6	12.011
Cerium	Ce	58	140.115
Chlorine	Cl	17	35.452 7
Chromium	Cr	24	51.996 1
Cobalt	Co	27	58.933 20
Copper	Cu	29	63.546
Curium	Cm	96	(247)
Dysprosium	Dy	66	162.50
Einsteinium	Es	99	(252)
Erbium	Er	68	167.26
Europium	Eu	63	151.965
Fermium	Fm	100	(257)
Fluorine	F	9	18.998 403
Francium	Fr	87	(223)
Gadolinium	Gd	64	157.25
Gallium	Ga	31	69.723
Germanium	Ge	32	72.61
Gold	Au	79	196.966 54
Hafnium	Hf	72	178.49
Helium	He	2	4.002 602
Holmium	Ho	67	164.930 32
Hydrogen	H	1	1.007 94
Indium	In	49	114.82
Iodine	I	53	126.904 47
Iridium	Ir	77	192.22
Iron	Fe	26	55.847
Krypton	Kr	36	83.80
Lanthanum	La	57	138.905 5
Lawrencium	Lr	103	(260)
Lead	Pb	82	207.2
Lithium	Li	3	6.941
Lutetium	Lu	71	174.967
Magnesium	Mg	12	24.305 0
Manganese	Mn	25	54.938 05
Mendelevium	Md	101	(258)
Mercury	Hg	80	200.59
Molybdenum	Mo	42	95.94
Neodymium	Nd	60	144.24
Neon	Ne	10	20.179 7
Neptunium	Np	93	(237)
Nickel	Ni	28	58.69

Name	Symbol	Atomic number	Atomic weight; or molar mass/g mol^{-1}
Niobium	Nb	41	92.906 38
Nitrogen	N	7	14.006 74
Nobelium	No	102	(259)
Osmium	Os	76	190.2
Oxygen	O	8	15.999 4
Palladium	Pd	46	106.42
Phosphorus	P	15	30.973 762
Platinum	Pt	78	195.09
Plutonium	Pu	94	(244)
Polonium	Po	84	(209)
Potassium (Kalium)	K	19	39.098 3
Praseodymium	Pr	59	140.907 65
Promethium	Pm	61	(145)
Protactinium	Pa	91	231.035 88
Radium	Ra	88	(226)
Radon	Rn	86	(222)
Rhenium	Re	75	186.207
Rhodium	Rh	45	102.905 50
Rubidium	Rb	37	85.467 8
Ruthenium	Ru	44	101.07
Samarium	Sm	62	150.36
Scandium	Sc	21	44.955 910
Selenium	Se	34	78.96
Silicon	Si	14	28.085 5
Silver	Ag	47	107.868 2
Sodium (Natrium)	Na	11	22.989 768
Strontium	Sr	38	87.62
Sulphur	S	16	32.066
Tantalum	Ta	73	180.947 9
Technetium	Tc	43	(98)
Tellurium	Te	52	127.60
Terbium	Tb	65	158.925 34
Thallium	Tl	81	204.383
Thorium	Th	90	232.038 1
Thulium	Tm	69	168.934 21
Tin	Sn	50	118.710
Titanium	Ti	22	47.88
Tungsten (Wolfram)	W	74	183.85
Unnilhexium	Unh	106	(263)
Unnilpentium	Unp	105	(262)
Unnilquadium	Unq	104	(261)
Uranium	U	92	238.028 9
Vanadium	V	23	50.941 5
Xenon	Xe	54	131.29
Ytterbium	Yb	70	173.04
Yttrium	Y	39	88.905 85
Zinc	Zn	30	65.38
Zirconium	Zr	40	91.22

Note. For elements without a characteristic terrestrial isotopic composition no value of the atomic weight is recommended, but the mass number of the most abundant isotopic species is given in brackets. Otherwise the uncertainty of the atomic weight is between 1 and 9 in the last digit.

PHYSICAL PROPERTIES OF MATERIALS

Melting and boiling points for some of the elements, and for a few selected organic compounds are shown below. They are given in degrees Celsius and also as absolute temperatures in degrees kelvin.

Melting and boiling points at 1 atm

Material	Melting point °C	K	Boiling point °C	K
Elements				
Aluminium	660.323[a]	933.473[a]	2 520	2 793
Antimony	630.63	903.78	1 600	1 873
Barium	730	1 003	1 640	1 913
Boron	2 130	2 403	3 700	3 973
Cadmium	321.069	594.219	770	1 043
Calcium	840	1 113	1 490	1 763
Carbon: graphite	3 652	3 925	4 827	5 100
diamond	3 550	3 823	4 827	5 100
Chlorine	−101	172	−34	239
Cobalt	1 495	1 768	2 900	3 200
Copper	1 084.62[a]	1 357.77[a]	2 590	2 863
Fluorine	−220	53	−188	85
Gold	1 064.18[a]	1 337.33[a]	2 850	3 123
Helium	−269.65	1	−268	5
Hydrogen	−259.347[b]	13.8	−252.88[a]	20.27[a]
Iron	1 540	1 813	2 760	3 033
Krypton	−157.3	115.85	−153.5	119.65
Lead	327.462	600.612	1 760	2 033
Magnesium	650	923	1 110	1 383
Mercury	−38.829[b]	234.321[b]	356.66	629.81
Molybdenum	2 623	2 896	4 630	4 903
Neon	−248.594[b]	24.556[b]	−246	27
Nickel	1 455	1 728	2 900	3 173
Nitrogen	−210	63	−195.80	77.35
Oxygen	−218.792[b]	55.358[b]	−183	90
Phosphorus	44	317	280	553
Platinum	1 768	2 041	3 820	4 093
Potassium	63.2	336.35	770	1 043
Radium	700	973	1 500	1 773
Silver	961.78[a]	1 234.93[a]	2 170	2 443
Sodium	97.9	371	900	1 173
Sulphur	115.3	388.45	444.67	719.85
Tin	231.928[a]	505.078[a]	2 720	2 993
Tungsten	3 420	3 693	5 700	5 973
Uranium	1 135	1 408	4 000	4 273
Vanadium	1 920	2 193	3 400	3 673
Zinc	419.527[a]	692.677[a]	910	1 183
Inorganic molecules				
Nitric acid	−42	231	86	359
Sulphuric acid	10.9	284	336.9	610
Water	0.01[b]	273.16[b]	99.974	373.124
Organic molecules				
Methane	−182	91	−164	109.1
Ethane	−183.3	90	−88.6	184.5
Propane	−189.7	83.4	−42.2	230.9
Butane	−138.1	135	−0.5	272.6
Pentane	−130	143.1	36.3	309.2
Hexane	−95	178.1	69	342.1

Material	Melting point °C	K	Boiling point °C	K
Hexadecane	18.2	291.6	287	560
Cyclohexane	6.5	279.6	80.7	353.8
Benzene	5.5	278.6	80.1	353.2
Methylbenzene	−95.0	178.1	111	384
Naphthalene	80.2	353.3	218	491
Anthracene	217	489	342	613
Chloromethane	−97.7	175.4	−24	249.3
Dichloromethane	−95.1	178	40.2	313.3
Trichloromethane	−63.5	209.6	61.2	334.3
Tetrachloromethane	−23.0	250.1	76.8	349.9
Methanol	−93.9	179.2	65.0	338.1
Ethanol	−117.3	155.8	78.5	351.6

[a] These values are recommended as fixed points to standardise thermometers on the ITS-90 (International Temperature Scale, 1990).
[b] These values are actually values of the triple point of the material concerned, the temperature at which solid, liquid and vapour are all in mutual equilibrium; this is generally close to but slightly different from the melting point at 1 atm.

RELATIVE DENSITY

The relationship between mass and volume is indicated by the density of a substance, measured usually in kilograms per cubic metre (kg/m^3) or kilograms per litre (kg/l). Relative density (RD), the internationally recognised term for specific gravity (sg), is the ratio of the mass of one substance to another for equal volumes and standard conditions of temperature and pressure. Relative densities are usually expressed in the form RD 15/4°C, where the first number refers to the temperature at which the density of a substance is measured, and the second to the temperature of water against the density of which it is compared; water is usually taken as the standard for solids and liquids. Since 1 litre of water has a mass of 1 kilogram at approximately 4°C, there is a direct relationship between relative density and density for water at that temperature.

Relative density of 1.0 = 1 kilogram per litre (kg/l)
= 1 000 kilograms (1 tonne) per cubic metre (t/m^3)
= 1 gram per millilitre (g/ml)
= 1 gram per cubic centimetre (g/cm^3 or g/cc)

For gases, relative density is usually compared with dry air of normal carbon dioxide content at the same temperature and pressure.

Variation with temperature

The maximum density of water is at 4°C (more accurately at 3.98°C or 277.13 K). The change in the density of water with temperature is as follows.

°C	Density: kg/l	°C	Density: kg/l	°C	Density: kg/l
0	0.999 87	4	1.000 00	10	0.999 72
1	0.999 93	5	0.999 99	15	0.999 13
2	0.999 97	6	0.999 97	20	0.998 22
3	0.999 99				

The relative densities of various substances are indicated in the table below; density in kilograms per litre is approximately the same as the relative density. In this table approximate average values are given at 4°C and relative to water at 4°C and under normal atmospheric temperature and pressure. By definition, a substance with relative density less than 1 will float on water (when it does not mix), and one with relative density greater than 1 will not float.

For any substance, density at t_1°C = mass/volume at t_1°C,

and relative density t_1/t_2°C $= \dfrac{\text{density of the substance at } t_1\text{°C}}{\text{density of water at } t_2\text{°C}}$

Since the density of water at 4°C is unity, relative densities compared with water at 4°C are equal to density whatever the temperature; eg, RD 15/4°C of a substance is the same as density at 15°C.

Densities of common materials

Material	Density in g/cm^3 or relative density
Acids: acetic	1.05
hydrochloric (40%)	1.20
nitric (91%)	1.50
sulphuric (90%)	1.81
(100%)	1.83
Alcohol: ethyl	0.79
methyl	0.80
Aluminium	2.7
Antimony	6.7
Asbestos	2.4
Ashes	0.7
Asphalt	1.4
Bismuth	9.8
Bone	1.8
Brass (60 Cu/40 Zn)	8.4
Brick: building	2.5
medium	1.8
Bromine	3.1
Bronze (90 Cu/10 Sn)	8.8
Butter	0.9
Carbon, graphite	2.3
Cellulose	1.3
Cement, Portland	3.1
Chalk	2.3
Charcoal	0.4
Chloroform	1.5
Chromium	7.2
Clay	2.2
Coal: anthracite	1.6
bituminous	1.4
lignite	2.2
Cobalt	8.8

Material	Density in g/cm^3 or relative density
Concrete: general	2.3
lightweight	1.6
Copper	8.9
Cork	0.24
Cotton	1.5
Diamonds	3.5
Ether	0.74
German silver	8.6
Glass: crown	2.6
crystal	3.0
flint	4.0
Glass wool	0.5
Gold	19.3
Gold coin	17.2
Granite	2.7
Ice	0.92
Iron: ingot	7.9
cast grey	7.2
malleable	7.3
Lard	0.9
Lead	11.34
Leather	0.95
Lime	0.9
Limestone	2.5
Magnesium	1.7
Manganese	7.4
Marble	2.7
Mercury	13.6
Monel (70 Ni/30 Cu)	8.9
Milk	1.03
Nickel	8.9
Nylon	1.15

Material	Density in g/cm³ or relative density
Oils, vegetable	0.95
Olive oil	0.92
Paper	0.9
Paraffin (kerosene)	0.81
Petrol (gasoline)	0.74
Petroleum	0.87
Platinum	21.4
Plutonium	19.8
Resin, epoxy	1.1

Material	Density in g/cm³ or relative density
Rubber	0.94
Rubber goods	1.5
Salt	0.77
Sand, loose	2.5
Shale	1.5
Silicon	2.3
Silver	10.5
Slag	2.0
Slate	2.8

Material	Density in g/cm³ or relative density
Sodium	0.97
Soil: dry, loose	1.2
Solder	8.3
Sulphur	2.1
Tar	1.0
Timber: ash	0.75
balsa wood	0.15
oak	0.75
pine	0.55
teak	0.85

Material	Density in g/cm³ or relative density
Tin	7.3
Titanium	4.5
Turpentine	0.87
Tungsten	19.3
Uranium	19.0
Water: distilled	1.0
sea	1.03
Wool	1.3
Zinc	7.1

Computers

Analogue computer

An analogue computer is a machine which performs functions upon numbers in other than digital form, eg, in electrical analogue computers numbers may be represented by voltages.

Digital computer

A digital computer is a machine which performs operations on data represented in digital, discrete or number form. In electronic digital computers the number system used is that of binary notation. Data are recorded in the form of bits (binary digits) 0 or 1. Bits are grouped into bytes (8 bits) or words (24–32 bits).

Units
1 kilobyte (kb or Kb) = 1 024 or 1 000 bits or bytes
1 megabyte (Mb) = 1 048 576 or 1 000 000 bits or bytes

Binary system

A system for representing numbers by two digits, 0 and 1.

In the usual decimal system, each addition of a numerical character means multiplication by 10; in the binary system addition of an extra character means multiplication by 2 as shown in the following table.

See also page 13.

Decimal 10^1	10^0	Binary 2^7	2^6	2^5	2^4	2^3	2^2	2^1	2^0
0	1	0	0	0	0	0	0	0	1
0	2	0	0	0	0	0	0	1	0
0	3	0	0	0	0	0	0	1	1
0	4	0	0	0	0	0	1	0	0
0	5	0	0	0	0	0	1	0	1
0	6	0	0	0	0	0	1	1	0
0	7	0	0	0	0	0	1	1	1
0	8	0	0	0	0	1	0	0	0
0	9	0	0	0	0	1	0	0	1
1	0	0	0	0	0	1	0	1	0

HARDWARE

Computer systems

Computers have generally been divided into three main groups, mainframe, minicomputers and microcomputers. In general terms, the mainframe computer is a large, fast, fixed installation which handles very large amounts of data and a high throughput of transactions through a variety of terminals or visual display units. A minicomputer is usually a computer of a lesser capacity and speed than a mainframe. Finally, the microcomputer is usually a smaller and more portable computer than either the mainframe or minicomputer and is most commonly found as a stand-alone unit used by one operator at a time. However, with the advent of new and faster processors and operating systems, there is a great deal of overlap in the capabilities of these three types of computer.

Central processing unit (CPU)

The core component of every computer. It executes the instructions which form a programme.

Input devices

The most commonly used input device is the keyboard, but mice, scanners and light pens are also used.

Output devices

Screens. The computer screen or monitor is the main output device. It can be a cathode ray (television type), which in turn can be single colour or multicolour and either low or high resolution. Other display types include gas plasma, as used in some portable computers, or liquid crystal display (LCD), as used in the more compact and lightweight portable computers.

Printers. Printers fall into two main groups: impact and non-impact. Impact printers include the daisy wheel printer where a spinning wheel of characters is struck against an inked ribbon on to paper, and the dot matrix printer where pins are pressed in the form of a character again using an inked ribbon on to paper. Non-impact printers include laser and liquid crystal printers which use light to form a static image on a drum. This in turn picks up and transfers a toner powder on to paper which is fixed by heat. Other examples are ink jet printers which form characters with ultra-fine jets of quick drying ink, and thermal printers which use heated pins on temperature sensitive paper.

Storage devices

Data are most commonly stored on a rigid or hard magnetic disk which is accessed by read heads moving across its surface. Most computers also have floppy disks which are relatively low capacity disks of a flexible material. Unlike most hard disks they can be removed from the computer. Magnetic tape is used on larger systems for day-to-day storage and can be used on all systems for taking secure back-ups.

Memory

The most common is random access memory (RAM) which is composed of solid state devices used for temporary manipulation of data and programmes by the CPU.

Read only memory (ROM) is pre-written during the manufacturing process. It usually contains programmes relating to the function of the computer's hardware or peripherals. This pre-programmed hardware is often called firmware.

There are also programmable read only memories (PROM) and erasable programmable read only memories (EPROM) which are generally used for the same purposes as the ROM.

Networking

The joining together of two or more separate computer systems on one site in the case of a local area network (LAN) or across two or more sites in the case of a wide area network (WAN), allowing the sharing of data and peripheral devices such as printers and high capacity hard disks.

SOFTWARE

Software is simply a synonym for programme and is a series of instructions to the computer on how to carry out a task such as the manipulation of data.

Programmes are written as problem solving algorithms in various programming languages. A programming language is a set of key words which are decoded by an interpreter or compiler into machine code which the computer can then execute.

GLOSSARY

Access time. The time taken to retrieve data from a storage device or memory.

Analogue. The representation of values by a continuously varying value, such as a voltage or sound.

Application programme. A programme which performs a user-oriented task rather than a system function.

American Standard Code for Information Interchange (ASCII) was introduced to offer a standard numeric representation of characters and instructions. It now exists in various non-standard forms.

Back-up. The copying of data from the working storage to a safe location.

Batch processing. The processing of several transactions at once.

Baud. A measure of the speed of data processing. The baud rate is the number of signal elements per second. A signal element can be more than a bit, so baud is not the same as bits per second. Typical baud rates are 110, 300, 1 200, 2 400, 4 800 and 9 600.

Bootstrap or boot programme. A programme which loads the initial system software into a computer.

BPI. The number of bits per inch held on a data tape.

Buffer. Temporary memory often used to allow a device such as a disk or a printer to catch up with computer output which is faster than it can process.

Bug. An error in a computer's hardware or software.

Character. A letter, number or symbol.

Controller. A piece of hardware dedicated to the handling of a device such as a disk or a printer.

Cursor. The symbol on a screen which shows the current location.

D to A, A to D. The conversion of digital to analogue signals and vice versa.

Database. A collection of data usually ordered in a manner allowing ease of access and manipulation.

Disk Operating System (DOS). A large set of programmes which form the interface between the application programmes and the hardware.

Error code. A number generated by a computer which corresponds to a particular error condition.

Format. The arrangement of data, most commonly associated with the preparation of disks, into pre-defined tracks and sectors ready to receive data.

Interface. A hardware or software link between two or more components of a computer system.

Light pen. An input device which detects its location while pointing at a screen and which can, therefore, be used to select items from a menu or to draw on to the screen.

Machine code. The native language of a computer system.

Macro. A technique adopted by some software packages for the recording and subsequent playback of frequently used or complex groups of keystrokes.

Menu. A list of operations available to a user.

MIPS. Millions of instructions per second.

MODEM. Modulator/demodulator: changes the digital signals of a computer into analogue sound signals which can be sent down a telephone wire and vice versa.

Multi-tasking. The ability to process a number of tasks simultaneously.

On-line. Under the control of the computer or in the case of a user with direct interactive connection with a computer.

Operating System. See Disk Operating System.

Optical fibre. A fibre through which digital signals are sent as light impulses.

Parity check. Binary error checking.

Port. An input or output socket from a computer.

Portability. The ability of a programme to be moved between different system types without modification.

Real time. Where a computer system is acting immediately on the instructions of an operator or external controller.

Register. A temporary storage location used by the CPU to store the components and results of a calculation or data manipulation.

Spreadsheet. An application programme which is usually used for financial modelling and is based on a matrix of data and calculation cells.

Stack. A series of registers which are written and read in strict sequence.

Subroutine. A self-contained routine within a larger programme which can be executed a number of times as the programme is run.

Syntax. The form or grammatical rules governing the design of a computer programme.

User friendly. Adjective adopted in computer terminology to describe a programme which can be easily used with little or no prior knowledge of computers.

Utility. A programme often included with the operating system software which is used to carry out commonly required tasks, such as backing up data, or security checks for errors, or general tidying up and housekeeping of data held on computer.

Virus. An invasive programme which in some ways impairs, and in some cases prevents, the normal running of a computer system. The virus is usually attached to an apparently innocuous programme. When the programme runs it activates the virus which in turn attaches itself to other programmes or disks which come into contact with the "infected" computer. The action of infecting other programmes and disks is the source of the analogy with a biological virus.

Word processing. The creation, editing and formatting of text on a computer system.

Construction

AGGREGATES

Aggregates are bulk materials used in the construction industry. They are used either with binders (eg, cement, bitumen, tar) in composite materials such as concrete, mortar or bituminous mixtures for roads, or on their own as road sub-bases, railway ballast or special fill. They are usually sold in bulk by the tonne. Relative density is about 2.1.

BRICKS

Measures

Bricks are sold by 1 000 in packs of 300–500, depending on weight.

Brickwork is measured by m^2 of the relevant thickness.

Sizes

UK standard "work size" of bricks is:
215 mm × 102.5 mm × 65 mm

Special shaped bricks are available for corners, curves, etc.

Weight

Bricks weigh 2–3 kg (4.5–7 lb) each; ie, 2–3 tonnes per 1 000. Brickwork weighs 1 400–2 400 kg/m^3.

Quantities of bricks and mortar

Wall thickness (mm)	Quantities per m^2	
	Bricks (no.)	Mortar (m^3)
102.5 (0.5 brick)	60	0.02–0.025
215 (1 brick)	120	0.05–0.06
327.5 (1.5 bricks)	180	0.07–0.10

When measuring quantities of bricks required per square metre of brickwork, a cutting and wastage factor should be added to the above figures.

Haulage

Lorries can carry 6 000–10 000 bricks.

CEMENT

Ordinary Portland cement is produced by heating together limestone and clay or shale and adding gypsum.

Rapid-hardening Portland cement is similar to ordinary, but more finely ground; there is a higher rate of gain of strength, leading to rapid hardening.

Sulphate-resistant cement has its composition adjusted to resist attack by sulphates, occurring in some types of soil and ground water.

Portland blast-furnace cement consists of a mixture of Portland cement clinker and granulated blast-furnace slag.

Portland pulverised-fuel ash cement comprises a mixture of Portland cement and pulverised-fuel ash.

Measures

UK and Europe
Cement is sold in bulk by the tonne, and in 50 kg (110 lb) bags; the bag was formerly 112 lb (50.8 kg) before the change to the metric system.

USA
Bushel = 80 or 100 lb (36 or 45 kg)
Barrel (net): masonry = 280 lb (127 kg)
Portland = 376 lb (170 kg)
Bag = 94 lb (43 kg)

Canada
Barrel = 350 lb (159 kg)

Density

Relative density of Portland cement is 3.0–3.2; bulk density of cement powder (allowing for air in between particles) is about 1.4.

CONCRETE

Composition

Concrete is made from cement, aggregates and water; chemical admixtures are also used to alter handling and placing characteristics and long-term durability. The proportions of the ingredients are varied to suit the required performance.

Ready mixed concrete

Supplied by volume of fully compacted concrete in cubic metres. Specification by compressive strength in newtons per square millimetre (N/mm^2) measured from standard cube specimens, or by prescribed proportions of the basic ingredients. A typical specified strength grade is C25.

Density

	kg/m^3	lb/ft^3
Normal concrete[a]	2 300	140
Lightweight concrete[b]	650–2 000	40–125

[a]With natural aggregates. [b]Made by incorporating air bubbles in the mix or using synthetic lightweight aggregates.

Target mean strength is the least strength for which a concrete may be designed making allowance for variability in materials, etc. Strength is usually measured in terms of newtons per square millimetre; average strength is about 10 N/mm^2 higher than the grade specified.

GLASS

Following the change to the metric system, UK standard thicknesses are as follows (with the old equivalent); the tolerance range and mass are also shown.

	Nominal thickness mm	Tolerance range mm	Mass kg/m^2
Sheet glass (clear)	2 (18 oz)	1.8–2.2	5.0
	3 (24 oz)	2.8–3.2	7.5
	4 (32 oz)	3.7–4.3	10.0
	5 (in)	4.7–5.3	12.5
	6 (in)	5.7–6.3	15.0
Float glass (clear)	3	2.8–3.2	7.5
	4	3.8–4.2	10.0
	5	4.8–5.2	12.5
	6	5.8–6.2	15.0
	10	9.7–10.3	25.0
	12	11.7–12.3	30.0
	15	14.5–15.5	37.5
	19	18.0–20.0	47.5
	25	24.0–26.0	63.5
Rough cast	5 (in)	4.5–5.5	12.5
	6 (in)	5.5–6.5	15.0
	10 (in)	9.7–10.8	25.0

Properties

Average values are as follows.

Density 2 560 kg/m^3
Refractive index 1.52

See Light, optics and photography, pages 107–110.

HEATING AND VENTILATING

General heat conversions are included on page 163, with temperature conversions on pages 187–188.
Some special units of measure are as follows.

Intensity of heat-flow rate. Measured in watts per square metre (W/m^2).

Thermal capacity. Per unit mass (specific heat capacity): kilojoules per kilogram kelvin (kJ/kg K). Per unit volume: kilojoules per cubic metre kelvin (kJ/m^3 K)

Thermal conductance (coefficient of thermal transmittance). Measured in watts per square metre kelvin (W/m^2 K).

Thermal conductivity. Measured in watts per metre kelvin (W/m K).

Thermal resistivity. Measured in metres kelvin per watt (m K/W). Thermal resistivity is the reciprocal of thermal conductivity.

The kelvin is the expression of thermodynamic temperature for which the absolute zero is the datum. It is also used for the expression of any temperature difference or temperature interval.

$K = °C + 273.15$

Old units

1 British thermal unit (Btu) = 1.055 kilojoules

1 langley = 41.84 kilojoules per square metre (kJ/m^2)

The clo is a dimensionless factor defined as:

$$1_{cl} = \frac{Rcl}{Rr}$$

where both R values are in the same units. 1 clo is the insulation given by a typical business suit with waistcoat.

PAINT

The following table shows the main standard range of containers for paint, following the UK change to the metric system. Also indicated is the approximate spreading capacity on non-porous surfaces.

Metric	Spreading capacity m^2 Primer undercoat	Gloss	Emulsion	yd^2 Primer undercoat	Gloss	Emulsion
500 ml	8	8.5	6	9.5	10	7
1 litre	16	17	12	19	20	14
2.5 litre	40	42	30	47	50	35
5 litre	80	84	60	94	100	70

WATER SUPPLY

Density

Distilled water at 4°C (maximum density)
1 millilitre weighs 1 gram
1 litre weighs 1 kilogram
1 cubic metre weighs 1 tonne
1 US gallon weighs 3.785 kg (8.345 lb)
1 US (short) ton contains 907.18 l (239.7 US gallons)

Salt water (with relative density of 1.027)
1 cubic metre weighs approximately 1.03 tonnes

Flow

A cumec represents a volume of water equivalent to the flow of 1 cubic metre of water for 1 second.

1 cumec = 86 400 cubic metres per day (m^3/d)
= 15.83 mn US gallons per day
= 1 000 litres per second
1 US gallon per minute = 0.063 litre per second
1 litre per second = 0.001 cumec

Coverage and drainage

An acre foot represents a volume of water sufficient to cover 1 acre to a depth of 1 foot.

1 acre foot = 43 560 cubic feet = 1 233.48 cubic metres
= 325 851 US gallons
1 acre foot per day = 0.014 cumec
1 cumec = 0.056 acre feet per day
1 hectare metre = 10 000 cubic metres = 353 147 cubic feet
= 8.107 1 acre feet
1 acre foot = 0.123 3 hectare metre

1 cubic foot per 1 000 acres	= 6.997 2 litres per square kilometre
	= 0.07 litre per hectare
	= 0.007 cubic metre per square kilometre
1 mn acre feet	= 43 560 mn cubic feet

Flow per unit area. Measured in litres per second per square kilometre ($l/s\ km^2$).

Transmissivity. Measured in cubic metres per day per metre ($m^3/d\ m$).

Hydraulic conductivity. Measured in cubic metres per day per square metre ($m^3/d\ m^2$).

Precipitation. 1 millimetre of rainfall on 1 square kilometre = 1 megalitre (10^6 litres).

Hardness of water. The hardness of water is usually measured by the amount of calcium carbonate in the water; this is expressed as parts per million (ppm).

The usual classification is shown in the following table.

	ppm		ppm
Soft	0–5	Moderately hard	10–15
Slightly hard	5–10	Very hard	over 15

BUILDING AND CONSTRUCTION MATERIALS

The following table shows densities of many materials in kg/m^3, their thermal conductivities in W/m°C and thermal resistivities in m°C/W.

Bulk densities and thermal properties

Bulk density kg/m^3	Material	Thermal conductivity k W/m°C	Thermal resistivity 1/k m°C/W
64	Expanded ebonite	0.03	34.48
20	Expanded polystyrene	0.03	29.44
32	Foamed polyurethane	0.03	33.65
32	Glass fibre quilt	0.04	28.13
48	Mineral & slag wools	0.04	25.00
120	Wool, hair & jute fibre felts	0.04	27.78
128	Corkboard, baked	0.04	29.15
160	Balsa	0.05	22.22
160	Sprayed asbestos	0.05	20.25
295	Insulated fibre building boards	0.05	20.00
112	Exfoliated vermiculite, loose	0.05	20.00
132	Rigid foamed glass slabs	0.05	20.00
575	Medium-fibre building boards	0.09	11.89
450	Wood-wool slabs	0.09	10.75
365	Compressed straw slabs	0.10	9.90
680	Expanded clay, loose	0.12	8.33
513	Softwoods & plywoods	0.12	8.06
510	Aerated concrete, low density	0.13	8.73
625	Particle board	0.13	8.12
721	Diatomaceous earth bricks	0.14	7.09
881	Asbestos-silica-lime insulating board	0.14	6.94
881	Standard & tempered hardboards	0.15	6.78
961	Plasterboard	0.16	6.25
769	Hardwoods	0.16	6.25
600	Exfoliated vermiculite concrete	0.18	5.55
641	Exfoliated vermiculite plaster	0.19	5.26
1 190	Perspex	0.21	4.76
1 620	Polyester glass fibre laminate	0.35	2.86
1 522	Asbestos cement	0.37	2.70
1 282	Clinker concrete	0.48	2.21
1 442	Plaster, dense	0.48	2.08
2 306	Cement/sand	0.53	1.89
1 480	Foamed blastfurnace slag concrete	0.58	2.62
1 240	Expanded clay & sintered PVA concretes	0.58	2.63
2 100	Mastic asphalt	0.60	1.67
1 698	Asbestos cement, fully compressed	0.65	1.54
1 602	Aerated concrete	0.65	1.54
1 492	No-fines concrete	1.09	1.56
1 700	Brickwork	0.66	0.92
2 520	Glass	1.05	0.95
2 500	Sandstone	1.29	0.78
2 260	Concrete; cement 1, sand 2, ballast 4	1.44	0.69
2 310	Limestone	1.53	0.65
2 590	Slate	1.88	0.53
2 662	Granite	2.93	0.34
7 850	Steel	57.00	0.02
2 700	Aluminium & alloys	214.00	0.005
9 000	Copper	400.00	0.003

Thermal conductivity (k) measures the rate of heat transfer through a material from face to face. Calculate for any material by multiplying the thickness in metres by the appropriate k value.

Thermal transmittance (U) is the rate of heat transfer through a structure from air to air. Calculate by finding the thermal resistance for each material (resistivity × thickness in metres), adding these together, and taking the reciprocal. The addition should include surface resistances, which may be taken as 0.05 m°C/W for external surfaces and 0.15 m°C/W for internal surfaces.

Country codes and currencies

In the following table, country codes are included for reference; the currency code is that introduced by the International Organisation for Standardisation (ISO), and refers to the main currency unit. The country position refers to end-1991.

CURRENCIES IN USE

Rates of exchange between currencies have in general been floating since the early 1970s. When one currency buys fewer units of another, the first currency is said to have depreciated if the change was the result of market forces, or to have been devalued if the rate is fixed by the authorities. A currency which buys more of another is said to have appreciated (if due to market forces) or been revalued or upvalued (for fixed-rate currencies).

For example, the exchange rate between the currencies of the UK and USA averaged $1.30 = £1 in 1985 and $1.78 = £1 in 1990. At the end of this period more dollars were needed to buy one pound; the dollar had depreciated by 1.78/1.30 = 37%. From the UK's point of view, the pound appreciated from $1 = £0.769 to £1 = 0.562. Fewer pounds were required to buy one dollar; the pound had appreciated by 0.562/0.769 = 27%.

For any depreciation or devaluation, the corresponding appreciation or revaluation can be determined from the percentage reversals table on page 165.

For example, the percentage reversal of 36% is 27% (from the above illustration).

Country codes UN/ISO 3-Digit	ISO Alpha-2	Alpha-3	Name	Code ISO		Currency unit and divisions
004	AF	AFG	Afghanistan	AFA	004	Afghāni = 100 puls
008	AL	ALB	Albania	ALL	008	Lek = 100 quintars
012	DZ	DZA	Algeria	DZD	012	Dinar = 100 centimes
			American Samoa: see Samoa, American			
020	AD	AND	Andorra	FRF	250	French franc
				ESP	020	Spanish peseta
024	AO	AGO	Angola	AON	024	New kwanza = 100 lwei
660	AI	AIA	Anguilla	XCD	951	East Caribbean dollar = 100 cents
028	AG	ATG	Antigua	XCD	951	East Caribbean dollar = 100 cents
			Antilles, Netherlands: see Netherlands Antilles			
032	AR	ARG	Argentina	ARA	032	Austral[a] = 100 centavos
051	AM	ARM	Armenia[b]			
533	AW	ABW	Aruba	AWG	533	Aruban guilder = 100 cents
036	AU	AUS	Australia	AUD	036	Australian dollar = 100 cents
040	AT	AUT	Austria	ATS	040	Schilling = 100 groschen
031	AZ	AZE	Azerbaijan[b]			
044	BS	BHS	Bahamas	BSD	044	Bahamian dollar = 100 cents
048	BH	BHR	Bahrain	BHD	048	Bahrain dinar = 1 000 fils
050	BD	BGD	Bangladesh	BDT	050	Taka = 100 poisha
052	BB	BRB	Barbados	BBD	052	Barbados dollar = 100 cents
112	BY	BLR	Belarus	SUR	810	Rouble = 100 kopeks
056	BE	BEL	Belgium	BEF	056	Belgian franc = 100 centimes
084	BZ	BLZ	Belize	BZD	084	Belize dollar = 100 cents
204	BJ	BEN	Benin	XOF	952	CFA franc = 100 centimes
060	BM	BMU	Bermuda	BMD	060	Bermuda dollar = 100 cents
064	BT	BTN	Bhutan	INR	356	Indian rupee
				BTN	064	Ngultrum = 100 chetrum
068	BO	BOL	Bolivia	BOB	068	Boliviano = 100 centavos
072	BW	BWA	Botswana	BWP	072	Pula = 100 thebes
074	BV	BVT	Bouvet Island	NOK	578	Norwegian krone = 100 øre
076	BR	BRA	Brazil	BRE	076	Cruzeiro = 100 centavos
086	IO	IOT	British Indian Ocean Territory	USD	840	US dollar = 100 cents
			British Virgin Islands: see Virgin Islands, British			
096	BN	BRN	Brunei	BND	096	Brunei dollar = 100 cents
100	BG	BGR	Bulgaria	BGL	100	Lev = 100 stótinki
854	BF	BFA	Burkina Faso	XOF	952	CFA franc = 100 centimes
			Burma: see Myanmar			
108	BI	BDI	Burundi	BIF	108	Burundi franc = 100 centimes
116	KH	KHM	Cambodia	KHR	116	Riel = 100 sen
120	CM	CMR	Cameroon	XAF	950	CFA franc = 100 centimes
124	CA	CAN	Canada	CAD	124	Canadian dollar = 100 cents
132	CV	CPV	Cape Verde	CVE	132	Cape Verde escudo = 100 centavos
136	KY	CYM	Cayman Islands	KYD	136	Cayman Islands dollar = 100 cents
140	CF	CAF	Central African Republic	XAF	950	CFA franc = 100 centimes
148	TD	TCD	Chad	XAF	950	CFA franc = 100 centimes

Country codes UN/ISO 3-Digit	ISO Alpha-2	Alpha-3	Name	Code ISO		Currency unit and divisions
152	CL	CHL	Chile	CLP	152	Chilean peso = 100 centavos
156	CN	CHN	China	CNY	156	Yuan (renminbi) = 10 chiao (jiao) = 100 fen
162	CX	CXR	Christmas Island	AUD	036	Australian dollar = 100 cents
166	CC	CCK	Cocos Islands	AUD	036	Australian dollar = 100 cents
170	CO	COL	Colombia	COP	170	Colombian peso = 100 centavos
174	KM	COM	Comoros	KMF	174	Comoros franc = 100 centimes
178	CG	COG	Congo	XAF	950	CFA franc = 100 centimes
184	CK	COK	Cook Islands	NZD	554	New Zealand dollar = 100 cents
188	CR	CRI	Costa Rica	CRC	188	Colón = 100 céntimos
192	CU	CUB	Cuba	CUP	192	Cuban peso = 100 centavos
196	CY	CYP	Cyprus	CYP	196	Cyprus pound = 100 cents
200	CS	CSK	Czechoslovakia	CSK	200	Koruna (crown) = 100 haleru
208	DK	DNK	Denmark	DKK	208	Danish krone = 100 øre
262	DJ	DJI	Djibouti	DJF	262	Djibouti franc = 100 centimes
212	DM	DMA	Dominica	XCD	951	East Caribbean dollar = 100 cents
214	DO	DOM	Dominican Republic	DOP	214	Dominican peso = 100 centavos
218	EC	ECU	Ecuador	ECS	218	Sucre = 100 centavos
818	EG	EGY	Egypt	EGP	818	Egyptian pound = 100 piastres = 1 000 millièmes
			Eire: see Ireland			
222	SV	SLV	El Salvador	SVC	222	Colón = 100 centavos
226	GQ	GNQ	Equatorial Guinea	XAF	950	CFA franc = 100 centimes
233	EE	EST	Estonia[b]			
230	ET	ETH	Ethiopia	ETB	230	Birr = 100 cents
238	FK	FLK	Falkland Islands	FKP	238	Falkland Island pound = 100 new pence
234	FO	FRO	Faroes	DKK	208	Danish krone = 100 øre
242	FJ	FJI	Fiji	FJD	242	Fiji dollar = 100 cents
246	FI	FIN	Finland	FIM	246	Markka = 100 penni
			Formosa: see Taiwan			
250	FR	FRA	France	FRF	250	French franc = 100 centimes
			French Polynesia: see Polynesia, French			
266	GA	GAB	Gabon	XAF	950	CFA franc = 100 centimes
270	GM	GMB	Gambia	GMD	270	Dalasi = 100 bututs
268	GE	GEO	Georgia[b]			
280	DE	DEU	Germany	DEM	280	Deutschemark = 100 pfennig
288	GH	GHA	Ghana	GHC	288	Cedi = 100 pesewas
292	GI	GIB	Gibraltar	GIP	292	Gibraltar pound = 100 new pence
300	GR	GRC	Greece	GRD	300	Drachma = 100 lepta
304	GL	GRL	Greenland	DKK	208	Danish krone = 100 øre
308	GD	GRD	Grenada	XCD	951	East Caribbean dollar = 100 cents
312	GP	GLP	Guadeloupe	FRF	250	French franc = 100 centimes
316	GU	GUM	Guam	USD	840	US dollar = 100 cents
320	GT	GTM	Guatemala	GTQ	320	Quetzal = 100 centavos
254	GF	GUF	Guiana, French	FRF	250	French franc = 100 centimes
324	GN	GIN	Guinea	GNF	324	Guinea franc = 100 centimes
624	GW	GNB	Guinea-Bissau	GWP	624	Guinea peso = 100 centavos
328	GY	GUY	Guyana	GYD	328	Guyana dollar = 100 cents
332	HT	HTI	Haiti	HTG	332	Gourde = 100 centimes
				USD	840	US Dollar = 100 cents
			Holland: see Netherlands			
340	HN	HND	Honduras	HNL	340	Lempira = 100 centavos
344	HK	HKG	Hong Kong	HKD	344	Hong Kong dollar = 100 cents
348	HU	HUN	Hungary	HUF	348	Forint = 100 fillér
352	IS	ISL	Iceland	ISK	352	Icelandic króna = 100 aurar (øre)
356	IN	IND	India	INR	356	Indian rupee = 100 paisa

Country codes UN/ISO 3-Digit	ISO Alpha-2	Alpha-3	Name	Code ISO		Currency unit and divisions
360	ID	IDN	Indonesia	IDR	360	Rupiah = 100 sen
364	IR	IRN	Iran	IRR	364	Rial = 100 dinars
368	IQ	IRQ	Iraq	IQD	368	Iraqi dinar = 20 dirhams = 1 000 fils
372	IE	IRL	Ireland	IEP	372	Punt = 100 pighne
376	IL	ISR	Israel	ILS	376	New shekel = 100 agorot
380	IT	ITA	Italy	ITL	380	Italian lira = 100 centesimi
384	CI	CIV	Ivory Coast	XOF	952	CFA franc = 100 centimes
388	JM	JAM	Jamaica	JMD	388	Jamaican dollar = 100 cents
392	JP	JPN	Japan	JPY	392	Yen = 100 sen
396	JT	JTN	Johnston Island	USD	840	US dollar = 100 cents
400	JO	JOR	Jordan	JOD	400	Jordan dinar = 1 000 fils
			Kampuchea: see Cambodia			
398	KZ	KAZ	Kazakhstan[b]			
404	KE	KEN	Kenya	KES	404	Kenya shilling = 100 cents
296	KI	KIR	Kiribati	AUD	036	Australian dollar = 100 cents
408	KP	PRK	Korea, North	KPW	408	North Korean Won = 100 chon (jun)
410	KR	KOR	Korea, South	KRW	410	South Korean Won = 100 chon (jun)
414	KW	KWT	Kuwait	KWD	414	Kuwaiti dinar = 10 dirhams = 1 000 fils
417	KG	KGZ	Kyrgyzstan[b]			
418	LA	LAO	Laos	LAK	418	Kip = 100 at
428	LV	LVA	Latvia[c]			
422	LB	LBN	Lebanon	LBP	422	Lebanese pound = 100 piastres
426	LS	LSO	Lesotho	LSL	426	Loti (maloti for 2 or more) = 100 lisente
430	LR	LBR	Liberia	LRD	430	Liberian dollar = 100 cents
434	LY	LBY	Libya	LYD	434	Libyan dinar = 1 000 dirhams
438	LI	LIE	Liechtenstein	CHF	756	Swiss franc = 100 centimes (rappen)
440	LT	LTU	Lithuania[c]	LTT		Litas
442	LU	LUX	Luxembourg	LUF	442	Luxembourg franc = 100 centimes
446	MO	MAC	Macao	MOP	446	Pataca = 100 avos
450	MG	MDG	Madagascar	MGF	450	Madagascar franc = 100 centimes
454	MW	MWI	Malawi	MWK	454	Kwacha = 100 tambala
458	MY	MYS	Malaysia	MYR	458	Ringgit = 100 sen
462	MV	MDV	Maldives	MVR	462	Maldivian rupee = 100 laris
466	ML	MLI	Mali	XOF	952	CFA franc = 100 centimes
470	MT	MLT	Malta	MTL	470	Maltese lira = 100 cents = 1 000 mils
			Marianas, Northern: see Pacific Islands, US			
474	MQ	MTQ	Martinique	FRF	250	French franc = 100 centimes
478	MR	MRT	Mauritania	MRO	478	Ouguiya = 5 khoums
480	MU	MUS	Mauritius	MUR	480	Mauritius rupee = 100 cents
484	MX	MEX	Mexico	MXP	484	Mexican peso = 100 centavos
488	MI	MID	Midway Islands	USD	840	US dollar = 100 cents
498	MD	MDA	Moldova[b]			
492	MC	MCO	Monaco	FRF	250	French franc = 100 centimes
496	MN	MNG	Mongolia	MNT	496	Tugrik or Tögrög = 100 möngö
500	MS	MSR	Montserrat	XCD	951	East Caribbean dollar = 100 cents
504	MA	MAR	Morocco	MAD	504	Dirham = 100 centimes
508	MZ	MOZ	Mozambique	MZM	508	Metical = 100 centavos
104	MM	MMR	Myanmar	MMK	104	Kyat = 100 pyas
516	NA	NAM	Namibia	ZAR	710	South African Rand = 100 cents
520	NR	NRU	Nauru	AUD	036	Australian dollar = 100 cents
524	NP	NPL	Nepal	NPR	524	Nepalese rupee = 2 mohur = 100 paisa (pice)
528	NL	NLD	Netherlands	NLG	528	Guilder (florin) = 100 cents
532	AN	ANT	Netherlands Antilles	ANG	532	Netherlands Antillian guilder (florin) = 100 cents
540	NC	NCL	New Caledonia	XPF	953	CFP franc = 100 centimes
554	NZ	NZL	New Zealand	NZD	554	New Zealand dollar = 100 cents

Country codes UN/ISO 3-Digit	ISO Alpha-2	Alpha-3	Name	Code ISO		Currency unit and divisions
558	NI	NIC	Nicaragua	NIO	558	Córdoba = 100 centavos
562	NE	NER	Niger	XOF	952	CFA franc = 100 centimes
566	NG	NGA	Nigeria	NGN	566	Naira = 100 kobo
570	NU	NIU	Niue	NZD	544	New Zealand dollar = 100 cents
574	NF	NFK	Norfolk Island	AUD	036	Australian dollar = 100 cents
578	NO	NOR	Norway	NOK	578	Norwegian krone = 100 øre
512	OM	OMN	Oman	OMR	512	Rial Omani = 1 000 baizas
582	PC	PCI	Pacific Islands, US	USD	840	US dollar = 100 cents
586	PK	PAK	Pakistan	PKR	586	Pakistan rupee = 100 paisa
590	PA	PAN	Panama	PAB	590	Balboa = 100 centésimos
598	PG	PNG	Papua New Guinea	PGK	598	Kina = 100 toea
600	PY	PRY	Paraguay	PYG	600	Guarani = 100 céntimos
604	PE	PER	Peru	PEN	604	Nuevo sol = 100 céntimos
608	PH	PHL	Philippines	PHP	608	Philippine peso = 100 centavos
612	PN	PCN	Pitcairn	NZD	554	New Zealand dollar = 100 cents
616	PL	POL	Poland	PLZ	616	Zloty = 100 groszy
258	PF	PYF	Polynesia, French	XPF	953	CFP franc = 100 centimes
620	PT	PRT	Portugal	PTE	620	Escudo = 100 centavos
630	PR	PRI	Puerto Rico	USD	840	US dollar = 100 cents
634	QA	QAT	Qatar	QAR	634	Qatar riyal = 100 dirhams
638	RE	REU	Réunion	FRF	250	French franc = 100 centimes
			Rhodesia: see Zimbabwe			
542	RO	ROM	Romania	ROL	642	Leu (plural lei) = 100 bani
643	RU	RUS	Russia[b]			
646	RW	RWA	Rwanda	RWF	646	Rwanda franc = 100 centimes
732	EH	ESH	Sahara, Western	MAD	504	Moroccan dirham = 100 centimes
659	KN	KNA	St Christopher (St Kitts)	XCD	951	East Caribbean dollar = 100 cents
654	SH	SHN	St Helena	SHP	654	St Helena pound = 100 new pence
662	LC	LCA	St Lucia	XCD	951	East Caribbean dollar = 100 cents
666	PM	SPM	St Pierre and Miquelon	FRF	250	French franc = 100 centimes
670	VC	VCT	St Vincent	XCD	951	East Caribbean dollar = 100 cents
			Salvador, El: see El Salvador			
016	AS	ASM	Samoa, American	USD	840	US dollar = 100 cents
				ESP	724	Spanish peseta = 100 céntimos
882	WS	WSM	Samoa, Western	WST	882	Tala (dollar) = 100 sene (cents)
674	SM	SMR	San Marino	ITL	380	Italian lira = 100 centesimi
678	ST	STP	São Tomé and Principe	STD	678	Dobra = 100 céntimos
682	SA	SAU	Saudi Arabia	SAR	682	Saudi riyal = 20 quirsh = 100 hallalas
686	SN	SEN	Senegal	XOF	952	CFA franc = 100 centimes
690	SC	SYC	Seychelles	SCR	690	Seychelles rupee = 100 cents
			Siam: see Thailand			
694	SL	SLE	Sierra Leone	SLL	694	Leone = 100 cents
702	SG	SGP	Singapore	SGD	702	Singapore dollar = 100 cents
090	SB	SLB	Solomon Islands	SBD	090	Solomon Islands dollar = 100 cents
706	SO	SOM	Somalia	SOS	706	Somali shilling = 100 centesimi
710	ZA	ZAF	South Africa	ZAR	710	Rand = 100 cents
810	SU	SUN	Soviet Union (former)	SUR	810	Rouble = 100 kopecks
724	ES	ESP	Spain	ESP	724	Peseta = 100 céntimos
144	LK	LKA	Sri Lanka	LKR	144	Sri Lanka rupee = 100 cents
736	SD	SDN	Sudan	SDP	736	Sudanese pound = 100 piastres = 1 000 millièmes
740	SR	SUR	Surinam	SRG	740	Surinam guilder (florin) = 100 cents
748	SZ	SWZ	Swaziland	SZL	748	Lilangeni (Emalangeni for 2 or more) = 100 cents
752	SE	SWE	Sweden	SEK	752	Swedish krona = 100 öre
756	CH	CHE	Switzerland	CHF	756	Swiss franc (franken) = 100 centimes (rappen)
760	SY	SYR	Syria	SYP	760	Syrian pound = 100 piastres

Country codes			Name	Code		Currency unit and divisions
N/ISO	ISO			ISO		
-Digit	Alpha-2	Alpha-3				
			Tahiti: see Polynesia, French			
01	TW	TWN	Taiwan	TWD	158	New Taiwan dollar = 100 cents
62	TJ	TJK	Tajikistan[b]			
34	TZ	TZA	Tanzania	TZS	834	Tanzanian shilling = 100 cents
64	TH	THA	Thailand	THB	764	Baht = 100 satang
26	TP	TMP	Timor, East	TPE	626	Timor escudo = 100 centavos
				IDR		
68	TG	TGO	Togo	XOF	360	Indonesian rupiah = 100 sen
72	TK	TKL	Tokelau	NZD	952	CFA franc = 100 centimes
76	TO	TON	Tonga	TOP	554	New Zealand dollar = 100 cents
80	TT	TTO	Trinidad and Tobago	TTD	776	Pa'anga = 100 seniti
88	TN	TUN	Tunisia	TND	780	Trinidad and Tobago dollar = 100 cents
92	TR	TUR	Turkey	TRL	788	Tunisian dinar = 1 000 millemes
95	TM	TKM	Turkmenistan[b]		792	Turkish lira = 100 kurus (piastres)
96	TC	TCA	Turks and Caicos Islands	USD	840	US dollar = 100 cents
98	TV	TUV	Tuvalu	AUD	036	Australian dollar = 100 cents
00	UG	UGA	Uganda	UGX	800	Uganda shilling = 100 cents
04	UA	UKR	Ukraine[b]			
84	AE	ARE	United Arab Emirates	AED	784	UAE dirham = 100 fils
26	GB	GBR	United Kingdom	GBP	826	Pound = 100 pence
40	US	USA	United States of America	USD	840	Dollar = 100 cents
54	HV	HVO	Upper Volta	XOF	952	CFA franc = 100 centimes
58	UY	URY	Uruguay	UYP	858	New Uruguayan peso = 100 centésimos
60	UZ	UZB	Uzbekistan[b]			
48	VU	VUT	Vanuatu	VUV	548	Vatu
36	VA	VAT	Vatican	ITL	380	Vatican or Italian lira = 100 centesimi
62	VE	VEN	Venezuela	VEB	862	Bolívar = 100 céntimos
04	VN	VNM	Vietnam	VND	704	Dong = 10 chao = 100 sau
92	VG	VGB	Virgin Islands, British	USD	840	US dollar = 100 cents
50	VI	VIR	Virgin Islands, US	USD	840	US dollar = 100 cents
72	WK	WAK	Wake Island	USD	840	US dollar = 100 cents
76	WF	WLF	Wallis & Futuna Islands	XPF	953	CFP franc = 100 centimes
			Western Sahara: see Sahara, Western			
			Western Samoa: see Samoa, Western			
87	YE	YEM	Yemen	YER	886	Yemeni rial = 100 fils
90	YU	YUG	Yugoslavia[d]	YUN	890	New Yugoslav dinar = 100 paras
80	ZR	ZAR	Zaire	ZRZ	180	Zaire = 100 makuta = 10 000 sengi
94	ZM	ZMB	Zambia	ZMK	894	Kwacha = 100 ngwee
			Zanzibar: see Tanzania			
16	ZW	ZWE	Zimbabwe	ZWD	716	Zimbabwe dollar = 100 cents

Likely to be replaced by the Argentine peso in 1992.
As of spring 1992 currency codes have not been agreed.
As of spring 1992 currency codes have been reserved but not officially confirmed.
As of spring 1992 codes for Croatia are HR, HRV, currency dinar; for Slovenia SI, SVN, currency Slovenian tollar.

Economics

NATIONAL ACCOUNTS

Definitions of basic items

The following definitions are based on the System of National Accounts (SNA) as formulated by the United Nations in 1968 (this replaced the former system which was formulated in 1952). Main differences in definitions as used in the UK national accounts are also indicated.

Factor cost and market value. The basis of valuation for the different items is usually either at factor values (factor cost) or at market prices (or purchasers' values, which is the cost at the point of delivery). Market price value is the factor cost plus taxes on expenditure net of subsidies falling on each item of expenditure.

Private final consumption expenditure is the outlay of resident non-government units (households and non-profit institutions serving households) on new durable and non-durable goods and services, less their net sales of second-hand goods, scraps and wastes. For valuations at market prices certain taxes (eg, motor vehicle licence duty) are classified in the UK system as taxes on expenditure whereas they are classified in the UN system as direct taxes.

Consumer durables are goods acquired by households which have an expected life of considerably more than one year and a relatively high value, such as motor cars, refrigerators and washing machines. Dwellings are excluded since they are classed as fixed assets.

Government final consumption expenditure is net current expenditure by both central government and local authorities; this excludes expenditure on grants, subsidies, interest payments and all other transfers, as well as stocks and fixed capital. The equivalent UK item, general government final consumption, uses a different basis of valuation to the UN system for imputed rent on buildings owned and occupied by public authorities.

Increase in stocks (inventories) is the market value of the physical change during the year in stocks of materials, supplies, work-in-progress, finished products, etc, held by trading enterprises or by government.

Gross fixed capital formation is net expenditure on fixed assets (buildings, vehicles, plant and machinery, etc) either for replacing or adding to the stock of existing fixed assets.

Exports of goods and services are all transfers of the ownership of goods to non-residents, and services provided by resident producers to non-residents. Valued fob.

Imports of goods and services are all transfers of the ownership of goods from non-residents to residents, and services provided by non-resident producers to residents. Valued fob.

Net property income from other countries is property and entrepreneurial income (including dividends, etc) from other countries, less property and entrepreneurial income paid to other countries.

Consumption of fixed capital is the value, at current replacement cost, of the fixed capital used up during the year as a result of normal wear and tear, foreseen obsolescence and the normal rate of accidental damage.

Stock appreciation or depreciation is that increase or fall in the value of stocks which has been due to the change in prices during the year. This item, used in the UK system, is not quantified in the UN system in which all items are measured net of any stock appreciation.

Compensation of employees is all payments by resident producers of wages and salaries to their employees, in kind and in cash, and of contributions, paid or imputed, in respect of their employees to social security schemes and to private pension, family allowance, casualty insurance, life insurance and similar schemes. The equivalent UK item, income from employment, excludes payments to non-resident employees of UK resident employers, but includes receipts by UK resident employees working for non-resident employers. Net receipts by resident employees from non-resident employers are shown in the UN system as compensation of employees receivable from the rest of the world.

Operating surplus is the excess of the value added of resident industries over the sum of their costs of employee compensation, consumption of fixed capital and indirect taxes reduced by subsidies; imputations are included in respect of rent, etc. In the UK system the operating surplus is equivalent to the sum of income from self-employment, gross trading profits of companies, gross trading surplus of public corporations and general government enterprises and rents of properties, less consumption of fixed capital and stock appreciation.

Indirect taxes are taxes and import duties assessed on producers in respect of the production, sale, purchase or use of goods and services, which they charge to the expenses of production. The equivalent UK item, taxes on expenditure, includes certain taxes which are classified as direct in the UN system.

Subsidies are all grants on current account made by government to private industries and public corporations.

Formulae

Final expenditure is:
private final consumption expenditure (consumers' expenditure)
+ government final consumption expenditure
+ increase in stocks
+ gross fixed capital formation
+ exports of goods and services

Gross domestic product (GDP) at market prices is:
final expenditure
− (ie, less) imports of goods and services

Gross national product (GNP) at market prices is:
gross domestic product at market prices
+ net property income from other countries

Gross domestic product at factor cost is:
gross domestic product at market prices
- indirect taxes
+ subsidies

National income at market prices is:
gross domestic product at market prices
+ net property income from other countries
- consumption of fixed capital
and
gross national product at market prices
- consumption of fixed capital
and
compensation of employees
+ compensation of employees receivable from the rest of the world
+ operating surplus
+ net property income from other countries
+ indirect taxes
- subsidies

National income at factor cost is:
national income at market prices
- indirect taxes
+ subsidies
and (in the UK system)
income from employment
+ income from self-employment
+ gross trading profits of companies
+ gross trading surplus of public corporations
+ gross trading surplus of general government enterprises
+ rents of property
+ imputed charge for consumption of non-trading capital
+ net property income from other countries
- consumption of fixed capital

FINANCIAL ACCOUNTS

Saving is current income less current expenditure for each sector, before providing for depreciation and stock appreciation.

Increase in the value of stocks is the value of the physical change in stocks, plus stock appreciation or less stock depreciation.

Net acquisition of financial assets is saving, plus capital transfers, less gross domestic fixed capital formation, less the increase in the value of stocks.

EXTERNAL (OR INTERNATIONAL) TRANSACTIONS ACCOUNTS

These are accounts setting out the current and capital transactions of a country with the rest of the world; they are associated with the national accounts, and are also referred to as the balance of payments.

Current external transactions account, or current balance of payments account

Current balance is
exports of goods and services
- imports of goods and services
+ net property income from other countries
- net current transfers to other countries,
where exports, imports and net property income are as defined above for the national accounts, and net current transfers to other countries equal current transfers of goods, services and financial assets to other countries, less transfers from other countries, such transfers being made without charge or right to compensation. The balance of exports and imports of goods only is referred to as the visible balance, and the balance of other current items (services, income and transfers) as the invisible balance.

Investment and financing account (investment or lending abroad)

The balance on current account shows whether a country has added to or consumed its net external assets in any period. These net external assets represent the net increase in physical assets, financial assets and gold and foreign currency reserves.

These assets are presented in the UK balance of payments in two groups.

Investment and other capital transactions which include official long-term capital transactions, investment flows, changes in the balances of other countries held in the UK, trade credit and other capital flows.

Official financing which covers changes in the official reserves, net borrowing from the International Monetary Fund (IMF) and net transactions with other overseas monetary authorities.

The currency flow is the net movement (allowing for a balancing item) of the current balance and investment and other capital flows. The relationships are as follows.

Financing of currency flow is:
official financing (= change in official reserves + net transactions with overseas monetary authorities)
+ allocation of special drawing rights by the IMF
- gold subscription to the IMF

Currency flow less balancing item is:
current balance
+ investment and other capital flows

Investment and other capital transactions include flows which are regarded as investment flows when of a long-term and other capital flows when of a short-term nature.

Investment and other capital transactions are:
official long-term capital flows (including intergovernment loans)
+ private investment flows (including direct and portfolio investment)
+ other capital flows (including changes in net borrowing or lending by UK banks in overseas currencies; changes in overseas holdings of sterling securities, bank deposits, etc; trade credit; and other official and private short-term flows)

PRICES

Constant prices

Estimates of items in the national accounts are first calculated in terms of current prices – actual prices for each period. Estimates at constant prices are obtained by revaluing each item included at the prices of a base date; this provides an indication of changes in volume when different years are compared.

Implicit price deflator is the term used to describe the price index implied by the difference between current and constant price estimates. For example, where the base date is 1975, the implicit price deflator or price index for national income is given by:

$$\frac{\text{National income at current prices}}{\text{National income at 1975 prices}} \times 100$$

This provides the price index for national income with base 1975 = 100.

Retail prices index

The general index of retail prices in the UK measures the changes month by month in the average level of prices of the commodities and services purchased by the great majority of UK households, including practically all wage earners and most small and medium salary earners. Weights for the index are based on information from the annual Family Expenditure Surveys. This index is less widely based than the price index given by the implicit price deflator for all consumers' expenditure.

See also Finance, page 89.

Purchasing power of money

Changes in the purchasing power of money between any two times can be defined as the inverse of changes in consumer prices between those two times. For example, taking the purchasing power of the pound to be 100p in 1975, its current value is given by:

$$\frac{\text{Index of consumer prices in 1975}}{\text{Current index of consumer prices}} \times 100\text{p}$$

The index used for this purpose may vary; the official UK measure of the purchasing power of the pound has been based as follows: from 1914 to 1938 on the Ministry of Labour's cost of living index; from 1938 to 1962 on the implicit price deflator for total consumers' expenditure; from 1962 on the general index of retail prices.

Index numbers

Index numbers are statistical constructions designed to provide comparisons for numbers or aggregates over a period of years. Where the item being measured is aggregated from a number of individual components, these are weighted to provide an estimate of the average.

The main types of weighted index are as follows.

The Laspeyres index, which uses base year weights to multiply against each of the items in the base year and in the year for which the index is being constructed. Where:

p_o is the base year price
p_t is the current year price
q_o is the base year quantity (weight)

the Laspeyres index is $\dfrac{\sum p_t q_o}{\sum p_o q_o} \times 100$

Thus the sum of the base year quantities multiplied by the current year prices, divided by the sum of the base year quantities multiplied by the base year prices, multiplied by 100, gives the price index for the current year.

The Paasche index, which uses current year weights to multiply against each of the items in the base year and in the year for which the index is being constructed. Where, in addition to the above:

q_t is the current year quantity (weight)

the Paasche index is $\dfrac{\sum p_t q_t}{\sum p_o q_t} \times 100$

Thus the sum of the current year quantities multiplied by the current year prices, divided by the sum of the current year quantities multiplied by the base year prices, multiplied by 100, gives the price index for the current year. The implicit price deflator is a Paasche type index number, while the retail price index is a Laspeyres type.

The Irving Fisher "ideal" index is the geometric mean of the Laspeyres and Paasche indices; using the above symbols, the ideal price index is:

$$\sqrt{\frac{\sum p_t q_o}{\sum p_o q_o} \times \frac{\sum p_t q_t}{\sum p_o q_t}} \times 100$$

RATES OF INCREASE OR GROWTH

Growth rates

The rate at which an amount is changing over time is usually expressed as a percentage change from year to year. When the change is measured over more than one year, the rate of increase or compound growth rate per annum is given by the following formula, where:

n is the number of years over which the increase is measured
A is the percentage increase over the period

$$\text{growth rate in \% pa} = \left[\left(\frac{100 + A}{100}\right)^{-n} \times 100\right] - 100$$

Tables for obtaining growth rates from percentage increases are provided on pages 208–215.

Acceleration of growth

Where a rate of increase or growth is increasing through time it is said to be accelerating and where it is decreasing it is said to be decelerating.

For example, a rate of inflation is the percentage change from year to year, but an increase in this rate is an acceleration and a fall is a deceleration.

Over the period of a business cycle the rate of growth is positive during expansion and accelerating during the early stages of recovery; then the rate of growth falls and is small or negative during recession. In terms of calculus, where dy/dt is the first differential (rate of change) and d^2y/dt^2 is the second differential (rate of acceleration), the changes in these rates are indicated in the following diagram (of a sine curve).

See also Mathematics and statistics, page 113.

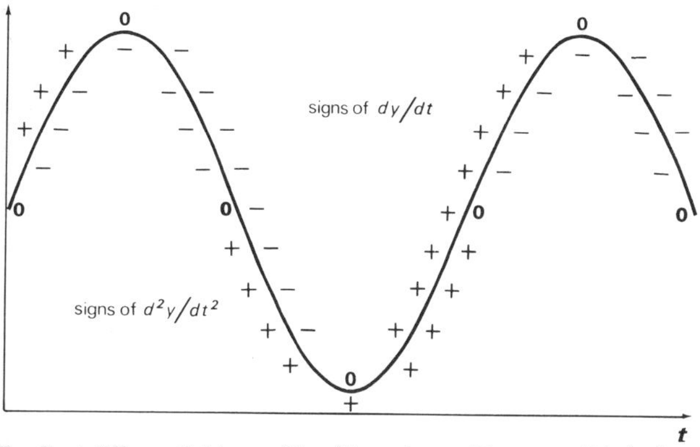

The first differential is positive (there is positive growth) during recovery from a trough; the second differential is at first positive (the rate of growth is increasing), then as recovery continues a point of inflexion is reached at which the second differential becomes zero (the rate of growth, while still positive, begins to slacken); at a peak the first differential becomes zero (the rate of growth changes from positive to negative), while the second differential is still negative; the rate of fall then increases until another point of inflexion is reached (when the second differential is zero), when the rate of fall begins to slow down, becoming zero at the bottom of the trough.

MONEY

There is no single universally accepted definition of money. Any definition must therefore to some extent be arbitrary and different monetary aggregates will be useful for different purposes.

Since the February 1990 issue of the Bank of England *Quarterly Bulletin*, only three definitions of money have been used in the UK. These are M0, M2 and M4. The narrow definition M0 may be thought of as representing the transactions demand for money. It comprises notes and coin in circulation outside of the Bank of England plus bankers' deposits with the Bank of England Banking Department.

M2 covers notes and coin in circulation with the public plus UK private sector sterling sight deposits with banks (less 60% of the net value of transit items) plus UK private sector retail deposits with banks and building societies.

The widest definition, M4, is M2 plus private sector sterling time deposits with banks and building societies less building society deposits with banks.

INTERNATIONAL MONEY

Definitions used in connection with the International Monetary Fund (IMF)

Quotas. Each member of the IMF has a quota which determines the voting power and subscription of that member, the member's share in an allocation of SDRs and the normal quantitative limitations on the member's use of Fund resources.

Subscriptions are equal to quotas; they are payable partly in reserve assets and partly in the member's currency, or they can be fully paid in a member's currency.

Reserve positions in the fund are unconditional drawing rights as a result of the payment of reserve assets and of the Fund's net use of their currencies including borrowing.

Credit tranche positions are conditional liquidity rights which can be drawn on if justification is sufficient. The liquidity of credit tranche positions can be enhanced through a stand-by arrangement which indicates the policies of the member on the basis of which the Fund allows the member to purchase a specific amount in a specified period; specific policies may be indicated, for example, in the fields of exchange, monetary and fiscal matters.

Special drawing rights (SDRs) are unconditional reserve assets created by the IMF to influence the total level of world reserves; member countries that are also participants in the special drawing account receive supplements of SDRs in proportion to their Fund quota. Provision for allocation of SDRs was first made on July 28th 1969.

The value of the SDR from its introduction until end-June 1974 was 0.888 671 gram of fine gold. This was also the par value of the US dollar from the formation of the Fund until November 1971. The value of the SDR was fixed by dividing the gold content of 1 troy ounce, namely 31.103 476 8 grams, by 35 and rounding the resulting number to six significant figures (it being established Fund practice to round values to six significant figures).

From July 1974 the SDR was defined as a weighted index (basket) of 16 currencies. The value of SDR is determined daily from the market exchange rate for each of the 16 currencies in terms of the US dollar, duly weighted. The rates for the SDR in terms of other currencies is determined by the market exchange rate for those currencies against the US dollar, and the US dollar rate against the SDR.

The relative weights for each of the 16 countries were based on relative exports, but also took account of the importance of a currency internationally. Initial weightings, used from July 1974 to end-June 1978, were determined for those countries whose share in the world exports of goods and services averaged more than 1% in the period 1968–72.

The initial weightings are shown in column A in the table below; column B lists the currency components, as calculated on June 28th 1974, which are estimated in such a way that the value of an SDR is the sum of each currency component multiplied by the actual number of US dollars per corresponding unit for any day. For June 28th 1974 the value as calculated was equal to $1.20635, identical with the value based on the old method of valuing the SDR.

	A	B		A	B
USA: dollars	33.0	0.400 0	**Belgium**: francs	3.5	1.600 0
Germany, West: D-marks	12.5	0.380 0	**Sweden**: krona	2.5	0.130 0
UK: pounds	9.0	0.045 0	**Australia**: dollars	1.5	0.012 0
France: francs	7.5	0.440 0	**Denmark**: krone	1.5	0.110 0
Japan: yen	7.5	26.000 0	**Norway**: krone	1.5	0.099 0
Canada: dollars	6.0	0.071 0	**Spain**: pesetas	1.5	1.100 0
Italy: lire	6.0	47.000 0	**Austria**: schillings	1.0	0.220 0
Netherlands: guilders	4.5	0.140 0	**South Africa**: rand	1.0	0.008 2

A revised basket of 16 currencies based on statistics for the period 1972–76 began on July 1st 1978. The currencies of Iran and Saudi Arabia replaced those of Denmark and South Africa, and weights of some countries were changed.. The revised weights were designed in such a way that the value of the SDR for June 30th 1978 was the same using both the old weightings and the new.

It was agreed in September 1980 that the SDR should be based on the currencies of the five members having the largest exports of goods and services. From January 1981 to December 1985 the weights for these five currencies reflected relative export shares in the period 1975–79 (column C below). From January 1st 1986 the weights have been based on exports in the period 1980–84 (column D below).

	C (%)	D (%)
USA: dollars	42	42
Germany, West: D-marks	19	19
Japan: yen	13	15
France: francs	13	12
UK: pounds	13	12

Thus the SDR now broadly reflects the relative importance of five major currencies in international trade.

EC units

Unit of account (UA). The first EC unit of account (gold-based) was defined in 1962 as equal in gold value to the US dollar, equal to 0.888 670 88 grams. The relationship between each member's currency and the unit of account was then equal to the relationship between the currency and the US dollar. At November 1st 1962 the values were as follows.

	Members' units per UA	UA per member's unit
Original six members		
Belgium/Luxembourg: francs	50	0.02
France: francs	4.937 06	0.202 549
Germany, West: D-marks	4	0.25
Italy: lire	625	0.001 6
Netherlands: guilders	3.62	0.276 243
New members (from Jan 1st 1973)		
Denmark: krone	7.5	0.133 333
Ireland: punts	0.416 667	2.40
UK: pounds	0.416 667	2.40

The gold-based unit of account was in use for most EC purposes until replaced in general by the European unit of account (EUA); it was in use for customs purposes up to December 31st 1978. Up to 1977 the EC Statistical Office used the Eur unit as a unit of common value in its publications; this was equal to the UA. In 1977 the Eur was replaced by the EUA.

European unit of account (EUA). In December 1974 the EC Commission introduced the EUA as a unit to replace progressively other EC units. A different unit to the UA had become necessary because members' exchange rates fluctuated away from the original gold-based parities. From January 1st 1978 the EUA started to be used for general budgetary purposes.

The value of the EUA is determined from a basket of currencies of EC members. The weighting of currencies in the basket is based on gross national product and intra-community trade importance. At the outset, the EUA was fixed so that EUA1 was equal to SDR1 equal to US$1.206 35 at June 28th 1974. At that date the weighting and corresponding quantity of each currency in the basket were as follows.

	Weight (%)	No. units
Belgium: francs	7.9	3.66
Denmark: krone	3.0	0.217
France: francs	19.5	1.15
Germany, West: D-marks	27.3	0.828
Ireland: punts	1.5	0.007 59
Italy: lire	14.0	109
Luxembourg: francs	0.3	0.14
Netherlands: guilders	9.0	0.286
UK: pounds	17.5	0.88 5

European currency unit (ecu). Introduced March 13th 1979 as a basket of currencies of EC members, this unit was designed for use within the European Monetary System (EMS). Currency rates for members of the system have a fixed central rate in terms of the ecu, and also upper and lower intervention limits. The various rates and the weights for each currency in the ecu vary when a change in the basic central rate is agreed within the system. At the beginning of the system, the composition and value of the ecu was the same as for EUA. Central rates of EMS members at the beginning of the system were as follows.

	Members' units per ecu
Belgium: francs	39.458 2
Denmark: krone	7.085 92
France: francs	5.798 31
Germany, West: D-marks	2.510 64
Ireland: punts	0.662 638
Italy: lire	1 148.15
Netherlands: guilders	2.720 77

Rates were revised eight times before the Greek drachma was included in the ecu on September 17th 1984. There were a further four changes before the Spanish peseta was included on June 19th 1989. On September 21st 1989 the Portuguese escudo was taken in. There was another change in central rates in January 1990, then on October 8th 1990 the UK pound was admitted, when central rates were as follows.

	Members' units per ecu
Belgium/Luxembourg: francs	42.403 2
Denmark: krone	7.841 95
Germany, West: D-marks	2.055 86
Greece: drachmas	205.311
Spain: pesetas	133.631
France: francs	6.895 09
Ireland: punts	0.767 417

	Members' units per ecu
aly: lire	1 538.24
letherlands: guilders	2.316 43
ortugal: escudos	178.735
K: pounds	0.696 904

he Greek drachma and Portuguese escudo are represented in e ecu, but they do not participate in the EMS exchange rate echanism. The currencies in the ERM are limited to a maximum divergence spread" of 2.25% or, for the UK pound nd the Greek drachma, 6% from the central rates against the cu.

gricultural representative (green) rates. The Common gricultural Policy (CAP) attempts to stabilise agricultural prices roughout the EC. Agricultural products in the EC are priced in e ecu (UA before the introduction of the ecu in 1970). To avoid rice fluctuations due to market-driven exchange rate novements, conversion into national currencies is at epresentative (or "green") rates fixed by administrative ecision from time to time. There are different representative ates for different products. In addition, monetary ompensatory amounts (MCAS) are imposed as taxes or paid as ubsidies to even out prices and avoid distortions caused by elative exchange rate movements between green fixings. It vas the European Commission's objective to abolish green ates and MCAS by 1992. Illustrative green rates fixed in lovember 1990 were as follows.

lational currency/sector	Value in national currency of 1 ecu
elgium/Luxembourg: francs	
ll products	48.556 3
enmark: krone	
ll products	8.979 89
ermany, West: D-mark	
ereals	2.373 60
ther products	2.354 18
reece: drachmas	
ggs, poultrymeat	212.503
ishery products	181.094
live oil	232.153
igmeat	237.081[a]
heepmeat, goatmeat	216.902
tructural measures	230.337
obacco, cereals, sugar, wine	230.472
ther crop products	222.905
ther products	204.710
ortugal: escudos	
heepmeat, goatmeat, fishery products	200.843
ther products	208.676
rance: francs	
heepmeat, goatmeat, fishery products	7.740 81
ther products	7.895 63
Netherlands: guilders	
Cereals	2.660 89
Other products	2.652 56
Ireland: punts	
Sheepmeat, goatmeat, fishery products	0.861 545
Other products	0.878 776
Italy: lire	
Sheepmeat, goatmeat, fishery products	1 718.00
Other products	1 761.45
Spain: pesetas	
Milk, milk products, structural measures, eggs, poultrymeat	154.794
Pigmeat	146.105
Rice, wine, oilseeds	152.896
Sheepmeat, goatmeat	153.315
Tobacco	153.498
Wine, olive oil	151.927
Other crop products	154.213
Other livestock products	155.786
UK: pounds	
Cereals, sugar, olive oil	0.779 553
Beef, veal	0.795 232
Pigmeat	0.794 820
Sheepmeat, goatmeat	0.702 276
Other crop products	0.704 335
Other products	0.758 185

[a] On November 19th 1990.

Definitions of other forms of international money

Eurodollars are dollar deposits held through banks outside the USA. The Eurodollar market is the market through which such dollars are borrowed and on-lent. The term is sometimes used loosely to refer to Eurocurrency markets in general; these include the Eurodollar market and markets in other currencies, such as the Deutschemark, Swiss franc or sterling, which are similarly defined in terms of the borrowing and lending of the currency in question by banks situated outside the country whose currency is being used.

The Eurobond market is the market through which medium and long-term bonds in Eurocurrencies are issued and traded.

EXTERNAL TRADE

Systems of trade

There are two main systems for recording trade.

General trade. Imports are goods entering for domestic consumption and goods entered into customs storage.
Exports are as follows.

a) Domestic or national goods, wholly or partly produced in the country.

b) Foreign goods, neither transformed nor declared for domestic consumption in the country, which move out of the country from customs storage.
c) Domesticised goods, ie, foreign goods declared for domestic consumption and having paid duty, which move outward without having been transformed.

Where re-exports are distinguished, these are the total of foreign and domesticised goods.

Special trade. Imports are goods entering for domestic consumption both direct from other countries and from customs storage. This is equal to general trade imports, less the items which move outwards from customs storage without entering for domestic consumption (equal to the amount under exports (b) above, but not necessarily the same amount for any one period, due to the time interval between entering and leaving customs). Exports are categories (a) and (c) above, ie, domestic and domesticised goods.

The special trade system is in use in most European countries, the main exceptions being the UK, Ireland and the Nordic countries.

Semi-special trade is also sometimes distinguished, being general trade less all re-exports.

Direct transit trade, consisting of goods entering or leaving for transport purposes only, is generally excluded from both import and export statistics.

Value of trade

External trade may be valued at different stages in its transportation from the seller to the buyer. The terms in common use are listed below. UK imports are recorded cif, exports fob. US imports and exports are both recorded fob.

Cost, insurance and freight (cif). The seller has agreed for the named price to bear all risks of the goods and all expenses up to and including their delivery upon an overseas vessel (or other means of international transport), and also to provide at their own risk and expense for transportation of the goods to the named destination and for insurance covering such transportation.

Free alongside ship (fas). The seller has agreed for the named price to bear all risks of the goods and all expenses up to and including their delivery upon an overseas vessel (or other vessel).

Free on board (fob). The seller has agreed for the named price to bear all risks of the goods and all expenses up to and including delivery of the goods upon an overseas vessel.

Cost and freight (c & f). The seller has agreed for the named price to bear all risk of the goods and all expenses up to and including their delivery upon an overseas vessel, and also to provide at their own risk and expense for transportation of the goods to the named destination.

Imports fob and cif. Most countries' exports are recorded fob and imports cif, except the countries listed below whose imports are recorded fob or have been so recorded in past years. The percentage to be added to imports fob to convert them to imports cif is shown in the following table, in which the estimates are those used by the International Monetary Fund.

Percentage addition to fob to obtain cif

	1950	1960	1970	1980	199
Australia	11	12	11	10	10
Bolivia	17	17	18	18	20
Canada	3	3	3	3	3
Dominican Republic	14	15	14	15	15
Ecuador	20	14	15	13	13
Guatemala	10	10	9	9	14
Honduras	10	10	11	11	11
New Zealand	13	12	7	9	8
Nicaragua	10	10	11	8	10
Panama	10	10	9	12	14
Paraguay	7	18	19	19	15
Philippines	11	10	11	7	7
South Africa	8	5	8	5	9
USA	7	9	7	5	4
Venezuela	12	12	11	11	11

[a]Estimate.

The IMF adds an average 5% to convert from fob to cif.

Balance of payments basis. Values of imports (cif) are converted to an fob basis for use in calculating the current balance of payments. The visible trade balance is then the difference between exports and imports of goods both valued on an fob basis, insurance and freight for both exports and imports being included as services.

Volume and unit value index numbers

Volume of imports and exports. Volume index numbers are designed to show movements in imports and exports after eliminating variations due to price changes. For the UK they are prepared by estimating what the value of the goods imported (or exported) in the current period would have been if their prices had been those of a base period. This estimate is then divided by the value of goods actually imported or exported in the base year, to provide an index (with base year = 100) of the changes in the value of imports and exports at constant prices. The volume index is a Laspeyres type, with base year prices as weights.

Unit values of imports and exports. Index numbers of unit values are intended as guides to changes in the prices of imports and exports and are sometimes referred to as import or export price indices. The unit values are obtained by dividing the value of trade recorded in the month for each selected heading by the corresponding quantity (numbers, tonnes, etc). As far as possible only those headings are used which cover a sufficiently homogeneous group of commodities, such that their unit values move in much the same way as true prices.

In the UK the indices are constructed by combining the unit values with the quantities recorded in the base year as weights (Laspeyres type), but unit value indices can also be constructed using current weights (Paasche type).

alance of payments basis. The import and export volume and nit value index numbers are calculated from trade statistics; dex numbers comparable with the value of trade on a alance of payments basis are also constructed for the UK. Veights for commodity groups are altered to allow for the ffects of balance of payments adjustments in the base year.

erms of trade. An index of the terms of trade is derived by ividing the total export unit value index by the total import nit value index, both being on a balance of payments basis. his index rises when the terms of trade become more vourable; ie, when export prices rise more quickly than nport prices. Conversely it falls when the terms of trade move gainst a country because import prices rise faster than export rices.

lassification of commodities

he Standard International Trade Classification, revision 3, SITC 3), has in general replaced the former SITC revisions; for the K the new classification was introduced on January 1st 1988.

utline of SITC sections, divisions and main groups. There are ine sections, given single digits 1–9; divisions within these ections have 2-digit numbers and groups within each division ave 3-digit numbers. In the list below all sections and ivisions are shown, together with selected groups. There are lso 4-digit subgroups in the full SITC list, eg, 072.3 for cocoa utter and cocoa paste as a subgroup of 072 (cocoa), and rther breakdowns for some items into a 5-digit level, eg, 72.32 for cocoa cake.

tandard International Trade Classification, SITC (R3)

	Food and live animals
0	Live animals other than animals of division 03
1	Meat and meat preparations
2	Dairy products and birds' eggs
22	Milk and cream
23	Butter
24	Cheese and curd
3	Fish, crustaceans, molluscs and aquatic invertebrates, and preparations thereof
4	Cereals and cereal preparations
41	Wheat (incl. spelt) and meslin, unmilled
42	Rice
43	Barley, unmilled
44	Maize (corn, not incl. sweet corn), unmilled
5	Vegetables and fruit
6	Sugar, sugar preparations and honey
7	Coffee, tea, cocoa, spices and manufactures thereof
71	Coffee and coffee substitutes
72	Cocoa
74	Tea and maté
8	Feeding stuff for animals (excl. unmilled cereals)
9	Miscellaneous edible products and preparations
	Beverages and tobacco
1	Beverages
12	Alcoholic beverages
2	Tobacco and tobacco manufactures
	Crude materials, inedible, except fuels
1	Hides, skins and furskins, raw
2	Oil seeds and oleaginous fruit
23	Crude rubber (incl. synthetic and reclaimed)
24	Cork and wood
25	Pulp and waste paper
26	Textile fibres (other than wool tops and other combed wool), and their wastes (not manufactured into yarn or fabric)
263	Cotton
266	Synthetic fibres suitable for spinning
267	Other man-made fibres suitable for spinning and wastes of man-made fibres
268	Wool and other animal hair (excl. wool tops)
27	Crude fertilisers other than those of division 56 and crude minerals (excl. coal, petroleum and precious stones)
28	Metalliferous ores and metal scrap
281	Iron ore and concentrates
29	Crude animal and vegetable materials, nes
3	Mineral fuels, lubricants and related materials
32	Coal, coke and briquettes
33	Petroleum, petroleum products and related materials
333	Petroleum oils, crude, and crude oils obtained from bituminous materials
334	Petroleum products, refined
34	Gas, natural and manufactured
35	Electric current
4	Animal and vegetable oils, fats and waxes
41	Animal oils and fats
42	Fixed vegetable oils and fats
43	Animal and vegetable oils and fats, processed, and waxes of animal or vegetable origin
5	Chemical and related products, nes
51	Organic chemicals
52	Inorganic chemicals
53	Dyeing, tanning and colouring materials
54	Medicinal and pharmaceutical products
55	Essential oils and perfume materials; toilet, polishing and cleansing preparations
56	Fertilisers, manufactured
57	Plastics in primary form
58	Plastics in non-primary form
59	Chemical materials and products, nes
6	Manufactured goods, classified chiefly by material
61	Leather, leather manufactures, nes and dressed furskins
62	Rubber manufacturers, nes
63	Cork and wood manufactures (excl. furniture)
64	Paper, paperboard and articles of paper pulp, of paper or of paperboard
65	Textile yarn, fabrics, made-up articles, nes, and related products
66	Non-metalllic mineral manufactures, nes
67	Iron and steel
68	Non-ferrous metals
681	Silver, platinum and other metals of the platinum group
682	Copper
683	Nickel
684	Aluminium
687	Tin
69	Manufactures of metal, nes

7	Machinery and transport equipment
71	Power generating machinery and equipment
713	Internal combustion piston engines, and parts thereof, nes
72	Machinery specialised for particular industries
721	Agricultural machinery (excl. tractors) and parts thereof, nes
724	Textile and leather machinery, and parts thereof, nes
73	Metalworking machinery
74	General industrial machinery and equipment, nes, and machine parts, nes
75	Office machines and automatic data processing equipment
76	Telecommunications and sound recording and reproducing apparatus and equipment
761	Television receivers (incl. video monitors and video projectors) whether or not combined in the same housing with radio broadcast receivers or sound or video recording or reproducing apparatus
77	Electrical machinery, apparatus and appliances, nes, and electrical parts thereof (incl. non-electrical counterparts, nes of electrical household type equipment)
78	Road vehicles (incl. air-cushion vehicles)
781	Passenger motor cars (other than public-service type vehicles) incl. vehicles designed for the transport of both passengers and goods
782	Motor vehicles for the transport of goods or materials and special purpose motor vehicles
79	Other transport equipment
791	Railway vehicles (incl. hovertrains) and associated equipment
792	Aircraft, spacecraft (incl. satellites) and spacecraft launc vehicles and parts thereof
793	Ships, boats (incl. hovercraft) and floating structures
8	Miscellaneous manufactured articles
81	Prefabricated buildings, sanitary, plumbing, heating and lighting fixtures and fittings, nes
82	Furniture and parts thereof
83	Travel goods, handbags and similar containers
84	Articles of apparel and clothing accessories
85	Footwear
87	Professional, scientific and controlling instruments and apparatus, nes
88	Photographic apparatus, equipment and supplies and optical goods, nes; watches and clocks
881	Photographic apparatus and equipment, nes
885	Watches and clocks
89	Miscellaneous manufactured articles, nes
9	Commodities and transactions not classified elsewhere in the SITC
911.0	Postal packages not classified according to kind
931.0	Special transactions and commodities not classified according to kind
961.0	Coin (other than gold coin), not being legal tender
971.0	Gold, non-monetary (excl. gold ores and concentrates
981.0	Military arms and ammunition

lectronics

LECTROMAGNETIC MEASURES

lectromagnetic spectrum

he main divisions are as follows.

requency (Hz)	Wavelength (m)	Description
$\times 10^3$ to 3×10^{12}	1×10^5 to 1×10^{-4}	Radio waves
$\times 10^{11}$ to 4×10^{14}	1×10^{-3} to 8×10^{-7}	Infra-red
$\times 10^{14}$ to 1×10^{15}	8×10^{-7} to 3×10^{-7}	Visible light
$\times 10^{15}$ to 6×10^{16}	3×10^{-7} to 5×10^{-9}	Ultra-violet
$\times 10^{16}$ to 3×10^{20}	5×10^{-9} to 1×10^{-12}	X-rays
$\times 10^{18}$ to 3×10^{24}	1×10^{-10} to 8×10^{-16}	Gamma rays

he relationship between frequency and wavelength is defined s wave velocity = frequency × wavelength. Wave velocity of ie electromagnetic spectrum is constant for a given medium, nd for the speed of light in a vacuum is approximately 3×10^8 ietres per second (more exactly $2.997\,924\,58\times 10^8$ m/s).
Hence, approximately:

requency in Hz = 3×10^8/wavelength in metres
requency in kHz = 3×10^5/wavelength in metres
requency in MHz = 3×10^2/wavelength in metres
requency in GHz = 3×10^{-1}/wavelength in metres

ld units
ngström (Å) = 10^{-10} metres = approx. 3×10^{18} Hz
Vave number = reciprocal of wavelength = 1/m or 1 m^{-1}
kayser (or rydberg) = 1/cm
X unit (or X-ray unit or Siegbahn unit) = $1.002\,02\times 10^{-4}$ nm

lectromagnetic units summary

summary of the relationships is as follows.

ate of flow of electric current: ampere (A) = watt (W)/volt (V)
uantity of electricity or electric charge: coulomb (C) = A s
ower rate: watt (W) = J/s
lectric potential: volt (V) = W/A
lectric resistance: ohm (Ω) = V/A
lectric conductance: siemens (S) = 1/ohm = A/V
lectric capacitance: farad (F) = A s/V = C/V
lectric field strength: volt per metre (V/m)
Aagnetic flux: weber (Wb) = V s
nductance: henry (H) = V s/A
Aagnetic flux density: tesla (T) = Wb/m^2
Aagnetic field strength: ampere per metre (A/m)

or definitions of the main SI units, see pages 13–17.

lectromagnetic and electrostatic units

lectromagnetic units (EMU)

EMU of current	= 10 A	1 EMU of conductance	= 1 GS
EMU of charge	= 10 C	1 EMU of capacitance	= 1 GF
EMU of potential	= 10 nV	1 EMU of inductance	= 1 nH
EMU of resistance	= 1 nΩ		

Electrostatic units (ESU)
(where c = velocity of light in free space = 299 792 458 m/s)

1 ESU of current	= $1/10c$ A	= 333.564 095 pA
1 ESU of charge	= $1/10c$ C	= 333.564 095 pC
1 ESU of potential	= $10^{-6}c$ V	= 299.792 458 V
1 ESU of resistance	= $10^{-5}c^2$ Ω	= 898.755 179 GΩ
1 ESU of conductance	= $10^5/c^2$ S	= 1.112 650 pS
1 ESU of capacitance	= $10^5/c^2$ F	= 1.112 650 pF
1 ESU of inductance	= $10^{-5}c^2$ H	= 898.755 179 GH

Old units

1 biot (bi)	= 10 amperes
1 faraday (based on carbon-12)	= 96 487 coulombs
1 faraday (chemical)	= 96 495.7 coulombs
1 faraday (physical)	= 96 521.9 coulombs
1 franklin (Fr)	= $(0.1/c)\ 10^{-9}$ coulomb
(where c = speed of light)	= $\frac{1}{3}\ 10^{-9}$ coulomb (approx.)
1 debye (D)	= 10^{-18} franklin centimetre
1 gamma	= 10^{-9} tesla
1 gauss (Gs)	= 10^{-4} tesla
1 gilbert (Gb)	= $10/4\pi$ ampere
1 maxwell (Mx)	= 10^{-8} weber
1 mho	= 1/ohm = 1 siemens
1 oersted (Oe)	= $1\,000/4\pi$ amperes per metre
1 unit pole	= 125.663 7 nanowebers

Electromagnetic constants

Where c = speed of light in a vacuum (or in free space)
= $2.997\,924\,58\times 10^8$ m/s
and μ_0 = magnetic constant (permeability of a vacuum or of free space)
= $4\pi\ 10^{-7}$ H/m = $12.566\,371\times 10^{-7}$ H/m
then ε_0 = electric constant (permittivity of a vacuum or of free space)
= $1/\mu_0 c^2 = 8.854\,187\,82\times 10^{-12}$ F/m

Diamagnetic substances have magnetic permeability less than μ_0. Paramagnetic substances have magnetic permeability slightly above μ_0. Ferromagnetic substances have magnetic permeability well above μ_0.

RADIO WAVE FREQUENCIES

Revisions to radio regulations were made in 1979 by the International Telecommunication Union (ITU) and came into effect in 1982.
For purposes of allocation, the ITU divides the world into three main regions.

Region 1: Europe, former Soviet Union, Mongolia, Middle East (excl. Iran), Africa
Region 2: America, Greenland, East Pacific
Region 3: Asia (incl. Iran; excl. former Soviet Union, Mongolia), West Pacific

The ITU controls allocations within the frequency range 9 kHz (9×10^3 Hz)–400 GHz (4×10^{11} Hz). The range 9–148.5 kHz is used mainly for telecommunications and radionavigation. Other frequencies are divided between many different users: public broadcasting; fixed or mobile telecommunications (including maritime); radionavigation (including aeronautical and maritime); amateur; space research; radio astronomy; satellites (including meteorological, radionavigation, etc); and so on.

Standard frequencies and time signals are at (central frequency) 2 500 kHz, 5 000 kHz, 10 000 kHz, 15 000 kHz, 20 000 kHz, 25 000 kHz, and (for satellites) 400.1 MHz; distress and calling frequencies are at 495–505 kHz (centred on 500 kHz) and 2 173.5–2 190.5 kHz (centred on 2 182 kHz). It may be noted, in connection with the above frequencies, that the ITU uses the multiple kilohertz up to 27 500 kHz (27.5 MHz), the multiple megahertz from 27.5 MHz up to 10 000 MHz (10 GHz), and the multiple gigahertz from 10 GHz up to the recognised end of radio waves or hertzian waves at 3 000 GHz.

Broadcasts are made using both AM (amplitude modulation) and FM (frequency modulation) signals. AM broadcasts are sent out on a single frequency or wavelength, whereas FM uses a band of frequencies to transmit a signal. The bandwidth allocated for FM signals is 87.5–108 MHz in Region 1.

Broadcasting frequencies are in general as shown in the following table (where kHz = 10^3 Hz, MHz = 10^6 Hz, GHz = 10^9 Hz; allocations as fixed in 1979, not all of which are exclusive to broadcasting).

Region 1	Region 2	Region 3
148.5–283.5 kHz		
526.5–1 606.5 kHz	525–1 705 kHz	526.5–1 605.5 kHz
2 300–2 498 kHz	2 300–2 495 kHz	2 300–2 495 kHz
3 200–3 400 kHz	3 200–3 400 kHz	3 200–3 400 kHz
3 950–4 000 kHz		3 900–4 000 kHz
4 750–4 995 kHz	4 750–4 995 kHz	4 750–4 995 kHz
5 005–5 060 kHz	5 005–5 060 kHz	5 005–5 060 kHz
5 950–6 200 kHz	5 950–6 200 kHz	5 950–6 200 kHz
7 100–7 300 kHz		7 100–7 300 kHz
9 500–9 900 kHz	9 500–9 900 kHz	9 500–9 900 kHz
11 650–12 050 kHz	11 650–12 050 kHz	11 650–12 050 kHz
13 600–13 800 kHz	13 600–13 800 kHz	13 600–13 800 kHz
15 100–15 600 kHz	15 100–15 600 kHz	15 100–15 600 kHz
17 550–17 900 kHz	17 550–17 900 kHz	17 550–17 900 kHz
21 450–21 850 kHz	21 450–21 850 kHz	21 450–21 850 kHz
25 670–26 100 kHz	25 670–26 100 kHz	25 670–26 100 kHz
47–68 MHz	54–72 MHz	47–50 MHz, 54–68 MHz
87.5–108 MHz	76–108 MHz	87–108 MHz
174–230 MHz	174–216 MHz	174–230 MHz
470–960 MHz	470–608 MHz, 614–890 MHz	470–960 MHz
2 500–2 690 MHz[a]	2 500 MHz–2 690 MHz[a]	2 500 MHz–2 690 MHz[a]
11.7–12.5 GHz[b]	12.1–12.7 GHz[b]	11.7–12.2 GHz[b]
		12.2–12.5 GHz
		12.5–12.75 GHz[a]
	22.5–23 GHz[a]	22.5–23 GHz[a]
40.5–42.5 GHz[b]	40.5–42.5 GHz[b]	40.5–42.5 GHz[b]
84–86 GHz[b]	84–86 GHz[b]	84–86 GHz[b]

[a]Broadcasting via satellite. [b]Also includes broadcasting via satellite.

The general classification of frequencies is as follows.

	Minimum	Maximum
Very low frequency (VLF)	3 kHz	30 kHz
Low frequency (LF)	30 kHz	300 kHz
Medium frequency (MF)	300 kHz	3 MHz
High frequency (HF)	3 MHz	30 MHz
Very high frequency (VHF)	30 MHz	300 MHz
Ultra high frequency (UHF)	300 MHz	3 GHz
Super high frequency (SHF)	3 GHz	30 GHz
Extra high frequency (EHF)	30 GHz	300 GHz

SOUND BROADCASTING

The main sound frequency ranges are as follows (see also above).

Band	Range (kHz)
Low frequency (LF)	148.5–283.5
Medium frequency (MF)	525–1 705
High frequency (HF)	2 300–26 100[a]
Very high frequency (VHF)	47–108[ab]

[a]Not all sections. [b]MHz.

The following table gives conversions between frequency and wavelength (metres) for main general sound ranges, using the customary approximation for wave velocity equal to 3×10^8 m/s. Since this is a reciprocal type of relationship, the kilohertz tables also apply for converting from metres to kilohertz; eg, 200 kHz = 1 500 m and 1 500 kHz = 200 m. A full range of conversions is shown, including some for frequencies not allocated to broadcasting.

kHz	m	kHz	m	kHz	m	kHz	m	kHz	m
Low frequency (long wave)									
150	2 000	180	1 667	210	1 429	240	1 250	270	1 11
155	1 935	185	1 622	215	1 395	245	1 224	275	1 09
160	1 875	190	1 579	220	1 364	250	1 200	280	1 07
165	1 818	195	1 538	225	1 333	255	1 176		
170	1 765	200	1 500	230	1 304	260	1 154		
175	1 714	205	1 463	235	1 277	265	1 132		
Medium frequency (medium wave)									
525	571	770	389	1 020	294	1 270	236	1 520	19
530	566	780	385	1 030	291	1 280	234	1 530	19
540	556	790	380	1 040	288	1 290	233	1 540	19
550	545	800	375	1 050	286	1 300	231	1 550	19
560	536	810	370	1 060	283	1 310	229	1 560	19
570	526	820	366	1 070	280	1 320	227	1 570	19
580	517	830	361	1 080	278	1 330	226	1 580	19
590	508	840	357	1 090	275	1 340	224	1 590	18
600	500	850	353	1 100	273	1 350	222	1 600	18
610	492	860	349	1 110	270	1 360	221	1 610	18
620	484	870	345	1 120	268	1 370	219	1 620	18
630	476	880	341	1 130	265	1 380	217	1 630	18
640	469	890	337	1 140	263	1 390	216	1 640	18
650	462	900	333	1 150	261	1 400	214	1 650	18
660	455	910	330	1 160	259	1 410	213	1 660	18
670	448	920	326	1 170	256	1 420	211	1 670	18
680	441	930	323	1 180	254	1 430	210	1 680	17
690	435	940	319	1 190	252	1 440	208	1 690	17
700	429	950	316	1 200	250	1 450	207	1 700	17
710	423	960	313	1 210	248	1 460	205	1 705	17

kHz	m	kHz	m	kHz	m	kHz	m	kHz	m
720	417	970	309	1 220	246	1 470	204		
730	411	980	306	1 230	244	1 480	203		
740	405	990	303	1 240	242	1 490	201		
750	400	1 000	300	1 250	240	1 500	200		
760	395	1 010	297	1 260	238	1 510	199		
High frequency (short wave)									
2 300	130.4	7 300	41.1	12 300	24.4	17 300	17.3	22 300	13.5
2 400	125.0	7 400	40.5	12 400	24.2	17 400	17.2	22 400	13.4
2 500	120.0	7 500	40.0	12 500	24.0	17 500	17.1	22 500	13.3
2 600	115.4	7 600	39.5	12 600	23.8	17 600	17.0	22 600	13.3
2 700	111.1	7 700	39.0	12 700	23.6	17 700	16.9	22 700	13.2
2 800	107.1	7 800	38.5	12 800	23.4	17 800	16.9	22 800	13.2
2 900	103.4	7 900	38.0	12 900	23.3	17 900	16.8	22 900	13.1
3 000	100.0	8 000	37.5	13 000	23.1	18 000	16.7	23 000	13.0
3 100	96.8	8 100	37.0	13 100	22.9	18 100	16.6	23 100	13.0
3 200	93.7	8 200	36.6	13 200	22.7	18 200	16.5	23 200	12.9
3 300	90.9	8 300	36.1	13 300	22.6	18 300	16.4	23 300	12.9
3 400	88.2	8 400	35.7	13 400	22.4	18 400	16.3	23 400	12.8
3 500	85.7	8 500	35.3	13 500	22.2	18 500	16.2	23 500	12.8
3 600	83.3	8 600	34.9	13 600	22.1	18 600	16.1	23 600	12.7
3 700	81.1	8 700	34.5	13 700	21.9	18 700	16.0	23 700	12.7
3 800	78.9	8 800	34.1	13 800	21.7	18 800	16.0	23 800	12.6
3 900	76.9	8 900	33.7	13 900	21.6	18 900	15.9	23 900	12.6
4 000	75.0	9 000	33.3	14 000	21.4	19 000	15.8	24 000	12.5
4 100	73.2	9 100	33.0	14 100	21.3	19 100	15.7	24 100	12.4
4 200	71.4	9 200	32.6	14 200	21.1	19 200	15.6	24 200	12.4
4 300	69.8	9 300	32.3	14 300	21.0	19 300	15.5	24 300	12.3
4 400	68.2	9 400	31.9	14 400	20.8	19 400	15.5	24 400	12.3
4 500	66.7	9 500	31.6	14 500	20.7	19 500	15.4	24 500	12.2
4 600	65.2	9 600	31.2	14 600	20.5	19 600	15.3	24 600	12.2
4 700	63.8	9 700	30.9	14 700	20.4	19 700	15.2	24 700	12.1
4 800	62.5	9 800	30.6	14 800	20.3	19 800	15.2	24 800	12.1
4 900	61.2	9 900	30.3	14 900	20.1	19 900	15.1	24 900	12.0
5 000	60.0	10 000	30.0	15 000	20.0	20 000	15.0	25 000	12.0
5 100	58.8	10 100	29.7	15 100	19.9	20 100	14.9	25 100	12.0
5 200	57.7	10 200	29.4	15 200	19.7	20 200	14.9	25 200	11.9
5 300	56.6	10 300	29.1	15 300	19.6	20 300	14.8	25 300	11.9
5 400	55.6	10 400	28.8	15 400	19.5	20 400	14.7	25 400	11.8
5 500	54.5	10 500	28.6	15 500	19.4	20 500	14.6	25 500	11.8
5 600	53.6	10 600	28.3	15 600	19.2	20 600	14.6	25 600	11.7
5 700	52.6	10 700	28.0	15 700	19.1	20 700	14.5	25 700	11.7
5 800	51.7	10 800	27.8	15 800	19.0	20 800	14.4	25 800	11.6
5 900	50.8	10 900	27.5	15 900	18.9	20 900	14.4	25 900	11.6
6 000	50.0	11 000	27.3	16 000	18.7	21 000	14.3	26 000	11.5
6 100	49.2	11 100	27.0	16 100	18.6	21 100	14.2	26 100	11.5
6 200	48.4	11 200	26.8	16 200	18.5	21 200	14.2		
6 300	47.6	11 300	26.5	16 300	18.4	21 300	14.1		
6 400	46.9	11 400	26.3	16 400	18.3	21 400	14.0		
6 500	46.2	11 500	26.1	16 500	18.2	21 500	14.0		
6 600	45.5	11 600	25.9	16 600	18.1	21 600	13.9		
6 700	44.8	11 700	25.6	16 700	18.0	21 700	13.8		
6 800	44.1	11 800	25.4	16 800	17.9	21 800	13.8		
6 900	43.5	11 900	25.2	16 900	17.8	21 900	13.7		
7 000	42.9	12 000	25.0	17 000	17.6	22 000	13.6		
7 100	42.3	12 100	24.8	17 100	17.5	22 100	13.6		
7 200	41.7	12 200	24.6	17 200	17.4	22 200	13.5		

MHz	m	MHz	m	MHz	m	MHz	m	MHz	m
Very high frequency (ultra short wave)									
47	6.38	60	5.00	73	4.11	86	3.49	99	3.03
48	6.25	61	4.92	74	4.05	87	3.45	100	3.00
49	6.12	62	4.84	75	4.00	88	3.41	101	2.97
50	6.00	63	4.76	76	3.95	89	3.37	102	2.94
51	5.88	64	4.69	77	3.90	90	3.33	103	2.91
52	5.77	65	4.62	78	3.85	91	3.30	104	2.88
53	5.66	66	4.55	79	3.80	92	3.26	105	2.86
54	5.56	67	4.48	80	3.75	93	3.23	106	2.83
55	5.45	68	4.41	81	3.70	94	3.19	107	2.80
56	5.36	69	4.35	82	3.66	95	3.16	108	2.78
57	5.26	70	4.29	83	3.61	96	3.13		
58	5.17	71	4.23	84	3.57	97	3.09		
59	5.08	72	4.17	85	3.53	98	3.06		

TELEVISION BROADCASTING

UK 625-line television channels have a bandwidth of 8 MHz. Television has been allocated two frequency bands in the UHF range: channels 21–34 in Band IV between 465 MHz and 585 MHz and channels 39–68 in Band V between 610 MHz and 855 MHz.

The frequencies are shown in the following table.

	Vision	Sound
Band IV		
Channel 21	471.25 MHz	477.25 MHz
Channel 22	479.25 MHz	485.25 MHz
increasing by 8 MHz per channel to		
Channel 34	575.25 MHz	581.25 MHz
Band V		
Channel 39	615.25 MHz	621.25 MHz
Channel 40	623.25 MHz	629.25 MHz
increasing by 8 MHz per channel to		
Channel 68	847.25 MHz	853.25 MHz

For each channel, the vision signal occupies a band of frequencies arranged asymmetrically around the vision carrier frequency shown above, while the sound signal covers a narrower band centred on the sound carrier frequency.

Until 1984 two bands of VHF frequencies, 41.5–66.75 MHz and 176.25–214.75 MHz, were allocated to 13 405-line television channels, each 5 MHz wide. This service no longer operates.

SATELLITE BROADCASTING

Higher-power DBS (direct broadcast by satellite) channels in Europe operate in the 11.7–12.5 GHz band. In addition, low-power telecommunications satellites are used for TV and radio broadcasting at frequencies between 10.95–11.2 GHz and 12.5–12.71 GHz.

Satellite television channels have a bandwidth of 27 MHz and are spaced 19 MHz apart. Interference is avoided by ensuring adjacent overlapping channels serve different geographical regions and use different polarisations.

Other frequencies where satellite broadcasting is permitted though not used are:

2.50–2.69 GHz
40.5–42.5 GHz
84–86 GHz

The 16 satellites used for broadcasting whose signals can be received in the UK are listed in the following table.

Satellite	Type	Position
Intelsat VB F15	Telecoms	60°E
DFS 1 Kopernikus	DBS	23.5°E
Astra	Telecoms	19.2°E
Eutelsat II F1	Telecoms	13°E
Eutelsat II F2	Telecoms	10°E
Eutelsat I F4	Telecoms	7°E
Tele-X	DBS	5°E
Intelsat VA F12	Telecoms	1°W
Telecom 1C	Telecoms	5°W
Telecom 1A	Telecoms	8°W
Olympus 1A	DBS	18.8°W
TDF 1A	DBS	19°W
TV Sat 2	DBS	19.2°W
Intelsat VI F4	Telecoms	27.5°W
Marcopolo 1	DBS	31°W
Panamsat 1 F1	Telecoms	45°W

MICROELECTRONICS

Materials

A semiconductor is a material whose conductivity can be altered by changes in temperature or the addition of impurities to its crystal structure (doping). When doping results in an increase of negative charge carriers, the material is n-type. When the number of positive charge carriers is increased, the material is p-type. The most common semiconductor is silicon. Others include gallium arsenide and germanium.

Semiconductors made possible the transistor electronic device. A semiconductor can be doped to produce a single discrete device such as a transistor or diode.

Alternatively, an entire circuit can be built on a single semiconductor wafer. This is known as an integrated circuit chip.

The integrated circuit was developed in 1958. Moore's Law (named after Gordon Moore of Intel Corporation) states that the number of transistors able to be built on a single chip will double every two years. In 1991 it was possible to integrate more than 1 mn transistors on a single chip.

Purposes

Integrated circuits perform several functions at the heart of modern computers. A microprocessor is the brain of a personal computer. It take data from a computer's memory, performs instructions on them, and returns the result to memory. Today's computers perform many millions of instructions per second.

Data and instructions used by a computer are stored in memory chips, of which there are various types; random access memory (RAM) is the most common. Data can be written to or read from any part of the chip. Read only memory (ROM) chips hold information which can be read from the chip but cannot be altered.

In general, RAM holds data that a user will create and alter whereas ROM holds instructions and information regarding the configuration of a computer that does not need to be changed.

Variants of ROM include programmable and erasable programmable devices, called respectively PROMS and EPROMS. These allow users to programme the devices with their own code, and to erase them completely if required. However, the devices must be removed from the equipment in which they are housed and the erasing process takes several minutes.

A more recent variant is electronically erasable PROM (EEPROM), which allows the contents of a chip to be erased without removing it from the circuit. However, it can only erase blocks of data at a time and is slower than RAM. Fast-erase FLASH devices, based on EEPROM technology, are becoming important in miniature portable computers.

Size

In the years listed below, the number of memory cells per single silicon chip was (and will be) as follows.

1970: 1 000 (1 Kbit)
1980: 64 000 (64 Kbit)
1990: 16 000 000 (16 Mbit)
1995: 64 000 000 (64 Mbit)

See also Computers, pages 51–53.

Energy

Measures

The main SI unit for measuring all forms of energy is the joule (J), which is supplemented (particularly for electricity, and in some countries also for gas) by the kilowatt hour (kWh). The calorie, therm and British thermal unit are also used. The petajoule (10^{15} joules) and the exajoule (10^{18} joules) are used in addition to the normal SI multiples. US statistics are sometimes expressed in "quads", one quad being 10^{15} British thermal units. Conversions between the various energy and power units are as follows.

See page 197 for conversion tables.

1 international table (IT) calorie	= 4.186 8 joules
1 15°C calorie	= 4.185 5 joules
1 thermochemical calorie	= 4.184 joules
1 kilocalorie (IT)	= 1 000 calories
	= 3.968 3 British thermal units
	= 1.163 watt hours
	= 0.001 thermie
1 kilowatt hour	= 3 412.14 British thermal units
	= 859.845 kilocalories (IT)
	= 3.6 megajoules
	= 1.341 0 horsepower hours
1 therm	= 100 000 British thermal units
	= 105.506 megajoules
	= 29.307 1 kilowatt hours
	= 25.199 6 thermies
1 metric horsepower (Pferdestärke or cheval vapeur)	= 735.499 watts
	= 542.476 foot pounds-force/second
	= 0.986 32 imperial horsepower
1 imperial horsepower	= 745.700 watts
	= 550 foot pounds-force/second
	= 1.013 9 metric horsepower
1 kilowatt	= 737.562 foot pounds-force/second
	= 1.359 6 metric horsepower
	= 1.341 0 imperial horsepower

Factors to convert between the less widely used energy units and the main units are given below.

1 joule = 10 000 000 ergs
= 1 000 000 microjoules
= 10 197.162 13 gram force centimetres
= 23.730 360 40 foot poundals
= 0.737 562 149 3 foot pound force
= 0.239 005 736 1 calorie
= 0.101 971 621 3 kilogram force metre
= 0.001 kilojoule
= 0.000 948 451 414 8 British thermal unit
= 0.000 277 777 777 8 watt hour
= 0.000 239 005 736 1 kilocalorie
= 0.000 001 megajoule
= $3.776\,726\,715 \times 10^{-7}$ metric horsepower hour
= $3.725\,061\,360 \times 10^{-7}$ horsepower hour
= $3.723\,562\,705 \times 10^{-7}$ electric horsepower hour
= $2.777\,777\,778 \times 10^{-7}$ kilowatt hour

1 kilowatt hour = 36 000 000 000 000 ergs
= 3 600 000 000 000 microjoules
= $3.670\,978\,367 \times 10^{10}$ gram-force centimetres
= 85 429 297.46 foot poundals
= 3 600 000 joules
= 2 655 223.737 foot pounds-force
= 860 420.650 1 calories
= 367 097.836 7 kilogram-force metres
= 3 600 kilojoules
= 3 414.425 093 British thermal units
= 1 000 watt hours
= 860.420 650 1 kilocalories
= 3.6 megajoules
= 1.359 621 617 metric horsepower hours
= 1.341 022 090 horsepower hours
= 1.340 482 574 electric horsepower hours

1 calorie = 41 840 000 ergs
= 4 184 000 microjoules
= 42 664.926 35 gram force centimetres
= 99.287 827 93 foot poundals
= 4.184 joules
= 3.085 960 033 foot pounds-force
= 0.426 649 263 5 kilogram-force metre
= 0.004 184 kilojoule
= 0.003 968 320 719 British thermal unit
= 0.001 162 222 222 watt hour
= 0.001 kilocalorie
= 0.000 004 184 megajoule
= 0.000 001 580 182 457 metric horsepower hour
= 0.000 001 558 565 673 horsepower hour
= 0.000 001 557 938 636 electric horsepower hour
= 0.000 001 162 222 222 kilowatt hour

1 British thermal unit = $1.054\,350\,264 \times 10^{10}$ ergs
= $1.054\,350\,264 \times 10^{9}$ microjoules
= 10 751 380.59 gram-force centimetres
= 25 020.111 77 foot poundals
= 1 054.350 264 joules
= 777.648 847 2 foot-pounds force
= 251.995 761 1 calories
= 107.513 805 9 kilogram-force metres
= 1.054 350 264 kilojoules
= 0.292 875 073 5 watt hour
= 0.251 995 761 1 kilocalorie
= 0.001 054 350 264 megajoule
= 0.000 398 198 281 1 metric horsepower hour
= 0.000 392 751 943 0 horsepower hour
= 0.000 392 593 932 3 electric horsepower hour
= 0.000 292 875 073 5 kilowatt hour

Energy equivalents

To facilitate comparisons of energy consumption, energy units are often converted to tonnes of oil equivalent (TOE) or tonnes of coal equivalent (TCE), also sometimes barrels of oil equivalent. Such comparisons cannot be precise because different grades of crude oil and coal have different calorific values (ie, different heat energy contents per unit weight).

Average calorific values often used in compiling international statistics are:

1 kilogram of hard coal = 29 307 kilojoules (or 7 000 kilocalories)
1 kilogram of crude oil = 41 868 kilojoules (or 10 000 kilocalories)

On this basis, the following table gives approximate oil equivalents for coal and oil products.

1 tonne	TOE
Hard coal, anthracite & bituminous	0.700
Hard coal (Denmark)	0.640
Lignite	0.200
Lignite (Greece)	0.138
BKB	0.480
Coke oven coke	0.670
Gas coke	0.670
Patent fuel	0.700
Crude oil	1.007
Liquefied petroleum gases (LPG)	1.140
Gasoline, naphtha	1.073
Kerosene, gas/diesel oil, fuel oil, jet oil	1.045
Residual fuel oil	0.969
Non-energy products (other than naphtha)	0.950

The following table gives approximate coal equivalents for coal and oil products.

1 tonne	TCE
Coal, anthracite & bituminous	1.00
Coal, low grade:	
New Zealand	0.84
Pakistan	0.70
Soviet Union (former)	0.81–0.84
Recovered slurries:	
France, Spain, UK	0.70
Czechoslovakia	0.60
Hungary	0.52
Turkey	0.50
Coal briquettes	1.00
Cokes of anthracite or bituminous coal	0.90
Cokes of brown coal or lignite	0.67
Lignite briquettes	0.67
Lignite & brown coal:	
Czechoslovakia, France, North Korea	0.60
Chile	0.59
USA	0.57
Canada	0.52
Albania, Austria, Bulgaria, New Zealand, Portugal, Soviet Union (former), Spain, Yugoslavia	0.50
Hungary	0.40
Italy	0.36
Australia, Denmark, Greece, India, Japan, South Korea, Mongolia, Romania, Thailand, Turkey	0.33
Germany, Poland	0.30
Peat briquettes	0.50
Peat for fuel:	
Burundi, Ireland	0.50
Soviet Union (former)	0.31–0.34
Crude petroleum	1.47
Natural gas liquids	1.67
Liquefied petroleum gases (LPG)	1.68
Natural gasoline	1.66
Motor spirit	1.61
Kerosene and jet fuels	1.59
Fuel oils	1.50

For natural gas, 1 000 cubic metres is taken to be equivalent to 1.7 TCE or 1 TOE.

For electricity, 1 000 kilowatt hours are taken to be equivalent to 0.135 TOE or 0.086 TOE.

Energy contents

The following table gives energy contents (calorific values) for various fuels.

	MJ/kg	Btu/lb
Cowdung (50% moisture)	8.6	3 700
Wood: green	10	4 400
dry	17	7 310
Peat: mild	11	4 790
sod	14	6 200
Lignite	21	9 000
Coke	29	12 500
Coal: bituminous	23.7–34.0	10 200–14 600
anthracite	34	14 500
Crude oil	42.6–45.4	18 300–19 500
Gasoline	47.7	20 500
Kerosene	46.1	19 800
Benzole	42.1	18 100
Ethanol	27.0	11 600
Gas oil	44.7	19 200
Fuel oil (bunker)	42.6	18 300
LNG	51.9	22 300

OIL

In the industry, crude oil and refined oil products are generally measured in barrels, but some countries use litres or cubic metres. Factors for converting between these units and into other volume units are given below. Note that the US gallon is smaller than the UK gallon. Japanese official statistics use kilolitres (1 000 litres).

1 barrel = 9 702 cubic inches
= 158.987 litres
= 42 US gallons
= 34.972 6 UK gallons
= 5.614 6 cubic feet
= 0.158 9 cubic metre

1 litre = 61.024 cubic inches
= 1.759 8 pints
= 1 cubic decimetre
= 0.264 2 US gallons
= 0.220 UK gallons
= 0.035 3 cubic foot

1 cubic metre = 1 000 litres
= 264.172 US gallons
= 219.969 UK gallons
= 35.314 7 cubic feet
= 6.289 8 US barrels

Crude oil is also measured in tonnes, but conversions from tonnes to volume units cannot be precise unless the specific gravity (relative density) of the particular grade of crude is known. An average conversion factor is 7.33 barrels per tonne.

For UK North Sea crudes the average factor is 7.49 barrels per tonne.

A quick and reasonably accurate way of converting from tonnes per year to barrels per day is to divide by 50. One barrel per day is equivalent to 50 tonnes per year.

The specific gravity of crude oil is measured in degrees API (American Petroleum Institute). This is defined as follows.

$$^{\circ}\text{API} = \frac{141.5}{\text{Relative density at } 60/60^{\circ}\text{F}} - 131.5$$

The following table gives barrels per tonne factors for crudes of known API gravity.

°API	Specific gravity	Barrels/ tonne	°API	Specific gravity	Barrels/ tonne
25	0.904	6.98	34	0.855	7.37
26	0.898	7.02	35	0.850	7.42
27	0.893	7.06	36	0.845	7.46
28	0.887	7.10	37	0.840	7.51
29	0.882	7.15	38	0.835	7.55
30	0.876	7.19	39	0.830	7.60
31	0 871	7.24	40	0.825	7.64
32	0.865	7.28	41	0.820	7.69
33	0.860	7.33	42	0.816	7.73

Barrels per tonne conversions for the main refined oil products are given below.

	Specific gravity	Barrels/ tonne
Aviation gasoline	0.70–0.78	9.1–8.2
Motor gasoline	0.71–0.79	9.0–8.1
Kerosene	0.78–0.84	8.2–7.6
Gas oil	0.82–0.90	7.8–7.1
Diesel oil	0.82–0.92	7.8–6.9
Lubricating oil	0.82–0.95	7.5–6.7
Fuel oil	0.92–0.99	6.9–6.5
Asphaltic bitumen	1.00–1.10	6.4–5.8

See pages 198–200 for conversions from barrels to tonnes and the relation between volume and mass.

Refined oil products

When refined, crude oil gives the following principal products.

Gas and LPG. Methane, ethane, propane and butane are produced during refining processes. Methane and ethane may be used as fuel at the refinery, but propane and butane are recovered for sale as liquified petroleum gases (LPG). Propane is used as a domestic fuel in bottled gas; butane is used in the production of gasoline and in petrochemicals.

Gasoline (motor spirit or petrol). Used as fuel for spark-ignition engines. Its grade is measured in terms of octane numbers, which indicate how prone the gasoline is to pre-ignition (knocking or pinking). Octane ratings are measured using a test engine, measuring the intensity of knocking and comparing the result with a reference fuel composed of iso-octane and normal-heptane. Pure iso-octane is regarded as having an octane number of 100 while pure normal-heptane is regarded as having an octane number of 0; the octane number of the gasoline under test is therefore the percentage of iso-octane in the blend which gives equivalent test characteristics.

There are two different test procedures for measuring octane numbers – research and motor. The research octane number (RON) is higher than the motor octane number (MON), usually by about 10. In Europe RON is used; in the USA an average of the two $\left(\frac{\text{RON} \times \text{MON}}{2}\right)$ is used.

As gasolines can have better anti-knock properties than pure iso-octane, octane numbers can be in excess of 100.

In the UK gasolines are given a star rating, but only one grade is now generally available: 4-star (minimum 97 octane). Unleaded and diesel do not have a star rating.

Lead additives can be used to increase the octane number, but unleaded gasoline is becoming increasingly popular worldwide. In Europe the standard grade of unleaded gasoline is 95 RON.

See also Transport, page 148.

Aviation gasoline. Very similar to motor gasoline. The generally available grade is 100 RON, low lead.

Aviation kerosene (jet fuel). A middle distillate used in turbine engines, also referred to as Avtur. The main grade is Jet-A1, used by all commercial jet aircraft and, increasingly, by military jet aircraft.

Kerosene. Also known as paraffin in the UK. A middle distillate used as a domestic fuel.

Gas oil/diesel oil. A middle distillate used as fuel for compression-ignition (diesel) engines. In the UK it is called Derv (diesel engined road vehicle) when duty-paid for use on public roads. Also used for heating systems.

Fuel oil. Heavy oil used in steam-raising and electricity generation.

NATURAL GAS

Natural gas can be extracted from oilfields or produced from fields containing only gas. It is also found in association with very light oil, termed condensate. Light hydrocarbons extracted from natural gas are referred to as natural gas liquids (NGL). Natural gas is methane, formula CH_4. It can be liquefied, for transportation or storage, by cooling to about −160°C, and is then referred to as liquefied natural gas (LNG).

For international trade or other large sale contracts, and also for many statistical purposes, quantities of natural gas are usually measured in cubic metres or cubic feet, at normal temperature and pressure (**see below**). Usual multiples are billion (thousand million) cubic metres and billion or trillion (thousand billion) cubic feet.

1 cubic metre = 35.314 7 cubic feet.

Contracts between gas producers and distribution companies or large consumers are usually on a take-or-pay basis. The buyer is required to pay for the volume contracted, even if actual offtake falls short of this volume.

In the USA millions of British thermal units (abbreviated

MMBtu or mBtu) are used. In most countries, when gas is sold to the consumer it is measured in energy units: therms in the UK, kilowatt hours in some countries.

In the UK pipeline gas supplied by British Gas has a calorific value of 38.0 megajoules per cubic metre (1 018 British thermal units per cubic foot). In the Netherlands gas from the Groningen field has a calorific value of 35.169 MJ/m^3, and in Dutch official statistics volumes of gas from other fields are often converted to "Groningen equivalents" on this basis. In Belgium volumes are expressed either as Groningen equivalent or as rich gas (the latter assuming 41.868 MJ/m^3).

As the volume of gas changes in line with changes in temperature and pressure, volumes are often expressed in normal cubic metres or cubic feet. Normal conditions are generally taken to be a temperature of 0°C and a pressure of 1.013 3 bar. Normal cubic metres are abbreviated to Nm^3. (Note that N in this context should not be confused with the SI symbol for newton, N.)

In a few countries – including the Netherlands – normal conditions are defined as 15°C and 1.0133 bar. As the reference temperature is higher the gas is less dense and its heating value is therefore lower. Approximately, 1 normal cubic metre at 0°C is equivalent to 1.055 normal cubic metre at 15°C. In the USA volumes are expressed in standard cubic feet, defined as a cubic foot at 60°F and 30 in of mercury pressure.

Liquefied natural gas conversion factors

The following table gives factors for converting weight, volume and energy units of LNG, and shows the volume of gas resulting from the regasification of LNG.

	Btu mn	Gas ft^3	LNG ft^3	Gas m^3	LNG m^3	LNG t
1 mn Btu	1	987.91	1.579 6	26.52	0.044 7	0.018 7
1 mn ft^3 (gas)	101.210	1 mn	1 599	26 847	45.27	18.91
1 m^3 (LNG)	63.29	625.43	1	16.789	0.028 3	0.011 8
1 mn m^3 (gas)	3.77 mn	37 252	59 562	1 mn	1 686	704.374
1 m^3 (LNG)	2 235.5	22 090	35.315	593	1	0.417 7
1 t (LNG)	5 352	52 886	84.56	1 419.7	2.394	1

COAL

Coal rank	Coal group	Basis of classification: Fixed carbon percentage[a]		
		Equal to or greater than	Less than	Agglomerating character
Coals classified by fixed carbon				
Anthracitic	Meta-anthracite	98	–	Non-agglomerating
	Anthracite	92	98	Non-agglomerating
	Semi-anthracite[b]	86	92	Non-agglomerating
Bituminous	Low-volatile bituminous	78	86	Commonly agglomerating[c]
	Medium-volatile bituminous	69[d]	78	Commonly agglomerating[c]
	High-volatile A bituminous	–	69[d]	Commonly agglomerating[c]
		Heat content (Btu/lb)[e]		
		Equal to or greater than	**Less than**	
Coals classified by heat content				
Bituminous	High-volatile B bituminous	13 000	14 000	Commonly agglomerating[c]
	High-volatile C bituminous	11 500	13 000	Commonly agglomerating[c]
	High-volatile C bituminous	10 500	11 500	Agglomerating
Sub-		10 500	11 500	Non-agglomerating
bituminous	Sub-bituminous A	9 500	10 500	Non-agglomerating
	Sub-bituminous B	8 300	9 500	Non-agglomerating
	Sub-bituminous C			
Lignitic	Lignite A	6 300	8 300	Non-agglomerating
	Lignite B	–	6 300	Non-agglomerating

[a]Percentages based on dry mineral-matter-free coal. Volatile matter (not shown) is the complement of fixed carbon; ie, the percentages of fixed carbon and volatile matter sum to 100%. As fixed carbon percentage decreases, therefore, volatile matter percentage increases by the same amount. [b]If agglomerating, classify in low-volatile group of the bituminous class. [c]There may be non-agglomerating varieties in the bituminous class, most notably in the high-volatile C bituminous group. [d]Coals having 69% or more fixed carbon are classified according to fixed carbon, regardless of Btu value. Coals with less than 69% fixed carbon, but with 14 000 or more Btu/lb, are classified as high-volatile A bituminous. [e]Calorific values in Btu/lb, on a moist mineral-matter-free basis.

The principal types of coal (referred to as ranks) in increasing order of energy content are: peat; lignite or brown coal; bituminous or soft coal; and anthracite or hard coal. The following table shows how coal types are classified.

The lower rank coals can be classified based on heat content. The heat content of the higher rank coals is generally above 14 000 Btu/lb for each coal rank group (except for meta-anthracite, which trends slightly lower), and heat content ranges vary within a relatively narrow range. Since heat content is not a dependable criterion for these higher rank coals, their rank categories are instead described by degree of metamorphism, or "coalification", a property that is measured by fixed carbon content. Finally, the agglomerating character of bituminous coals is a critical attribute for certain coal consumers, and thus agglomerating character has come to define the distinctions between certain adjacent coal groups. Some high-volatile C bituminous and sub-bituminous A coals can be distinguished only on the basis of agglomerating character.

Anthracite, or hard coal, is the highest rank of economically usable coal. It is jet black with a high lustre. The moisture content is generally less than 15%. Anthracite contains approximately 22–28 mn British thermal units per ton as received, averaging about 25 mBtu/t. Its ignition temperature is approximately 925–970°F. It is used for heating and electricity generation.

Bituminous coal, or soft coal, is the most common type. It is dense black, with a moisture content usually less than 20%. Its heating value is in the range 19–30 mBtu/t as received, and averages about 24 mBtu/t. Ignition temperature is in the range 700–900°F. It is used for heating, electricity generation, steam-raising and making coke.

Sub-bituminous coal, or black lignite, is dull black and generally contains 20–30% moisture. The heat content is in the range 16–24 mBtu/t as received, averaging about 18 mBtu/t. It is used for electricity generation and heating.

Lignite, the poorest quality of coal, is brownish black and has a high moisture content, sometimes as high as 45%. It tends to crumble when exposed to the weather. Heat content is in the range 9–17 mBtu/t as received, averaging 14 mBtu/t. Ignition temperature is about 600°F. Lignite often has a high sulphur content, leading to air pollution when burned, so its use is declining.

Coke is usually made from bituminous coal by baking in an oven to drive off the volatile constituents and to fuse the fixed carbon and ash together. It is hard and porous, and grey in colour. Heat content is 24.8 mBtu/t. Coke is used for heating and for smelting iron in the manufacture of steel.

ELECTRICITY

In statistics electricity is considered to be either primary or secondary. Primary electricity is that generated from nuclear power stations, hydroelectric power stations, and from wind, tides, etc; imports and exports of electricity are also included in this category. Secondary electricity is that generated by burning other fuels: coal, oil and gas.

Conversion factors for electricity measurement units are given in the energy measures section above. See also the table below. 1 terawatt hour of electricity is taken to be equivalent to 86 000 tonnes of oil equivalent.

In statistics the primary energy value given to the output of nuclear power stations is calculated from gross generation, assuming that only 33% of the primary energy appears as electricity. The abbreviation MW(e) stands for megawatts of electricity; MW(h) stands for megawatts of heat.

The main types of nuclear power stations are as follows.

AGR	Advanced gas-cooled reactor
BWR	Boiling water reactor
Candu	Canadian deuterium reactor
FBR	Fast (breeder) reactor
HTR	High temperature reactor
LWR	Light water reactor (includes BWR and PWR)
Magnox	Gas-cooled reactor
PWR	Pressurised water reactor
RBMK	Example: Chernobyl

Conversion factors for electricity measurement units

From To	electron-volt multiply by	joule	calorie	Btu	kWh	thermie	TCE[a]	TOE[a]	quad
electronvolt	1	6.24×10^{8}	–	–	–	–	–	–	
joule	–	1	4.184	1 055	3.6×10^{6}	4.184×10^{6}	30×10^{9}	44×10^{9}	1.055×10^{18}
calorie	–	0.239	1	252.5	–	10^{6}	7.17×10^{9}	10.52×10^{9}	2.525×10^{17}
Btu	–	9.48×10^{-4}	3.96×10^{-3}	1	3 412	3.96×10^{3}	2.85×10^{7}	4.17×10^{7}	10^{15}
kWh	–	2.78×10^{-7}	6.64×10^{-8}	2.93×10^{-4}	1	1.163	8.34×10^{3}	1.22×10^{4}	2.93×10^{12}
thermie	–	2.39×10^{-7}	1×10^{-6}	2.52×10^{-5}	–	1	1.25×10^{5}	1.84×10^{5}	2.525×10^{11}
TCE[a]	–	3.33×10^{-11}	7.96×10^{-12}	3.51×10^{-8}	1.198×10^{-4}	7.96×10^{-6}	1	1.467	3.51×10^{7}
TOE[a]	–	2.27×10^{-11}	5.43×10^{-12}	2.39×10^{-8}	8.174×10^{-5}	5.43×10^{-6}	0.68	1	2.39×10^{7}
quad	–	9.479×10^{-19}	3.96×10^{-18}	10^{-15}	3.41×10^{-13}	3.96×10^{-12}	2.85×10^{-8}	4.184×10^{-10}	1

[a] Assume TCE $= 30 \times 10^{9}$ J or 30 GJ/tonne; TOE $= 44 \times 10^{9}$ J or 44 GJ/tonne.

Engineering

Measures

Engineering industries in the UK have in general changed over to SI metric measures, but about 50% still use imperial measures. Some measures of special interest are listed below.

Power. The basic SI unit of power is the watt; the most frequently used unit is the kilowatt (1 000 watts). The following table gives a summary of conversions for the different types of horsepower. The UK measure of horsepower, at 550 ft lbf/s, is also 33 000 ft lbf/min; this is approximately equal to the original estimate of the power of 1 horse in pulling a load.

See also pages 17 and 19.

1 unit of	Equals (units of) ft lbf/s	kgf m/s	kW (kJ/s)
UK horsepower	550	76.040 2	0.745 7
Metric horsepower	542.476	75	0.735 5
Electric horsepower[a]	550.221	76.071	0.746

[a]Special unit based on UK horsepower, value approx. 0.746 kW.

Metric horsepower is referred to as "cheval vapeur" (ch or CV) in France, and "Pferdestärke" (PS) in Germany; other names for metric horsepower are "cavallo vapore" (cv) and "Paardekracht" (pk). In France a "poncelet" is 100 kgf m/s.

Brake horsepower (bhp), or brake power, is the horsepower generated by an engine which does useful work; this is usually measured at the crankshaft or flywheel. The main European standard is the German DIN (Deutsche Industrie Normen) rating, which measures the power available at the flywheel of an engine when it is in an installed condition (with all ancillaries fitted). The term brake is used, as the force can be measured by the braking power necessary to stop the engine. Thus:

where ihp = indicated horsepower of the engine
mechanical efficiency = (brake power/ihp × 100) %

See page 201 for conversions between kilowatts and UK and metric horsepowers.

Torque (moment of force). Torque is force applied at a right angle at a distance, measured in the UK system by the pound-force foot (lbf ft). The product force by length used as a torque unit is the same as the product length by force used as an energy unit. In the UK the convention is to express the torque unit as lbf ft and the energy unit as ft lbf; there is not a similar convention in the metric system, but there is a corresponding general usage of N m (force by distance) for torque units and J (which equals N m) for energy. Because torque and energy units are equal in this way, conversions are numerically equal; eg, the torque conversion from lbf ft to N m on **page 162** is the same as the energy conversion from ft lbf to J on **page 163**.

Summary of torque conversions

From	To lbf ft	kgf m multiply by	N m
lbf ft	1	0.138 3	1.355 8
kgf m	7.233	1	9.806 65
N m	0.737 56	0.101 972	1

Pressure. The main SI unit for pressure is the pascal, but the bar (100 kPA) is used in parts of the engineering industry (eg, machine tools and hydraulics), being approximately equal to normal atmospheric pressure.

Details of the various units of pressure are included on page 16, with summary conversions on pages 162–163.

Pounds-force per square inch is usually abbreviated to psi.

Rotational frequency. The revolution per second is the main SI unit, but revolutions per minute (rev/min or rpm) is also a standard unit; 60 rev/min = 1/s = 1 Hz.

Friction. The coefficient of friction measures the relationship between a force and the load it can move: coefficient of friction = lbf/lbf = kgf/kgf = N/N.

BOLTS, SCREWS AND STUDS

Threads

Pitch is the distance between the crest of 1 thread and that of the next, parallel to the axis. Threads per inch is the reciprocal of pitch measured in inches. The usual angle of thread with reference to the pitch line is 55° or 60°.

The ISO recommendation for international use is as follows (showing a selected list of the "first choice" only); the international standard is based on an angle of 60°. All measures in the following table are in millimetres.

Nominal dia.	Pitches	Nominal dia.	Pitches	Nominal dia.	Pitches
1	0.2, 0.25	16	1, 1.5, 2	90	2, 3, 4, 6
1.2	0.2, 0.25	20	1, 1.5, 2, 3.5	100	2, 3, 4, 6
1.6	0.2, 0.35	24	1, 1.5, 2, 3	110	2, 3, 4, 6
2	0.25, 0.4	30	1, 1.5, 2, 3.5	125	2, 3, 4, 6
2.5	0.35, 0.45	36	1.5, 2, 3, 4	140	2, 3, 4, 6
3	0.35, 0.5	42	1.5, 2, 3, 4, 4.5	160	3, 4, 6
4	0.5, 0.7	48	1.5, 2, 3, 4, 5	180	3, 4, 6
5	0.5, 0.8	56	1.5, 2, 3, 4, 5.5	200	3, 4, 6
6	0.75, 1	64	1.5, 2, 3, 4, 6	220	3, 4, 6
8	0.75, 1, 1.25	72	1.5, 2, 3, 4, 6	250	3, 4, 6
10	0.75, 1, 1.25, 1.5	80	1.5, 2, 3, 4, 6	280	4, 6
12	1, 1.25, 1.5, 1.75				

Up to a nominal diameter of 64 mm, the largest pitch is referred to as a coarse pitch, the others being fine. Where a thread is required with a pitch larger than 6 mm, in the diameter range 150–300 mm, a pitch of 8 mm is preferred. A screw thread in conformity with the International Standard is designated by the letter M, followed by the values of the nominal diameter and the pitch, expressed in millimetres and separated by the sign ×; eg, M6 × 0.75. No indication for pitch means that a coarse pitch is specified.

UK industry uses British Standards Institution (BSI) regulations BS 580, Parts 1 and 2, 1962.

COMPRESSED AIR

Pressure

In the metric system gauges are in general calibrated in bar or mbar, in place of pounds-force per square inch.

Absolute and gauge pressure. Absolute pressure is expressed with zero pressure as the datum, and gauge pressure with atmospheric pressure as the datum. For clarity absolute and gauge pressure are specified; eg, at a gauge pressure of 1 bar. Symbols used in the UK and USA are "a" for absolute and "g" for gauge, so that pounds-force per square inch absolute is psia, and gauge psig. In Germany the technical atmosphere symbol (at) becomes ata for absolute and atü (for über) for gauge.

Most compressed air equipment operates at about 6 or 7 bar gauge.

Flow

Air and gas flow in the metric system use cubic capacity per second as follows.

	Unit used
Large compressors	m^3/s
Pneumatic controls, tools, up to medium-sized compressors	dm^3/s (=l/s)
Fluidics	cm^3/s (=ml/s)

The usual imperial measure, cubic feet per minute, relates to the metric system as follows.

1 ft^3/min (cfm) = 0.47 dm^3/s
1 dm^3/s = 2.1 ft^3/min

Usual size ranges of compressors

Size	l/s
Small	under 40
Medium	40–300
Large	over 300

Kinematic viscosity

Centistokes is the metric replacement for Redwood seconds, Saybolt seconds and Engler degrees. Quotation at 20°C has the advantage that it is close to atmospheric temperature, and at the equivalent 68°F is close to a standard Redwood viscosity temperature of 70°F.

See Chemicals, industrial, page 43, for definitions.

Specific power consumption

The shaft power input per unit of compressor capacity is measured as follows.

kW s/m^3 = 1 000 J/m^3 = J/dm^3 = J/litre

A high degree of efficiency gives a low specific power consumption. Required power decreases with altitude, as shown in the following table.

Power consumption by altitude

Altitude (m)	Pressure 4 bar (gauge) single stage[a] J/l	two stage[b] J/l	7 bar (gauge) single stage[a] J/l	two stage[b] J/l
0	258	232	349	302
300	254	229	342	296
600	251	226	336	290
900	248	221	330	284
1 200	243	218	325	280
1 500	237	214	320	273
1 800	232	210	316	268
2 100	229	205	309	262
2 400	226	200	304	256
2 700	222	197	298	251
3 000	206	186	283	237

[a]Compression from initial to final pressure is in a single step or stage.
[b]Compression from initial to final pressure is in two stages or steps with cooling between the stages.

GEARS

Module = D/N where D is diameter in millimetres
Diametral pitch = $N/D = \pi \times$ reciprocal of circular pitch
Circular pitch = circumference/number of teeth
= $\pi D/N$ where D is diameter and N number of teeth

See page 195 for a table of π.

Some close equivalents are as follows.

Module mm	Diametral pitch in	Circular pitch in
2	12	0.25
4	7	0.50
6	4	0.75
8	1	1.00
10	1.25	1.25
12	1.50	1.50
16	2.00	2.00

Pressure angle. Angle at the pitch line made by the surface of teeth with the radius passing through the same point on the pitch line. This is usually 20°.

Angle depression. 90° – pressure angle (usually 70°).

HYDRAULICS

Recommended practical metric units incude the following.

Pressure: MPa
Stress: N/mm^2
Rotational frequency: rev/min (SI unit is 1/s)
Volumetric flow: l/min (SI unit is m^3/s)

MOTOR VEHICLES

Engine capacity is cylinder capacity × number of cylinders (for cars usually 4 or 6). In Europe, capacity is mainly expressed in terms of litres or cc (cubic centimetres or SI unit symbol cm^3):

1 litre = 1 000 millilitres = 1 000 cubic centimetres (cc or cm^3)

In the USA engine capacity is also quoted in cubic inches.

See page 179 for conversion from cubic inches to cubic centimetres (cm^3 or cc).

Cylinder capacity (for 1 cylinder) = swept volume = area of cylinder bore × piston stroke (length of sweep) = $R^2 \times S$, where R is radius of the cylinder (= $\frac{1}{2}$ bore) and S is the piston stroke.

For area from radius see pages 171–174; **also $= \pi \times D^2 \times S/4$, where D is the diameter or bore.**

Compression ratio $= \frac{V+v}{v} = \frac{\text{Maximum volume}}{\text{Minimum volume}}$

where V is the swept volume, and v = volume of space above the piston at the top of the stroke (combustion chamber). The compression ratio is the amount by which the fuel is compressed before combustion. The usual compression ratio for cars is 8–9.5, but ratios can be higher for use with special fuels.

See also Energy, page 77.

Engine power. There is no direct relationship between swept volume or compression ratio and output, since this is affected by engine duty and endurance, as well as tolerances of construction, age, materials and design. However, the output of a normal road-going engine in 1992 would be 50–70 bhp per litre, and tuning could give outputs of up to 175 bhp (a Honda 1 000 motorcycle can achieve this without high octane fuel).

A turbocharger, recycling engine exhaust gas flow, can give a power output up to approx. 150 bhp per litre.

SIEVES

The recommended ISO main sizes, based on rounded preferred numbers, are as follows.

Micrometre series (μm)

20[a]	90	250	710
45	125	355	
63	180	500	

[a]Lowest supplementary size.

Millimetre series (mm)

1.00	2.80	8.0	22.4	63.0
1.40	4.00	11.2	31.5	90.0
2.00	5.60	16.0	45.0	125.0

Recommended nominal sizes for woven metal wire cloth (with square apertures) are 20 μm–125 mm, and for perforated plate are 4 mm–125 mm for square apertures and 1 mm–125 mm for round apertures.

TUBES

Nominal and outside diameter

In specifying size of tubes, nominal diameter is used as a convenient round number; this is normally only related to the manufacturing size. ISO recommendations for sizes are largely based on imperial dimensions as these have been important internationally. In the following table a selection of size recommendations are given for nominal and corresponding outside diameter. The dimensions in millimetres and inches are corresponding values, and are not necessarily exact equivalents.

Nominal size		Outside diameter		Nominal size		Outside diameter	
mm	in	mm	in	mm	in	mm	in
6	$\frac{1}{8}$	10.2	0.402	350	14	355.6	14.0
8	$\frac{1}{4}$	13.5	0.531	400	16	406.4	16.0
10	$\frac{3}{8}$	17.2	0.677	450	18	457	18.0
15	$\frac{1}{2}$	21.3	0.840	500	20	508	20.0
20	$\frac{3}{4}$	26.9	1.059	550	22	559	22.0
25	1	33.7	1.327	600	24	610	24.0
32	$1\frac{1}{4}$	42.4	1.669	650	26	660	26.0
40	$1\frac{1}{2}$	48.3	1.900	700	28	711	28.0
50	2	60.3	2.375	750	30	762	30.0
65	$2\frac{1}{2}$	76.1	3.000	800	32	813	32.0
80	3	88.9	3.500	850	34	864	34.0
90	$3\frac{1}{2}$	101.6	4.000	900	36	914	36.0
100	4	114.3	4.500	1 000	40	1 016	40.0
125	5	139.7	5.500	1 200	48	1 220	48.0
150	6	168.3	6.625	1 400	56	1 420	55.9
175[a]	7[a]	193.7[a]	7.625[a]	1 600	64	1 620	63.8
200	8	219.1	8.625	1 800	72	1 820	71.7
225[a]	9[a]	244.5[a]	9.625[a]	2 000	80	2 020	79.5
250	10	273	10.750	2 200	88	2 220	87.4
300	12	323.9	12.750				

[a]Sizes to be avoided if possible.

Thickness

The range of thicknesses of wall for general UK use is from 1.2 mm (0.048 in) to 32.0 mm (1.26 in).

VACUUM SYSTEMS

Old units for the measurement of the rate of leak

1 clusec = 1 centilitre per second at a pressure of 1 millitorr (mtorr cl/s)
1 lusec = 1 litre per second at a pressure of 1 millitorr (mtorr l/s)
100 clusec = 1 lusec
1 000 lusec = 1 torr litre per second (torr l/s)

Metric equivalents

1 clusec = 1.333 22 μN m/s
1 lusec = 133.322 μN m/s
1 torr l/s = 0.133 322 N m/s

WIRE

A special measure, the circular mil, is used for wire.

See page 18; and for the weight of steel wire see page 227.

Wire gauges (also for sheet metal and wall thickness of tubes)

BG	Birmingham Sheet and Hoop Iron Gauge (former legal system in UK)
BWG	Birmingham Wire Gauge (also called Stubs Iron Wire Gauge)
SWG	British Standard Wire Gauge (former legal system in UK)
USG	US standard gauge for sheet and plate
AWG	American Wire Gauge (also called B & S – Brown & Sharpe), for electric wire
Stubs' SW	Stubs' Steel Wire Gauge, for soft wire

International standards do not recognise gauge systems, and gauges have in general been replaced in the UK by the internationally agreed metric series based on preferred numbers. The following table shows the international range for wire diameters, based on the series of R40 preferred numbers; an approximate equivalent in the BG and SWG systems is shown for comparison.

Metric standard R40		BG			SWG		
mm	in	gauge no.	in	mm	gauge no.	in	mm
0.020 0	0.000 79						
0.021 2	0.000 83						
0.022 4	0.000 88						
0.023 6	0.000 93	52	0.000 95	0.024 1			
0.025 0	0.000 98				50	0.001 0	0.025 4
0.026 5	0.001 04	51	0.001 07	0.027 2			
0.028 0	0.001 10						
0.030 0	0.001 18	50	0.001 20	0.030 5	49	0.001 2	0.030 5
0.031 5	0.001 24						
0.033 5	0.001 32	49	0.001 35	0.034 3			
0.035 5	0.001 40						
0.037 5	0.001 48	48	0.001 52	0.038 6			
0.040 0	0.001 57				48	0.001 6	0.040 6
0.042 5	0.001 67	47	0.001 70	0.043 2			
0.045 0	0.001 77						
0.047 5	0.001 87	46	0.001 92	0.049			
0.050	0.001 97				47	0.002 0	0.051
0.053	0.002 09	45	0.002 15	0.055			
0.056	0.002 20						
0.060	0.002 36	44	0.002 42	0.061	46	0.002 4	0.061
0.063	0.002 48						
0.067	0.002 64	43	0.002 72	0.069			
0.071	0.002 80				45	0.002 8	0.071
0.075	0.002 95	42	0.003 06	0.078			
0.080	0.003 15				44	0.003 2	0.081
0.085	0.003 35	41	0.003 43	0.087			
0.090	0.003 54				43	0.003 6	0.091
0.095	0.003 74	40	0.003 86	0.098			
0.100	0.003 9				42	0.004 0	0.102
0.106	0.004 2	39	0.004 3	0.109			
0.112	0.004 4				41	0.004 4	0.112
0.118	0.004 6	38	0.004 8	0.122	40	0.004 8	0.122
0.125	0.004 9						
0.132	0.005 2	37	0.005 4	0.137	39	0.005 2	0.132
0.140	0.005 5						
0.150	0.005 9	36	0.006 1	0.155	38	0.006 0	0.152
0.160	0.006 3						
0.170	0.006 7	35	0.006 9	0.175	37	0.006 8	0.173
0.180	0.007 1						
0.190	0.007 5	34	0.007 7	0.196	36	0.007 6	0.193
0.200	0.007 9						
0.212	0.008 3				35	0.008 4	0.213
0.224	0.008 8	33	0.0087	0.221			
0.236	0.009 3				34	0.009 2	0.237
0.250	0.009 8	32	0.009 8	0.249	33	0.010 0	0.254
0.265	0.010 4						
0.280	0.011 0	31	0.011 0	0.279	32	0.010 8	0.274
0.300	0.011 8				31	0.011 6	0.295
0.315	0.012 4	30	0.012 3	0.312	30	0.012 4	0.315
0.335	0.013 2				29	0.013 6	0.345
0.355	0.014 0	29	0.013 9	0.353			
0.375	0.014 8				28	0.014 8	0.376
0.400	0.015 7	28	0.015 6	0.397			
0.425	0.016 7				27	0.016 4	0.417
0.450	0.017 7	27	0.017 4	0.443	26	0.018	0.457
0.475	0.018 7						
0.50	0.019 7	26	0.019 6	0.498	25	0.020	0.508
0.53	0.020 9						
0.56	0.022 0	25	0.022 0	0.560	24	0.022	0.559
0.60	0.023 6						
0.63	0.024 8	24	0.024 8	0.629	23	0.024	0.610
0.67	0.026 4						
0.71	0.028 0	23	0.027 8	0.707	22	0.028	0.711
0.75	0.029 5						
0.80	0.031 5	22	0.031 2	0.794	21	0.032	0.813
0.85	0.033 5						
0.90	0.035 4	21	0.034 9	0.886	20	0.036	0.914
0.95	0.037 4						
1.00	0.039 4	20	0.039 2	0.996	19	0.040	1.016
1.06	0.041 7						
1.12	0.044 1	19	0.044 0	1.118			
1.18	0.046 5				18	0.048	1.219
1.25	0.049 2	18	0.049 5	1.257			
1.32	0.052 0						
1.40	0.055 1	17	0.055 6	1.412	17	0.056	1.422
1 50	0.059 1						
1.60	0.063 0	16	0.062 5	1.588	16	0.064	1.626
1.70	0.066 9						
1.80	0.070 9	15	0.069 9	1.775	15	0.072	1.829
1.90	0.074 8						
2.00	0.078 7	14	0.078 5	1.994	14	0.080	2.032
2.12	0.083 5						
2.24	0.088 2	13	0.088 2	2.240			
2.36	0.092 9				13	0.092	2.337
2.50	0.098 4	12	0.099 1	2.517			
2.65	0.104 3				12	0.104	2.642
2.80	0.110 2	11	0.111 3	2.827			
3.00	0.118 1				11	0.116	2.946
3.15	0.124 0	10	0.125 0	3.175	10	0.128	3.251
3.35	0.131 9						
3.55	0.139 8	9	0.139 8	3.551	9	0.144	3.658
3.75	0.147 6						
4.00	0.157 5	8	0.157 0	3.988	8	0.160	4.064
4.25	0.167 3						
4.50	0.177 2	7	0.176 4	4.481	7	0.176	4.470
4.75	0.187 0				6	0.192	4.877
5.00	0.196 9	6	0.198 1	5.032			
5.30	0.208 7				5	0.212	5.385

Metric standard R40 mm	in	BG gauge no.	BG in	BG mm	SWG gauge no.	SWG in	SWG mm
5.60	0.220 5	5	0.222 5	5.652			
6.00	0.236 2				4	0.232	5.893
6.30	0.248 0	4	0.250 0	6.350			
6.70	0.263 8				3	0.252	6.401
7.10	0.279 5	3	0.280 4	7.122	2	0.276	7.010
7.50	0.295 3				1	0.300	7.620
8.00	0.315 0	2	0.314 7	7.993	0	0.324	8.230
8.50	0.334 6				2/0	0.348	8.839
9.00	0.354 3	1	0.353 2	8.971			
9.50	0.374 0				3/0	0.372	9.449
10.00	0.393 7	0	0.396 4	10.07	4/0	0.4	10.16

Finance

MONEY MARKET

Bank of England's minimum lending rate (MLR)

This is the minimum rate at which members of the discount market have a right to discount British government Treasury bills or other approved bills at the Bank of England. In practice bills are usually discounted at market rates, but the Bank, acting as a lender of last resort, lends at the official discount rate to the discount market against security of such bills or of short-term British government stocks with five years or less to final maturity. Before October 13th 1972 it was known as the Bank Rate. The MLR was, from that date until May 25th 1978, normally 0.5% higher than the average rate of discount for Treasury bills established at the weekly tender, rounded to the nearest 0.25% above.

From May 25th 1978 to August 20th 1981 MLR was fixed by administrative decision. The UK then switched to a system of monetary control that did not have a declared formal interest rate and the Bank of England no longer continuously posts a minimum lending rate. MLR was reintroduced on January 14th 1985 for one day at 12% per annum, and again on October 8th 1990 at 14% per annum.

Base rates

Each London clearing bank posts a base rate linked loosely to short-term market rates. Customer deposit and lending rates are set at margins below or above base rate.

London interbank offered rate (LIBOR)

Some bank and Euromarket lending is set at a margin over the market-determined London interbank offered rate (LIBOR) which fluctuates daily. LIBOR is the rate at which top banks lend cash to each other.

US rates

The US equivalent to MLR is the discount rate. This is fixed by the Federal Reserve Bank, which has a similar role to the Bank of England. The US interbank market is known as the Federal Funds market. Instead of base rates, US banks each post a prime rate, which is the lowest interest rate at which they will lend to first-class borrowers.

Treasury and commercial bills

Bills bear no interest, but are payable at a fixed sum after a certain period, usually 30, 60, 91, 120 or 181 days.

Bills are traded on a discount per year basis, where a year is counted as 365 days in general, but as 360 days for bills expressed in US dollars and other foreign currencies. Where:

F is the final or principal amount of the bill
D is the discount amount
r is the per cent rate of discount
d is the number of days

$$D = F \times \frac{r}{100} \times \frac{d}{365 \text{ (or 360)}}$$

The true yield, y, is higher than the discount rate, and is given by:

$$y = r \times \frac{F}{P}, \text{ where } P \text{ is the net proceeds} = F - D$$

Also, $P \times 100/F$ is the price per 100 of the bill. For example, where £100 000 is discounted at 15% for 91 days:

$$D = 100\,000 \times \frac{15}{100} \times \frac{91}{365} = 3\,739.73$$

$$P = 100\,000 - 3\,739.73 = 96\,260.27$$

$$\text{price} = 96.260$$

$$y = 15 \times \frac{100\,000}{96\,260.27} = 15.582\,8$$

Certificates of deposit

Certificates of deposit have a fixed interest rate, and are payable after a fixed period.

Short-term. Certificates of deposit for up to one year are short-term certificates. Where:

F is the final amount or principal
P is the proceeds from sale within the period during which the certificate runs
r is the rate at which the certificate was issued
r_x is the rate at which the certificate is quoted for sale
d is the number of days at which the certificate was issued
d_x is the number of days to run until maturity

$$P = F \times \frac{1 + \left(\frac{r}{100} \times \frac{d}{365^a}\right)}{1 + \left(\frac{r_x}{100} \times \frac{d_x}{365^a}\right)}$$

[a]Or 360 for US dollar certificates.

Medium-term. Certificates of deposit for periods of 1–5 years are medium-term certificates. Proceeds are determined by successive discounting of the final amount at maturity year by year, with addition of annual interest payments.

Letters of credit

The following terms are sometimes used.

Beginning of month	1st–10th inclusive
Middle of month	11th–20th inclusive
End of month	21st–last day

CONSUMER CREDIT

Rates of interest quoted and charged for consumer credit in the UK must be accompanied by the annual equivalent percentage rate (APR). Where:

x is the rate of interest quoted for a period less than a year
y is the number of such periods in a year

$$\text{APR} = 100 \times \left[\left(1 + \frac{x}{100}\right)^y - 1\right]$$

For example, a rate of 2.25% per month, with $x = 2.25$, $y = 12$, gives

$\text{APR} = 100 \times (1.0225^{12} - 1) = 100 \times (1.306 - 1) = 30.6.$

A table of main rates is included on page 206 for conversion from rates quoted monthly to annual percentage rates.

When a sum is borrowed and repayable in a lump sum after a specified period, the annual percentage rate equivalent is determined as follows. Where:

P is the amount borrowed and repayable
C is the additional amount repayable for credit
n is the period from borrowing to repayment (in years)

$$\text{APR} = 100 \times \left[\left(1 + \frac{C}{P}\right)^{1/n} - 1\right]$$

For example, an amount of £100, to be repaid after six months ($n = 0.5$) by £200 ($C = 100$) gives an APR of $100 \times (2^2 - 1) = 100 \times (4 - 1) = 300$.

A table of annual percentage rates for fixed sum repayments for monthly periods up to one year is included on page 207.

MORTGAGES

Mortgage repayments are usually repayments of a total fixed sum by regular fixed sum instalments which include both repayment of capital and interest.

For general estimation of the amount required to pay off a mortgage at different rates of interest, see below and the tables on pages 220–223. Examples of the way in which the fixed instalment is divided between payment of capital and interest are included on pages 203–205 for various rates of interest.

Interest payment is high in the early years and capital repayment low, with interest amounts gradually falling and capital repayments rising. The tables assume that interest is paid at the end of the year on the balance at the beginning; the monthly rate makes no allowance for any interest within the year, but assumes that the monthly payments are only applied at the end of the year as an annual payment.

Such mortgage repayments result in a variable amount of capital being repaid each year. An alternative method provides for repayment of a fixed capital sum each year, the amount of interest varying according to the balance outstanding.

For fixed capital repayments, it can be seen that interest payments are lower in total, the instalment paid being higher in the earlier years.

Examples of the payments when fixed capital repayments are made are included in the table on page 205.

INSURANCE

Adjustment: a settlement of a loss incurred by an insured person.

Average: in marine insurance, the apportionment of loss incurred in transactions between the person suffering the loss and other persons concerned or interested; in other insurance, if the sum insured does not represent the full value of the property at risk, the insurers' liability is limited to the proportion of loss which the sum insured bears to the full value. "Special condition of average" allows 25% underinsurance before average applies.

Average, general: liability for contributions to cover loss of property (ship and cargo) and any expenditure incurred.

Average, particular: partial loss due to accident, act of God, or stress of weather; not general average and not shared generally.

Average adjuster: a person who officially calculates the contribution due from each beneficiary as a consequence of a general average act.

For risk, see also Probability (pages 116–117); for shipping terms, see also Transport (pages 149–153).

Expectation of life

The following table gives the average number of years persons, at any age level specified, can expect to live in the UK (1986–88 tables).

Age (years)	Males	Females	Age (years)	Males	Females
0	72.2	77.9	45	74.6	79.6
5	72.0	78.6	50	75.1	80.0
10	73.1	78.7	55	75.9	80.5
15	73.2	78.7	60	77.0	81.3
20	73.4	78.8	65	78.6	82.5
25	73.6	78.9	70	80.6	83.9
30	73.8	79.0	75	83.2	85.7
35	74.0	79.1	80	86.2	87.9
40	74.3	79.3	85	89.6	90.7

INTEREST

Simple interest

Definition. If interest is computed on the original principal during the whole life of a transaction, the interest due at the end of the time is called simple interest. Where:

P is the principal
n is the number of years the sum P is invested
r is the % rate of interest
I is the total interest after n years
F is the final amount,

$$I = \frac{Prn}{100}$$

$$F = P + I$$

$$F = P\left[1 + \frac{rn}{100}\right]$$

$$P = \frac{100I}{rn}$$

Compound interest

Definition. If at stated intervals during the term of an investment, the interest due is added to the principal and therefore earns interest, the sum by which the original principal has increased by the end of the term of the

investment is called compound interest. Where:
P is the principal
n is the number of years the sum P is invested
r is the % rate of interest (paid once a year)
I is the total interest after n years
F is the final amount

$$F = P\left[1 + \frac{r}{100}\right]^n$$

For estimation of r from F and n (with $P = 1$) see the tables on pages 208–215. For estimation of F from r and n (with $P = 1$) see the tables on pages 216–219.

$$I = F - P = P\left[\left(1 + \frac{r}{100}\right)^n - 1\right]$$

$$P = F\left[1 + \frac{r}{100}\right]^{-n}$$

For estimation of the principal or present value P from r and n (with $F = 1$), the reciprocal of the figure from the tables on pages 216–219 can be used.

$$n = \frac{\log F - \log P}{\log\left[1 + \frac{r}{100}\right]}$$

To find the amount x to pay off 1 unit in equal instalments of principal and interest (paid once a year)

$$x = \frac{\frac{r}{100}}{1 - \left[1 + \frac{r}{100}\right]^{-n}}$$

For estimation of x from r and n see the tables on pages 220–223.

The effect on the number of years payment of changing the interest rate r can be seen from these tables; eg, where the interest rate is 9.5% repayment (say, of a mortgage) of 1 unit over 11 years is 0.150 44 per year. Raising the interest rate to 12% means that the repayment period is extended to 14 years for approximately the same amount (in the table 0.150 87); an interest rate of 14% raises the period to 20 years (0.150 99 in the table) and a rate of 15% raises the period to 36 years for 0.150 99, and to 42 years for 0.150 42.

To find the final amount (F) after n years, if 1 unit is invested at r % compound interest and 1 unit is added every year

$$F = \frac{\left[1 + \frac{r}{100}\right]^n - 1}{\frac{r}{100}}$$

To find present value (P) to yield 1 unit per year over n years

$$P = \frac{1 - \left[1 + \frac{r}{100}\right]^{-n}}{\frac{r}{100}}$$

To find the number (n_2) of years it takes a sum to double itself

$$n_2 = \frac{\log 2}{\log\left[1 + \frac{r}{100}\right]}$$

Very approximately $n_2 = 70/r$

To find the number (n_3) of years it takes a sum to treble itself replace the 2 in the above formula with 3, and so on for quadrupling, etc.

The following table gives number of years to double, etc, for various rates of interest.

Rate of compound interest %	No. years it takes a sum to: double	treble	quadruple	quintuple	sextuple
0.25	277.6	440.0	555.2	644.6	717.6
0.50	139.0	220.3	278.0	322.7	359.2
0.75	92.8	147.0	185.5	215.4	239.8
1.00	69.7	110.4	139.3	161.7	180.1
1.50	46.6	73.8	93.1	108.1	120.3
2.00	35.0	55.5	70.0	81.3	90.5
2.50	28.1	44.5	56.1	65.2	72.6
3.00	23.4	37.2	46.9	54.4	60.6
3.50	20.1	31.9	40.3	46.8	52.1
4.00	17.7	28.0	35.3	41.0	45.7
4.50	15.7	25.0	31.5	36.6	40.7
5.00	14.2	22.5	28.4	33.0	36.7
5.50	12.9	20.5	25.9	30.1	33.5
6.00	11.9	18.9	23.8	27.6	30.7
6.50	11.0	17.4	22.0	25.6	28.5
7.00	10.2	16.2	20.5	23.8	26.5
7.50	9.6	15.2	19.2	22.3	24.8
8.00	9.0	14.3	18.0	20.9	23.3
8.50	8.5	13.5	17.0	19.7	22.0
9.00	8.0	12.7	16.1	18.7	20.8
9.50	7.6	12.1	15.3	17.7	19.7
10.00	7.3	11.5	14.5	16.9	18.8
11.00	6.6	10.5	13.3	15.4	17.2
12.00	6.1	9.7	12.2	14.2	15.8
13.00	5.7	9.0	11.3	13.2	14.7
14.00	5.3	8.4	10.6	12.3	13.7
15.00	5.0	7.9	9.9	11.5	12.8
16.00	4.7	7.4	9.3	10.8	12.1
17.00	4.4	7.0	8.8	10.3	11.4
18.00	4.2	6.6	8.4	9.7	10.8
19.00	4.0	6.3	8.0	9.3	10.3
20.00	3.8	6.0	7.6	8.8	9.8
21.00	3.6	5.8	7.3	8.4	9.4
22.00	3.5	5.5	7.0	8.1	9.0
23.00	3.3	5.3	6.7	7.8	8.7
24.00	3.2	5.1	6.4	7.5	8.3
25.00	3.1	4.9	6.2	7.2	8.0
26.00	3.0	4.8	6.0	7.0	7.8
27.00	2.9	4.6	5.8	6.7	7.5
28.00	2.8	4.5	5.6	6.5	7.3
29.00	2.7	4.3	5.4	6.3	7.0
30.00	2.6	4.2	5.3	6.1	6.8

INVESTMENT

Fixed interest securities

The gross flat yield on a security is the annual amount receivable as interest expressed as a percentage of the purchase price. The net flat yield is the gross flat yield less income tax at the standard rate (for the UK). These yields are used mainly for irredeemable or undated stocks, where the absence of a fixed redemption date does not permit the calculation of any certain capital gain or loss; they are comparable with rates of interest obtainable on deposits, mortgages and other investments that offer no capital gain or loss.

For a description of formulae concerning accumulation from interest rates, etc, see above, and for tables see pages 208–223.

The gross redemption yield comprises the gross flat yield together with an apportionment of the calculated capital gain or loss on dated securities held to redemption; more precisely it is the rate of interest which if used to discount future dividends and the sum due at redemption will make their present value equal to the present price of the stock. This is the same rate of interest as the DCF solution rate.

See Accountancy, page 26.

Ordinary shares

Nominal share capital is the value of the capital with which the company is registered. The nominal value of a share is the par rate at which it is valued for registration. For other than UK shares, shares may be npv (no par value).

Issued share capital is the value of the capital actually issued.

The asset value of an ordinary share is the total net assets of a company, divided by the number of ordinary shares in issue.

See Accountancy, page 25.

Where there is more than one class of share in issue, the net assets belonging to shareholders must be allocated according to the class of preference of capital.

Preference capital is the main type of share capital other than ordinary shares, and usually has preference as to capital on winding up. Hence the value of preference capital, where it occurs, is deducted from net assets to determine the value belonging to ordinary shareholders:

Assets value per ordinary share

$$= \frac{\text{Net assets} - \text{preference shares (value)}}{\text{Number of ordinary shares}}$$

Gearing is the amount of leverage exerted by the existence of fixed interest capital; where there is a fixed interest payment any increase in profits accrues to the shareholders and any fall in profits reduces the amount attributable to them by the total amount of the fall.

Earnings are profits for shareholders, after payment of interest, etc; and in the case of ordinary shareholders, after payment of any preference dividends. Following the introduction of a changed system of corporation tax in the UK from April 1973, there are two main methods of assessing earnings for shareholders. This follows because tax paid overseas, while it can be set off against corporation tax on companies, cannot be set off against the tax paid on dividends; the latter can, however, be set off against UK corporation tax paid. Tax paid on dividends is at the standard income tax rate, and a part of this is paid in advance of payment of corporation tax and is called advance corporation tax (ACT).

	No overseas tax paid		All tax paid overseas	
Profits before tax		100		100
less tax (at 33%)		33		33
Profit after tax		67[a]		67[a]
less unrelieved ACT		0		10
Profit after tax and ACT		48[b]		38
Dividend paid gross:	30		30	
less tax (at 33%)	10		10	
		20		20
Retentions		28		18

Profits after corporation tax (marked[a] on table) are referred to as earnings on a nil distribution basis, ie, where no dividends are paid and allowed for. Profits after corporation tax and any unrelieved ACT (marked[b]) are referred to as earnings on a net distribution basis, ie, after allowing for the deduction of the ACT which cannot be set off because there are insufficient taxes paid in the UK against which to offset.

Earnings per share are the total of earnings (on either a nil or net distribution basis) divided by the number of ordinary shares to which those earnings are attributable. Earnings are also sometimes expressed as a percentage of the nominal value of the share.

$$\text{Hence: earnings per share} = \frac{\text{earnings for ordinary shareholders}}{\text{number of ordinary shares}}$$

$$\%\ \text{earnings rate} = \frac{\text{earnings per share}}{\text{nominal value per share}} \times 100$$

Dividends, like earnings, are usually expressed either as a value per share or as a percentage rate per nominal value of the share.

Dividend cover is earnings per share/dividend per share, where earnings per share is usually taken as the value for a full distribution of dividends – full distribution basis. This is usually the same as the net distribution basis, the main exception being the case where payment of additional dividends may involve the company in the payment of further taxation either in the UK or overseas; cover is then the theoretical maximum dividend which could be paid, after allowing for such additional taxation, divided by the actual dividend.

Price/earnings ratio (P/E ratio) is the number of years' earnings in the share price of an ordinary share.

$$\text{P/E ratio} = \frac{\text{price per share}}{\text{earnings per share}}$$

$$\textbf{Earnings yield} = \frac{\text{earnings per share}}{\text{price per share}} \times 100$$

$$= \text{\% earnings rate} \times \frac{\text{nominal value per share}}{\text{market price per share}}$$

$$\textbf{Dividend yield} = \frac{\text{gross dividend per share}}{\text{price per share}} \times 100$$

$$= \text{\% rate of gross dividend} \times \frac{\text{nominal value per share}}{\text{market price per share}}$$

Scrip issue or bonus issue is shares issued to shareholders for which no payment is required. The price is adjusted in proportion: where the scrip issue is a for b, the new price = old price × $b/(a+b)$. For example, with a 1 for 3 scrip issue, and a price of 100p before the issue is made ex-scrip, the new price = 100p × 3/4 = 75p.

Rights issue is shares issued to shareholders for which payment is made. The price adjustment makes allowance for the amount of the payment made to the company by the shareholders. Where the issue is a for b at x pence per share,

$$\text{the new price} = \frac{(\text{old price} \times b) + (\text{payment} \times a)}{a+b}$$

For example, with an issue of 1 share at 20p for each 3, and price of 100p, the new price = (300 + 20)p/4 = 80p.

Adjustment of previous dividend and earnings rates to the new basis can be made by using the ratio as calculated for the price, taking the estimate of new price/old price as the multiplier to apply to previous earnings and dividends. For example, in the 1 for 3 scrip, the multiplier is 75/100 = 0.75, and a previous dividend of 10p per share would be equivalent after the scrip issue to 10p × 0.75 = 7.5p per share.

Rates of growth. Where dividend and earnings rates have been fully adjusted for all share issues, growth rates can be obtained by using the tables on **pages 208–215**. For example, where a dividend has gone up from 1.00p to 1.33p per share over six years the table on **page 208** indicates the growth rate for the dividend as 4.87% pa (column for six years, 1.33 at the side of the line).

TAXATION

Income tax

Under the unified income tax system in the UK, the amount of tax due is based on various rates applying to each band of income, after deducting the various allowances. The main rate of tax is called the standard or basic rate.

Income tax is payable on taxable income (total net income less various allowances such as the personal allowance of £3 295 and the married couples allowance of £1 720). Taxable income up to £23 700 is taxed at 25%, while all income over this threshold is taxed at 40%. (All rates and allowances correct for 1991–92.)

Tax may be calculated as follows.

Taxable income £	Tax due £
up to 23 700	0.25 × taxable income
23 700 and over	£5 925 + [0.4 × (taxable income – 23 700)]

For example, tax due on taxable income of £10 000 is 0.25 × £10 000 = £2 500. Tax due on taxable income of £30 000 is £5 925 + [0.4 × (£30 000 – 23 700)] = £5 925 + £2 520 = £8 445.

Corporation tax

The main rate of corporation tax for 1991–92 was 33%, with a rate of 25% for companies with profits of £250 000 or below and marginal relief for profits between £250 000 and £1.25 mn.

Capital gains tax (CGT)

Capital gains tax is payable on inflation-adjusted capital gains at the highest rate of income tax or corporation tax to which an individual or company is liable. For 1991–92 the capital gains tax annual exempt amount was £5 500 for individuals and £2 750 for trusts.

The capital gain is the asset's sale price less its indexed purchase price. The purchase price is indexed by multiplying it

Retail prices index, January 1987 = 100

	1982	1983	1984	1985	1986	1987	1988	1989	1990	1991
Jan		82.6	86.8	91.2	96.3	100.0	103.3	111.0	119.5	130.2
Feb		83.0	87.2	91.9	96.6	100.4	103.7	111.8	120.2	130.9
Mar	79.4	83.1	87.5	92.8	96.7	100.6	104.1	112.3	121.4	131.4
Apr	81.0	84.3	88.6	94.8	97.7	101.8	105.8	114.3	125.1	133.1
May	81.6	84.6	89.0	95.2	97.9	101.9	106.2	115.0	126.2	133.5
Jun	81.9	84.8	89.2	95.4	97.8	101.9	106.6	115.4	126.7	134.1
Jul	81.9	85.3	89.1	95.2	97.5	101.8	106.7	115.5	126.8	133.8
Aug	81.9	85.7	89.9	95.5	97.8	102.1	107.9	115.8	128.1	134.1
Sep	81.9	86.1	90.1	95.4	98.3	102.4	108.4	116.6	129.3	134.6
Oct	82.3	86.4	90.7	95.6	98.5	102.9	109.5	117.5	130.3	135.1
Nov	82.7	86.7	91.0	95.9	99.3	103.4	110.0	118.5	130.0	135.6
Dec	82.5	86.9	90.9	96.1	99.6	103.3	110.3	118.8	129.9	135.7

by the Inland Revenue's indexation allowance for the month of purchase and sale. Since indexation allowances are based on the retail prices index (RPI), the indexation allowance can be calculated by dividing the RPI for the month of sale by the RPI for the month of purchase. For example, for shares bought in January 1983 and sold in March 1991, the indexation allowance is 131.4 ÷ 82.6 = 1.591. If the shares were bought for £1 000, the indexed purchase price is £1 000 × 1.591 = £1 591. If the shares were sold for £7 000, the indexed capital gain is £7 000 – £1 591 = £5 409; which is just below the 1991–92 CGT allowance.

Inheritance tax

The threshold for inheritance tax was £140 000 from April 6th 1991. The excess over this amount is taxed at 40%.

Value added tax (VAT)

VAT (sales tax) in the UK is charged at 17.5% from April 1st 1991.

To calculate VAT due, multiply the sale price by 0.175. For example, a VAT-rated sale of £50 is liable to VAT of £50 × 0.175 = £8.75.

To calculate the sale price including VAT, multiply by 1.175. For example, the VAT-inclusive price for a £50 item is £50 × 1.175 = £58.75.

To calculate the VAT included in a VAT-inclusive price, divide by 1.175. For example, the tax element in a VAT-inclusive price of £58.75 is £58.75 ÷ 1.175 = £50.

Food and drink

FOOD

Measures in the UK

The food industry in the UK is expected to be completely metric by the end of 1994. At present there is a legal obligation for foodstuffs to be marked by metric weights, following the 1985 Weights and Measures Act. The old pack sizes for prepacked foods have mostly been replaced:

125 g replacing 4 oz (113 g)
250 g replacing 8 oz (227 g)
500 g replacing 1 lb (454 g)

However, in some cases, especially canned or tinned foods, old pack sizes are still being phased out while machinery and packaging equipment are replaced. Certain foods, such as milk, jam and beer, have been relieved of metrication because of the high costs involved. Products sold by number rather than weight must be displayed to the customer.

See also Paper, packaging and printing, pages 125–126.

Prescribed quantities. These have been set by the government in the Price Marking Order 1991 for many foodstuffs. This means that foods have to be sold in specified quantities to enable direct price comparisons. The EC has been attempting to co-ordinate a similar range of product prescribed quantities which is expected to come into effect in the mid-1990s.

Unit pricing. Uses the same basis, except that it matches the prices of differently packaged foods by expressing the price of a named quantity of the product; eg, the price per 100 g of the product. It has been adopted by some outlets and, although it is not a legal obligation for most products, the EC is in favour of this means of pricing.

Net weights. Must be given if a product is packaged.

Drained weight. Must be given if a product is sold in a liquid medium.

Size of equipment

UK

1 teaspoon	= 5 ml	1 tablespoon	= 15 ml
½ teaspoon	= 2.5 ml	1 teacup	= 150 ml
¼ teaspoon	= 1.25 ml	1 cup or "tumbler"	= 300 ml
⅛ teaspoon	= 0.6 ml		

The 150 ml size is roughly the teacup size of 5 fl oz and the 300 ml size the tumbler size of 10 fl oz. Also, roughly, the 5 ml spoon (used in pharmaceutical measures) is the teaspoon of 0.125 fl oz, and the 15 ml spoon the tablespoon of 0.5 fl oz.

The 150 ml cup holds roughly 150 g sugar and 100 g flour.

USA

The US system uses cups as the standard measurement guide, measuring by volume rather than weight, which creates difficulties in conversions.

1 cup	= 237 ml	1 teaspoon	= 4.6 ml
1 cup plain flour	= 150 g	1 tablespoon	= 13.7 ml
1 cup caster sugar	= 200 g		

Additives

Many foods contain additives. In the UK about 300 additives and over 3 000 flavourings are listed. Safety tests are examined by the Committee on Toxicity of Chemicals in Food, Consumer Products and the Environment (COT) which then advises the government on whether the additive should be permitted. COT sets an "acceptable daily intake" for each additive. Most additives must obtain EC clearance in advance of UK proposals.

E numbers. Show that an additive is accepted as safe throughout the EC. Any additive allowed in the UK is considered safe for almost everyone, although a few people may react badly to it as they might to any everyday food. In general the absence of an E number for an additive indicates that it has been approved by the UK but not yet by the EC.

Anti-oxidants. Stop fatty foods from going rancid and protect fat-soluble vitamins from the harmful effects of oxidation.

Colours. Make food more colourful and compensate for colour lost in processing.

Emulsifiers and stabilisers. Enable oils and fats to mix with water in foods; add to smoothness and creaminess of texture; retard baked goods going stale.

Flavour enhancers. Widely used in savoury foods to make flavours seem stronger.

Preservatives. Protect against microbes which cause spoilage and food poisoning and increase the food's storage life.

Sweeteners. Are being used more widely as sugar in food is reduced. Artificial sweeteners are very low in calories and safer for teeth.

Others. Acids, anti-caking and anti-foaming agents, bases, buffers, bulking and firming agents, flavour modifiers, flour improvers, glazing agents, humectants, liquid freezants, packaging gases, propellants, release agents, sequestrants and solvents.

Content

British or EC standards exist for a range of manufactured food products.

In the UK government regulations lay down statutory limits for the amount of arsenic, lead and other heavy metals in food; eg, the general permitted level of lead is 1 milligram per kilogram (1 mg/kg). A regulation limiting the amount of tin in food was to be introduced in early 1992 to help combat poor canning practices.

The regulations also lay down lists of permitted anti-oxidants, colouring matter, emulsifiers and stabilisers, preservatives, carrier solvents and sweeteners with specifications of purity for each substance. The use of chloroform and mineral hydrocarbons (with certain exceptions) is prohibited. The potassium bromate regulations control by permitted list 15 classes of food additives: acids, anti-caking and anti-foaming agents, bases, buffers, bulking aids, firming agents, flavour modifiers, glazing agents, humectants, liquid freezants, packaging gases, propellants, release agents and sequestrants.

Labelling

In the UK the food labelling regulations lay down that prepacked food must be labelled with the following details.

- The name of the food.
- A list of ingredients.
- An appropriate durability indication.
- Any special storage conditions or conditions of use.
- The name or business name and an address or registered office of the manufacturer or packer, or of a seller established within the EC.
- Particulars of the place of origin if failure to give such particulars might mislead a purchaser to a material degree as to the true origin of the food.
- Instructions for use if it would be difficult to make appropriate use of the food without such instructions.

There are less onerous rules for foods which are non-prepacked or prepacked for direct sale.

New labelling regulations were introduced in January 1991. The main changes are as follows.

- A "Use by" date has been introduced to help ensure that highly perishable food is used safely.
- "Best before" dates must be used for other foods to help ensure that they are used at their best.
- "Sell by" dates have been phased out for all food.
- Datemarking will be introduced for frozen foods, all cheeses and long-life foods from June 20th 1992.
- It is illegal to sell any food after its "Use by" date.
- It is illegal for anyone other than the manufacturer to change a datemark after it has been set.

Food with no datemark. A few foods do not hâve to carry a datemark, such as fresh fruit, vegetables and some cakes which are normally bought for use within a very short period and it is obvious when their quality is deteriorating. Food such as meat bought from a butcher is also unlikely to carry a datemark. Other goods such as alcoholic drinks, sugar, salt and vinegar last for so long that a datemark is unnecessary.

List of ingredients. Required for all products and must include additives and added water. Ingredients are listed in order of weight. There are rules for words and pictures. For instance, a food label cannot say "reduced calorie" unless the product is much lower in calories than the ordinary version; a yoghurt cannot show strawberries on the pot unless the flavour comes mainly from strawberries.

Nutritional information. Must be displayed if the food is for a special dietary purpose or is making nutritional claims. The labels on food packaging must not mislead the consumer.

BEER

Beer is an alcoholic beverage produced from the fermentation of a liquid extract prepared mainly from a malted (germinated) cereal, usually barley, and normally flavoured with hops. The process of fermentation turns the sugar in the cereal into alcohol and carbon dioxide.

Barley is malted by soaking in water to encourage germination, followed by drying in a kiln. The malted barley, or malt, is then ready to be milled into a powder and mashed with hot water in the brewery. The resultant liquid mixture is known as wort, to which may be added other cereals (such as unmalted barley or wheat) and sugar, before being boiled with hops to impart a bitter flavour. After boiling, the hopped wort is cooled and yeast added. The yeast converts the carbohydrates in the wort into alcohol and flavours. The resultant beer needs a further period of conditioning before it is ready to be packaged and drunk.

The most common types of beer are ales (the traditional British style of brewing) and lagers, but there are many other lesser-known types, often speciality products peculiar to one country or region. Beers can be brewed with rice, wheat and roasted barley to produce different styles and in some countries can be flavoured with herbs and spices or even fruit, rather than hops.

Ale-brewing is essentially a faster process than lager-brewing. An ale brew can be fermented and conditioned within two weeks, although some strong ales require a much longer maturation period. Lager beers are fermented at lower temperatures and are conditioned ("lagered") over longer periods, usually at least six weeks. Ale is, today, quintessentially a British beer style, although there has been a great revival of interest in it among new microbrewers in the USA. Blonde, lager type beers originated in Czechoslovakia in the 19th century and with the invention of refrigeration equipment spread all over the world. At least 90% of the world's beer is now lager style and the most common is that of Pilsner, named after the school of brewing which originated in the Czech town of Pilsen.

Total world beer production is estimated at more than 1 115 mn hectolitres. The USA remains the biggest single brewing country, producing 233 mn hectolitres per year.

Measures

In most countries beer production is measured in hectolitres.

1 hectolitre = 21.996 9 UK gallons = 26.417 2 US gallons

In the UK and USA brewers use barrels – but not the same ones.

1 UK barrel = 1.636 6 hectolitres = 1.394 7 US barrels
1 US barrel = 1.173 5 hectolitres = 0.717 UK barrels
1 UK barrel = 26 UK gallons
1 US barrel = 31 US gallons

Legal measures for the retail of beer or cider, in the UK, other than in a container are: $\frac{1}{3}$ pint, $\frac{1}{2}$ pint or a multiple of $\frac{1}{2}$ pint.

There are no standard measures in the USA.

Common trade measures

	Cans (ml)	Bottles (ml)	Bottles (l)
Beer, cider	330	275	1
	440	330	2
	500	660	3
Mineral water		330	1
		750	2
			5
Tonic, soda water, etc	330	500	1

Strength

By law, all countries in the EC now display the alcoholic strength of beers (and wines and spirits) in terms of alcohol by volume. In the USA beer strengths tend to be expressed in terms of alcohol by weight, which would give a lower percentage figure. A regular beer in the USA would be, on average, 3.5% alcohol by weight. The European equivalent would be 4.4% alcohol by volume.

WINES AND SPIRITS

Wines

Within the EC wine is defined as: "the product obtained exclusively from the total or partial alcoholic fermentation of fresh grapes, whether or not crushed, or of grape must". Wine is about 70% of the weight of crushed grapes. The sugar content of a grape varies between about 12% and 27% by weight. The grapes are broken and crushed to form must (unfermented grape juice); yeast which has settled on the skins of grapes before gathering (or added where necessary) produces fermentation, and as alcohol is formed it releases the red colour in the skins where the grapes are coloured (and also from the pulp in Teinturier grapes, as this is also coloured).

Classification of wines. Within the EC wines are either "quality wine", a reserved term expressed formally as "vin de qualité produit dans des régions déterminées" (VQPRD) in France, for example, and "quality wine produced in specified regions" in the UK, or "table wine", another reserved term, expressed in France as "vin de table" and in Spain as "vino de mesa". Table wines, which come from delimited areas and comply with certain criteria, can be called "vin de pays", "vino tipico", "vino de la tierra", etc.

Those wines which can lay claim to having come from particular parts of countries outside the EC are recognised as "being equivalent in quality to VQPRD". All other imported wines are regarded as equivalent to table wines. Quality wines and their imported equivalents have certain labelling advantages.

The best known gradings within VQPRD are as follows.

France. AC or AOC (Appellation d'Origine Contrôlée). All top quality wines are subject to strict laws of origin and content. The main areas are in Alsace, Bordeaux, Burgundy, Champagne, Loire, Rhône Valley, etc. Limitations include those on quantity (in terms of hectolitres per hectare), sugar content of must (in terms of grams per litre) and strength (in terms of percentage strength of alcohol by volume).

Examples of maximum yield for AC (AOC) wines

Area	hl/ha	Area	hl/ha
Bordeaux		**Burgundy**	
Médoc	45	Côte de Nuits	35
Margaux	40	Côte de Beaune	35
Sauternes	25	Mâcon	50
Entre-deux-mers	50	Mâcon Villages	45
Bordeaux	50	Beaujolais	50
		Beaujolais (the growths)	40

Area	hl/ha	Area	hl/ha
Corsica		**Loire Valley**	
Vin de Corse: Coteaux d'Ajaccio	45	Touraine	45
Patrimonio	45	Chinon	40
		Saumur: still white	45
		sparkling	60
Côtes du Rhône	40	red	40
Hermitage	32	Anjou: white	45
Château Grillet	35	rosé	45
Châteauneuf du Pape	50	red	40
Côtes du Rhône		Muscadet	40
		South-east	
		Fitou	40
		Corbières	50

VDQS (Vins délimités de qualité supérieure) include limitations on region, type of vine, methods of growing the vine and making the wine, maximum yield, alcohol content and taste.

Germany. Qualitätswein has limitations on region, type of grape, alcoholic content (a minimum alcoholic content of 8.5%) and taste.

Qualitätswein mit Prädikat has similar limitations to Qualitätswein, plus a minimum alcoholic content of 9% obtained from the original sugar content with no added sugar.

US classification. AVA (American Viticultural Area) is the system of appellation of origin. This guarantees that a minimum of 85% of the wine in the bottle comes from grapes grown in the region named on the label. 95% of any wine using a vineyard name must come from grapes grown in that vineyard and from a recognised AVA.

Australian classification. LIP (Label Integrity Program) was introduced in 1990, which states that 80% of wine in the bottle must come from the variety or area specified on the label. If a vintage is declared, the level must be 95%.

Spirits

Because alcohol has a lower boiling point (78°C, 173°F) than water (100°C, 212°F), it can be separated from its carrier (whether it is wine *per se*, fruit, or fermented cereal mash) simply by the application of heat to the host liquid.

The main types of whisky are as follows.

Scotland
- malt whisky, made from malted barley;
- grain whisky, made from barley and matured for at least three years.

Ireland
- Irish whiskey: made with a wider range of cereals than Scotch.

Most commercial brands are blends of about 40% malt and 60% grain. 1.016 tonnes (1 ton) of barley is estimated to produce about 477.3 litres (105 proof gallons) of whisky (272.8 litres or 60 gallons of pure alcohol).

USA
- bourbon whisky, made from at least 51% corn (maize),

distilled at not more than 160 US proof, and aged for not less than four years;
- corn whisky, made from a mash of at least 80% corn;
- rye whisky, made from at least 51% rye.

Measures: retail

Usual measures in the UK of gin, rum, vodka and whisky (but not other spirits) for retail supply, other than in a container, are: 25 ml or any multiples thereof or $\frac{1}{6}, \frac{1}{5}, \frac{1}{4}$ gill, giving approximately 32, 26 or 21 singles per bottle respectively; the smaller singles are more usual in the South of the UK and the larger in the North and Scotland. Usually 1 tot = 35.5 ml = $\frac{1}{4}$ gill.

However, the UK is being obliged increasingly to accommodate the practices of its EC partners. After December 31st 1994 any establishment in the UK will be required to choose between only the 25 ml and the 35 ml measure; to use the chosen size throughout the premises; and to display notices showing the quantities chosen at the point of sale.

In 1975 the EC drew up a programme to regulate by prescription the sizes in which all wines and spirits can be held and offered for sale to the final consumer; implementation of this programme is almost complete. Throughout the EC, therefore, the standard bottle size for still and sparkling wine is 75 cl, but for spirits it is 70 cl. Even the size of the carafe, where wine is sold "loose", is regulated and the sizes permitted generally mirror the sizes in which wine may be sold by the bottle (eg, 25, 50, 75 cl, or 1 litre). Notice of the quantity in which wine is offered for sale (and its typical strength) must be posted at the point of sale.

Sizes for champagne

Name	No. bottles	Name	No. bottles
Magnum	2	Salmanezah	12
Jeroboam[a]	4	Balthazar	16
Rehoboam	6	Nebuchadnezzar	20
Methuselah[b]	8		

[a]In Burgundy a jeroboam is 4 bottles and in Bordeaux 5 or 6 bottles.
[b]Impériale in Bordeaux.

In the UK a jeroboam is usually 6 bottles and a rehoboam 8 bottles. Wine is not usually matured in sizes above one bottle.

Measures: wholesale

Today most of the wine sold in the UK and USA is packaged abroad. Even the quantities which are imported for packaging travel in stainless steel containers: the traditional casks, developed by the production region and – via their quaint names – regarded almost as old friends, have virtually disappeared. Nonetheless, most of them together with their capacities and conversion values are listed below.

	Litres	UK gallons	US gallons
Aum or Ohm			
Rhenish (Alsatian, Hock, Moselle)	150	33	40
Barrique			
Anjou, Touraine	232	51	61
Bordeaux	225	49	59
Burgundy, Nantes	228	50	60
Butt or Bota			
Lisbon	530	117	141
Sherry	491	108	130
Whisky	500	110	132
Feuillette			
Burgundy:			
Saône et Loire, Côte d'Or	114	25	20
Yonne (Chablis)	132	29	35
Hogshead			
Australia, South Africa	295	65	78
Brandy	273	60	72
Claret	209–225	46–49	55–59
Madeira, Marsala	209	46	55
Port	260	57	70
Sherry	246	54	66
Whisky	255	56	67
Leaguer			
South Africa	577	127	153
Muid			
Aisne	260	57	68
Hérault	685	151	181
Montpellier	608	134	161
Octave			
Sherry	62.5	13.75	16.5
Whisky	64	14	17
Pièce			
Burgundy: Côte d'Or	228	50	60
Mâcon	216	47.5	57
Beaujolais	214	47	56.5
Pipe			
Madeira	418	92	110
Marsala	423	93	112
Port or Tarragona	522–535	115–117	138–141
Teneriffe	455	100	120
Puncheon			
Brandy, rum	509–546	112–120	135–144
Whisky	432–546	95–120	114–144
Quarter			
Brandy	136	30	36
Port	132	29	35
Sherry	125	27.5	33
Whisky	127	28	34
Queue			
Burgundy	456	100	120
Champagne	216	47.5	57
Stück			
Hock	1200	264	317

	Litres	UK gallons	US gallons
erçon			
nguedoc	228	50	60
onneau			
ordeaux	900	198	238

ote. All measures are approximate.

sual general relationships are (or were) as follows.

octaves	= 1 quarter	2 feuilletes	= 1 pièce
quarters	= 1 hogshead	2 pièces	= 1 queue
hogsheads	= 1 butt, pipe or puncheon	3 tierçons	= 1 muid
		4 barriques	= 1 tonneau
pipes	= 1 tonne, tonneau or tun		

trength

he process of fermentation in wine stops when the original ugar content is used up in producing alcohol (when the wine totally dry), or when the alcohol level rises to the point at hich the yeasts cannot survive (even though, for particularly weet wines like Sauternes, a good level of sugar is still resent) and fermentation stops.

When there is not enough sugar in the juice, sugar is ometimes added to help increase the alcoholic content (this is alled chaptalisation). Fortified wines, such as port and sherry, ave had brandy or pure alcohol added to arrest fermentation efore all sugar has been used up, and to increase alcoholic ontent (such wines are usually called dessert wines in the SA).

Must contains about 70–85% water; the remainder is mainly arbohydrates. Alcohol is about 48% of the weight of sugar rmented.

The detailed relationship between sugar content of must and ubsequent alcohol content (without adding sugar) is pproximately as shown in the following table (at 15°C); the xcess gravity shown is the number of grams by which 1 litre f the must is heavier than 1 litre of distilled water (also called ust-weight). Excess gravity for zero sugar content is taken in is table as 11; values for this measure can vary.

ugar ontent /l	Excess gravity g	Alcohol content % by volume	Sugar content g/l	Excess gravity g	Alcohol content % by volume
0	11	0.0	150	68	8.8
8	18	1.1	160	71	9.4
0	30	3.0	170	75	10.0
0	34	3.5	180	79	10.6
70	37	4.1	190	83	11.2
30	41	4.7	200	87	11.8
90	45	5.3	210	90	12.4
00	49	5.9	220	94	13.0
10	52	6.5	230	98	13.6
20	56	7.1	240	101	14.2
30	60	7.7	250	105	14.7
40	64	8.3	255	107	15.0

For general conversions between weight and volume, the FAO takes the specific gravity (relative density) of wine as 1 000 (excess gravity = 0), so that, as with water, 1 litre weighs 1 kilogram, 1 hectolitre weighs 1 quintal, and 1 kilolitre weighs 1 tonne.

UK measures. Official UK measures for alcohol changed to the metric system in 1980. Litres and hectolitres replaced the gallon, the Celsius temperature scale replaced Fahrenheit, and the Sikes proof system for ascertaining the alcoholic strength of spirits and other liquids was replaced by a system of measurement by reference to percentages of alcohol by volume, as established by the Organisation Internationale de Métrologie Légale (OIML) and laid down in EC regulations for use in the EC.

The official definitions of alcoholic strength are as follows.

- Alcoholic strength by volume. The ratio of the volume of alcohol present in a mixture of water and ethanol at 20°C to the total volume of the mixture at the same temperature expressed as parts of alcohol per 100 parts of the mixture (with symbol: % vol).
- Alcoholic strength by mass. The ratio of the mass of alcohol present in a mixture of water and ethanol to the total mass of the mixture expressed as parts of alcohol per 100 parts of the mixture (with symbol: % mas).

For mixtures of alcohol (ethyl alcohol or ethanol) and water, the table on **page 224** gives the relationship between density (kg/m^3 in air at 20°C) and strength by volume (at 20°C) and by mass. These are the official UK relationships; for the purpose of estimating duty, figures beyond the first decimal place are disregarded whatever their value: eg, 46.37% vol is taken as 46.3% vol.

Other measures of strength

- Tralles (used in some European countries): a scale at 60°F, expressed as percentages of alcohol by volume.
- US proof spirit: a scale by volume at 60°F, where 100% alcohol is 200% proof spirit and percentage of proof spirit is throughout double the actual percentage of alcohol by volume, so that 50% alcohol, for example, is 100% proof spirit. Hence US proof spirit = Tralles × 2. US proof is sometimes expressed, as Sikes used to be, in terms of percentages above or below 100 degrees proof – which is 50% by volume in US terms.
- Gay-Lussac (°GL used in France and Belgium): a scale in degrees at 15°C (59°F), expressed as percentages of alcohol by volume. Hence Gay-Lussac is approximately the same as Tralles, but based on 59°F instead of 60°F.

A detailed table showing the relationship between Sikes and some other systems of measuring alcohol content is given on **page 225**; it may be noted that there is only a very small difference in the level of accuracy shown between Gay-Lussac and the percentage by volume at 20°C. Tralles measure is the same as Gay-Lussac in the table, except for strengths marked*, which are 0.1 higher for Tralles.

difference in the level of accuracy shown between Gay-Lussac and the percentage by volume at 20°C. Tralles measure is the same as Gay-Lussac in the table, except for strengths marked*, which are 0.1 higher for Tralles.

The following table shows the approximate strengths of some alcoholic drinks as consumed in the UK using the OIML system of alcohol by volume.

See pages 224–225 for tables.

	Alcohol content (% vol)		**Alcohol content (% vol)**
Whisky	40	Burgundy	
Gin, rum, vodka	37.5	white	10.5–14
Brandy	36	red	10–14
Sherry, port, madeira	15.5–22	Champagne	12.5–13
Bordeaux			
Sauternes	13 min.		
other white	9–13		
red	10–13		

Since January 1976 wine has been classified for duty purposes according to a three-strength structure determined by the percentage of alcohol by volume at 20°C: lower (15% and under), middle (over 15% and up to 18%) and higher (over 18% and up to 22%); over 22%, duty is charged on each 1% or part of 1%. Before 1976 a two-strength structure was used. Wine was classified as either "light" or "heavy", using the Sikes proof strengths. The old light classification was 27° proof or under (under about 15.5% vol) for British and Commonwealth wines and 25° proof or under (under about 14.4% vol) for other wines. Hence the new lower wine classification corresponds roughly to the old light classification.

Health

BLOOD

Properties of human blood

Relative density (at 25°C) = 1.05–1.06
Relative viscosity (at 18°C) = 4.75 (times that of water)
Average temperature = 37°C
Acidity = 7.35–7.45 pH (where 7 is neutral, 0–7 means acidic, 7–14 alkaline)
Coagulation time = 5–11 min

Volume. Blood makes up 5.5–8.0% of a person's body weight. Someone weighing 70 kg contains about 4.9 kg of blood. Each red cell contains millions of haemoglobin molecules. The haemoglobin increases the blood's ability to carry oxygen by a factor of more than 200. The life span of a red blood cell is 120 days plus or minus 30 days.

Blood content

Blood component	Adult males	Adult females
Haemoglobin (g/dl)	13.5–17.5	12.0–16.0
Red blood cells ($\times 10^{12}$ per litre)	4.6–6.5	3.9–5.6
White blood cells ($\times 10^{9}$ per litre)	4.0–10.0	
Platelets ($\times 10^{9}$ per litre)	140–130	

Groups. The main blood groups are determined by the presence or absence of inherited substances (antigens) A and B.

Group	Antigens present	Possible donors	Incidence (approx. %) UK	USA
A	A	A & O	43	41
B	B	B & O	9	10
AB	A & B	Any	3	4
O	Neither	O	45	45

Alcohol content. Under the UK Road Traffic Act the prescribed limit of alcohol over which it is not permissible to drive is 80 mg of alcohol per 100 ml of blood. A single whisky or half-pint of beer produces about 15–20 mg per 100 ml, a bottle of whisky about 600 mg per 100 ml. The body can eliminate about 15–20 mg of alcohol per 100 ml of blood in 1 hour.

CONCENTRATION OF SUBSTANCES

With the change to SI units substance concentration, traditionally measured in grams or submultiples of grams per litre (or cubic decimetre) or submultiples of litres (or cubic decimetres), is to be measured in moles or submultiples of moles per litre (or cubic decimetre), where the relative molecular or atomic mass is known.

Examples of the main types of units used are shown in the following table.

Traditional form	New form
ng/dl	pmol/l
µg/dl	µmol/l
mg/dl	µmol/l or mmol/l
g/dl	µmol/l or mmol/l
g/l	mmol/l

The actual conversion rate depends on the substance concerned, and its atomic or molecular mass. Examples of conversion rates are shown in the following table.

Substance	Conversion rates	Atomic or molecular mass[a]
Cholesterol	1 g/l = 2.586 mmol/l	386.660
	1 mmol/l = 0.386 7 g/l	
Glucose	1 mg/dl = 0.055 5 mmol/l	180.157
	1 mmol/l = 18.02 mg/dl	
Iron	1 µg/dl = 0.1791 µmol/l	55.847
	1 µmol/l = 5.585 µg/dl	
Lead	1 µg/l = 0.004 8 µmol/l	207.2
	1 µmol/l = 207.2 µg/l	

[a]Or atomic weight.

See pages 47–48 for a list of atomic weights for all elements.

It may be noted that, for the same multiples of grams and moles, the conversion between moles and grams is the atomic mass or weight, and the conversion between grams and moles its reciprocal (see table, for example, for lead conversions).

GENETICS

In humans and other multicellular organisms, chromosomes are linear structures found inside the nucleus of each cell. They contain DNA (deoxyribonucleic acid), the blueprint of life, which transmits genetic information from one generation to the next.

Most human body cells contain 23 pairs of chromosomes, the exception being sperm and egg cells, which contain only 23 single chromosomes. When the sperm fertilises the egg, the full complement of 23 pairs is restored. Subsequent cell division increases the number of cells to about 2×10 to the power of 11 (ie, 2×10^{11}) by the time of birth.

The sex ratio is not equal at birth; about 106 boys are born to every 100 girls.

There are about 3 500 genetic diseases caused by defects in single genes. About 40% of infant deaths are due to genetic disease.

HEART

Properties

Normal heart beat = 70–72 beats per min (range: 50–90; in the newborn, 130–150 per minute)
Blood propelled = 80 ml per beat (range: 60–100 ml)
Oxygen consumption of the body = 250 ml per minute for an average man at rest

Blood pressure

Average human blood pressures

	mm Hg	kPa
Diastolic[a]	70–90	9–12
Systolic:[b] children	100	13
young adults	100–140	13–19
adults over 40 years	100 + age	13 + (age/7) approx.

[a]When the heart is relaxed. [b]When the heart is contracted at each heart beat, forcing blood through the arteries. These values refer to a resting individual; strenuous activity can increase systolic blood pressure above this "normal" level by 60–80 mm Hg (8–11 kPa).

Blood pressures are usually written with the systolic over the diastolic; eg, as 140/90. Traditionally blood pressures have been measured in millimetres of mercury (using a sphygmomanometer); the SI unit recommended as a replacement is the kilopascal (kPa).

A table of conversions is shown on page 226.

Vascular resistance is measured in peripheral resistance units (PRU; millimetre of mercury minute per litre, mm Hg min/l) or dynes second per cm^5 (dyn s/cm^5). The recommended SI unit is kilopascal second per litre (kPa s/l), where:
1 mm Hg min/l = 8 kPa s/l
1 dyn s/cm^5 = 0.1 kPa s/l

RESPIRATION

Respiratory pressure and resistance to flow (in airways) are measured in kilopascals. The traditional unit of measurement, centimetre of water, is still used in the USA.

DISEASES

Figures from the World Health Organisation (WHO) show that about 50 mn people die in the world each year from all causes, including disease. About 80% of these deaths occur in developing countries.

Within this total, each year 14.6 mn children under the age of five die in developing countries from disease and other causes. More than 8 000 children die each day because they are not immunised; almost 11 000 a day die of dehydration caused by diarrhoea and about 8 000 a day die of pneumonia.

Disease	Nos affected (bn)	Disease	Nos affected (bn)
Hepatitis B	2	Vaccine-preventable diseases	1.8
Intestinal worms	2.2	Anaemia	1.5

Global deaths from diseases

Illness	Annual deaths (mn)	Illness	Annual deaths (mn)
Cardiovascular diseases	12.00	Measles	1.50
Diarrhoeal diseases	5.00	Malaria	1–2
Cancer	4.80	Pertussis (whooping cough)	0.50
Pneumonia	4.80	Maternal mortality	0.50
Tuberculosis	3.00	Rabies	0.04

Worldwide average life expectancy is 61.5 years; 73.4 years for developed countries and 59.7 years for developing countries.

Acquired immune deficiency syndrome (AIDS)

By October 1st 1991 a cumulative total of 418 403 cases of AIDS had been reported to the WHO from 163 countries. Taking into account underdiagnosis, underreporting and delays in reporting, the WHO estimates that more than 1 mn adult AIDS cases may have occurred worldwide since the pandemic began. By April 1991 8–10 mn infections with the human immunodeficiency virus were estimated to have occurred. 10–20 mn new infections are expected among adults during the 1990s.

Viruses

The smallest viruses (also known as micro-organisms) are those that infect plants, causing wilting diseases and mottle leaf diseases. Average diameter: 20–30 nanometres (1 nm = $\frac{1}{1000}$ micrometre.)

The largest viruses are the pox viruses, causing diseases such as cowpox and smallpox, and the herpes viruses, causing cold sores, shingles and genital warts. Average diameter: 250–400 nanometres.

Bacteria vary greatly in size and shape. The average rod-shaped bacterium, such as Escherichia coli, which lives in the gut, is 2 000 nm in diameter.

The smallest spherical bacteria include staphylococci, which cause boils, and streptococci, which cause sore throats and tooth decay. Their average diameter is 400 nm. For comparison, it is possible to get 250,000 average-sized bacteria on a full stop. The diameter of a red blood cell is 7 000 nm.

ENERGY AND NUTRIENT REQUIREMENTS

The dieticians' "calorie" (Cal) is the same as the kilocalorie (kcal), the heat energy required to raise the temperature of 1 kilogram of water through 1 degree celsius from 14.5°C to 15.5°C. The equivalent SI units are kilojoules and megajoules.

See also Energy, page 75.

1 000 calories = 1 Cal = 1 kcal = 4.184 kJ
1 000 Cal = 4.184 MJ

Energy sources

The diet consists of carbohydrates (sugar, starch and cellulose), fats and proteins. Fats can be divided into unsaturated fats, which can possess more than only fat atoms, and saturated, which cannot. The average diet should consist of around 60% carbohydrate, and 20% of both fat and protein. The diet must also include water, which is present in most foodstuffs.

- Metabolisable energy (ME) is the energy available for use by the body after making allowances for energy losses during the process of digesting food.
- BMR (basic metabolic rate) is the rate at which the resting body uses energy to support life.
- RMR (resting metabolic rate) is the measurement used to approximate BMR for practical purposes.
- Thermogenesis is the warming of the body other than as a result of physical movement, eg, emotive responses.

Average approximate estimates for the energy values ("calorific" values) of different nutrients are shown in the following table.

	kcal/oz	kcal/g	kJ/g
Protein	113	4.0	17
Fat	250	9.0	37
Carbohydrate	106	3.7	16
Ethyl alcohol	200	7.0	29

Energy expenditure

Energy expenditure of various activities of moderate duration grouped according to physical activity ratio (PAR) are as follows. (Physical activity ratio is a way of expressing the energy cost of an activity in terms of multiples of BMR).

PAR 1.0–1.4. Reading, watching TV, writing, playing cards, eating, standing at rest.

PAR 1.5–1.8. Sitting while sewing, knitting, playing the piano, driving; standing while preparing vegetables, washing dishes, ironing, general office work.

PAR 1.9–2.4. Mixed household chores such as dusting and cleaning, washing small clothes, cooking activities, hairdressing, bowling.

PAR 2.5–3.3. Making beds, showering, vacuum cleaning, playing cricket, walking at 3–4 km/h; work activities such as tailoring, shoemaking, operating machine tools, painting and decorating.

PAR 3.4–4.4. Mopping the floor, gardening, cleaning windows, playing table tennis, sailing; walking at 4–6 km/h; playing golf; work activities such as motor vehicle repairs, carpentry, joinery, bricklaying.

PAR 4.5–5.9. Polishing furniture, chopping wood, heavy gardening, playing volley ball; walking at 6–7 km/h; dancing, moderate swimming, gentle cycling, slow jogging; work activities such as labouring, hoeing, road construction, digging and shovelling, felling trees.

PAR 6.0–7.9. Walking uphill with load or cross-country; climbing stairs; average jogging, cycling, football, energetic swimming, tennis, skiing.

Estimated average requirements (EARs) for energy

Age	Males MJ/day	Males kcal/day	Females MJ/day	Females kcal/day
0–3 months	2.28	545	2.16	515
4–6 months	2.89	690	2.69	645
7–9 months	3.44	825	3.20	765
10–12 months	3.85	920	3.61	865
1–3 years	5.15	1 230	4.86	1 165
4–6 years	7.16	1 715	6.46	1 545
7–10 years	8.24	1 970	7.28	1 740
11–14 years	9.27	2 220	7.92	1 845
15–18 years	11.51	2 755	8.83	2 110
19–50 years	10.60	2 550	8.10	1 940
51–59 years	10.60	2 550	8.00	1 900
60–64 years	9.93	2 380	7.99	1 900
65–74 years	9.71	2 330	7.96	1 900
75+ years	8.77	2 100	7.61	1 810

Estimated daily energy expenditures of men and women aged 25 years and of median weight in light activity occupations and three categories of non-occupational activities are as follows.

Males. Total energy expenditure ranges from 10.08 MJ/d (2 400 kcal/d) for a man who spends 10.5 hours a day on non-occupational activities classified as "inactive", to 11.36 MJ/d (2 710 kcal/d) for a man whose non-occupational activities are classified as "very active".

Females. Total energy expenditure ranges from 7.77 MJ/d (1 850 kcal/d) for a woman who spends 10.5 hours a day on non-occupational activities classified as "inactive", to 8.75 MJ/d (2 090 kcal/d) for a woman whose non-occupational activities are classified as "very active".

Dietary reference values for fat and carbohydrate for adults (% daily total energy intake[a])

Saturated fatty acids	10
Cis-polyunsaturated fatty acids	6
Cis-mono-unsaturated fatty acids	12
Trans fatty acids	2
Total fatty acids	30
TOTAL fat	33
Non-milk extrinsic sugars	10
Intrinsic milk sugars & starch	37
TOTAL carbohydrate	47
Non-starch polysaccharide (g/day)	18

Note. The average percentage contribution to total energy does not total 100% because figures for protein and alcohol are excluded. Protein intakes average 15% of total energy, which is above the reference nutrient intake. The energy derived from alcohol is assumed to average 5%.

[a]Population averages.

Ideal weights

The following table shows weight limits for each height. A smaller framed person will weigh towards the lower end of the ideal range, a larger framed person towards the higher end.

Height ft	cm	Weight lb	kg
Men			
5′1	155	105–134	46–59
5′2	157	108–137	47–61
5′3	160	111–141	49–63
5′4	163	114–145	50–64
5′5	165	117–149	52–66
5′6	168	121–154	54–67

Height ft	cm	Weight lb	kg
5'7	170	125–159	55–70
5'8	173	129–163	57–72
5'9	175	133–167	60–74
5'10	178	137–172	61–77
5'11	180	141–177	63–80
6'0	183	145–182	64–83
6'1	185	149–187	66–85
6'2	188	153–192	69–87
6'3	190	157–197	71–89
Women			
4'10	147	92–121	42–55
4'11	150	95–124	43–56
5'0	152	98–127	44–58
5'1	155	101–130	46–59
5'2	157	104–134	47–61
5'3	160	107–138	49–63
5'4	163	110–142	50–64
5'5	165	114–146	52–66
5'6	168	118–150	54–67
5'7	170	122–154	55–70
5'8	173	126–159	57–72
5'9	175	130–164	60–74
5'10	178	134–169	61–77

Nutrient requirements

Reference nutrient intakes for protein[a]

Age	g/day
0–3 months	12.5
4–6 months	12.7
7–9 months	13.7
10–12 months	14.9
1–3 years	15.5
4–6 years	19.7
7–10 years	28.3
Males	
11–14 years	42.1
15–18 years	55.2
19–50 years	55.5
50+ years	53.3
Females	
11–14 years	41.2
15–18 years	45.0
19–50	45.0
50+ years	46.5

[a]These figures, based on egg and milk protein, assume complete digestibility.

Reference nutrient intakes for vitamins and minerals

	Males	Females	Children (7–10 yrs
Calcium (mg/d)	700.0	700.0	550.0
Chloride (mg/d)	2 500.0	2 500.0	1 800.0
Copper (mg/d)	1.2	1.2	0.7
Folate (μg/d)[a]	200.0	200.0	150.0
Iodine (μg/d)	140.0	140.0	110.0
Iron (mg/d)[b]	8.7	14.8	8.7
Magnesium (mg/d)	300.0	270.0	200.0
Niacin (nicotinic acid equivalent; mg/d)[c]	17.0	13.0	12.0
Phosphorus (mg/d)	550.0	550.0	450.0
Potassium (mg/d)	3 500.0	3 500.0	2 000.0
Riboflavin (mg/d)	1.3	1.1	1.0
Selenium (μ/d)	75.0	60.0	30.0
Sodium (mg/d)	1 600.0	1 600.0	1 200.0
Thiamin (mg/d)[d]	1.0	0.8	0.7
Vitamin A (μg/d)[e]	700.0	600.0	500.0
Vitamin B6 (mg/d)[f]	1.4	1.2	1.0
Vitamin B12 (μg/d)	1.5	1.5	1.0
Vitamin C (mg/d)	40.0	40.0	30.0
Vitamin D (μg/d)[g]	10.0	10.0	–
Zinc (mg/d)	9.5	7.0	7.0

Note. Alcohol, the contraceptive pill, caffeine, smoking and food processing slow the absorption of some vitamins and minerals, thus raising daily needs. Pregnant or lactating women may require a little more than indicated.

[a]Human milk provides 5 μg folate/100 ml.

[b]Insufficient for women with high menstrual losses where the most practical way of meeting iron requirements is to take iron supplements.

[c]1 nicotonic acid equivalent = 1 unit of available niacin or 60 units of tryptophan.

[d]Thiamin requirements are closely related to energy intake; the usual recommendation is 0.4 mg per 1 000 kcal.

[e]In terms of retinol equivalent, where 1 retinol equivalent = 1 μg retinol or 6 μg B-carotene or 12 μg of other biologically active carotenoids.

[f]Based on protein providing 14.7% of estimated average requirement for energy.

[g]The main source of vitamin D is from the action of ultraviolet light on the skin; the amounts shown are for people with little exposure to sunlight, such as people over 65.

Vitamin E is necessary for normal metabolism; it is found in small amounts in many foods and larger amounts are found in vegetable oils, some margarines, wheat germ and eggs. Most diets provide 10 mg/day; recommended intake has not been established, but a safe level is above 4 mg a day for men and 3 mg a day for women.

Vitamin K is essential for the clotting of blood; it is found in green vegetables (cabbage, spinach, etc), cauliflower, peas and cereals, and can also be synthesised by bacteria in the intestine. Deficiency of the vitamin is unlikely in a healthy person. A recommended intake has not been established but a safe level for adults is 1 μg/kg body weight/day.

Other vitamins include pantothenic acid found in meat, vegetables and grains, biotin found in meat and vegetables.

Other minerals are also required. Sodium is a necessary mineral but is so commonly found in foods in the form of salt that it is rarely deficient. Both phosphorus and iodine are important for growing children.

Protein is also vital for health. A diet lacking in protein will eventually lead to a condition known as kwashiorkor, where the body swells and a child's development will be affected.

Salt in large quantities can lead to hypertension and high blood pressure, which increase the risk of heart disease and strokes.

Cholesterol is also linked to heart disease and strokes. It is present in saturated fats, usually found in animal fats or dairy products. A high intake can cause arteriosclerosis, which hardens the arteries.

Obesity is when the body weighs 20% over its ideal weight; it carries extra health risks. Although being overweight can be hereditary, most obesity cases result from overeating.

The main vitamins and their uses

Vitamin	Uses	Important sources
A	Promotes night vision, healthy eyes, skin, hair, nails, internal mucous membranes. Helps utilisation of fat, vitamin C & action of liver & thyroid.	Liver, eggs, whole-milk products, yellow-orange & dark green leafy vegetables
B_1 (thiamin)	Helps to metabolise carbohydrates. Keeps the nervous system, brain, muscles, heart functioning well. Some losses with cooking.	Pork, legumes, green peas, some green vegetables, whole & enriched grains
B_2 (riboflavin)	Keeps skin, eyes, nails, hair & lips healthy. With thiamin, helps to metabolise carbohydrates. Helps thyroid function.	Liver, meat, most dairy products, broccoli, spinach, enriched grains
B_3 (niacin)	Keeps brain & nervous system functioning well. Helps to metabolise food and to synthesise hormones.	Sources of high quality protein (meat, milk), nuts, seeds, enriched grains
B_6	Helps the body to use protein, fats & iron. Important in nerve, brain, blood & muscle functioning. Controls cholesterol levels. Activates enzymes.	Liver, meat, legumes, green peppers, potatoes, other vegetables
B_{12}	Helps to form blood cells & metabolise food. Prevents pernicious anaemia. Works with folic acid. Vegetarians, especially vegans, may be deficient.	Found only in animal products (meat, milk)
C	Helps to prevent disease & infection, increases anti-bodies, energy levels. Aids calcium & oxygen metabolism, iron absorption, lowers cholesterol.	Citrus fruit, strawberries, green vegetables, tomatoes, potatoes, other fruits & vegetables
D	Helps in absorption of calcium, phosphorus. Keeps heart, nervous system, eyes, bones, teeth healthy.	Only reliable sources are fish-liver oil, fortified milk; small amounts in egg yolk, butter, liver
E	Protects cell walls. Helps wounds to heal quickly. Relieves heart conditions. Stimulates immune system. Deficiency very rare.	Vegetable oils, nuts, whole grains, green vegetables
Folic acid	Helps form red blood cells, genetic material, metabolise protein & sugars, make antibodies. Promotes healthy skin, wards off anaemia.	Liver, legumes, some nuts, green vegetables, citrus fruits, whole grains, wheat germ

The main minerals and their uses

Mineral	Uses	Important sources
Iron	Essential for the formation of haemoglobin & to carry oxygen. Vegans, vegetarians, children may be deficient.	Liver, sardines, raisins, dried fruits, rice, nuts
Calcium	Works with vitamin D to promote healthy bones, teeth, nerves. Deficiency can cause osteoporosis in older people.	Cheese, milk, yoghurt, fish with edible bones (sardines, anchovies), watercress, figs, seeds, beans
Magnesium	Helps synthesis of protein, fats & use of calcium, potassium, sodium, Vitamin B_6. Maintains healthy heart beat.	Nuts, wholemeal flour
Potassium	Acts with sodium to regulate body fluids, maintain acid/alkali balance & to transport nerve impulses to muscles. Dietary deficiency rare.	Dried fruits, yeast extract
Zinc	Essential for enzyme action. Aids vision, bone growth. Zinc absorption is reduced by a high-fibre diet.	Wheatgerm, brewer's yeast, seeds, eggs, seafood

RADIATION

Radiation is a general term used to describe all waves or rays in the electromagnetic spectrum and also some types of atomic particles. There are two main types of radiation, ionising and non-ionising.

Ionising radiation

Ionising radiation can knock an orbital electron out of an atom to leave a positive ion (charged atom or molecule). Since the orbital electrons are involved in bonding atoms into molecules, ionising radiation can lead to the disruption of the molecule. In living tissue, this can interfere with normal cell biochemistry. In other materials, changes in colour or shape can occur.

Non-ionising radiation

Non-ionising radiation can interact with living tissues in several ways. Overexposure to ultraviolet radiation can produce photochemical damage; overexposure to visible and infra-red radiation can produce progressive effects from photochemical damage through to thermal damage; overexposure to microwave and radio-frequency radiation can cause thermal damage; overexposure to low-frequency electric or magnetic fields can cause muscle stimulation and/or electric shock.

The two main kinds of ionising radiation are directly ionising radiation, such as charged particles (alpha and beta particles, fission fragments, protons, etc), and indirectly ionising radiation, which carries no electric charge, such as neutrons and electromagnetic radiation. Electromagnetic radiation exists in discrete packets called photons.

Whether electromagnetic radiation is ionising or not depends on whether it has sufficient energy to remove an outer orbital electron from an atom. The average energy required for this in tissue is about 30 eV. For electromagnetic radiation, the relationship between frequency and the energy of the photon is given by the equation $E = hy$, where E is the energy of the photon, y is the frequency of the electromagnetic radiation and h is the Planck constant:

$$h = 6.63 \times 10^{-34}\ \mathrm{J\ Hz^{-1}} = 4.14 \times 10^{-15}\ \mathrm{eV\ Hz^{-1}}$$

The ionising minimum level of 30 eV corresponds to a frequency of about 7×10^{15} Hz, ie, between the ultraviolet and the X-ray range; lower frequency radiations (light, infra-red and radio waves) have too little energy to cause ionisation, although ultraviolet radiation and blue visible light can initiate photochemical reactions in the body. Energy per photon for the ionising levels of radiation is shown in the following table.

	Frequency (hertz)	Energy per photon
Ultraviolet	1×10^{15} to 6×10^{16}	3 eV to 250 eV
X-rays	6×10^{16} to 3×10^{20}	250 eV to 1 200 000 eV
Gamma rays	3×10^{18} to 6×10^{24}	12 000 eV to 12 000 MeV

Measures

Radioactivity. Radioactive substances are those in which the nuclei of atoms are disintegrating spontaneously, emitting ionising radiation. Radioactivity occurs naturally (eg, in uranium and thorium, potassium-40 and carbon-14) or can be induced artificially by bombardment with radiation (eg, by neutrons in a reactor). Each radioactive nucleus (radioisotope) has a characteristic half-life, the time taken for any amount of radioactivity to be reduced to half that amount by radioactive disintegration. Hence in two half-lives the radioactivity is reduced to a quarter of the original level, etc. There are many different radioisotopes and their half-lives vary from fractions of a second to millions of years; eg, radium-216 has a half-life of 0.18 microseconds and another isotope of the same element, radium-226, has a half-life of 1 600 years.

The main unit of measurement for radioactivity has been the Curie (Ci), originally defined as the disintegration rate of the quantity of radon gas in equilibrium with 1 gram of radium. Later a precise disintegration rate was fixed at a level close to that of the earlier definition:

$$1\ \mathrm{Ci} = 3.7 \times 10^{10}\ \text{disintegrations per second}$$

In 1975 a new unit was recommended for use as an SI unit in this field: the becquerel (Bq) = 1 atomic disintegration per second. Relationships are as follows.

$$1\ \mathrm{Ci} = 3.7 \times 10^{10}\ \mathrm{Bq} = 3.7 \times 10^{4}\ \mathrm{MBq}$$
$$1\ \mathrm{Bq} = 2.7 \times 10^{-11}\ \mathrm{Ci} = 0.027\ \mathrm{nCi}$$

Concentration of radioactivity in SI terms is usually expressed in Bq m^3 or Bq kg^{-1}. On average each cubic metre of air in houses in the UK contains enough radon such that 20 atoms disintegrate every second; so the radioactivity per cubic metre of air is 20 bequerels.

Exposure. The International Commission on Radiological Protection (ICRP) recognises three classes of exposure: occupational, medical and public. Dose limits apply to occupational and public exposures.

The absorbed dose is measured in grays, symbol Gy. A gray is the quantity of energy imparted by ionising radiation to a unit mass of matter such as tissue. 1 gray is equal to 1 joule per kilogram. Absorbed dose used to be expressed in rads (1 rad = 0.01 Gy).

Because some types of radiation are more harmful to tissue than others, equal absorbed doses may not have equal biological effects. To allow comparison another quantity, the dose equivalent, has been introduced. This is expressed in sieverts, symbol Sv. The dose equivalent is obtained by multiplying the absorbed dose by a factor that reflects the degree of harm that a particular type of radiation can cause. This factor is 1 for gamma-rays, x-rays and beta particles, 10 for fission neutrons and protons and 20 for alpha particles. Someone who has experienced an absorbed dose of 1 Gy from alpha radiation has therefore had a dose equivalent of 20 Sv. Dose equivalent used to be expressed in rems (1 rem = 0.01 Sv).

Dose equivalent is now the basic quantity used when discussing radiation protection. However, the risk of fatal malignancy per sievert differs according to which tissues of the body have been exposed. To overcome this problem, the ICRP has introduced a system of taking the dose equivalent experienced by the major organs and tissues of the body, and multiplying it by a weighting factor related to the risk associated with that organ. Adding up these weighted dose equivalents gives rise to the effective dose equivalent. This measure indicates the risk to health from exposure to ionising radiation, regardless of the type and energy of the radiation.

‹isk weighting factor

·issue or organ	Factor
onads	0.20
one surfaces	0.01
kin	0.01
reast	0.05
ladder	0.05
iver	0.05
esophagus	0.05
hyroid	0.05
olon	0.12
ung	0.12
ed bone marrow	0.12
tomach	0.12
emainder	0.05[a]
Vhole body total	1.00

Veighting factor for remainder is 0.05. This is applied to the average ose to all organs which do not have their own weighting factor unless ne of the remainder organs receives the highest dose of any organ, in vhich case its weighting factor is 0.025, with 0.025 for the mean of the ther remainder organ doses.

‹mounts of radiation

Radioactivity. Examples of amounts of radioactivity are as ollows.

- Most types of smoke detector contain about 1 μCi (1×10^{-6} Ci) = 37 kBq. Radiotherapy sources used in hospitals range up to about 2 000 Ci = 74 TBq (tera Becquerels).
- A nuclear accident may produce radiation of about 30 000 curies (3×10^4 Ci) = 1 petabecquerel (1×10^{15} Bq).
- A nuclear weapon can produce in a nuclear fission detonation, per kiloton of bomb power, 300 mn curies (3×10^8 Ci) = 10 exabecquerel (1×10^{19} Bq).

See also Weapons

Dose. The average dose to the UK population is about 2.5 millisieverts per year (mSv/yr) or 250 millirem per year; some details are shown in the following table.

	mSv/yr
Natural background	2.20[a]
of which: cosmic radiation	0.25
Man-made	0.32
of which: medical (X-rays, etc)	0.30
weapon test fallout	0.01
nuclear power	0.0005
TOTAL	2.50

[a]Varies geographically; eg, London 1.7 mSv/yr, Cornwall 7.4 mSv/yr.

1 milliSievert = 1 000 microSieverts (μSv). According to the National Radiological Protection Board, 1 μSv is:

- $\frac{1}{10}$ of the dose that would be incurred by flying from the UK to Spain in a jet aircraft;
- $\frac{1}{20}$ of the average dose from a single film chest x-ray;
- $\frac{1}{5}$ of the average yearly dose from radioactive fallout in the UK;
- twice the annual average dose to the UK population due to discharges from existing nuclear installations.

For radiological protection, the ICRP recommends the following limits.

	mSv/yr
Members of the public	1[a]
People exposed to radiation at work	20[b]

[a]Averaged over 5 years in special circumstances.
[b]Averaged over 5 years with no more than 50 mSv in a single year.

Effects at high doses include nausea and reduction of white blood cells at 500 mSv. The threshold for early death is 2 000 mSv, with only 50% survival after 4 000 mSv.

Iron and steel

See also Minerals and alloys, pages 120–123.

STEEL PRODUCTION

World production is approximately 780 mn tonnes per annum.

Raw materials

Iron ore. Widely distributed in the Earth's crust. Main deposits are to be found in Australia, the former Soviet Union, India, North and South America. Mining in the UK has virtually ceased because the ore is generally of poor quality and low in iron content.

Coke. Made by heating coal in air-tight ovens at about 1 300°C. Coke oven gas and other byproducts are recovered from the volatile material driven off.

Limestone. Good quality deposits are available in the UK.

Sinter. Nowadays a significant proportion of the blast furnace burden. It is produced by igniting a mixture of coke breeze, fine ore and limestone. Combustion of the coke partially melts the mixture, producing a porous clinker or sinter.

The following table shows world producers of ore with averages of iron content and production figures for 1989; they are as indicated by the International Iron and Steel Institute.

Country	% iron	mn tonnes
France	33	9.3
West Germany	28	0.1
Spain	48	4.6
Other EC	–	1.5
TOTAL EC		15.6
Austria	32	2.4
Norway	65	2.4
Sweden	63	21.8
Other Western Europe	–	8.6
TOTAL Western Europe		50.7
Canada	63	40.4
USA	60	57.9
TOTAL North America		98.3
Brazil	66	153.7
Chile	61	8.5
Mexico	65	7.4
Peru	60	4.2
Venezuela	64	18.1
Other Latin America	–	1.2
TOTAL Latin America		193.0
Liberia	68	12.3
Mauritania	65	12.0
South Africa	65	30.0
Other Africa	–	6.4
TOTAL Africa		60.6
India	61	51.4
Japan	57	0.3
Other Asia	–	1.0
TOTAL Asia		52.7
Australia	65	109.0
New Zealand	–	2.6
TOTAL Western World		566.6
Soviet Union & other CMEA	60	246.7
China & North Korea	28	173.5
TOTAL World		986.9

Ironmaking

Pig iron or hot metal is produced by smelting iron ore with the other raw materials in a blast furnace. The preheated blast may be enriched with oxygen to improve thermal efficiency and output. Fuel oil or powdered coal may also be injected to reduce the consumption of costly metallurgical coke.

Blast furnace gas, containing carbon monoxide, is a useful fuel. Slag, the other major byproduct, has various uses, notably as roadstone or in cement production.

Hot metal composition

Typically about 4.5% carbon, 0.5% silicon, 0.5% manganese, 0.05% sulphur, 0.07% phosphorus.

Steelmaking

The process by which hot metal and/or scrap are converted to steel by melting and refining by the injection of oxygen. Most of the impurities present are more readily oxidised than iron and are absorbed into a lime-based slag.

Production by the bessemer process has effectively ceased and the open hearth process is in decline, accounting for about 15% of world production (mainly in Eastern Europe and India).

Basic Oxygen Steelmaking (BOS) process. Accounts for about 57% of world steel production. A supersonic jet of oxygen gas (approx. 99.9% pure) is blown on to the hot metal and scrap in a cylindrical converter. Lime is added to flux with the oxidised impurities and form a slag. The normal practice is to reduce the carbon content (as CO) to less than 0.1%. This ensures that conditions have become sufficiently oxidising to remove the phosphorus. The crude steel is then "tapped" into a ladle, care being taken to minimise transfer of impurity-rich slag with it.

Electric Arc Furnace (EAF) process. Used to produce steel from scrap. Constituting about 28% of world steel output, EAF steelmaking is probably the world's largest scale recycling process.

74% of UK output is by the BOS process and 26% by the EAF.

Secondary steelmaking

In the past the normal practice was to take a sample of the crude steel prior to tapping the furnace and then throw measured amounts of alloying additions into the ladle during tapping. Ever growing demand for higher quality steels has led to the widespread use of secondary refining processes to ensure satisfactory levels of purity and composition control. These processes, usually carried out in the ladle, include the use of vacuum treatment for control of dissolved gases and carbon content, and the use of special refining slags to remove sulphur. Temperature adjustment to tight limits, to ensure good quality in the cast product, can also be carried out in the ladle.

Casting

Ingot casting. A mass of steel, usually 2–20 tonnes, is formed by pouring the molten metal into a mould. This is then rolled down to an intermediate bloom or slab which, after inspection, is reheated and rolled to the product required by the customer, ie, sheet, bar, joist, etc.

Continuous casting. In this process the liquid steel is poured into a water-cooled mould having a base that can be lowered as the steel solidifies. In this way a long continuous strand can be formed. Typically the cross-section of the strand is of similar dimensions to that of the intermediate product from the ingot route. Thus the process removes a rolling step and in doing so improves the yield of useful product by about 10%, as well as saving energy and shortening delivery time.

In some countries all steel is now continuously cast. Worldwide, 64% of steel produced was cast by this method in 1990 and the proportion is rising.

Rolling

Rolling mills form the cast steel into plates, slabs, rounds, etc. The primary mills hitherto widely used to convert ingots into an intermediate product are now much less in evidence. Continuously cast steel is hot rolled directly to the final product (plates, joists, etc), or it may then be finished rolled in a cold mill. The latter, operating at room temperature, strengthens the steel to a desired level and enables more accurate dimensional control to be achieved.

The major steel-producing countries, 1990–91[a] (mn tonnes crude steel)

Country	1990 Rank	Tonnage	1991 Rank	Tonnage
Soviet Union	1	154.4	1	132.8
Japan	2	110.3	2	109.6
USA	3	88.9	3	79.2
China	4	67.2	4	70.4
West Germany[b]	5	38.4	5	42.2
Italy	6	25.5	7	25.1
South Korea	7	23.1	6	26.0
Brazil	8	20.6	8	22.6
France	9	19.0	9	18.4
UK	10	17.8	11	16.5
India	11	15.0	10	17.1
Czechoslovakia	12	14.9	14	12.1
Poland	13	13.6	17	10.4
Spain	14	12.9	13	12.9
Canada	15	12.3	12	13.0
Belgium	16	11.4	15	11.3
Taiwan	17	9.7	16	11.0
Romania	18	9.7	21	7.1
Turkey	19	9.3	19	9.3
Mexico	20	8.7	20	7.9
South Africa	21	8.6	18	9.4
North Korea	22	7.0	22	7.0
Australia	23	6.7	23	6.1
East Germany[b]	24	5.6		
Netherlands	25	5.4	24	5.2
Sweden	26	4.5	25	4.3
Austria	27	4.3	26	4.2
Argentina	28	3.6	31	3.0
Yugoslavia	29	3.6	27	3.8
Luxembourg	30	3.6	28	3.4
Venezuela	31	3.2	29	3.1
Hungary	32	2.9	35	1.9
Finland	33	2.9	32	2.9
Indonesia	34	2.6	30	3.0
Bulgaria	35	2.4	36	1.6
Egypt	36	2.1	33	2.6
Iran			34	2.2
Other countries		18.4		17.5
TOTAL		770.1		736.2

[a]This table lists all countries producing more than 2 mn tonnes of crude steel in either year shown: source *World Steel in Figures 1991*, © International Iron and Steel Institute, 1991. [b]Merged in 1990.

TYPES OF STEEL

Mild steel

Soft, non-alloy steel (ie, with a low carbon content, about 0.12–0.25% by weight).

Carbon steels

Plain carbon steels represent the most important group of engineering materials. They can be classified as hypoeutectoid: those having a carbon content less than about 0.8% (mild steels fall into this group); or as hypereutectoid: those having a carbon content of about 0.8%. A wide range of properties can be obtained by varying the carbon content, working the metal or by heat treatment.

Alloy steels

All steels contain carbon and small amounts of silicon, manganese, sulphur and phosphorus. Alloying elements are deliberately added to produce certain properties in the product. In government statistics alloy steel figures relate to steel, other than high-speed steel, containing any of the following elements: chromium or nickel (0.4% or more); molybdenum, tungsten or vanadium (0.1% or more); manganese (10% or more).

High speed steels

An alloy steel, usually containing 0.6–0.7% carbon, 12–18% tungsten, 3–4% chromium and small amounts of other elements, eg, vanadium and molybdenum. After heat treatment these steels retain their hardness up to about 700°C and so can be used for metal-cutting tools at high speeds.

Stainless steels

A group of alloy steels having greatly improved corrosion-resistance essentially due to their containing by weight, 11.5% or more of chromium. Corrosion resistance can be further enhanced by additions of nickel and molybdenum. There are three main sub-groups.

Ferritic stainless steels. 16–30% chromiuim and less than 0.1% carbon. They are ferritic in structure and very malleable.

Martensitic stainless steels. 11–14% chromium and about 0.1–0.45% carbon. These steels can be hardened and tempered.

Austenitic stainless steels. 16–26% chromium and 6–20% nickel. These steels have an essentially austenitic structure at room temperature and below. They are non-magnetic and while very malleable, are greatly strengthened by cold working.

Tinplate

Low carbon steel usually less than 1 mm thick, coated with tin. Widely used in food and beverage packaging. The coat is applied either by dipping in molten tin or by electrodeposition.

FINISHED STEEL PRODUCTS

Ingots are rolled into semi-finished products (billets, blooms and slabs). These in turn are rolled into finished products (bars, plates, sheets, etc). Processing in this way involves scrapping part of the material at each stage. The yield loss from crude steel to finished product is quite large but varies according to the product.

As noted earlier, the equivalent yield loss when producing material via the continuous casting process is much smaller than that from the ingot route.

The use of continuous casting has increased progressively since the early 1970s and this has had an important effect on product yield. The crude steel : product yield varies according to product type (slab, strip, rails, forgings, etc), but in 1978 with continuous casting accounting for 15% of UK steel output, the average all-items yield was about 75%. In 1990, with 85% of production by the continuous casting route, the average yield was 80%. This can be expected to rise further as the proportion of continuous casting increases, and as other detailed process improvements are introduced.

Finished steel may be supplied in the hot rolled, cold rolled and/or heat treated condition according to end use. A range of metallic or organic coatings can also be applied, again according to customer requirements.

WEIGHT (MASS) OF STEEL

The density of steel is based internationally on a standard weight (mass) of 7 850 kilograms per cubic metre.

The conversion tables on pages 227–229 indicate the weight (mass) for wire, plate, sheet and strip based on this density.

For wire, figures are shown in terms of kilograms per 100 metre length, for varying diameters of wire. For plate sheet and strip, figures are shown in terms of kilograms per metre length for varying thickness and width.

As the weight (mass) of different types of steel will vary, the tables can be used for different densities to the standard by using multipliers, ie, by multiplying by the actual density divided by 7 850. A table of multipliers for densities from 7 500 to 8 690 is given on **page 227**. Since products other than steel will usually have a lower density (water has a density of 1 000 kg/m^3 at 4°C), a table of multipliers is given below for densities in the range 500–2 500 so that the steel tables can also be used for other products. For example, with a density for timber of 700 kg/m^3 (**page 40**) the weight (mass) for planks of timber can be obtained by multiplying the figures in the steel tables by 700/7 850 or 0.089.

See also page 120 for multipliers of main non-ferrous metals.

The tables include a selection of various sizes, not all of which are standard recommended sizes for steel. Standard thicknesses of sheet and strip available from the UK steel industry are, in millimetres: 0.6, 0.7, 0.8, 0.9, 1.0, 1.2, 1.6, 2.0, 2.5, 3.0, 4.0, 5.0, 6.0, 8.0, 10.0, 12.5. In the tables of plate, sheet and strip any sizes for which weights are shown, but which are outside the thickness/width range available from the UK steel industry, are marked with an asterisk (*). For use of the tables with centimetres, note that 1 cm = 10 mm, and divide millimetres by 10 (delete the last zero or move the decimal point 1 place to the left).

Multipliers for use with tables on steel density for products other than steel
(showing multipliers for different levels of density, kg/m^3)

kg/m^3		kg/m^3		kg/m^3	
500	0.064	1 200	0.153	1 900	0.242
600	0.076	1 300	0.166	2 000	0.255
700	0.089	1 400	0.178	2 100	0.268
800	0.102	1 500	0.191	2 200	0.280
900	0.115	1 600	0.204	2 300	0.293
1 000	0.127	1 700	0.217	2 400	0.306
1 100	0.140	1 800	0.229	2 500	0.318

Light, optics and photography

LIGHT

Range

Light is the part of the electromagnetic spectrum which can be distinguished by human vision; the range is approximately 300–700 nm, divided as shown in the following table. The table shows wavelength in the old unit of the ångström and the modern unit of the nanometre, and also shows frequency in 10^{12} Hz, the unit used in the 1979 definition of the candela. 10 ångström = 1 nanometre.

The exact relationship between wavelength and frequency is: frequency in hertz = speed of light (in m/s)/wavelength in metres

frequency in hertz = $2.992\,927 \times 10^8$/wavelength in metres
frequency in 10^{12} Hz = $2.997\,925 \times 10^{-4}$/wavelength in metres
= $2.997\,925 \times 10^5$/wavelength in nanometres
= 299 792.5/wavelength in nanometres

Colour	Wavelength 10^{-10} m or Å	10^{-9} m or nm	Frequency 10^{12} Hz
(Infra-red[a])	(over 7 600[b])	(over 760[b])	(under 400[b])
Red	6 300–7 600	630–760	480–400
Yellow	5 800–6 300	580–630	520–480
Green	4 800–5 800	480–580	620–520
Blue	4 000–4 800	400–480	750–620
Violet	3 000–4 000	300–400	1 000–750
(Ultra-violet)	(under 3 000[c])	(under 300)[c]	(over 1 000[c])

[a]Wavelengths in this range can give a sensation of light up to about 1 050 nm (10 500 Å) or down to about 3×10^{14} Hz. [b]The full infra-red range extends to about 1 000 000 nm (10 000 000 Å) or 3×10^{11} Hz. [c]The effective visible limit is usually about 360 nm (3 600 Å) or 8.3×10^{14} Hz; the full ultra-violet range extends to about 5 nm (50 Å) or 6×10^{16} Hz.

Relative visibility changes according to wavelength, with a peak near the centre and a gradually falling away to either end of the visual range. The brightest colour, as indicated by a light meter, is at 555 nm (5.4×10^{14} Hz).

The range which can be distinguished by the eye varies from about 1 nm or 10^{12} Hz in the central yellow-green-blue area to about 10 nm or 10^{13} Hz at the deep red and violet edges of the visible spectrum.

White is the colour of sunlight and of a substance which reflects sunlight with no absorption of any of the visible rays. Black is the absence of any visible rays and the colour of a substance which absorbs all visible rays.

Measurement of electromagnetic radiation in general is called radiometry; measurement of the portion which can be distinguished by human vision is called photometry.

See Electronics, page 71, for further details and for the full electromagnetic spectrum.

Doppler effect. Where the source of light is approaching, the wavelength appears lower and the light becomes more blue; where the source of light is moving away, the wavelength appears higher and the light becomes more red. The latter phenomenon is known as the red shift. The red shift of the hydrogen emission spectrum of stars is critical to the determination of the distances of stellar objects, and hence the size of the known universe. The amount of change is:

wavelength observed = $w \times V/(V - v)$
where w = wavelength of the light
V = velocity of light
v = velocity at which the source of the light is moving away from the observer

See Electronics, page 71, concerning the velocity of light; and Sound and music, page 128, concerning the Doppler effect.

Measures

Luminous intensity. The candela (cd) is the SI unit for measuring luminous intensity (I or I_v). The candela was first defined internationally in 1946 and was at that time called the new candle. It replaced the former various candle measures in use at the following approximate rates.

1 candela = 0.98 former international candle
= 0.95 former British standard candle

The former British candle was defined as light from a candle burning under certain conditions.

In 1967 the candela was defined as "the luminous intensity, in the perpendicular direction, of a surface of 1/600 000 square metre of a black body at the temperature of freezing platinum under a pressure of 101 325 newtons per square metre". In 1979 it was redefined as "the luminous intensity, in a given direction, of a source which emits monochromatic radiation of frequency 5.4×10^{14} hertz and which has a radiant intensity in that direction of 1/683 watt per steradian".

Examples of the amount of luminous intensity are: a 100 watt tungsten filament bulb has an intensity of about 130 cd, and the sun has a luminous intensity of about 2×10^{27} cd.

Luminous flux (Φ). The rate of flow of light from a source or received by a surface indicating the intensity of a source (which is measured in candela). Luminous flux is measured in SI terms by the lumen (lm), which is "the luminous flux emitted within the solid angle of 1 steradian by a point source having a uniform luminous intensity of 1 candela". Thus:

$$1\ \text{lm} = 1\ \text{cd sr} = \frac{1}{4\pi}\ \text{cd; also } 1\ \text{cd} = 4\pi\ \text{lm and } 1\ \text{cd} = 1\ \text{lm/sr}$$

The steradian (sr), an SI unit, is the solid angle at the centre of a sphere arising from an area on the surface of the sphere equal to a square with sides equal to the radius of the sphere. The surface area giving a solid angle of 1 steradian is r^2 where r is the radius of the sphere. Since the total surface area of a sphere is $4\pi r^2$ (**see page 112**), the total area arising from the solid total angle at the centre is equal to 4π steradians or approximately 12.566 sr. The solid angle of 1 steradian is the following fraction of the total angle at the centre of the sphere and of the surface area:

$r^2/4\pi r^2 = 1/4\pi = 1/12.566 = 0.079\,6 = 8\%$ of total surface area (approx.)

The total luminous flux emitted by a source emitting uniformly in all directions is equal to luminous intensity $\times 4\pi$ = 12.566 lumens. If 92% of the area of a sphere is blacked out, the amount of light remaining from a 1 candela source at the centre is 1 lumen.

Examples of amounts of luminous flux are: an ordinary light bulb = 1 500 lm, and a flashlight bulb = 1–3 mn lm.

The quantity of light emitted by a source is the amount of luminous flux over time, and is measured in SI terms by lumen seconds or lumen hours.

Luminous efficacy (efficiency). The flow of light from a source of light obtained from a known flow of power will vary according to the efficiency with which the power is turned into light. This is measured in terms of lumen per watt of power consumed. For an average 100 watt bulb with an intensity of 130 candela, the luminous flux for a complete sphere of light would be 1 630 lm ($130 \times 4\pi$); the average actual flux in a downwards direction is usually about 1 200 lm giving a luminous efficacy of 12 lm/W. Thus, for an average bulb, 1 watt of power gives (in a downward direction) about 12 lumen. Fluorescent lights may attain an efficacy of up to about 80 lm/W.

The maximum flow of monochromatic light from a given power source occurs in the brightest colour range at 5.4×10^{14} Hz (555 nm); this amount is 683 lm/W. For light which is a mixture of colours, the weighted average for that mixture must be determined by multiplying the value of 683 lm/W by the estimated relative visibility for each wavelength in the mixture. For example, daylight has a maximum flow of about 240 lm/W when the differing wavelengths are allowed for (assuming all power goes into the light wavelengths and not other radiations).

Illuminance. The illuminance or illumination (E) of a surface receiving light is measured by the amount of light reaching it per unit area. In SI terms this is measured by the special unit called the lux (lx), which is an illuminance of 1 lumen per square metre. 1 lx = 1 lm = 1 cd sr/m^2

The illuminance of a room is normally about 200–500 lux; general minimum recommendations are as follows.

	lx
Working space continuously occupied	200
Casual work	300
Other (incl. reading)	500
Critical colour matching	1 000

The relationship between the SI unit and old units is as follows.

1 lux = 1 lm/m^2
= 0.092 9 lm/ft^2
= 10^{-4} phot (ph) or fot
1 lm/ft^2 = 10.763 9 lx
1 phot (ph) = 10^4 lx = 10 klx = 10 000 lx

The quantity of light received by a surface, or light exposure (also formerly called quantity of illumination) is measured in SI terms by lux seconds or lux hours.

Luminance. Luminance (L or Lv) or surface brightness of a source or of reflected light is measured in SI terms by candela per unit of apparent area as viewed from a given direction, the SI unit being candela per square metre (cd/m^2).

If all the light falling on a surface were perfectly reflected by the surface, then the amount of luminance would be the same as the amount of illuminance of the light reaching the surface. The reflection factor or reflectance measures the degree to which a surface is not a perfect reflector; it is the ratio reflected light/incident light. Examples of approximate reflectances for different building finishes are given in the table below.

Finish	Reflectance
White emulsion paint on plain plaster surface	0.8
Concrete (light grey)	0.4
Bricks (fletton)	0.3
Timber panelling: medium oak	0.2

For SI units, where unit illuminance is that of a flat uniform diffuser emitting π lumens per square metre, luminance (cd/m^2) = (illuminance × reflectance)/π, illuminance being measured in lux.

Luminance of a reflecting surface is sometimes called luminous exitance, and the SI unit for measurement is lumen per square metre.

The luminance of the sun is about 2 000 million cd/m^2, of a lighted electric bulb about 5 million cd/m^2, and of a lighted candle about 5 000 cd/m^2.

The relationship between the SI unit and old units is as follows.

1 cd/m^2 = 1 nit (nt)
= 0.092 9 cd/ft^2
= 0.000 6 cd/in^2
= $\pi \times$ 0.092 9 (0.291 9) foot-lambert (ft-L or fL)
= $\pi \times 10^{-4}$ lambert = 0.000 3 lambert (L)
= 0.314 millilambert (mL)
= 0.000 1 stilb (sb)
1 nit = 1 cd/m^2
1 cd/ft^2 = 10.763 9 cd/m^2 (= π ft-L)
1 cd/in^2 = 1 550.00 cd/m^2
1 lambert = 1 lm/cm^2 = ($10^4/\pi$) cd/m^2 = 3 183.1 cd/m^2
1 foot-lambert = 3.426 3/m^2
1 stilb = 1 cd/cm^2 = 10 000 cd/m^2 = 10 000 nt

OPTICS

Measures

Power

The unit of refractive power is called the diopter or dioptre (di or dpt or D), where 1 di = 1 m^{-1} = 1/m. This unit is acceptable with SI units.

Refractive index

Where light passes through two different materials, the direction of light changes according to the nature of the materials. The angle of change is dependent on the index of refraction = velocity of light in a vacuum/velocity of light in the material.

Where light passes from medium 1 to medium 2, the index of refraction is given by:

$$n_{1,2} = \frac{\sin A_i}{\sin A_r} = \frac{b_1}{b_2}$$

where $n_{1,2}$ is the index of refraction between medium 1 and 2

A_i is the angle of incidence (in medium 1)
A_r is the angle of refraction (in medium 2)
b_1 is the phase velocity of medium 1
b_2 is the phase velocity of medium 2

Examples of refractive indexes are given in the table below.

Medium	Refractive index
Water	1.33
Human eye (cornea)	1.337 6
Crown glass	1.52

Radius of curvature

The radius of curvature of a lens, as related to the distance of the lens from the image and from the object focused on, is:

$$1/r_1 - 1/r_2 = (1/i - 1/d)/(n - 1)$$

where r_1 and r_2 are the radii of curvature of the lens,
i = distance of the lens from the image
d = distance of the object observed from the lens
n = index of refraction of the lens

Polarised light

Light is a transverse wave motion; ie, the vibrations are at right angles to the direction of propagation. Polarised light is light which has been changed from natural (or unpolarised) light to waves where the vibrations are restricted to one plane only. This change occurs when light is reflected twice.

When natural light waves are first reflected from a flat surface, such as glass or water, the intensity of the reflected beam varies with the angle of incidence of the light. If the reflected light is reflected again from another surface, the light coming from the second surface varies in intensity according to the relative angle which the second surface bears to the first, the intensity being greatest when the surfaces are parallel and least when they are at right angles. The light wave vibrations are in one plane only. Such light reflected from a second surface is called polarised light.

Polarised light can be measured by a polariser or polariscope, in which a beam of light enters at one end and is reflected twice to emerge as polarised light at the other end. The polariscope can be used to determine, for example, the concentration of a dissolved substance which has optical activity, as it causes a rotation of the direction of vibration of polarised light traversing the medium. The amount of optical rotation is proportional to the degree of concentration, so that the polariscope can be used to estimate, for example, the concentration of sugar in a solution. The quality of sugar for international comparisons is usually based on a test of 96 sugar degrees by a polariscope. To convert 1 unit of refined or unrefined sugar to a basis of 96° polarisation the formula used is $[(2 \times P) - 100]/92$, where P = degrees of polarisation as tested by the polariscope.

Laser and maser

When it has the energy to do so, an atom emits a photon of light in about 1 microsecond, and at random. If a photon of the same wavelength passes at the same time as emission is occurring, the atom emits its photon in phase with the other photon – there is stimulated emission.

A laser is a device for arranging the stimulated emission so that there is a high intensity of light: **l**ight **a**mplification by **s**timulated **e**mission of **r**adiation. Similarly, a maser is a device used to amplify other forms of electromagnetic radiation, especially microwaves: **m**icrowave **a**mplification by **s**timulated **e**mission of **r**adiation.

The concentration of light intensity by lasers can produce very short pulses of light (10^{-14} s or 10 femtoseconds) with very intense peak power of 10^{14} watts or 100 US billion kilowatts.

PHOTOGRAPHY

Film

Size. The nominal size of a camera is usually that of the film taken by the camera; the image area is usually smaller than the size of the film. Examples of some usual sizes are shown in the following tables.

Still cameras

Film size designation	Image size
110	13 × 17 mm
135 (35 mm half-frame)	18 × 24 mm
135 (35 mm full-frame)	24 × 36 mm
126	28 × 28 mm
127	$1\frac{13}{16} \times 1\frac{9}{16}$ in
127	$1\frac{5}{8} \times 1\frac{5}{8}$ in
127	$1\frac{5}{8} \times 2\frac{1}{2}$ in
120, 620	$1\frac{1}{4} \times 2\frac{1}{4}$ in
120, 220, 70 mm	$2\frac{1}{4} \times 1\frac{3}{4}$ in
120, 620, 220, 70 mm	$2\frac{1}{4} \times 2\frac{1}{4}$ in
120, 220, 70 mm	$2\frac{1}{4} \times 2\frac{3}{4}$ in
120, 620, 220, 70 mm	$2\frac{1}{4} \times 3\frac{1}{4}$ in

Motion-picture cameras

Film size designation (mm)	Image size (mm) height width
8	3.68 × 4.88
16	7.49 × 10.26
35	16.03 × 22.05
35	18.67 × 24.89
65	23.01 × 52.63

Film speed. The measure of response of photographic material to radiant energy under specified conditions. Exposure (usually designated by H) is the quantity of radiant energy, measured in lux seconds. It is often expressed in $\log_{10}H$ units. The formulae for determining speed are as follows.

where S or S° = speed
H_m = exposure in lux
$S = 0.8/H_m$ or
$S^\circ = 1 + 10 \log_{10}(0.8/H_m)$

The designation of film speeds has been standardised by the ISO.

ISO speed scales

Arithmetic	Logarithmic	Arithmetic	Logarithmic
3 200	36°	100	21°
2 500	35°	80	20°
2 000	34°	64	19°
1 600	33°	50	18°
1 250	32°	40	17°
1 000	31°	32	16°
800	30°	25	15°
640	29°	20	14°
500	28°	16	13°
400	27°	12	12°
320	26°	10	11°
250	25°	8	10°
200	24°	6	9°
160	23°	5	8°
125	22°	4	7°

The designation is, for example, ISO 125/22° (where both types of number are shown). The arithmetic number replaces the old ASA (American Standards Association) value and the logarithmic number replaces the old DIN (Deutsche Industrie Normen) value.

Camera stops. In the arithmetic scale, doubling or halving of the film speed is given by equivalent doubling or halving of the numbers; for the logarithmic scale, doubling or halving of speed is given by adding or subtracting 3 (a change of 0.30 or $\log_{10}2$ in $\log_{10}$ units). The scales coincide at 12.

Lens

Angle of view. A normal camera lens gives an angle of view of 45–55°; extremes can be as low as 15° for a telephoto long distance view and as high as 100° for wideranging views such as those for architectural purposes.

Focal length. The distance between the centre of a lens and the plane of the image when the lens is focused on infinity.

Where F = focal length
v = lens to image distance
u = lens to object distance

$$\frac{1}{F}=\frac{1}{v}+\frac{1}{u}$$

This general formula gives the value of F for other than small values of v and u, when the F value may be inaccurate. Where u = infinity, $F=v$.

The focal length is also defined in the formula $F=h/\tan A$, where h = image size and A = the angle subtended by the object at the lens.

f-number

The *f*-number (or *f*-stop) is the ratio of the focal length of the lens and the effective diameter of the lens opening or aperture: *f*-number $=F/d$, where F is the focal length and d the aperture diameter. Hence for a given focal length, the *f*-number is larger for a smaller aperture, and smaller for a larger aperture. The *f*-number is usually expressed in the form *f*/2, meaning $f=2$. The usual *f*-numbers are: *f*/1.4, *f*/2, *f*/2.8, *f*/4, *f*/5.6, *f*/8, *f*/11, *f*/16, *f*/22, *f*/32 and *f*/45. Each lens in this series transmits half as much light as the preceding lens opening; ie, the *f*-number series is a series of the square root of a number series where each number is doubled.

Area of lens (amount of light)	Square root	Area of lens (amount of light)	Square root
1	1.00	64	8.0
2	1.41	128	11.3
4	2.00	256	16.0
8	2.83	512	22.6
16	4.00	1 024	32.0
32	5.66	2 048	45.3

Sometimes *f*-numbers are used which are not full *f*-stops derived from a doubling of the lens area, *f*/3.5 and *f*/4.5. For most cameras, where the focal length is fixed, the *f*-number effectively measures the aperture size.

Colour temperature

Colours of light, especially in photographic use, are sometimes expressed in terms of colour temperatures, rated in kelvin (K). These are based on the variation in radiations emitted when the temperature of a substance with a high melting point is raised: the radiations emitted begin with those in the infra-red range, then the frequency increases with temperature (wavelength falls) and the colour moves through the visible spectrum from red to blue and into ultra-violet. The temperature, for a given substance, provides a measure of the colour, with lower temperatures (colder) relating to the higher wavelength or red end of the spectrum, and higher temperatures (hotter) relating to the lower wavelength or blue end of the spectrum.

Examples of colour temperature are shown in the table.

Source	K
Warm white lamp (for hotels, restaurants and homes)	2 700
Photographic daylight	5 500
North-light fluorescent (emphasising blues)	6 500

Flashlight bulbs are sometimes rated in kelvin to indicate whether they are suitable for use with daylight film or film balanced for a lower colour temperature light source.

Filters used, for example, to change the balance of a colour source from daylight (5 500 K) towards a different colour such as 3 200 K, are sometimes given a shift value in terms of the mired (microreciprocal degree), where the number of mireds = 1 000 000/K (10^6/K).

The daylight value is 182 mireds, and a shift to 3 200 K (313 mireds) is a shift of 131 mireds (313 − 182).

Mathematics and statistics

LENGTH, AREA AND VOLUME

In this section h = height (vertical), r = radius, d = diameter.

2-dimensional

Circle
Length of circumference $= 2\pi r = \pi d$
Area $= \pi r^2 = \pi d^2/4$
Radius $= r = \sqrt{\text{area}/\pi}$

π = circumference/diameter = 3.141 592 653 589 793 . . .
= approx. $3\frac{1}{7}$
$1/\pi$ = diameter/circumference = 0.318 309 886 183 791 . . .

Tables of π and $1/\pi$ are included on **page 195**, giving conversions between diameter and circumference in connection with the girth of timber.

Tables for obtaining areas from radii and radii from areas are on pages 171–178.

A complete revolution of a line in a clockwise direction back to its original position gives a plane angle of 360°; hence the complete angle at the centre of a circle is 360 degrees, where:

60 seconds (″) = 1 minute (′)
60 minutes = 1 degree
90 degrees = 1 quadrant = 1 right angle
4 quadrants = 360 degrees = 1 circle

In France 1 grade (^{g} or gr) = 1/100 right angle, and 100 grades = 1 right angle. 1 grade = (π/200) rad. Centigrade, in this connection, means 1/10 000 right angle.

The same system is also used in Germany, where the grade is called the gon or new grade. 1 gon = (π/200) rad; 100 gon = 1 Rechter.

Also, 1 new minute (^{c}) = 1/100 gon = 10^{-2} gon
1 new second (^{cc}) = 1/10 000 gon = 10^{-4} gon

The grade or gon = (π/200) rad has been recognised for use in the UK since 1980.

In Belgium 1 gon = 1/400 circumference.

The radian (rad) is defined as an SI unit **(page 14).**
1 rad = angle at centre of circle × (radius/circumference)
= 360°/2π
= 180°/π
= 57.295 779 513 082° approx. = 57° 17′ 44.8″ approx.

1° = π/180 rad
= 0.017 453 292 520 rad approx.

Radians to degrees rad	°	Degrees to radians °	rad	°	rad
1	= 57.295 8 = 57° 17′ 45″	1	0.017 453 3	10	0.174 532 9
2	= 114.591 6 = 114° 35′ 30″	2	0.034 906 6	20	0.349 065 9
3	= 171.887 3 = 171° 53′ 14″	3	0.052 359 9	30	0.523 598 8
4	= 229.183 1 = 229° 10′ 59″	4	0.069 813 2	40	0.698 131 7
5	= 286.478 9 = 286° 28′ 44″	5	0.087 266 5	50	0.872 664 6
6	= 343.774 7 = 343° 46′ 29″	6	0.104 719 8	60	1.047 197 6
7	= 401.070 5 = 401° 4′ 14″	7	0.122 173 0	70	1.221 730 5
8	= 458.366 2 = 458° 21′ 58″	8	0.139 626 3	80	1.396 263 4
9	= 515.662 0 = 515° 39′ 43″	9	0.157 079 6	90	1.570 796 3

Ellipse
Area $= \pi ab$ where a and b are the lengths of semi-major and semi-minor axes respectively ($2a$ and $2b$ are the lengths of the full axes).

Triangle
Area $= \frac{1}{2}$ base $\times h$

Pythagoras's theorem states that in a right-angled triangle the square of the hypotenuse (longest side) equals the sum of the squares of the other two sides.

Two triangles are similar if the angles of one are equal to the angles of the other.

The relationship between sides and angles (basic trigonometry) is as follows.

Where A is an angle of a right-angled triangle
tangent of A ($\tan A$) = opposite side/adjacent side
sine of A ($\sin A$) = opposite side/hypotenuse
cosine of A ($\cos A$) = adjacent side/hypotenuse
cotangent of A ($\cot A$) = $1/\tan A$
cosecant of A (cosec A[a]) = $1/\sin A$
secant of A ($\sec A$) = $1/\cos A$

[a] Cosec A is sometimes written csc A.

Where $\sin A = y$, A is the angle whose sine is y, and this is written as $\sin^{-1} y$. Other functions can be expressed in the same way, and these are referred to as inverse forms.

Where a, b and c denote the lengths of the sides opposite the angles A, B and C respectively (and when dealing with a triangle $A + B + C = 180°$), then:

cosine rule is $\cos A = \dfrac{b^2 + c^2 - a^2}{2bc}$ and similarly for $\cos B$ and $\cos C$

sine rule is $\dfrac{a}{\sin A} = \dfrac{b}{\sin B} = \dfrac{c}{\sin C}$

area $= \frac{1}{2}bc \sin A = \frac{1}{2}ac \sin B = \frac{1}{2}ab \sin C$
$= \sqrt{s(s-a)(s-b)(s-c)}$
where $s = \frac{1}{2}(a + b + c)$ = semi-perimeter of the triangle.

Trapezium

Area $= h \times \dfrac{\text{sum of the parallel sides}}{2}$

Regular polygons Where n is the number of sides of a regular polygon, and a the length of a side, then:

area $= \frac{1}{4}na^2 \cot \dfrac{180°}{n} = \frac{1}{4}n \cot \dfrac{180°}{n} \times$ the square of the length of one of the sides (a^2). The multiplier, $\frac{1}{4}n \cot 180°/n$, to apply to a^2, is as follows for various polygons.

Name of polygon	No. sides	Multiplier	Name of polygon	No. sides	Multiplier
Square	4	1.0	Nonagon	9	6.182
Pentagon	5	1.720	Decagon	10	7.694
Hexagon	6	2.598	Undecagon	11	9.366
Heptagon	7	3.634	Duodecagon	12	11.196
Octagon	8	4.828			

Also, area = $\frac{1}{2}$ perimeter of sides × radius of the inscribed circle. The inscribed circle is the circle within the sides, and

$$\text{radius} = \frac{a}{2} \cot \frac{180^\circ}{n}$$

The circumscribed circle is the circle passing through the points of the polygon, and

$$\text{radius of circumscribed circle} = \frac{a}{2} \operatorname{cosec} \frac{180^\circ}{n}$$

3-dimensional

Sphere
Surface area = $4\pi r^2 = \pi d^2$

The steradian (sr) is defined as an SI unit (**page 14**).

A complete sphere subtends a solid angle of 4π sr (approx. 12.566 371 sr) at the centre.

1 spat (sp) = 4π = unit of solid angle

Volume = $\frac{4}{3}\pi r^3 = \frac{1}{6}\pi d^3$

Cube
Where a is the length of a side and b is the length of a diagonal, then:

surface area = $6a^2$ volume = a^3 $b = a\sqrt{3}$

Cylinder
Surface area of curved surface = perimeter of base × height = $2\pi rh$;
plus one end = $\pi r(r+2h)$;
plus both ends = $2\pi r(r+h)$
Volume = area of base × height = $\pi r^2 h$

Tables for volumes of timber as shown on page 196 can be used for volumes of cylinders.

Barrel or cask. Where the edges are straight, the formula for a cylinder applies. For curved edges, taking d as the internal diameter at the ends and D as the internal diameter at the widest part, the following apply.

Measured in metres, volume = $0.261\,8\,(2D^2+d^2)h$ cubic metres
= $261.8\,(2D^2+d^2)h$ litres

Measured in inches, volume = $\frac{\pi}{12}(2D^2+d^2)h$ cubic inches
= $0.261\,8\,(2D^2+d^2)h$ cubic inches
= $0.000\,943\,7\,(2D^2+d^2)h$ UK gallons
= $0.001\,133\,(2D^2+d^2)h$ US gallons
= $0.004\,290\,(2D^2+d^2)h$ litres

Cone or pyramid
Surface area of curved surface = $\frac{1}{2}$ perimeter of base × slant height;
plus base = ($\frac{1}{2}$perimeter of base × slant height) + area of base
Volume = $\frac{1}{3}$ area of base × height

For a cone, the perimeter of the base is $2\pi r$; the area of the base is πr^2.

TRIGONOMETRIC FUNCTIONS

Basic functions related to triangles are defined in the previous section.

Where a general angle greater than 90° is concerned, the following relationships apply.

Quadrant between 90° and 180°	Quadrant between 270° and 360°
$\tan A = -\tan(180^\circ - A)$	$\tan A = -\tan(360^\circ - A)$
$\sin A = \sin(180^\circ - A)$	$\sin A = -\sin(360^\circ - A)$
$\cos A = -\cos(180^\circ - A)$	$\cos A = \cos(360^\circ - A)$

Quadrant between 180° and 270°
$\tan A = \tan(A - 180^\circ)$
$\sin A = -\sin(A - 180^\circ)$
$\cos A = -\cos(A - 180^\circ)$

Values for special angles

	0°	30°	45°	60°	90°	180°	270°	360°
tan	0	$\sqrt{3}/3$	1	$\sqrt{3}$	∞	0	∞	0
sin	0	1/2	$\sqrt{2}/2$	$\sqrt{3}/2$	1	0	−1	0
cos	1	$\sqrt{3}/2$	$\sqrt{2}/2$	1/2	0	−1	0	1
cot	∞	$\sqrt{3}$	1	$\sqrt{3}/3$	0	∞	0	∞
cosec	∞	2	$\sqrt{2}$	$2\sqrt{3}/3$	1	∞	−1	∞
sec	1	$2\sqrt{3}/3$	$\sqrt{2}$	2	∞	−1	∞	1

Fundamental identities

$\tan A = \sin A/\cos A$
$\cot A = \cos A/\sin A$
$\sin^2 A + \cos^2 A = 1$

where $\sin^2 A$ means the square of $\sin A$ and $\cos^2 A$ the square of $\cos A$

$1 + \tan^2 A = \sec^2 A$
$1 + \cot^2 A = \operatorname{cosec}^2 A$
$\sin^2 A = \frac{1}{2}(1 - \cos 2A)$
$\cos^2 A = \frac{1}{2}(1 + \cos 2A)$

$$\tan^2 A = \frac{1 - \cos 2A}{1 + \cos 2A}$$

$\sin 2A = 2 \sin A \cos A$
$\cos 2A = \cos^2 A - \sin^2 A$

$$\tan 2A = \frac{2 \tan A}{1 - \tan^2 A}$$

$\sin \frac{1}{2}A = \pm\sqrt{\frac{1}{2}(1 - \cos A)}$, positive for $\frac{1}{2}A$ between 0° and 180°

$\cos \frac{1}{2}A = \pm\sqrt{\frac{1}{2}(1+\cos A)}$, positive for $\frac{1}{2}A$ between 0° and 90°, 270° and 360°

$\tan \frac{1}{2}A = \pm\sqrt{\frac{1-\cos A}{1+\cos A}}$, positive for $\frac{1}{2}A$ between 0° and 90°, 180° and 270°

More than one angle

$\sin (A \pm B) = \sin A \cos B \pm \cos A \sin B$
$\cos (A + B) = \cos A \cos B - \sin A \sin B$
$\cos (A - B) = \cos A \cos B + \sin A \sin B$
$\tan (A + B) = (\tan A + \tan B)/(1 - \tan A \tan B)$
$\tan (A - B) = (\tan A - \tan B)/(1 + \tan A \tan B)$
$\sin A + \sin B = 2 \sin \frac{1}{2}(A+B) \cos \frac{1}{2}(A-B)$
$\sin A - \sin B = 2 \cos \frac{1}{2}(A+B) \sin \frac{1}{2}(A-B)$
$\cos A + \cos B = 2 \cos \frac{1}{2}(A+B) \cos \frac{1}{2}(A-B)$
$\cos A - \cos B = -2 \sin \frac{1}{2}(A+B) \sin \frac{1}{2}(A-B)$
$\sin A \sin B = \frac{1}{2} \cos (A-B) - \frac{1}{2} \cos (A+B)$
$\cos A \cos B = \frac{1}{2} \cos (A-B) + \frac{1}{2} \cos (A+B)$
$\sin A \cos B = \frac{1}{2} \sin (A+B) + \frac{1}{2} \sin (A-B)$

INDICES

$x^m \times x^n = x^{m+n}$
$x^m/x^n = x^{m-n}$
$x^{-m} = 1/x^m$
$x^{1/n} = \sqrt[n]{x}$
$x^0 = 1$

LOGARITHMS

The logarithm y of a number x is the power to which a base a must be raised to equal x; this can be written: $y = \log_a x \quad x = a^y$

Where there are two different bases, $\log_b x = \log_a x/\log_a b$

For any system: $\log_a XY = \log_a X + \log_a Y$
$\log_a X/Y = \log_a X - \log_a Y$

There are two main systems of logarithms in use.

1. Common (or Briggsian) which uses 10 as a base.
2. Natural (or Naperian) which uses e as a base where $e = 2.718\,281\,828\,459\ldots$
   $\log_{10}$ is usually described symbolically as log
   $\log_e$ is usually described symbolically as ln

To convert from one system to the other, multiply by the following:

from common to natural: 2.302 585 092 994 ($\log_e 10$)
from natural to common: 0.434 294 481 903 ($\log_{10} e$)

$\log_{10} 2 = 0.301\,029\,995\,664$

Naperian logarithms form the basis of the neper sound scale.
For the neper sound scale, see page 129.

Actual logarithms to base *e* from 1 to 10

1	0.000 0	4	1.386 3	7	1.945 9	10	2.302 6
2	0.693 1	5	1.609 4	8	2.079 4		
3	1.098 6	6	1.791 8	9	2.197 2		

Logarithms to base 10 from 1 to 10

1	0.000 0	4	0.602 1	7	0.845 1	10	1.000 0
2	0.301 0	5	0.699 0	8	0.903 1		
3	0.477 1	6	0.778 2	9	0.954 2		

RATIOS

If $\frac{a}{b} = \frac{x}{y}$

then $\frac{a}{b} = \frac{ma+nx}{mb+ny} = \frac{ma-nx}{mb-ny}$, where m and n are real quantities

EQUATIONS AND CURVES

$(a \pm b)^2 = a^2 \pm 2ab + b^2$
$(a+b+c)^2 = a^2 + b^2 + c^2 + 2ab + 2ac + 2bc$
$a^2 - b^2 = (a-b)(a+b)$

Straight line

$y = mx + c$, where m = slope of the line, and c is the intercept on the y-axis (where the x-axis is horizontal in a graph and the y-axis vertical)

also $\frac{x}{a} + \frac{y}{b} = 1$, where a and b are the intercepts on the x and y axes respectively

and $\frac{y-y_1}{x-x_1} = \frac{y_2-y_1}{x_2-x_1}$, where x_1, y_1 and x_2, y_2 are two points defining the line, measured with respect to the x and y axes.

Simultaneous

For two simultaneous equations $a_1x + b_1y = c_1$ and $a_2x + b_2y = c_2$

$x = (b_2c_1 - b_1c_2)/(a_2b_1 - a_1b_2)$

and

$y = (a_2c_1 - a_1c_2)/(a_2b_1 - a_1b_2)$

Quadratic

Where $ax^2 + bx + c = 0$, then $x = \frac{-b \pm \sqrt{b^2 - 4ac}}{2a}$, being the roots of the equation.

Logarithmic and exponential

$y = \log_a x$ for logarithmic ($x = a^y$); $x = \log_a y$ for exponential ($y = a^x$).

Sine curve

$y = a \sin (bx + c)$, where a = amplitude = the height of the sine wave, $2\pi/b$ = wavelength = distance from the peak of one wave to the next (also = pitch of thread).

See also Economics (page 65) for a chart of the sine curve and page 80 for pitch of thread.

Motion

For uniformly accelerated motion:

$v = u + at$, where v is the velocity at time t, a is the acceleration, and u is the initial velocity. This is the velocity-time relationship which adds to initial velocity the acceleration increase through time.

Where s is the distance travelled,

$s = ut + \frac{1}{2}at^2$
and $v^2 = u^2 + 2as$

The SI unit for velocity is metres per second.
For standard gravitational acceleration see page 15.

COMBINATIONS AND PERMUTATIONS

The number of combinations is the number of ways in which r objects can be selected from n objects without account of the order in which the r objects are selected.

The number of permutations is the number of different ways in which r objects can be selected from n objects when account is taken of the order of selection of the r objects.

For example, there are four combinations of three letters out of A, B, C and D:

ABC *BCD* *CDA* *DAB*

but 24 permutations:

ABC	*BCD*	*CDA*	*DAB*
ACB	*BDC*	*CAD*	*DBA*
BAC	*CDB*	*ACD*	*ABD*
BCA	*CBD*	*ADC*	*ADB*
CAB	*DBC*	*DAC*	*BAD*
CBA	*DCB*	*DCA*	*BDA*

Where $n!$ (factorial n) $= 1 \times 2 \times 3 \times \ldots (n-1) \times n$
eg $7! = 1 \times 2 \times 3 \times 4 \times 5 \times 6 \times 7$
$= 5\,040$

$$\text{Combination} = C_r^n = \frac{n!}{r!(n-r)!}$$

$$\text{Permutation} = P_r^n = \frac{n!}{(n-r)!}$$

Notes
$C_r^n = C_{n-r}^n$
0! may be taken as equal to 1.
Factorial n may also be written as $\lfloor n$
C_r^n may be written as C and P_r^n as P
When n is large the Stirling approximation is useful:
$n! =$ approximately $\sqrt{2\pi n}\, n^n e^{-n}$

The first ten factorials are as follows.

1!	1	6!	720
2!	2	7!	5 040
3!	6	8!	40 320
4!	24	9!	362 880
5!	120	10!	3 628 800

DIFFERENTIATION AND INTEGRATION (CALCULUS)

The slope of a straight line, as noted above, is m in the equation $y = mx + c$. The slope or gradient of a straight line is also the angle made with the horizontal axis. The gradient of a curve is the gradient of the tangent to the curve at any point.

The gradient is generalised as the differentiation of the line of curve. Where $y = f(x)$, (ie, y is a function of x),

$$\text{differentiation} = \frac{dy}{dx} = \frac{d(f(x))}{dx} = f'(x), \text{ where } f'(x) \text{ is a symbol for } \frac{dy}{dx}$$

$$\text{For a straight line, } \frac{d(mx+c)}{dx} = m = \text{the slope of the line.}$$

dx and dy are called differentials, and $\frac{dy}{dx}$, also written as dy/dx, is called the differential coefficient.

The derivative of dy/dx is called the second differential of $f(x)$ and denoted by d^2y/dx^2 or $f''(x)$, and so on with the nth differential coefficient d^ny/dx^n or $f^n(x)$.

Where a function is increasing, the slope is positive and the first differential coefficient positive; where it is decreasing the first differential coefficient is negative.

For signs of the first and second differentials see pages 64–65.

Integral of a function $f(x)$ from a to b is the area under the curve between $x = a$ and $x = b$; the symbol is $\int_a^b f(x)\,dx$. For a general integration the symbol is $\int f(x)\,dx$. Integration is the reverse process of differentiation; since the differential of any constant is zero, integration of any function includes an unknown constant amount.

Summary of differentials and integrals

y	$\frac{dy}{dx}$	$\int y\,dx$ = integral (with C a constant, unknown)
x^n	nx^{n-1}	$\frac{x^{n+1}}{n+1} + C$ except for $n = -1$
x^{-1}		$\log_e x + C$
e^x	e^x	$e^x + C$
e^{ax}	ae^{ax}	$\frac{e^{ax}}{a} + C$
a^x	$a^x \log_e a$	$\frac{a^x}{\log_e a} + C$ except for $a \leq 0, a = 1$
$\log_e x$	$1/x$	$x(\log_e x - 1) + C$
$\sin ax$	$a \cos ax$	$-\cos \frac{ax}{a} + C$
$\cos ax$	$-a \sin ax$	$\sin \frac{ax}{a} + C$
$\tan ax$	$a \sec^2 ax$	$-\log \cos \frac{ax}{a} + C$

SERIES

Arithmetic progression

A series of numbers such that the difference between one number and the next is constant.

Where a is the first term
d is the common difference
l is the last term
The series is: $a, a+d, a+2d, a+3d, \ldots$

Sum of n terms $=\frac{n}{2}[2a+(n-1)d]$

$=\frac{n}{2}(a+l)$

Last term l $=a+(n-1)d$

Geometric progression

A series of numbers such that the ratio between one number and the next is constant; the constant ratio is called the common ratio.

Where a is the first term
r is the common ratio
The series is: $a, ar, ar^2, ar^3, \ldots$

Sum of n terms:
when r is less than 1 $=\frac{a(1-r^n)}{1-r}$

when r is greater than 1 $=\frac{a(r^n-1)}{r-1}$

Last term $=ar^{n-1}$

The series of preferred numbers (**see page 118**) is an example of geometric progression; the common ratios are:

$\sqrt[5]{10}, \sqrt[10]{10}, \sqrt[20]{10}, \sqrt[40]{10}, \sqrt[80]{10}$

which are approximately 1.58 for R 5 (the series with the fifth root of 10 as the common ratio), 1.26 for R 10, 1.12 for R 20, 1.06 for R 40 and 1.03 for R 80. Thus successive terms in the preferred series increase by the constant amount of approximately 58%, 26%, 12%, 6% and 3% respectively.

Harmonic progression

A series of numbers whose reciprocals form an arithmetic progression.

The series is $\frac{1}{a}, \frac{1}{a+d}, \frac{1}{a+2d}, \ldots$

Power series

$$e^x=1+x+\frac{x^2}{2!}+\frac{x^3}{3!}+\ldots$$

$$e=e^1=1+1+\frac{1}{2!}+\frac{1}{3!}+\ldots$$

$$\log_e(1+x)=x-\frac{x^2}{2}+\frac{x^3}{3}-\frac{x^4}{4}+\ldots \text{ for } x \text{ between } -1 \text{ and } +1$$

$$\sin x=x-\frac{x^3}{3!}+\frac{x^5}{5!}+\frac{x^7}{7!}+\ldots$$

$$\cos x=1-\frac{x^2}{2!}+\frac{x^4}{4!}-\frac{x^6}{6!}+\ldots$$

Binomial (Bernoulli)

Where n is a positive integer, then:

$$(x+a)^n=x^n+C_1^n x^{n-1}a+C_2^n x^{n-2}a^2+C_3^n x^{n-3}a^3+\ldots+C_{n-1}^n xa^{n-1}+a^n$$

where, as noted above,

$$C_1^n=\frac{n!}{1!(n-1)!}=n,\ C_2^n=\frac{n!}{2!(n-2)!}=\frac{n(n-1)}{2!}, \text{ etc.}$$

For the cases where $a=1$, and $n=1$–10, binomial coefficients are as follows.

n	Coefficients										
1	1	1									
2	1	2	1								
3	1	3	3	1							
4	1	4	6	4	1						
5	1	5	10	10	5	1					
6	1	6	15	20	15	6	1				
7	1	7	21	35	35	21	7	1			
8	1	8	28	56	70	56	28	8	1		
9	1	9	36	84	126	126	84	36	9	1	
10	1	10	45	120	210	252	210	120	45	10	1

Expansion in differentials

Taylor's expansion:

$$f(a+x)=f(a)+xf'(a)+\frac{x^2}{2!}f''(a)+\frac{x^3}{3!}f'''(a)+\ldots$$

Maclaurin's expansion is the special case where $a=0$.

STATISTICS

Summation notation

Where there is a series of n values, denoted by $x_1, x_2, x_3, \ldots x_n$, the symbol Σ (sigma) is used to denote their sum; in full the notation is:

$$\sum_{i=1}^{n} x_i=x_1+x_2+x_3+\ldots x_n,$$

where $\sum_{i=1}^{n} x_i$ means the sum of all the x_i

for i increasing from 1 to n. Where the meaning is clear it is usually abbreviated to Σx_i or Σx.

Measures of central tendency

Arithmetic mean, also called the average, of a series of quantities, is obtained by finding the sum of the quantities (Σx) and dividing it by the number of quantities (n).

Mean $=\Sigma x/n$, also written as $\bar{x}$ (x bar). Where not otherwise qualified, mean usually means the arithmetic mean, and is here referred to in that way. For example, in the series 1, 3, 5, 18, 19, 20, 25, the mean is 13, ie, 91 ÷ 7.

See page 64 for a weighted average, used for index numbers.

Geometric mean is the nth root of the product of the n items in the group:

$${}^{n}\sqrt{x_1 x_2 x_3 \ldots x_n}$$

For example, in the series 3, 4, 15 the geometric mean is 5.65, ie, ${}^{3}\sqrt{180}$.

Harmonic mean is the reciprocal of the arithmetic mean of the reciprocals of the numbers: $n/(\Sigma 1/x)$. For example, in the series 1, 3, 5 the harmonic mean is 1.96, ie, $3/(1+1/3+1/5) = 3/1.533$.

Median of a series is that point which so divides it that half the quantities are on one side, half on the other. For example, in the series 1, 3, 6, 18, 19, 20, 25, the median is 18.

If there is an even number of items in the series, the median is the point midway between the two central items. For example, in the series 1, 3, 6, 18, 19, 20, the median is 12.

Mode is the most frequently recurring item in any distribution. For example, in a series of letters where there are 2 *A*s, 3 *B*s, 4 *C*s, 8 *D*s, 6 *E*s and 1 *F*, *D* would be the mode.

For unimodal frequency curves which are fairly symmetrical:
mean – mode = 3(mean – median) approximately
mode = 3 median – 2 mean

Marginal and average. A marginal increase is the increment to a sum of quantities; hence for n quantities $x_1, x_2, \ldots x_n$, where $\Sigma x = x_1 + x_2 + \ldots x_n$ an increment of x_{n+1} gives:

$$\text{marginal increase, expressed as a percentage} = \frac{x_{n+1}}{\Sigma x}$$

$$\text{while average} = \frac{\Sigma x + x_{n+1}}{n+1}$$

Measures of dispersion

Range of a set of numbers is the smallest number subtracted from the largest.

Mean absolute deviation is the mean of the sum of the deviations of a series of quantities from the arithmetic mean of those quantities, without regard to the sign of the deviation. For example, in the series 1, 3, 5 the arithmetic mean is 3 and the deviations are –2, 0, 2; the mean absolute deviation is 2 + 0 + 2 = 4 divided by 3 = 1.3.

Standard deviation is the square root of the mean of the sum of the squares of the deviations of a series from the arithmetic mean of those quantities; ie, as for the mean absolute deviation, but using the squares of the deviations, and the square root of the result. For example, in the series 1, 3, 5 above, the sum of the squares of the deviations from the arithmetic mean is 4 + 0 + 4 = 8, and the standard deviation is the square root of

2.67 (8/3), which is 1.6. Symbolically, $s = \sqrt{\sum_{i=1}^{n} (x_i - \bar{x})^2/n}$

The variance is the sum $\sum_{i=1}^{n} (x_i - \bar{x})^2/n$, so standard deviation = $\sqrt{\text{variance}}$

The symbol σ (sigma) is often used for standard deviation of a total population, *s* being then used as the symbol for the standard deviation of a sample.

Coefficient of variation (V) is a measure of relative variation; it equals the standard deviation divided by the mean and multiplied by 100. For example, in the above series, V = (1.6/3) × 100 = 53.

Skewness is said to occur in a frequency distribution when it is not symmetrical about the mean (arithmetic); skewness is positive (to the right) if the mean exceeds the median and negative (to the left) if the median exceeds the mean. There are several measures of skewness.

- Pearson's first coefficient = (mean – mode)/standard deviation.
- Pearson's second coefficient = 3(mean – median)/standard deviation.
- Coefficient of skewness is the mean of the sum of the cubes of the deviations of a series from the mean, divided by the cube of the standard deviation;

symbolically, equals $\sum_{i=1}^{n} (x_i - \bar{x})^3/ns^3$

A skewed curve is sometimes referred to as a J-shaped curve.

Kurtosis or peakedness is said to occur in a frequency distribution when it is markedly flat (platykurtic) or markedly peaked (leptokurtic), compared with a normal distribution. Coefficient of kurtosis is the mean of the sum of the fourth powers of the deviations of a series from the mean, divided by the fourth power of the standard deviation;

symbolically, equals $\sum_{i=1}^{n} (x_i - \bar{x})^4/ns^4$.

A coefficient of 3 indicates a normal distribution. A coefficient greater than 3 indicates a leptokurtic distribution; one of less than 3 indicates a platykurtic distribution.

Probability

Where E is an event which can happen in r ways out of a total of n equally likely ways, then the probability of the event (its success) $p = r/n$. For example, the probability of throwing a 2 or 3 from a die (which has 6 equally likely ways to fall) is 2 ways/6 ways = 1/3. The probability of the event not occurring (its failure) is $q = 1 - p = 2/3$ in the example.

If p is the probability that an event will occur, then the odds in favour of it happening are $p:q$ (p to q) and the odds against it happening are $q:p$.

Bayes' theorem. For a finite number of mutually exclusive events $B_1, B_2, B_3, \ldots$ where A is an event with non-zero probability, for each B_i the probability of B_i given A, written $P(B_i|A)$, is:

$$P(B_i|A) = \frac{P(A|B_i)P(B_i)}{P(A|B_1)P(B_1) + P(A|B_2)P(B_2) + P(A|B_3)P(B_3) \ldots}$$

Probability distributions

Discrete. If p is the probability that an event will occur in a single trial, and q the probability that it will fail, the probabiity of r successes in n independent trials is equal to the number of combinations of n items selected r at a time, multiplied by the probability of a success raised to the power of r and by the probability of a failure raised to the power $(n-r)$.

Thus the probability that the event will happen r times in n trials is $C_r^n p^r q^{n-r}$ where $r=0, 1, 2, 3, \ldots n$. This is the binomial distribution for $(q+p)^n$, which is outlined above for $x=q$, $a=p$.

In the binomial probability distribution, the mean number of favourable events is np, of unfavourable events nq and the standard deviation $=\sqrt{npq}$ (variance $=npq$).

The Poisson distribution is defined by $p(x)=\dfrac{g^x}{x!}e^{-g}$

where $g=$ mean rate of occurrence of an event $=$ variance; standard deviation $=\sqrt{g}$

If $n>50$, $np<5$, the binomial distribution is approximated by a Poisson distribution with $g=np$.

Continuous. The normal distribution (Gaussian distribution) is defined by the formula:

Proportions of the normal distribution

z	Single tail	Body–1 tail	Both tails	Body–2 tails
0.0	0.500 0	0.500 0	1.000 0	0.000 0
0.1	0.460 2	0.539 8	0.920 4	0.079 6
0.2	0.420 7	0.579 3	0.841 4	0.158 6
0.3	0.382 1	0.617 9	0.764 2	0.235 8
0.4	0.344 6	0.655 4	0.689 2	0.310 8
0.5	0.308 5	0.691 5	0.617 0	0.383 0
0.6	0.274 3	0 725 7	0.548 6	0.451 4
0.7	0.242 0	0.758 0	0.484 0	0.516 0
0.8	0.211 9	0.788 1	0.423 8	0.576 2
0.9	0.184 1	0.815 9	0.368 2	0.631 8
1.0	0.158 7	0.841 3	0.317 4	0.682 6
1.1	0.135 7	0.864 3	0.271 4	0.728 6
1.2	0.115 1	0.884 9	0.230 2	0.769 8
1.3	0.096 8	0.903 2	0.193 6	0.806 4
1.4	0.080 8	0.919 2	0.161 6	0.838 4
1.5	0.066 8	0.933 2	0.133 6	0.866 4
1.6	0.054 8	0.945 2	0.109 6	0.890 4
1.7	0.044 6	0.955 4	0.089 2	0.910 8
1.8	0.035 9	0.964 1	0.071 8	0.928 2
1.9	0.028 7	0.971 3	0.057 4	0.942 6
2.0	0.022 8	0.977 2	0.045 6	0.954 4
2.1	0.017 9	0.982 1	0.035 8	0.964 2
2.2	0.013 9	0.986 1	0.027 8	0.972 2
2.3	0.010 7	0.989 3	0.021 4	0.978 6
2.4	0.008 2	0.991 8	0.016 4	0.983 6
2.5	0.006 2	0.993 8	0.012 4	0.987 6
2.6	0.004 7	0.995 3	0.009 4	0.990 6
2.7	0.003 5	0.996 5	0.007 0	0.993 0
2.8	0.002 6	0.997 4	0.005 2	0.994 8
2.9	0.001 9	0.998 1	0.003 8	0.996 2
3.0	0.001 4	0.998 6	0.002 7	0.997 3
3.1	0.001 0	0.999 0	0.002 0	0.998 0

$\dfrac{1}{s\sqrt{2\pi}}e^{-\frac{1}{2}(x-\bar{x})^2/s^2}$ where $\bar{x}$ is the mean and s the standard deviation.

For the normal distribution the coefficient of skewness is 0, the coefficient of kurtosis is 3, and the area bounded by the curve and the x axis (the integral) is 1. The probability that x will lie between x_1 and x_2 is the integral from x_1 to x_2 of the above function; ie, the area under the curve between the ordinates x_1 and x_2.

The standard form of the normal distribution has mean $x=0$ and variance $=$ standard deviation $=1$; the formula is

$\dfrac{1}{\sqrt{2\pi}}e^{-\frac{1}{2}z^2}$ where $z=(x-\bar{x})/s$

For the standard normal curve, 68.27% lies in the area within z equal to plus or minus 1, 95.45% between $z=\pm2$, and 99.73% between $z=\pm3$.

For a sampling distribution of a statistic S which is approximately normal, it is to be expected that the mean of the sampling distribution will lie in the intervals $S\pm s$, $S\pm 2s$, and $S\pm 3s$ about 68.27%, 95.45% and 99.73% of the time respectively, where s is the standard deviation (or standard error) of the sampling distribution.

The intervals are called confidence intervals, and the points confidence limits or levels.

If $np>5$ and $nq>5$, the binomial distribution is approximated by a normal distribution with mean np and standard deviation $\sqrt{npq}$ (variance $=npq$).

Curve fitting

See also Equations and curves, page 113.

Modified exponential: $y=ba^x+C$
Gompertz: $y=ba^{dx}$
Modified Gompertz: $y=ba^{dx}+C$
Logistic: $y=1/(ba^x+C)$

Method of least squares is the method by which, in curve-fitting, the sum of the squares of the deviations of the actual from the curve value is a minimum; the "best fit" is given by the curve with a least squares minimum.

Interpolation

If a function $f(x)$ is approximately linear, interpolation for an unknown x_a between two known values x_0 and x_1 is given by

$$f(x_a)\approx\frac{1}{x_1-x_0}[(x_1-x_a)f(x_0)-(x_0-x_a)f(x_1)]$$

For example, where $f(x)$ is $\sin x$ in radians, interpolation of sin 0.53 (x_a) between sin 0.5 (x_0) with value 0.479 426 and sin 0.6 (x_1) with value 0.564 642, is given by: $\frac{1}{0.10}[(0.07)(0.479\,426)-(-0.03)(0.564\,642)]=0.504\,991$. Since actual sin 0.53 = 0.505 533, the error = −0.107%.

Correlation

For the two series, $x_1, x_2, \ldots x_n$, and $y_1, y_2, \ldots y_n$, the

$$\text{correlation coefficient} = r = \frac{\sum_{j=1}^{n} (x_i - \bar{x})(y_i - \bar{y})}{n s_x s_y}$$

or

$$r = \frac{n\,\Sigma xy - \Sigma x\,\Sigma y}{\sqrt{[\{n\,\Sigma x^2 - (\Sigma x)^2\}\{n\,\Sigma y^2 - (\Sigma y)^2\}]}}$$

where $\bar{x}$ and $\bar{y}$ are the means and s_x, s_y the standard deviations of the two series.

The sum $\sum_{j=1}^{n} (x_i - \bar{x})(y_i - \bar{y})$ divided by n is called the covariance and can be written cov (x, y).

The least square "regression" lines for the two series are:

$$y = \bar{y} = \frac{rs_y}{s_x}(x - \bar{x}) \quad \text{and} \quad x = \bar{x} = \frac{rs_x}{s_y}(y - \bar{y})$$

r varies between -1 and $+1$, $r = +1$ meaning completely positive correlation, $r = -1$ completely negative correlation, and $r = 0$ no correlation.

Where the regression line is $y = a + bx$:

$$b = \frac{n\,\Sigma xy - \Sigma x\,\Sigma y}{n\,\Sigma x^2 - (\Sigma x)^2}$$

$$a = \frac{\Sigma y - b\,\Sigma x}{n}$$

NUMBERS

Preferred numbers

The following table gives the series of preferred numbers recommended by the ISO for use where a range of sizes is required. These are designated R 5, R 10, R 20, R 40 and R 80 in order of preference; the R 80 series is to be used only exceptionally. The R stands for Renard and the number indicates the particular root of 10 on which the series is based; the numbers in the series are not exact theoretical values but are rounded.

See Wire, pages 83–84; and page 114.

Basic series				Serial number
R 5	R 10	R 20	R 40	
1.00	1.00	1.00	1.00	0
			1.06	1
		1.12	1.12	2
			1.18	3
	1.25	1.25	1.25	4
			1.32	5
		1.40	1.40	6
			1.50	7
1.60	1.60	1.60	1.60	8
			1.70	9
		1.80	1.80	10
			1.90	11
	2.00	2.00	2.00	12
			2.12	13
		2.24	2.24	14
			2.36	15
2.50	2.50	2.50	2.50	16
			2.65	17
		2.80	2.80	18
			3.00	19
	3.15	3.15	3.15	20
			3.35	21
		3.55	3.55	22
			3.75	23
4.00	4.00	4.00	4.00	24
			4.25	25
		4.50	4.50	26
			4.75	27
	5.00	5.00	5.00	28
			5.30	29
		5.60	5.60	30
			6.00	31
6.30	6.30	6.30	6.30	32
			6.70	33
		7.10	7.10	34
			7.50	35
	8.00	8.00	8.00	36
			8.50	37
		9.00	9.00	38
			9.50	39
10.00	10.00	10.00	10.00	40

Exceptional R 80 series

1.00	1.40	2.00	2.80	4.00	5.60	8.00
1.03	1.45	2.06	2.90	4.12	5.80	8.25
1.06	1.50	2.12	3.00	4.25	6.00	8.50
1.09	1.55	2.18	3.07	4.37	6.15	8.75
1.12	1.60	2.24	3.15	4.50	6.30	9.00
1.15	1.65	2.30	3.25	4.62	6.50	9.25
1.18	1.70	2.36	3.35	4.75	6.70	9.50
1.22	1.75	2.43	3.45	4.87	6.90	9.75
1.25	1.80	2.50	3.55	5.00	7.10	
1.28	1.85	2.58	3.65	5.15	7.30	
1.32	1.90	2.65	3.75	5.30	7.50	
1.36	1.95	2.72	3.87	5.45	7.75	

Other numbers

Roman numerals

I	1	X	10	C	100	M	1 000
V	5	L	50	D	500		

To make up numbers, start from the left with the symbol of the largest number. The symbols I X C may each be repeated up to three times; the symbols V L D are each written once only. A maller number placed after a larger is to be added to it, and a maller number placed before a larger number is to be taken om it. For example:

1	VI	6	XX	20	LXX	70
2	VII	7	XXX	30	LXXX	80
3	VIII	8	XL	40	XC	90
4	IX	9	L	50	C	100
5	X	10	LX	60	CM	900

nglo-Asian (Bangladesh, India, Pakistan)
lac or lakh = 1,00,000 = 100 000 = one hundred thousand
0 lacs or lakhs = 10,00,000 = 1 000 000 = one million
crore = 100 lacs or lakhs = 1,00,00,000 = 10 000 000 = ten illion
arab (or arb) = 100 crores = 1,00,00,00,000 = 1 000 000 000 one thousand million

ortugal
conto = 1 000 escudos

eneral

items		= 1 pair
2 items	= 6 pairs	= 1 dozen[a]
) items	= 10 pairs	= 1 score[b]
44 items	= 12 dozen	= 1 gross
728 items	= 12 gross	= 1 great gross

long or baker's dozen is 13 items. [b] 1 long score is items.

)0 items = 1 short hundred
20 items = 1 long hundred

Mathematical symbols

+	plus or positive	⩾	equal to or greater than
−	minus or negative	⩽	equal to or less than
±	plus or minus, positive or negative	≫	much greater than
×	multiplied by	≪	much less than
÷ /	divided by	r! ⌊r	factorial *r*
=	equal to	√	square root
≡	identically equal to	$^r\sqrt{}$	*r*th root
≠	not equal to	r^n	*r* to the power of *n*
≢	not identically equal to	∝	is proportional to or varies with
≙ ≈ ≅	approximately equal to	∞	infinity
∼	of the order of or similar to	%	per cent
>	greater than	‰	per mille (thousand)
<	less than	Σ	sum of
≯	not greater than	Π	product of
≮	not less than	Λ	difference
		∴	therefore

See also pages 111–113 for trigonometric symbols.

Greek alphabet

A	α	alpha	I	ι	iota	P	ϱ	rho
B	β	beta	K	ϰ	kappa	Σ	σ or ς	sigma
Γ	γ	gamma	Λ	λ	lambda	T	τ	tau
Δ	δ	delta	M	μ	mu	Y	υ	upsilon
E	ε	epsilon	N	ν	nu	Φ	ϕ	phi
Z	ζ	zeta	Ξ	ξ	xi	X	χ	chi
H	η	eta	O	ο	omicron	Ψ	ψ	psi
Θ	θ	theta	Π	π	pi	Ω	ω	omega

Minerals and alloys

Measures

Gold and silver are usually measured in troy weights (**see page 19**). 1 metric carat = 200 milligrams. The UK symbol for metric carat is CM. 100 points = 1 metric carat (1 point = 2 mg).

Hardness scales are listed below.

Scratch hardness. The basis of Moh's scale is that each substance can be scratched by those higher in the series.

Moh's scale

Substance	Hardness	Substance	Hardness
Talc	1	Feldspar	6
Gypsum	2	Quartz	7
Calcite	3	Topaz	8
Fluorite	4	Corundum	9
Apatite	5	Diamond	10
Levels for other substances			
Thumb nail	2.5	Mild steel	4–5
Aluminium	2–3	Glass	4.5–6.5
Copper	2.5–3	Knife-blade	5

Note. Generally, 1–3 is soft, 4–7 is intermediate and 8–10 is hard.

There is a modified scale which is the same up to scale 6, but extends it so that diamond = 15.

Indentation hardness. This is based on the size of the indentation from a given load, or on the ability of a load to make a certain sized indentation. There are a number of different scales, including the following.

	Based on an indenter of: shape	material
Brinell	Sphere	Hardened steel or tungsten carbide
Rockwell	Sphere	Hardened steel
	Cone	Diamond
Vickers	Square-based pyramid	Diamond

Brinell hardness (HB) = $F/\pi Dh$

where F = force applied (measured in kilograms-force)

D = diameter (in mm) of the sphere acting as indenter

h = depth of indentation

Rockwell hardness (HR) = $E - e$

where E = 100 or 130 according to the Rockwell system used

$e = h_1 - h_2$, h_1 being the indentation when increasing from an initial force to a total force, and h_2 the indentation left when the force is removed

Forces applied for some Rockwell systems

System	*E*	Initial force N	Initial force kgf	Force applied N	Force applied kgf	Total force N	Total force kgf
C	100	98	10	1 372	140	1 470	150
A	100	98	10	490	50	588	60
B	130	98	10	882	90	980	100
F	100	98	10	490	50	588	60
15 N	100	29.4	3	117.6	12	147	15
15 T	100	29.4	3	117.6	12	147	15
30 N	100	29.4	3	264.6	27	294	30
30 T	100	29.4	3	264.6	27	294	30
45 N	100	29.4	3	411.6	42	441	45
45 T	100	29.4	3	411.6	42	441	45

Vickers hardness (HV) = $2F \sin \theta / d^2$

where F = force applied to the indenter (in kgf, chosen as 1, 2.5, 5, 10, 20, 30, 50 or 100)

$\theta = \frac{1}{2}$ angle of the taper of the indenter (2θ = standard value of 136°)

d = arithmetic mean diagonal diameter of indentation (in mm)

Density comparisons

Relation between volume and weight (mass) of various metals

	To obtain kg multiply no. cubic decimetres (litres) by[a]	Weight relative to steel = 1[b]
Cast iron	7.20	0.917
Steel	7.85	1.000
Aluminium	2.70	0.344
Zinc	7.10	0.904
Tin (white)	7.31	0.931
Manganese	7.40	0.943
Brass	8.40	1.070
Nickel	8.90	1.134
Copper	8.92	1.136
Lead	11.34	1.445
Mercury	13.55	1.726
Uranium	18.70	2.382
Tungsten	19.30	2.459

[a]Equals relative density; for kilograms per cubic metre also multiply by 1 000. [b]Weights for various sizes can be obtained from the tables for steel on **pages 227–229** by applying the weight relative to steel as a multiplier.

MINERALS AND ALLOYS LISTING

The alloy percentages included in the following list of minerals are intended as rough guides; the exact proportions will vary according to the nature of the finished product and the purpose for which it is intended.

See also Iron and steel, pages 104–106.

Aluminium

Derived mainly from bauxite. The typical composition of bauxite is Al_2O_3 (alumina) 40–60%; Fe_2O_3 5–30%; water 12–30%; with small amounts of SiO_2 and TiO_2. Aluminium can be alloyed so that it is as strong as steel and only one-third the weight. A simple alloy would be 4% copper, less than 1% each of magnesium and manganese, and the rest aluminium.

Duralumin alloys (average) of 94–95% aluminium, 4% copper, 0.5% manganese, 0.5% magnesium, 0.4% silicon, and not more than 0.5% iron, are used in aircraft and structural applications.

Anhydrite

See gypsum.

Antimony

Used to impart hardness and stiffness to lead alloys. Antimonial lead (hard lead) is 1–12% antimony.

Arsenic

Up to 0.5% arsenic added to lead or copper imparts hardness.

Asbestos

Fibrous varieties of some silicate minerals; the main variety is chrysotile. The fibre can be very fine; as small in diameter as 0.000 02 mm (compare with wool 0.025 mm, cotton 0.010 2 mm and nylon 0.007 6 mm). Tensile strength of asbestos fabrics is about 7 000 kgf/cm^2 (100 000 lbf/in^2).

Barium

The main form is barytes (chiefly barium sulphate). It is used as a pigment in white paint, and in paper and textile industries and oil-well drilling muds. Lithopone (white paint pigment) is 67–73% barium sulphate, 26–32% zinc sulphide.

Beryllium

Can be commercial beryl or gem variety (emeralds or aquamarines); it is very light with a relative density of 1.85. It is used in nuclear reactors as a moderator and as canning material for fuel elements because it reflects neutrons.

Beryllium aluminium is 72% beryllium, 28% aluminium; it is very strong with a relative density of 2.0.

Beryllium copper alloys (beryllium bronzes) have a copper base with about 2.5% beryllium; this increases strength about 6 times.

Bismuth

As an alloy it has a low melting point; bismuth amalgam (with mercury in varying proportions) is used for silvering globes, etc.

Wood's metal is 50% bismuth, 25% lead, 12.5% tin, 12.5% cadmium, and melts at 70°C.

Borates

In the glass industry 15–50 parts of borax (sodium tetraborate) may be mixed with 1 000 parts of quartz sand to brighten and strengthen the glass. Boron is used for control rods in nuclear reactors, often alloyed with steel. Pyrex is borax-silicate glass.

Cadmium

Used as an alloy it gives strength, enables the withstanding of higher temperatures, and gives a high electrical resistance; used in electro-plating of iron and steel, in bearing metals, and for some types of nuclear reactor rods, etc.

Cadmium-nickel alloy	= 98.5% cadmium, 1–1.5% nickel
Cadmium-silver alloy	= 96.25% cadmium, 3% silver, 0.75% copper
Cadmium-copper alloy	= copper alloy with 1% cadmium

China clay (kaolin)

46% silica (SiO_2), 40% alumina (Al_2O_3) and 14% water. It is used in paper manufacture, pottery, paint, etc.

Chromium

As an alloy it increases the hardness, tenacity, ductility, resistance to wear and corrosion of steel, and gives a high electrical resistance. Alloys of less than 3% chromium are used in the automobile industry and for rails. Alloys of more than 12% produce stainless and rustless steels.

Chromium iron = 65–70% iron, 25–30% chromium, 5% nickel

Cobalt

Used for heat-resisting and rustless alloys and steel. Stellite alloys are 35–80% cobalt, 10–40% chromium, 0.25 tungsten, 0.1% molybdenum.

Copper

The composition of copper alloys can vary widely.

Bronze, modern (average)	= 88% copper, 10% tin, 0.1–2% zinc; usual range 5–15% tin
Gunmetal	= 88–90% copper, 8–10% tin, 2–6% zinc
Brass	= 60–80% copper, 15–20% zinc, 0.1–5% lead (**see also Zinc, below**)
Cartridge brass	= 70% copper, 30% zinc

Diamonds

Almost pure carbon with a relative density of 3.5, they are the hardest mineral (10 on Moh's scale). Unit of weight is metric carat; a brilliant cut diamond weighing 1 carat has a diameter of about 6 mm. The carat count is the number of near equal size diamonds per carat, and is a measure of diamond size. Industrial diamonds range in size from about 120 per carat (120-count) to 4 or more carats per stone.

Fluorspar

Used mainly as a flux for open hearth steel; 2.25–3.5 kg (5–8 lb) are needed for every tonne (or ton) of steel. For electric steel smelting 6–18 kg (14–40 lb) are used per tonne (or ton).

Fuller's earth

Comprises clay-like minerals, mainly hydrated silicates of aluminium. Typical composition is 60% silica (SiO_2) and 20% alumina (Al_2O_3). Absorbs grease and is used for detergents and cat litter.

Gold

The purity of gold is expressed as parts of 1 000, so that a fineness of 800 is 80% gold. Pure gold is defined as 24 carats (1 000 fine), but usually the highest degree of fineness in use is 22 carats. Dental gold is usually 16 or 20 carat (62.5% or 83.33%); gold in jewellery is usually in the range 9–22 carat (37.5–91.66%). A golden sovereign is 22 carat (91.66% gold, 8.33% copper).

White gold is 12% palladium, 15% nickel or 20–25% platinum.

A standard international bar of gold is 400 troy ounces; bars of 250 troy ounces are also used.

Graphite ("black lead")

The "lead" in pencils is about 50% graphite, 50% fine clay. Graphite is used as a moderator in nuclear reactors.

Graphite bronze is 89% copper, 10% tin, 1% graphite; for use in bearings.

Gypsum and anhydrite

These are calcium sulphates used for plaster of paris and hard finish plasters; also used in pigments, cement, etc.

Iron

See Iron and steel, pages 104–106.

Lead

Used with 1–4% antimony for sheet and foil. (See also antimony.)

Limestone

Mainly calcium carbonate; usually has 22–56% lime (CaO), 0–21% magnesia (MgO). Those with 5–20% MgO are called magnesian limestones, and those with over 20% MgO dolomites. It is used for aggregates, cement, building lime, glass, paper industries, etc.

Magnesium

The lightest of all metals, two-thirds of the weight of aluminium; when alloyed combines mechanical strength with lightness. An incendiary bomb is 93% magnesium, 7% aluminium.

Manganese

A deoxydiser and desulphuriser for steel. If a fraction of 1% of manganese is added to the steel melt the elastic limit and tenacity is increased; 12% in steel gives high tensile strength and abrasion resistance.

Ferro-manganese is 80% manganese, 20% iron and 0.1–7% carbon.

Mercury (quicksilver)

Sold in wrought-iron flasks; the standard flask contains 76 lb (34.473 kg) of mercury and is the market unit of quantity. Mercury is used in production of chemicals, drugs, scientific instruments and ammunition, and in extracting gold and silver. In combination it is called an amalgam.

Mica

Usually a silicate of aluminium. The value of mica lies in its perfect cleavage – it can be separated easily into sheets 1/1 000 inch thick (1 mil). It is used for electrical insulation and, when ground, as a dusting powder for rubber and in paint.

Molybdenum

Principally used for special steels, such as high speed cutting steels; it has a similar effect to chromium or tungsten. 1% or less in steel increases the hardness.

Nickel

When alloyed to steel nickel increases strength with less reduction in ductility than is caused when carbon is used. Steel alloys usually have 0.2–9% nickel; high nickel (stainless) steels have 7–35%, while up to 50% is used for very high resistance to corrosion. With 13% nickel steel is so strong it can hardly be cut or drilled; with 25% it has a high electrical resistance and is used for resistance wire. Nickel steel or invar is 36% nickel, and does not expand or contract appreciably with temperature variations. Added to iron, 10–15% of nickel increases the strength, hardness and corrosion resistance, and makes it non-magnetic. 48–80% of nickel with iron is highly magnetic.

Platinum

The metal and alloys are very resistant to corrosion and are unaffected by normal atmospheric exposure; uses are for instruments, crucibles, electrical contacts, as a catalyst in chemical engineering and for motor vehicles.

Platinum-iridium alloy = 65–95% platinum, 5–35% iridium
Platinum-nickel alloy = 80–95% platinum, 5–20% nickel

Silicon

Useful in alloys as it is fluid when molten and not brittle after casting. Silicon-aluminium alloy is 10–13% silicon, 86–89% aluminium, 0.5% manganese, 0.5% iron, 0.1% zinc.

Silver

Next to gold, the most malleable and ductile of metals; 1 gram of pure silver can be drawn into a wire more than 1.5 kilometres long, and silver leaf can be 6 micrometres thick. It is used for electrical contacts, etc. Electrum metal is a natural gold/silver alloy with 55–88% gold.

Sulphur

Pyrites contains 53% sulphur, 47% iron; in the paper industry 50–150 kg (110–300 lb) of sulphur is used in the manufacture of 1 tonne (ton) of wood pulp.

Talc

Hydrated silicate of magnesium with 63.5% SiO_2, 31.7% MgO and 4.8% water. Prepared talc is sometimes called French chalk. Has extreme softness and smoothness (1 on Moh's scale).

Tantalum and niobium (columbium)

May be alloyed with iron, nickel, tungsten, molybdenum and chromium to give tenacity, ductility, tensile strength, hardness and resistance to corrosion by most acids.

0.5–0.8% of niobium in steel makes it resistant to high temperatures; it is useful as a material in nuclear reactors.

"Tantaloy" = 92% tantalum, 7.5% tungsten

Thorium and cerium (rare earths)

Obtained mainly from monazite (thoria 0–30%, cerium group oxides 39–74%). Thorium is used in magnesium alloys, and in production of nuclear energy fuel. Cerium and other rare earth oxides are called lanthanons; they are used for lighter flints and in electric arc carbons (for cinema projectors, etc).

Tin

The main ore is cassiterite; the principal use is in tinplating. Tinplate is mild steel up to 0.49 mm thick, coated very thinly with tin metal. Tin can is 1.5% tin, 98.5% steel.

Solder: soft tin = 63% tin, 37% lead
other = 25–50% tin, 50–75% lead

Titanium

Rutile is titanium dioxide, used mainly in pigments. Titanium paints have twice the opacity of zinc, and three times the opacity of white lead paints. Sometimes used as a mixture; eg 30% TiO_2 with 70% $CaSO_4$ (calcium sulphate).

Tungsten (wolfram)

Strengthens steel at ordinary and high temperatures. Less than 2 tons of tungsten supply filaments for 100 mn electric bulbs.

1 tonne tungsten (W)	= 1.261 tonnes tungsten trioxide (WO_3)
Ferro-tungsten	= 75–80% tungsten with iron (and small amounts of silicon, manganese, etc)
Tungsten steel	= 18% tungsten, 4% chromium, 1% vanadium, 77% steel

Vanadium

Mainly found as vanadium pentoxide (V_2O_5); 1 ton of vanadium (V) = 1.785 tons vanadium pentoxide. Usually less than 1% vanadium is added to steel to increase the toughness and high temperature resistance.

Zinc

Used in paint (see also barium). Resists corrosion: rolled zinc alloy (for roofing, etc) contains 1% copper; galvanizing is depositing a thin coat of zinc on iron and steel to prevent rusting. Copper-zinc alloy is used in the electrical industry.

Zinc amalgam = 89% zinc, 11% mercury

Zirconium

Imparts hardness when alloyed with iron, copper, aluminium and magnesium, etc. Used in production of nuclear power reactor cores.

Cooperite is a nickel-zirconium alloy, acid resisting and very hard.

Paper, packaging and printing

PAPER

Sizes of printing paper

The UK paper industry in general converted to the use of international paper units during the 1970s. The main size classifications, including the former British units, are as follows.

International paper sizes (ISO). International paper sizes are trimmed sizes based on the A0 sheet which is 1 m^2 in area, and with sides such that when the larger side is halved the relationship is retained; the relationships between the sides is then in the ratio of $\sqrt{2}:1$.

ISO A series of trimmed sizes

A series	mm	in
4A0	1 682 × 2 378	66.22 × 93.62
2A0	1 189 × 1 682	46.81 × 66.22
A0	841 × 1 189	33.11 × 46.81
A1	594 × 841	23.39 × 33.11
A2	420 × 594	16.54 × 23.39
A3	297 × 420	11.69 × 16.54
A4	210 × 297	8.27 × 11.69
A5	148 × 210	5.83 × 8.27
A6	105 × 148	4.13 × 5.83
A7	74 × 105	2.91 × 4.13
A8	52 × 74	2.05 × 2.91
A9	37 × 52	1.46 × 2.05
A10	26 × 37	1.02 × 1.46

There is also an ISO B series (trimmed sizes), little used, which has as a starting point a sheet with 1 m on one side and $\sqrt{2}$ m (1.414 m) on the other.

ISO B series of trimmed sizes

B series	mm	in
B0	1 000 × 1 414	39.37 × 55.67
B1	707 × 1 000	27.83 × 38.37
B2	500 × 707	19.68 × 27.83
B3	353 × 500	13.90 × 19.68
B4	250 × 353	9.84 × 13.90
B5	176 × 250	6.93 × 9.84
B6	125 × 176	4.92 × 6.93
B7	88 × 125	3.46 × 4.92
B8	62 × 88	2.44 × 3.46
B9	44 × 62	1.73 × 2.44
B10	31 × 44	1.22 × 1.73

Main envelope sizes (trimmed sizes)

	mm	in
C4	229 × 324	9.02 × 12.76
C5	162 × 229	6.38 × 9.02
C6	114 × 162	4.49 × 6.38
DL	101 × 220	4.33 × 8.66

The series for untrimmed stock sizes are the RA series for normal trims and the SRA series for extra trims.

	mm	in
RA series		
RA0	860 × 1 220	33.86 × 48.03
RA1	610 × 860	24.02 × 33.86
RA2	430 × 610	16.93 × 24.02
SRA series		
SRA0	900 × 1 280	35.43 × 50.39
SRA1	640 × 900	25.20 × 35.43
SRA2	450 × 640	17.72 × 25.20

Books
Untrimmed equivalents for book papers have been established, based on multiples of 24 mm. These are as follows.

	mm	in
Metric quad crown	768 × 1 008	30.24 × 39.68
Metric large quad crown	816 × 1 056	32.13 × 41.57
Metric quad demy	888 × 1 128	34.96 × 44.41
Metric small quad royal	960 × 1 272	37.80 × 50.08

Trimmed book sizes normally allow for trims from head, tail and fore-edge of a page; for the metric sizes above a trim of 3 mm is standard ($\frac{1}{8}$ inch for traditional UK sizes).

	Untrimmed size mm	Trimmed size mm
Metric crown 8vo	126 × 192	123 × 186
Metric large crown 8vo	132 × 204	129 × 198
Metric demy 8vo	141 × 222	138 × 216
Metric royal 8vo	159 × 240	156 × 234

Old UK sizes. These sizes, now obsolete, were the basis for the metric sizes described above.

	in	mm
Trimmed		
Octavo	8 × 5	203 × 127
Quarto	8 × 10	203 × 254
Foolscap	8 × 13	203 × 330
Untrimmed[a]		
Crown	15 × 20	381 × 508
Large post	16½ × 21	419 × 533
Double foolscap	17 × 27	432 × 686
Demy	17½ × 22½	445 × 572
Medium	18 × 23	457 × 584
Royal	20 × 25	508 × 635
Double crown	20 × 30	508 × 762
Imperial	22 × 30	559 × 762
Double demy	22½ × 35	572 × 890
Quad crown	30 × 40	762 × 1 016
Large crown	32 × 42	813 × 1 067
Quad demy	35 × 45	890 × 1 144

[a]Full sheet.

ubdivisions of the above full sheets for UK and metric sizes re described as follows.

Folio means a full sheet folded or cut in half.
Quarto (or 4to) means a full sheet folded or cut into 4.
Octavo (or 8vo) means a full sheet folded or cut into 8.
16mo means a full sheet folded or cut into 16.

aper substances

/ith the change to the metric system, paper substance rammage) in the UK is expressed in terms of grams per quare metre. Stock weights are expressed in terms of kg per 000 sheets (formerly in terms of lb per ream). Grammage was t first expressed in a range based on the R20 and R40 series of referred numbers, but this range has been changed to a range ased on a series rounded to 5 g/m². Some paper substances re shown in the table below.

rammage /m²	kg/'000 sheets SRA1	SRA2	RA1	RA2	A4
25	14.4	7.2	13.1	6.6	1.56
30	17.3	8.6	15.7	7.9	1.87
45	25.9	13.0	23.6	11.8	2.81
60	34.6	17.3	31.5	15.7	3.74
70	40.3	20.2	36.7	18.4	4.37
80	46.1	23.0	42.0	21.0	4.99
85	49.0	24.5	44.6	22.3	5.30
90	51.8	25.9	47.2	23.6	5.61
00	57.6	28.8	52.5	26.2	6.24
05	60.5	30.2	55.1	27.5	6.55
15	66.2	33.1	60.3	30.2	7.17
35	77.8	38.9	70.8	35.4	8.42
55	89.3	44.6	81.3	40.7	9.67
60	92.2	46.1	83.9	42.0	9.98
70	97.9	49.0	89.2	44.6	10.60

aper measures

ream = 500 sheets
reams = 1 bundle = 1 000 sheets
reams = 1 bale = 2 500 sheets
Old measures: 1 ream = 480 sheets for writing and 516 sheets or printing; 1 ream = 20 quires.)

ULP

Voodpulp

Voodpulp is paper-making wood (pulpwood) after it has been nade into a fibrous mass by mechanical or chemical means.

ulping yield. The wood input in cubic metres per tonne of air-ry pulp is as follows, varying according to the chemical omposition of the wood and the nature of the pulping rocess.

Type of pulp	Coniferous	Non-coniferous
Mechanical	1.7–3.3	
Semi-chemical		1.7–4.0
Sulphite: unbleached	3.4–6.5	2.6–5.3
bleached	3.7–7.1	2.7–5.7
Sulphate: unbleached	3.6–7.0	2.6–5.4
bleached	3.9–7.5	2.9–5.9
Dissolving	4.8–10.1	4.0–9.0

Wood input in terms of tonnes of oven-dry pulp per tonne of oven-dry wood is as follows.

Type of pulp	Coniferous	Non-coniferous
Mechanical	0.90–0.95	
Semi-chemical		0.70–0.83
Sulphite: unbleached	0.48–0.51	0.52–0.55
bleached	0.44–0.47	0.49–0.52
Sulphate: unbleached	0.45–0.48	0.51–0.54
bleached	0.42–0.45	0.47–0.50
Dissolving	0.31–0.36	0.31–0.36

While mechanical pulp yields are generally over 90%, those of dissolving pulp are about 34%.

Other pulps

Pulp yields from other materials are approximately as follows.

Straw 46–53%
Esparto grass 40–45%
Rags (cotton, linen) 60–75%
Waste paper: bond 90%
coated 50%

Products

Paper. Consumption of pulp per tonne of finished product in manufacture of paper is as follows.

Newsprint	0.19 tonne chemical pulp, 0.83 tonne mechanical pulp
Kraft paper	1.03 tonnes chemical pulp
Other paper & board	0.40 tonne chemical pulp, 0.10 tonne mechanical pulp

Other. Dissolving pulp is used in manufacture of rayon and acetate fibres, cellophane and cellulose film and other cellulose derivatives.

100 units of dissolving pulp produces 95 units of rayon and acetate fibres, or 100 units of cellophane.

PACKAGING

Systems

Under the minimum system, applicable under law in the UK to all packages before 1980, a container marked with a statement as to the quantity of goods contained had to contain at least that quantity.

Under the average system, applicable in law for certain packages within the UK (and the EC) from January 1st 1980, the average contents of packages must not be less than the stated quantity (where a package or prepackage is the combination of a container and the goods it contains, and the nominal quantity is the weight or volume of the contents); a certain proportion of the packages can contain less (up to a point) than the nominal quantity.

Packaging rules

Three rules have been established to help the packer conform to the average standards laid down.

1. The actual contents of the packages shall not be less, on average, than the nominal quantity.
2. Not more than 2.5% of the packages may be non-standard, ie, have negative errors larger than the tolerable negative error (TNE) specified for the nominal quantity.
3. No package may be inadequate, ie, have a negative error larger than twice the specified TNE.

Tolerable negative error (TNE)

Nominal quantity of package (g or ml)	TNE % nominal quantity	g or ml
5–50	9	–
50–100	–	4.5
100–200	4.5	–
200–300	–	9
300–500	3	–
500–1 000	–	15
1 000–10 000	1.5	–
10 000–15 000	–	150
>15 000	1	–

In calculating the error as a percentage of nominal quantity, in units of weight or volume, the amount of a tolerable error in the cases shown in the above table shall be rounded up to the nearest one-tenth of a gram or millilitre as the case may be.

A non-standard package is one where the quantity of the goods it contains is less by more than the prescribed amount than the nominal quantity on the package.

An inadequate package is one where the quantity of the goods it contains is less by more than twice the prescribed amount than the nominal quantity on the package.

Packaging ranges

The ranges established by the EC for nominal quantities of contents of prepackages are shown in the table for some main items.

See also Food and drink, page 91, for metric package sizes in the UK.

Product	Range of nominal quantities
Sold by weight	**Quantity (gm)**
Barley kernels, pearl barley, rice (incl. ground rice & rice flakes), sago, semolina, tapioca	125, 250, 375, 500 or multiple of 500
Bread (in form of whole loaf)	400 or multiple of 400
Butter	125, 250, 1 000, 1 500, 2 000, 2 500, 5 000
Cereals (ready-to-serve)	250, 375, 500, 750, 1 000, 1 500, 2 000
Frozen fruit & vegetables	150, 300, 450, 600, 750, 1 000, 1 500, 2 000, 2 500
Solid toilet & household soaps	25, 50, 75, 100, 150, 200, 250, 300, 400, 500, 1 000
Sugar	125, 250, 500, 750, 1 000, 1 500, 2 000, 2 500, 3 000, 4 000, 5 000
Sold by volume	**Quantity (ml)**
Ice cream[a]	300, 500, 750, 1 000, 1 500, 2 000, 2 500, 3 000, 4 000, 5 000
Lubricating oils	125, 250, 500, 1 000, 2 000, 2 500, 3 000, 4 000, 5 000, 10 000
Milk[b]	200, 250, 500, 750, 1 000, 2 000 or thereafter single multiple of 500
Paints & varnishes	25, 50, 125, 250, 375, 500, 750, 1 000, 2 000, 2 500, 4 000, 5 000, 10 000
Toothpaste	25, 50, 75, 100, 125, 150, 200, 250, 300

[a]For quantities over 250 ml. [b]In the UK still sold by the pint.

PRINTING

Sizes of type

The basis of the Anglo-US system is the 12-point (pica) em, which measures 0.166 of an inch (4.217 6 mm). The point, one-twelfth of the em, is 0.013 9 of an inch (0.351 5 mm); there are approximately 72 points to an inch (a closer approximation is 72.25 points to the inch).

The Didot point, used in continental Europe, is generally defined as 0.376 mm, equal to 0.014 8 in approximately (for Germany it is defined as 1.000 333/2 660 m = 0.376 1 m approx.). Other points are as follows.

Fournier 0.348 8 mm (0.013 7 in)
Casion 0.351 6 mm (0.013 8 in)
German 0.376 5 (0.014 8 in)
1 cicero = 12 Didot points = 4.512 mm (0.178 in)

Point comparisons

Anglo-US points	in	mm	Didot points
1	0.014	0.351	0.935
2	0.028	0.703	1.869
3	0.042	1.054	2.804
4	0.055	1.406	3.739
5	0.069	1.757	4.674
6	0.083	2.109	5.608
7	0.097	2.460	6.543
8	0.111	2.812	7.478
9	0.125	3.163	8.413
0	0.138	3.515	9.347
1	0.152	3.866	10.282
2	0.166	4.218	11.217
4	0.194	4.920	13.086
6	0.221	5.623	14.956
8	0.249	6.326	16.825
0	0.277	7.029	18.695
4	0.332	8.435	22.434
0	0.415	10.544	28.042
6	0.498	12.653	33.650

Anglo-US points	in	mm	Didot points
42	0.581	14.761	39.259
48	0.664	16.870	44.867
60	0.830	21.088	56.084
72	0.996	25.305	67.301

Old UK sizes of type bore individual names; the equivalents in Anglo-US point sizes of these names are as follows.

Brilliant	$3\frac{1}{2}$	Emerald	$6\frac{1}{2}$	Small pica	11
Diamond	$4\frac{1}{2}$	Minion	7	Pica	12
Pearl or agate	5	Brevier	8	English	14
Ruby	$5\frac{1}{2}$	Bourgeois	9	Great primer	18
Nonpareil	6	Long primer	10	Double pica	22

A metric system is not internationally agreed, but some use is made of a system with 0.025 mm as basic unit for width, and 0.25 mm as a basic unit for character depth.

Sound and music

SOUND

Range

The limits of human audibility are for frequency of vibrations from about 15 Hz to 20 000 Hz. The range decreases with age, particularly in the high frequency register; a condition known as presbyacusis. The typical range of a male voice is 100–9 000 Hz, and of a female voice 150–10 000 Hz.

Below 15 Hz (sometimes 20 Hz) frequencies are described as infrasonic. Above 20 000 Hz frequencies are described as ultrasonic. An example of an ultrasonic frequency is that used by a bat as a type of sound radar: the frequency is about 50 000 Hz.

Velocity

The velocity of sound in air at sea level, and at 0°C = 331.5 metres per second
At 15°C (ICAO standard atmosphere) = 340.294 m/s

The velocity of sound waves in air is proportional to the square root of absolute temperature; where T is temperature in kelvin (°C + 273.15), speed of sound equals:

$$S \times \sqrt{1 + (T/273.15)}$$

where $S = 331.5$ m/s

The velocity of sound in water is approximately 1 450 m/s at 10°C and 1 480 m/s at 20°C; actual velocity varies with the salinity of water.

The term supersonic usually means above the speed of sound. In terms of Mach numbers:

Mach 1 = the speed of sound
Mach 2 = twice the speed of sound, etc.

A sonic boom, created when a plane passes the speed of sound, has a pressure of about 3–4 kPa at ground level (30–40 millibars).

Doppler effect. Where the source of a sound is moving relative to the listener, the frequency observed by the listener is different from that created by the source; this is the Doppler effect (which also applies to light frequencies).

Where f = frequency of the sound (in Hz)
S = velocity of sound
v = velocity at which source of sound is moving towards the observer then frequency observed (in Hz) $= f \times S/(S - v)$

Where the sound source is approaching, the frequency (or pitch) is higher, and where the sound source is moving away, the frequency (or pitch) is lower than the source frequency (pitch).

See Music section below for further information on pitch. See also Light, optics and photography, page 107.

Perception

Physical perception of sound is measured by the amplitude of a vibration creating sound; loudness is sound perception as heard by the human ear.

Physical. This can be measured objectively either as a pressure measurement, in terms of newtons per square metre (pascal), or as a power measurement, in terms of the power creating th sound, in terms of watts per square metre.

The threshold of hearing or audibility is the sound level which is just audible for an average listener. For an average note of frequency taken at 1 000 Hz, the usually accepted level of audibility is taken as 0.000 2 microbar (2×10^{-5} Pa or 0.000 02 Pa); in other words, that is the minimum effective sound pressure which can be heard. In power terms, the threshold is 1 pW/m^2 (10^{-12} W/m^2). Sound is measured above the threshold in terms of ratios relative to the threshold.

The basic unit of interval is the bel:

bel $= \log_{10}(W_1/W_0)$ where W_1 and W_0 are two power levels.

In practice the decibel (dB), equal to one-tenth of a bel, is used

decibel $= 10 \log_{10}(W_1/W_0)$

W_0 is normally a reference value given in terms of rayls. A rayl is a unit of specific acoustical impedence, equal to a pressure of 0.1 pascal divided by a sound particle velocity of 10^{-2} metres per second. It is also known as the specific acoustical ohm (Ω_s) or unit-area acoustical ohm.

Since the apparent loudness of a sound also depends on the frequency (pitch) of a sound, sound levels are sometimes weighted to standardise in terms of frequency. Standard frequency responses have been established, the most usual being designated as the A response; this discriminates against low and high frequencies in favour of average frequencies. A sound level weighted according to this system is usually shown as dB(A).

Typical sound levels

	dB(A)
Quiet whisper	30
Conversation	60
Typical machine shop	65
Motor-car horn	100
Heavy lorry at 1 m	105
Jet taking off	120
UK ship maximum limit[a]	135
Threshold of pain	140

[a]For parts of a ship other than sleeping quarters (maximum of 60 dB) and living quarters (maximum of 65 dB).

In general damaging noise is considered to begin at the 80–90 dB(A) level; a hearing impediment may occur above 90 dB(A) for an 8-hour day.

See Transport, page 148, for details of permitted noise levels for vehicles in the UK.

Loudness. Loudness, as subjective measure for the listener, is sometimes expressed in measures other than the decibel.

Measures of loudness are:

- the phon (p), the subjective equivalent of the decibel, produced by a 1 000 Hz tone (1 phon = 1 dB); and
- the sone, which has a loudness level of 40 phons (physical intensity of 40 dB(A)). Loudness, N, in sones of any sound is

given by $N = 2^{0.1(p-40)}$ where p is the loudness level expressed in phons. Some equivalents are shown in the table below.

phons	sones	phons	sones
40	1.00	80	16.0
50	2.00	90	32.0
60	4.00	100	64.0
65	5.66	105	90.5
70	8.00		

The above formulae for decibels show ratios using common logarithms (base of 10); natural logarithms (base e) are also used, with a basic unit called a neper or napier, with symbol Np or Nep:

$$\text{neper} = \log_e \sqrt{(W_1/W_0)} = \tfrac{1}{2} \log_e (W_1/W_0)$$

To determine the number of decibels equivalent to various voltage or current ratios, multiply the number of decibels by 2; since, for voltage or current ratios: decibel $= 20 \log_{10}(V_1/V_0)$. The reference level for voltage or current ratios, where dB = 0, is the picowatt (dBp), the milliwatt (dBm), watt (dBW), kilowatt (dBk), etc.

Reverberation. A sound in an enclosed space is reflected repeatedly by the boundaries of the enclosure, even after the source ceases to emit sound. A certain amount of reverberation adds a pleasing characteristic to the acoustical properties of a room. However, excessive reverberation can ruin the acoustical properties of an otherwise well-designed room. Because of the importance of the proper control of reverberations in rooms, reverberation time, t_{60}, has been defined as the time required for sound to die away to one-thousandth of its initial pressure, that is to drop 60 dB in sound pressure level.

MUSIC

Pitch

The normal range of sound which can be heard is 20–20 000 Hz (although some people can detect sounds at 15 Hz). Of this, the practical musical range is usually regarded as 40–4 000 Hz.

The international standard musical pitch is 440 Hz for the note A in the treble stave (ie, A above middle C on a piano). Previously the French, continental or Vienna standard was 436 Hz, and up to 1896 the Philharmonic standard was 439 Hz. In earlier times, pitch standards have varied by as much as +/− a quarter (ie, by three semitones, see below).

Intervals

An interval in music is the difference in pitch between any two notes. The most fundamental pitch relationship, used in virtually all music and throughout documented history, is the octave (English terminology). This represents a doubling in the frequency of the sound vibrations, and can be achieved by halving the length of vibrating string or pipe, or by causing it to vibrate with a node (still point) at its mid-point.

Scales

The range of frequencies falling within the limits of any given octave is divided into a number of smaller steps, whose number and size varies. The two most familiar scales, on which all 16th–early 20th century Western music as well as popular music and jazz are based, are known as the major and minor scales. Both have eight steps (hence the expression octave), and most of the notes are common to both.

Much folk music is based on simpler, pentatonic, scales, which use only the five most important notes from the ordinary major scale, corresponding to the black notes on the piano (starting on F sharp).

Some non-Western cultures divide the octave into unequal or smaller steps in an extremely complex manner.

The steps used in Western scales were also originally uneven, and the frequency relationships rather complex, deriving from naturally occurring sounds (known as the notes of the harmonic series) arising in vibrating vessels, rather than by any scientific or theoretical process. The most important natural frequency relationship is 3:2 (approximately 1.5 octaves), when the vessel has two still points, the octave being generated with a single node, halfway along its length.

However, if a succession of notes is built up using the 3:2 ratio, they gradually diverge from; and thus become more out of tune from, those deriving from the octave ratio 2:1. In order to overcome the problem, at around the beginning of the 18th century theorists forced the complex relationships of naturally derived scales into a uniform pattern, by dividing each octave into 12 exactly equal intervals. Thus the frequency relationship of any note to the one immediately beneath it is 1.059, being the 12th root of 2.

This method of tuning, known as the equally tempered chromatic scale, is the one by which all modern pianos and orchestral instruments are tuned. It enables music to be played beginning on any note (ie, in any key), all sounding equally, but only very slightly, out of tune. (The ear more readily accepts the compromises involved here than under earlier tuning systems, where certain keys became painfully out of tune.)

Each interval of $\frac{1}{12}$ of an octave is known as a semitone, two adjacent semitones forming a tone. The 12 notes contained in the chromatic scale can be arranged to provide all the notes required to play music in any major or minor key. The eight steps of the scales, in ascending order, are made up of tones (*T*) and semitones (*S*) in the following order.

Major keys: *T–T–S–T–T–T–S*
Minor keys: *T–S–T–T–S–T–T*

The minor scale is actually more complicated than this, its exact form varying according to whether the melody is rising or falling, and is sometimes further dependent upon the underlying harmony.

The table lists the terms used to describe the intervals in Western musical scales.

Intervals greater than an octave are known as compound intervals, and use the same terminological convention; eg, an octave plus a minor third is known as a minor tenth, and comprises 15 semitones.

The frequency of any note can be calculated from any other given note (whether or not on the international pitch standard) by counting the number of semitones which separates them and applying the ratio 1.059 raised to the appropriate power. The frequency of notes which are an exact number of octaves

Intervals in Western musical scales

Interval	No. semitones	Pitch ratio	Note reached if counting upwards from C	Frequency (Hz)
Unison (same note)	0	1.000	C	261.63
Minor second	1	1.059	C sharp or D flat	277.18
Major second	2	1.122	D	293.66
Minor third	3	1.189	D sharp or E flat	311.13
Major third	4	1.260	E	329.63
Perfect fourth	5	1.335	F	349.23
Augmented fourth (or diminished fifth)	6	1.414	F sharp	369.99
Perfect fifth	7	1.498	G	392.00
Minor sixth	8	1.587	G sharp or A flat	415.30
Major sixth	9	1.682	A	440.00[a]
Minor seventh	10	1.782	A sharp or B flat	466.16
Major seventh	11	1.888	B	493.88
Octave	12	2.000	C	523.25

[a]International standard musical pitch.

apart can be calculated by applying whole number ratios as shown in the following table.

Ratio	Note	Frequency	Note	Frequency
1	C_0	16.35	A_0	27.5
2	C_1[a]	32.70	A_1	55
3	C_2	65.41	A_2	110
4	C_3	130.81	A_3	220
5	C_4[b]	261.63	A_4	440
6	C_5	523.25	A_5	880
7	C_6	1 046.50	A_6	1 760
8	C_7	2 093.00	A_7	3 520
9	C_8	4 185.01	A_8	7 040[c]
10	C_9	8 372.02	A_9	14 080
11	C_{10}	16 744.04	A_{10}	28 160[d]

[a]Lowest note on piano. [b]Middle C. [c]Highest note on piano.
[d]Inaudible.

For more complex tunings, the semitone is divided into 100 parts, known as cents. There are 1 200 cents to the octave. A savart is reckoned to be the smallest musical interval that the human ear is capable of distinguishing, and is equal to 4 cents. The term milloctave is also occasionally used, and is one thousandth of an octave.

Harmonics

The frequency of vibration of a string (the fundamental note) is determined by $f_a = T/(2 \times m \times h)$, where:

f_a = frequency
T = tension of the string
m = mass per unit length
h = length of string

Hence, if a string is dampened at a point $1/f$ of its length from a fixed end, the note emitted has a frequency f times that of the fundamental note; this is called the $(f-1)$th overtone or harmonic of the fundamental note. For example, where $f = 2$, the length of string is halved, and the frequency doubled.

Space, time and the Earth

SPACE

The solar system

	Distance from the sun AU	km (mn)	mi (mn)	Diameter (equatorial) relative to earth (=1)	km ('000)	mi ('000)	Mass (excl. satellites) relative to earth (=1)	kg	tons	Gravity relative to earth (=1)	m/s^2
Sun	0	0	0	109.00	1 392.140	865.040	332 946.040	1.989×10^{30}	1.958×10^{27}	28.00	274.0
Mercury	0.39	58	36	0.38	4.880	3.032	0.056	3.302×10^{23}	3.250×10^{21}	0.38	3.7
Venus	0.72	108	67	0.95	12.103	7.520	0.815	4.869×10^{24}	4.794×10^{21}	0.90	9.0
Earth	1	150[a]	93[a]	1	12.756	7.926	1	5.974×10^{24}	5.879×10^{21}	1	9.8
Moon	–	150	93	0.27	3.475	2.159	0.012	7.343×10^{22}	7.232×10^{19}	0.16	1.6
Mars	1.52	228	142	0.53	6.794	4.221	0.107	6.419×10^{23}	6.317×10^{20}	0.38	3.7
Jupiter	5.20	778	483	11.21	142.984	88.846	317.828	1.899×10^{27}	1.869×10^{24}	2.63	26.4
Saturn	9.54	1 429	888	9.45	120.536	74.898	95.161	5.685×10^{26}	5.595×10^{26}	1.14	11.4
Uranus	19.19	2 875	1 786	4.00	51.118	31.763	14.536	8.683×10^{25}	8.546×10^{22}	0.92	9.2
Neptune	30.07	4 504	2 798	3.89	49.600	30.820	17.132	1.023×10^{26}	1.007×10^{23}	1.15	11.8
Pluto	39.46	5 913	3 674	0.18	2.284	1.419	0.002	1.29×10^{22}	1.27×10^{19}	0.06	4.2

[a]Or 8.3 light minutes. Average distance; for the Earth the perihelion distance (at the point nearest to the sun) is 147.1×10^6 km $= 91.4 \times 10^6$ mi = 8.2 light minutes, and the aphelion distance (at the point farthest from the sun) is 153.1×10^6 km $= 95.1 \times 10^6$ mi = 8.5 light minutes.

By early 1991 61 satellites or moons had been discovered in the solar system orbiting the following planets.

Planet	No. moons	Planet	No. moons
Earth	1	Neptune	8
Jupiter	16	Pluto	1
Mars	2	Uranus	15

Diameters of largest moons (excl. Earth)

Name	Planet	km	mi
Ganymede	Jupiter	5 262	3 270
Titan	Saturn	5 150	3 200
Callisto	Jupiter	4 800	2 983
Io	Jupiter	3 642	2 263
Europa	Jupiter	3 138	1 950
Triton	Neptune	2 720	1 690
Titania	Uranus	1 578	980
Rhea	Saturn	1 528	949
Oberon	Uranus	1 523	946
Iapetus	Saturn	1 463	892
Chaxon	Pluto	1 192	741
Umbriel	Uranus	1 169	727

Measures

Newton's law of gravity: $F = Gm_1m_2/r^2$
where F is the force exerted by the masses m_1 and m_2 at a distance apart of r, and G = gravitational constant $= 6.672 \times 10^{-11}$ $m/kg/s^2$

Astronomical unit (AU) = mean sun to earth distance
= 149.597 9 mn kilometres (1.496×10^{11} m)
= approximately 92.956 mn miles
The above is the international value.

Parsec (pc or psc) = the distance at which 1 astronomical unit (AU) subtends an angle of 1 second of arc
= 206 265 AU
= approximately $3.085\,7 \times 10^{13}$ km
= approximately 1.917×10^{13} miles
= 3.26 light years, so no stars are as close as 1 parsec

Light (in a vacuum) travels at approx. 300 000 km/s (186 286 mi/s)

Light year = approximate distance travelled by light in 1 year
$= 9.460\,5 \times 10^{12}$ km
$= 5.875 \times 10^{12}$ miles

Light second $= 2.997\,9 \times 10^5$ km or approx. 300 000 km (186 286 mi)

Light minute $= 1.798\,8 \times 10^7$ km or approx. 18 000 000 km (11 177 0C

Light hour $= 1.079\,3 \times 10^9$ km or approx. 1 079 mn km (671 mn mi)

Solar energy. The photon energy from the sun's radiation is mainly in the wavelength range 300–2 700 nanometres ($3–27 \times 10^{-7}$ m) or $1 \times 10^{15}–1 \times 10^{14}$ hertz; ie, the visible light range and just into the infra-red range.

Energy radiated by the sun is equal to about 1 400 watts per square metre of cross section through which the rays pass; this is called the solar constant = 1 400 W/m^2 = 1.4 kW/m^2.

See also Electronics, page 71.

The universe

The limit of the observable universe is about $1.5–2 \times 10^{23}$ km or 15 000–20 000 mn light years. The mass of the observable universe is about 10^{23} solar masses or 10^{50} tonnes.

The farthest quasar yet detected, PKS 2000-300, is about 13 000 mn light years away.

The nearest star to the Earth, other than the sun, is Proxima Centauri which is about 4.3 light years away (4×10^{13} km).

TIME

Geological eras

The following table gives a broad outline of the main ages of the universe and the Earth.

Era, period, epoch	Years ago[a] (mn)	Characteristics
Origin of the universe (estimates vary)	20 000–10 000	
Origin of the sun	5 000	
Origin of the Earth	4 600	
Pre-Cambrian		
Archean	4 000	First signs of fossilised microbes
Proterozoic	2 500	
Palaeozoic		
Cambrian	570	First appearance of abundant fossils
Ordovician[b]	500	Vertebrates emerge
Silurian	440	Fishes emerge
Devonian	400	Primitive plants emerge
Carboniferous	350	Amphibians emerge
Permian	270	Reptiles emerge
Mesozoic		
Triassic	250	Seed plants emerge
Jurassic	210	Age of dinosaurs
Cretaceous	145	Flowering plants emerge; Dinosaurs extinct at end of this period
Cenozoic		
Palaeocene	65	
Tertiary: Eocene	55	Mammals emerge
Oligocene	40	
Miocene	25	
Pliocene	5	
Quaternary:		
Pleistocene or Glacial	2	Ice ages; stone age man emerges
Holocene or Recent	10 000[c]	Modern man emerges

[a]Year at beginning; all times are approximate. [b]Obsolete.
[c]10 000, not 10 000 mn.

Time scales

Several time scales are in use which are distinct but for many purposes interchangeable; the main scales are as follows.

Universal time (UT) is a time scale based on the rotation of the Earth about its axis, and is directly related to the alternation of day and night. 1200 UT is mean noon on the Greenwich meridian. Time scales for civil use must not drift in the long term relative to UT. The universal time calculated directly from immediately observed sidereal time (based on the rotation of the Earth) is denoted by UT0. For more precise work, UT0 is adjusted for observed polar motion and denoted by UT1; UT1 corrected for extrapolated seasonal variation in the rate of rotation of the Earth is denoted by UT2.

UT is now known to be very slightly irregular and unpredictable, so that other time scales described below are normally used in very precise work, unless rotation of the Earth is a factor – as, for example, in work by surveyors and astronomers.

The terms UT and universal time are sometimes used to mean UTC (see below).

Atomic time (TA) is any time scale formed by counting from some initial instant in SI seconds (ie, atomic seconds, as defined on **page 13**). International atomic time (TAI) is the atomic time scale recognised by the Conférence Générale des Poids et Mesures (CGPM) in 1971. It is formed by the Bureau International de l'Heure on the basis of atomic clock data contributed by establishments in many countries, and its unit is the SI second at sea level.

Coordinated universal time (UTC) is the time scale that is made available by radio signals. It was introduced in its present form on January 1st 1972 and was designed to make both UT1 and TAI accessible with appropriate accuracy. UTC differs from TAI by a whole number of exact seconds and never differs from UT1 by more than 0.9 seconds. The relationship with UT1 is maintained by inserting or deleting a leap-second in the UTC scale as the last second of a calendar month if astronomical observations show that one is needed. The decision to introduce a leap-second is taken by the Bureau International de l'Heure and is announced at least eight weeks in advance.

The CGPM recognised and recommended the use of UTC as the basis of national civil time scales in 1975.

Ephemeris time (ET) is a time scale determined from astronomical observations of the orbital motions of the Earth, moon and planets in the solar system. In the period 1960–67 the second was defined in terms of ephemeris time, which is more uniform than UT1, but less precise and less accessible than TA. The ephemeris second was defined as the fraction 1/31 556 925.974 7 of the tropical year for 1900, January 0 at

12 h ET. It is equal to 1/86 400 part of a day of that tropical year, which is defined as equal to 365.242 198 78 days, decreasing at the rate of 0.000 006 14 days per century (about 400 mn years ago there were about 400 days to the year). A tropical year is the time between two consecutive passages in the same direction of the sun through the Earth's equatorial plane. ET is not in general use.

Greenwich mean time (GMT) was the original basis for UT; it now usually means UTC. GMT has been the basis of legal time in the UK since 1880. Before 1925 0000 GMT meant Greenwich noon, but since then it has meant Greenwich midnight.

Time units

10 nanoseconds	= 1 shake
1 000 nanoseconds	= 1 microsecond
1 000 microseconds	= 1 millisecond
864 milliseconds (10^{-5} day)	= 1 blink
1 000 milliseconds	= 1 second
60 seconds	= 1 minute (min)
3 600 seconds	= 1 hour (h)
60 minutes	= 1 hour
86 400 seconds	= 1 day (d)
1 440 minutes	= 1 day
24 hours	= 1 day
604 800 seconds	= 1 week
10 080 minutes	= 1 week
168 hours	= 1 week
7 days	= 1 week
28 days	= 1 lunar month
28–31 days	= 1 calendar month[a]
31 556 925 seconds (approx.)	= 1 year
365 days	= 1 standard year
366 days	= 1 leap year
12 calendar months	= 1 calendar year
10 years	= 1 decade
25 years	= 1 generation
100 years	= 1 century
1 000 years	= 1 millennium
1 000 000 years	= 1 cron or aeon

[a] For calendar months in the Gregorian system, April, June, September and November have 30 days; all other months except February have 31 days. February has 28 days except in leap years, when it has 29.

For Christian years AD, a year is a leap year in the Gregorian calendar if its year number is divisible by 4 unless it is also divisible by 100 (ie, ends in 00); then it is only a leap year if divisible by 400.

Hourly time systems

24-hour	12-hour am	Marine watches (bells)	24-hour	12-hour pm	Marine watches (bells)
		Middle			Afternoon
0030	12.30	1	1230	12.30	1
0100	1.00	2	1300	1.00	2
0130	1.30	3	1330	1.30	3
0200	2.00	4	1400	2.00	4
0230	2.30	5	1430	2.30	5
0300	3.00	6	1500	3.00	6
0330	3.30	7	1530	3.30	7
0400	4.00	8	1600	4.00	8
		Morning			First dog
0430	4.30	1	1630	4.30	1
0500	5.00	2	1700	5.00	2
0530	5.30	3	1730	5.30	3
0600	6.00	4	1800	6.00	4
0630	6.30	5			Second dog
0700	7.00	6	1830	6.30	1
0730	7.30	7	1900	7.00	2
0800	8.00	8	1930	7.30	3
		Forenoon	2000	8.00	8
0830	8.30	1			First
0900	9.00	2	2030	8.30	1
0930	9.30	3	2100	9.00	2
1000	10.00	4	2130	9.30	3
1030	10.30	5	2200	10.00	4
1100	11.00	6	2230	10.30	5
1130	11.30	7	2300	11.00	6
1200	12.00 (noon)	8	2330	11.30	7
			2400 = 0000	12.00 (midnight)	8

Calendars

Roman, Julian and Gregorian calendars. The Roman calendar is usually taken as dating from 753 BC in terms of the Gregorian calendar, that being the date of the founding of Rome. The Julian calendar was established by Julius Caesar in the Roman year 707 (46 BC), the main feature being the insertion of an extra day every four years, to allow for the fact that every year has about 365.25 days, and not 365 days.

The Christian era numbering system was established about AD 525 (Roman year 1278). In this system the era begins with AD 1, the preceding year being 1 BC; there is no year 0 in the chronological reckoning, so the first century (100 years) ended on December 31st AD 100. According to this system, the century closes with the end of the year ending in 00, and not with the year ending in 99, so that the end of the 20th century would be December 31st 2000, and not December 31st 1999. That is the position for the Christian calendar; in general, common usage takes the position that the century ends on, for the above example, December 31st 1999, and that January 1st 2000 starts a new century – in the same way that common usage considers that the decade of the 1980s started on January 1st 1980. For astronomical purposes, the common sense view is taken, with the year before AD 1 being the year 0, and the year before that the year −1. Hence the year 1 BC = 0, 2 BC = −1, 2001 BC = −2000, etc.

The mean Julian calendar year was established as 365.25 days, whereas in fact the year is slightly less; using 365.25 days leads to an excess number of days amounting to about 3 days every 400 years. In 1582 Pope Gregory corrected this by establishing his calendar in which leap years occur in centurial years only where they are divisible by 400, instead of in every centurial year which was the position under the Julian calendar. Hence, leap years occur in the Gregorian calendar in

1600 and 2000, but not in 1700, 1800 and 1900, which were leap years under the Julian calendar. The reform consisted of changing October 5th 1582 to October 15th 1582, ie, losing 10 days. The British government changed to the Gregorian calendar in 1752, changing September 3rd 1752 to September 14th 1752, a loss of 11 days (there having been an extra day lost after 1582 in the year 1700, which was a leap year for the Julian calendar but not for the Gregorian).

To change from the Julian to the Gregorian calendar, 11 days should be added to the date from September 3rd 1752 up to February 28th 1800; 12 days up to February 28th 1900, and 13 days up to February 28th 2100 (2000 being a leap year in both systems).

Julian period. The Julian period lasts 7 980 years, being the common multiple of the 28-year solar cycle, 19-year lunar cycle, and 15-year cycle of indiction (a Roman accounting year). The Julian epoch began when all three cycles began together; this was established as 4713 BC, January 1st being day 0, and the count of days from Greenwich noon on that day ($0^d\ 12^h$) is known as a Julian day number (JD).

Some Julian day numbers[a]

Julian period	Julian calendar	Julian Day number (January 1)	Gregorian calendar	Julian Day number (January 1)
1	4713 BC	0		
2713	2001 BC	99 0558		
4613	101 BC	168 4533		
4713	1 BC	172 1058		
4714	1 AD	172 1424		
4813	100 AD	175 1058		
6213	1500 AD	226 8933	1500 AD	226 8924
6613	1900 AD	241 5033	1900 AD	241 5021
6713	2000 AD	245 1558	2000 AD	245 1545

[a]Day commencing at Greenwich noon.

Muslim. The *Hejira* calendar is used principally in Egypt, parts of India, Iran, Saudi Arabia, Malaysia, Turkey and some Arab states. It is based on lunar years beginning with the year of the *Hejira* (622 Julian calendar) when Mohammed travelled to Medina. The year consists of 12 months containing alternately 29 and 30 days with the intercalation of 1 day at the end of the 12th month in a leap year. Years run in cycles of 30, of which 19 are common (354 days) and 11 intercalary (known as *kabishah* – 355 days). To ascertain the type of year divide by 30; the quotient gives the number of completed cycles and the remainder shows the place of the year in the current cycle. The remainders 2, 5, 7, 10, 13, 16, 18, 21, 24, 26, 29 = leap (*kabishah*) years of 355 days. The names of the months are as follows.

Muharram	Rahab
Safar	Shaaban
Rabia I	Ramadan
Rabia II	Shawwal
Jumada I	Dhu al-Kadah
Jumada II	Dhu al-Hijah

Muslim years begin on the following dates of the Gregorian calendar (1993–96 are approximate).

1412 July 13th 1991	1415 June 9th 1994
1413 July 2nd 1992	1416 May 30th 1995
1414 June 20th 1993	1417 May 18th 1996

Jewish. A luni-solar calendar has been used by Jews from about 9 BCE based on biblical calculations that place creation in 3761 BC (954 Julian calendar). BCE = before common era; CE = common era; ie, BC and AD respectively. Complicated rules with regard to feasts and festivals resulted in a calendar scheme in which the Jewish year can be one of the following six types.

Year	No. days	Year	No. days
Minimal common	353	Minimal leap	383
Regular	354	Regular leap	384
Full common	355	Full leap	385

Regular years contain 29 and 30 days alternately. In full years (common or leap) Chesvan has 30 days instead of 29. A 13th month, called Ve-Adar (leap years) or Adar Sheni (other years), is intercalated into the calendar every 3rd, 6th, 8th, 11th, 14th, 17th and 19th year of the 19-year cycle. It contains all the religious observances that normally occur in Adar. When the two Adars occur they always contain 30 days, but this does not change the number of days in other months which follow the alternation of the normal 12.

The full leap year 5752 began on September 9th 1991 and the minimal common year 5753 on September 28th 1992.

Coptic. Used in Ethiopia and parts of Egypt, the Coptic calendar dates from August 29th 284 of the Gregorian calendar. Years contain 12 months of 30 days, plus 5 complementary days (6 in a leap year) in the last month.

Indian. The Saka (Hindu) calendar dates from March 3rd 78 of the Gregorian calendar. It is based on the solar year beginning with the spring equinox. Years contain 365 days (366 in leap years) divided into 12 months. The first 5 contain 31 days and the remaining 7 contain 30 days. In 1957 the Saka was declared the national calendar of India to run concurrently with the Gregorian.

Japanese. The Gregorian calendar is used in Japan but the numeration of years is based on imperial epochs. As the Gregorian calculates years from one religious date, the Japanese calendar calculates each epoch from the accession of the emperor. Each year of a period closes on December 31st. Months are not named but numbered; ie, first month = January.

Recent epochs	Start	End
Meiji	Oct 13th 1886	Jul 31st 1912
Taisho	Aug 1st 1912	Dec 25th 1926
Showa	Dec 26th 1926	Jan 7th 1989
Heisei	Jan 8th 1989	. . .

Heisei 4 began on January 1st 1992.

Main solar calendars

Gregorian	Hindu[a]
January (31)	
February (28 or 29)	
March (31)	Caitra (30)
April (30)	Vaisakha (31)
May (31)	Jyaistha (31)
June (30)	Asadha (31)
July (31)	Sravana (31)
August (31)	Bhadrapada (31)
September (30)	Asvina (30)
October (31)	Karttika (30)
November (30)	Margasirsa (30)
December (31)	Pausa (30)
(January)	Magha (30)
(February)	Phalguna (30)

Gregorian	Ethiopian[b]	Jewish[c]
September	Maskerem (30)	Tishri (30)
October	Tikimit (30)	Cheshvan (29 or 30)
November	Hidar (30)	Kislev (29 or 30)
December	Tahsas (30)	Tebet (29)
January	Tir (30)	Shebat (30)
February	Yekatit (30)	Adar (29)
March	Megabit (30)	Nisan (30)
April	Miazia (30)	Iyyar (29)
May	Guenbot (30)	Sivan (30)
June	Sene (30)	Tammuz (39)
July	Hamle (30)	Ab (30)
August	Nahassie (30+5 or 6)	Elul (29)

Note Figures in brackets denote the number of days in that month.
[a]Months begin about the 22nd of the corresponding Gregorian month. [b]Months begin about the 11th of the corresponding Gregorian month.
[c]The date of the new year varies, but normally falls in the second half of September in the Gregorian calendar.

Standard times

Since the Earth makes one complete revolution in 24 hours, 1 hour corresponds to a longitude of 360/24 = 15 degrees, and 30 minutes to 7.5 degrees.

Under the system of zone time, zones are established within which national standards are in general the same, and differ from other zones by 30 minutes or 1 hour; ideal time zones are centred on meridians at multiples of 15° east or west of Greenwich. Since the apparent motion of the sun is from east to west, time in zones east of Greenwich is ahead of (a later time than) Greenwich Mean Time (GMT) and in zones west of Greenwich it is behind (an earlier time than) GMT. At longitude 180° E or W of Greenwich there is a time difference of 1 day on either side of the line. An international date line is established defining the day to which countries near the line adhere; the date line does not keep to the 180° line exactly but varies to include, for example, Tonga, which then has a time 13 hours ahead of GMT. In the following list countries and areas are shown with standard times fast (+) or slow (−) in hours on GMT. In the list the hour is marked with an asterisk (*) where summer time is generally kept (usually 1 hour in advance of standard time).

See map (page 137) for date line and time zones.

Afghanistan	+4½
Albania	+1*
Algeria	+1
Andaman Islands	+5½
Andorra	+1*
Angola	+1
Antigua	−4
Argentina	−3*
Aruba	−4
Ascension Island	GMT
Australia:	
Canberra, New South Wales[a], Queensland, Tasmania, Victoria	+10*
South Australia	+9½*
Northern Territory	+9½
Western Australia	+8
Austria	+1*
Azores	−1*
Bahamas	−5*
Bahrain	+3
Balearic Islands	+1*
Bangladesh	+6
Barbados	−4
Belgium	+1*
Belize	−6
Benin	+1
Bermuda	−4*
Bhutan	+6
Bolivia	−4
Botswana	+2
Brazil:	
Fernando de Noronha	−2*
East[b], Brasilia	−3*
West	−4*
Acre	−5*
British Indian Ocean Territory	+5
Brunei	+8
Bulgaria	+2*
Burma: see Myanmar	
Burkina Faso	GMT
Burundi	+2
Cambodia	+7
Cameroon	+1
Canada[c]:	
Newfoundland	−3½*
Atlantic: Labrador, New Brunswick, Nova Scotia, Prince Edward Is., Quebec (East of Pte des Monts)	−4*
Eastern: North West Territory (East), Ontario, Ottawa, Quebec (West of Pte des Monts)	−5*
Central: Manitoba, North-West Territory (Central), Saskatchewan (East)	−6*
Mountain: Alberta, North-West Territory (Mountain), Saskatchewan (West)	−7*
Pacific: British Columbia, Yukon	−8*
Canary Islands	GMT*
Cape Verde	−1
Cayman Islands	−5
Central African Republic	+1
Chad	+1
Channel Islands	GMT*
Chile	−4*
China	+8*
Christmas Island	+7
Cocos-Keeling Islands	+6½
Colombia	−5
Commonwealth of Independent States (CIS): see Soviet Union	
Comoros	+3
Congo	+1
Cook Islands	−10½
Costa Rica	−6
Côte d'Ivoire	GMT
Cuba	−5*
Cyprus	+2*
Czechoslovakia	+1*
Denmark	+1*
Djibouti	+3
Dominica	−4*
Dominican Republic	−4
Ecuador[d]	−5
Egypt	+2*
El Salvador	−6*
Equatorial Guinea	+1
Estonia	+2
Ethiopia	+3
Falkland Islands[e]	−4
Faroe Islands	GMT
Fiji	+12
Finland	+2*
France	+1*
Gabon	+1

Gambia	GMT
Germany	+1*
Ghana	GMT
Gibraltar	+1*
Greece	+2*
Greenland:	
Scoresby Sound	−1*
Angmagssalik, West Coast except Thule	−3*
Thule area	−4
Grenada	−4
Guadeloupe	−4
Guam	+10
Guatemala	−6
Guiana, French	−3
Guinea	GMT
Guinea-Bissau	GMT
Guyana	−3
Haiti	−5*
Honduras	−6
Hong Kong	+8
Hungary	+1*
Iceland	GMT
India	$+5\frac{1}{2}$
Indonesia	
Western: Java, Sumatra, Bali, Bangka, Billiton, Madura	+7
Central: Kalimantan, Sulawesi, Flores, Soembawa, Soemba, Timor, Lombok	+8
Eastern: Molucca Islands, Tanimbar, Kai, Aroe, West Irian	+9
Iran	$+3\frac{1}{2}$*
Iraq	+3*
Ireland	GMT*
Israel	+2*
Italy	+1*
Jamaica	−5*
Japan	+9
Jordan	+2*
Kenya	+3
Kiribati:	
Ocean Island	$+11\frac{1}{2}$
Gilbert Islands	+12
Phoenix Islands	−11
Line Islands	−10
Korea, North	+9
Korea, South	+9
Kuwait	+3
Laos	+7
Latvia	+2
Lebanon	+2*
Lesotho	+2
Liberia	GMT
Libya	+1*
Liechtenstein	+1*
Lithuania	+2
Luxembourg	+1*
Macao	+8
Madagascar	+3
Madeira	GMT*
Malawi	+2
Malaysia	+8
Maldives	+5
Mali	GMT
Malta	+1*
Martinique	−4
Mauritania	GMT
Mauritius	+4
Mexico:	
Mexico City	−6
Baja California Sur, Sonara, Sinaloa, Nayarit	−7
Baja California Norte	−8*
Midway Islands	−11
Monaco	+1*
Mongolia	+8*
Montserrat	−4
Morocco	GMT*
Mozambique	+2
Myanmar	$+6\frac{1}{2}$
Namibia	+2
Nauru	+1
Nepal	$+5\frac{3}{4}$
Netherlands	+1*
Netherlands Antilles	−4
New Caledonia	+11
New Zealand	+12*
Nicaragua	−6
Niger	+1
Nigeria	+1
Niue	−11
Norfolk Island	$+11\frac{1}{2}$
Norway	+1*
Oman	+4
Pacific Islands, US:	
Northern Marianas, Western Caroline Islands	+10
Truk Island	+11
Eastern Caroline Islands, Marshall Islands	+12
Pakistan	+5
Panama	−5
Papua New Guinea	+10
Paraguay	−4*
Peru	−5*
Philippines	+8
Pitcairn Islands	$-8\frac{1}{2}$
Poland	+1*
Polynesia, French	−10
Portugal	GMT*
Puerto Rico	−4
Qatar	+3
Réunion	+4
Romania	+2*
Rwanda	+2
St Christopher and Nevis	−4
St Helena	GMT
St Lucia	−4
St Pierre and Miquelon	−3*
St Vincent and The Grenadines	−4
Samoa, US	−11
Samoa, Western	−11
San Marino	+1*
São Tomé and Principe	GMT
Saudi Arabia	+3
Senegal	GMT
Seychelles	+4
Sierra Leone	GMT
Singapore	+8
Solomon Islands	+11
Somalia	+3
South Africa	+2
Soviet Union (former) (chief towns):	
Kiev, St Petersburg, Moscow, Odessa	+3*
Archangel, Volgograd, Tiflis	+4
Ashkhabad, Sverdlovsk	+5
Alma-Ata, Karaganda, Omsk	+6*
Novosibirsk, Krasnoyarsk	+7
Irkutsk	+8
Yakutsk	+9
Khabarovsk, Vladivostok	+10*
Magadan, Yuzhno-Sakhalinsk (Sakhalin Island)	+11
Petropavlovsk-Kamchatskiy	+12
Anadyr	+12*
Spain	+1*
Sri Lanka	$+5\frac{1}{2}$
Sudan	+2
Surinam	−3
Swaziland	+2
Sweden	+1*
Switzerland	+1*
Syria	+2*
Taiwan	+8
Tanzania	+3
Thailand	+7
Timor, East	+8
Togo	GMT
Tonga	+13
Trinidad and Tobago	−4
Tunisia	+1*
Turkey	+2*
Turks and Caicos Islands	−5*
Tuvalu	+12
Uganda	+3
United Arab Emirates	+4
UK	GMT*
USA:	
Eastern: Connecticut, Delaware, District of Columbia (Washington), Indiana, Florida, Georgia, Maine, Maryland, Massachusetts, Michigan, New Hampshire, New Jersey, New York, North Carolina, Ohio, Pennsylvania, Rhode Island, South Carolina, Vermont, Virginia, West Virginia	−5*
Central: Alabama, Arkansas, Illinois, Iowa, Kansas, Kentucky, Louisiana, Minnesota, Mississippi, Missouri, Nebraska, North Dakota, Oklahoma, South Dakota, Tennessee, Texas, Wisconsin	−6*
Mountain: Arizona[f], Colorado, Idaho, Montana, New Mexico, Utah, Wyoming	−7
Pacific: California, Nevada, Oregon, Washington State	−8*
Alaska:	
Ketchikan to Skagway	−8*
Skagway to 141° West long.	−9*
141° West long. to 162° West long.	−10
162° West long. to Hawaii	−10
Westernmost point	−11*
Uruguay	−3*
Vanuatu	+11*
Vatican	+1*
Venezuela	−4
Vietnam	+7
Virgin Islands, British and US	−4
Wallis and Futuna Islands	+12
Yemen	+3
Yugoslavia	+1*
Zaire:	
Kinshasa	+1
Shaba	+2
Zambia	+2
Zimbabwe	+2

[a]Except Lord Howe Island: $10\frac{1}{2}$ (summer time as rest of NSW). [b]Including all the coast. [c]Summer time (daylight saving time) is at the discretion of individual provinces and cities. [d]Except Galapagos Islands: −6. [e]Summer time is used in Port Stanley. [f]Does not keep summer time.

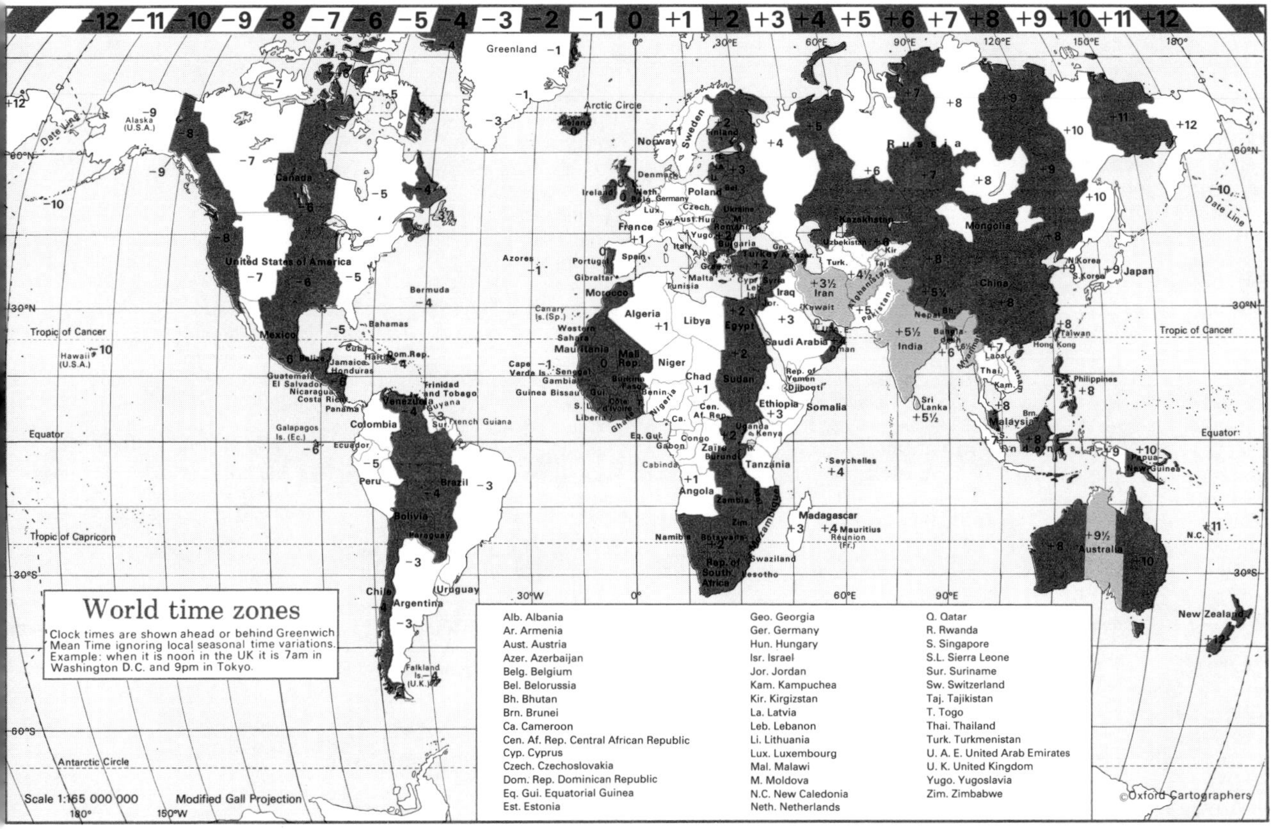

THE EARTH

Measures

Circumference

	km	mi
At equator	40 075	24 902
At poles	40 008	24 860

Diameter

	km	mi
At equator	12 756	7 926
At poles	12 713	7 899

Length of 1° of latitude or longitude (1/360 of circumference)

	km	mi	nautical mi (international)
Latitude			
0° (equator)	110.57	68.70	59.70
45°	111.13	69.05	60.01
90° (poles)	111.70	69.41	60.31

	km	mi	nautical mi (international)
Longitude at latitude of:			
0	111.32	69.17	60.11
5	110.90	68.91	59.88
10	109.64	68.13	59.20
15	107.55	66.83	58.07
20	104.65	65.03	56.51
25	100.95	62.73	54.51
30	96.49	59.60	52.10
35	91.29	56.72	49.29
40	85.40	53.06	46.11
45	78.85	48.99	42.58
50	71.70	44.55	38.71
55	64.00	39.77	34.56
60	55.80	34.67	30.13
65	47.18	29.31	25.47
70	38.19	23.73	20.62
75	28.90	17.96	15.61
80	19.39	12.05	10.47
85	9.74	6.05	5.26
90	0.00	0.00	0.00

Structure
Volume: 1.08×10^{21} m^3 = 1.41×10^{21} yd^3
Density: 5 520 kg/m^3 = relative density of 5.5
Mass: 5.974×10^{21} tonnes
Atmosphere: weighs 5.24×10^{15} tonnes
= 0.000 09% of total mass
Density increases as the Earth picks up cosmic dust; estimates vary widely: upper limit = 30 000 tonnes/year
Greatest height: Mt Everest = 8 863 m = 29 078 ft
Greatest depth: Marianas Trench = 11 002 m = 36 160 ft

Surface area

	km^2 (mn)	mi^2 (mn)		km^2 (mn)	mi^2 (mn)
The Earth	510.07	196.94	**Main land areas**		
of which: water	361.64	139.63	Asia	44.03	17.00
land	148.43	57.31	Africa	30.26	11.68
			America: North	24.19	9.34
Main seas			South	17.82	6.88
Pacific	166.24	64.19	Antarctica	13.21	5.10
Atlantic	86.56	33.42	Europe	10.40	4.02
Indian	73.43	28.35	Australia	7.69	2.97
Arctic	13.23	5.11			

Velocity
Average speed in orbit around the sun
= 29.78 km/s
= 18.5 mile/s
= 66 600 miles per hour
Escape speed at surface = 11.2 km/s
= 7.0 mile/s
= 25 200 miles per hour
Rotational speed at equator = 0.465 km/s
= 0.29 mile/s
= 1 670 km per hour
= 1 040 miles per hour

Moon
Average distance from Earth = 0.002 57 AU
= 384 000 km
= 239 000 mi
= 1.28 light seconds
At the mean perigee (nearest point) the distance is 363 000 km = 227 700 mi; at the mean apogee (farthest point) the distance is 405 500 km = 252 000 mi.

Atmosphere

The atmosphere is the gaseous envelope surrounding the Earth which protects it from excessive radiation and cosmic particles. It is important in maintaining the Earth's heat balance. The lower atmosphere is composed of the gases listed in the following table together with various amounts of water vapour.

Gas	% by volume
Nitrogen (N_2)	78.084
Oxygen (O_2)	20.946
Argon (Ar)	0.934
Carbon dioxide (CO_2)	0.033
Neon (Ne)	0.001 82
Helium (He)	0.000 53
Krypton (Kr)	0.000 12
Xenon (Xe)	0.000 09
Hydrogen (H_2)	0.000 05
Methane (CH_4)	0.000 02
Nitrous oxide (N_2O)	0.000 05
Ozone (O_3)	0–0.000 007 (summer)
	0–0.000 002 (winter)
Sulphur dioxide (SO_2)	0–0.000 1
Nitrogen dioxide (NO_2)	0–0.000 002
Ammonia (NH_3)	0–trace
Carbon monoxide (CO)	0–trace
Iodine (I_2)	0–0.000 001

Some of the sea-level values of the ICAO Standard Atmosphere are as follows.

	Metric	UK (Imperial) equivalent
Temperature	288.15 K (15°C)	518.67°R (59°F)
Pressure	1 013.25 millibars	2 116 lbf/ft^2
Gravitational acceleration	9.806 65 m/s^2	32.174 ft/s^2
Density	1.225 0 kg/m^3	0.076 474 lb/ft^3
Viscosity:		
dynamic	$1.789\,4 \times 10^{-5}$ kg m^{-1} s^{-1}	$1.202\,4 \times 10^{-5}$ lb ft^{-1} s^{-1}
kinematic	$1.460\,7 \times 10^{-5}$ m^2/s	$1.572\,3 \times 10^{-4}$ ft^2/s
Particle speed	458.94 m/s	1 505.7 ft/s
Speed of sound	340.294 m/s	1 116.45 ft/s

The following layers make up the ionosphere, which is the region of the upper atmosphere that includes the highly ionised Appleton and Kennelly-Heaviside layers.

- Troposphere: lowest layer whose thickness varies by approx. 7–16 km above the equator; air temperature gradually decreases with height. The boundary between the troposphere and the stratosphere is called the tropopause which is about 16 km above the equator, 11 km above 50° and 9 km above the poles.
- Stratosphere: 16–50 km; air temperature fairly constant.
- Mesosphere: 50–85 km; air temperature decreases with height.
- Thermosphere: 86–700 km; air temperature increases with height.

The outermost layer, from approx. 700 km, is called the exosphere.

Ozone layer (ozonosphere). The zone in the upper atmosphere in which gas ozone (triatomic oxygen – O_3) forms in its greatest concentrations. Generally 10–50 km above the surface, it protects the Earth from excessive ultraviolet radiation. The current thinning of the ozone layer is caused by highly stable synthetic chemicals (products of the petrochemical industry including chlorofluorocarbons – CFCs) rising into the atmosphere and partly decomposing into methyl chloroform and carbon tetrachloride which destroy the ozone molecules. This causes the temperature of the Earth to rise.

The greenhouse effect. The Earth's temperature has increased by 0.5°C (0.9°F) since records began in 1860. However, it is the rate of temperature change – now faster than at any time in the past – that is causing concern. This trend is called global warming.

The main reason for the greenhouse effect is a significant increase in so-called greenhouse gases such as carbon dioxide (CO_2), methane (CH_4), nitrous oxide (N_2O), chlorofluorocarbons (CFCs) and, most recently, benzene (C_6H_6; symbol not usually used). These restrict the loss of long-wave radiation and cause the atmosphere to warm.

The amount of CO_2 in the atmosphere has increased by 28%, from 265 parts per million (ppm) in 1850 to 340 ppm by 1987; it is expected to rise to 600 ppm by 2050. CO_2 is currently responsible for 57% of the global warming trend, with 80% of the gas coming from the burning of fossil fuels.

Relative contributions to greenhouse effect

Gas	%
Carbon dioxide	50
Methane	18
CFCS	14
Surface ozone	12
Nitrous oxide	6

Global warming is a controversial subject and there is considerable disagreement as to its extent and severity. However, in 1987 the developed countries reached agreement with the developing countries on the use of CFCs and halons (haloginated aliphatic hydrocarbons used in fire-fighting). The Montreal Protocol stated that their use should be restricted to 1986 levels by 1992. By July 1990 scientific evidence showed these levels to be insufficient and the figures were revised as follows.

- CFCs: 50% reduction by 1995, 85% by 1997, total ban by 2000.
- Halons: total ban by 2000.

Other air pollutants include sulphur dioxide (SO_2) – the principle component of acid rain – carbon monoxide (CO) and lead compounds.

Air density

The following tables show the variation in air density with varying air pressure and temperature, and with varying altitude.

Density for different pressures and temperatures[a]

Air pressure (kPa = 10 mb)	Air temperature (°C) 10 kg/m³	20 kg/m³	30 kg/m³
95	1.167	1.124	1.083
96	1.179	1.136	1.094
97	1.191	1.148	1.106
98	1.203	1.160	1.117
99	1.216	1.172	1.129
100	1.228	1.184	1.140
101	1.240	1.196	1.152
102	1.253	1.207	1.163
103	1.265	1.219	1.175
104	1.277	1.231	1.186
105	1.290	1.243	1.198

[a]In typical laboratory air with 50% humidity.

Density and pressure for varying altitudes[a]

Altitude	Pressure (kPa)	Density (kg/m³)
metres		
−250	104.3	1.255
−100	102.5	1.237
−50	101.9	1.231
0 (sea level)	101.3	1.225
50	100.7	1.219
100	100.1	1.213
250	98.4	1.196
500	95.5	1.167
750 (0.75 km)	92.6	1.139
kilometres		
1	89.9	1.112
2.5	74.7	0.957
5	54.0	0.736
7.5	38.3	0.557
10	26.5	0.414
20	5.5	0.089
30	1.2	0.018
40	0.3	0.004
50	0.1	0.001

[a]For a standard atmosphere.

Gravity variation

The internationally agreed standard value for gravity on Earth (g_n), 9.806 65 metres per second per second, is the acceleration of a freely falling body on to the rotating earth; it is the value which approximates to that applying at 45° latitude. Actual gravity values vary according to latitude, altitude, etc. For Greenwich the approximate value is 9.811 88 m/s² (local gravity or g_L). Variations need to be allowed for where accuracy is required; eg, for barometers or "weighing" machines (which measure the effect of gravitational force on mass).

The following table gives a standard set of variations by latitude and altitude (height above sea level); actual gravities will vary according to local geological conditions, so this table is approximate.

Latitude (°)	Altitude (m) 0 m/s²	500 m/s²	1 000 m/s²	10 000 m/s²	20 000 m/s²	30 000 m/s²
0	9.7805	9.7789	9.7774	9.7496	9.7188	9.6879
5	9.7809	9.7793	9.7778	9.7500	9.7192	9.6883
10	9.7820	9.7805	9.7790	9.7512	9.7203	9.6895
15	9.7840	9.7824	9.7809	9.7531	9.7222	9.6914
20	9.7865	9.7850	9.7835	9.7557	9.7248	9.6940
25	9.7897	9.7882	9.7866	9.7589	9.7280	9.6971
30	9.7934	9.7919	9.7903	9.7626	9.7317	9.7008
35	9.7975	9.7960	9.7944	9.7666	9.7358	9.7049
40	9.8018	9.8003	9.7987	9.7709	9.7401	9.7092
41	9.8027	9.8011	9.7996	9.7718	9.7410	9,7101
42	9.8036	9.8020	9.8005	9.7727	9.7419	9.7110
43	9.8045	9.8029	9.8014	9.7736	9.7428	9.7119
44	9.8054	9.8038	9.8023	9.7745	9.7437	9.7128
45	9.8063	9.8047	9.8032	9.7754	9.7446	9.7137
46	9.8072	9.8056	9.8041	9.7763	9.7455	9.7146
47	9.8081	9.8066	9.8050	9.7772	9.7464	9.7155
48	9.8090	9.8075	9.8059	9.7781	9.7473	9.7164
49	9.8099	9.8083	9.8068	9.7790	9.7482	9.7173
50	9.8108	9.8092	9.8077	9.7799	9.7491	9.7182
51	9.8117	9.8101	9.8086	9.7808	9.7499	9.7191
52	9.8125	9.8110	0.8095	9.7817	9.7508	9.7200
53	9.8134	9.8119	9.8103	9.7826	9.7517	9.7208
54	9.8143	9.8127	9.8112	9.7834	9.7526	9.7217
55	9.8151	9.8136	9.8120	9.7843	9.7534	9.7226
60	9.8192	9.8177	9.8161	9.7884	9.7575	9.7266
65	9.8230	9.8214	9.8199	9.7921	9.7613	9.7304
70	9.8262	9.8246	9.8231	9.7953	9.7644	9.7336
75	9.8287	9.8272	9.8257	9.7979	9.7670	9.7362
80	9.8307	9.8291	9.8276	9.7998	9.7689	9.7381
85	9.8318	9.8303	9.8287	9.8010	9.7701	9.7392
90	9.8322	9.8307	9.8291	9.8013	9.7705	9.7396

The % correction for divergence from standard gravity is then as shown in the following table.

Latitude (°)	Altitude (m) 0 %	500 %	1 000 %	10 000 %	20 000 %	30 000 %
0	−0.27	−0.28	−0.30	−0.58	−0.90	−1.21
5	−0.26	−0.28	−0.29	−0.58	−0.89	−1.21
10	−0.25	−0.27	−0.28	−0.57	−0.88	−1.19
15	−0.23	−0.25	−0.26	−0.55	−0.86	−1.18
20	−0.21	−0.22	−0.24	−0.52	−0.83	−1.15
25	−0.17	−0.19	−0.20	−0.49	−0.80	−1.12
30	−0.13	−0.15	−0.17	−0.45	−0.76	−1.08
35	−0.09	−0.11	−0.12	−0.41	−0.72	−1.04
40	−0.05	−0.07	−0.08	−0.36	−0.68	−0.99
41	−0.04	−0.06	−0.07	−0.36	−0.67	−0.98
42	−0.03	−0.05	−0.06	−0.35	−0.66	−0.98
43	−0.02	−0.04	−0.05	−0.34	−0.65	−0.97
44	−0.01	−0.03	−0.04	−0.33	−0.64	−0.96
45	0.00	−0.02	−0.04	−0.32	−0.63	−0.95
46	0.01	−0.01	−0.03	−0.31	−0.62	−0.94
47	0.01	0.00	−0.02	−0.30	−0.61	−0.93
48	0.02	0.01	−0.01	−0.29	−0.61	−0.92
49	0.03	0.02	0.00	−0.28	−0.60	−0.91
50	0.04	0.03	0.01	−0.27	−0.59	−0.90
51	0.05	0.04	0.02	−0.26	−0.58	−0.89
52	0.06	0.04	0.03	−0.25	−0.57	−0.88
53	0.07	0.05	0.04	−0.25	−0.56	−0.88
54	0.08	0.06	0.05	−0.24	−0.55	−0.87
55	0.09	0.07	0.06	−0.23	−0.54	−0.86
60	0.13	0.11	0.10	−0.19	−0.50	−0.82
65	0.17	0.15	0.13	−0.15	−0.46	−0.78
70	0.20	0.18	0.17	−0.12	−0.45	−0.75
75	0.23	0.21	0.19	−0.09	−0.40	−0.72
80	0.24	0.23	0.21	−0.07	−0.38	−0.70
85	0.26	0.24	0.23	−0.06	−0.37	−0.69
90	0.26	0.24	0.23	−0.05	−0.37	−0.68

Temperature

Temperature intervals
kelvin (K) = degree Celsius (°C) or centigrade
degree Rankine (°R) = degree Fahrenheit (°F)

Temperature scales. The thermodynamic scales of kelvin and Rankine are fixed such that the zero on the scale is the theoretical zero of temperature (absolute zero); this is the level at which any gas would theoretically be reduced to zero volume – since gases at constant pressure lose approximately 0.004 of their volume at 0°C for each fall of 1°C in their temperature.

Where K, °C, °R, °F refer to temperatures on their scales:

°C = K − 273.15 K = °C + 273.15
°F = °R − 459.67 °R = °F + 459.67
°C = 0.56(°F − 32) °F = 1.8°C + 32
K = 0.56°R °R = 1.8 K

Some notable temperatures

	°C	°F	K	°R
Theoretical zero	−273.15	−459.67	0.00	0.00
Space	−270.00	−454.00	3.00	5.00
Ice point of water	0.00	32.00	273.15	491.67
Triple point of water	0.01	32.02	273.16	491.69
Atmosphere:				
FAO reference	10.00	50.00	283.15	509.67
ICAO	15.00	59.00	288.15	518.67
Fine summer day (UK)	20.00	68.00	293.15	527.67
Blood, human	37.00	98.60	310.15	558.27
Boiling point of water	100.00	212.00	373.15	671.67
White heat (approx.)	1 300.00	2 370.00	1 570.00	2 830.00

Standard temperature and pressure (stp) is 0°C and 1.013 25 bar.

Curie point (or Curie temperature) is the temperature at which ferromagnetic material loses its magnetism (becomes paramagnetic); this varies according to the mixture of metals.

Degree days. A degree day usually means a period of 24 hours during which the outside temperature is 1 degree below an accepted base. In the UK the base outside temperature is 15.5°C (60°F approx.); this is considered consistent with an inside temperature of 18.3°C (65°F) – comfortable for normal domestic purposes – the difference being made up by other heat sources such as people, lights, cooking applicances, etc. In New York the base used is 20.6°C (69°F).

Hence, for the UK 1 degree day = a 24-hour period during which the outside temperature is at an average of 14.5°C compared with the base of 15.5°C. Official figures are published for the UK for different regions on a monthly basis. For example, if for December 1991 the number of degree days was 280 for south-east England, the average would be 9 degrees below the base per day (the month being 31 days). This is equivalent to a temperature of approx. 6°C, compared with a usual average daily temperature for December of approx. 5°C.

Wind speed

Beaufort scale. Consists of numbers 0–17 each representing a certain strength or velocity of wind at 10 m (33 ft) above ground in the open.

The Beaufort scale is related to wind speed by the formula $v = kN^1$, where

v = average wind speed
N = Beaufort number
k = 3.0 for kilometres per hour, 0.83 for metres per second, and 1.87 for miles per hour

General scale

Force	Description	Conditions[a] on land	at sea	Equivalent speed at 10 m height km/h	knots	mph
0	Calm	Smoke rises vertically	Sea like a mirror	0–2	0–1	0–1
1	Light air	Smoke drifts	Ripples	2–5	1–3	1–3
2	Light breeze	Leaves rustle	Small wavelets	6–11	4–6	4–7
3	Gentle breeze	Wind extends light flag	Large wavelets, crests break	12–19	7–10	8–12
4	Moderate breeze	Raises paper and dust	Small waves, some white horses	20–29	11–16	13–18
5	Fresh breeze	Small trees in leaf sway	Moderate waves, many white horses	30–39	17–21	19–24
6	Strong breeze	Large branches in motion	Large waves form, some spray	40–50	22–27	25–31
7	Near gale	Whole trees in motion	Sea heaps up, white foam streaks	51–61	28–33	32–38
8	Gale	Breaks twigs off trees	Moderately high waves, well-marked foam streaks	62–74	34–40	39–46
9	Strong gale	Slight structural damage	High waves, crests start to tumble over	75–87	41–47	47–54
10	Storm	Trees uprooted, considerable structural damage	Very high waves, white sea tumbles	88–101	48–55	55–63
11	Violent storm	Very rarely exprienced, widespread damage	Exceptionally high waves, edges of wave crests blow to froth	102–117	56–63	64–73
12	Hurricane	–	Sea completely white with driving spray	118–132	64–71	74–82
13[b]	–	–	–	133–148	72–80	83–92
14	–	–	–	149–166	81–89	93–103
15	–	–	–	167–184	90–99	104–114
16	–	–	–	185–201	100–108	115–125
17	–	–	–	202–219	109–118	126–136

[a]Abbreviated. [b]13–17 added in 1955 by US Weather Bureau but not in international use since they are regarded as impractical.

Revised scale[a]

Force	m/s interval	mean	Force	m/s interval	mean	Force	m/s interval	mean	Force	m/s interval	mean
0	0–1.3	0.8	4	6.7–8.9	7.8	8	16.5–19.2	17.8	12	30.1 and over	32.2
1	1.4–2.7	2.0	5	9.0–11.3	10.2	9	19.3–22.4	20.8			
2	2.8–4.5	3.6	6	11.4–13.8	12.6	10	22.5–26.0	24.2			
3	4.6–6.6	5.6	7	13.9–16.4	15.1	11	26.1–30.0	28.0			

[a]As used in the climatological summaries of the WMO (World Meteorological Organisation) Historical Sea Surface Temperature Data Project.

Wave height

The approximate height of average waves for different strengths of wind is shown in the following table, which indicates for each wind strength the average wave height and the likely maximum wave height.

Beaufort scale force	Height of waves m average	m maximum	ft average	ft maximum
0	0	0	0	0
1	0.1	0.1	0.25	0.25
2	0.2	0.3	0.5	1.0
3	0.6	1.0	2.0	3.0
4	1.0	1.5	3.5	5.0
5	2.0	2.5	6.0	8.5
6	3.0	4.0	9.5	13.0
7	4.0	5.5	13.5	19.0
8	5.5	7.5	18.0	25.0
9	7.0	10.0	23.0	32.0
10	9.0	12.5	29.0	41.0
11	11.5	16.0	37.0	52.0
12	>14[a]		>45[a]	

[a]For the North Sea, wave heights can reach 17–30 m (55–100 ft); in general, the maximum height is reached once in 50 years (30 m is a "50 year wave").

Earthquake measurement

The Richter scale defines the magnitude of an earthquake in terms of the energy released; this has usually been measured by means of a seismometer which determines the amplitude of the seismic waves resulting from an earthquake. The Richter scale was first formulated in 1935 and there have been subsequent revisions; the main types are as follows.

- Local magnitude scale (M_L)
- Surface-wave magnitude scale (M_S)
- Body-wave magnitude scale (M_b)

Of these the surface-wave scale has been the most generally used.

One estimate of the energy equivalents of the Richter scale, showing also the equivalent in terms of explosions, is given in the following table.

Scale	Joules[a]	Explosion equivalent TNT terms[b]	Nuclear weapon terms[c]
0[d]	7.9×10^2	175 mg	
1	6.0×10^4	13 g	
2	4.0×10^6	0.89 kg	
3	2.4×10^8	53 kg	
4	1.3×10^{10}	3 tons	
5[e]	6.3×10^{11}	140 tons	
6[f]	2.7×10^{13}	6 kilotons	$ atomic bomb
7	1.1×10^{15}	240 kilotons	12 atomic bombs
8	3.7×10^{16}	8) megatons	$ hydrogen bomb
9	1.1×10^{18}	250 megatons	13 hydrogen bombs
10	3.2×10^{19}	7 000 megatons	350 hydrogen bombs

[a]Using the approx. relationship $\log_{10}(J \times 10^7) = 9.9 + 1.9\,M - 0.024\,M^2$ where M is the scale number and J is the energy in joules. Other formulae used to give the energy relationship are: $\log_{10}(J \times 10^7) = 1.5\,M + 11.8$ and $\log_{10}(J \times 10^7) = 2.4\,M - 1.2$. [b]Using the standard that 1 kg of TNT produces 4.5×10^6 J. [c]One atomic bomb is equivalent to 6.3 on the Richter scale, and one hydrogen bomb to 8.2. [d]Approximately equivalent to the shock caused by an average man jumping from a table; negative values on the Richter scale are possible (for energy less than 7.9×10^2 J). [e]Potentially damaging to structures. [f]Potentially capable of general destruction; widespread damage is usually caused above magnitude 6.5.

Examples of earthquake magnitudes

Place	Year	Richter scale (surface-wave or M_S scale)[a]
UK	1984	5.5
Armenia	1989	6.9
San Francisco	1989	7.1
Japan	1983	7.7
Iran	1978	7.7
Mexico City	1985	8.1
San Francisco	1906	8.3
Chile	1960	8.3
Alaska	1964	8.4
Soviet Union	1952	8.5
Colombia	1906	8.6
Krakatoa	1883	9.9[b]

[a]Another magnitude scale, the seismic moment scale (M_0) was introduced in the late 1970s. This measures directly the energy of an earthquake in terms of the area of the fault, the average displacement on the fault, and the shear strength of the faulted rock. With this new scale, the Chile 1960 earthquake is rated 9.5, the Alaska 1964 earthquake 9.2, and the Colombia 1906 earthquake 8.8. [b]Estimate.

The frequency of occurrence of large earthquakes throughout the world is approximately as follows.

Richter scale	No. earthquakes per year
6.0–6.9	266
7.0–7.9	18
8.0–8.9	1.5

Mercalli scale. The effect of any earthquake depends not only on its magnitude as measured by the Richter scale, but also on the nearness of the epicentre to centres of population and on other factors such as the depth of the epicentre.

The Mercalli scale and its modifications measure earthquakes in terms of the effect they have at any particular point.

Mercalli intensity scale[a]

Scale	Effect[b]
I	Not noticeable
II	Scarcely noticeable
III	Partially observed only
IV	Widely observed, rattles windows and doors
V	Sleeping people awakened
VI	Frightening

Scale	Effect[b]
VII	Damage to buildings
VIII	Some panic; destruction of buildings
IX	General panic; general damage to buildings
X	General destruction of buildings
XI	Catastrophe; severe damage and distortion of ground
XII	Landscape changes; virtually all structures are destroyed

[a]MSK 1964 modification. [b]Abbreviated description.

Earth satellites

Definition. A satellite is a body which revolves around another body of preponderant mass and which has a motion primarily and permanently determined by the force of attraction of that body.

Man-made satellites. Within 160 km of the Earth's surface a satellite will burn up within a few months. Above approx. 1 500 km (1 000 mi) a satellite is generally free of air drag. Above approx. 36 000–40 000 km the gravitational effects of the sun and moon become relatively more important.

A geosynchronous satellite is an Earth satellite whose period of revolution is equal to the period of rotation of the Earth about its axis.

Geostationary orbit. An equatorial orbit with an orbital period equal to the sidereal period of the Earth's rotation (23 hours 56 minutes). A satellite in geostationary orbit thus remains fixed relative to the Earth.

Most communications and many meteorological satellites are in geostationary orbit at an altitude of approx. 36 000 km (22 369 mi). The orbit is thus in danger of overcrowding, although the congestion is not uniform. The most crowded areas are 50–90°E longitude over the Indian Ocean; 0–35°W longitude over the Atlantic Ocean; 85–135°W longitude over North America. In order to avoid radio interference the International Telecommunications Union regulates the position and operating frequency of every satellite either operating or planning to operate in geostationary orbit.

The Intelsat global satellite system provides an international space telecommunications service. It has 109 member states, serves 170 countries and provides two-thirds of intercontinental telecommunications from its geostationary satellite network. The Intelsat 5 type satellite weighs nearly 2 000 kg and can handle 2 TV channels and 12 000 telephone calls simultaneously.

Low Earth orbit (LEO). The parameters of this orbit depend on the satellite's mass, density, lifetime and other variables. Many spy satellites use LEO, as does the Hubble Space Telescope which was launched in 1990 by space shuttle at 28.5° inclination. It has a mass of 11 tonnes, is over 13 m long and carries a 2.4 m telescope. It is hoped the telescope can be maintained in orbit for 15 years.

Sun-synchronous orbit. A polar orbit at an orbital inclination such that a satellite passes over a given site at the same local time throughout the year. Many meteorological satellites travel in this orbit at altitudes of 600–1 600 km to complement the work of their geostationary counterparts.

Some examples of meteorological satellites

Polar

Name	Country	Year	Weight (kg)	Perigee[a] (km)	Apogee[b] (km)	Orbital (°)
NOAA II	USA	1988	1 030	850	875	98.9
Meteor III	Soviet Union	1988	. . .	1 198	1 221	82.5
Fengyun I	China	1988	. . .	881	904	99.1

Geostationary (apogee = perigee = 36 000 km; 0°)

Name	Country	Year	Weight (kg)	Position
GOES 7	USA	1987	834	107.9°W then 135°W
Meteosat 4	Europe	1989	720	0°
GMS 3	Japan	1984	296	140°E
Insat 1B	India	1983	580	74°E

[a]Shortest orbital distance from Earth. [b]Greatest orbital distance from Earth.

Other uses

- Military. Over 2 000 satellites have been launched for military purposes, accounting for 70% of all satellites. They are used for electronic intelligence, early warning of nuclear attack, reconnaissance, etc, and include the USAF Big Bird and KH-11, and Soviet Cosmos.
- Navigation. A constellation of satellites broadcasts signals which can be used by an unlimited number of users; eg, US GPS Navistar and Soviet Glosnass emit precisely timed radio signals for ships, aircraft and land vehicles.
- Remote sensing. Satellites in mainly near-polar sun-synchronous orbits are used for topographical and geological mapping, mineral exploration, evaluating damage caused by natural disasters, etc. They include the US Landsat (705 km) and French SPOT (832 km).
- Search and rescue. The Cospas–Sarsat system relays distress signals from emergency radio beacons and ships, aircraft and land vehicles to rescue co-ordination centres.
- Space flight. Early manned spacecraft were little more than simple satellites fitted with life support systems. The current US Space Shuttle and Soviet Buran are true reusable aerospacecraft which can re-enter the Earth's atmosphere and land. Various space stations have also been launched. These are large modular satellites which can accommodate crews for long stays in space. They include the US Skylab and Soviet Salyut and Mir. At present the USA is collaborating with Canada, Europe and Japan on an international space station for the 1990s called Freedom, where the partners can learn to live and work productively in space for long periods of time.

There is increasing concern about the amount of man-made material orbiting the Earth, which in addition to operating satellites includes such things as dead satellites, spent upper stages, fragments of exploded spacecraft and sundry "space rubbish".

See also Electronics, pages 73–74.

Textiles

Main definitions

Man-made fibres are all fibres manufactured by man as distinct from those occurring naturally. Man-made fibres include: non-cellulosic fibres, such as polyamide (nylon), polyester, acrylic (or polyester fibre), etc, made from synthetic polymers (called synthetic fibres), natural polymers or inorganic materials (glass, etc); cellulosic fibres made from regenerated cellulose (cuprammonium rayon, viscose) or cellulose esters (acetates and triacetates). Regenerated cellulose fibres were formerly known by the name rayon but the use of this term is not allowed under EC law.

For natural fibres, see Agriculture, fishing and forestry, pages 34–37. For synthetic fibres, see Chemicals, industrial, page 44.

Continuous filament yarn is a yarn composed of one or more filaments that run the whole length of the yarn (yarn of one filament is called monofilament).

Discontinuous fibres are short or staple fibres; man-made staple fibre is usually prepared by cutting or breaking filaments into suitable lengths, generally 5–46 cm (0.2–20 in).

Tow is a large number of parallel continuous filaments with little or no twist.

Twist is the spiral disposition of the component(s) of a yarn, which is usually the result of relative rotation of the extremities of the yarn.

Warp is threads lengthways in a fabric as woven.

Chain is a term used for warp only in relation to carpets.

Weft, woof or filling is threads widthways in a fabric as woven.

Wale is a column of loops along the length of knitted fabric.

Course is a row of loops across the width of knitted fabric.

Yarn count systems

These measure the thickness of yarn and there are many systems. There are two main ways of expressing the fineness or coarseness of a yarn: direct systems and indirect systems. (The term that covers both types of system is "grist".) One system measures weight (mass) per unit length of the fibre, and the other length per unit weight (mass). The first system gives the linear density of the fibre, and this system is now the internationally agreed standard system, using as a unit the tex which measures in grams per kilometre (10^{-6} kg/m).

100 millitex (mtex)	= 1 decitex (dtex)
1 000 millitex	= 1 tex (tex)
10 decitex	= 1 tex
1 000 tex	= 1 kilotex (ktex)

The symbol for linear density expressed in the tex system is Tt.

In the tex and other weight per length systems the count is higher for thicker yarns, while in length per weight systems the count is higher for finer yarns and lower for thicker yarns.

The tables below give definitions of the main count systems. In the first table, for linear density systems, conversion from numbers or titres (terms used to express yarn fineness) to tex values can be made by multiplying by the factor given; in the second table, for length per unit systems, conversion to tex is made by dividing the constant shown by the count to be converted. For example, the equivalent of 800 denier is:

$800 \times 0.111\,1 = 88.9$ tex = 889 decitex

and the equivalent of a worsted yarn count of 20 is:

$885.8/20 = 44.3$ tex.

Linear density values of folded yarns can be designated by using "R" (resultant) after the overall value. Alternatively, where the linear densities of the components are similar, they can be designated by including "x" and then the number of components after the linear density. For example, a two-fold yarn consisting of two yarns of 20 tex each can be designated as "R 40 tex" or as "20 tex × 2".

A range of equivalent yarn counts is included in the table on page 230.

This shows values for each of the main count systems corresponding to a range of tex values. For decitex, multiply the number in the tex column by 10.

Measures

Wales or courses per unit length are measured in terms of the number per inch or centimetre.

Gauge is the number of needles per inch along a needle bed or needle bar in a weft or warp knitting machine (an example of nomenclature is E10 = 10 needles per inch); for knitted fabric it refers to the gauge of machine on which it is made and is a measure of the density of knit measured across the wales.

Threads in cloth are measured in terms of the number of picks (for length) or ends (for width) per inch or centimetre; for coarse fabrics, such as jute, threads per 10 centimetres is the main unit.

Twist is measured as the number of turns per inch or metre (for some sectors turns per centimetre). The twist factor or multiplier, when multiplied by the square root of the count for indirect systems, or divided by the square root of the linear density in the case of direct systems, gives the twist.

Cover factor (woven fabrics) is the extent to which an area of fabric is covered by a set of threads. Separate factors are used for warp threads and for weft threads. Under the English cotton count system, cover factor is the ratio of the number of threads per inch to the square root of the cotton count.

Linear density or direct systems (weight per unit length)

	Symbol	Unit of weight (mass)	Unit of length	Unit of yarn number	Multiplying factor for conversion to tex values
Tex	Tt	gram	kilometre	g/km	1
Denier	Td	gram	9 000 metres	g/9 000 m	0.111 1
Linen (dry spun), hemp, jute	Tj	pound	14 400 yards (spyndle)	lb/14 400 yd	34.45
Woollen (Aberdeen)	Ta	pound	14 400 yards	lb/14 400 yd	34.45
Woollen (US grain)	–	grain	20 yards	grain/20 yd	3.543

Indirect systems (length per unit weight)

	Symbol	Unit of length	Unit of weight (mass)	Unit of yarn count	Constant for conversion to tex values
Asbestos (US)	Na_A	100 yards (cut)	pound	100 yd/lb	4 961
Asbestos (UK)	Ne_A	50 yards	pound	50 yd/lb	9 921
Cotton (bump yarn)	N_B	yard	ounce	yd/oz	31 003
Cotton (UK)	Ne_C	840 yards (hank)	pound	840 yd/lb	590.5
Glass (US & UK)	N_G	100 yards	pound	100 yd/lb	4 961
Linen (wet or dry spun)	Ne_L	300 yards (lea)	pound	300 yd/lb	1 654
Metric	Nm	kilometre	kilogram	km/kg	1 000
Spun silk	N_S	840 yards (hank)	pound	840 yd/lb	590.5
Typp ('000 yd/lb)	Nt	1 000 yards	pound	1 000 yd/lb	496.1
Woollen (Alloa)	Na1	11 520 yards (spyndle)	24 pounds	11 520 yd/24 lb	1 033
Woollen (American cut)	Nac	300 yards (cut)	pound	300 yd/lb	1 654
Woollen (American run)	Nar	100 yards	ounce	100 yd/oz	310
Woollen (Dewsbury)	Nd	yard	ounce	yd/oz	31 003
Woollen (Galashiels)	Ng	300 yards (cut)	24 ounces	300 yd/24 oz	2 480
Woollen (Hawick)	Nh	300 yards (cut)	26 ounces	300 yd/26 oz	2 687
Woollen (Irish)	Ni_W	yard	0.25 ounce	yd/0.25 oz	7 751
Woollen (West of England)	Nwe	320 yards (snap)	pound	320 yd/lb	1 550
Woollen (Yorkshire)	Ny	256 yards (skein) or yard	pound or dram	256 yd/lb or yd/dram	1 938
Worsted	Ne_W	560 yards (hank)	pound	560 yd/lb	885.8

FABRIC AND CLOTHING

Size: clothing (UK)

Approximate equivalents of a range of sizes

Increasing by intervals of:

1 in		1½ in		2 in		4 cm	
in	cm	in	cm	in	cm	cm	in
29	74	29	74	28	71	72	28½
30	76	30½	77	30	76	76	30
31	79	32	81	32	81	80	31½
32	81	33½	85	34	86	84	33
33	84	35	89	36	91	88	34½
34	86	36½	93	38	97	92	36
35	89	38	97	40	102	96	38
36	91	39½	100	42	107	100	39½
37	94	41	104	44	112	104	41
38	97	42½	108	46	117	108	42½
39	99	44	112	48	122	112	44
40	102	45½	116			116	45½
41	104	47	119			120	47
42	107	48½	123			124	49
43	109						
44	112						
45	114						
46	117						
47	119						
48	122						
49	124						
50	127						

Collar sizes

in	cm	in	cm
14½	37	16½	42
15	38	17	43
15½	39–40	17½	44
16	41		

Brassière sizes[a]

in	cm	in	cm
32	70	38	85
34	75	40	90
36	80	42	95

[a]European continental measurement is of underbust size (with separate specification of cup size), while UK measurement is across the bust; hence the continental size indicated is smaller than the standard conversion, eg, 92 cm for a 36 in brassière.

Equivalents for UK and metric sizes for knitting needles

UK	metric (mm)	UK	metric (mm)	UK	metric (mm)
14	2	8	4	2	7
13	2.25	7	4.5	1	7.5
12	2.75	6	5	0	8
11	3	5	5.5	00	9
10	3.25	4	6	000	10
9	3.75	3	6.5		

Wool blankets
1 full size blanket = 5.75 square metres (6.88 square yards)
1 cot blanket = 1.5 square metres (1.79 square yards)

Conversions: area

Conversion from linear metres to square metres can be made approximately by multiplying by the following factors (allowing for average width).

Material	Factor	Material	Facto
100% cotton	1.09	Man-made fibre and filament mixtures	1.66
100% spun man-made fibre	1.6	100% man-made filament fabrics (excluding glass fibre and tyre cord)	1.54
silk fabrics	0.8		

Conversions: weight and area

Conversion factors
1 ounce per square yard (oz/yd^2) = 33.905 5 grams per square metre (g/m^2)
1 gram per square metre = 0.029 5 ounce per square yard
1 pound per square yard (lb/yd^2) = 0.542 5 kilogram per square metre (kg/m^2)
1 square yard per pound (yd^2/lb) = 1 843.3 square metres per tonne (m^2/t)
1 square metre per tonne = 0.000 5 square yard per pound

Conversions: number and area

Average conversions

	m^2/item	m^2/dozen items
Men's & women's wool-type coats	3.76	45.1
Men's & women's anoraks	2.88	34.5
Men's woven suits	3.76	45.1
Men's woven shirts	1.68	20.1
Men's woven trousers	1.24	14.9
Women's cotton dresses	3.16	37.9
Women's cotton skirts	1.24	14.9
Women's cotton blouses	1.01	12.1
Knitted T-shirts	0.5	6.0
Track suits	4.12	49.4
Sweaters	2.57	30.8

FOOTWEAR

Heavy leather is measured in irons in the UK, footwear and clothing leathers in millimetres, and light flexible leathers in ounces; where 1 iron = 1/48 in, 1 ounce = 1/64 in.

A summary of the relationships is shown in the following table.

See page 166 for a detailed table showing the conversion from fractions of an inch to millimetres.

Fractions of an in	mm	Irons	oz
1/64	0.4	¾	1
1/32	0.8	1½	2
3/64	1.2	2¼	3
1/16	1.6	3	4
5/64	2.0	3¾	5

Fractions of an in	mm	Irons	oz
3/32	2.4	4½	6
7/64	2.8	5¼	7
1/8	3.2	6	8
9/64	3.6	6¾	9
5/32	4.0	7½	10
11/64	4.4	8¼	11
3/16	4.8	9	12
13/64	5.2	9¾	13
7/32	5.6	10½	14
15/64	6.0	11¼	15
1/4	6.4	12	16
17/64	6.7	12¾	17
9/32	7.1	13½	18

Mondopoint shoe sizes

The Mondopoint shoe sizing system is an internationally agreed standard, providing length and width of the foot in millimetres.

Length is defined as the distance between the end of the most prominent toe and the most prominent part of the heel, measured with the person standing (with weight equally distributed) and wearing appropriate hose.

Width is defined as the horizontal distance between the outside of the foot at the first and fifth metatarsophalangeal joints, which is generally the broadest part of the foot.

Length markings are expressed in whole numbers in millimetres; these are in multiples of 5 mm or of 7.5 mm (0.5 being rounded down). The origin of the scale is zero, and the main 5 mm series runs from 105 by 5 mm to 300 mm. The main part of the series of 7.5 mm intervals is as follows.

120	150	180	210	240	270	300
127	157	187	217	247	277	
135	165	195	225	255	285	
142	172	202	232	262	292	

Width markings are also expressed in whole numbers, in millimetres. Measurements are expressed with the length first; eg, 215/82.

Shoe sizes

European continental sizes are usually measured by the Paris-point (PP).

3 Paris-points = 20 millimetres
1 Paris-point = 6.7 millimetres = approximately 4/15 inch

A broad comparison of UK and European continental sizes

UK sizes	European continental sizes	mm length
Infants		
½	15.87	106
1	16.51	110
1½	17.14	114
2	17.78	118
2½	18.41	123
3	19.05	127
3½	19.68	131
4	20.32	136
4½	20.95	140
5	21.59	144
5½	22.22	148
6	22.86	152
Children		
6½	23.49	157
7	24.13	161
7½	24.76	165
8	25.40	169
8½	26.03	174
9	26.67	178
9½	27.30	182
10	27.94	186
Boys or girls		
10½	28.57	190
11	29.21	195
11½	29.84	199
12	30.48	203
12½	31.11	207
13	31.75	212
13½	32.38	216
½	33.02	220

UK sizes	European continental sizes	mm length
Teenagers		
1½	33.65	224
2	34.29	229
2½	34.92	233
3	35.56	237
3½	36.19	241
Men or ladies		
4	36.83	246
4½	37.46	250
5	38.10	254
5½	38.73	258
6	39.37	262
6½	40.00	267
7	40.64	271
7½	41.27	275
8	41.91	279
8½	42.54	284
9	43.18	288
9½	43.81	292
10	44.45	296
10½	45.08	301
11	45.72	305
11½	46.35	309
12	46.99	313
12½	47.62	318
13	48.26	322
13½	48.89	326
14	49.53	330

US women's sizes are approximately 1½ up on the UK sizes, eg, 5 UK equals 6½ US. US men's sizes are approximately ½ higher than the UK equivalent.

Transport

Measures

1 passenger-kilometre = 0.621 4 passenger-mile
1 passenger-mile = 1.609 4 passenger-kilometres
1 tonne-kilometre = 0.611 6 UK (long) ton-mile
1 UK (long) ton-mile = 1.635 2 tonne-kilometres
1 tonne-kilometre = 0.684 9 US (short) ton-mile
1 US (short) ton-mile = 1.460 tonne-kilometres
1 tonne-kilometre/litre = 2.780 2 UK (long) ton-miles/UK gallon
1 UK (long) ton-mile/UK gallon = 0.359 7 tonne-kilometre/litre
1 tonne-kilometre/litre = 2.592 8 US (short) ton-miles/US gallon
1 US (short) ton-mile/US gallon = 0.385 7 tonne-kilometre/litre

See page 167 for conversion of kilometres to miles, and miles to kilometres. The tables can also be used for passenger-distance conversions.

ROAD

Fuel

Petrol in the UK is sold in litres. Three types are available: 4 star, unleaded and diesel.

See tables on pages 231–232, for conversion factors between kilometres per litre and miles per gallon.

Lead in petrol. The maximum permissible level is 0.15 grams per litre. The average lead content of petrol in the UK in 1990 was 0.143 g/l (4-star) and 0.002 g/l (unleaded).

See also Energy, page 77.

UK motor vehicle dimensions

	m
Maximum length	
Wheeled vehicle	12.00
Track laying vehicle	9.20
Motor vehicle & trailer	18.00
Motor vehicle & trailer[a]	18.35
Motor vehicle & two or more trailers	25.90
Maximum width	
Motor vehicle	2.50
Refrigerated vehicle	2.60
Locomotive	2.75
Trailer drawn by motor vehicle[b]	2.50
Other trailers	2.30
Agricultural trailer or appliance	2.50
Maximum height[c]	
Tractive unit & semi-trailer[d]	4.20

[a] If one or both are goods vehicles.
[b] Maximum weight exceeding 3 500 kg.
[c] Other vehicles not subject to height limits except buses.
[d] Exceeding 32 520 kg.

Tyre tread depth. From January 1st 1992 the minimum tread depth of tyres fitted to cars and light goods vehicles up to 3 500 kg maximum gross weight and trailers must be a minimum of 1.6 mm in depth throughout a continuous band situated in the central three quarters of the breadth of tread and round the entire outer circumference of the tyre.

UK noise limits for vehicles

	dB(A)
Cars	
Passenger	77
Direct injection diesel engines	78
Large buses and coaches	
Engine power <150 kW	80
Engine power ≥150 kW	83
Small buses/light goods	
GVW[a] <2 t	78
GVW[a] >2 t, ≤3.5 t	79
Direct injection diesel engines	80
Heavy goods vehicles	
Engine power <75 kW	81
Engine power, ≥75 kW, <150 kW	83
Engine power ≥150 kW	84

[a] Gross vehicle weight.

Motorcycles. The first European legislation for motorcycle noise limits was Directive 78/1015/EEC, which the UK mandated for all machines first used on or after April 1st 1983. The Commission subsequently adopted a two-stage amending directive 87/56/EEC. The UK has required compliance with Stage I, which revised the test procedure and lowered the noise limits, since April 1st 1991. Stage II, intended for the mid-1990s, has not yet been adopted by the UK as the limits may be reviewed before the end of 1994.

Engine capacity (cm^3)	78/1015/EEC dB(A) April 1st 1983	87/56/EEC Stage I dB(A) April 1st 1991	87/56/EEC Stage II dB(A) –
C≤80	78	77	75
C≤125	80	79	77
C≤175	83	79	77
C≤350	83	82	80
C≤500	85	82	80
C>500	86	82	

The UK also imposes a noise limit of 73 dB(A) on mopeds first used on or after April 1st 1983.

RAILWAYS

UK permanent way

Track gauge. 1 435 mm (nominal); 1 432 mm (since 1966).

Rail. Standard British Rail flat bottom rail (FB 113A).

Height = 159 mm
Width = 140 mm

Nominal weight = 55.8 kg/m
Rolled in 18.3 m lengths

London Transport: bullhead rail.
Weight = 47.6 kg/m

US permanent way

Track gauge. 4 ft $8\frac{1}{2}$ inches (same as UK).

Loading gauge

UK	European standard	Channel Tunnel
Height = 3 860 mm	Height = 4 279 mm	Height = 5 400 mm
Width = 2 692 mm	Width = 3 150 mm	Width = 4 000 mm

AIR

The Civil Aviation Authority in the UK follows closely the statistical practices of the International Civil Aviation Organisation for its measures and computation and uses the following definitions.

Aircraft days available. The sum of the number of days each aircraft is available for use. This figure includes days required for maintenance and overhaul but it does not include days between the date of purchase and the date actually placed in service, days out of the service due to major accidents or conversion, days when an aircraft is in the possession of others or is not available because of government action such as grounding by government regulatory agencies.

Aircraft hours. An aircraft hour is said to be performed when an aircraft operates 1 hour. Aircraft hours are measured on the basis of block-to-block times, ie, measured from the time the aircraft moves from the loading point until it stops at the unloading point.

Average daily utilisation per aircraft (hours). This is the total number of aircraft hours flown (passenger and cargo) divided by the number of aircraft days available for the period in question.

Aircraft kilometres are calculated by multiplying the number of flights performed by the stage distance.

All cargo services are scheduled or non-scheduled flights performed by aircraft carrying loads other than passengers, ie, cargo, baggage, mail.

Freight (or mail) tonne-kilometres used are calculated by multiplying the number of tonnes of cargo and diplomatic bags carried over each stage flight by the stage distance. Mail tonne-kilometres used are computed in a similar way.

Cargo. The weight of property carried on an aircraft including, for example, the weight of freight, mail, excess baggage and diplomatic bags, but excluding passengers' and crews' permitted baggage.

Cargo tonnes uplifted are calculated by counting each tonne of revenue cargo or mail on a particular journey (with one flight number) once only and not repeatedly on each individual stage of that flight.

Distance flown per passenger. The average distance flown per passenger is calculated by dividing the seat kilometres used by the number of passengers carried.

Passenger load factor is calculated by dividing seat-kilometres used by seat-kilometres available and expressing it as a percentage.

Passenger tonne kilometres used are calculated by multiplying the weight of passengers carried over each stage flight by the stage distance.

Passengers uplifted are calculated by counting each revenue passenger on a particular flight (with one flight number) once only and not repeatedly on each individual stage of that flight.

Payload capacity. Total of aircraft capacity available for the carriage of revenue load (passengers, baggage, cargo and mail) measured in tonnes.

Payload carried. The revenue load of passengers, baggage, cargo and mail carried in the aircraft measured in tonnes.

Revenue passengers. Those who pay 25% or more of the normal applicable fare.

Seat-kilometres available are calculated by multiplying the number of seats available for sale on each stage flight by the stage distance. Seats not available for the carriage of passengers because of the weight of fuel or other load are excluded from the calculations.

Seat-kilometres used are calculated by multiplying the number of revenue passengers carried on each stage flight by the stage distance.

Stage flight is operated from when an aircraft takes off to when it next lands (including technical stops).

Stage flights average distance is calculated by dividing the aircraft kilometres flown by the related number of stage flights.

Tonne-kilometres available are calculated by multiplying the number of tonnes available for the carriage of revenue load (passengers, cargo and mail) on each flight stage by the stage distance.

Tonne-kilometres used are calculated by multiplying the number of tonnes of revenue load carried on each flight stage by the stage distance.

Tonnes available. The capacity of the aircraft available for the carriage of payload measured in tonnes.

Weight load factor is calculated by dividing tonne-kilometres used by tonne-kilometres available expressing it as a percentage.

SHIPPING

Note. In this section the commonly used measure is quoted first with the equivalent in brackets.

Ship carrying capacity

There are two ways to measure the carrying capacity of ships:

- the weight of cargo loaded (up to the loadline);
- the cubic capacity of cargo spaces.

The main design criterion is that a ship should be as full as possible when it is charged up to its loadline and that it should not be too light and high above the water mark when its cargo spaces are full.

Cargo freight

Cargo freight – the payment made by shippers to shipowners or shipping lines for the carriage of cargo – is influenced by market conditions.

Market-related factors include: the value of the commodity carried; the degree of competition from other carriers; the importance of the commodity to the carrier to achieve a balanced load; the viability/profitability on a particular round voyage or in a particular trade. Shippers of large volumes may negotiate volume discounts; eg, under a service contract (SC) with a shipping line.

The cost side of cargo freight is computed from the cost of the ship's carrying capacity, in weight or volume, taken up by the cargo carried, over the period of time required for the voyage.

Cost-based cargo freight

In the general cargo liner trade (ie, ships operating on regular itineraries to predetermined schedules carrying various cargoes for a multiplicity of shippers) cost-related freight is normally computed on the basis of cubic capacity for lighter, more voluminous cargoes of low specific gravity having relatively high stowage factors and weight (eg, $ per tonne) for heavier cargoes.

Shipping or measurement tons. Sometimes used for the computation of freight. Until about 1965–70 1 standard measurement ton = 40 or 42 cubic feet (1.133 or 1.189 cubic metres) which approximated the average stowage factor (cubic feet of space occupied by a UK ton of cargo) in most liner trades. The progressive loss of the heavier liner cargoes, such as coal, grain, meat, minerals and metals, to bulk and specialised shipping, the spread of containerisation and the increased sophistication of cargo packaging have increased the average stowage factor in the liner trades to 50, 70 and 100 cubic feet or more in some trades. The measurement ton has been redefined as a result of these changes, but not uniformly in all trades, in the range 1–3 cubic metres per tonne. It is therefore no longer a standard, uniquely defined and generally accepted measure of the space occupied by 1 ton of cargo.

Containerised cargo. This constitutes most of the general cargo liner trade and is predominantly charged per container unit (per twenty-foot or forty-foot unit); ie, on a volume basis ("freight all kinds" – FAK). It can also be charged according to a commodity tariff which takes into account the volume : weight ratios. Terms may be on a port-to-port, quay-to-quay basis or from inland point of origin to inland port of delivery.

Dry bulk and liquid bulk cargoes. These include coal, grain, crude oil and petroleum products, and liquid petroleum gas, which are generally charged on a weight basis; eg, $ per tonne from A to B.

Roll-on/roll off (ro-ro) trades. Where wheeled cargo is loaded horizontally over ramps the critical dimension is length of cargo deck and cargo. Charging is based on, or takes into account, the linear length of cargo deck occupied by the vehicle.

Stowage

Stowage is the cubic space, measured in cubic feet or cubic metres, occupied by 1 ton or tonne of cargo. It is a key factor when estimating the utilisation and freight earning potential of a ship with regard to a particular cargo.

Stowage factors of a wide range of commodities entering seaborne trade are published and updated from time to time for the convenience of shippers, shipping agents and brokers. Care is required in the compilation and use of stowage factors. The cubic spaces in a ship's hold taken up by 1 ton of a commodity varies depending on the commodity's grade, precise chemical composition and physical characteristics and, in the general cargo liner trades, on primary and secondary packaging; eg 1 ton of coffee beans in sacks loaded on pallets or coffee beans loaded directly into 20-foot containers, **see page 151**; garments on rails in containers or garments in cartons. Some examples of stowage factors are shown below.

Commodity	ft^3/t	m^3/t
Bauxite	32	0.9
Iron ore	16–25	0.4–0.7
Oranges (in boxes)	85	2.4
Tea (in chests)	70	2.0
Wheat	45	1.3

Ship charters

Small shippers entrust relatively small parcels of cargo to a shipping line for transportation. Larger shippers and traders can contract with a shipowner to charter a ship on a bareboat, time, trip or voyage charter basis. They may also conclude a contract of affreightment whereby specified quantities of cargo are transported in specified quantities at specified intervals in ships nominated before each shipment. Large shippers, including other shipping lines, freight forwarders and cargo consolidators, may also contract to space charter cubic capacity on ships on particular routes.

Bareboat charter. Similar to a lease with the charterer paying the owner for the hire of the vessel only. The charterer is responsible for operating the ship, including hiring of crew, arranging insurance and maintenance. Bareboat charters are normally arranged for periods of several years, sometimes with the charterer having the option to buy the vessel at stages throughout the charter at a pre-specified price.

Time charter. The charterer hires a particular vessel for a specified period, from a few days to several years. The charterer pays for the costs incurred during voyages undertaken, ie, fuel costs, port costs, canal dues and cargo handling, and the owner pays capital and operating costs. Payment of hire is usually on the basis of $ per day or $/dwt per month (dwt is deadweight), sometimes with an allowance for escalation over time, particularly for charters over 12 months.

Trip charter. A form of time charter used only in the dry cargo market, whereby a named ship is hired on a time charter basis or one voyage with specified delivery point, loading port, discharge port and redelivery point.

Voyage charter. The charter of a named ship to transport a given quantity of a specified cargo from a port or range of loading ports to a port or range of discharge ports. Consecutive voyage charters are sometimes arranged, where two or more voyages are fixed at the same time. Tanker voyage charters are discussed below. For dry cargoes, the charter payment is generally expressed in $ per tonne, less often as a lump sum, and covers all ship costs including fuel, canal dues and port charges; eg, vessel XY to carry 50 000 tonnes of grain from A to B at a rate of $16.50 per tonne. The cost of cargo handling may be borne by either the owner or the charterer according to the terms of the charter, but generally charters are "free in and out" (FIO) and handling costs are paid by the charterer.

Tanker voyage freight rates: Worldscale

In the crude oil and petroleum product trades voyage freight rates in $ per tonne are generally expressed Worldscale (W), which is an index permitting direct comparison of the level of tanker freight rates on voyages of different lengths and at different times of the year. This is achieved by calculating the cost (in $) of carrying 1 tonne of cargo in a standard tanker on each of a large number of recognised crude and petroleum product voyages, adding variable voyage cost (ie, fuel, canal transit dues and port charges) and equating the resulting total voyage cost to W100 (Worldscale flat); eg, Ras Tanura to Yokohama: $10.16 = W100; Curaçao to New York: $3.76 = W100 (1992 Worldscale rates). An actual voyage fixture from Ras Tanura to Yokohama at W80 converts into $8.13 per tonne (10.16 × 0.8). Rates are occasionally expressed in terms of a lump sum.

The Worldscale index is updated and published annually on January 1st by the Worldscale Association of London and New York, a panel of tanker brokers. The annual updating takes into account changes in fuel costs and port charges. At less frequent intervals changes are made to representative tanker operating cost and the size of the notional standard tanker.

The standard Worldscale tanker is at present a ship of 75 000 dwt tonnes with a speed of 14.5 knots, daily fuel oil consumption of 55 tonnes, and total fixed operating costs of $12 000 per day.

Oil tankers (and the corresponding freight rates) are of two kinds: clean tankers intended primarily for the carriage of refined products (C); and dirty tankers, designed and primarily suitable for the carriage of crude oil, residual fuel and certain other unrefined or semi-refined materials and refinery feedstocks (D). The cargo holds of clean tankers are usually coated to prevent corrosion and to facilitate cleaning to prevent contamination by previous cargoes.

Containers

Most seaborne containerised trade is shipped in twenty-foot equivalent (TEU) or forty-foot equivalent (FEU) ISO freight containers having the following nominal external measurements (length × width × height).

	Imperial (ft)	Metric (m)
TEU	20 × 8 × 8	6 × 2.438 × 2.438
	20 × 8 × 8 ft 6 in	6 × 2.438 × 2.591
FEU	40 × 8 × 8	12 × 2.438 × 2.438
	40 × 8 × 8 ft 6 in	12 × 2.438 × 2.591
	40 × 8 × 9 ft 6 in	12 × 2.438 × 2.896

The recent trend has been away from 8 ft high containers. The 9 ft 6 in high FEU is known as a high cube container. Other dimensions are less common and appear only in some trades and for some cargoes; eg, lengths of 10 ft, 30 ft, 45 ft, 53 ft, height of 4 ft, width of 2.5 m (8 ft 2 in).

In certain countries the overall length and height of vehicles, and hence overland transportation of freight containers in excess of certain maximum length and height, is restricted by law, chiefly to meet bridge and tunnel clearances.

Precise external and internal measurements and tolerances and other details of ISO freight containers are obtainable from the International Organisation for Standardisation.

Gross tonnage

Gross tonnage is a ship's volumetric capacity. Until the 1969 International Convention on Tonnage Measurement of Ships came into force in 1982 the widely accepted volumetric unit of ship capacity was the gross registered ton (grt) or Moorsom ton. This was broadly, and for some ships and purposes remains, the capacity in cubic feet of the spaces within the hull and of enclosed spaces above deck available for cargo, stores, fuel, passengers and crew divided by 100. Thus 100 cubic feet of capacity = 1 gross registered ton.

Under the 1969 convention a new definition of gross tonnage became applicable to merchant ships of 24 metres or longer, the keel of which was laid after July 18th 1982 ("new ships"). This, with certain exceptions, will become applicable as of July 18th 1994 to other ("existing") ships. The new gross tonnage (gt) definition is all spaces bounded by the hull and cargo spaces above deck (more comprehensively defined than formerly) in cubic metres multiplied by a coefficient K_1. Thus:

$gt = K_1 V$
where $K_1 = 0.2 + 0.02 \log_{10} V$
and V = enclosed spaces in cubic metres

The values of coefficient K_1 lie in the range 0.22 (when $V = 10\ m^3$) to 0.32 (when $V = 10^6\ m^3$).

Some ships therefore are measured according to old regulations and others according to the requirements of the convention, a situation which will continue until July 18th 1994 and in some respects beyond that date. Primary sources give old or new measurements as appropriate. Ships built on the shelter deck principle with large exempt spaces under the old measurement regulations, such as roll-on/roll-off ferries, car carriers and general cargo ships (smaller vessels in particular), are liable to have their gross tonnage substantially increased under the new rules. There is no general formula to convert old gross registered tonnage into new gross tonnage.

Net tonnage

Net tonnage is the volumetric capacity of a ship's useful spaces designated for the carriage of cargo. Before the 1969 convention came into effect net tonnage or net registered tonnage (nrt) was obtained by deducting from gross tonnage the spaces used for the accommodation of the master, officers and crew, navigation and propelling machinery. This still applies for older ships and in some respects for all ships. Under the 1969 convention (Regulation 4) net tonnage is calculated according to a complex formula, the variables of which are the volume of spaces designated as cargo compartments in cubic metres multiplied by a coefficient K_c (analogous to K_1) and by a factor derived from the ratio of the ship's draught to its depth, plus a term taking into account the number of passengers the ship is permitted to carry. Primary sources give old or new net tonnage measurements for each ship listed as appropriate.

Net tonnage according to the convention, like the new gross tonnage, may differ considerably from pre-convention measurements; eg, the net tonnage of ships designed for the carriage of high density cargoes such as bulk carriers may be considerably reduced when measured in accordance with the convention.

Gross or net tonnages serve as bases for levying port dues, registration fees and other charges on ships. Some ships, for example ore/oil carriers designed to carry either ore or oil cargoes, may have two gross and two net tonnages. Ships of the shelter-deck construction capable of converting the greater part of the upper deck from the open (OSD) to the closed shelter deck condition (CSD) have two tonnage measurements, the higher tonnages corresponding to the closed condition.

Suez and Panama Canal tonnages

Suez and Panama net tonnages are defined in the regulations of the two waterways and recorded for each ship listed in some annual ship registers. They serve as bases for levying transit tolls on laden ships and, at a lower rate, on ships in ballast. For certain types of ships, eg, containerships carrying tiers of containers on deck, surcharges may be levied. For charging purposes ships are classified according to type. Tolls are levied at a decreasing rate on successive canal tonnage bands.

Both waterways' net tonnages are generally higher than the pre-1969 convention net (registered) tonnage. The Suez Canal net tonnage, derived from the British Moorsom registered ton, is usually higher than the Panama net tonnage. The definition of ships' spaces excluded from gross tonnage in the 1969 convention (Regulation 2(5)) was influenced by Panama Canal tonnage regulations and there is an affinity between the convention and Panama Canal tonnages. There is no general formula for converting the convention or the pre-convention tonnages into Suez or Panama Canal tonnages. According to a rule of thumb an average of pre-convention gross and net tonnage approximates the Panama net tonnage; multiplied by 1.1, the Suez net tonnage. A laden bulk carrier with a Suez net tonnage of 30 000 (about 60 000 dwt) would pay a Suez toll of about $140 000 (at 1992 rates).

The critical dimension of ships passing through the canals is, for the Suez Canal, the maximum draught of 53 ft (16.15 m) corresponding to a fully laden tanker of approximately 150 000 dwt ("Suezmax"), and the Panama Canal extreme breadth (beam) of 32.26 m (107 ft), dictated by the 110 ft (33.53 m) width of the locks, corresponding to a bulk carrier of up to about 78 000 dwt ("Panamax"). Tankers of any size can transit the Suez Canal in a ballast condition.

Deadweight

Deadweight (dwt) is the weight in tons (2 240 lbs) or tonnes (1 000 kg) of cargo, stores, fuel, passengers and crew carried by the ship when loaded to maximum summer loadline. Deadweight plus lightweight equal total displacement tonnage. In a typical laden cargo ship, stores, fuel, passengers and crew account for about 5% of the deadweight and cargo for 95%.

The relationship between a ship's deadweight (carrying capacity in weight) and gross tonnage (carrying capacity in cubic metres) varies depending on the design, ship type and size. According to a rule of thumb, the ratio of dwt to gt is about 2.1 for very large crude carriers (VLCC), 1.6 for smaller tankers, 1.8 for bulk and ore carriers (ranging from 1.6 for small bulk carriers of 25 000 dwt to 2.0 for large bulk carriers of 150 000 dwt and over) and about 1.2 for various general cargo ships. In 1990 the fleets of fully cellular container ships of the top 20 world operators averaged a dwt : gt ratio of 1.06.

Lightweight

Lightweight tonnage (lwt) or lightweight displacement ton (ldt) is the weight of the ship and its machinery and equipment as represented by the weight of the water displaced:
1 displacement ton of 2 240 lbs = approx. 35 cubic feet of salt water. Ships sold to scrapyards for demolition are sold on a lightweight ton basis. The ratio of dwt : ldt ranges from as little as 1 and sometimes less for small cargo ships to 7 or more for very large tankers.

Compensated gross tonnage

Compensated gross tonnage (cgt) is obtained by multiplying gross tonnage by coefficients of compensation (cc). These were developed in the late 1960s by organisations of West European and Japanese shipbuilders under the auspices of the Organisation for Economic Cooperation and Development (OECD, Directorate III, Working Party 6–Shipbuilding) for different ship size groups within over a dozen principal ship types to reflect differences in labour inputs and in value added. This provides a more balanced measure of shipbuilding capacity and output from an economic and political point of view than technical–engineering measures of ship capacity and shipyard production such as gross tonnage or deadweight. The 74 coefficients of compensation valid on July 1st 1991 range from 0.20 for VLCCs over 250 000 dwt to 6.00 for small passenger vessels under 1 000 gt. The basis coefficient for a general cargo ship of 10 000–20 000 dwt = 1.00. Examples of other coefficients are shown in the following table.

	dwt	Coefficient
Bulk carrier	50 000–80 000[a]	0.50
Petroleum product carrier	30 000–50 000	0.75
Containership	20 000–30 000	0.80
Passenger ship	3 000–10 000[b]	3.00
Roll-on/roll-off vessel	Up to 4 000	1.50

[a]Panamax. [b]grt.

Speed

A ship's speed is measured in knots. Most cargo ships travel at 10–20 knots (passenger ships and some containerships travel faster), where 1 knot = 1 international nautical mile of 1 852 metres per hour (0.514 4 m/s).

Loadline

The loadline is the mark on the ship's side showing the maximum permitted loaded draught (the vertical distance from the keel to the waterline) of the vessel according to the seasons and waters in which it is trading. Ships must be so loaded that the loadline corresponding to the zone in which they are travelling must not be submerged.

International loadline of cargo vessel
(not to scale)

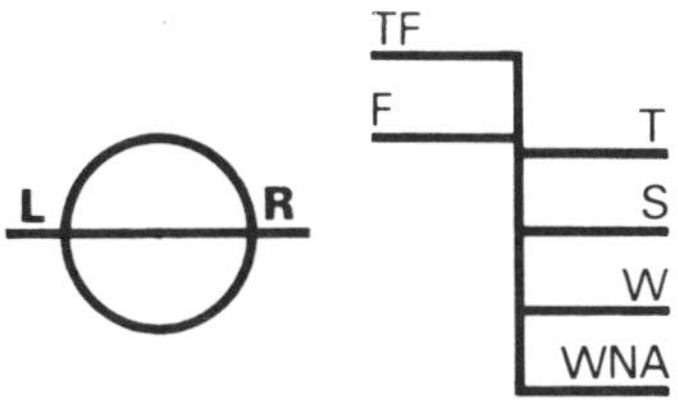

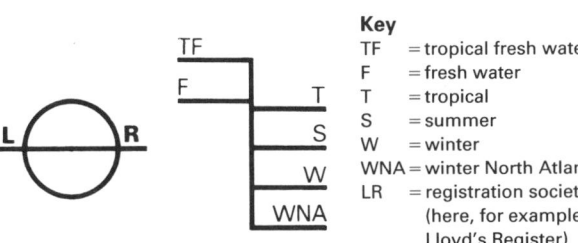

Key
TF = tropical fresh water
F = fresh water
T = tropical
S = summer
W = winter
WNA = winter North Atlantic
LR = registration society (here, for example, Lloyd's Register)

LAND FREIGHT: CONTAINERS

The universally accepted standard for the construction and safety of containers is the ISO standard. All containers have to be type tested and approved and to undergo periodic examination throughout their working life. These requirements are set out in the International Convention for Safe Containers (CSC). All containers as defined in CSC are required to carry a safety approval plate showing safe working load or gross weight. This must correspond with details elsewhere on the container.
The first examination of a container after manufacture must occur within a period not exceeding five years. Subsequent examinations should be at intervals not exceeding 30 months. The date of the next examination must be marked on the Safety Approval Plate, if practicable. Alternatively, coloured decals may be applied to the container indicating the next year of examination.

Brown	Blue	Yellow	Red	Black	Green
1992	1993	1994	1995	1996	1997
1998	1999	2000	2001	2002	2003

External dimensions, permissible tolerances and ratings for series 1 freight containers

Freight container designation	Length mm (tol.)		Length ft	Length in	Length in (tol.)	Width mm (tol.)		Width ft	Width in (tol.)	Height mm (tol.)		Height ft	Height in	Height (tol.)	Rating (gross mass) kg	Rating (gross mass) lb
1AA	12 192	$^{-0}_{-10}$	40		$^{-0}_{-3/8}$	2 438	$^{-0}_{-5}$	8	$^{-0}_{-3/16}$	2 591[a]	$^{-0}_{-5}$	8	6[a]	$^{-0}_{-3/16}$	30 480	67 200
1A	12 192	$^{-0}_{-10}$	40		$^{-0}_{-3/8}$	2 438	$^{-0}_{-5}$	8	$^{-0}_{-3/16}$	2 438	$^{-0}_{-5}$	8		$^{-0}_{-3/16}$	30 480	67 200
1AX	12 192	$^{-0}_{-10}$	40		$^{-0}_{-3/8}$	2 438	$^{-0}_{-5}$	8	$^{-0}_{-3/16}$	<2 438		<8			30 480	67 200
1BB	9 125	$^{-0}_{-10}$	29	$11\frac{1}{4}$	$^{-0}_{-3/8}$	2 438	$^{-0}_{-5}$	8	$^{-0}_{-3/16}$	2 591[a]	$^{-0}_{-5}$	8	6[a]	$^{-0}_{-3/16}$	25 400	56 000
1B	9 125	$^{-0}_{-10}$	29	$11\frac{1}{4}$	$^{-0}_{-3/8}$	2 438	$^{-0}_{-5}$	8	$^{-0}_{-3/16}$	2 438	$^{-0}_{-5}$	8		$^{-0}_{-3/16}$	25 400	56 000
1BX	9 125	$^{-0}_{-10}$	29	$11\frac{1}{4}$	$^{-0}_{-3/8}$	2 438	$^{-0}_{-5}$	8	$^{-0}_{-3/16}$	<2 438		<8			25 400	56 000
1CC	6 058	$^{-0}_{-6}$	19	$10\frac{1}{2}$	$^{-0}_{-1/4}$	2 438	$^{-0}_{-5}$	8	$^{-0}_{-3/16}$	2 591[a]	$^{-0}_{-5}$	8	6[a]	$^{-0}_{-3/16}$	24 000	52 900
1C	6 058	$^{-0}_{-6}$	19	$10\frac{1}{2}$	$^{-0}_{-1/4}$	2 438	$^{-0}_{-5}$	8	$^{-0}_{-3/16}$	2 438	$^{-0}_{-5}$	8		$^{-0}_{-3/16}$	24 000	52 900
1CX	6 058	$^{-0}_{-6}$	19	$10\frac{1}{2}$	$^{-0}_{-1/4}$	2 438	$^{-0}_{-5}$	8	$^{-0}_{-3/16}$	<2 438		<8			24 000	52 900
1D	2 991	$^{-0}_{-5}$	9	$9\frac{3}{4}$	$^{-0}_{-3/16}$	2 438	$^{-0}_{-5}$	8	$^{-0}_{-3/16}$	2 438	$^{-0}_{-5}$	8		$^{-0}_{-3/16}$	10 160	22 400
1DX	2 991	$^{-0}_{-5}$	9	$9\frac{3}{4}$	$^{-0}_{-3/16}$	2 438	$^{-0}_{-5}$	8	$^{-0}_{-3/16}$	<2 438		<8			10 160	22 400

[a]In certain countries there are legal limitations to the overall height of vehicle and load.

Minimum internal dimensions for series 1 freight containers

Freight container designation	Minimum height	Minimum width mm	Minimum width in	Minimum length mm	Minimum length ft	Minimum length in
1A	Nominal container	2 330	$91\frac{3}{4}$	11 998	39	$4\frac{3}{8}$
1AA	external height			11 998	39	$4\frac{3}{8}$
1B	minus 241 mm ($9\frac{1}{2}$ in)			8 931	29	$3\frac{5}{8}$
1BB				8 931	29	$3\frac{5}{8}$
1C				5 867	19	3
1CC				5 867	19	3
1D				2 802	9	$2\frac{5}{16}$

Note. The dimensions apply when measured at a temperature of 20°C (68°F). Measurements taken at other temperatures should be adjusted accordingly. Where a top corner fitting projects into the internal space specified by the table, that part of the corner fitting projecting into the container should not be considered to be reducing the size of the container.

Weapons

SMALL ARMS

Bore diameter usually means the diameter from land to land of a rifled barrel (minimum diameter), but sometimes means groove diameter which is measured from groove to groove of a rifled barrel (maximum diameter).

Nominal or designated calibre does not usually correspond exactly to actual bore diameter, although it may do so; the following table gives some illustrative values.

Calibre (nominal) mm	Other[a]	Actual bore diameter mm	in
	22	5.50	0.216
6.35		6.35	0.250
7.50		7.823	0.308
7.62	30	7.823	0.308
	303	7.925	0.312
7.92		8.204	0.323
8.00		8.204	0.323
	38	8.89	0.350
9.00		9.02	0.355
	45	11.30	0.445
	455	11.60	0.455
	50	12.70	0.500

[a]Nominal inch calibre, measured in hundredths or thousandths, but frequently referred to as the number of hundredths or thousandths; eg, 22 and 303.

Shotguns

The bore or gauge number for shotguns was originally the number of solid round lead balls, of a bore diameter size which could be taken by the gun, required to make a pound (avoirdupois). The smallest bore is now described by the actual size (0.410). Some usual sizes are as follows.

Bore or gauge (nominal)	Actual bore diam mm	in
410	10.4	0.410
28	14.0	0.550
20	15.6	0.615
16	16.8	0.662

Bore or gauge (nominal)	Actual bore diam mm	in
12	18.5	0.729
10	19.7	0.775
8	21.2	0.835
4	26.7	1.052

GUNS

Examples of the range of sizes

UK mm	in	USA mm	in	Soviet Union[a] mm	in
8.1	3.2	20	0.8	76	3.0
84	3.3	105[b]	4.1	82	3.2
105	4.1	120[b]	4.7	85	3.3
114[c]	4.5	127[c]	5	100[cb]	3.9
120[b]	4.7	155	6.1	115[b]	4.5
155	6.1	203	8	120	4.7
175	6.9			122	4.8
203	8			125[b]	4.9
				130[c]	5.1
				152	6
				160	6.3
				203	8
				240	9.4

[a]Former name.
[b]Typical tank main guns. [c]Typical naval guns.

BOMBS AND WARHEADS

Trinitrotoluene (TNT)

The energy released by TNT is used as the basis of measures of explosions. The standard used here is that 1 kilogram of TNT produces 4.5×10^6 J (1 ton or tonne produces 4.5×10^9 J); the relationship 1 kg TNT = 4.2×10^6 J is also in use.

Atomic (fission) weapons

Energy released by nuclear explosion – fission of all atoms of the fuel within a fraction of a second – is close to the maximum possible for fission (the splitting of each atom into two not quite equal parts). Thus, for 1 kilogram of U-235 it is about 8×10^7 MJ or 8×10^{13} J.

The magnitude of atomic explosion is usually expressed in terms of the ton of TNT; hence for 1 kilogram of U-235, the magnitude in tons of TNT is: $(8.2 \times 10^{13}\ \text{J})/(4.5 \times 10^9\ \text{J}) = 2 \times 10^4$ tons approximately = 20 000 tons. Larger multiples used in this connection are as follows.

1 kiloton (kT or kt) = 1 000 tons = 4.5×10^{12} J
1 megaton (MT or Mt) = 1 000 kilotons = 1 000 000 tons = 4.5×10^{15} J

Hence 1 kilogram of U-235 produces an explosion of 20 kilotons.

Uranium and plutonium are the main nuclear fuels; thorium-233 is a possible future fuel for atomic explosions.

Atomic bombs normally use enriched uranium with over 40% and up to 97% of U-235, or plutonium with over 90% Pu-239.

Hydrogen or thermonuclear (fusion) weapons

A hydrogen or thermonuclear bomb (H-bomb) is produced by a process of nuclear fusion – the merging of nuclei as compared with the splitting (fission) of atoms in the atomic bomb. Extreme heat – of the order of 100 mn °C – is required, and so fusion weapons need a small atomic (fission) charge as an initiator.

Energy released by a thermonuclear bomb is of the order of 20 megatons. Main fuels for the thermonuclear bomb are certain kinds of hydrogen atoms: hydrogen-deuterium and hydrogen-tritium.

Neutron bombs or warheads

A neutron bomb is an atomic bomb which releases more of its energy in the form of immediate radiation (a high-intensity ast of neutrons and gamma rays) than the "conventional" uclear weapon. An approximate comparison of the type of amage is shown in the table.

se of energy released (%)

	Blast	Heat	"Prompt" radiation	Other radiation
-bomb	45	35	5	15
eutron warhead	34	24	40	2

uclear delivery

elivery systems. Nuclear weapons can be delivered by the ollowing:

- land-based systems – missiles or artillery;
- sea-based systems – submarines (ICBMS), submarines or surface ships (tactical land attack missiles – TOMAHAWK – mines and torpedoes);
- air-based systems – SBRMS, air-launched cruise missiles and bombs.

lissiles

itials	Full name	Range (km)
RBM	Short range ballistic missile	Under 1 100
RBM	Medium range ballistic missile	1 100–2 750
BM	Intermediate range ballistic missile	2 750–5 500
BM	Intercontinental ballistic missile	Over 5 500

ubmarines. A UK Polaris submarine carries 16 missiles, each vith 3 thermonuclear warheads.

A US Trident 2 submarine carries 24 missiles, each with ither 12 MIRV or 7 MARV thermonuclear warheads.

A Soviet Delta IV class ballistic missile submarine carries 16 nissiles, each with 10 MIRV thermonuclear warheads.

luclear damage

The effects of nuclear explosions depend on the nature of the veapon and its power. The following tables show the effects or three levels of power, using ground burst weapons:

- 20 kilotons = atomic bomb dropped on Hiroshima
- 1 megaton = modern atomic bomb
- 20 megatons = hydrogen bomb

ersons. The following table shows the effect on people exposed to initial radiation and heat blast in the open. The able takes into account the inverse square law, whereby the ntensity of radiation and heat decreases by a factor which is proportional to the square of the distance from the source of he explosion; eg, if distance is trebled, intensity falls to a ninth ($\frac{1}{3^2}$). The distances shown are those beyond which the person vill in general not suffer the effects indicated.

Initial effects	Weapon power (ground burst) 20 kilotons km	mi	1 megaton km	mi	20 megatons km	mi
Death (50–50 chance)[a]	1.25	0.75	2.50	1.50	3.75	2.25
Radiation sickness[b]	1.50	1.00	2.75	1.75	4.00	2.50
Charring of skin[c]	1.50	1.00	8.00	5.00	26.00	16.00

[a]There is a 50–50 chance of death or survival; this is called an LD 50, signifying that there is a lethal dose for 50% of people. This level is taken as 4.5 sieverts (450 rem); for nuclear weapon purposes, the röntgen is regarded as about equal to the rad and to the rem. [b]Taken at the UK "War Emergency Dose" (WED) level of 0.75 sievert (75 rem). [c]The effect of thermal radiation or heat flash which consists almost entirely, beyond the immediate dangerous blast area, of intense visible light and infra-red rays. The distance is shown (for a clear atmosphere) for serious charring of the full thickness of the skin, extending to underlying tissue; reddening of the skin, similar to sunburn, can be suffered up to nearly double the distance shown for charring.

The distances are shown for a ground burst nuclear weapon; for an air burst weapon the distances are about the same for death and radiation sickness effects, and about 50% greater for the effect of heat blast.

For further information about radiation and radiation measures see Health, pages 102–103.

Shielding for defence against radiation is usually measured in terms of the "half-value" thickness; this is the thickness of the shield needed to reduce the dose rate in a beam of gamma rays by half, so that, in general, defence against radiation is given for twice the weapon power indicated in the above table where there is shielding at half-value thickness. Approximate values are as follows.

Shielding material	Half-value thickness against initial gamma radiation cm	in
Steel	4	1½
Concrete	15	6
Earth	20	7½
Water	33	13

The table above refers to initial effects on people. The effect of downwind fallout depends on atmospheric conditions (especially cloud dimensions and height) and speed of wind, in relation to the time after the explosion occurs; a standard reference time is defined in the UK to be either $H+1$ or $H+7$, meaning 1 hour or 7 hours after detonation. Since the amount of radiation decays over time, the dose rate is defined on the same time scale as, for example, DR1 and DR7, meaning the dose rate after 1 hour and after 7 hours. The general decay law is that radiation falls by a factor of 10 as time lengthens by a factor of 7; more exactly, $R_t = R_1 t^{-1.2}$, where R_1 is the nominal dose rate at 1 hour after burst, and R_t is the dose rate at time t (in hours). The following table gives approximate dose rates for various times after burst, starting from a nominal rate of 100 (sievert per second or, say, rem per hour, since the rate of decay does not depend on the unit used).

Time after burst	Dose rate	Time after burst	Dose rate
1 hour	100.00	2 days	1.00
1.75 hours	50.00	2 weeks	0.10
7 hours	10.00	14 weeks	0.01

The area of downwind fallout depends on wind conditions; approximate areas which will be contaminated downwind, under average conditions, are given in the following table.

Dose rate at edge of area specified at DR1		Downwind contamination area (by weapon power)					
		20 kilotons		1 megaton		20 megatons	
rem per hour	sievert per hour	km^2	mi^2	km^2	mi^2	km^2	mi^2
1 000	10.0	3.4	1.3	230	90	5 000	1 900
100	1.0	41.0	16.0	2 300	900	47 000	18 000
10	0.1	500.0	200.0	12 000	4 500	240 000	93 000

Houses. Pressure from the shock wave is likely to cause slight damage to average UK houses at about 5 kPa(0.75 lbf/in^2), reparable damage (houses remaining habitable) at about 10 kPa (1.5 lbf/in^2), and irreparable damage at about 40 kPa (6 lbf/in^2).

The average range of estimated blast damage to average UK houses is shown in the following table, giving very approximate limits in kilometres and miles.

Type of damage up to range specified	Range of blast damage (by weapon power)					
	20 kilotons		1 megaton		20 megatons	
	km	mi	km	mi	km	mi
Total destruction	0.6	0.4	2.4	1.5	7.2	4.5
Irreparable	1.0	0.6	3.6	2.2	10.0	6.0
Severe to moderate	2.5	1.5	9.0	5.5	25.0	15.0
Light	4.0	2.5	14.5	9.0	40.0	25.0

PART III

CONVERSION TABLES

USE OF CONVERSION TABLES

From the summary tables for conversions, which give the equivalent number for converting 1 unit, it is possible to determine the equivalent for 10, 100, 1 000, etc, units by moving the decimal point one place to the right for each 0; eg:

1 pound = 0.453 592 37 kilogram
10 pounds = 4.535 923 7 kilograms
1 000 (one thousand) pounds = 453.592 37 kilograms
1 000 000 (one million) pounds = 453 592.37 kilograms

In the same way, the equivalent conversion for 0.1, 0.01, 0.001, etc, can be obtained by moving the decimal point one place to the left for each decimal place in the unit to be converted; eg:

0.1 pound = 0.045 359 237 kilogram
0.01 pound = 0.004 535 923 7 kilogram

Further, since 1 000 kilograms equals 1 tonne (or megagram), then from 1 000 pounds = 453.592 37 kilograms the new conversion rate of 1 000 pounds = 0.453 592 37 tonne (megagram) and of 1 000 000 pounds = 453.592 37 tonnes (megagrams), can be obtained by moving the decimal point relating to kilograms three places to the left.

See also page 14, Metric system, for the relationship between metric multiples and submultiples.

Detailed conversions for some of the main units in use, usually up to the number of 100 or 1 000, are provided on **pages 166–186**. The tables are set out mainly with 10s at the side and single units at the top; so the first row, with 0 at the side, is the conversion for numbers from 0 to 9, and the second row for numbers from 10 to 19. Thus, the number to be converted is the number at the side of a line, 10, added to the number at the top of a column. For example, to convert 11, it is necessary to find the 10 line and the 1 column, and the conversion of 11 is, as indicated below by the figures *4.990* (shown here in italics), the number in the position where line and column meet (example from **page 183**).

lb → ↓	0	1	2
	kg	kg	kg
0	0.000	0.454	0.907
10	4.536	*4.990*	5.443
20	9.072	9.525	9.979

Conversion for some numbers other than those included in the tables can be obtained by adding together (or subtracting) the conversions for other numbers; eg, the conversion for 1 011 can be obtained from the table on **page 183** by adding together the conversion for 1 000 and that for 11; this equals 453.592 kg plus 4.990 kg or 458.582 kg. However, the rounding is not always accurate to the last decimal place after making this calculation.

In general, the number to be converted, which is made up by adding the unit at the side of a line to the unit at the head of a column, is converted to the number in the position where the line and column meet. An example is given at the top of each table.

Summary

Exact values are shown in bold type: other values are generally shown to six significant figures.

Numbers are shown in full. Where the shorthand notation using numbers equal to or larger than 1 and under 10 associated with powers of 10 is preferred, these can be obtained as follows: a positive power as suffix to the 10 indicates the number of digits to the left of the decimal point minus 1, and a negative power the number of noughts between the decimal point and the first real number, plus 1. For example, 304.8 mm $= 3.048 \times 10^2$ mm and 0.003 048 mm $= 3.048 \times 10^{-3}$ mm. Non-metric units are UK (imperial) unless otherwise stated.

Length

Multiply number of	by	to obtain equivalent number of
Milli-inches (mils or 'thou')	**25.4**	micrometres (μm)
Inches (in)	**25.4**	millimetres (mm)
	2.54	centimetres (cm)
	0.025 4	metres (m)
Hands	**101.6**	millimetres
Links (lk)	**0.201 168**	metres
Feet (ft)	**304.8**	millimetres
	30.48	centimetres
	0.304 8	metres
US survey feet	0.304 801	metres
Yards (yd)	**0.914 4**	metres
Fathoms	**1.828 8**	metres
Rods	**5.029 2**	metres
Chains (ch)	**20.116 8**	metres
Engineers' chains	**30.48**	metres
Furlongs	**201.168**	metres
Miles, statute (mi)	**1 609.344**	metres
Miles, international nautical	**1 852**	metres
Miles, UK nautical	**1 853.184**	metres
Miles, telegraph nautical	**1 855.317 6**	metres
Chains	**0.020 116 8**	kilometres (km)
Engineers' chains	**0.030 48**	kilometres (km)
Furlongs	**0.201 168**	kilometres (km)
Miles, statute	**1.609 344**	kilometres (km)
Miles, international nautical	**1.852**	kilometres (km)
Miles, UK nautical	**1.853 184**	kilometres (km)
Miles, telegraph nautical	**1.855 317 6**	kilometres (km)
Miles, statute	0.868 976	miles, international nautical

Multiply number of	by	to obtain equivalent number of
Micrometres	0.039 370 1	milli-inches
Millimetres	0.039 370 1	inches
Centimetres	0.393 701	inches
	0.049 709 7	links
	0.032 808 4	feet
	0.032 808 3	US survey feet
Metres	39.370 1	inches
	4.970 97	links
	3.280 84	feet
	3.280 83	US survey feet
	1.093 61	yards
	0.546 807	fathoms
	0.198 839	rods
	0.049 709 7	chains
	0.004 970 97	furlongs
Kilometres	49.709 7	chains
	32.808 4	engineers' chains
	4.970 97	furlongs
	0.621 371	miles, statute
	0.539 957	miles, international nautical
	0.539 612	miles, UK nautical
	0.538 991	miles, telegraph nautical
Miles, international nautical	1.150 78	miles, statute

Area

Multiply number of	by	to obtain equivalent number of
Circular mils	506.707	square micrometres (μm^2)
Square inches (in^2)	**645.16**	square millimetres (mm^2)
	6.451 6	square centimetres (cm^2)
Square feet (ft^2)	**929.030 4**	square centimetres
	0.092 903 04	square metres
Square yards (yd^2)	**0.836 127 36**	square metres (m^2)
	0.008 361 273 6	ares (a)
Square chains (ch^2)	**404.685 642 24**	square metres
	4.046 856 422 4	ares
	0.404 685 642 24	dekares (daa)
Roods	**1 011.714 105 6**	square metres
	10.117 141 056	ares
	1.011 714 105 6	dekares
	0.101 171 410 56	hectares (ha)
Acres	**4 046.856 422 4**	square metres
	40.468 564 224	ares
	0.404 685 642 24	hectares
Square miles (mi^2)	**258.998 811 033 6**	hectares
	2.589 988 110 336	sq. kilometres (km^2)
US townships	**93.239 571 972 096**	square kilometres

Multiply number of	by	to obtain equivalent number of
Square micrometres	0.001 973 53	circular mils
Square millimetres	0.001 550 00	square inches
Square centimetres	0.155 000	square inches
	0.001 076 39	square feet
Square metres	10.763 9	square feet
	1.195 99	square yards
	0.002 471 05	square chains
Ares	119.599	square yards
	0.247 105	square chains
	0.098 842 2	roods
	0.024 710 5	acres
Dekares	2.471 05	square chains
	0.988 422	roods
	0.247 105	acres
Hectares	9.884 22	roods
	2.471 05	acres
	0.003 861 02	square miles
Square kilometres	247.105	acres
	0.386 102	square miles
	0.010 725 1	US townships

In this section no distinction is made between UK or metric units hich are no longer authorised and those which remain authorised. **See pages 13–19 for further information. More detailed conversions r main units are given in the tables on pages 166–186.**

	Multiply number of	by	to obtain equivalent number of
Volume and capacity	Cubic inches (in^3)	0.576 744	UK fluid ounces (UK fl oz)
		0.554 113	US liquid ounces (US liq oz)
		0.028 837 20	UK pints (UK pt)
		0.003 604 65	UK gallons (UK gal)
	Cubic inches	**16.387 064**	cubic centimetres (cm^3) *also* SI millilitres (ml)
	UK fluid ounces	**28.413 062 5**	
	US liquid ounces	29.573 5	
	US liquid pints (US liq pt)	**473.176 473**	
	UK pints	**568.261 25**	
	US liquid quarts (US liq qt)	**946.352 946**	
	UK quarts (UK qt)	**1 136.522 5**	
	US liquid gallons (US liq gal)	**3 785.411 784**	
	UK gallons	**4 546.09**	
	Cubic inches	**0.016 387 064**	cubic decimetres (dm^3) *also* SI litres (l or L)
	US liquid pints	**0.473 176 473**	
	UK pints	**0.568 261 25**	
	US liquid quarts	**0.946 352 946**	
	Litres (1901 definition)	1.000 028	
	UK quarts	**1.136 522 5**	
	US liquid gallons	**3.785 411 784**	
	UK gallons	**4.546 09**	
	UK gallons (1963 definition)	4.546 091 88	
	Cubic feet (ft^3)	**28.316 846 592**	
	Cubic feet	7.480 52	US liquid gallons
		6.228 84	UK gallons
		0.803 564	US bushels (US bu)
		0.778 604	UK bushels (UK bu)
	UK gallons	**0.045 460 9**	SI hectolitres (hl)
	US bushels	0.352 391	
	UK bushels	**0.363 687 2**	
	US liquid gallons	**0.003 785 411 784**	cubic metres (m^3) *also* kilolitres kl)
	US dry gallons	0.004 404 88	
	UK gallons	**0.004 546 09**	
	Cubic feet	**0.028 316 846 592**	
	US bushels	0.035 239 1	
	UK bushels	**0.036 368 72**	
	Barrels, bulk (36 UK gallons)	**0.163 659 24**	
	Barrels, petroleum (42 US gallons)	**0.158 987 294 928**	
	Cubic yards (yd^3)	**0.764 554 857 984**	
Weight (mass)	Grains (gr)	**64.798 91**	milligrams (mg)
		0.323 994 55	metric carats
		0.064 798 91	grams (g)
	Scruples	**1.295 978 2**	grams
	Pennyweights (dwt)	**1.555 173 84**	
	Drams (dr)	1.771 85	
	Drachms (drm)	**3.887 934 6**	
	Ounces (oz)	**28.349 523 125**	
	Ounces troy (oz tr)	**31.103 476 8**	
	Ounces	0.911 458	ounces troy
	Ounces troy	**155.517 384**	metric carats
	Ounces	**0.028 349 523 125**	kilograms (kg)
	Pounds (lb)	**0.453 592 37**	
	Stones	**6.350 293 18**	
	US (short) hundredweights (US cwt)	**45.359 237**	
	UK (long) hundredweights (UK cwt)	**50.802 345 44**	
	US (short) tons	**907.184 74**	
	UK (long) tons	**1 016.046 908 8**	
	Slugs	14.593 9	kilograms
		1.488 16	hyls (metric slugs)

Multiply number of	by	to obtain equivalent number of
Cubic centimetres *also* SI millilitres (ml)	0.061 023 7	cubic inches
	0.035 195 1	UK fluid ounces
	0.033 814 0	US liquid ounces
	0.002 113 38	US liquid pints
	0.001 759 75	UK pints
	0.001 056 69	US liquid quarts
	0.000 879 877	UK quarts
	0.000 264 172	US liquid gallons
	0.000 219 969	UK gallons
UK fluid ounces	1.733 87	cubic inches
UK pints	34.677 4	
UK quarts	69.354 9	
UK gallons	277.419	
Cubic decimetres *also* SI litres	61.023 7	cubic inches
	35.195 1	UK fluid ounces
	33.814 0	US liquid ounces
	2.113 38	US liquid pints
	1.759 75	UK pints
	1.056 69	US liquid quarts
	0.999 972	litres (1901 definition)
	1.056 69	US liquid quarts
	0.879 877	UK quarts
	0.264 172	US liquid gallons
	0.219 969	UK gallons
	0.035 314 7	cubic feet
US liquid gallons	0.133 681	cubic feet
UK gallons	0.160 544	
US bushels	1.244 46	
UK bushels	1.284 35	
SI hectolitres	26.417 2	US liquid gallons
	21.996 9	UK gallons
	2.837 76	US bushels
	2.749 62	UK bushels
Cubic metres	264.172	US liquid gallons
	227.021	US dry gallons
	219.969	UK gallons
	35.314 7	cubic feet
	28.377 6	US bushels
	27.496 2	UK bushels
	6.110 26	barrels, bulk (36 UK gallons)
	6.289 81	barrels, petroleum (42 US gallons)
	1.307 95	cubic yards
Milligrams	0.015 432 4	grains
Metric carats	3.086 47	
Grams	15.432 4	
Metric carats	0.006 430 15	ounces troy
Grams	0.771 618	scruples
	0.643 015	pennyweights
	0.564 383	drams
	0.257 206	drachms
	0.035 274 0	ounces
	0.032 150 7	ounces troy
Ounces troy	1.097 14	ounces
Kilograms	35.274 0	ounces
	32.150 7	ounces troy
	2.204 62	pounds
	0.157 473	stones
	0.022 046 2	US (short) hundredweights
	0.019 684 1	UK (long) hundredweights
	0.001 102 31	US (short) tons
	0.000 984 207	UK (long) tons
Hyls (metric slugs)	9.806 65	kilograms
	0.671 969	slugs

	Multiply number of	by	to obtain equivalent number of	Multiply number of	by	to obtain equivalent number of
Weight (mass) cont.	US (short) hundred-weights	**0.453 592 37**	metric quintals (q)	Metric quintals	2.204 62	US (short) hundred-weights
	UK (long) hundred-weights	**0.508 023 454 4**	metric quintals (q)		1.968 41	UK (long) hundred-weights
	Pounds	**0.000 453 592 37**	megagrams (Mg) = tonnes (t)	Megagrams = tonnes	2 204.62	pounds
	US (short) tons	**0.907 184 74**			1.102 31	US (short) tons
	UK (long) tons	**1.016 046 908 8**			0.984 207	UK (long) tons
Velocity	Inches per minute (in/min)	0.423 333	millimetres per second (mm/s)	Millimetre per second	2.362 20	inches per minute
	Feet per minute (ft/min)	**5.08**			0.196 850	feet per minute
				Kilometres per hour	0.621 371	miles per hour
				Metres per second	2.236 94	miles per hour
	Miles per hour (mph)	**1.609 344**	kilometres per hour (km/h)	Kilometres per hour	0.539 957	international knots
		0.447 04	metres per second (m/s)	Miles per hour	0.868 976	
				UK knots	1.000 64	
				Metres per second	1.943 84	
	International knots	1.150 78	miles per hour			
		0.999 361	UK knots			
		0.514 444	metres per second			
Fuel consumption	Miles per UK gallon	0.354 006	kilometres per SI litre (km/l)	Kilometre per SI litre	2.824 81	miles per UK gallon
	Miles per US gallon	0.425 144			2.352 15	miles per US gallon
	UK gallons per mile	282.481	SI litres per 100 kilometres (l/100 km)	SI litres per 100 kilometres	0.003 540 06	UK gallons per mile
	US gallons per mile	235.215			0.004 251 44	US gallons per mile
Weight (mass) per unit length or area	UK (long) tons per mile (UK ton/mile)	0.631 342	tonnes per kilometre (t/km) *also* kilograms per metre kg/m)	Tonnes per kilometre *also* Kilograms per metre	1.583 93	UK (long) tons per mile
	Pounds per foot (lb/ft)	1.488 16			0.671 969	pounds per foot
	Pounds per square inch (lb/in²)	70.307 0	grams per sq. centimetre (g/cm²)	Grams per sq. centimetre	0.014 223 3	pounds per square inch
	Pounds per acre (lb/acre)	1.120 85	kilograms per hectare (kg/ha)	Kilograms per hectare	0.892 179	pounds per acre
Density and concentration	Ounces per UK gallon (oz/UK gal)	6.236 02	kilograms per cubic metre (kg/m³) *also* grams per SI SI litre (g/l)	Kilograms per cubic metre *also* Grams per SI litre	0.160 359	ounces per UK gallon
	Ounces per US liquid gallon (oz/US liq gal)	7.489 15			0.133 526	ounces per US liquid gallon
	Pounds per cubic foot (lb/ft³)	16.018 5			0.062 428 0	pounds per cubic foot
Force	Poundals (pdl)	0.138 255	newtons (N)	Newtons	7.233 01	poundals
	Ounces-force (ozf)	0.278 014			3.596 94	ounces-force
	Pounds-force (lbf)	4.448 22			0.224 809	pounds-force
	Newtons	0.101 972	kilograms-force (kgf) *or* kiloponds (kp)	Kilograms-force *or* Kiloponds	**9.806 65**	newtons
	Pounds-force	**0.453 592 37**			2.204 62	pounds-force
	US (short) tons-force (US tonf)	8.896 44	kilonewtons (kN)	Kilonewtons	0.112 404	US (short) tons-force
	UK (long) tons-force (UK tonf)	9.964 02			0.100 361	UK (long) tons-force
Torque (moment of force)	Poundals foot (pdl ft)	0.042 140 1	newton metres (N m)	Newton metres	23.730 4	poundals foot
	Pounds-force foot (lbf ft)	1.355 82			0.737 562	pounds-force foot
Pressure and stress	Poundals per sq. foot (pdl/ft²)	1.488 16	pascals (Pa) *also* newtons per square metre (N/m²)	Pascals *also* Newtons per square metre	0.671 969	poundals per sq. foot
	Pounds-force per sq. foot (lbf/ft²)	47.880 3			0.020 885 4	pounds-force per square foot
	Pounds-force per sq. foot	0.478 803	millibars (mbar)	Millibars	2.088 54	pounds-force per sq. foc
	Inches of water (in H_2O)	**2.490 889 1**			0.401 463	inches of water
	Inches of mercury (in Hg)	33.863 9			0.029 530 0	inches of mercury
	Pounds-force per sq. inch (lbf/in²)	68.947 6			0.014 503 8	pounds-force per sq. inc
	Pounds-force per sq. inch	6.894 76	kilopascals (kPa) *also* kilonewtons per sq. metre (kN/m²)	Kilopascals *also* Kilonewtons per square metre	0.145 038	pounds-force per sq. inc

	Multiply number of	by	to obtain equivalent number of	Multiply number of	by	to obtain equivalent number of
ressure nd stress ont.	Pounds-force per sq. inch	0.070 307 0	kilograms-force per sq. centimetre (kgf/cm²)	Kilograms-force per square centimetre	14.223 3	pounds-force per sq. inch
	Pounds-force per sq. inch	0.068 947 6	bars (bar)	Bars	14.503 8	pounds-force per sq. inch
	UK tons-force per sq. foot (UK tonf/ft²)	1.072 52			0.932 385	UK tons-force per sq. foot
	Pounds-force per sq. inch	0.006 894 76	megapascals (MPa) *also* newtons per sq. millimetre (N/mm²)	Megapascals *also* Newtons per square millimetre	145.038	pounds-force per sq. inch
	UK tons-force per sq. foot	0.107 252			9.323 85	UK tons-force per sq. foot
	UK tons-force per sq. inch UK tonf/in²)	15.444 3			0.064 749 0	UK tons-force per sq. inch
	Pounds-force per sq. inch	0.000 703 07	kilograms-force per sq. millimetre (kgf/mm²)	Kilograms-force per square millimetre	1 422.33	pounds-force per sq. inch
	UK tons-force per sq. inch	1.574 88			0.634 971	UK tons-force per sq. inch
	UK tons-force per sq. foot	0.010 725 2	hectobars(hbar)	Hectobars	93.238 5	UK tons-force per sq. foot
	UK tons-force per sq. inch	1.544 43			0.647 490	UK tons-force per sq. inch
nergy, ork, uantity of eat	Foot poundals (ft pdl)	0.042 140 1	joules (J)	Joules	23.730 4	foot poundals
	Foot pounds-force (ft lbf)	1.355 82			0.737 562	foot pounds-force
	Calories, thermochemical or defined (cal_{th})	**4.184**			0.239 006	calories, thermochemical or defined
	Calories, 15°C (cal_{15})	4.185 5			0.238 920	calories, 15°C
	Calories, international table (cal_{IT})	**4.186 8**			0.238 846	calories, international table
	Kilograms-force metre (kgf/m)	**9.806 65**			0.101 972	kilograms-force metre
	British thermal units (Btu)	1.055 06	Kilojoules (kJ)	Kilojoules	0.947 817	British thermal units
	Watt hours (W h)	**3.6**			0.277 778	watt hours
	Kilocalories, international table ($kcal_{IT}$)	**4.186 8**			0.238 846	kilocalories, international table
	UK horsepower hours (hph)	0.745 700	kilowatt hours (kW h)	Kilowatt hours	1.341 02	UK horsepower hours
	UK horsepower hours	2.684 52	megajoules (MJ)	Megajoules	0.372 506	UK horsepower hours
	Kilowatt hours	**3.6**			0.277 778	kilowatt hours
	Thermies, international table (th_{IT})	**4.186 8**			0.238 846	thermies, international table
	Therms	105.506			0.009 478 17	therms
ower	Foot pounds-force per second (ft lbf/s)	1.355 82	watts (W)	Watts	0.737 562	foot pounds-force per second
	Metric horsepower (ch or PS)	735.499			0.001 359 62	metric horsepower
	UK horsepower (hp)	745.700			0.001 341 02	UK horsepower
	Metric horsepower	0.735 499	kilowatts (kW)	Metric horsepower	0.986 320	UK horsepower
	UK horsepower	0.745 700		Kilowatts	1.359 62	metric horsepower
	UK horsepower	1.013 87	metric horsepower		1.341 02	UK horsepower
leat flow ate	British thermal units per hour (Btu/h)	0.293 071	watts	Watts	3.412 14	British thermal units per hour
	Kilocalories, international table, per hour ($kcal_{IT}$/h)	**1.163**			0.859 845	kilocalories, international table, per hour
	Tons of refrigeration (12 000 Btu/h)	3516.85			0.000 284 345	tons of refrigeration
eat nergy ontent	British thermal units per pound (Btu/lb)	**2.326**	joules per gram (J/g) *also* kilojoules per kilogram (kJ/kg)	Joules per gram *also* kilojoules per kilogram	0.429 923	British thermal units per pound
	Kilocalories, international table, per kilogram ($kcal_{IT}$/kg)	**4.186 8**			0.238 846	kilocalories, international table, per kilogram
ight	Foot-lamberts	3.426 26	candelas per sq. metre(cd/m²)	Candelas per sq. metre	0.291 864	foot-lamberts
	Candelas per square foot (cd/ft²)	10.763 9			0.092 903 0	candelas per square foot
	Lumens per square foot (lm/ft²) foot-candles	10.763 9	lux (lx) *also* lumens per sq. metre (lm/m²)	Lux	0.092 903 0	lumens per square foot *also* foot-candles
lane angle	Degrees (°)	0.017 453 3	radians(rad)	Radians	57.295 8	degrees
	Grades (^{g}) or gons	0.015 708 0			63.662 0	grades or gons

Fractions to decimals

Fraction	Decimal equivalent	Fraction	Decimal equivalent
1/2	0.5	1/37	0.027 027
1/3	0.333 333	1/38	0.026 316
1/4	0.25	1/39	0.025 641
1/5	0.2	1/40	0.025
1/6	0.166 667	1/41	0.024 390
1/7	0.142 857	1/42	0.023 810
1/8	0.125	1/43	0.023 256
1/9	0.111 111	1/44	0.022 727
1/10	0.1	1/45	0.022 222
1/11	0.090 909	1/46	0.021 739
1/12	0.083 333	1/47	0.021 277
1/13	0.076 923	1/48	0.020 833
1/14	0.071 429	1/49	0.020 408
1/15	0.066 667	1/50	0.02
1/16	0.062 5	1/51	0.019 608
1/17	0.058 824	1/52	0.019 231
1/18	0.055 556	1/53	0.018 868
1/19	0.052 632	1/54	0.018 519
1/20	0.05	1/55	0.018 182
1/21	0.047 619	1/56	0.017 857
1/22	0.045 455	1/57	0.017 544
1/23	0.043 478	1/58	0.017 241
1/24	0.041 667	1/59	0.016 949
1/25	0.04	1/60	0.016 667
1/26	0.038 462	1/61	0.016 393
1/27	0.037 037	1/62	0.016 129
1/28	0.035 714	1/63	0.015 873
1/29	0.034 483	1/64	0.015 625
1/30	0.033 333	1/65	0.015 385
1/31	0.032 258	1/66	0.015 152
1/32	0.031 25	1/67	0.014 925
1/33	0.030 303	1/68	0.014 706
1/34	0.029 412	1/69	0.014 493
1/35	0.028 571	1/70	0.014 286
1/36	0.027 778		

Fractions 3rds	6ths	12ths	24ths	Decimal equivalent
			1	0.041 667
		1	2	0.083 333
			3	0.125
	1	2	4	0.166 667
			5	0.208 333
		3	6	0.25
			7	0.291 667
1	2	4	8	0.333 333
			9	0.375
		5	10	0.416 667
			11	0.458 333
	3	6	12	0.5
			13	0.541 667
		7	14	0.583 333
			15	0.625
2	4	8	16	0.666 667
			17	0.708 333
		9	18	0.75
			19	0.791 667
	5	10	20	0.833 333
			21	0.875
		11	22	0.916 667
			23	0.958 333
3	6	12	24	1

Fractions 1/2's	1/4's	8ths	16ths	32nds	64ths	Decimal equivalent (all figures are exact)
					1	0.015 625
				1	2	0.031 25
					3	0.046 875
			1	2	4	0.062 5
					5	0.078 125
				3	6	0.093 75
					7	0.109 375
		1	2	4	8	0.125
					9	0.140 625
				5	10	0.156 25
					11	0.171 875
			3	6	12	0.187 5
					13	0.203 125
				7	14	0.218 75
					15	0.234 375
	1	2	4	8	16	0.25
					17	0.265 625
				9	18	0.281 25
					19	0.296 875
			5	10	20	0.312 5
					21	0.328 125
				11	22	0.343 75
					23	0.359 375
		3	6	12	24	0.375
					25	0.390 625
				13	26	0.406 25
					27	0.421 875
			7	14	28	0.437 5
					29	0.453 125
				15	30	0.468 75
					31	0.484 375
1	2	4	8	16	32	0.5
					33	0.515 625
				17	34	0.531 25
					35	0.546 875
			9	18	36	0.562 5
					37	0.578 125
				19	38	0.593 75
					39	0.609 375
		5	10	20	40	0.625
					41	0.640 625
				21	42	0.656 25
					43	0.671 875
			11	22	44	0.687 5
					45	0.703 125
				23	46	0.718 75
					47	0.734 375
	3	6	12	24	48	0.75
					49	0.765 625
				25	50	0.781 25
					51	0.796 875
			13	26	52	0.812 5
					53	0.828 125
				27	54	0.843 75
					55	0.859 375
		7	14	28	56	0.875
					57	0.890 625
				29	58	0.906 25
					59	0.921 875
			15	30	60	0.937 5
					61	0.953 125
				31	62	0.968 75
					63	0.984 375
2	4	8	16	32	64	1

Percentage reversals

ercentage reversal is the term used here for the value which brings a gross amount, including a percentage, back to the net figure before the ercentage was added. For example, 100 + 10% = 110; 110 − 9.1% = 100, where 9.1% is the percentage reversal of 10%.

se of the table. The unit at the side of a line for each section, added to the unit at the head of a column, makes up the number for which the ercentage reversal is shown in the position where line and column meet. For example, 10 + 0.1 = 10.1; the percentage reversal of 10.1% is 9.2%.

%	% 0.0	% 0.1	% 0.2	% 0.3	% 0.4	% 0.5	% 0.6	% 0.7	% 0.8	% 0.9
0	0.0	0.1	0.2	0.3	0.4	0.5	0.6	0.7	0.8	0.9
1	1.0	1.1	1.2	1.3	1.4	1.5	1.6	1.7	1.8	1.9
2	2.0	2.1	2.2	2.2	2.3	2.4	2.5	2.6	2.7	2.8
3	2.9	3.0	3.1	3.2	3.3	3.4	3.5	3.6	3.7	3.8
4	3.8	3.9	4.0	4.1	4.2	4.3	4.4	4.5	4.6	4.7
5	4.8	4.9	4.9	5.0	5.1	5.2	5.3	5.4	5.5	5.6
6	5.7	5.7	5.8	5.9	6.0	6.1	6.2	6.3	6.4	6.5
7	6.5	6.6	6.7	6.8	6.9	7.0	7.1	7.1	7.2	7.3
8	7.4	7.5	7.6	7.7	7.7	7.8	7.9	8.0	8.1	8.2
9	8.3	8.3	8.4	8.5	8.6	8.7	8.8	8.8	8.9	9.0
10	9.1	9.2	9.3	9.3	9.4	9.5	9.6	9.7	9.7	9.8
11	9.9	10.0	10.1	10.2	10.2	10.3	10.4	10.5	10.6	10.6
12	10.7	10.8	10.9	11.0	11.0	11.1	11.2	11.3	11.3	11.4
13	11.5	11.6	11.7	11.7	11.8	11.9	12.0	12.0	12.1	12.2
14	12.3	12.4	12.4	12.5	12.6	12.7	12.7	12.8	12.9	13.0
15	13.0	13.1	13.2	13.3	13.3	13.4	13.5	13.6	13.6	13.7
16	13.8	13.9	13.9	14.0	14.1	14.2	14.2	14.3	14.4	14.5
17	14.5	14.6	14.7	14.7	14.8	14.9	15.0	15.0	15.1	15.2
18	15.3	15.3	15.4	15.5	15.5	15.6	15.7	15.8	15.8	15.9
19	16.0	16.0	16.1	16.2	16.2	16.3	16.4	16.5	16.5	16.6
20	16.7	16.7	16.8	16.9	16.9	17.0	17.1	17.1	17.2	17.3
21	17.4	17.4	17.5	17.6	17.6	17.7	17.8	17.8	17.9	18.0
22	18.0	18.1	18.2	18.2	18.3	18.4	18.4	18.5	18.6	18.6
23	18.7	18.8	18.8	18.9	19.0	19.0	19.1	19.2	19.2	19.3
24	19.4	19.4	19.5	19.5	19.6	19.7	19.7	19.8	19.9	19.9
25	20.0	20.1	20.1	20.2	20.3	20.3	20.4	20.4	20.5	20.6
26	20.6	20.7	20.8	20.8	20.9	20.9	21.0	21.1	21.1	21.2
27	21.3	21.3	21.4	21.4	21.5	21.6	21.6	21.7	21.8	21.8
28	21.9	21.9	22.0	22.1	22.1	22.2	22.2	22.3	22.4	22.4
29	22.5	22.5	22.6	22.7	22.7	22.8	22.8	22.9	23.0	23.0
30	23.1	23.1	23.2	23.3	23.3	23.4	23.4	23.5	23.5	23.6
31	23.7	23.7	23.8	23.8	23.9	24.0	24.0	24.1	24.1	24.2
32	24.2	24.3	24.4	24.4	24.5	24.5	24.6	24.6	24.7	24.8
33	24.8	24.9	24.9	25.0	25.0	25.1	25.1	25.2	25.3	25.3
34	25.4	25.4	25.5	25.5	25.6	25.7	25.7	25.8	25.8	25.9
35	25.9	26.0	26.0	26.1	26.1	26.2	26.3	26.3	26.4	26.4
36	26.5	26.5	26.6	26.6	26.7	26.7	26.8	26.8	26.9	27.0
37	27.0	27.1	27.1	27.2	27.2	27.3	27.3	27.4	27.4	27.5
38	27.5	27.6	27.6	27.7	27.7	27.8	27.8	27.9	28.0	28.0
39	28.1	28.1	28.2	28.2	28.3	28.3	28.4	28.4	28.5	28.5
40	28.6	28.6	28.7	28.7	28.8	28.8	28.9	28.9	29.0	29.0
41	29.1	29.1	29.2	29.2	29.3	29.3	29.4	29.4	29.5	29.5
42	29.6	29.6	29.7	29.7	29.8	29.8	29.9	29.9	30.0	30.0
43	30.1	30.1	30.2	30.2	30.3	30.3	30.4	30.4	30.5	30.5
44	30.6	30.6	30.7	30.7	30.7	30.8	30.8	30.9	30.9	31.0
45	31.0	31.1	31.1	31.2	31.2	31.3	31.3	31.4	31.4	31.5
46	31.5	31.6	31.6	31.6	31.7	31.7	31.8	31.8	31.9	31.9
47	32.0	32.0	32.1	32.1	32.2	32.2	32.2	32.3	32.3	32.4
48	32.4	32.5	32.5	32.6	32.6	32.7	32.7	32.8	32.8	32.8
49	32.9	32.9	33.0	33.0	33.1	33.1	33.2	33.2	33.2	33.3
50	33.3	33.4	33.4	33.5	33.5	33.6	33.6	33.6	33.7	33.7
51	33.8	33.8	33.9	33.9	33.9	34.0	34.0	34.1	34.1	34.2
52	34.2	34.3	34.3	34.3	34.4	34.4	34.5	34.5	34.6	34.6
53	34.6	34.7	34.7	34.8	34.8	34.9	34.9	34.9	35.0	35.0
54	35.1	35.1	35.1	35.2	35.2	35.3	35.3	35.4	35.4	35.4
55	35.5	35.5	35.6	35.6	35.6	35.7	35.7	35.8	35.8	35.9
56	35.9	35.9	36.0	36.0	36.1	36.1	36.1	36.2	36.2	36.3
57	36.3	36.3	36.4	36.4	36.5	36.5	36.5	36.6	36.6	36.7
58	36.7	36.7	36.8	36.8	36.9	36.9	36.9	37.0	37.0	37.1
59	37.1	37.1	37.2	37.2	37.3	37.3	37.3	37.4	37.4	37.5
60	37.5	37.5	37.6	37.6	37.7	37.7	37.7	37.8	37.8	37.8
61	37.9	37.9	38.0	38.0	38.0	38.1	38.1	38.2	38.2	38.2
62	38.3	38.3	38.3	38.4	38.4	38.5	38.5	38.5	38.6	38.6
63	38.7	38.7	38.7	38.8	38.8	38.8	38.9	38.9	38.9	39.0
64	39.0	39.1	39.1	39.1	39.2	39.2	39.2	39.3	39.3	39.4
65	39.4	39.4	39.5	39.5	39.5	39.6	39.6	39.6	39.7	39.7
66	39.8	39.8	39.8	39.9	39.9	39.9	40.0	40.0	40.0	40.1
67	40.1	40.2	40.2	40.2	40.3	40.3	40.3	40.4	40.4	40.4
68	40.5	40.5	40.5	40.6	40.6	40.7	40.7	40.7	40.8	40.8
69	40.8	40.9	40.9	40.9	41.0	41.0	41.0	41.1	41.1	41.1
70	41.2	41.2	41.2	41.3	41.3	41.3	41.4	41.4	41.5	41.5
71	41.5	41.6	41.6	41.6	41.7	41.7	41.7	41.8	41.8	41.8
72	41.9	41.9	41.9	42.0	42.0	42.0	42.1	42.1	42.1	42.2
73	42.2	42.2	42.3	42.3	42.3	42.4	42.4	42.4	42.5	42.5
74	42.5	42.6	42.6	42.6	42.7	42.7	42.7	42.8	42.8	42.8
75	42.9	42.9	42.9	43.0	43.0	43.0	43.1	43.1	43.1	43.1
76	43.2	43.2	43.2	43.3	43.3	43.3	43.4	43.4	43.4	43.5
77	43.5	43.5	43.6	43.6	43.6	43.7	43.7	43.7	43.8	43.8
78	43.8	43.9	43.9	43.9	43.9	44.0	44.0	44.0	44.1	44.1
79	44.1	44.2	44.2	44.2	44.3	44.3	44.3	44.4	44.4	44.4
80	44.4	44.5	44.5	44.5	44.6	44.6	44.6	44.7	44.7	44.7
81	44.8	44.8	44.8	44.8	44.9	44.9	44.9	45.0	45.0	45.0
82	45.1	45.1	45.1	45.1	45.2	45.2	45.2	45.3	45.3	45.3
83	45.4	45.4	45.4	45.4	45.5	45.5	45.5	45.6	45.6	45.6
84	45.7	45.7	45.7	45.7	45.8	45.8	45.8	45.9	45.9	45.9
85	45.9	46.0	46.0	46.0	46.1	46.1	46.1	46.1	46.2	46.2
86	46.2	46.3	46.3	46.3	46.4	46.4	46.4	46.4	46.5	46.5
87	46.5	46.6	46.6	46.6	46.6	46.7	46.7	46.7	46.8	46.8
88	46.8	46.8	46.9	46.9	46.9	46.9	47.0	47.0	47.0	47.1
89	47.1	47.1	47.1	47.2	47.2	47.2	47.3	47.3	47.3	47.3
90	47.4	47.4	47.4	47.5	47.5	47.5	47.5	47.6	47.6	47.6
91	47.6	47.7	47.7	47.7	47.8	47.8	47.8	47.8	47.9	47.9
92	47.9	47.9	48.0	48.0	48.0	48.1	48.1	48.1	48.1	48.2
93	48.2	48.2	48.2	48.3	48.3	48.3	48.3	48.4	48.4	48.4
94	48.5	48.5	48.5	48.5	48.6	48.6	48.6	48.6	48.7	48.7
95	48.7	48.7	48.8	48.8	48.8	48.8	48.9	48.9	48.9	49.0
96	49.0	49.0	49.0	49.1	49.1	49.1	49.1	49.2	49.2	49.2
97	49.2	49.3	49.3	49.3	49.3	49.4	49.4	49.4	49.4	49.5
98	49.5	49.5	49.5	49.6	49.6	49.6	49.6	49.7	49.7	49.7
99	49.7	49.8	49.8	49.8	49.8	49.9	49.9	49.9	49.9	50.0

Length

Use of the table. The number of inches to be converted, which is made up by the number of inches at the head of a column and the fraction at the side of a line, is converted to the number in the position where line and column meet. For example, 1 1/64 in = 1 in + 1/64 in = 25.797 mm.

Inches and fractions of an inch to millimetres

1 in = 25.4 mm

in → ↓	0	1	2	3	4	5	6	7	8	9	10	11
	mm	mm	mm	mm	mm	mm	mm	mm	mm	mm	mm	mm
0	0.000	25.400	50.800	76.200	101.600	127.000	152.400	177.800	203.200	228.600	254.000	279.400
1/64	0.397	25.797	51.197	76.597	101.997	127.397	152.797	178.197	203.597	228.997	254.397	279.797
1/32	0.794	26.194	51.594	76.994	102.394	127.794	153.194	178.594	203.994	229.394	254.794	280.194
3/64	1.191	26.591	51.991	77.391	102.791	128.191	153.591	178.991	204.391	229.791	255.191	280.591
1/16	1.588	26.988	52.388	77.788	103.188	128.588	153.988	179.388	204.788	230.188	255.588	280.988
5/64	1.984	27.384	52.784	78.184	103.584	128.984	154.384	179.784	205.184	230.584	255.984	281.384
3/32	2.381	27.781	53.181	78.581	103.981	129.381	154.781	180.181	205.581	230.981	256.381	281.781
7/64	2.778	28.178	53.578	78.978	104.378	129.778	155.178	180.578	205.978	231.378	256.778	282.178
1/8	3.175	28.575	53.975	79.375	104.775	130.175	155.575	180.975	206.375	231.775	257.175	282.575
9/64	3.572	28.972	54.372	79.772	105.172	130.572	155.972	181.372	206.772	232.172	257.572	282.972
5/32	3.969	29.369	54.769	80.169	105.569	130.969	156.369	181.769	207.169	232.569	257.969	283.369
11/64	4.366	29.766	55.166	80.566	105.966	131.366	156.766	182.166	207.566	232.966	258.366	283.766
3/16	4.762	30.162	55.562	80.962	106.362	131.762	157.162	182.562	207.962	233.362	258.762	284.162
13/64	5.159	30.559	55.959	81.359	106.759	132.159	157.559	182.959	208.359	233.759	259.159	284.559
7/32	5.556	30.956	56.356	81.756	107.156	132.556	157.956	183.356	208.756	234.156	259.556	284.956
15/64	5.953	31.353	56.753	82.153	107.553	132.953	158.353	183.753	209.153	234.553	259.953	285.353
1/4	6.350	31.750	57.150	82.550	107.950	133.350	158.750	184.150	209.550	234.950	260.350	285.750
17/64	6.747	32.147	57.547	82.947	108.347	133.747	159.147	184.547	209.947	235.347	260.747	286.147
9/32	7.144	32.544	57.944	83.344	108.744	134.144	159.544	184.944	210.344	235.744	261.144	286.544
19/64	7.541	32.941	58.341	83.741	109.141	134.541	159.941	185.341	210.741	236.141	261.541	286.941
5/16	7.938	33.338	58.738	84.138	109.538	134.938	160.338	185.738	211.138	236.538	261.938	287.338
21/64	8.334	33.734	59.134	84.534	109.934	135.334	160.734	186.134	211.534	236.934	262.334	287.734
11/32	8.731	34.131	59.531	84.931	110.331	135.731	161.131	186.531	211.931	237.331	262.731	288.131
23/64	9.128	34.528	59.928	85.328	110.728	136.128	161.528	186.928	212.328	237.728	263.128	288.528
3/8	9.525	34.925	60.325	85.725	111.125	136.525	161.925	187.325	212.725	238.125	263.525	288.925
25/64	9.922	35.322	60.722	86.122	111.522	136.922	162.322	187.722	213.122	238.522	263.922	289.322
13/32	10.319	35.719	61.119	86.519	111.919	137.319	162.719	188.119	213.519	238.919	264.319	289.719
27/64	10.716	36.116	61.516	86.916	112.316	137.716	163.116	188.516	213.916	239.316	264.716	290.116
7/16	11.112	36.512	61.912	87.312	112.712	138.112	163.512	188.912	214.312	239.712	265.112	290.512
29/64	11.509	36.909	62.309	87.709	113.109	138.509	163.909	189.309	214.709	240.109	265.509	290.909
15/32	11.906	37.306	62.706	88.106	113.506	138.906	164.306	189.706	215.106	240.506	265.906	291.306
31/64	12.303	37.703	63.103	88.503	113.903	139.303	164.703	190.103	215.503	240.903	266.303	291.703
1/2	12.700	38.100	63.500	88.900	114.300	139.700	165.100	190.500	215.900	241.300	266.700	292.100
33/64	13.097	38.497	63.897	89.297	114.697	140.097	165.497	190.897	216.297	241.697	267.097	292.497
17/32	13.494	38.894	64.294	89.694	115.094	140.494	165.894	191.294	216.694	242.094	267.494	292.894
35/64	13.891	39.291	64.691	90.091	115.491	140.891	166.291	191.691	217.091	242.491	267.891	293.291
9/16	14.288	39.688	65.088	90.488	115.888	141.288	166.688	192.088	217.488	242.888	268.288	293.688
37/64	14.684	40.084	65.484	90.884	116.284	141.684	167.084	192.484	217.884	243.284	268.684	294.084
19/32	15.081	40.481	65.881	91.281	116.681	142.081	167.481	192.881	218.281	243.681	269.081	294.481
39/64	15.478	40.878	66.278	91.678	117.078	142.478	167.878	193.278	218.678	244.078	269.478	294.878
5/8	15.875	41.275	66.675	92.075	117.475	142.875	168.275	193.675	219.075	244.475	269.875	295.275
41/64	16.272	41.672	67.072	92.472	117.872	143.272	168.672	194.072	219.472	244.872	270.272	295.672
21/32	16.669	42.069	67.469	92.869	118.269	143.669	169.069	194.469	219.869	245.269	270.669	296.069
43/64	17.066	42.466	67.866	93.266	118.666	144.066	169.466	194.866	220.266	245.666	271.066	296.466
11/16	17.462	42.862	68.262	93.662	119.062	144.462	169.862	195.262	220.662	246.062	271.462	296.862
45/64	17.859	43.259	68.659	94.059	119.459	144.859	170.259	195.659	221.059	246.459	271.859	297.259
23/32	18.256	43.656	69.056	94.456	119.856	145.256	170.656	196.056	221.456	246.856	272.256	297.656
47/64	18.653	44.053	69.453	94.853	120.253	145.653	171.053	196.453	221.853	247.253	272.653	298.053
3/4	19.050	44.450	69.850	95.250	120.650	146.050	171.450	196.850	222.250	247.650	273.050	298.450
49/64	19.447	44.847	70.247	95.647	121.047	146.447	171.847	197.247	222.647	248.047	273.447	298.847
25/32	19.844	45.244	70.644	96.044	121.444	146.844	172.244	197.644	223.044	248.444	273.844	299.244
51/64	20.241	45.641	71.041	96.441	121.841	147.241	172.641	198.041	223.441	248.841	274.241	299.641
13/16	20.638	46.038	71.438	96.838	122.238	147.638	173.038	198.438	223.838	249.238	274.638	300.038
53/64	21.034	46.434	71.834	97.234	122.634	148.034	173.434	198.834	224.234	249.634	275.034	300.434
27/32	21.431	46.831	72.231	97.631	123.031	148.431	173.831	199.231	224.631	250.031	275.431	300.831
55/64	21.828	47.228	72.628	98.028	123.428	148.828	174.228	199.628	225.028	250.428	275.828	301.228
7/8	22.225	47.625	73.025	98.425	123.825	149.225	174.625	200.025	225.425	250.825	276.225	301.625
57/64	22.622	48.022	73.422	98.822	124.222	149.622	175.022	200.422	225.822	251.222	276.622	302.022
29/32	23.019	48.419	73.819	99.219	124.619	150.019	175.419	200.819	226.219	251.619	277.019	302.419
59/64	23.416	48.816	74.216	99.616	125.016	150.416	175.816	201.216	226.616	252.016	277.416	302 816
15/16	23.812	49.212	74.612	100.012	125.412	150.812	176.212	201.612	227.012	252.412	277.812	303.212
61/64	24.209	49.609	75.009	100.409	125.809	151.209	176.609	202.009	227.409	252.809	278.209	303.609
31/32	24.606	50.006	75.406	100.806	126.206	151.606	177.006	202.406	227.806	253.206	278.606	304.006
63/64	25.003	50.403	75.803	101.203	126.603	152.003	177.403	202.803	228.203	253.603	279.003	304.403

e of the tables. 11 miles = 10 miles + 1 mile = 17.703 km.

ilometres to miles 1 km = 0.621 371 mile

km	0	1	2	3	4	5	6	7	8	9
	miles	miles	miles	miles	miles	miles	miles	miles	miles	miles
0	0.000	0.621	1.243	1.864	2.485	3.107	3.728	4.350	4.971	5.592
10	6.214	6.835	7.456	8.078	8.699	9.321	9.942	10.563	11.185	11.806
20	12.427	13.049	13.670	14.292	14.913	15.534	16.156	16.777	17.398	18.020
30	18.641	19.263	19.884	20.505	21.127	21.748	22.369	22.991	23.612	24.233
40	24.855	25.476	26.098	26.719	27.340	27.962	28.583	29.204	29.826	30.447
50	31.069	31.690	32.311	32.933	33.554	34.175	34.797	35.418	36.040	36.661
60	37.282	37.904	38.525	39.146	39.768	40.389	41.010	41.632	42.253	42.875
70	43.496	44.117	44.739	45.360	45.981	46.603	47.224	47.846	48.467	49.088
80	49.710	50.331	50.952	51.574	52.195	52.817	53.438	54.059	54.681	55.302
90	55.923	56.545	57.166	57.788	58.409	59.030	59.652	60.273	60.894	61.516
100	62.137									

km	0	10	20	30	40	50	60	70	80	90
	miles	miles	miles	miles	miles	miles	miles	miles	miles	miles
0	0.000	6.214	12.427	18.641	24.855	31.069	37.282	43.496	49.710	55.923
100	62.137	68.351	74.565	80.778	86.992	93.206	99.419	105.633	111.847	118.061
200	124.274	130.488	136.702	142.915	149.129	155.343	161.557	167.770	173.984	180.198
300	186.411	192.625	198.839	205.052	211.266	217.480	223.694	229.907	236.121	242.335
400	248.548	254.762	260.976	267.190	273.403	279.617	285.831	292.044	298.258	304.472
500	310.686	316.899	323.113	329.327	335.540	341.754	347.968	354.182	360.395	366.609
600	372.823	379.036	385.250	391.464	397.678	403.891	410.105	416.319	422.532	428.746
700	434.960	441.174	447.387	453.601	459.815	466.028	472.242	478.456	484.670	490.883
800	497.097	503.311	509.524	515.738	521.952	528.166	534.379	540.593	546.807	553.020
900	559.234	565.448	571.661	577.875	584.089	590.303	596.516	602.730	608.944	615.157
1000	621.371									

iles to kilometres 1 mile = 1.609 344 km

miles	0	1	2	3	4	5	6	7	8	9
	km	km	km	km	km	km	km	km	km	km
0	0.000	1.609	3.219	4.828	6.437	8.047	9.656	11.265	12.875	14.484
10	16.093	17.703	19.312	20.921	22.531	24.140	25.750	27.359	28.968	30.578
20	32.187	33.796	35.406	37.015	38.624	40.234	41.843	43.452	45.062	46.671
30	48.280	49.890	51.499	53.108	54.718	56.327	57.936	59.546	61.155	62.764
40	64.374	65.983	67.592	69.202	70.811	72.420	74.030	75.639	77.249	78.858
50	80.467	82.077	83.686	85.295	86.905	88.514	90.123	91.733	93.342	94.951
60	96.561	98.170	99.779	101.389	102.998	104.607	106.217	107.826	109.435	111.045
70	112.654	114.263	115.873	117.482	119.091	120.701	122.310	123.919	125.529	127.138
80	128.748	130.357	131.966	133.576	135.185	136.794	138.404	140.013	141.622	143.232
90	144.841	146.450	148.060	149.669	151.278	152.888	154.497	156.106	157.716	159.325
100	160.934									

miles	0	10	20	30	40	50	60	70	80	90
	km	km	km	km	km	km	km	km	km	km
0	0.000	16.093	32.187	48.280	64.374	80.467	96.561	112.654	128.748	144.841
100	160.934	177.028	193.121	209.215	225.308	241.402	257.495	273.588	289.682	305.775
200	321.869	337.962	354.056	370.149	386.243	402.336	418.429	434.523	450.616	466.710
300	482.803	498.897	514.990	531.084	547.177	563.270	579.364	595.457	611.551	627.644
400	643.738	659.831	675.924	692.018	708.111	724.205	740.298	756.392	772.485	788.579
500	804.672	820.765	836.859	852.952	869.046	885.139	901.233	917.326	933.420	949.513
600	965.606	981.700	997.793	1013.887	1029.980	1046.074	1062.167	1078.260	1094.354	1110.447
700	1126.541	1142.634	1158.728	1174.821	1190.915	1207.008	1223.101	1239.195	1255.288	1271.382
800	1287.475	1303.569	1319.662	1335.756	1351.849	1367.942	1384.036	1400.129	1416.223	1432.316
900	1448.410	1464.503	1480.596	1496.690	1512.783	1528.877	1544.970	1561.064	1577.157	1593.251
1000	1609.344									

Area

Use of the tables. 11 in^2 = 10 in^2 + 1 in^2= 70.968 cm^2.

Square centimetres to square inches 1 cm^2 = 0.155 000 in^2

cm² → ↓	0	1	2	3	4	5	6	7	8	9
	in²	in²	in²	in²	in²	in²	in²	in²	in²	in²
0	0.000	0.155	0.310	0.465	0.620	0.775	0.930	1.085	1.240	1.395
10	1.550	1.705	1.860	2.015	2.170	2.325	2.480	2.635	2.790	2.945
20	3.100	3.255	3.410	3.565	3.720	3.875	4.030	4.185	4.340	4.495
30	4.650	4.805	4.960	5.115	5.270	5.425	5.580	5.735	5.890	6.045
40	6.200	6.355	6.510	6.665	6.820	6.975	7.130	7.285	7.440	7.595
50	7.750	7.905	8.060	8.215	8.370	8.525	8.680	8.835	8.990	9.145
60	9.300	9.455	9.610	9.765	9.920	10.075	10.230	10.385	10.540	10.695
70	10.850	11.005	11.160	11.315	11.470	11.625	11.780	11.935	12.090	12.245
80	12.400	12.555	12.710	12.865	13.020	13.175	13.330	13.485	13.640	13.795
90	13.950	14.105	14.260	14.415	14.570	14.725	14.880	15.035	15.190	15.345
100	15.500									

cm² → ↓	0	10	20	30	40	50	60	70	80	90
	in²	in²	in²	in²	in²	in²	in²	in²	in²	in²
0	0.000	1.550	3.100	4.650	6.200	7.750	9.300	10.850	12.400	13.950
100	15.500	17.050	18.600	20.150	21.700	23.250	24.800	26.350	27.900	29.450
200	31.000	32.550	34.100	35.650	37.200	38.750	40.300	41.850	43.400	44.950
300	46.500	48.050	49.600	51.150	52.700	54.250	55.800	57.350	58.900	60.450
400	62.000	63.550	65.100	66.650	68.200	69.750	71.300	72.850	74.400	75.950
500	77.500	79.050	80.600	82.150	83.700	85.250	86.800	88.350	89.900	91.450
600	93.000	94.550	96.100	97.650	99.200	100.750	102.300	103.850	105.400	106.950
700	108.500	110.050	111.600	113.150	114.700	116.250	117.800	119.350	120.900	122.450
800	124.000	125.550	127.100	128.650	130.200	131.750	133.300	134.850	136.400	137.950
900	139.500	141.050	142.600	144.150	145.700	147.250	148.800	150.350	151.900	153.450
1000	155.000									

Square inches to square centimetres 1 in^2 = 6.451 6 cm^2

in² → ↓	0	1	2	3	4	5	6	7	8	9
	cm²	cm²	cm²	cm²	cm²	cm²	cm²	cm²	cm²	cm²
0	0.000	6.452	12.903	19.355	25.806	32.258	38.710	45.161	51.613	58.064
10	64.516	70.968	77.419	83.871	90.322	96.774	103.226	109.677	116.129	122.580
20	129.032	135.484	141.935	148.387	154.838	161.290	167.742	174.193	180.645	187.096
30	193.548	200.000	206.451	212.903	219.354	225.806	232.258	238.709	245.161	251.612
40	258.064	264.516	270.967	277.419	283.870	290.322	296.774	303.225	309.677	316.128
50	322.580	329.032	335.483	341.935	348.386	354.838	361.290	367.741	374.193	380.644
60	387.096	393.548	399.999	406.451	412.902	419.354	425.806	432.257	438.709	445.160
70	451.612	458.064	464.515	470.967	477.418	483.870	490.322	496.773	503.225	509.676
80	516.128	522.580	529.031	535.483	541.934	548.386	554.838	561.289	567.741	574.192
90	580.644	587.096	593.547	599.999	606.450	612.902	619.354	625.805	632.257	638.708
100	645.160									

in² → ↓	0	10	20	30	40	50	60	70	80	90
	cm²	cm²	cm²	cm²	cm²	cm²	cm²	cm²	cm²	cm²
0	0.000	64.516	129.032	193.548	258.064	322.580	387.096	451.612	516.128	580.644
100	645.160	709.676	774.192	838.708	903.224	967.740	1032.256	1096.772	1161.288	1255.804
200	1290.320	1354.836	1419.352	1483.868	1548.384	1612.900	1677.416	1741.932	1806.448	1870.964
300	1935.480	1999.996	2064.512	2129.028	2193.544	2258.060	2322.576	2387.092	2451.608	2516.124
400	2580.640	2645.156	2709.672	2774.188	2838.704	2903.220	2967.736	3032.252	3096.768	3161.284
500	3225.800	3290.316	3354.832	3419.348	3483.864	3548.380	3612.896	3677.412	3741.928	3806.444
600	3870.960	3935.476	3999.992	4064.508	4129.024	4193.540	4258.056	4322.572	4387.088	4451.604
700	4516.120	4580.636	4645.152	4709.668	4774.184	4838.700	4903.216	4967.732	5032.248	5096.764
800	5161.280	5225.796	5290.312	5354.828	5419.344	5483.860	5548.376	5612.892	5677.408	5741.924
900	5806.440	5870.956	5935.472	5999.988	6064.504	6129.020	6193.536	6258.052	6322.568	6387.084
1000	6451.600									

Use of the tables. 11 acres = 10 acres + 1 acre = 4.452 ha.

Hectares to acres 1 ha = 2.471 054 acres

ha → ↓	0 acres	1 acres	2 acres	3 acres	4 acres	5 acres	6 acres	7 acres	8 acres	9 acres	← ha ↓
0	0.000	2.471	4.942	7.413	9.884	12.355	14.826	17.297	19.768	22.239	0
10	24.711	27.182	29.653	32.124	34.595	37.066	39.537	42.008	44.479	46.950	10
20	49.421	51.892	54.363	56.834	59.305	61.776	64.247	66.718	69.190	71.661	20
30	74.132	76.603	79.074	81.545	84.016	86.487	88.958	91.429	93.900	96.371	30
40	98.842	101.313	103.784	106.255	108.726	111.197	113.668	116.140	118.611	121.082	40
50	123.553	126.024	128.495	130.966	133.437	135.908	138.379	140.850	143.321	145.792	50
60	148.263	150.734	153.205	155.676	158.147	160.618	163.090	165.561	168.032	170.503	60
70	172.974	175.445	177.916	180.387	182.858	185.329	187.800	190.271	192.742	195.213	70
80	197.684	200.155	202.626	205.097	207.569	210.040	212.511	214.982	217.453	219.924	80
90	222.395	224.866	227.337	229.808	232.279	234.750	237.221	239.692	242.163	244.634	90
100	247.105										100

ha → ↓	0 acres	10 acres	20 acres	30 acres	40 acres	50 acres	60 acres	70 acres	80 acres	90 acres	← ha ↓
0	0.000	24.711	49.421	74.132	98.842	123.553	148.263	172.974	197.684	222.395	0
100	247.105	271.816	296.526	321.237	345.948	370.658	395.369	420.079	444.790	469.500	100
200	494.211	518.921	543.632	568.342	593.053	617.763	642.474	667.185	691.895	716.606	200
300	741.316	766.027	790.737	815.448	840.158	864.869	889.579	914.290	939.000	963.711	300
400	988.422	1013.132	1037.843	1062.553	1087.264	1111.974	1136.685	1161.395	1186.106	1210.816	400
500	1235.527	1260.237	1284.948	1309.659	1334.369	1359.080	1383.790	1408.501	1433.211	1457.922	500
600	1482.632	1507.343	1532.053	1556.764	1581.474	1606.185	1630.896	1655.606	1680.317	1705.027	600
700	1729.738	1754.448	1779.159	1803.869	1828.580	1853.290	1878.001	1902.711	1927.422	1952.133	700
800	1976.843	2001.554	2026.264	2050.975	2075.685	2100.396	2125.106	2149.817	2174.527	2199.238	800
900	2223.948	2248.659	2273.370	2298.080	2322.791	2347.501	2372.212	2396.922	2421.633	2446.343	900
1000	2471.054										1000

Acres to hectares 1 acre = 0.404 686 ha

acres → ↓	0 ha	1 ha	2 ha	3 ha	4 ha	5 ha	6 ha	7 ha	8 ha	9 ha	← acres ↓
0	0.000	0.405	0.809	1.214	1.619	2.023	2.428	2.833	3.237	3.642	0
10	4.047	4.452	4.856	5.261	5.666	6.070	6.475	6.880	7.284	7.689	10
20	8.094	8.498	8.903	9.308	9.712	10.117	10.522	10.927	11.331	11.736	20
30	12.141	12.545	12.950	13.355	13.759	14.164	14.569	14.973	15.378	15.783	30
40	16.187	16.592	16.997	17.401	17.806	18.211	18.616	19.020	19.425	19.830	40
50	20.234	20.639	21.044	21.448	21.853	22.258	22.662	23.067	23.472	23.876	50
60	24.281	24.686	25.091	25.495	25.900	26.305	26.709	27.114	27.519	27.923	60
70	28.328	28.733	29.137	29.542	29.947	30.351	30.756	31.161	31.565	31.970	70
80	32.375	32.780	33.184	33.589	33.994	34.398	34.803	35.208	35.612	36.017	80
90	36.422	36.826	37.231	37.636	38.040	38.445	38.850	39.255	39.659	40.064	90
100	40.469										100

acres → ↓	0 ha	10 ha	20 ha	30 ha	40 ha	50 ha	60 ha	70 ha	80 ha	90 ha	← acres ↓
0	0.000	4.047	8.094	12.141	16.187	20.234	24.281	28.328	32.375	36.422	0
100	40.469	44.515	48.562	52.609	56.656	60.703	64.750	68.797	72.843	76.890	100
200	80.937	84.984	89.031	93.078	97.125	101.171	105.218	109.265	113.312	117.359	200
300	121.406	125.453	129.499	133.546	137.593	141.640	145.687	149.734	153.781	157.827	300
400	161.874	165.921	169.968	174.015	178.062	182.109	186.155	190.202	194.249	198.296	400
500	202.343	206.390	210.437	214.483	218.530	222.577	226.624	230.671	234.718	238.765	500
600	242.811	246.858	250.905	254.952	258.999	263.046	267.093	271.139	275.186	279.233	600
700	283.280	287.327	291.374	295.421	299.467	303.514	307.561	311.608	315.655	319.702	700
800	323.749	327.795	331.842	335.889	339.936	343.983	348.030	352.077	356.123	360.170	800
900	364.217	368.264	372.311	376.358	380.405	384.451	388.498	392.545	396.592	400.639	900
1000	404.686										1000

Use of the tables. 11 mile^2 = 10 mile^2 + 1 mile^2 = 28.490 km^2.

Square kilometres to square miles   1 km^2 = 0.386 102 mile^2

km^2 → ↓	0	1	2	3	4	5	6	7	8	9
	mile^2	mile^2	mile^2	mile^2	mile^2	mile^2	mile^2	mile^2	mile^2	mile^2
0	0.000	0.386	0.772	1.158	1.544	1.931	2.317	2.703	3.089	3.475
10	3.861	4.247	4.633	5.019	5.405	5.792	6.178	6.564	6.950	7.336
20	7.722	8.108	8.494	8.880	9.266	9.653	10.039	10.425	10.811	11.197
30	11.583	11.969	12.355	12.741	13.127	13.514	13.900	14.286	14.672	15.058
40	15.444	15.830	16.216	16.602	16.988	17.375	17.761	18.147	18.533	18.919
50	19.305	19.691	20.077	20.463	20.850	21.236	21.622	22.008	22.394	22.780
60	23.166	23.552	23.938	24.324	24.711	25.097	25.483	25.869	26.255	26.641
70	27.027	27.413	27.799	28.185	28.572	28.958	29.344	29.730	30.116	30.502
80	30.888	31.274	31.660	32.046	32.433	32.819	33.205	33.591	33.977	34.363
90	34.749	35.135	35.521	35.908	36.294	36.680	37.066	37.452	37.838	38.224
100	38.610									

km^2 → ↓	0	10	20	30	40	50	60	70	80	90
	mile^2	mile^2	mile^2	mile^2	mile^2	mile^2	mile^2	mile^2	mile^2	mile^2
0	0.000	3.861	7.722	11.583	15.444	19.305	23.166	27.027	30.888	34.749
100	38.610	42.471	46.332	50.193	54.054	57.915	61.776	65.637	69.498	73.359
200	77.220	81.081	84.942	88.803	92.665	96.526	100.387	104.248	108.109	111.970
300	115.831	119.692	123.553	127.414	131.275	135.136	138.997	142.858	146.719	150.580
400	154.441	158.302	162.163	166.024	169.885	173.746	177.607	181.468	185.329	189.190
500	193.051	196.912	200.773	204.634	208.495	212.356	216.217	220.078	223.939	227.800
600	231.661	235.522	239.383	243.244	247.105	250.966	254.827	258.688	262.549	266.410
700	270.272	274.133	277.994	281.855	285.716	289.577	293.438	297.299	301.160	305.021
800	308.882	312.743	316.604	320.465	324.326	328.187	332.048	335.909	339.770	343.631
900	347.492	351.353	355.214	359.075	362.936	366.797	370.658	374.519	378.380	382.241
1000	386.102									

Square miles to square kilometres   1 mile^2 = 2.589 988 km^2

mile^2 → ↓	0	1	2	3	4	5	6	7	8	9
	km^2	km^2	km^2	km^2	km^2	km^2	km^2	km^2	km^2	km^2
0	0.000	2.590	5.180	7.770	10.360	12.950	15.540	18.130	20.720	23.310
10	25.900	28.490	31.080	33.670	36.260	38.850	41.440	44.030	46.620	49.210
20	51.800	54.390	56.980	59.570	62.160	64.750	67.340	69.930	72.520	75.110
30	77.700	80.290	82.880	85.470	88.060	90.650	93.240	95.830	98.420	101.010
40	103.600	106.190	108.780	111.369	113.959	116.549	119.139	121.729	124.319	126.909
50	129.499	132.089	134.679	137.269	139.859	142.449	145.039	147.629	150.219	152.809
60	155.399	157.989	160.579	163.169	165.759	168.349	170.939	173.529	176.119	178.709
70	181.299	183.889	186.479	189.069	191.659	194.249	196.839	199.429	202.019	204.609
80	207.199	209.789	212.379	214.969	217.559	220.149	222.739	225.329	227.919	230.509
90	233.099	235.689	238.279	240.869	243.459	246.049	248.639	251.229	253.819	256.409
100	258.999									

mile^2 → ↓	0	10	20	30	40	50	60	70	80	90
	km^2	km^2	km^2	km^2	km^2	km^2	km^2	km^2	km^2	km^2
0	0.000	25.900	51.800	77.700	103.600	129.499	155.399	181.299	207.199	233.099
100	258.999	284.899	310.799	336.698	362.598	388.498	414.398	440.298	466.198	492.098
200	517.998	543.898	569.797	595.697	621.597	647.497	673.397	699.297	725.197	751.097
300	776.996	802.896	828.796	854.696	880.596	906.496	932.396	958.296	984.195	1010.095
400	1035.995	1061.895	1087.795	1113.695	1139.595	1165.495	1191.395	1217.294	1243.194	1269.094
500	1294.994	1320.894	1346.794	1372.694	1398.594	1424.493	1450.393	1476.293	1502.193	1528.093
600	1553.993	1579.893	1605.793	1631.693	1657.592	1683.492	1709.392	1735.292	1761.192	1787.092
700	1812.992	1838.892	1864.791	1890.691	1916.591	1942.491	1968.391	1994.291	2020.191	2046.091
800	2071.990	2097.890	2123.790	2149.690	2175.590	2201.490	2227.390	2253.290	2279.190	2305.089
900	2330.989	2356.889	2382.789	2408.689	2434.589	2460.489	2486.389	2512.288	2538.188	2564.088
1000	2589.988									

Areas of circles from radii

se of the table. The unit at the side of a line added to the unit at the head of a column makes up the radius of a circle for which the area is shown in e position where line and column meet. For example, 0.1 + 0.01 = 0.11; the area of a circle with radius 0.11 is 0.0238.

	0.00	0.01	0.02	0.03	0.04	0.05	0.06	0.07	0.08	0.09	
0	0.000	0.000	0.001	0.003	0.005	0.008	0.011	0.015	0.020	0.025	0.0
1	0.031	0.038	0.045	0.053	0.062	0.071	0.080	0.091	0.102	0.113	0.1
2	0.126	0.139	0.152	0.166	0.181	0.196	0.212	0.229	0.246	0.264	0.2
3	0.283	0.302	0.322	0.342	0.363	0.385	0.407	0.430	0.454	0.478	0.3
4	0.503	0.528	0.554	0.581	0.608	0.636	0.665	0.694	0.724	0.754	0.4
5	0.785	0.817	0.849	0.882	0.916	0.950	0.985	1.021	1.057	1.094	0.5
6	1.131	1.169	1.208	1.247	1.287	1.327	1.368	1.410	1.453	1.496	0.6
7	1.539	1.584	1.629	1.674	1.720	1.767	1.815	1.863	1.911	1.961	0.7
8	2.011	2.061	2.112	2.164	2.217	2.270	2.324	2.378	2.433	2.488	0.8
9	2.545	2.602	2.659	2.717	2.776	2.835	2.895	2.956	3.017	3.079	0.9
0	3.142	3.205	3.269	3.333	3.398	3.464	3.530	3.597	3.664	3.733	1.0
1	3.801	3.871	3.941	4.011	4.083	4.155	4.227	4.301	4.374	4.449	1.1
2	4.524	4.600	4.676	4.753	4.831	4.909	4.988	5.067	5.147	5.228	1.2
3	5.309	5.391	5.474	5.557	5.641	5.726	5.811	5.896	5.983	6.070	1.3
4	6.158	6.246	6.335	6.424	6.514	6.605	6.697	6.789	6.881	6.975	1.4
5	7.069	7.163	7.258	7.354	7.451	7.548	7.645	7.744	7.843	7.942	1.5
6	8.042	8.143	8.245	8.347	8.450	8.553	8.657	8.762	8.867	8.973	1.6
7	9.079	9.186	9.294	9.402	9.511	9.621	9.731	9.842	9.954	10.066	1.7
8	10.179	10.292	10.406	10.521	10.636	10.752	10.869	10.986	11.104	11.222	1.8
9	11.341	11.461	11.581	11.702	11.824	11.946	12.069	12.192	12.316	12.441	1.9
0	12.566	12.692	12.819	12.946	13.074	13.203	13.332	13.461	13.592	13.723	2.0
1	13.854	13.987	14.120	14.253	14.387	14.522	14.657	14.793	14.930	15.067	2.1
2	15.205	15.344	15.483	15.623	15.763	15.904	16.046	16.188	16.331	16.475	2.2
3	16.619	16.764	16.909	17.055	17.202	17.349	17.497	17.646	17.795	17.945	2.3
4	18.096	18.247	18.398	18.551	18.704	18.857	19.012	19.167	19.322	19.478	2.4
5	19.635	19.792	19.950	20.109	20.268	20.428	20.589	20.750	20.912	21.074	2.5
6	21.237	21.401	21.565	21.730	21.896	22.062	22.229	22.396	22.564	22.733	2.6
7	22.902	23.072	23.243	23.414	23.586	23.758	23.931	24.105	24.279	24.454	2.7
8	24.630	24.806	24.983	25.161	25.339	25.518	25.697	25.877	26.058	26.239	2.8
9	26.421	26.603	26.786	26.970	27.155	27.340	27.525	27.712	27.899	28.086	2.9
0	28.274	28.463	28.653	28.843	29.033	29.225	29.417	29.609	29.802	29.996	3.0
1	30.191	30.386	30.582	30.778	30.975	31.172	31.371	31.570	31.769	31.969	3.1
2	32.170	32.371	32.573	32.776	32.979	33.183	33.388	33.593	33.799	34.005	3.2
3	34.212	34.420	34.628	34.837	35.046	35.257	35.467	35.679	35.891	36.103	3.3
4	36.317	36.531	36.745	36.961	37.176	37.393	37.610	37.828	38.046	38.265	3.4
5	38.485	38.705	38.926	39.147	39.369	39.592	39.815	40.039	40.264	40.489	3.5
6	40.715	40.942	41.169	41.396	41.625	41.854	42.084	42.314	42.545	42.776	3.6
7	43.008	43.241	43.475	43.709	43.943	44.179	44.415	44.651	44.888	45.126	3.7
8	45.365	45.604	45.843	46.084	46.325	46.566	46.808	47.051	47.295	47.539	3.8
9	47.784	48.029	48.275	48.522	48.769	49.017	49.265	49.514	49.764	50.014	3.9
0	50.265	50.517	50.769	51.022	51.276	51.530	51.785	52.040	52.296	52.553	4.0
1	52.810	53.068	53.327	53.586	53.846	54.106	54.367	54.629	54.891	55.154	4.1
2	55.418	55.682	55.947	56.212	56.478	56.745	57.012	57.280	57.549	57.818	4.2
3	58.088	58.359	58.630	58.901	59.174	59.447	59.720	59.995	60.270	60.545	4.3
4	60.821	61.098	61.375	61.653	61.932	62.211	62.491	62.772	63.053	63.335	4.4
5	63.617	63.900	64.184	64.468	64.753	65.039	65.325	65.612	65.899	66.187	4.5
6	66.476	66.765	67.055	67.346	67.637	67.929	68.222	68.515	68.808	69.103	4.6
7	69.398	69.693	69.990	70.287	70.584	70.882	71.181	71.480	71.780	72.081	4.7
8	72.382	72.684	72.987	73.290	73.594	73.898	74.203	74.509	74.815	75.122	4.8
9	75.430	75.738	76.047	76.356	76.666	76.977	77.288	77.600	77.913	78.226	4.9

Use of the table. 5.1 + 0.01 = 5.11; the area of a circle with radius 5.11 is 82.034.

	0.00	0.01	0.02	0.03	0.04	0.05	0.06	0.07	0.08	0.09
5.0	78.540	78.854	79.169	79.485	79.801	80.118	80.436	80.754	81.073	81.393
5.1	81.713	82.034	82.355	82.677	83.000	83.323	83.647	83.971	84.296	84.622
5.2	84.949	85.276	85.603	85.932	86.261	86.590	86.920	87.251	87.583	87.915
5.3	88.247	88.581	88.915	89.249	89.584	89.920	90.257	90.594	90.932	91.270
5.4	91.609	91.948	92.289	92.630	92.971	93.313	93.656	93.999	94.343	94.688
5.5	95.033	95.379	95.726	96.073	96.421	96.769	97.118	97.468	97.818	98.169
5.6	98.520	98.873	99.225	99.579	99.933	100.287	100.643	100.999	101.355	101.713
5.7	102.070	102.429	102.788	103.148	103.508	103.869	104.231	104.593	104.956	105.319
5.8	105.683	106.048	106.413	106.779	107.146	107.513	107.881	108.250	108.619	108.988
5.9	109.359	109.730	110.102	110.474	110.847	111.220	111.594	111.969	112.345	112.721
6.0	113.097	113.475	113.853	114.231	114.610	114.990	115.371	115.752	116.133	116.516
6.1	116.899	117.282	117.666	118.051	118.437	118.823	119.210	119.597	119.985	120.374
6.2	120.763	121.153	121.543	121.934	122.326	122.718	123.111	123.505	123.899	124.294
6.3	124.690	125.086	125.483	125.880	126.278	126.677	127.076	127.476	127.877	128.278
6.4	128.680	129.082	129.485	129.889	130.293	130.698	131.104	131.510	131.917	132.324
6.5	132.732	133.141	133.550	133.960	134.371	134.782	135.194	135.607	136.020	136.433
6.6	136.848	137.263	137.678	138.095	138.512	138.929	139.347	139.766	140.185	140.605
6.7	141.026	141.447	141.869	142.292	142.715	143.139	143.563	143.988	144.414	144.840
6.8	145.267	145.695	146.123	146.552	146.981	147.411	147.842	148.273	148.705	149.138
6.9	149.571	150.005	150.440	150.875	151.310	151.747	152.184	152.621	153.060	153.499
7.0	153.938	154.378	154.819	155.260	155.702	156.145	156.588	157.032	157.477	157.922
7.1	158.368	158.814	159.261	159.709	160.157	160.606	161.056	161.506	161.957	162.408
7.2	162.860	163.313	163.766	164.220	164.675	165.130	165.586	166.042	166.499	166.957
7.3	167.415	167.874	168.334	168.794	169.255	169.717	170.179	170.642	171.105	171.569
7.4	172.034	172.499	172.965	173.431	173.898	174.366	174.835	175.304	175.773	176.244
7.5	176.715	177.186	177.658	178.131	178.605	179.079	179.553	180.029	180.505	180.981
7.6	181.458	181.936	182.415	182.894	183.374	183.854	184.335	184.816	185.299	185.782
7.7	186.265	186.749	187.234	187.719	188.205	188.692	189.179	189.667	190.156	190.645
7.8	191.134	191.625	192.116	192.608	193.100	193.593	194.086	194.581	195.075	195.571
7.9	196.067	196.563	197.061	197.559	198.057	198.557	199.056	199.557	200.058	200.560
8.0	201.062	201.565	202.068	202.573	203.078	203.583	204.089	204.596	205.103	205.611
8.1	206.120	206.629	207.139	207.650	208.161	208.672	209.185	209.698	210.212	210.726
8.2	211.241	211.756	212.272	212.789	213.307	213.825	214.343	214.863	215.383	215.903
8.3	216.424	216.946	217.469	217.992	218.515	219.040	219.565	220.090	220.616	221.143
8.4	221.671	222.199	222.728	223.257	223.787	224.318	224.849	225.381	225.913	226.446
8.5	226.980	227.514	228.049	228.585	229.121	229.658	230.196	230.734	231.273	231.812
8.6	232.352	232.893	233.434	233.976	234.519	235.062	235.606	236.150	236.695	237.241
8.7	237.787	238.334	238.882	239.430	239.979	240.528	241.078	241.629	242.180	242.732
8.8	243.285	243.838	244.392	244.947	245.502	246.057	246.614	247.171	247.728	248.287
8.9	248.846	249.405	249.965	250.526	251.087	251.649	252.212	252.775	253.339	253.904
9.0	254.469	255.035	255.601	256.168	256.736	257.304	257.873	258.443	259.013	259.584
9.1	260.155	260.727	261.300	261.873	262.447	263.022	263.597	264.173	264.750	265.327
9.2	265.904	266.483	267.062	267.641	268.222	268.803	269.384	269.966	270.549	271.132
9.3	271.716	272.301	272.886	273.472	274.059	274.646	275.234	275.822	276.411	277.001
9.4	277.591	278.182	278.774	279.366	279.959	280.552	281.146	281.741	282.336	282.932
9.5	283.529	284.126	284.724	285.322	285.921	286.521	287.121	287.722	288.324	288.926
9.6	289.529	290.133	290.737	291.342	291.947	292.553	293.160	293.767	294.375	294.983
9.7	295.592	296.202	296.813	297.424	298.035	298.648	299.261	299.874	300.488	301.103
9.8	301.719	302.335	302.951	303.569	304.187	304.805	305.424	306.044	306.665	307.286
9.9	307.907	308.530	309.153	309.776	310.401	311.026	311.651	312.277	312.904	313.531

Use of the table. 11 + 0.01 = 11.1; the area of a circle with radius 11.1 is 387.076.

0.0	0.1	0.2	0.3	0.4	0.5	0.6	0.7	0.8	0.9	
314.159	320.474	326.851	333.292	339.795	346.361	352.989	359.681	366.435	373.253	10
380.133	387.076	394.081	401.150	408.281	415.476	422.733	430.053	437.435	444.881	11
452.389	459.961	467.595	475.292	483.051	490.874	498.759	506.707	514.719	522.792	12
530.929	539.129	547.391	555.716	564.104	572.555	581.069	589.646	598.285	606.987	13
615.752	624.580	633.471	642.424	651.441	660.520	669.662	678.867	688.134	697.465	14
706.858	716.315	725.834	735.415	745.060	754.768	764.538	774.371	784.267	794.226	15
804.248	814.332	824.480	834.690	844.963	855.299	865.697	876.159	886.683	897.270	16
907.920	918.633	929.409	940.247	951.149	962.113	973.140	984.230	995.382	1006.598	17
1017.876	1029.217	1040.621	1052.088	1063.618	1075.210	1086.865	1098.584	1110.365	1122.208	18
1134.115	1146.084	1158.117	1170.212	1182.370	1194.591	1206.874	1219.221	1231.630	1244.102	19
1256.637	1269.235	1281.895	1294.619	1307.405	1320.254	1333.166	1346.141	1359.179	1372.279	20
1385.442	1398.668	1411.957	1425.309	1438.724	1452.201	1465.741	1479.345	1493.010	1506.739	21
1520.531	1534.385	1548.303	1562.283	1576.326	1590.431	1604.600	1618.831	1633.126	1647.483	22
1661.903	1676.385	1690.931	1705.539	1720.210	1734.945	1749.741	1764.601	1779.524	1794.509	23
1809.557	1824.668	1839.842	1855.079	1870.379	1885.741	1901.166	1916.654	1932.205	1947.819	24
1963.495	1979.235	1995.037	2010.902	2026.830	2042.821	2058.874	2074.991	2091.170	2107.412	25
2123.717	2140.084	2156.515	2173.008	2189.564	2206.183	2222.865	2239.610	2256.418	2273.288	26
2290.221	2307.217	2324.276	2341.398	2358.582	2375.829	2393.140	2410.513	2427.948	2445.447	27
2463.009	2480.633	2498.320	2516.070	2533.883	2551.759	2569.697	2587.698	2605.763	2623.890	28
2642.079	2660.332	2678.648	2697.026	2715.467	2733.971	2752.538	2771.167	2789.860	2808.615	29
2827.433	2846.314	2865.258	2884.265	2903.334	2922.467	2941.662	2960.920	2980.240	2999.624	30
3019.071	3038.580	3058.152	3077.787	3097.485	3117.245	3137.069	3156.955	3176.904	3196.916	31
3216.991	3237.128	3257.329	3277.592	3297.918	3318.307	3338.759	3359.274	3379.851	3400.491	32
3421.194	3441.960	3462.789	3483.681	3504.635	3525.652	3546.732	3567.875	3589.081	3610.350	33
3631.681	3653.075	3674.532	3696.052	3717.635	3739.281	3760.989	3782.760	3804.594	3826.491	34
3848.451	3870.474	3892.559	3914.707	3936.918	3959.192	3981.529	4003.928	4026.381	4048.916	35
4071.504	4094.155	4116.869	4139.645	4162.485	4185.387	4208.352	4231.380	4254.470	4277.624	36
4300.840	4324.120	4347.462	4370.866	4394.334	4417.865	4441.458	4465.114	4488.833	4512.615	37
4536.460	4560.367	4584.338	4608.371	4632.467	4656.626	4680.847	4705.132	4729.479	4753.889	38
4778.362	4802.898	4827.497	4852.158	4876.883	4901.670	4926.520	4951.433	4976.408	5001.447	39
5026.548	5051.712	5076.939	5102.229	5127.582	5152.997	5178.476	5204.017	5229.621	5255.288	40
5281.017	5306.810	5332.665	5358.583	5384.564	5410.608	5436.715	5462.884	5489.116	5515.411	41
5541.769	5568.190	5594.674	5621.220	5647.830	5674.502	5701.237	5728.034	5754.895	5781.819	42
5808.805	5835.854	5862.966	5890.141	5917.378	5944.679	5972.042	5999.468	6026.957	6054.509	43
6082.123	6109.801	6137.541	6165.344	6193.210	6221.139	6249.130	6277.185	6305.302	6333.482	44
6361.725	6390.031	6418.399	6446.831	6475.325	6503.882	6532.502	6561.185	6589.930	6618.739	45
6647.610	6676.544	6705.541	6734.601	6763.723	6792.909	6822.157	6851.468	6880.842	6910.279	46
6939.778	6969.341	6998.966	7028.654	7058.405	7088.218	7118.095	7148.034	7178.037	7208.102	47
7238.229	7268.420	7298.674	7328.990	7359.369	7389.811	7420.316	7450.884	7481.514	7512.208	48
7542.964	7573.783	7604.665	7635.610	7666.617	7697.687	7728.821	7760.017	7791.275	7822.597	49
7853.982	7885.429	7916.939	7948.512	7980.148	8011.847	8043.608	8075.433	8107.320	8139.270	50
8171.282	8203.358	8235.497	8267.698	8299.962	8332.289	8364.679	8397.132	8429.647	8462.225	51
8494.867	8527.571	8560.337	8593.167	8626.059	8659.015	8692.033	8725.114	8758.258	8791.464	52
8824.734	8858.066	8891.461	8924.919	8958.440	8992.024	9025.670	9059.379	9093.151	9126.986	53
9160.884	9194.845	9228.868	9262.955	9297.104	9331.316	9365.590	9399.928	9434.328	9468.792	54
9503.318	9537.907	9572.558	9607.273	9642.051	9676.891	9711.794	9746.760	9781.789	9816.880	55
9852.035	9887.252	9922.532	9957.875	9993.281	10028.749	10064.281	10099.875	10135.532	10171.252	56
10207.035	10242.880	10278.789	10314.760	10350.794	10386.891	10423.050	10459.273	10495.558	10531.907	57
10568.318	10604.792	10641.328	10677.928	10714.590	10751.315	10788.104	10824.954	10861.868	10898.845	58
10935.884	10972.986	11010.151	11047.379	11084.670	11122.023	11159.440	11196.919	11234.461	11272.066	59

Use of the table. 61 + 0.1 = 61.1; the area of a circle with radius 561.1 is 11728.225.

	0.0	0.1	0.2	0.3	0.4	0.5	0.6	0.7	0.8	0.9
60	11309.734	11347.464	11385.257	11423.114	11461.033	11499.015	11537.059	11575.167	11613.337	11651.570
61	11689.866	11728.225	11766.647	11805.131	11843.679	11882.289	11920.962	11959.698	11998.496	12037.358
62	12076.282	12115.269	12154.319	12193.432	12232.608	12271.846	12311.148	12350.512	12389.939	12429.429
63	12468.981	12508.597	12548.275	12588.016	12627.820	12667.687	12707.617	12747.609	12787.664	12827.783
64	12867.964	12908.207	12948.514	12988.883	13029.316	13069.811	13110.369	13150.990	13191.673	13232.420
65	13273.229	13314.101	13355.036	13396.034	13437.094	13478.218	13519.404	13560.653	13601.965	13643.340
66	13684.778	13726.278	13767.841	13809.467	13851.156	13892.908	13934.723	13976.600	14018.540	14060.543
67	14102.609	14144.738	14186.930	14229.184	14271.501	14313.882	14356.324	14398.830	14441.399	14484.030
68	14526.724	14569.482	14612.301	14655.184	14698.130	14741.138	14784.209	14827.343	14870.540	14913.800
69	14957.123	15000.508	15043.956	15087.467	15131.041	15174.678	15218.377	15262.140	15305.965	15349.853
70	15393.804	15437.818	15481.894	15526.034	15570.236	15614.501	15658.829	15703.219	15747.673	15792.189
71	15836.769	15881.411	15926.115	15970.883	16015.714	16060.607	16105.563	16150.582	16195.664	16240.809
72	16286.016	16331.287	16376.620	16422.016	16467.475	16512.996	16558.581	16604.228	16649.938	16695.711
73	16741.547	16787.446	16833.407	16879.432	16925.519	16971.669	17017.882	17064.157	17110.496	17156.897
74	17203.361	17249.888	17296.478	17343.131	17389.846	17436.625	17483.466	17530.370	17577.337	17624.366
75	17671.459	17718.614	17765.832	17813.113	17860.457	17907.864	17955.333	18002.865	18050.460	18098.118
76	18145.839	18193.623	18241.469	18289.379	18337.351	18385.386	18433.483	18481.644	18529.867	18578.154
77	18626.503	18674.915	18723.390	18771.927	18820.528	18869.191	18917.917	18966.706	19015.558	19064.472
78	19113.450	19162.490	19211.593	19260.759	19309.988	19359.279	19408.634	19458.051	19507.531	19557.074
79	19606.680	19656.348	19706.080	19755.874	19805.731	19855.651	19905.634	19955.679	20005.788	20055.959
80	20106.193	20156.490	20206.850	20257.272	20307.758	20358.306	20408.917	20459.591	20510.327	20561.127
81	20611.989	20662.915	20713.903	20764.954	20816.067	20867.244	20918.483	20969.785	21021.150	21072.578
82	21124.069	21175.623	21227.239	21278.918	21330.660	21382.465	21434.333	21486.263	21538.257	21590.313
83	21642.432	21694.614	21746.858	21799.166	21851.536	21903.969	21956.465	22009.024	22061.646	22114.330
84	22167.078	22219.888	22272.761	22325.697	22378.695	22431.757	22484.881	22538.068	22591.318	22644.631
85	22698.007	22751.445	22804.947	22858.511	22912.138	22965.828	23019.580	23073.396	23127.274	23181.215
86	23235.219	23289.286	23343.416	23397.608	23451.863	23506.182	23560.563	23615.006	23669.513	23724.082
87	23778.715	23833.410	23888.168	23942.989	23997.872	24052.819	24107.828	24162.900	24218.035	24273.233
88	24328.494	24383.817	24439.203	24494.652	24550.164	24605.739	24661.377	24717.077	24772.840	24828.666
89	24884.555	24940.507	24996.522	25052.599	25108.739	25164.943	25221.208	25277.537	25333.929	25390.383
90	25446.900	25503.481	25560.123	25616.829	25673.598	25730.429	25787.323	25844.281	25901.300	25958.383
91	26015.529	26072.737	26130.008	26187.342	26244.739	26302.199	26359.722	26417.307	26474.955	26532.666
92	26590.440	26648.277	26706.176	26764.139	26822.164	26880.252	26938.403	26996.617	27054.893	27113.233
93	27171.635	27230.100	27288.628	27347.218	27405.872	27464.588	27523.368	27582.210	27641.114	27700.082
94	27759.113	27818.206	27877.362	27936.581	27995.863	28055.208	28114.615	28174.086	28233.619	28293.215
95	28352.874	28412.595	28472.380	28532.227	28592.137	28652.110	28712.146	28772.245	28832.406	28892.631
96	28952.918	29013.268	29073.681	29134.156	29194.695	29255.296	29315.960	29376.687	29437.477	29498.330
97	29559.245	29620.224	29681.265	29742.369	29803.536	29864.765	29926.058	29987.413	30048.831	30110.312
98	30171.856	30233.462	30295.132	30356.864	30418.659	30480.517	30542.438	30604.422	30666.468	30728.577
99	30790.750	30852.985	30915.282	30977.643	31040.066	31102.553	31165.102	31227.714	31290.388	31353.126
100	31415.927	31478.790	31541.716	31604.705	31667.757	31730.871	31794.049	31857.289	31920.592	31983.958

Radii of circles from areas

Use of the table. The unit at the side of a line added to the unit at the head of a column makes up the area of a circle for which the radius is shown in the position were line and column meet. For example, 0.1 + 0.01 = 0.11; the radius of a circle with area 0.11 is 0.1871.

	0.00	0.01	0.02	0.03	0.04	0.05	0.06	0.07	0.08	0.09	
0.0	0.0000	0.0564	0.0798	0.0977	0.1128	0.1262	0.1382	0.1493	0.1596	0.1693	0.0
0.1	0.1784	0.1871	0.1954	0.2034	0.2111	0.2185	0.2257	0.2326	0.2394	0.2459	0.1
0.2	0.2523	0.2585	0.2646	0.2706	0.2764	0.2821	0.2877	0.2932	0.2985	0.3038	0.2
0.3	0.3090	0.3141	0.3192	0.3241	0.3290	0.3338	0.3385	0.3432	0.3478	0.3523	0.3
0.4	0.3568	0.3613	0.3656	0.3700	0.3742	0.3785	0.3827	0.3868	0.3909	0.3949	0.4
0.5	0.3989	0.4029	0.4068	0.4107	0.4146	0.4184	0.4222	0.4260	0.4297	0.4334	0.5
0.6	0.4370	0.4406	0.4442	0.4478	0.4514	0.4549	0.4583	0.4618	0.4652	0.4687	0.6
0.7	0.4720	0.4754	0.4787	0.4820	0.4853	0.4886	0.4918	0.4951	0.4983	0.5015	0.7
0.8	0.5046	0.5078	0.5109	0.5140	0.5171	0.5202	0.5232	0.5262	0.5293	0.5323	0.8
0.9	0.5352	0.5382	0.5412	0.5441	0.5470	0.5499	0.5528	0.5557	0.5585	0.5614	0.9
1.0	0.5642	0.5670	0.5698	0.5726	0.5754	0.5781	0.5809	0.5836	0.5863	0.5890	1.0
1.1	0.5917	0.5944	0.5971	0.5997	0.6024	0.6050	0.6077	0.6103	0.6129	0.6155	1.1
1.2	0.6180	0.6206	0.6232	0.6257	0.6283	0.6308	0.6333	0.6358	0.6383	0.6408	1.2
1.3	0.6433	0.6457	0.6482	0.6507	0.6531	0.6555	0.6580	0.6604	0.6628	0.6652	1.3
1.4	0.6676	0.6699	0.6723	0.6747	0.6770	0.6794	0.6817	0.6840	0.6864	0.6887	1.4
1.5	0.6910	0.6933	0.6956	0.6979	0.7001	0.7024	0.7047	0.7069	0.7092	0.7114	1.5
1.6	0.7136	0.7159	0.7181	0.7203	0.7225	0.7247	0.7269	0.7291	0.7313	0.7334	1.6
1.7	0.7356	0.7378	0.7399	0.7421	0.7442	0.7464	0.7485	0.7506	0.7527	0.7548	1.7
1.8	0.7569	0.7590	0.7611	0.7632	0.7653	0.7674	0.7695	0.7715	0.7736	0.7756	1.8
1.9	0.7777	0.7797	0.7818	0.7838	0.7858	0.7878	0.7899	0.7919	0.7939	0.7959	1.9
2.0	0.7979	0.7999	0.8019	0.8038	0.8058	0.8078	0.8098	0.8117	0.8137	0.8156	2.0
2.1	0.8176	0.8195	0.8215	0.8234	0.8253	0.8273	0.8292	0.8311	0.8330	0.8349	2.1
2.2	0.8368	0.8387	0.8406	0.8425	0.8444	0.8463	0.8482	0.8500	0.8519	0.8538	2.2
2.3	0.8556	0.8575	0.8593	0.8612	0.8630	0.8649	0.8667	0.8686	0.8704	0.8722	2.3
2.4	0.8740	0.8759	0.8777	0.8795	0.8813	0.8831	0.8849	0.8867	0.8885	0.8903	2.4
2.5	0.8921	0.8938	0.8956	0.8974	0.8992	0.9009	0.9027	0.9045	0.9062	0.9080	2.5
2.6	0.9097	0.9115	0.9132	0.9150	0.9167	0.9184	0.9202	0.9219	0.9236	0.9253	2.6
2.7	0.9271	0.9288	0.9305	0.9322	0.9339	0.9356	0.9373	0.9390	0.9407	0.9424	2.7
2.8	0.9441	0.9458	0.9474	0.9491	0.9508	0.9525	0.9541	0.9558	0.9575	0.9591	2.8
2.9	0.9608	0.9624	0.9641	0.9657	0.9674	0.9690	0.9707	0.9723	0.9739	0.9756	2.9
3.0	0.9772	0.9788	0.9805	0.9821	0.9837	0.9853	0.9869	0.9885	0.9901	0.9918	3.0
3.1	0.9934	0.9950	0.9966	0.9982	0.9997	1.0013	1.0029	1.0045	1.0061	1.0077	3.1
3.2	1.0093	1.0108	1.0124	1.0140	1.0155	1.0171	1.0187	1.0202	1.0218	1.0233	3.2
3.3	1.0249	1.0265	1.0280	1.0295	1.0311	1.0326	1.0342	1.0357	1.0372	1.0388	3.3
3.4	1.0403	1.0418	1.0434	1.0449	1.0464	1.0479	1.0495	1.0510	1.0525	1.0540	3.4
3.5	1.0555	1.0570	1.0585	1.0600	1.0615	1.0630	1.0645	1.0660	1.0675	1.0690	3.5
3.6	1.0705	1.0720	1.0734	1.0749	1.0764	1.0779	1.0794	1.0808	1.0823	1.0838	3.6
3.7	1.0852	1.0867	1.0882	1.0896	1.0911	1.0925	1.0940	1.0955	1.0969	1.0984	3.7
3.8	1.0998	1.1013	1.1027	1.1041	1.1056	1.1070	1.1085	1.1099	1.1113	1.1128	3.8
3.9	1.1142	1.1156	1.1170	1.1185	1.1199	1.1213	1.1227	1.1241	1.1256	1.1270	3.9
4.0	1.1284	1.1298	1.1312	1.1326	1.1340	1.1354	1.1368	1.1382	1.1396	1.1410	4.0
4.1	1.1424	1.1438	1.1452	1.1466	1.1480	1.1493	1.1507	1.1521	1.1535	1.1549	4.1
4.2	1.1562	1.1576	1.1590	1.1604	1.1617	1.1631	1.1645	1.1658	1.1672	1.1686	4.2
4.3	1.1699	1.1713	1.1726	1.1740	1.1754	1.1767	1.1781	1.1794	1.1808	1.1821	4.3
4.4	1.1835	1.1848	1.1861	1.1875	1.1888	1.1902	1.1915	1.1928	1.1942	1.1955	4.4
4.5	1.1968	1.1982	1.1995	1.2008	1.2021	1.2035	1.2048	1.2061	1.2074	1.2087	4.5
4.6	1.2101	1.2114	1.2127	1.2140	1.2153	1.2166	1.2179	1.2192	1.2205	1.2218	4.6
4.7	1.2231	1.2244	1.2257	1.2270	1.2283	1.2296	1.2309	1.2322	1.2335	1.2348	4.7
4.8	1.2361	1.2374	1.2386	1.2399	1.2412	1.2425	1.2438	1.2451	1.2463	1.2476	4.8
4.9	1.2489	1.2502	1.2514	1.2527	1.2540	1.2552	1.2565	1.2578	1.2590	1.2603	4.9

Use of the table. 5.1 + 0.01 = 5.11; the radius of a circle with area 5.11 is 1.2754.

	0.00	0.01	0.02	0.03	0.04	0.05	0.06	0.07	0.08	0.09
5.0	1.2616	1.2628	1.2641	1.2653	1.2666	1.2679	1.2691	1.2704	1.2716	1.2729
5.1	1.2741	1.2754	1.2766	1.2779	1.2791	1.2803	1.2816	1.2828	1.2841	1.2853
5.2	1.2866	1.2878	1.2890	1.2903	1.2915	1.2927	1.2940	1.2952	1.2964	1.2976
5.3	1.2989	1.3001	1.3013	1.3025	1.3038	1.3050	1.3062	1.3074	1.3086	1.3098
5.4	1.3111	1.3123	1.3135	1.3147	1.3159	1.3171	1.3183	1.3195	1.3207	1.3219
5.5	1.3231	1.3243	1.3255	1.3267	1.3279	1.3291	1.3303	1.3315	1.3327	1.3339
5.6	1.3351	1.3363	1.3375	1.3387	1.3399	1.3411	1.3422	1.3434	1.3446	1.3458
5.7	1.3470	1.3482	1.3493	1.3505	1.3517	1.3529	1.3541	1.3552	1.3564	1.3576
5.8	1.3587	1.3599	1.3611	1.3623	1.3634	1.3646	1.3658	1.3669	1.3681	1.3692
5.9	1.3704	1.3716	1.3727	1.3739	1.3750	1.3762	1.3774	1.3785	1.3797	1.3808
6.0	1.3820	1.3831	1.3843	1.3854	1.3866	1.3877	1.3889	1.3900	1.3912	1.3923
6.1	1.3934	1.3946	1.3957	1.3969	1.3980	1.3991	1.4003	1.4014	1.4026	1.4037
6.2	1.4048	1.4060	1.4071	1.4082	1.4093	1.4105	1.4116	1.4127	1.4139	1.4150
6.3	1.4161	1.4172	1.4184	1.4195	1.4206	1.4217	1.4228	1.4240	1.4251	1.4262
6.4	1.4273	1.4284	1.4295	1.4306	1.4318	1.4329	1.4340	1.4351	1.4362	1.4373
6.5	1.4384	1.4395	1.4406	1.4417	1.4428	1.4439	1.4450	1.4461	1.4472	1.4483
6.6	1.4494	1.4505	1.4516	1.4527	1.4538	1.4549	1.4560	1.4571	1.4582	1.4593
6.7	1.4604	1.4615	1.4625	1.4636	1.4647	1.4658	1.4669	1.4680	1.4691	1.4701
6.8	1.4712	1.4723	1.4734	1.4745	1.4755	1.4766	1.4777	1.4788	1.4799	1.4809
6.9	1.4820	1.4831	1.4842	1.4852	1.4863	1.4874	1.4884	1.4895	1.4906	1.4916
7.0	1.4927	1.4938	1.4948	1.4959	1.4970	1.4980	1.4991	1.5002	1.5012	1.5023
7.1	1.5033	1.5044	1.5054	1.5065	1.5076	1.5086	1.5097	1.5107	1.5118	1.5128
7.2	1.5139	1.5149	1.5160	1.5170	1.5181	1.5191	1.5202	1.5212	1.5223	1.5233
7.3	1.5244	1.5254	1.5264	1.5275	1.5285	1.5296	1.5306	1.5316	1.5327	1.5337
7.4	1.5348	1.5358	1.5368	1.5379	1.5389	1.5399	1.5410	1.5420	1.5430	1.5441
7.5	1.5451	1.5461	1.5472	1.5482	1.5492	1.5502	1.5513	1.5523	1.5533	1.5543
7.6	1.5554	1.5564	1.5574	1.5584	1.5595	1.5605	1.5615	1.5625	1.5635	1.5645
7.7	1.5656	1.5666	1.5676	1.5686	1.5696	1.5706	1.5717	1.5727	1.5737	1.5747
7.8	1.5757	1.5767	1.5777	1.5787	1.5797	1.5807	1.5817	1.5828	1.5838	1.5848
7.9	1.5858	1.5868	1.5878	1.5888	1.5898	1.5908	1.5918	1.5928	1.5938	1.5948
8.0	1.5958	1.5968	1.5978	1.5988	1.5998	1.6007	1.6017	1.6027	1.6037	1.6047
8.1	1.6057	1.6067	1.6077	1.6087	1.6097	1.6107	1.6116	1.6126	1.6136	1.6146
8.2	1.6156	1.6166	1.6176	1.6185	1.6195	1.6205	1.6215	1.6225	1.6235	1.6244
8.3	1.6254	1.6264	1.6274	1.6283	1.6293	1.6303	1.6313	1.6323	1.6332	1.6342
8.4	1.6352	1.6361	1.6371	1.6381	1.6391	1.6400	1.6410	1.6420	1.6429	1.6439
8.5	1.6449	1.6458	1.6468	1.6478	1.6487	1.6497	1.6507	1.6516	1.6526	1.6536
8.6	1.6545	1.6555	1.6565	1.6574	1.6584	1.6593	1.6603	1.6612	1.6622	1.6632
8.7	1.6641	1.6651	1.6660	1.6670	1.6679	1.6689	1.6698	1.6708	1.6718	1.6727
8.8	1.6737	1.6746	1.6756	1.6765	1.6775	1.6784	1.6794	1.6803	1.6812	1.6822
8.9	1.6831	1.6841	1.6850	1.6860	1.6869	1.6879	1.6888	1.6897	1.6907	1.6916
9.0	1.6926	1.6935	1.6944	1.6954	1.6963	1.6973	1.6982	1.6991	1.7001	1.7010
9.1	1.7019	1.7029	1.7038	1.7047	1.7057	1.7066	1.7075	1.7085	1.7094	1.7103
9.2	1.7113	1.7122	1.7131	1.7141	1.7150	1.7159	1.7168	1.7178	1.7187	1.7196
9.3	1.7205	1.7215	1.7224	1.7233	1.7242	1.7252	1.7261	1.7270	1.7279	1.7289
9.4	1.7298	1.7307	1.7316	1.7325	1.7334	1.7344	1.7353	1.7362	1.7371	1.7380
9.5	1.7389	1.7399	1.7408	1.7417	1.7426	1.7435	1.7444	1.7453	1.7463	1.7472
9.6	1.7481	1.7490	1.7499	1.7508	1.7517	1.7526	1.7535	1.7544	1.7553	1.7563
9.7	1.7572	1.7581	1.7590	1.7599	1.7608	1.7617	1.7626	1.7635	1.7644	1.7653
9.8	1.7662	1.7671	1.7680	1.7689	1.7698	1.7707	1.7716	1.7725	1.7734	1.7743
9.9	1.7752	1.7761	1.7770	1.7779	1.7788	1.7797	1.7806	1.7814	1.7823	1.7832

Use of the table. 11 + 0.1 = 11.1; the radius of a circle with area 11.1 is 1.8797.

	0.0	0.1	0.2	0.3	0.4	0.5	0.6	0.7	0.8	0.9	
10	1.7841	1.7930	1.8019	1.8107	1.8195	1.8282	1.8369	1.8455	1.8541	1.8627	10
11	1.8712	1.8797	1.8881	1.8965	1.9049	1.9133	1.9216	1.9298	1.9381	1.9462	11
12	1.9544	1.9625	1.9706	1.9787	1.9867	1.9947	2.0027	2.0106	2.0185	2.0264	12
13	2.0342	2.0420	2.0498	2.0576	2.0653	2.0730	2.0806	2.0883	2.0959	2.1035	13
14	2.1110	2.1185	2.1260	2.1335	2.1409	2.1484	2.1558	2.1631	2.1705	2.1778	14
15	2.1851	2.1924	2.1996	2.2068	2.2140	2.2212	2.2284	2.2355	2.2426	2.2497	15
16	2.2568	2.2638	2.2708	2.2778	2.2848	2.2917	2.2987	2.3056	2.3125	2.3194	16
17	2.3262	2.3330	2.3399	2.3466	2.3534	2.3602	2.3669	2.3736	2.3803	2.3870	17
18	2.3937	2.4003	2.4069	2.4135	2.4201	2.4267	2.4332	2.4398	2.4463	2.4528	18
19	2.4592	2.4657	2.4722	2.4786	2.4850	2.4914	2.4978	2.5041	2.5105	2.5168	19
20	2.5231	2.5294	2.5357	2.5420	2.5482	2.5545	2.5607	2.5669	2.5731	2.5793	20
21	2.5854	2.5916	2.5977	2.6038	2.6099	2.6160	2.6221	2.6282	2.6342	2.6403	21
22	2.6463	2.6523	2.6583	2.6643	2.6702	2.6762	2.6821	2.6881	2.6940	2.6999	22
23	2.7058	2.7116	2.7175	2.7233	2.7292	2.7350	2.7408	2.7466	2.7524	2.7582	23
24	2.7640	2.7697	2.7754	2.7812	2.7869	2.7926	2.7983	2.8040	2.8096	2.8153	24
25	2.8209	2.8266	2.8322	2.8378	2.8434	2.8490	2.8546	2.8602	2.8657	2.8713	25
26	2.8768	2.8823	2.8879	2.8934	2.8989	2.9043	2.9098	2.9153	2.9207	2.9262	26
27	2.9316	2.9370	2.9425	2.9479	2.9533	2.9586	2.9640	2.9694	2.9747	2.9801	27
28	2.9854	2.9907	2.9961	3.0014	3.0067	3.0119	3.0172	3.0225	3.0278	3.0330	28
29	3.0383	3.0435	3.0487	3.0539	3.0591	3.0643	3.0695	3.0747	3.0799	3.0850	29
30	3.0902	3.0953	3.1005	3.1056	3.1107	3.1158	3.1209	3.1260	3.1311	3.1362	30
31	3.1413	3.1463	3.1514	3.1564	3.1615	3.1665	3.1715	3.1765	3.1815	3.1865	31
32	3.1915	3.1965	3.2015	3.2065	3.2114	3.2164	3.2213	3.2263	3.2312	3.2361	32
33	3.2410	3.2459	3.2508	3.2557	3.2606	3.2655	3.2704	3.2752	3.2801	3.2849	33
34	3.2898	3.2946	3.2994	3.3042	3.3091	3.3139	3.3187	3.3235	3.3282	3.3330	34
35	3.3378	3.3426	3.3473	3.3521	3.3568	3.3615	3.3663	3.3710	3.3757	3.3804	35
36	3.3851	3.3898	3.3945	3.3992	3.4039	3.4086	3.4132	3.4179	3.4225	3.4272	36
37	3.4318	3.4365	3.4411	3.4457	3.4503	3.4549	3.4595	3.4641	3.4687	3.4733	37
38	3.4779	3.4825	3.4870	3.4916	3.4962	3.5007	3.5052	3.5098	3.5143	3.5188	38
39	3.5234	3.5279	3.5324	3.5369	3.5414	3.5459	3.5504	3.5548	3.5593	3.5638	39
40	3.5682	3.5727	3.5772	3.5816	3.5860	3.5905	3.5949	3.5993	3.6038	3.6082	40
41	3.6126	3.6170	3.6214	3.6258	3.6302	3.6345	3.6389	3.6433	3.6477	3.6520	41
42	3.6564	3.6607	3.6651	3.6694	3.6737	3.6781	3.6824	3.6867	3.6910	3.6953	42
43	3.6996	3.7039	3.7082	3.7125	3.7168	3.7211	3.7254	3.7296	3.7339	3.7382	43
44	3.7424	3.7467	3.7509	3.7551	3.7594	3.7636	3.7678	3.7721	3.7763	3.7805	44
45	3.7847	3.7889	3.7931	3.7973	3.8015	3.8057	3.8098	3.8140	3.8182	3.8224	45
46	3.8265	3.8307	3.8348	3.8390	3.8431	3.8473	3.8514	3.8555	3.8597	3.8638	46
47	3.8679	3.8720	3.8761	3.8802	3.8843	3.8884	3.8925	3.8966	3.9007	3.9047	47
48	3.9088	3.9129	3.9170	3.9210	3.9251	3.9291	3.9332	3.9372	3.9413	3.9453	48
49	3.9493	3.9534	3.9574	3.9614	3.9654	3.9694	3.9734	3.9774	3.9814	3.9854	49
50	3.9894	3.9934	3.9974	4.0014	4.0053	4.0093	4.0133	4.0173	4.0212	4.0252	50
51	4.0291	4.0331	4.0370	4.0410	4.0449	4.0488	4.0528	4.0567	4.0606	4.0645	51
52	4.0684	4.0723	4.0762	4.0801	4.0840	4.0879	4.0918	4.0957	4.0996	4.1035	52
53	4.1074	4.1112	4.1151	4.1190	4.1228	4.1267	4.1305	4.1344	4.1382	4.1421	53
54	4.1459	4.1498	4.1536	4.1574	4.1613	4.1651	4.1689	4.1727	4.1765	4.1803	54
55	4.1841	4.1879	4.1917	4.1955	4.1993	4.2031	4.2069	4.2107	4.2145	4.2182	55
56	4.2220	4.2258	4.2295	4.2333	4.2371	4.2408	4.2446	4.2483	4.2521	4.2558	56
57	4.2595	4.2633	4.2670	4.2707	4.2745	4.2782	4.2819	4.2856	4.2893	4.2930	57
58	4.2967	4.3004	4.3041	4.3078	4.3115	4.3152	4.3189	4.3226	4.3263	4.3299	58
59	4.3336	4.3373	4.3410	4.3446	4.3483	4.3519	4.3556	4.3593	4.3629	4.3666	59

Use of the table. 61 + 0.1 = 61.1; the radius of a circle with area 61.1 is 4.4101.

	0.0	0.1	0.2	0.3	0.4	0.5	0.6	0.7	0.8	0.9	
60	4.3702	4.3738	4.3775	4.3811	4.3847	4.3884	4.3920	4.3956	4.3992	4.4028	60
61	4.4065	4.4101	4.4137	4.4173	4.4209	4.4245	4.4281	4.4317	4.4353	4.4388	61
62	4.4424	4.4460	4.4496	4.4532	4.4567	4.4603	4.4639	4.4674	4.4710	4.4746	62
63	4.4781	4.4817	4.4852	4.4888	4.4923	4.4959	4.4994	4.5029	4.5065	4.5100	63
64	4.5135	4.5170	4.5206	4.5241	4.5276	4.5311	4.5346	4.5381	4.5416	4.5451	64
65	4.5486	4.5521	4.5556	4.5591	4.5626	4.5661	4.5696	4.5731	4.5765	4.5800	65
66	4.5835	4.5870	4.5904	4.5939	4.5974	4.6008	4.6043	4.6077	4.6112	4.6146	66
67	4.6181	4.6215	4.6250	4.6284	4.6319	4.6353	4.6387	4.6422	4.6456	4.6490	67
68	4.6524	4.6558	4.6593	4.6627	4.6661	4.6695	4.6729	4.6763	4.6797	4.6831	68
69	4.6865	4.6899	4.6933	4.6967	4.7001	4.7035	4.7068	4.7102	4.7136	4.7170	69
70	4.7203	4.7237	4.7271	4.7305	4.7338	4.7372	4.7405	4.7439	4.7472	4.7506	70
71	4.7539	4.7573	4.7606	4.7640	4.7673	4.7707	4.7740	4.7773	4.7807	4.7840	71
72	4.7873	4.7906	4.7940	4.7973	4.8006	4.8039	4.8072	4.8105	4.8138	4.8171	72
73	4.8204	4.8237	4.8270	4.8303	4.8336	4.8369	4.8402	4.8435	4.8468	4.8501	73
74	4.8533	4.8566	4.8599	4.8632	4.8664	4.8697	4.8730	4.8762	4.8795	4.8828	74
75	4.8860	4.8893	4.8925	4.8958	4.8990	4.9023	4.9055	4.9088	4.9120	4.9153	75
76	4.9185	4.9217	4.9250	4.9282	4.9314	4.9346	4.9379	4.9411	4.9443	4.9475	76
77	4.9507	4.9540	4.9572	4.9604	4.9636	4.9668	4.9700	4.9732	4.9764	4.9796	77
78	4.9828	4.9860	4.9892	4.9924	4.9955	4.9987	5.0019	5.0051	5.0083	5.0115	78
79	5.0146	5.0178	5.0210	5.0241	5.0273	5.0305	5.0336	5.0368	5.0400	5.0431	79
80	5.0463	5.0494	5.0526	5.0557	5.0589	5.0620	5.0652	5.0683	5.0714	5.0746	80
81	5.0777	5.0808	5.0840	5.0871	5.0902	5.0934	5.0965	5.0996	5.1027	5.1058	81
82	5.1090	5.1121	5.1152	5.1183	5.1214	5.1245	5.1276	5.1307	5.1338	5.1369	82
83	5.1400	5.1431	5.1462	5.1493	5.1524	5.1555	5.1586	5.1616	5.1647	5.1678	83
84	5.1709	5.1740	5.1770	5.1801	5.1832	5.1862	5.1893	5.1924	5.1954	5.1985	84
85	5.2016	5.2046	5.2077	5.2107	5.2138	5.2168	5.2199	5.2229	5.2260	5.2290	85
86	5.2321	5.2351	5.2382	5.2412	5.2442	5.2473	5.2503	5.2533	5.2564	5.2594	86
87	5.2624	5.2654	5.2685	5.2715	5.2745	5.2775	5.2805	5.2835	5.2865	5.2896	87
88	5.2926	5.2956	5.2986	5.3016	5.3046	5.3076	5.3106	5.3136	5.3166	5.3196	88
89	5.3226	5.3255	5.3285	5.3315	5.3345	5.3375	5.3405	5.3434	5.3464	5.3494	89
90	5.3524	5.3553	5.3583	5.3613	5.3643	5.3672	5.3702	5.3731	5.3761	5.3791	90
91	5.3820	5.3850	5.3879	5.3909	5.3938	5.3968	5.3997	5.4027	5.4056	5.4086	91
92	5.4115	5.4145	5.4174	5.4203	5.4233	5.4262	5.4291	5.4321	5.4350	5.4379	92
93	5.4408	5.4438	5.4467	5.4496	5.4525	5.4555	5.4584	5.4613	5.4642	5.4671	93
94	5.4700	5.4729	5.4758	5.4787	5.4816	5.4845	5.4875	5.4904	5.4932	5.4961	94
95	5.4990	5.5019	5.5048	5.5077	5.5106	5.5135	5.5164	5.5193	5.5221	5.5250	95
96	5.5279	5.5308	5.5337	5.5365	5.5394	5.5423	5.5452	5.5480	5.5509	5.5538	96
97	5.5566	5.5595	5.5623	5.5652	5.5681	5.5709	5.5738	5.5766	5.5795	5.5823	97
98	5.5852	5.5880	5.5909	5.5937	5.5966	5.5994	5.6023	5.6051	5.6079	5.6108	98
99	5.6136	5.6164	5.6193	5.6221	5.6249	5.6278	5.6306	5.6334	5.6363	5.6391	99
100	5.6419	5.6447	5.6475	5.6504	5.6532	5.6560	5.6588	5.6616	5.6644	5.6672	100

Volume and capacity

Use of the tables. 11 in^3 = 10 in^3 + 1 in^3 = 180.258 cm^3.

Cubic centimetres to cubic inches   1 cm^3 = 0.061 024 in^3

cm³ →	0	1	2	3	4	5	6	7	8	9	← cm³
↓	in³	in³	in³	in³	in³	in³	in³	in³	in³	in³	↓
0	0.000	0.061	0.122	0.183	0.244	0.305	0.366	0.427	0.488	0.549	0
10	0.610	0.671	0.732	0.793	0.854	0.915	0.976	1.037	1.098	1.159	10
20	1.220	1.281	1.343	1.404	1.465	1.526	1.587	1.648	1.709	1.770	20
30	1.831	1.892	1.953	2.014	2.075	2.136	2.197	2.258	2.319	2.380	30
40	2.441	2.502	2.563	2.624	2.685	2.746	2.807	2.868	2.929	2.990	40
50	3.051	3.112	3.173	3.234	3.295	3.356	3.417	3.478	3.539	3.600	50
60	3.661	3.722	3.783	3.844	3.906	3.967	4.028	4.089	4.150	4.211	60
70	4.272	4.333	4.394	4.455	4.516	4.577	4.638	4.699	4.760	4.821	70
80	4.882	4.943	5.004	5.065	5.126	5.187	5.248	5.309	5.370	5.431	80
90	5.492	5.553	5.614	5.675	5.736	5.797	5.858	5.919	5.980	6.041	90
100	6.102										100

cm³ →	0	10	20	30	40	50	60	70	80	90	← cm³
↓	in³	in³	in³	in³	in³	in³	in³	in³	in³	in³	↓
0	0.000	0.610	1.220	1.831	2.441	3.051	3.661	4.272	4.882	5.492	0
100	6.102	6.713	7.323	7.933	8.543	9.154	9.764	10.374	10.984	11.595	100
200	12.205	12.815	13.425	14.035	14.646	15.256	15.866	16.476	17.087	17.697	200
300	18.307	18.917	19.528	20.138	20.748	21.358	21.969	22.579	23.189	23.799	300
400	24.409	25.020	25.630	26.240	26.850	27.461	28.071	28.681	29.291	29.902	400
500	30.512	31.122	31.732	32.343	32.953	33.563	34.173	34.784	35.394	36.004	500
600	36.614	37.224	37.835	38.445	39.055	39.665	40.276	40.886	41.496	42.106	600
700	42.717	43.327	43.937	44.547	45.158	45.768	46.378	46.988	47.599	48.209	700
800	48.819	49.429	50.039	50.650	51.260	51.870	52.480	53.091	53.701	54.311	800
900	54.921	55.532	56.142	56.752	57.362	57.973	58.583	59.193	59.803	60.414	900
1000	61.024										1000

Cubic inches to cubic centimetres   1 in^3 = 16.387 064 cm^3

in³ →	0	1	2	3	4	5	6	7	8	9	← in³
↓	cm³	cm³	cm³	cm³	cm³	cm³	cm³	cm³	cm³	cm³	↓
0	0.000	16.387	32.774	49.161	65.548	81.935	98.322	114.709	131.097	147.484	0
10	163.871	180.258	196.645	213.032	229.419	245.806	262.193	278.580	294.967	311.354	10
20	327.741	344.128	360.515	376.902	393.290	409.677	426.064	442.451	458.838	475.225	20
30	491.612	507.999	524.386	540.773	557.160	573.547	589.934	606.321	622.708	639.095	30
40	655.483	671.870	688.257	704.644	721.031	737.418	753.805	770.192	786.579	802.966	40
50	819.353	835.740	852.127	868.514	884.901	901.289	917.676	934.063	950.450	966.837	50
60	983.224	999.611	1015.998	1032.385	1048.772	1065.159	1081.546	1097.933	1114.320	1130.707	60
70	1147.094	1163.482	1179.869	1196.256	1212.643	1229.030	1245.417	1261.804	1278.191	1294.578	70
80	1310.965	1327.352	1343.739	1360.126	1376.513	1392.900	1409.288	1425.675	1442.062	1458.449	80
90	1474.836	1491.223	1507.610	1523.997	1540.384	1556.771	1573.158	1589.545	1605.932	1622.319	90
100	1638.706										100

in³ →	0	10	20	30	40	50	60	70	80	90	← in³
↓	cm³	cm³	cm³	cm³	cm³	cm³	cm³	cm³	cm³	cm³	↓
0	0.000	163.871	327.741	491.612	655.483	819.353	983.224	1147.094	1310.965	1474.836	0
100	1638.706	1802.577	1966.448	2130.318	2294.189	2458.060	2621.930	2785.801	2949.672	3113.542	100
200	3277.413	3441.283	3605.154	3769.025	3932.895	4096.766	4260.637	4424.507	4588.378	4752.249	200
300	4916.119	5079.990	5243.860	5407.731	5571.602	5735.472	5899.343	6063.214	6227.084	6390.955	300
400	6554.826	6718.696	6882.567	7046.438	7210.308	7374.179	7538.049	7701.920	7865.791	8029.661	400
500	8193.532	8357.403	8521.273	8685.144	8849.015	9012.885	9176.756	9340.626	9504.497	9668.368	500
600	9832.238	9996.109	10159.980	10323.850	10487.721	10651.592	10815.462	10979.333	11143.204	11307.074	600
700	11470.945	11634.815	11798.686	11962.557	12126.427	12290.298	12454.169	12618.039	12781.910	12945.781	700
800	13109.651	13273.522	13437.392	13601.263	13765.134	13929.004	14092.875	14256.746	14420.616	14584.487	800
900	14748.358	14912.228	15076.099	15239.970	15403.840	15567.711	15731.581	15895.452	16059.323	16223.193	900
1000	16387.064										1000

Use of the tables. 11 UK gal = 10 UK gal + 1 UK gal = 13.210 US gal.

UK gallons to US gallons 1 UK gal = 1.200 950 US gal

UK gal → ↓	0	1	2	3	4	5	6	7	8	9	← UK gal ↓
	US gal	US gal	US gal	US gal	US gal	US gal	US gal	US gal	US gal	US gal	
0	0.000	1.201	2.402	3.603	4.804	6.005	7.206	8.407	9.608	10.809	0
10	12.009	13.210	14.411	15.612	16.813	18.014	19.215	20.416	21.617	22.818	10
20	24.019	25.220	26.421	27.622	28.823	30.024	31.225	32.426	33.627	34.828	20
30	36.028	37.229	38.430	39.631	40.832	42.033	43.234	44.435	45.636	46.837	30
40	48.038	49.239	50.440	51.641	52.842	54.043	55.244	56.445	57.646	58.847	40
50	60.047	61.248	62.449	63.650	64.851	66.052	67.253	68.454	69.655	70.856	50
60	72.057	73.258	74.459	75.660	76.861	78.062	79.263	80.464	81.665	82.866	60
70	84.066	85.267	86.468	87.669	88.870	90.071	91.272	92.473	93.674	94.875	70
80	96.076	97.277	98.478	99.679	100.880	102.081	103.282	104.483	105.684	106.885	80
90	108.085	109.286	110.487	111.688	112.889	114.090	115.291	116.492	117.693	118.894	90
100	120.095										100

US gallons to UK gallons 1 US gal = 0.832 674 UK gal

US gal → ↓	0	1	2	3	4	5	6	7	8	9	← US gal ↓
	UK gal	UK gal	UK gal	UK gal	UK gal	UK gal	UK gal	UK gal	UK gal	UK gal	
0	0.000	0.833	1.665	2.498	3.331	4.163	4.996	5.829	6.661	7.494	0
10	8.327	9.159	9.992	10.825	11.657	12.490	13.323	14.155	14.988	15.821	10
20	16.653	17.486	18.319	19.152	19.984	20.817	21.650	22.482	23.315	24.148	20
30	24.980	25.813	26.646	27.478	28.311	29.144	29.976	30.809	31.642	32.474	30
40	33.307	34.140	34.972	35.805	36.638	37.470	38.303	39.136	39.968	40.801	40
50	41.634	42.466	43.299	44.132	44.964	45.797	46.630	47.462	48.295	49.128	50
60	49.960	50.793	51.626	52.458	53.291	54.124	54.956	55.789	56.622	57.455	60
70	58.287	59.120	59.953	60.785	61.618	62.451	63.283	64.116	64.949	65.781	70
80	66.614	67.447	68.279	69.112	69.945	70.777	71.610	72.443	73.275	74.108	80
90	74.941	75.773	76.606	77.439	78.271	79.104	79.937	80.769	81.602	82.435	90
100	83.267										100

UK bushels to US bushels 1 UK bu = 1.032 057 US bu

UK bu → ↓	0	1	2	3	4	5	6	7	8	9	← UK bu ↓
	US bu	US bu	US bu	US bu	US bu	US bu	US bu	US bu	US bu	US bu	
0	0.000	1.032	2.064	3.096	4.128	5.160	6.192	7.224	8.256	9.289	0
10	10.321	11.353	12.385	13.417	14.449	15.481	16.513	17.545	18.577	19.609	10
20	20.641	21.673	22.705	23.737	24.769	25.801	26.833	27.866	28.898	29.930	20
30	30.962	31.994	33.026	34.058	35.090	36.122	37.154	38.186	39.218	40.250	30
40	41.282	42.314	43.346	44.378	45.410	46.443	47.475	48.507	49.539	50.571	40
50	51.603	52.635	53.667	54.699	55.731	56.763	57.795	58.827	59.859	60.891	50
60	61.923	62.955	63.988	65.020	66.052	67.084	68.116	69.148	70.180	71.212	60
70	72.244	73.276	74.308	75.340	76.372	77.404	78.436	79.468	80.500	81.532	70
80	82.565	83.597	84.629	85.661	86.693	87.725	88.757	89.789	90.821	91.853	80
90	92.885	93.917	94.949	95.981	97.013	98.045	99.077	100.110	101.142	102.174	90
100	103.206										100

US bushels to UK bushels 1 US bu = 0.968 939 UK bu

US bu → ↓	0	1	2	3	4	5	6	7	8	9	← US bu ↓
	UK bu	UK bu	UK bu	UK bu	UK bu	UK bu	UK bu	UK bu	UK bu	UK bu	
0	0.000	0.969	1.938	2.907	3.876	4.845	5.814	6.783	7.752	8.720	0
10	9.689	10.658	11.627	12.596	13.565	14.534	15.503	16.472	17.441	18.410	10
20	19.379	20.348	21.317	22.286	23.255	24.223	25.192	26.161	27.130	28.099	20
30	29.068	30.037	31.006	31.975	32.944	33.913	34.882	35.851	36.820	37.789	30
40	38.758	39.726	40.695	41.664	42.633	43.602	44.571	45.540	46.509	47.478	40
50	48.447	49.416	50.385	51.354	52.323	53.292	54.261	55.230	56.198	57.167	50
60	58.136	59.105	60.074	61.043	62.012	62.981	63.950	64.919	65.888	66.857	60
70	67.826	68.795	69.764	70.733	71.701	72.670	73.639	74.608	75.577	76.546	70
80	77.515	78.484	79.453	80.422	81.391	82.360	83.329	84.298	85.267	86.236	80
90	87.205	88.173	89.142	90.111	91.080	92.049	93.018	93.987	94.956	95.925	90
100	96.894										100

Use of the tables. 11 UK bu = 10 UK bu + 1 UK bu = 4.001 hl.

SI hectolitres to UK bushels 1 hl = 2.749 616 UK bu

hl → ↓	0	1	2	3	4	5	6	7	8	9	← hl ↓
	UK bu	UK bu	UK bu	UK bu	UK bu	UK bu	UK bu	UK bu	UK bu	UK bu	
0	0.000	2.750	5.499	8.249	10.998	13.748	16.498	19.247	21.997	24.747	0
10	27.496	30.246	32.995	35.745	38.495	41.244	43.994	46.743	49.493	52.243	10
20	54.992	57.742	60.492	63.241	65.991	68.740	71.490	74.240	76.989	79.739	20
30	82.488	85.238	87.988	90.737	93.487	96.237	98.986	101.736	104.485	107.235	30
40	109.985	112.734	115.484	118.233	120.983	123.733	126.482	129.232	131.982	134.731	40
50	137.481	140.230	142.980	145.730	148.479	151.229	153.978	156.728	159.478	162.227	50
60	164.977	167.727	170.476	173.226	175.975	178.725	181.475	184.224	186.974	189.723	60
70	192.473	195.223	197.972	200.722	203.472	206.221	208.971	211.720	214.470	217.220	70
80	219.969	222.719	225.468	228.218	230.968	233.717	236.467	239.217	241.966	244.716	80
90	247.465	250.215	252.965	255.714	258.464	261.213	263.963	266.713	269.462	272.212	90
100	274.962										100

UK bushels to SI hectolitres 1 UK bu = 0.363 687 hl

UK bu → ↓	0	1	2	3	4	5	6	7	8	9	← UK bu ↓
	hl	hl	hl	hl	hl	hl	hl	hl	hl	hl	
0	0.000	0.364	0.727	1.091	1.455	1.818	2.182	2.546	2.909	3.273	0
10	3.637	4.001	4.364	4.728	5.092	5.455	5.819	6.183	6.546	6.910	10
20	7.274	7.637	8.001	8.365	8.728	9.092	9.456	9.820	10.183	10.547	20
30	10.911	11.274	11.638	12.002	12.365	12.729	13.093	13.456	13.820	14.184	30
40	14.547	14.911	15.275	15.639	16.002	16.366	16.730	17.093	17.457	17.821	40
50	18.184	18.548	18.912	19.275	19.639	20.003	20.366	20.730	21.094	21.458	50
60	21.821	22.185	22.549	22.912	23.276	23.640	24.003	24.367	24.731	25.094	60
70	25.458	25.822	26.185	26.549	26.913	27.277	27.640	28.004	28.368	28.731	70
80	29.095	29.459	29.822	30.186	30.550	30.913	31.277	31.641	32.004	32.368	80
90	32.732	33.096	33.459	33.823	34.187	34.550	34.914	35.278	35.641	36.005	90
100	36.369										100

SI hectolitres to US bushels 1 hl = 2.837 759 US bu

hl → ↓	0	1	2	3	4	5	6	7	8	9	← hl ↓
	US bu	US bu	US bu	US bu	US bu	US bu	US bu	US bu	US bu	US bu	
0	0.000	2.838	5.676	8.513	11.351	14.189	17.027	19.864	22.702	25.540	0
10	28.378	31.215	34.053	36.891	39.729	42.566	45.404	48.242	51.080	53.917	10
20	56.755	59.593	62.431	65.268	68.106	70.944	73.782	76.620	79.457	82.295	20
30	85.133	87.971	90.808	93.646	96.484	99.322	102.159	104.997	107.835	110.673	30
40	113.510	116.348	119.186	122.024	124.861	127.699	130.537	133.375	136.212	139.050	40
50	141.888	144.726	147.563	150.401	153.239	156.077	158.915	161.752	164.590	167.428	50
60	170.266	173.103	175.941	178.779	181.617	184.454	187.292	190.130	192.968	195.805	60
70	198.643	201.481	204.319	207.156	209.994	212.832	215.670	218.507	221.345	224.183	70
80	227.021	229.859	232.696	235.534	238.372	241.210	244.047	246.885	249.723	252.561	80
90	255.398	258.236	261.074	263.912	266.749	269.587	272.425	275.263	278.100	280.938	90
100	283.776										100

US bushels to SI hectolitres 1 US bu = 0.352 391 hl

US bu → ↓	0	1	2	3	4	5	6	7	8	9	← US bu ↓
	hl	hl	hl	hl	hl	hl	hl	hl	hl	hl	
0	0.000	0.352	0.705	1.057	1.410	1.762	2.114	2.467	2.819	3.172	0
10	3.524	3.876	4.229	4.581	4.933	5.286	5.638	5.991	6.343	6.695	10
20	7.048	7.400	7.753	8.105	8.457	8.810	9.162	9.515	9.867	10.219	20
30	10.572	10.924	11.277	11.629	11.981	12.334	12.686	13.038	13.391	13.743	30
40	14.096	14.448	14.800	15.153	15.505	15.858	16.210	16.562	16.915	17.267	40
50	17.620	17.972	18.324	18.677	19.029	19.381	19.734	20.086	20.439	20.791	50
60	21.143	21.496	21.848	22.201	22.553	22.905	23.258	23.610	23.963	24.315	60
70	24.667	25.020	25.372	25.725	26.077	26.429	26.782	27.134	27.486	27.839	70
80	28.191	28.544	28.896	29.248	29.601	29.953	30.306	30.658	31.010	31.363	80
90	31.715	32.068	32.420	32.772	33.125	33.477	33.830	34.182	34.534	34.887	90
100	35.239										100

Weight (mass)

Use of the tables. 11 gr = 10 gr + 1 gr = 0.713 g.

Grams to grains   1 g = 15.432 358 gr

g → ↓	0	1	2	3	4	5	6	7	8	9	← g ↓
	gr	gr	gr	gr	gr	gr	gr	gr	gr	gr	
0	0.000	15.432	30.865	46.297	61.729	77.162	92.594	108.027	123.459	138.891	0
10	154.324	169.756	185.188	200.621	216.053	231.485	246.918	262.350	277.782	293.215	10
20	308.647	324.080	339.512	354.944	370.377	385.809	401.241	416.674	432.106	447.538	20
30	462.971	478.403	493.835	509.268	524.700	540.133	555.565	570.997	586.430	601.862	30
40	617.294	632.727	648.159	663.591	679.024	694.456	709.888	725.321	740.753	756.186	40
50	771.618	787.050	802.483	817.915	833.347	848.780	864.212	879.644	895.077	910.509	50
60	925.942	941.374	956.806	972.239	987.671	1003.103	1018.536	1033.968	1049.400	1064.833	60
70	1080.265	1095.697	1111.130	1126.562	1141.995	1157.427	1172.859	1188.292	1203.724	1219.156	70
80	1234.589	1250.021	1265.453	1280.886	1296.318	1311.750	1327.183	1342.615	1358.048	1373.480	80
90	1388.912	1404.345	1419.777	1435.209	1450.642	1466.074	1481.506	1496.939	1512.371	1527.803	90
100	1543.236										100

Grains to grams   1 gr = 0.064 799 g

gr → ↓	0	1	2	3	4	5	6	7	8	9	← gr ↓
	g	g	g	g	g	g	g	g	g	g	
0	0.000	0.065	0.130	0.194	0.259	0.324	0.389	0.454	0.518	0.583	0
10	0.648	0.713	0.778	0.842	0.907	0.972	1.037	1.102	1.166	1.231	10
20	1.296	1.361	1.426	1.490	1.555	1.620	1.685	1.750	1.814	1.879	20
30	1.944	2.009	2.074	2.138	2.203	2.268	2.333	2.398	2.462	2.527	30
40	2.592	2.657	2.722	2.786	2.851	2.916	2.981	3.046	3.110	3.175	40
50	3.240	3.305	3.370	3.434	3.499	3.564	3.629	3.694	3.758	3.823	50
60	3.888	3.953	4.018	4.082	4.147	4.212	4.277	4.342	4.406	4.471	60
70	4.536	4.601	4.666	4.730	4.795	4.860	4.925	4.990	5.054	5.119	70
80	5.184	5.249	5.314	5.378	5.443	5.508	5.573	5.638	5.702	5.767	80
90	5.832	5.897	5.961	6.026	6.091	6.156	6.221	6.285	6.350	6.415	90
100	6.480										100

Grams to ounces (avoirdupois)   1 g = 0.035 274 oz

g → ↓	0	1	2	3	4	5	6	7	8	9	← g ↓
	oz	oz	oz	oz	oz	oz	oz	oz	oz	oz	
0	0.000	0.035	0.071	0.106	0.141	0.176	0.212	0.247	0.282	0.317	0
10	0.353	0.388	0.423	0.459	0.494	0.529	0.564	0.600	0.635	0.670	10
20	0.705	0.741	0.776	0.811	0.847	0.882	0.917	0.952	0.988	1.023	20
30	1.058	1.093	1.129	1.164	1.199	1.235	1.270	1.305	1.340	1.376	30
40	1.411	1.446	1.482	1.517	1.552	1.587	1.623	1.658	1.693	1.728	40
50	1.764	1.799	1.834	1.870	1.905	1.940	1.975	2.011	2.046	2.081	50
60	2.116	2.152	2.187	2.222	2.258	2.293	2.328	2.363	2.399	2.434	60
70	2.469	2.504	2.540	2.575	2.610	2.646	2.681	2.716	2.751	2.787	70
80	2.822	2.857	2.892	2.928	2.963	2.998	3.034	3.069	3.104	3.139	80
90	3.175	3.210	3.245	3.280	3.316	3.351	3.386	3.422	3.457	3.492	90
100	3.527										100

Ounces (avoirdupois) to grams   1 oz = 28.349 523 g

oz → ↓	0	1	2	3	4	5	6	7	8	9	← oz ↓
	g	g	g	g	g	g	g	g	g	g	
0	0.000	28.350	56.699	85.049	113.398	141.748	170.097	198.447	226.796	255.146	0
10	283.495	311.845	340.194	368.544	396.893	425.243	453.592	481.942	510.291	538.641	10
20	566.990	595.340	623.690	652.039	680.389	708.738	737.088	765.437	793.787	822.136	20
30	850.486	878.835	907.185	935.534	963.884	992.233	1020.583	1048.932	1077.282	1105.631	30
40	1133.981	1162.330	1190.680	1219.029	1247.379	1275.729	1304.078	1332.428	1360.777	1389.127	40
50	1417.476	1445.826	1474.175	1502.525	1530.874	1559.224	1587.573	1615.923	1644.272	1672.622	50
60	1700.971	1729.321	1757.670	1786.020	1814.369	1842.719	1871.069	1899.418	1927.768	1956.117	60
70	1984.467	2012.816	2041.166	2069.515	2097.865	2126.214	2154.564	2182.913	2211.263	2239.612	70
80	2267.962	2296.311	2324.661	2353.010	2381.360	2409.709	2438.059	2466.409	2494.758	2523.108	80
90	2551.457	2579.807	2608.156	2636.506	2664.855	2693.205	2721.554	2749.904	2778.253	2806.603	90
100	2834.952										100

Use of the tables. 11 lb = 10 lb + 1 lb = 4.990 kg.

Kilograms to pounds[a] 1 kg = 2.204 623 lb

kg →	0	1	2	3	4	5	6	7	8	9 ←	kg
↓	lb	lb	lb	lb	lb	lb	lb	lb	lb	lb	↓
0	0.000	2.205	4.409	6.614	8.818	11.023	13.228	15.432	17.637	19.842	0
10	22.046	24.251	26.455	28.660	30.865	33.069	35.274	37.479	39.683	41.888	10
20	44.092	46.297	48.502	50.706	52.911	55.116	57.320	59.525	61.729	63.934	20
30	66.139	68.343	70.548	72.753	74.957	77.162	79.366	81.571	83.776	85.980	30
40	88.185	90.390	92.594	94.799	97.003	99.208	101.413	103.617	105.822	108.027	40
50	110.231	112.436	114.640	116.845	119.050	121.254	123.459	125.663	127.868	130.073	50
60	132.277	134.482	136.687	138.891	141.096	143.300	145.505	147.710	149.914	152.119	60
70	154.324	156.528	158.733	160.937	163.142	165.347	167.551	169.756	171.961	174.165	70
80	176.370	178.574	180.779	182.984	185.188	187.393	189.598	191.802	194.007	196.211	80
90	198.416	200.621	202.825	205.030	207.235	209.439	211.644	213.848	216.053	218.258	90
100	220.462										100

kg →	0	10	20	30	40	50	60	70	80	90 ←	kg
↓	lb	lb	lb	lb	lb	lb	lb	lb	lb	lb	↓
0	0.000	22.046	44.092	66.139	88.185	110.231	132.277	154.324	176.370	198.416	0
100	220.462	242.508	264.555	286.601	308.647	330.693	352.740	374.786	396.832	418.878	100
200	440.925	462.971	485.017	507.063	529.109	551.156	573.202	595.248	617.294	639.341	200
300	661.387	683.433	705.479	727.525	749.572	771.618	793.664	815.710	837.757	859.803	300
400	881.849	903.895	925.942	947.988	970.034	992.080	1014.126	1036.173	1058.219	1080.265	400
500	1102.311	1124.358	1146.404	1168.450	1190.496	1212.542	1234.589	1256.635	1278.681	1300.727	500
600	1322.774	1344.820	1366.866	1388.912	1410.958	1433.005	1455.051	1477.097	1499.143	1521.190	600
700	1543.236	1565.282	1587.328	1609.375	1631.421	1653.467	1675.513	1697.559	1719.606	1741.652	700
800	1763.698	1785.744	1807.791	1829.837	1851.883	1873.929	1895.975	1918.022	1940.068	1962.114	800
900	1984.160	2006.207	2028.253	2050.299	2072.345	2094.391	2116.438	2138.484	2160.530	2182.576	900
1000	2204.623										1000

[a] This table can also be used for the conversion of kilograms-force (kiloponds) to pounds-force.

Pounds to kilograms[a] 1 lb = 0.453 592 kg

lb →	0	1	2	3	4	5	6	7	8	9 ←	lb
↓	kg	kg	kg	kg	kg	kg	kg	kg	kg	kg	↓
0	0.000	0.454	0.907	1.361	1.814	2.268	2.722	3.175	3.629	4.082	0
10	4.536	4.990	5.443	5.897	6.350	6.804	7.257	7.711	8.165	8.618	10
20	9.072	9.525	9.979	10.433	10.886	11.340	11.793	12.247	12.701	13.154	20
30	13.608	14.061	14.515	14.969	15.422	15.876	16.329	16.783	17.237	17.690	30
40	18.144	18.597	19.051	19.504	19.958	20.412	20.865	21.319	21.772	22.226	40
50	22.680	23.133	23.587	24.040	24.494	24.948	25.401	25.855	26.308	26.762	50
60	27.216	27.669	28.123	28.576	29.030	29.484	29.937	30.391	30.844	31.298	60
70	31.751	32.205	32.659	33.112	33.566	34.019	34.473	34.927	35.380	35.834	70
80	36.287	36.741	37.195	37.648	38.102	38.555	39.009	39.463	39.916	40.370	80
90	40.823	41.277	41.730	42.184	42.638	43.091	43.545	43.998	44.452	44.906	90
100	45.359										100

lb →	0	10	20	30	40	50	60	70	80	90 ←	lb
↓	kg	kg	kg	kg	kg	kg	kg	kg	kg	kg	↓
0	0.000	4.536	9.072	13.608	18.144	22.680	27.216	31.751	36.287	40.823	0
100	45.359	49.895	54.431	58.967	63.503	68.039	72.575	77.111	81.647	86.183	100
200	90.718	95.254	99.790	104.326	108.862	113.398	117.934	122.470	127.006	131.542	200
300	136.078	140.614	145.150	149.685	154.221	158.757	163.293	167.829	172.365	176.901	300
400	181.437	185.973	190.509	195.045	199.581	204.117	208.652	213.188	217.724	222.260	400
500	226.796	231.332	235.868	240.404	244.940	249.476	254.012	258.548	263.084	267.619	500
600	272.155	276.691	281.227	285.763	290.299	294.835	299.371	303.907	308.443	312.979	600
700	317.515	322.051	326.587	331.122	335.658	340.194	344.730	349.266	353.802	358.338	700
800	362.874	367.410	371.946	376.482	381.018	385.554	390.089	394.625	399.161	403.697	800
900	408.233	412.769	417.305	421.841	426.377	430.913	435.449	439.985	444.521	449.056	900
1000	453.592										1000

[a] This table can also be used for the conversion of pounds-force to kilograms-force (kiloponds).

Pressure and stress

Use of the tables. 11 $lbf/in^2 = 10\ lbf/in^2 + 1\ lbf/in^2 = 0.773\ kgf/cm^2$.

Kilograms-force per square centimetre to pounds-force (pounds) per square inch 1 kgf/cm² = 14.223 343 lbf/in²

kgf/cm² → ↓	0	1	2	3	4	5	6	7	8	9	← kgf/cm² ↓
	lbf/in²	lbf/in²	lbf/in²	lbf/in²	lbf/in²	lbf/in²	lbf/in²	lbf/in²	lbf/in²	lbf/in²	
0	0.000	14.223	28.447	42.670	56.893	71.117	85.340	99.563	113.787	128.010	0
10	142.233	156.457	170.680	184.903	199.127	213.350	227.573	241.797	256.020	270.244	10
20	284.467	298.690	312.914	327.137	341.360	355.584	369.807	384.030	398.254	412.477	20
30	426.700	440.924	455.147	469.370	483.594	497.817	512.040	526.264	540.487	554.710	30
40	568.934	583.157	597.380	611.604	625.827	640.050	654.274	668.497	682.720	696.944	40
50	711.167	725.391	739.614	753.837	768.061	782.284	796.507	810.731	824.954	839.177	50
60	853.401	867.624	881.847	896.071	910.294	924.517	938.741	952.964	967.187	981.411	60
70	995.634	1009.857	1024.081	1038.304	1052.527	1066.751	1080.974	1095.197	1109.421	1123.644	70
80	1137.867	1152.091	1166.314	1180.537	1194.761	1208.984	1223.208	1237.431	1251.654	1265.878	80
90	1280.101	1294.324	1308.548	1322.771	1336.994	1351.218	1365.441	1379.664	1393.888	1408.111	90
100	1422.334										100

Pounds-force (pounds) per square inch to kilograms-force per square centimetre 1 lbf/in² = 0.070 307 kgf/cm²

lbf/in² → ↓	0	1	2	3	4	5	6	7	8	9	← lbf/in² ↓
	kgf/cm²	kgf/cm²	kgf/cm²	kgf/cm²	kgf/cm²	kgf/cm²	kgf/cm²	kgf/cm²	kgf/cm²	kgf/cm²	
0	0.000	0.070	0.141	0.211	0.281	0.352	0.422	0.492	0.562	0.633	0
10	0.703	0.773	0.844	0.914	0.984	1.055	1.125	1.195	1.266	1.336	10
20	1.406	1.476	1.547	1.617	1.687	1.758	1.828	1.898	1.969	2.039	20
30	2.109	2.180	2.250	2.320	2.390	2.461	2.531	2.601	2.672	2.742	30
40	2.812	2.883	2.953	3.023	3.094	3.164	3.234	3.304	3.375	3.445	40
50	3.515	3.586	3.656	3.726	3.797	3.867	3.937	4.007	4.078	4.148	50
60	4.218	4.289	4.359	4.429	4.500	4.570	4.640	4.711	4.781	4.851	60
70	4.921	4.992	5.062	5.132	5.203	5.273	5.343	5.414	5.484	5.554	70
80	5.625	5.695	5.765	5.835	5.906	5.976	6.046	6.117	6.187	6.257	80
90	6.328	6.398	6.468	6.539	6.609	6.679	6.749	6.820	6.890	6.960	90
100	7.031										100

Newtons per square millimetre to pounds-force (pounds) per square inch 1 N/mm² = 145.037 738 lbf/in²

N/mm² → ↓	0	1	2	3	4	5	6	7	8	9	← N/mm² ↓
	lbf/in²	lbf/in²	lbf/in²	lbf/in²	lbf/in²	lbf/in²	lbf/in²	lbf/in²	lbf/in²	lbf/in²	
0	0.000	145.038	290.075	435.113	580.151	725.189	870.226	1015.264	1160.302	1305.340	0
10	1450.377	1595.415	1740.453	1885.491	2030.528	2175.566	2320.604	2465.642	2610.679	2755.717	10
20	2900.755	3045.792	3190.830	3335.868	3480.906	3625.943	3770.981	3916.019	4061.057	4206.094	20
30	4351.132	4496.170	4641.208	4786.245	4931.283	5076.321	5221.359	5366.396	5511.434	5656.472	30
40	5801.510	5946.547	6091.585	6236.623	6381.660	6526.698	6671.736	6816.774	6961.811	7106.849	40
50	7251.887	7396.925	7541.962	7687.000	7832.038	7977.076	8122.113	8267.151	8412.189	8557.227	50
60	8702.264	8847.302	8992.340	9137.377	9282.415	9427.453	9572.491	9717.528	9862.566	10007.604	60
70	10152.642	10297.679	10442.717	10587.755	10732.793	10877.830	11022.868	11167.906	11312.944	11457.981	70
80	11603.019	11748.057	11893.094	12038.132	12183.170	12328.208	12473.245	12618.283	12763.321	12908.359	80
90	13053.396	13198.434	13343.472	13488.510	13633.547	13778.585	13923.623	14068.661	14213.698	14358.736	90
100	14503.774										100

Pounds-force (pounds) per square inch to newtons per square millimetre 1 lbf/in² = 0.006 895 N/mm²

lbf/in² → ↓	0	100	200	300	400	500	600	700	800	900	← lbf/in² ↓
	N/mm²	N/mm²	N/mm²	N/mm²	N/mm²	N/mm²	N/mm²	N/mm²	N/mm²	N/mm²	
0	0.000	0.689	1.379	2.068	2.758	3.447	4.137	4.826	5.516	6.205	0
1000	6.895	7.584	8.274	8.963	9.653	10.342	11.032	11.721	12.411	13.100	1000
2000	13.790	14.479	15.168	15.858	16.547	17.237	17.926	18.616	19.305	19.995	2000
3000	20.684	21.374	22.063	22.753	23.442	24.132	24.821	25.511	26.200	26.890	3000
4000	27.579	28.269	28.958	29.647	30.337	31.026	31.716	32.405	33.095	33.784	4000
5000	34.474	35.163	35.853	36.542	37.232	37.921	38.611	39.300	39.990	40.679	5000
6000	41.369	42.058	42.747	43.437	44.126	44.816	45.505	46.195	46.884	47.574	6000
7000	48.263	48.953	49.642	50.332	51.021	51.711	52.400	53.090	53.779	54.469	7000
8000	55.158	55.848	56.537	57.226	57.916	58.605	59.295	59.984	60.674	61.363	8000
9000	62.053	62.742	63.432	64.121	64.811	65.500	66.190	66.879	67.569	68.258	9000
10000	68.948										10000

Use of the tables. 11 lbf/in^2 = 10 lbf/in^2 + 1 lbf/in^2 = 0.758 bar.

Bars to pounds-force (pounds) per square inch   1 bar = 14.503 774 lbf/in^2

bar →	0.0	0.1	0.2	0.3	0.4	0.5	0.6	0.7	0.8	0.9	← bar
↓	lbf/in^2	lbf/in^2	lbf/in^2	lbf/in^2	lbf/in^2	lbf/in^2	lbf/in^2	lbf/in^2	lbf/in^2	lbf/in^2	↓
0	0.000	1.450	2.901	4.351	5.802	7.252	8.702	10.153	11.603	13.053	0
1	14.504	15.954	17.405	18.855	20.305	21.756	23.206	24.656	26.107	27.557	1
2	29.008	30.458	31.908	33.359	34.809	36.259	37.710	39.160	40.611	42.061	2
3	43.511	44.962	46.412	47.862	49.313	50.763	52.214	53.664	55.114	56.565	3
4	58.015	59.465	60.916	62.366	63.817	65.267	66.717	68.168	69.618	71.068	4
5	72.519	73.969	75.420	76.870	78.320	79.771	81.221	82.672	84.122	85.572	5
6	87.023	88.473	89.923	91.374	92.824	94.275	95.725	97.175	98.626	100.076	6
7	101.526	102.977	104.427	105.878	107.328	108.778	110.229	111.679	113.129	114.580	7
8	116.030	117.481	118.931	120.381	121.832	123.282	124.732	126.183	127.633	129.084	8
9	130.534	131.984	133.435	134.885	136.335	137.786	139.236	140.687	142.137	143.587	9
10	145.038										10

Pounds-force (pounds) per square inch to bars   1 lbf/in^2 = 0.068 948 bar

lbf/in^2 →	0	1	2	3	4	5	6	7	8	9	← lbf/in^2
↓	bar	bar	bar	bar	bar	bar	bar	bar	bar	bar	↓
0	0.000	0.069	0.138	0.207	0.276	0.345	0.414	0.483	0.552	0.621	0
10	0.689	0.758	0.827	0.896	0.965	1.034	1.103	1.172	1.241	1.310	10
20	1.379	1.448	1.517	1.586	1.655	1.724	1.793	1.862	1.931	1.999	20
30	2.068	2.137	2.206	2.275	2.344	2.413	2.482	2.551	2.620	2.689	30
40	2.758	2.827	2.896	2.965	3.034	3.103	3.172	3.241	3.309	3.378	40
50	3.447	3.516	3.585	3.654	3.723	3.792	3.861	3.930	3.999	4.068	50
60	4.137	4.206	4.275	4.344	4.413	4.482	4.551	4.619	4.688	4.757	60
70	4.826	4.895	4.964	5.033	5.102	5.171	5.240	5.309	5.378	5.447	70
80	5.516	5.585	5.654	5.723	5.792	5.861	5.929	5.998	6.067	6.136	80
90	6.205	6.274	6.343	6.412	6.481	6.550	6.619	6.688	6.757	6.826	90
100	6.895										100

Kilopascals to pounds-force (pounds) per square inch   1 kPa = 0.145 038 lbf/in^2

kPa →	0	1	2	3	4	5	6	7	8	9	← kPa
↓	lbf/in^2	lbf/in^2	lbf/in^2	lbf/in^2	lbf/in^2	lbf/in^2	lbf/in^2	lbf/in^2	lbf/in^2	lbf/in^2	↓
0	0.000	0.145	0.290	0.435	0.580	0.725	0.870	1.015	1.160	1.305	0
10	1.450	1.595	1.740	1.885	2.031	2.176	2.321	2.466	2.611	2.756	10
20	2.901	3.046	3.191	3.336	3.481	3.626	3.771	3.916	4.061	4.206	20
30	4.351	4.496	4.641	4.786	4.931	5.076	5.221	5.366	5.511	5.656	30
40	5.802	5.947	6.092	6.237	6.382	6.527	6.672	6.817	6.962	7.107	40
50	7.252	7.397	7.542	7.687	7.832	7.977	8.122	8.267	8.412	8.557	50
60	8.702	8.847	8.992	9.137	9.282	9.427	9.572	9.718	9.863	10.008	60
70	10.153	10.298	10.443	10.588	10.733	10.878	11.023	11.168	11.313	11.458	70
80	11.603	11.748	11.893	12.038	12.183	12.328	12.473	12.618	12.763	12.908	80
90	13.053	13.198	13.343	13.489	13.634	13.779	13.924	14.069	14.214	14.359	90
100	14.504										100

Pounds-force (pounds) per square inch to kilopascals   1 lbf/in^2 = 6.894 757 kPa

lbf/in^2 →	0	1	2	3	4	5	6	7	8	9	← lbf/in^2
↓	kPa	kPa	kPa	kPa	kPa	kPa	kPa	kPa	kPa	kPa	↓
0	0.000	6.895	13.790	20.684	27.579	34.474	41.369	48.263	55.158	62.053	0
10	68.948	75.842	82.737	89.632	96.527	103.421	110.316	117.211	124.106	131.000	10
20	137.895	144.790	151.685	158.579	165.474	172.369	179.264	186.158	193.053	199.948	20
30	206.843	213.737	220.632	227.527	234.422	241.317	248.211	255.106	262.001	268.896	30
40	275.790	282.685	289.580	296.475	303.369	310.264	317.159	324.054	330.948	337.843	40
50	344.738	351.633	358.527	365.422	372.317	379.212	386.106	393.001	399.896	406.791	50
60	413.685	420.580	427.475	434.370	441.264	448.159	455.054	461.949	468.843	475.738	60
70	482.633	489.528	496.423	503.317	510.212	517.107	524.002	530.896	537.791	544.686	70
80	551.581	558.475	565.370	572.265	579.160	586.054	592.949	599.844	606.739	613.633	80
90	620.528	627.423	634.318	641.212	648.107	655.002	661.897	668.791	675.686	682.581	90
100	689.476										100

Use of the tables. 11 tonf/in^2 = 10 tonf/in^2 + 1 tonf/in^2 = 169.887 N/mm^2.

Newtons per square millimetre to UK tons-force (tons) per square inch

1 N/mm^2 = 0.064 749 tonf/in^2

N/mm² → ↓	0	1	2	3	4	5	6	7	8	9 ← N/mm² ↓
	tonf/in²	tonf/in²	tonf/in²	tonf/in²	tonf/in²	tonf/in²	tonf/in²	tonf/in²	tonf/in²	tonf/in²
0	0.000	0.065	0.129	0.194	0.259	0.324	0.388	0.453	0.518	0.583
10	0.647	0.712	0.777	0.842	0.906	0.971	1.036	1.101	1.165	1.230
20	1.295	1.360	1.424	1.489	1.554	1.619	1.683	1.748	1.813	1.878
30	1.942	2.007	2.072	2.137	2.201	2.266	2.331	2.396	2.460	2.525
40	2.590	2.655	2.719	2.784	2.849	2.914	2.978	3.043	3.108	3.173
50	3.237	3.302	3.367	3.432	3.496	3.561	3.626	3.691	3.755	3.820
60	3.885	3.950	4.014	4.079	4.144	4.209	4.273	4.338	4.403	4.468
70	4.532	4.597	4.662	4.727	4.791	4.856	4.921	4.986	5.050	5.115
80	5.180	5.245	5.309	5.374	5.439	5.504	5.568	5.633	5.698	5.763
90	5.827	5.892	5.957	6.022	6.086	6.151	6.216	6.281	6.345	6.410
100	6.475									

UK tons-force (tons) per square inch to newtons per square millimetre

1 tonf/in^2 = 15.444 256 N/mm^2

tonf/in² → ↓	0	1	2	3	4	5	6	7	8	9 ← tonf/in² ↓
	N/mm²	N/mm²	N/mm²	N/mm²	N/mm²	N/mm²	N/mm²	N/mm²	N/mm²	N/mm²
0	0.000	15.444	30.889	46.333	61.777	77.221	92.666	108.110	123.554	138.998
10	154.443	169.887	185.331	200.775	216.220	231.664	247.108	262.552	277.997	293.441
20	308.885	324.329	339.774	355.218	370.662	386.106	401.551	416.995	432.439	447.883
30	463.328	478.772	494.216	509.660	525.105	540.549	555.993	571.437	586.882	602.326
40	617.770	633.215	648.659	664.103	679.547	694.992	710.436	725.880	741.324	756.769
50	772.213	787.657	803.101	818.546	833.990	849.434	864.878	880.323	895.767	911.211
60	926.655	942.100	957.544	972.988	988.432	1003.877	1019.321	1034.765	1050.209	1065.654
70	1081.098	1096.542	1111.986	1127.431	1142.875	1158.319	1173.763	1189.208	1204.652	1220.096
80	1235.541	1250.985	1266.429	1281.873	1297.318	1312.762	1328.206	1343.650	1359.095	1374.539
90	1389.983	1405.427	1420.872	1436.316	1451.760	1467.204	1482.649	1498.093	1513.537	1528.981
100	1544.426									

Bars to UK tons-force (tons) per square foot

1 bar = 0.932 385 tonf/ft^2

bar → ↓	0	1	2	3	4	5	6	7	8	9 ← bar ↓
	tonf/ft²	tonf/ft²	tonf/ft²	tonf/ft²	tonf/ft²	tonf/ft²	tonf/ft²	tonf/ft²	tonf/ft²	tonf/ft²
0	0.000	0.932	1.865	2.797	3.730	4.662	5.594	6.527	7.459	8.391
10	9.324	10.256	11.189	12.121	13.053	13.986	14.918	15.851	16.783	17.715
20	18.648	19.580	20.512	21.445	22.377	23.310	24.242	25.174	26.107	27.039
30	27.972	28.904	29.836	30.769	31.701	32.633	33.566	34.498	35.431	36.363
40	37.295	38.228	39.160	40.093	41.025	41.957	42.890	43.822	44.755	45.687
50	46.619	47.552	48.484	49.416	50.349	51.281	52.214	53.146	54.078	55.011
60	55.943	56.876	57.808	58.740	59.673	60.605	61.537	62.470	63.402	64.335
70	65.267	66.199	67.132	68.064	68.997	69.929	70.861	71.794	72.726	73.658
80	74.591	75.523	76.456	77.388	78.320	79.253	80.185	81.118	82.050	82.982
90	83.915	84.847	85.779	86.712	87.644	88.577	89.509	90.441	91.374	92.306
100	93.239									

UK tons-force (tons) per square foot to bars

1 tonf/ft^2 = 1.072 518 bar

tonf/ft² → ↓	0	1	2	3	4	5	6	7	8	9 ← tonf/ft² ↓
	bar	bar	bar	bar	bar	bar	bar	bar	bar	bar
0	0.000	1.073	2.145	3.218	4.290	5.363	6.435	7.508	8.580	9.653
10	10.725	11.798	12.870	13.943	15.015	16.088	17.160	18.233	19.305	20.378
20	21.450	22.523	23.595	24.668	25.740	26.813	27.885	28.958	30.030	31.103
30	32.176	33.248	34.321	35.393	36.466	37.538	38.611	39.683	40.756	41.828
40	42.901	43.973	45.046	46.118	47.191	48.263	49.336	50.408	51.481	52.553
50	53.626	54.698	55.771	56.843	57.916	58.988	60.061	61.134	62.206	63.279
60	64.351	65.424	66.496	67.569	68.641	69.714	70.786	71.859	72.931	74.004
70	75.076	76.149	77.221	78.294	79.366	80.439	81.511	82.584	83.656	84.729
80	85.801	86.874	87.946	89.019	90.091	91.164	92.237	93.309	94.382	95.454
90	96.527	97.599	98.672	99.744	100.817	101.889	102.962	104.034	105.107	106.179
100	107.252									

Temperature

Use of the table. Corresponding degrees on the Fahrenheit and Celsius scales are shown where, for example, 32 °F = 0 °C and 212 °F = 100 °C. The degree Celsius has been converted to the degree Fahrenheit by multiplying by 9, dividing by 5 and 32. The degree Fahrenheit has been converted to the degree Celsius by subtracting 32, multiplying by 5 and dividing by 9.

Fahrenheit and Celsius (centigrade)

°F	°C	°F	°C	°F	°C	°F	°C	°F	°C	°F	°C
−459.67	−273.15	0	−17.8	20	−6.7	40	4.4	60	15.6	80	26.7
−450	−267.8	0.5	−17.5	20.3	−6.5	40.1	4.5	60.5	15.8	80.5	26.9
−418	−250	1	−17.2	20.5	−6.4	40.5	4.7	60.8	16	80.6	27
−400	−240	1.4	−17	21	−6.1	41	5	61	16.1	81	27.2
−350	−212.2	1.5	−16.9	21.2	−6	41.5	5.3	61.5	16.4	81.5	27.5
−328	−200	2	−16.7	21.5	−5.8	41.9	5.5	61.7	16.5	82	27.8
−300	−184.4	2.3	−16.5	22	−5.6	42	5.6	62	16.7	82.4	28
−250	−156.7	2.5	−16.4	22.1	−5.5	42.5	5.8	62.5	16.9	82.5	28.1
−238	−150	3	−16.1	22.5	−5.3	42.8	6	62.6	17	83	28.3
−200	−128.9	3.2	−16	23	−5	43	6.1	63	17.2	83.3	28.5
−150	−101.1	3.5	−15.8	23.5	−4.7	43.5	6.4	63.5	17.5	83.5	28.6
−148	−100	4	−15.6	23.9	−4.5	43.7	6.5	64	17.8	84	28.9
−140	−95.6	4.1	−15.5	24	−4.4	44	6.7	64.4	18	84.2	29
−130	−90	4.5	−15.3	24.5	−4.2	44.5	6.9	64.5	18.1	84.5	29.2
−120	−84.4	5	−15	24.8	−4	44.6	7	65	18.3	85	29.4
−112	−80	5.5	−14.7	25	−3.9	45	7.2	65.3	18.5	85.1	29.5
−110	−78.9	5.9	−14.5	25.5	−3.6	45.5	7.5	65.5	18.6	85.5	29.7
−100	−73.3	6	−14.4	25.7	−3.5	46	7.8	66	18.9	86	30
−95	−70.6	6.5	−14.2	26	−3.3	46.4	8	66.2	19	86.5	30.3
−94	−70	6.8	−14	26.5	−3.1	46.5	8.1	66.5	19.2	86.9	30.5
−90	−67.8	7	−13.9	26.6	−3	47	8.3	67	19.4	87	30.6
−85	−65	7.5	−13.6	27	−2.8	47.3	8.5	67.1	19.5	87.5	30.8
−80	−62.2	7.7	−13.5	27.5	−2.5	47.5	8.6	67.5	19.7	87.8	31
−76	−60	8	−13.3	28	−2.2	48	8.9	68	20	88	31.1
−75	−59.4	8.5	−13.1	28.4	−2	48.2	9	68.5	20.3	88.5	31.4
−70	−56.7	8.6	−13	28.5	−1.9	48.5	9.2	68.9	20.5	88.7	31.5
−67	−55	9	−12.8	29	−1.7	49	9.4	69	20.6	89	31.7
−65	−53.9	9.5	−12.5	29.3	−1.5	49.1	9.5	69.5	20.8	89.5	31.9
−60	−51.1	10	−12.2	29.5	−1.4	49.5	9.7	69.8	21	89.6	32
−58	−50	10.4	−12	30	−1.1	50	10	70	21.1	90	32.2
−55	−48.3	10.5	−11.9	30.2	−1	50.5	10.3	70.5	21.4	90.5	32.5
−50	−45.6	11	−11.7	30.5	−0.8	50.9	10.5	70.7	21.5	91	32.8
−49	−45	11.3	−11.5	31	−0.6	51	10.6	71	21.7	91.4	33
−45	−42.8	11.5	−11.4	31.1	−0.5	51.5	10.8	71.5	21.9	91.5	33.1
−40	−40	12	−11.1	31.5	−0.3	51.8	11	71.6	22	92	33.3
−35	−37.2	12.2	−11	32	0	52	11.1	72	22.2	92.3	33.5
−31	−35	12.5	−10.8	32.5	0.3	52.5	11.4	72.5	22.5	92.5	33.6
−30	−34.4	13	−10.6	32.9	0.5	52.7	11.5	73	22.8	93	33.9
−25	−31.7	13.1	−10.5	33	0.6	53	11.7	73.4	23	93.2	34
−22	−30	13.5	−10.3	33.5	0.8	53.5	11.9	73.5	23.1	93.5	34.2
−20	−28.9	14	−10	33.8	1	53.6	12	74	23.3	94	34.4
−15	−26.1	14.5	−9.7	34	1.1	54	12.2	74.3	23.5	94.1	34.5
−13	−25	14.9	−9.5	34.5	1.4	54.5	12.5	74.5	23.6	94.5	34.7
−10	−23.3	15	−9.4	34.7	1.5	55	12.8	75	23.9	95	35
−9.4	−23	15.5	−9.2	35	1.7	55.4	13	75.2	24	95.5	35.3
−9	−22.8	15.8	−9	35.5	1.9	55.5	13.1	75.5	24.2	95.9	35.5
−8	−22.2	16	−8.9	35.6	2	56	13.3	76	24.4	96	35.6
−7.6	−22	16.5	−8.6	36	2.2	56.3	13.5	76.1	24.5	96.5	35.8
−7	−21.7	16.7	−8.5	36.5	2.5	56.5	13.6	76.5	24.7	96.8	36
−6	−21.1	17	−8.3	37	2.8	57	13.9	77	25	97	36.1
−5.8	−21	17.5	−8.1	37.4	3	57.2	14	77.5	25.3	97.5	36.4
−5	−20.6	17.6	−8	37.5	3.1	57.5	14.2	77.9	25.5	97.7	36.5
−4	−20	18	−7.8	38	3.3	58	14.4	78	25.6	98	36.7
−3	−19.4	18.5	−7.5	38.3	3.5	58.1	14.5	78.5	25.8	98.5	36.9
−2.2	−19	19	−7.2	38.5	3.6	58.5	14.7	78.8	26	98.6	37
−2	−18.9	19.4	−7	39	3.9	59	15	79	26.1	99	37.2
−1	−18.3	19.5	−6.9	39.2	4	59.5	15.3	79.5	26.4	99.5	37.5
−0.4	−18			39.5	4.2	59.9	15.5	79.7	26.5		

Fahrenheit and Celsius (centigrade) cont.

°F	°C	°F	°C	°F	°C	°F	°C	°F	°C	°F	°C
100	37.8	120	48.9	140	60	160	71.1	200	93.3	240	115.6
100.4	38	120.2	49	140.5	60.3	161	71.7	201	93.9	245	118.3
100.5	38.1	120.5	49.2	140.9	60.5	161.6	72	201.2	94	248	120
101	38.3	121	49.4	141	60.6	162	72.2	202	94.4	250	121.1
101.3	38.5	121.1	49.5	141.5	60.8	163	72.8	203	95	255	123.9
101.5	38.6	121.5	49.7	141.8	61	163.4	73	204	95.6	257	125
102	38.9	122	50	142	61.1	164	73.3	204.8	96	260	126.7
102.2	39	122.5	50.3	142.5	61.4	165	73.9	205	96.1	265	129.4
102.5	39.2	122.9	50.5	142.7	61.5	165.2	74	206	96.7	266	130
103	39.4	123	50.6	143	61.7	166	74.4	206.6	97	270	132.2
103.1	39.5	123.5	50.8	143.5	61.9	167	75	207	97.2	275	135
103.5	39.7	123.8	51	143.6	62	168	75.6	208	97.8	280	137.8
104	40	124	51.1	144	62.2	168.8	76	208.4	98	284	140
104.5	40.3	124.5	51.4	144.5	62.5	169	76.1	209	98.3	285	140.6
104.9	40.5	124.7	51.5	145	62.8	170	76.7	210	98.9	290	143.3
105	40.6	125	51.7	145.4	63	170.6	77	210.2	99	293	145
105.5	40.8	125.5	51.9	145.5	63.1	171	77.2	211	99.4	295	146.1
105.8	41	125.6	52	146	63.3	172	77.8	212	100	300	148.9
106	41.1	126	52.2	146.3	63.5	172.4	78	213	100.6	302	150
106.5	41.4	126.5	52.5	146.5	63.6	173	78.3	213.8	101	305	151.7
106.7	41.5	127	52.8	147	63.9	174	78.9	214	101.1	310	154.4
107	41.7	127.4	53	147.2	64	174.2	79	215	101.7	311	155
107.5	41.9	127.5	53.1	147.5	64.2	175	79.4	215.6	102	315	157.2
107.6	42	128	53.3	148	64.4	176	80	216	102.2	320	160
108	42.2	128.3	53.5	148.1	64.5	177	80.6	217	102.8	325	162.8
108.5	42.5	128.5	53.6	148.5	64.7	177.8	81	217.4	103	329	165
109	42.8	129	53.9	149	65	178	81.1	218	103.3	330	165.6
109.4	43	129.2	54	149.5	65.3	179	81.7	219	103.9	335	168.3
109.5	43.1	129.5	54.2	149.9	65.5	179.6	82	219.2	104	338	170
110	43.3	130	54.4	150	65.6	180	82.2	220	104.4	340	171.1
110.3	43.5	130.1	54.5	150.5	65.8	181	82.8	221	105	345	173.9
110.5	43.6	130.5	54.7	150.8	66	181.4	83	222	105.6	347	175
111	43.9	131	55	151	66.1	182	83.3	222.8	106	350	176.7
111.2	44	131.5	55.3	151.5	66.4	183	83.9	223	106.1	355	179.4
111.5	44.2	131.9	55.5	151.7	66.5	183.2	84	224	106.7	356	180
112	44.4	132	55.6	152	66.7	184	84.4	224.6	107	360	182.2
112.1	44.5	132.5	55.8	152.5	66.9	185	85	225	107.2	365	185
112.5	44.7	132.8	56	152.6	67	186	85.6	226	107.8	370	187.8
113	45	133	56.1	153	67.2	186.8	86	226.4	108	374	190
113.5	45.3	133.5	56.4	153.5	67.5	187	86.1	227	108.3	375	190.6
113.9	45.5	133.7	56.5	154	67.8	188	86.7	228	108.9	380	193.3
114	45.6	134	56.7	154.4	68	188.6	87	228.2	109	383	195
114.5	45.8	134.5	56.9	154.5	68.1	189	87.2	229	109.4	385	196.1
114.8	46	134.6	57	155	68.3	190	87.8	230	110	390	198.9
115	46.1	135	57.2	155.3	68.5	190.4	88	231	110.6	392	200
115.5	46.4	135.5	57.5	155.5	68.6	191	88.3	231.8	111	395	201.7
115.7	46.5	136	57.8	156	68.9	192	88.9	232	111.1	400	204.4
116	46.7	136.4	58	156.2	69	192.2	89	233	111.7	450	232.2
116.5	46.9	136.5	58.1	156.5	69.2	193	89.4	233.6	112	482	250
116.6	47	137	58.3	157	69.4	194	90	234	112.2	500	260
117	47.2	137.3	58.5	157.1	69.5	195	90.6	235	112.8	572	300
117.5	47.5	137.5	58.6	157.5	69.7	195.8	91	235.4	113	600	315.6
118	47.8	138	58.9	158	70	196	91.1	236	113.3	700	371.1
118.4	48	138.2	59	158.5	70.3	197	91.7	237	113.9	752	400
118.5	48.1	138.5	59.2	158.9	70.5	197.6	92	237.2	114	932	500
119	48.3	139	59.4	159	70.6	198	92.2	238	114.4	1000	537.8
119.3	48.5	139.1	59.5	159.5	70.8	199	92.8	239	115	1832	1000
119.5	48.6	139.5	59.7	159.8	71	199.4	93			2000	1093.3

Agriculture

For other measures see Agriculture, fishing and forestry, pages 27–41.

Note. Conversions are given for the weight of the UK or US wheat bushel (of 60 pounds), or international corn bushel (of 60 pounds), relating to tonnes. These can be used for any bushel containing 60 pounds.

Tonnes to UK or US bushels (of 60 pounds) 1 t = 36.743 710 bu

t → ↓	0	1	2	3	4	5	6	7	8	9 ←	t ↓
	bu	bu	bu	bu	bu	bu	bu	bu	bu	bu	
0	0.00	36.74	73.49	110.23	146.97	183.72	220.46	257.21	293.95	330.69	0
10	367.44	404.18	440.92	477.67	514.41	551.16	587.90	624.64	661.39	698.13	10
20	734.87	771.62	808.36	845.11	881.85	918.59	955.34	992.08	1028.82	1065.57	20
30	1102.31	1139.06	1175.80	1212.54	1249.29	1286.03	1322.77	1359.52	1396.26	1433.00	30
40	1469.75	1506.49	1543.24	1579.98	1616.72	1653.47	1690.21	1726.95	1763.70	1800.44	40
50	1837.19	1873.93	1910.67	1947.42	1984.16	2020.90	2057.65	2094.39	2131.14	2167.88	50
60	2204.62	2241.37	2278.11	2314.85	2351.60	2388.34	2425.08	2461.83	2498.57	2535.32	60
70	2572.06	2608.80	2645.55	2682.29	2719.03	2755.78	2792.52	2829.27	2866.01	2902.75	70
80	2939.50	2976.24	3012.98	3049.73	3086.47	3123.22	3159.96	3196.70	3233.45	3270.19	80
90	3306.93	3343.68	3380.42	3417.17	3453.91	3490.65	3527.40	3564.14	3600.88	3637.63	90
100	3674.37										100

UK or US bushels (of 60 pounds) to tonnes 1 bu = 0.027 216 t

bu → ↓	0	10	20	30	40	50	60	70	80	90 ←	bu ↓
	t	t	t	t	t	t	t	t	t	t	
0	0.00	0.27	0.54	0.82	1.09	1.36	1.63	1.91	2.18	2.45	0
100	2.72	2.99	3.27	3.54	3.81	4.08	4.35	4.63	4.90	5.17	100
200	5.44	5.72	5.99	6.26	6.53	6.80	7.08	7.35	7.62	7.89	200
300	8.16	8.44	8.71	8.98	9.25	9.53	9.80	10.07	10.34	10.61	300
400	10.89	11.16	11.43	11.70	11.97	12.25	12.52	12.79	13.06	13.34	400
500	13.61	13.88	14.15	14.42	14.70	14.97	15.24	15.51	15.79	16.06	500
600	16.33	16.60	16.87	17.15	17.42	17.69	17.96	18.23	18.51	18.78	600
700	19.05	19.32	19.60	19.87	20.14	20.41	20.68	20.96	21.23	21.50	700
800	21.77	22.04	22.32	22.59	22.86	23.13	23.41	23.68	23.95	24.22	800
900	24.49	24.77	25.04	25.31	25.58	25.85	26.13	26.40	26.67	26.94	900
1000	27.22										1000

bu → ↓	0	100	200	300	400	500	600	700	800	900 ←	bu ↓
	t	t	t	t	t	t	t	t	t	t	
0	0.00	2.72	5.44	8.16	10.89	13.61	16.33	19.05	21.77	24.49	0
1000	27.22	29.94	32.66	35.38	38.10	40.82	43.54	46.27	48.99	51.71	1000
2000	54.43	57.15	59.87	62.60	65.32	68.04	70.76	73.48	76.20	78.93	2000
3000	81.65	84.37	87.09	89.81	92.53	95.25	97.98	100.70	103.42	106.14	3000
4000	108.86	111.58	114.31	117.03	119.75	122.47	125.19	127.91	130.63	133.36	4000
5000	136.08	138.80	141.52	144.24	146.96	149.69	152.41	155.13	157.85	160.57	5000
6000	163.29	166.01	168.74	171.46	174.18	176.90	179.62	182.34	185.07	187.79	6000
7000	190.51	193.23	195.95	198.67	201.40	204.12	206.84	209.56	212.28	215.00	7000
8000	217.72	220.45	223.17	225.89	228.61	231.33	234.05	236.78	239.50	242.22	8000
9000	244.94	247.66	250.38	253.10	255.83	258.55	261.27	263.99	266.71	269.43	9000
10000	272.16										10000

The tables for conversion between US (short) hundredweights per acre and quintals per hectare can also be used for conversions between pounds per acre and kilograms per hectare. The tables for conversions using quintals per hectare can also be used as follows: for conversions from tonnes per hectare, by moving the decimal point in the table one place to the right, and for conversions from kilograms per hectare by moving the decimal point two places to the left; conversions to tonnes per hectare can be obtained by moving the decimal point one place to the left, and to kilograms per hectare by moving the decimal point two places to the right.

See pages 180–181 for conversions between the capacity measures of UK bushels, US bushels and hectolitres.

Please note that for capacity measurement: 1 hectolitre per hectare = 1.112 730 UK bushels per acre; 1 UK bushel per acre = 0.898 691 hectolitre per hectare.

Quintals (100 kilograms) per hectare to UK or US bushels (of 60 pounds) per acre 1 q/ha = 1.486 965 bu/acre

q/ha →	0	1	2	3	4	5	6	7	8	9	← q/ha
↓	bu/acre	bu/acre	bu/acre	bu/acre	bu/acre	bu/acre	bu/acre	bu/acre	bu/acre	bu/acre	↓
0	0.000	1.487	2.974	4.461	5.948	7.435	8.922	10.409	11.896	13.383	0
10	14.870	16.357	17.844	19.331	20.818	22.304	23.791	25.278	26.765	28.252	10
20	29.739	31.226	32.713	34.200	35.687	37.174	38.661	40.148	41.635	43.122	20
30	44.609	46.096	47.583	49.070	50.557	52.044	53.531	55.018	56.505	57.992	30
40	59.479	60.966	62.453	63.940	65.426	66.913	68.400	69.887	71.374	72.861	40
50	74.348	75.835	77.322	78.809	80.296	81.783	83.270	84.757	86.244	87.731	50
60	89.218	90.705	92.192	93.679	95.166	96.653	98.140	99.627	101.114	102.601	60
70	104.088	105.575	107.061	108.548	110.035	111.522	113.009	114.496	115.983	117.470	70
80	118.957	120.444	121.931	123.418	124.905	126.392	127.879	129.366	130.853	132.340	80
90	133.827	135.314	136.801	138.288	139.775	141.262	142.749	144.236	145.723	147.210	90
100	148.697										100

UK or US bushels (of 60 pounds) per acre to quintals (100 kilograms) per hectare 1 bu/acre = 0.672 511 q/ha

bu/acre →	0	1	2	3	4	5	6	7	8	9	← bu/acre
↓	q/ha	q/ha	q/ha	q/ha	q/ha	q/ha	q/ha	q/ha	q/ha	q/ha	↓
0	0.000	0.673	1.345	2.018	2.690	3.363	4.035	4.708	5.380	6.053	0
10	6.725	7.398	8.070	8.743	9.415	10.088	10.760	11.433	12.105	12.778	10
20	13.450	14.123	14.795	15.468	16.140	16.813	17.485	18.158	18.830	19.503	20
30	20.175	20.848	21.520	22.193	22.865	23.538	24.210	24.883	25.555	26.228	30
40	26.900	27.573	28.245	28.918	29.590	30.263	30.935	31.608	32.281	32.953	40
50	33.626	34.298	34.971	35.643	36.316	36.988	37.661	38.333	39.006	39.678	50
60	40.351	41.023	41.696	42.368	43.041	43.713	44.386	45.058	45.731	46.403	60
70	47.076	47.748	48.421	49.093	49.766	50.438	51.111	51.783	52.456	53.128	70
80	53.801	54.473	55.146	55.818	56.491	57.163	57.836	58.508	59.181	59.853	80
90	60.526	61.198	61.871	62.543	63.216	63.889	64.561	65.234	65.906	66.579	90
100	67.251										100

Quintals (100 kilograms) per hectare to US (short) hundredweights per acre 1 q/ha = 0.892 179 US cwt/acre

q/ha →	0	1	2	3	4	5	6	7	8	9	← q/ha
↓	US cwt/acre	US cwt/acre	US cwt/acre	US cwt/acre	US cwt/acre	US cwt/acre	US cwt/acre	US cwt/acre	US cwt/acre	US cwt/acre	↓
0	0.000	0.892	1.784	2.677	3.569	4.461	5.353	6.245	7.137	8.030	0
10	8.922	9.814	10.706	11.598	12.491	13.383	14.275	15.167	16.059	16.951	10
20	17.844	18.736	19.628	20.520	21.412	22.304	23.197	24.089	24.981	25.873	20
30	26.765	27.658	28.550	29.442	30.334	31.226	32.118	33.011	33.903	34.795	30
40	35.687	36.579	37.472	38.364	39.256	40.148	41.040	41.932	42.825	43.717	40
50	44.609	45.501	46.393	47.285	48.178	49.070	49.962	50.854	51.746	52.639	50
60	53.531	54.423	55.315	56.207	57.099	57.992	58.884	59.776	60.668	61.560	60
70	62.453	63.345	64.237	65.129	66.021	66.913	67.806	68.698	69.590	70.482	70
80	71.374	72.267	73.159	74.051	74.943	75.835	76.727	77.620	78.512	79.404	80
90	80.296	81.188	82.080	82.973	83.865	84.757	85.649	86.541	87.434	88.326	90
100	89.218										100

US (short) hundredweights per acre to quintals (100 kilograms) per hectare 1 US cwt/acre = 1.120 851 q/ha

US cwt/acre →	0	1	2	3	4	5	6	7	8	9	← US cwt/acre
↓	q/ha	q/ha	q/ha	q/ha	q/ha	q/ha	q/ha	q/ha	q/ha	q/ha	↓
0	0.000	1.121	2.242	3.363	4.483	5.604	6.725	7.846	8.967	10.088	0
10	11.209	12.329	13.450	14.571	15.692	16.813	17.934	19.054	20.175	21.296	10
20	22.417	23.538	24.659	25.780	26.900	28.021	29.142	30.263	31.384	32.505	20
30	33.626	34.746	35.867	36.988	38.109	39.230	40.351	41.471	42.592	43.713	30
40	44.834	45.955	47.076	48.197	49.317	50.438	51.559	52.680	53.801	54.922	40
50	56.043	57.163	58.284	59.405	60.526	61.647	62.768	63.889	65.009	66.130	50
60	67.251	68.372	69.493	70.614	71.734	72.855	73.976	75.097	76.218	77.339	60
70	78.460	79.580	80.701	81.822	82.943	84.064	85.185	86.306	87.426	88.547	70
80	89.668	90.789	91.910	93.031	94.151	95.272	96.393	97.514	98.635	99.756	80
90	100.877	101.997	103.118	104.239	105.360	106.481	107.602	108.723	109.843	110.964	90
100	112.085										100

Quintals (100 kilograms) per hectare to UK (long) hundredweights per acre 1 q/ha = 0.796 589 UK cwt/acre

q/ha → ↓	0	1	2	3	4	5	6	7	8	9	← q/ha ↓
	UK cwt/acre	UK cwt/acre	UK cwt/acre	UK cwt/acre	UK cwt/acre	UK cwt/acre	UK cwt/acre	UK cwt/acre	UK cwt/acre	UK cwt/acre	
0	0.000	0.797	1.593	2.390	3.186	3.983	4.780	5.576	6.373	7.169	0
10	7.966	8.762	9.559	10.356	11.152	11.949	12.745	13.542	14.339	15.135	10
20	15.932	16.728	17.525	18.322	19.118	19.915	20.711	21.508	22.304	23.101	20
30	23.898	24.694	25.491	26.287	27.084	27.881	28.677	29.474	30.270	31.067	30
40	31.864	32.660	33.457	34.253	35.050	35.846	36.643	37.440	38.236	39.033	40
50	39.829	40.626	41.423	42.219	43.016	43.812	44.609	45.406	46.202	46.999	50
60	47.795	48.592	49.388	50.185	50.982	51.778	52.575	53.371	54.168	54.965	60
70	55.761	56.558	57.354	58.151	58.948	59.744	60.541	61.337	62.134	62.930	70
80	63.727	64.524	65.320	66.117	66.913	67.710	68.507	69.303	70.100	70.896	80
90	71.693	72.490	73.286	74.083	74.879	75.676	76.472	77.269	78.066	78.862	90
100	79.659										100

UK (long) hundredweights per acre to quintals (100 kilograms) per hectare 1 UK cwt/acre = 1.255 353 q/ha

UK cwt/acre → ↓	0	1	2	3	4	5	6	7	8	9	← UK cwt/acre ↓
	q/ha	q/ha	q/ha	q/ha	q/ha	q/ha	q/ha	q/ha	q/ha	q/ha	
0	0.000	1.255	2.511	3.766	5.021	6.277	7.532	8.787	10.043	11.298	0
10	12.554	13.809	15.064	16.320	17.575	18.830	20.086	21.341	22.596	23.852	10
20	25.107	26.362	27.618	28.873	30.128	31.384	32.639	33.895	35.150	36.405	20
30	37.661	38.916	40.171	41.427	42.682	43.937	45.193	46.448	47.703	48.959	30
40	50.214	51.469	52.725	53.980	55.236	56.491	57.746	59.002	60.257	61.512	40
50	62.768	64.023	65.278	66.534	67.789	69.044	70.300	71.555	72.810	74.066	50
60	75.321	76.577	77.832	79.087	80.343	81.598	82.853	84.109	85.364	86.619	60
70	87.875	89.130	90.385	91.641	92.896	94.151	95.407	96.662	97.918	99.173	70
80	100.428	101.684	102.939	104.194	105.450	106.705	107.960	109.216	110.471	111.726	80
90	112.982	114.237	115.493	116.748	118.003	119.259	120.514	121.769	123.025	124.280	90
100	125.535										100

Quintals (100 kilograms) per hectare to UK (long) tons per acre 1 q/ha = 0.039 829 UK ton/acre

q/ha → ↓	0	10	20	30	40	50	60	70	80	90	← q/ha ↓
	UK ton/acre	UK ton/acre	UK ton/acre	UK ton/acre	UK ton/acre	UK ton/acre	UK ton/acre	UK ton/acre	UK ton/acre	UK ton/acre	
0	0.000	0.398	0.797	1.195	1.593	1.991	2.390	2.788	3.186	3.585	0
100	3.983	4.381	4.780	5.178	5.576	5.974	6.373	6.771	7.169	7.568	100
200	7.966	8.364	8.762	9.161	9.559	9.957	10.356	10.754	11.152	11.551	200
300	11.949	12.347	12.745	13.144	13.542	13.940	14.339	14.737	15.135	15.533	300
400	15.932	16.330	16.728	17.127	17.525	17.923	18.322	18.720	19.118	19.516	400
500	19.915	20.313	20.711	21.110	21.508	21.906	22.304	22.703	23.101	23.499	500
600	23.898	24.296	24.694	25.093	25.491	25.889	26.287	26.686	27.084	27.482	600
700	27.881	28.279	28.677	29.075	29.474	29.872	30.270	30.669	31.067	31.465	700
800	31.864	32.262	32.660	33.058	33.457	33.855	34.253	34.652	35.050	35.448	800
900	35.846	36.245	36.643	37.041	37.440	37.838	38.236	38.635	39.033	39.431	900
1000	39.829										1000

UK (long) tons per acre to quintals (100 kilograms) per hectare 1 UK ton/acre = 25.107 066 q/ha

UK ton/acre → ↓	0	0.5	1.0	1.5	2.0	2.5	3.0	3.5	4.0	4.5	← UK ton/acre ↓
	q/ha	q/ha	q/ha	q/ha	q/ha	q/ha	q/ha	q/ha	q/ha	q/ha	
0	0.000	12.554	25.107	37.661	50.214	62.768	75.321	87.875	100.428	112.982	0
5	125.535	138.089	150.642	163.196	175.749	188.303	200.857	213.410	225.964	238.517	5
10	251.071	263.624	276.178	288.731	301.285	313.838	326.392	338.945	351.499	364.052	10
15	376.606	389.160	401.713	414.267	426.820	439.374	451.927	464.481	477.034	489.588	15
20	502.141	514.695	527.248	539.802	552.355	564.909	577.463	590.016	602.570	615.123	20
25	627.677	640.230	652.784	665.337	677.891	690.444	702.998	715.551	728.105	740.658	25
30	753.212	765.766	778.319	790.873	803.426	815.980	828.533	841.087	853.640	866.194	30
35	878.747	891.301	903.854	916.408	928.961	941.515	954.069	966.622	979.176	991.729	35
40	1004.283	1016.836	1029.390	1041.943	1054.497	1067.050	1079.604	1092.157	1104.711	1117.264	40
45	1129.818	1142.371	1154.925	1167.479	1180.032	1192.586	1205.139	1217.693	1230.246	1242.800	45
50	1255.353	1267.907	1280.460	1293.014	1305.567	1318.121	1330.674	1343.228	1355.782	1368.335	50

Plant spacing

Square or rectangular plant spacing

The number of seeds or plants required for planting in different spacings are shown in terms of both hectares and acres. For usual square or rectangular spacing, with even spacing within rows and between rows, the number of seeds or plants is the number per row multiplied by the number of rows. Here, the number is shown to one decimal place for the number of rows (assuming an area in the form of a square); this applies only where there is more than 1 hectare or acre involved. If only 1 hectare or acre is to be planted, then only the actual whole number of rows should be used. For example, with spacing at 1.5 m intervals and rows at 1.5 m intervals there are 66.7 rows for a hectare in the shape of a square, giving 4 444 plants per hectare. For only 1 hectare, it would only be possible to use 66 rows and space 66 plants per row, so that the actual number would be 66 × 666 = 4 356.

Plants per hectare: spacing between plants and rows in centimetres

No. rows per ha	Spacing of rows	Spacing within rows											
	cm → ↓	10	12	14	16	18	20	25	30	35	40	45	50
1000.0	10	1000000	833333	714286	625000	555556	500000	400000	333333	285714	250000	222222	200000
833.3	12	833333	694444	595238	520833	462963	416667	333333	277778	238095	208333	185185	166667
714.3	14	714286	595238	510204	446429	396825	357143	285714	238095	204082	178571	158730	142857
625.0	16	625000	520833	446429	390625	347222	312500	250000	208333	178571	156250	138889	125000
555.6	18	555556	462963	396825	347222	308642	277778	222222	185185	158730	138889	123457	111111
500.0	20	500000	416667	357143	312500	277778	250000	200000	166667	142857	125000	111111	100000
400.0	25	400000	333333	285714	250000	222222	200000	160000	133333	114286	100000	88889	80000
333.3	30	333333	277778	238095	208333	185185	166667	133333	111111	95238	83333	74074	66667
285.7	35	285714	238095	204082	178571	158730	142857	114286	95238	81633	71429	63492	57143
250.0	40	250000	208333	178571	156250	138889	125000	100000	83333	71429	62500	55556	50000
222.2	45	222222	185185	158730	138889	123457	111111	88889	74074	63492	55556	49383	44444
200.0	50	200000	166667	142857	125000	111111	100000	80000	66667	57143	50000	44444	40000

Plants per hectare: spacing between plants and rows in metres

No. rows per ha	Spacing of rows	Spacing within rows												
	m → ↓	0.5	0.6	0.7	0.8	0.9	1.0	1.1	1.2	1.3	1.4	1.5	5.0	10.0
200.0	0.5	40000	33333	28571	25000	22222	20000	18182	16667	15385	14286	13333	4000	2000
166.7	0.6	33333	27778	23810	20833	18519	16667	15152	13889	12821	11905	11111	3333	1667
142.9	0.7	28571	23810	20408	17857	15873	14286	12987	11905	10989	10204	9524	2857	1429
125.0	0.8	25000	20833	17857	15625	13889	12500	11364	10417	9615	8929	8333	2500	1250
111.1	0.9	22222	18519	15873	13889	12346	11111	10101	9259	8547	7937	7407	2222	1111
100.0	1.0	20000	16667	14286	12500	11111	10000	9091	8333	7692	7143	6667	2000	1000
90.9	1.1	18182	15152	12987	11364	10101	9091	8264	7576	6993	6494	6061	1818	909
83.3	1.2	16667	13889	11905	10417	9259	8333	7576	6944	6410	5952	5556	1667	833
76.9	1.3	15385	12821	10989	9615	8547	7692	6993	6410	5917	5495	5128	1538	769
71.4	1.4	14286	11905	10204	8929	7937	7143	6494	5952	5495	5102	4762	1429	714
66.7	1.5	13333	11111	9524	8333	7407	6667	6061	5556	5128	4762	4444	1333	667
50.0	2.0	10000	8333	7143	6250	5556	5000	4545	4167	3846	3571	3333	1000	500
40.0	2.5	8000	6667	5714	5000	4444	4000	3636	3333	3077	2857	2667	800	400
33.3	3.0	6667	5556	4762	4167	3704	3333	3030	2778	2564	2381	2222	667	333
28.6	3.5	5714	4762	4082	3571	3175	2857	2597	2381	2198	2041	1905	571	286
25.0	4.0	5000	4167	3571	3125	2778	2500	2273	2083	1923	1786	1667	500	250
22.2	4.5	4444	3704	3175	2778	2469	2222	2020	1852	1709	1587	1481	444	222
20.0	5.0	4000	3333	2857	2500	2222	2000	1818	1667	1538	1429	1333	400	200
16.7	6.0	3333	2778	2381	2083	1852	1667	1515	1389	1282	1190	1111	333	167
14.3	7.0	2857	2381	2041	1786	1587	1429	1299	1190	1099	1020	952	286	143
12.5	8.0	2500	2083	1786	1562	1389	1250	1136	1042	962	893	833	250	125
11.1	9.0	2222	1852	1587	1389	1235	1111	1010	926	855	794	741	222	111
10.0	10.0	2000	1667	1429	1250	1111	1000	909	833	769	714	667	200	100

Number of plants per acre $= \frac{43560}{D}$

D = area occupied by one plant = $\frac{1}{2}$ × distance between plants in row × distance between rows × 2.
Distance between rows = $\frac{1}{2}$ tan 60° × distance between plants in row.
This may be calculated to at least ten places.

·lants per acre: spacing between plants and rows in inches

lo. ows ·er acre	Spacing of rows in →	Spacing within rows 4	5	6	7	8	9	10	11	12	15	18	21	24
26.1	4	392040	313632	261360	224023	196020	174240	156816	142560	130680	104544	87120	74674	65340
00.9	5	313632	250906	209088	179218	156816	139392	125453	114048	104544	83635	69696	59739	52272
17.4	6	261360	209088	174240	149349	130680	116160	104544	95040	87120	69696	58080	49783	43560
57.8	7	224023	179218	149349	128013	112011	99566	89609	81463	74674	59739	49783	42671	37337
13.1	8	196020	156816	130680	112011	98010	87120	78408	71280	65340	52272	43560	37337	32670
78.3	9	174240	139392	116160	99566	87120	77440	69696	63360	58080	46464	38720	33189	29040
50.5	10	156816	125453	104544	89609	78408	69696	62726	57024	52272	41818	34848	29870	26136
27.7	11	142560	114048	95040	81463	71280	63360	57024	51840	47520	38016	31680	27154	23760
08.7	12	130680	104544	87120	74674	65340	58080	52272	47520	43560	34848	29040	24891	21780
67.0	15	104544	83635	69696	59739	52272	46464	41818	38016	34848	27878	23232	19913	17424
39.1	18	87120	69696	58080	49783	43560	38720	34848	31680	29040	23232	19360	16594	14520
19.3	21	74674	59739	49783	42671	37337	33189	29870	27154	24891	19913	16594	14224	12446
04.4	24	65340	52272	43560	37337	32670	29040	26136	23760	21780	17424	14520	12446	10890

·lants per acre: spacing between plants and rows in feet

lo. ows er acre	Spacing of rows ft →	Spacing within rows 1	2	3	4	5	6	7	8	9	10	15	20	25	30	35	40
08.7	1	43560	21780	14520	10890	8712	7260	6223	5445	4840	4356	2904	2178	1742	1452	1245	1089
04.4	2	21780	10890	7260	5445	4356	3630	3111	2723	2420	2178	1452	1089	871	726	622	545
69.6	3	14520	7260	4840	3630	2904	2420	2074	1815	1613	1452	968	726	581	484	415	363
52.2	4	10890	5445	3630	2723	2178	1815	1556	1361	1210	1089	726	545	436	363	311	272
41.7	5	8712	4356	2904	2178	1742	1452	1245	1089	968	871	581	436	348	290	249	218
34.8	6	7260	3630	2420	1815	1452	1210	1037	908	807	726	484	363	290	242	207	182
29.8	7	6223	3111	2074	1556	1245	1037	889	778	691	622	415	311	249	207	178	156
26.1	8	5445	2723	1815	1361	1089	908	778	681	605	545	363	272	218	182	156	136
23.2	9	4840	2420	1613	1210	968	807	691	605	538	484	323	242	194	161	138	121
20.9	10	4356	2178	1452	1089	871	726	622	545	484	436	290	218	174	145	124	109
13.9	15	2904	1452	968	726	581	484	415	363	323	290	194	145	116	97	83	73
10.4	20	2178	1089	726	545	436	363	311	272	242	218	145	109	87	73	62	54
8.3	25	1742	871	581	436	348	290	249	218	194	174	116	87	70	58	50	44
7.0	30	1452	726	484	363	290	242	207	182	161	145	97	73	58	48	41	36
6.0	35	1245	622	415	311	249	207	178	156	138	124	83	62	50	41	36	31
5.2	40	1089	545	363	272	218	182	156	136	121	109	73	54	44	36	31	27

:quilateral triangle plant spacing

Vhere each plant is placed at the corner of an equilateral triangle more ·lants can be used per hectare or acre. The number of plants for the ame area is in general increased with equilateral spacing by about 5%; this derives from ½ tan 60° (each angle of an equilateral triangle ·eing 60°) or 0.866, this being the distance between rows where the spacing is a unit of 1.0: ie, an increase in the ratio of 1.0/0.866 or 1.155 or 15.5% (there is, however, 1 fewer plant per row every second row, which is allowed for here). Where there is not an exact number of rows, then for 1 hectare or acre the number of plants will be fewer; eg, with spacing at 1.0 m, there are 115.5 rows for a square hectare, which would be only 115 actual rows for 1 hectare.

·lants per hectare: spacing between plants and ·ows in metres

No. rows per ha[a]	Distance between rows[b] (m)	Distance between plants in a row[c] (m)	No. plants per ha
154.7	0.087	0.1	1 154 123
577.4	0.173	0.2	288 386
384.9	0.260	0.3	128 108
288.7	0.346	0.4	72 024
230.9	0.433	0.5	46 073
192.5	0.520	0.6	31 979
165.0	0.606	0.7	23 483
144.3	0.693	0.8	17 970
128.3	0.779	0.9	14 191
115.5	0.866	1.0	11 489
23.1	4.330	5.0	450
11.5	8.660	10.0	110

Plants per acre: spacing between plants and rows in feet

No. rows per acre[a]	Distance between rows[b] (ft)	Distance between plants in a row[c] (ft)	No. plants per acre
241.0	0.866 (10.4 in)	1	50 191
120.5	1.732 (20.8 in)	2	12 517
80.3	2.598	3	5 549
60.2	3.464	4	3 114
48.2	4.330	5	1 988
40.2	5.196	6	1 377
34.4	6.062	7	1 004
30.1	6.928	8	771
26.8	7.794	9	608
24.1	8.660	10	490
16.1	12.990	15	216
12.0	17.321	20	120
8.0	25.981	30	52
6.0	34.641	40	28

[a]Assuming a square area. [b]In which plants are spaced out to form equilateral triangles. [c]Also distance between plants as spaced in rows.

Cubic metres to board feet 1 m^3 = 423.776 001 bd ft

m^3 → ↓	0	1	2	3	4	5	6	7	8	9	← m^3 ↓
	bd ft	bd ft	bd ft	bd ft	bd ft	bd ft	bd ft	bd ft	bd ft	bd ft	
0	0.000	423.776	847.552	1271.328	1695.104	2118.880	2542.656	2966.432	3390.208	3813.984	0
10	4237.760	4661.536	5085.312	5509.088	5932.864	6356.640	6780.416	7204.192	7627.968	8051.744	10
20	8475.520	8899.296	9323.072	9746.848	10170.624	10594.400	11018.176	11441.952	11865.728	12289.504	20
30	12713.280	13137.056	13560.832	13984.608	14408.384	14832.160	15255.936	15679.712	16103.488	16527.264	30
40	16951.040	17374.816	17798.592	18222.368	18646.144	19069.920	19493.696	19917.472	20341.248	20765.024	40
50	21188.800	21612.576	22036.352	22460.128	22883.904	23307.680	23731.456	24155.232	24579.008	25002.784	50
60	25426.560	25850.336	26274.112	26697.888	27121.664	27545.440	27969.216	28392.992	28816.768	29240.544	60
70	29664.320	30088.096	30511.872	30935.648	31359.424	31783.200	32206.976	32630.752	33054.528	33478.304	70
80	33902.080	34325.856	34749.632	35173.408	35597.184	36020.960	36444.736	36868.512	37292.288	37716.064	80
90	38139.840	38563.616	38987.392	39411.168	39834.944	40258.720	40682.496	41106.272	41530.048	41953.824	90
100	42377.600										100

Board feet to cubic metres 1 bd ft = 0.002 360 m^3

bd ft → ↓	0	100	200	300	400	500	600	700	800	900	← bd ft ↓
	m^3	m^3	m^3	m^3	m^3	m^3	m^3	m^3	m^3	m^3	
0	0.000	0.236	0.472	0.708	0.944	1.180	1.416	1.652	1.888	2.124	0
1000	2.360	2.596	2.832	3.068	3.304	3.540	3.776	4.012	4.248	4.484	1000
2000	4.719	4.955	5.191	5.427	5.663	5.899	6.135	6.371	6.607	6.843	2000
3000	7.079	7.315	7.551	7.787	8.023	8.259	8.495	8.731	8.967	9.203	3000
4000	9.439	9.675	9.911	10.147	10.383	10.619	10.855	11.091	11.327	11.563	4000
5000	11.799	12.035	12.271	12.507	12.743	12.979	13.215	13.451	13.686	13.922	5000
6000	14.158	14.394	14.630	14.866	15.102	15.338	15.574	15.810	16.046	16.282	6000
7000	16.518	16.754	16.990	17.226	17.462	17.698	17.934	18.170	18.406	18.642	7000
8000	18.878	19.114	19.350	19.586	19.822	20.058	20.294	20.530	20.766	21.002	8000
9000	21.238	21.474	21.710	21.946	22.182	22.418	22.653	22.889	23.125	23.361	9000
10000	23.597										10000

Cubic metres to hoppus feet 1 m^3 = 27.736 074 h ft

m^3 → ↓	0	1	2	3	4	5	6	7	8	9	← m^3 ↓
	h ft	h ft	h ft	h ft	h ft	h ft	h ft	h ft	h ft	h ft	
0	0.000	27.736	55.472	83.208	110.944	138.680	166.416	194.153	221.889	249.625	0
10	277.361	305.097	332.833	360.569	388.305	416.041	443.777	471.513	499.249	526.985	10
20	554.721	582.458	610.194	637.930	665.666	693.402	721.138	748.874	776.610	804.346	20
30	832.082	859.818	887.554	915.290	943.027	970.763	998.499	1026.235	1053.971	1081.707	30
40	1109.443	1137.179	1164.915	1192.651	1220.387	1248.123	1275.859	1303.595	1331.332	1359.068	40
50	1386.804	1414.540	1442.276	1470.012	1497.748	1525.484	1553.220	1580.956	1608.692	1636.428	50
60	1664.164	1691.901	1719.637	1747.373	1775.109	1802.845	1830.581	1858.317	1886.053	1913.789	60
70	1941.525	1969.261	1996.997	2024.733	2052.470	2080.206	2107.942	2135.678	2163.414	2191.150	70
80	2218.886	2246.622	2274.358	2302.094	2329.830	2357.566	2385.302	2413.038	2440.775	2468.511	80
90	2496.247	2523.983	2551.719	2579.455	2607.191	2634.927	2662.663	2690.399	2718.135	2745.871	90
100	2773.607										100

Hoppus feet to cubic metres 1 h ft = 0.036 054 m^3

h ft → ↓	0	1	2	3	4	5	6	7	8	9	← h ft ↓
	m^3	m^3	m^3	m^3	m^3	m^3	m^3	m^3	m^3	m^3	
0	0.00000	0.03605	0.07211	0.10816	0.14422	0.18027	0.21632	0.25238	0.28843	0.32449	0
10	0.36054	0.39660	0.43265	0.46870	0.50476	0.54081	0.57687	0.61292	0.64897	0.68503	10
20	0.72108	0.75714	0.79319	0.82924	0.86530	0.90135	0.93741	0.97346	1.00952	1.04557	20
30	1.08162	1.11768	1.15373	1.18979	1.22584	1.26189	1.29795	1.33400	1.37006	1.40611	30
40	1.44217	1.47822	1.51427	1.55033	1.58638	1.62244	1.65849	1.69454	1.73060	1.76665	40
50	1.80271	1.83876	1.87481	1.91087	1.94692	1.98298	2.01903	2.05509	2.09114	2.12719	50
60	2.16325	2.19930	2.23536	2.27141	2.30746	2.34352	2.37957	2.41563	2.45168	2.48773	60
70	2.52379	2.55984	2.59590	2.63195	2.66801	2.70406	2.74011	2.77617	2.81222	2.84828	70
80	2.88433	2.92038	2.95644	2.99249	3.02855	3.06460	3.10066	3.13671	3.17276	3.20882	80
90	3.24487	3.28093	3.31698	3.35303	3.38909	3.42514	3.46120	3.49725	3.53330	3.56936	90
100	3.60541										100

Note. The standard detailed tables for converting radius (one-half diameter) to area, given on **pages 171–174**, can be used for obtaining volume from mid-diameter outside the range of diameter shown in this section. Volume is then multiplied by area of a cross-section (circle), area of the circle having been obtained from radius in those tables.

Girth (circumference) to diameter

1 unit girth is equivalent to 0.318 ($1/\pi$) unit diameter

Girth → ↓	0	1	2	3	4	5	6	7	8	9	← Girth ↓
0	0.000	0.318	0.637	0.955	1.273	1.592	1.910	2.228	2.546	2.865	0
10	3.183	3.501	3.820	4.138	4.456	4.775	5.093	5.411	5.730	6.048	10
20	6.366	6.685	7.003	7.321	7.639	7.958	8.276	8.594	8.913	9.231	20
30	9.549	9.868	10.186	10.504	10.823	11.141	11.459	11.777	12.096	12.414	30
40	12.732	13.051	13.369	13.687	14.006	14.324	14.642	14.961	15.279	15.597	40
50	15.915	16.234	16.552	16.870	17.189	17.507	17.825	18.144	18.462	18.780	50
60	19.099	19.417	19.735	20.054	20.372	20.690	21.008	21.327	21.645	21.963	60
70	22.282	22.600	22.918	23.237	23.555	23.873	24.192	24.510	24.828	25.146	70
80	25.465	25.783	26.101	26.420	26.738	27.056	27.375	27.693	28.011	28.330	80
90	28.648	28.966	29.285	29.603	29.921	30.239	30.558	30.876	31.194	31.513	90
100	31.831	32.149	32.468	32.786	33.104	33.423	33.741	34.059	34.377	34.696	100
110	35.014	35.332	35.651	35.969	36.287	36.606	36.924	37.242	37.561	37.879	110
120	38.197	38.515	38.834	39.152	39.470	39.789	40.107	40.425	40.744	41.062	120
130	41.380	41.699	42.017	42.335	42.654	42.972	43.290	43.608	43.927	44.245	130
140	44.563	44.882	45.200	45.518	45.837	46.155	46.473	46.792	47.110	47.428	140
150	47.746	48.065	48.383	48.701	49.020	49.338	49.656	49.975	50.293	50.611	150
160	50.930	51.248	51.566	51.885	52.203	52.521	52.839	53.158	53.476	53.794	160
170	54.113	54.431	54.749	55.068	55.386	55.704	56.023	56.341	56.659	56.977	170
180	57.296	57.614	57.932	58.251	58.569	58.887	59.206	59.524	59.842	60.161	180
190	60.479	60.797	61.115	61.434	61.752	62.070	62.389	62.707	63.025	63.344	190
200	63.662	63.980	64.299	64.617	64.935	65.254	65.572	65.890	66.208	66.527	200
210	66.845	67.163	67.482	67.800	68.118	68.437	68.755	69.073	69.392	69.710	210
220	70.028	70.346	70.665	70.983	71.301	71.620	71.938	72.256	72.575	72.893	220
230	73.211	73.530	73.848	74.166	74.485	74.803	75.121	75.439	75.758	76.076	230
240	76.394	76.713	77.031	77.349	77.668	77.986	78.304	78.623	78.941	79.259	240

Diameter to girth (circumference)

1 unit diameter is equivalent to 3.142 (π) units girth

Diameter → ↓	0	1	2	3	4	5	6	7	8	9	← Diameter ↓
0	0.000	3.142	6.283	9.425	12.566	15.708	18.850	21.991	25.133	28.274	0
10	31.416	34.558	37.699	40.841	43.982	47.124	50.265	53.407	56.549	59.690	10
20	62.832	65.973	69.115	72.257	75.398	78.540	81.681	84.823	87.965	91.106	20
30	94.248	97.389	100.531	103.673	106.814	109.956	113.097	116.239	119.381	122.522	30
40	125.664	128.805	131.947	135.088	138.230	141.372	144.513	147.655	150.796	153.938	40
50	157.080	160.221	163.363	166.504	169.646	172.788	175.929	179.071	182.212	185.354	50
60	188.496	191.637	194.779	197.920	201.062	204.204	207.345	210.487	213.628	216.770	60
70	219.911	223.053	226.195	229.336	232.478	235.619	238.761	241.903	245.044	248.186	70
80	251.327	254.469	257.611	260.752	263.894	267.035	270.177	273.319	276.460	279.602	80
90	282.743	285.885	289.027	292.168	295.310	298.451	301.593	304.734	307.876	311.018	90
100	314.159	317.301	320.442	323.584	326.726	329.867	333.009	336.150	339.292	342.434	100
110	345.575	348.717	351.858	355.000	358.142	361.283	364.425	367.566	370.708	373.850	110
120	376.991	380.133	383.274	386.416	389.557	392.699	395.841	398.982	402.124	405.265	120
130	408.407	411.549	414.690	417.832	420.973	424.115	427.257	430.398	433.540	436.681	130
140	439.823	442.965	446.106	449.248	452.389	455.531	458.673	461.814	464.956	468.097	140
150	471.239	474.380	477.522	480.664	483.805	486.947	490.088	493.230	496.372	499.513	150
160	502.655	505.796	508.938	512.080	515.221	518.363	521.504	524.646	527.788	530.929	160
170	534.071	537.212	540.354	543.496	546.637	549.779	552.920	556.062	559.203	562.345	170
180	565.487	568.628	571.770	574.911	578.053	581.195	584.336	587.478	590.619	593.761	180
190	596.903	600.044	603.186	606.327	609.469	612.611	615.752	618.894	622.035	625.177	190
200	628.319	631.460	634.602	637.743	640.885	644.026	647.168	650.310	653.451	656.593	200
210	659.734	662.876	666.018	669.159	672.301	675.442	678.584	681.726	684.867	688.009	210
220	691.150	694.292	697.434	700.575	703.717	706.858	710.000	713.142	716.283	719.425	220
230	722.566	725.708	728.849	731.991	735.133	738.274	741.416	744.557	747.699	750.841	230
240	753.982	757.124	760.265	763.407	766.549	769.690	772.832	775.973	779.115	782.257	240

Use of the table. A sawlog 2.0 m long, with mid-diameter 160 mm, has a volume of 0.040 cubic metre.

Diameter, mid, in millimetres,[a] by length in metres, to volume in cubic metres

Length in m → Mid diameter in mm ↓	1.0	1.5	2.0	2.5	3.0	3.5	4.0	4.5	5.0	6.0	7.0	8.0	9.0	10.0	← Length in m Mid diameter in mm ↓
	m^3	m^3	m^3	m^3	m^3	m^3	m^3	m^3	m^3	m^3	m^3	m^3	m^3	m^3	
70	0.004	0.006	0.008	0.010	0.012	0.013	0.015	0.017	0.019	0.023	0.027	0.031	0.035	0.038	70
80	0.005	0.008	0.010	0.013	0.015	0.018	0.020	0.023	0.025	0.030	0.035	0.040	0.045	0.050	80
90	0.006	0.010	0.013	0.016	0.019	0.022	0.025	0.029	0.032	0.038	0.045	0.051	0.057	0.064	90
100	0.008	0.012	0.016	0.020	0.024	0.027	0.031	0.035	0.039	0.047	0.055	0.063	0.071	0.079	100
110	0.010	0.014	0.019	0.024	0.029	0.033	0.038	0.043	0.048	0.057	0.067	0.076	0.086	0.095	110
120	0.011	0.017	0.023	0.028	0.034	0.040	0.045	0.051	0.057	0.068	0.079	0.090	0.102	0.113	120
130	0.013	0.020	0.027	0.033	0.040	0.046	0.053	0.060	0.066	0.080	0.093	0.106	0.119	0.133	130
140	0.015	0.023	0.031	0.038	0.046	0.054	0.062	0.069	0.077	0.092	0.108	0.123	0.139	0.154	140
150	0.018	0.027	0.035	0.044	0.053	0.062	0.071	0.080	0.088	0.106	0.124	0.141	0.159	0.177	150
160	0.020	0.030	0.040	0.050	0.060	0.070	0.080	0.090	0.101	0.121	0.141	0.161	0.181	0.201	160
170	0.023	0.034	0.045	0.057	0.068	0.079	0.091	0.102	0.113	0.136	0.159	0.182	0.204	0.227	170
180	0.025	0.038	0.051	0.064	0.076	0.089	0.102	0.115	0.127	0.153	0.178	0.204	0.229	0.254	180
190	0.028	0.043	0.057	0.071	0.085	0.099	0.113	0.128	0.142	0.170	0.198	0.227	0.255	0.284	190
200	0.031	0.047	0.063	0.079	0.094	0.110	0.126	0.141	0.157	0.188	0.220	0.251	0.283	0.314	200
210	0.035	0.052	0.069	0.087	0.104	0.121	0.139	0.156	0.173	0.208	0.242	0.277	0.312	0.346	210
220	0.038	0.057	0.076	0.095	0.114	0.133	0.152	0.171	0.190	0.228	0.266	0.304	0.342	0.380	220
230	0.042	0.062	0.083	0.104	0.125	0.145	0.166	0.187	0.208	0.249	0.291	0.332	0.374	0.415	230
240	0.045	0.068	0.090	0.113	0.136	0.158	0.181	0.204	0.226	0.271	0.317	0.362	0.407	0.452	240
250	0.049	0.074	0.098	0.123	0.147	0.172	0.196	0.221	0.245	0.295	0.344	0.393	0.442	0.491	250
260	0.053	0.080	0.106	0.133	0.159	0.186	0.212	0.239	0.265	0.319	0.372	0.425	0.478	0.531	260
270	0.057	0.086	0.115	0.143	0.172	0.200	0.229	0.258	0.286	0.344	0.401	0.458	0.515	0.573	270
280	0.062	0.092	0.123	0.154	0.185	0.216	0.246	0.277	0.308	0.369	0.431	0.493	0.554	0.616	280
290	0.066	0.099	0.132	0.165	0.198	0.231	0.264	0.297	0.330	0.396	0.462	0.528	0.594	0.661	290
300	0.071	0.106	0.141	0.177	0.212	0.247	0.283	0.318	0.353	0.424	0.495	0.565	0.636	0.707	300
310	0.075	0.113	0.151	0.189	0.226	0.264	0.302	0.340	0.377	0.453	0.528	0.604	0.679	0.755	310
320	0.080	0.121	0.161	0.201	0.241	0.281	0.322	0.362	0.402	0.483	0.563	0.643	0.724	0.804	320
330	0.086	0.128	0.171	0.214	0.257	0.299	0.342	0.385	0.428	0.513	0.599	0.684	0.770	0.855	330
340	0.091	0.136	0.182	0.227	0.272	0.318	0.363	0.409	0.454	0.545	0.636	0.726	0.817	0.908	340
350	0.096	0.144	0.192	0.241	0.289	0.337	0.385	0.433	0.481	0.577	0.673	0.770	0.866	0.962	350
360	0.102	0.153	0.204	0.254	0.305	0.356	0.407	0.458	0.509	0.611	0.713	0.814	0.916	1.018	360
370	0.108	0.161	0.215	0.269	0.323	0.376	0.430	0.484	0.538	0.645	0.753	0.860	0.968	1.075	370
380	0.113	0.170	0.227	0.284	0.340	0.397	0.454	0.510	0.567	0.680	0.794	0.907	1.021	1.134	380
390	0.119	0.179	0.239	0.299	0.358	0.418	0.478	0.538	0.597	0.717	0.836	0.956	1.075	1.195	390
400	0.126	0.188	0.251	0.314	0.377	0.440	0.503	0.565	0.628	0.754	0.880	1.005	1.131	1.257	400
410	0.132	0.198	0.264	0.330	0.396	0.462	0.528	0.594	0.660	0.792	0.924	1.056	1.188	1.320	410
420	0.139	0.208	0.277	0.346	0.416	0.485	0.554	0.623	0.693	0.831	0.970	1.108	1.247	1.385	420
430	0.145	0.218	0.290	0.363	0.436	0.508	0.581	0.653	0.726	0.871	1.017	1.162	1.307	1.452	430
440	0.152	0.228	0.304	0.380	0.456	0.532	0.608	0.684	0.760	0.912	1.064	1.216	1.368	1.521	440
450	0.159	0.239	0.318	0.398	0.477	0.557	0.636	0.716	0.795	0.954	1.113	1.272	1.431	1.590	450
460	0.166	0.249	0.332	0.415	0.499	0.582	0.665	0.748	0.831	0.997	1.163	1.330	1.496	1.662	460
470	0.173	0.260	0.347	0.434	0.520	0.607	0.694	0.781	0.867	1.041	1.214	1.388	1.561	1.735	470
480	0.181	0.271	0.362	0.452	0.543	0.633	0.724	0.814	0.905	1.086	1.267	1.448	1.629	1.810	480
490	0.189	0.283	0.377	0.471	0.566	0.660	0.754	0.849	0.943	1.131	1.320	1.509	1.697	1.886	490
500	0.196	0.295	0.393	0.491	0.589	0.687	0.785	0.884	0.982	1.178	1.374	1.571	1.767	1.963	500
600	0.283	0.424	0.565	0.707	0.848	0.990	1.131	1.272	1.414	1.696	1.979	2.262	2.545	2.827	600
700	0.385	0.577	0.770	0.962	1.155	1.347	1.539	1.732	1.924	2.309	2.694	3.079	3.464	3.848	700
800	0.503	0.754	1.005	1.257	1.508	1.759	2.011	2.262	2.513	3.016	3.519	4.021	4.524	5.027	800
900	0.636	0.954	1.272	1.590	1.909	2.227	2.545	2.863	3.181	3.817	4.453	5.089	5.726	6.362	900
1000	0.785	1.178	1.571	1.963	2.356	2.749	3.142	3.534	3.927	4.712	5.498	6.283	7.069	7.854	1000
1100	0.950	1.425	1.901	2.376	2.851	3.326	3.801	4.276	4.752	5.702	6.652	7.603	8.553	9.503	1100
1200	1.131	1.696	2.262	2.827	3.393	3.958	4.524	5.089	5.655	6.786	7.917	9.048	10.179	11.310	1200
1300	1.327	1.991	2.655	3.318	3.982	4.646	5.309	5.973	6.637	7.964	9.291	10.619	11.946	13.273	1300
1400	1.539	2.309	3.079	3.848	4.618	5.388	6.158	6.927	7.697	9.236	10.776	12.315	13.854	15.394	1400
1500	1.767	2.651	3.534	4.418	5.301	6.185	7.069	7.952	8.836	10.603	12.370	14.137	15.904	17.671	1500
1600	2.011	3.016	4.021	5.027	6.032	7.037	8.042	9.048	10.053	12.064	14.074	16.085	18.096	20.106	1600

[a]For diameter in centimetres delete the last zero from the number of millimetres.

Energy

For other measures see Energy, pages 75–79.

Use of the tables. 11 ft lbf = 10 ft lbf + 1 ft lbf = 14.914 J.

Joules to foot pounds-force 1 J = 0.737 562 ft lbf

J → ↓	0	1	2	3	4	5	6	7	8	9	← J ↓
	ft lbf	ft lbf	ft lbf	ft lbf	ft lbf	ft lbf	ft lbf	ft lbf	ft lbf	ft lbf	
0	0.000	0.738	1.475	2.213	2.950	3.688	4.425	5.163	5.900	6.638	0
10	7.376	8.113	8.851	9.588	10.326	11.063	11.801	12.539	13.276	14.014	10
20	14.751	15.489	16.226	16.964	17.701	18.439	19.177	19.914	20.652	21.389	20
30	22.127	22.864	23.602	24.340	25.077	25.815	26.552	27.290	28.027	28.765	30
40	29.502	30.240	30.978	31.715	32.453	33.190	33.928	34.665	35.403	36.141	40
50	36.878	37.616	38.353	39.091	39.828	40.566	41.303	42.041	42.779	43.516	50
60	44.254	44.991	45.729	46.466	47.204	47.942	48.679	49.417	50.154	50.892	60
70	51.629	52.367	53.104	53.842	54.580	55.317	56.055	56.792	57.530	58.267	70
80	59.005	59.743	60.480	61.218	61.955	62.693	63.430	64.168	64.905	65.643	80
90	66.381	67.118	67.856	68.593	69.331	70.068	70.806	71.544	72.281	73.019	90
100	73.756										100

Foot pounds-force to joules 1 ft lbf = 1.355 818 J

ft lbf → ↓	0	1	2	3	4	5	6	7	8	9	← ft lbf ↓
	J	J	J	J	J	J	J	J	J	J	
0	0.000	1.356	2.712	4.067	5.423	6.779	8.135	9.491	10.847	12.202	0
10	13.558	14.914	16.270	17.626	18.981	20.337	21.693	23.049	24.405	25.761	10
20	27.116	28.472	29.828	31.184	32.540	33.895	35.251	36.607	37.963	39.319	20
30	40.675	42.030	43.386	44.742	46.098	47.454	48.809	50.165	51.521	52.877	30
40	54.233	55.589	56.944	58.300	59.656	61.012	62.368	63.723	65.079	66.435	40
50	67.791	69.147	70.503	71.858	73.214	74.570	75.926	77.282	78.637	79.993	50
60	81.349	82.705	84.061	85.417	86.772	88.128	89.484	90.840	92.196	93.551	60
70	94.907	96.263	97.619	98.975	100.331	101.686	103.042	104.398	105.754	107.110	70
80	108.465	109.821	111.177	112.533	113.889	115.245	116.600	117.956	119.312	120.668	80
90	122.024	123.379	124.735	126.091	127.447	128.803	130.159	131.514	132.870	134.226	90
100	135.582										100

Kilojoules to British thermal units 1 kJ = 0.947 817 Btu

kJ → ↓	0	1	2	3	4	5	6	7	8	9	← kJ ↓
	Btu	Btu	Btu	Btu	Btu	Btu	Btu	Btu	Btu	Btu	
0	0.000	0.948	1.896	2.843	3.791	4.739	5.687	6.635	7.583	8.530	0
10	9.478	10.426	11.374	12.322	13.269	14.217	15.165	16.113	17.061	18.009	10
20	18.956	19.904	20.852	21.800	22.748	23.695	24.643	25.591	26.539	27.487	20
30	28.435	29.382	30.330	31.278	32.226	33.174	34.121	35.069	36.017	36.965	30
40	37.913	38.861	39.808	40.756	41.704	42.652	43.600	44.547	45.495	46.443	40
50	47.391	48.339	49.286	50.234	51.182	52.130	53.078	54.026	54.973	55.921	50
60	56.869	57.817	58.765	59.712	60.660	61.608	62.556	63.504	64.452	65.399	60
70	66.347	67.295	68.243	69.191	70.138	71.086	72.034	72.982	73.930	74.878	70
80	75.825	76.773	77.721	78.669	79.617	80.564	81.512	82.460	83.408	84.356	80
90	85.304	86.251	87.199	88.147	89.095	90.043	90.990	91.938	92.886	93.834	90
100	94.782										100

British thermal units to kilojoules 1 Btu = 1.055 056 kJ

Btu → ↓	0	1	2	3	4	5	6	7	8	9	← Btu ↓
	kJ	kJ	kJ	kJ	kJ	kJ	kJ	kJ	kJ	kJ	
0	0.000	1.055	2.110	3.165	4.220	5.275	6.330	7.385	8.440	9.496	0
10	10.551	11 606	12.661	13.716	14.771	15.826	16.881	17.936	18.991	20.046	10
20	21.101	22.156	23.211	24.266	25.321	26.376	27.431	28.487	29.542	30.597	20
30	31.652	32.707	33.762	34.817	35.872	36.927	37.982	39.037	40.092	41.147	30
40	42.202	43.257	44.312	45.367	46.422	47.478	48.533	49.588	50.643	51.698	40
50	52.753	53.808	54.863	55.918	56.973	58.028	59.083	60.138	61.193	62.248	50
60	63.303	64.358	65.413	66.469	67.524	68.579	69.634	70.689	71.744	72.799	60
70	73.854	74.909	75.964	77.019	78.074	79.129	80.184	81.239	82.294	83.349	70
80	84.404	85.460	86.515	87.570	88.625	89.680	90.735	91.790	92.845	93.900	80
90	94.955	96.010	97.065	98.120	99.175	100.230	101.285	102.340	103.395	104.451	90
100	105.506										100

Note. These tables apply for conversions where densities and volumes are expressed at the same temperature. The standard reference temperature in the UK is 15°C.

Petroleum: barrels to tonnes, for varying densities

Density (kg/l) →	0.80	0.81	0.82	0.83	0.84	0.85	0.86	0.87	0.88	0.89	0.90	0.92	0.94	0.96	0.98	1.00	Density ← (kg/l)
Barrels ↓	t	t	t	t	t	t	t	t	t	t	t	t	t	t	t	t	Barrels
10	1.3	1.3	1.3	1.3	1.3	1.4	1.4	1.4	1.4	1.4	1.4	1.5	1.5	1.5	1.6	1.6	10
20	2.5	2.6	2.6	2.6	2.7	2.7	2.7	2.8	2.8	2.8	2.9	2.9	3.0	3.1	3.1	3.2	20
30	3.8	3.9	3.9	4.0	4.0	4.1	4.1	4.1	4.2	4.2	4.3	4.4	4.5	4.6	4.7	4.8	30
40	5.1	5.2	5.2	5.3	5.3	5.4	5.5	5.5	5.6	5.7	5.7	5.9	6.0	6.1	6.2	6.4	40
50	6.4	6.4	6.5	6.6	6.7	6.8	6.8	6.9	7.0	7.1	7.2	7.3	7.5	7.6	7.8	7.9	50
60	7.6	7.7	7.8	7.9	8.0	8.1	8.2	8.3	8.4	8.5	8.6	8.8	9.0	9.2	9.3	9.5	60
70	8.9	9.0	9.1	9.2	9.3	9.5	9.6	9.7	9.8	9.9	10.0	10.2	10.5	10.7	10.9	11.1	70
80	10.2	10.3	10.4	10.6	10.7	10.8	10.9	11.1	11.2	11.3	11.4	11.7	12.0	12.2	12.5	12.7	80
90	11.4	11.6	11.7	11.9	12.0	12.2	12.3	12.4	12.6	12.7	12.9	13.2	13.5	13.7	14.0	14.3	90
100	12.7	12.9	13.0	13.2	13.4	13.5	13.7	13.8	14.0	14.1	14.3	14.6	14.9	15.3	15.6	15.9	100
110	14.0	14.2	14.3	14.5	14.7	14.9	15.0	15.2	15.4	15.6	15.7	16.1	16.4	16.8	17.1	17.5	110
120	15.3	15.5	15.6	15.8	16.0	16.2	16.4	16.6	16.8	17.0	17.2	17.6	17.9	18.3	18.7	19.1	120
130	16.5	16.7	16.9	17.2	17.4	17.6	17.8	18.0	18.2	18.4	18.6	19.0	19.4	19.8	20.3	20.7	130
140	17.8	18.0	18.3	18.5	18.7	18.9	19.1	19.4	19.6	19.8	20.0	20.5	20.9	21.4	21.8	22.3	140
150	19.1	19.3	19.6	19.8	20.0	20.3	20.5	20.7	21.0	21.2	21.5	21.9	22.4	22.9	23.4	23.8	150
160	20.4	20.6	20.9	21.1	21.4	21.1	21.9	22.1	22.4	22.6	22.9	23.4	23.9	24.4	24.9	25.4	160
170	21.6	21.9	22.2	22.4	22.7	23.0	23.2	23.5	23.8	24.1	24.3	24.9	25.4	25.9	26.5	27.0	170
180	22.9	23.2	23.5	23.8	24.0	24.3	24.6	24.9	25.2	25.5	25.8	26.3	26.9	27.5	28.0	28.6	180
190	24.2	24.5	24.8	25.1	25.4	25.7	26.0	26.3	26.6	26.9	27.2	27.8	28.4	29.0	29.6	30.2	190
200	25.4	25.8	26.1	26.4	26.7	27.0	27.3	27.7	28.0	28.3	28.6	29.3	29.9	30.5	31.2	31.8	200
210	26.7	27.0	27.4	27.7	28.0	28.4	28.7	29.0	29.4	29.7	30.0	30.7	31.4	32.1	32.7	33.4	210
220	28.0	28.3	28.7	29.0	29.4	29.7	30.1	30.4	30.8	31.1	31.5	32.2	32.9	33.6	34.3	35.0	220
230	29.3	29.6	30.0	30.4	30.7	31.1	31.4	31.8	32.2	32.5	32.9	33.6	34.4	35.1	35.8	36.6	230
240	30.5	30.9	31.3	31.7	32.1	32.4	32.8	33.2	33.6	34.0	34.3	35.1	35.9	36.6	37.4	38.2	240
250	31.8	32.2	32.6	33.0	33.4	33.8	34.2	34.6	35.0	35.4	35.8	36.6	37.4	38.2	39.0	39.7	250
260	33.1	33.5	33.9	34.3	34.7	35.1	35.5	36.0	36.4	36.8	37.2	38.0	38.9	39.7	40.5	41.3	260
270	34.3	34.8	35.2	35.6	36.1	36.5	36.9	37.3	37.8	38.2	38.6	39.5	40.4	41.2	42.1	42.9	270
280	35.6	36.1	36.5	36.9	37.4	37.8	38.3	38.7	39.2	39.6	40.1	41.0	41.8	42.7	43.6	44.5	280
290	36.9	37.3	37.8	38.3	38.7	39.2	39.7	40.1	40.6	41.0	41.5	42.4	43.3	44.3	45.2	46.1	290
300	38.2	38.6	39.1	39.6	40.1	40.5	41.0	41.5	42.0	42.4	42.9	43.9	44.8	45.8	46.7	47.7	300
310	39.4	39.9	40.4	40.9	41.4	41.9	42.4	42.9	43.4	43.9	44.4	45.3	46.3	47.3	48.3	49.3	310
320	40.7	41.2	41.7	42.2	42.7	43.2	43.8	44.3	44.8	45.3	45.8	46.8	47.8	48.8	49.9	50.9	320
330	42.0	42.5	43.0	43.5	44.1	44.6	45.1	45.6	46.2	46.7	47.2	48.3	49.3	50.4	51.4	52.5	330
340	43.2	43.8	44.3	44.9	45.4	45.9	46.5	47.0	47.6	48.1	48.7	49.7	50.8	51.9	53.0	54.1	340
350	44.5	45.1	45.6	46.2	46.7	47.3	47.9	48.4	49.0	49.5	50.1	51.2	52.3	53.4	54.5	55.6	350
360	45.8	46.4	46.9	47.5	48.1	48.7	49.2	49.8	50.4	50.9	51.5	52.7	53.8	54.9	56.1	57.2	360
370	47.1	47.6	48.2	48.8	49.4	50.0	50.6	51.2	51.8	52.4	52.9	54.1	55.3	56.5	57.6	58.8	370
380	48.3	48.9	49.5	50.1	50.7	51.4	52.0	52.6	53.2	53.8	54.4	55.6	56.8	58.0	59.2	60.4	380
390	49.6	50.2	50.8	51.5	52.1	52.7	53.3	53.9	54.6	55.2	55.8	57.0	58.3	59.5	60.8	62.0	390
400	50.9	51.5	52.1	52.8	53.4	54.1	54.7	55.3	56.0	56.6	57.2	58.5	59.8	61.1	62.3	63.6	400
410	52.1	52.8	53.5	54.1	54.8	55.4	56.1	56.7	57.4	58.0	58.7	60.0	61.3	62.6	63.9	65.2	410
420	53.4	54.1	54.8	55.4	56.1	56.8	57.4	58.1	58.8	59.4	60.1	61.4	62.8	64.1	65.4	66.8	420
430	54.7	55.4	56.1	56.7	57.4	58.1	58.8	59.5	60.2	60.8	61.5	62.9	64.3	65.6	67.0	68.4	430
440	56.0	56.7	57.4	58.1	58.8	59.5	60.2	60.9	61.6	62.3	63.0	64.4	65.8	67.2	68.6	70.0	440
450	57.2	58.0	58.7	59.4	60.1	60.8	61.5	62.2	63.0	63.7	64.4	65.8	67.3	68.7	70.1	71.5	450
460	58.5	59.2	60.0	60.7	61.4	62.2	62.9	63.6	64.4	65.1	65.8	67.3	68.7	70.2	71.7	73.1	460
470	59.8	60.5	61.3	62.0	62.8	63.5	64.3	65.0	65.8	66.5	67.3	68.7	70.2	71.7	73.2	74.7	470
480	61.1	61.8	62.6	63.3	64.1	64.9	65.6	66.4	67.2	67.9	68.7	70.2	71.7	73.3	74.8	76.3	480
490	62.3	63.1	63.9	64.7	65.4	66.2	67.0	67.8	68.6	69.3	70.1	71.7	73.2	74.8	76.3	77.9	490
500	63.6	64.4	65.2	66.0	66.8	67.6	68.4	69.2	70.0	70.7	71.5	73.1	74.7	76.3	77.9	79.5	500
510	64.9	65.7	66.5	67.3	68.1	68.9	69.7	70.5	71.4	72.2	73.0	74.6	76.2	77.8	79.5	81.1	510
520	66.1	67.0	67.8	68.6	69.4	70.3	71.1	71.9	72.8	73.6	74.4	76.1	77.7	79.4	81.0	82.7	520
530	67.4	68.3	69.1	69.9	70.8	71.6	72.5	73.3	74.2	75.0	75.8	77.5	79.2	80.9	82.6	84.3	530
540	68.7	69.5	70.4	71.3	72.1	73.0	73.8	74.7	75.6	76.4	77.3	79.0	80.7	82.4	84.1	85.9	540
550	70.0	70.8	71.7	72.6	73.5	74.3	75.2	76.1	76.9	77.8	78.7	80.4	82.2	83.9	85.7	87.4	550
560	71.2	72.1	73.0	73.9	74.8	75.7	76.6	77.5	78.3	79.2	80.1	81.9	83.7	85.5	87.3	89.0	560
570	72.5	73.4	74.3	75.2	76.1	77.0	77.9	78.8	79.7	80.7	81.6	83.4	85.2	87.0	88.8	90.6	570
580	73.8	74.7	75.6	76.5	77.5	78.4	79.3	80.2	81.1	82.1	83.0	84.8	86.7	88.5	90.4	92.2	580
590	75.0	76.0	76.9	77.9	78.8	79.7	80.7	81.6	82.5	83.5	84.4	86.3	88.2	90.1	91.9	93.8	590
600	76.3	77.3	78.2	79.2	80.1	81.1	82.0	83.0	83.9	84.9	85.9	87.8	89.7	91.6	93.5	95.4	600

Petroleum: barrels per day (b/d) to tonnes per year (t/yr), for varying densities

Density (kg/l) →	0.80	0.81	0.82	0.83	0.84	0.85	0.86	0.87	0.88	0.89	0.90	0.92	0.94	0.96	0.98	1.00	Density ← (kg/l)
b/d ↓	t/yr	t/yr	t/yr	t/yr	t/yr	t/yr	t/yr	t/yr	t/yr	t/yr	t/yr	t/yr	t/yr	t/yr	t/yr	t/yr	b/d ↓
0.1	4.6	4.7	4.8	4.8	4.9	4.9	5.0	5.0	5.1	5.2	5.2	5.3	5.5	5.6	5.7	5.8	0.1
0.2	9.3	9.4	9.5	9.6	9.7	9.9	10.0	10.1	10.2	10.3	10.4	10.7	10.9	11.1	11.4	11.6	0.2
0.3	13.9	14.1	14.3	14.4	14.6	14.8	15.0	15.1	15.3	15.5	15.7	16.0	16.4	16.7	17.1	17.4	0.3
0.4	18.6	18.8	19.0	19.3	19.5	19.7	20.0	20.2	20.4	20.7	20.9	21.4	21.8	22.3	22.7	23.2	0.4
0.5	23.2	23.5	23.8	24.1	24.4	24.7	25.0	25.2	25.5	25.8	26.1	26.7	27.3	27.9	28.4	29.0	0.5
0.6	27.9	28.2	28.6	28.9	29.2	29.6	29.9	30.3	30.6	31.0	31.3	32.0	32.7	33.4	34.1	34.8	0.6
0.7	32.5	32.9	33.3	33.7	34.1	34.5	34.9	35.3	35.7	36.2	36.6	37.4	38.2	39.0	39.8	40.6	0.7
0.8	37.1	37.6	38.1	38.5	39.0	39.5	39.9	40.4	40.9	41.3	41.8	42.7	43.6	44.6	45.5	46.4	0.8
0.9	41.8	42.3	42.8	43.3	43.9	44.4	44.9	45.4	46.0	46.5	47.0	48.0	49.1	50.1	51.2	52.2	0.9
1.0	46.4	47.0	47.6	48.2	48.7	49.3	49.9	50.5	51.1	51.6	52.2	53.4	54.5	55.7	56.9	58.0	1.0
1.1	51.1	51.7	52.3	53.0	53.6	54.3	54.9	55.5	56.2	56.8	57.5	58.7	60.0	61.3	62.6	63.8	1.1
1.2	55.7	56.4	57.1	57.8	58.5	59.2	59.9	60.6	61.3	62.0	62.7	64.1	65.5	66.9	68.2	69.6	1.2
1.3	60.4	61.1	61.9	62.6	63.4	64.1	64.9	65.6	66.4	67.1	67.9	69.4	70.9	72.4	73.9	75.4	1.3
1.4	65.0	65.8	66.6	67.4	68.2	69.1	69.9	70.7	71.5	72.3	73.1	74.7	76.4	78.0	79.6	81.2	1.4
1.5	69.6	70.5	71.4	72.2	73.1	74.0	74.9	75.7	76.6	77.5	78.3	80.1	81.8	83.6	85.3	87.0	1.5
1.6	74.3	75.2	76.1	77.1	78.0	78.9	79.8	80.8	81.7	82.6	83.6	85.4	87.3	89.1	91.0	92.8	1.6
1.7	78.9	79.9	80.9	81.9	82.9	83.9	84.8	85.8	86.8	87.8	88.8	90.8	92.7	94.7	96.7	98.7	1.7
1.8	83.6	84.6	85.7	86.7	87.7	88.8	89.8	90.9	91.9	93.0	94.0	96.1	98.2	100.3	102.4	104.5	1.8
1.9	88.2	89.3	90.4	91.5	92.6	93.7	94.8	95.9	97.0	98.1	99.2	101.4	103.6	105.8	108.1	110.3	1.9
2.0	92.8	94.0	95.2	96.3	97.5	98.7	99.8	101.0	102.1	103.3	104.5	106.8	109.1	111.4	113.7	116.1	2.0
2.1	97.5	98.7	99.9	101.1	102.4	103.6	104.8	106.0	107.2	108.5	109.7	112.1	114.6	117.0	119.4	121.9	2.1
2.2	102.1	103.4	104.7	106.0	107.2	108.5	109.8	111.1	112.3	113.6	114.9	117.5	120.0	122.6	125.1	127.7	2.2
2.3	106.8	108.1	109.4	110.8	112.1	113.4	114.8	116.1	117.5	118.8	120.1	122.8	125.5	128.1	130.8	133.5	2.3
2.4	111.4	112.8	114.2	115.6	117.0	118.4	119.8	121.2	122.6	124.0	125.3	128.1	130.9	133.7	136.5	139.3	2.4
2.5	116.1	117.5	119.0	120.4	121.9	123.3	124.8	126.2	127.7	129.1	130.6	133.5	136.4	139.3	142.2	145.1	2.5
2.6	120.7	122.2	123.7	125.2	126.7	128.2	129.8	131.3	132.8	134.3	135.8	138.8	141.8	144.8	147.9	150.9	2.6
2.7	125.3	126.9	128.5	130.0	131.6	133.2	134.7	136.3	137.9	139.4	141.0	144.1	147.3	150.4	153.5	156.7	2.7
2.8	130.0	131.6	133.2	134.9	136.5	138.1	139.7	141.4	143.0	144.6	146.2	149.5	152.7	156.0	159.2	162.5	2.8
2.9	134.6	136.3	138.0	139.7	141.4	143.0	144.7	146.4	148.1	149.8	151.5	154.8	158.2	161.6	164.9	168.3	2.9
3.0	139.3	141.0	142.8	144.5	146.2	148.0	149.7	151.5	153.2	154.9	156.7	160.2	163.6	167.1	170.6	174.1	3.0
3.1	143.9	145.7	147.5	149.3	151.1	152.9	154.7	156.5	158.3	160.1	161.9	165.5	169.1	172.7	176.3	179.9	3.1
3.2	148.6	150.4	152.3	154.1	156.0	157.8	159.7	161.6	163.4	165.3	167.1	170.8	174.6	178.3	182.0	185.7	3.2
3.3	153.2	155.1	157.0	158.9	160.9	162.8	164.7	166.6	168.5	170.4	172.4	176.2	180.0	183.8	187.7	191.5	3.3
3.4	157.8	159.8	161.8	163.8	165.7	167.7	169.7	171.7	173.6	175.6	177.6	181.5	185.5	189.4	193.4	197.3	3.4
3.5	162.5	164.5	166.5	168.6	170.6	172.6	174.7	176.7	178.7	180.8	182.8	186.9	190.9	195.0	199.0	203.1	3.5
3.6	167.1	169.2	171.3	173.4	175.5	177.6	179.7	181.8	183.8	185.9	188.0	192.2	196.4	200.6	204.7	208.9	3.6
3.7	171.8	173.9	176.1	178.2	180.4	182.5	184.7	186.8	188.9	191.1	193.2	197.5	201.8	206.1	210.4	214.7	3.7
3.8	176.4	178.6	180.8	183.0	185.2	187.4	189.6	191.8	194.1	196.3	198.5	202.9	207.3	211.7	216.1	220.5	3.8
3.9	181.1	183.3	185.6	187.8	190.1	192.4	194.6	196.9	199.2	201.4	203.7	208.2	212.7	217.3	221.8	226.3	3.9
4.0	185.7	188.0	190.3	192.7	195.0	197.3	199.6	201.9	204.3	206.6	208.9	213.6	218.2	222.8	227.5	232.1	4.0
4.1	190.3	192.7	195.1	197.5	199.9	202.2	204.6	207.0	209.4	211.8	214.1	218.9	223.6	228.4	233.2	237.9	4.1
4.2	195.0	197.4	199.9	202.3	204.7	207.2	209.6	212.0	214.5	216.9	219.4	224.2	229.1	234.0	238.9	243.7	4.2
4.3	199.6	202.1	204.6	207.1	209.6	212.1	214.6	217.1	219.6	222.1	224.6	229.6	234.6	239.5	244.5	249.5	4.3
4.4	204.3	206.8	209.4	211.9	214.5	217.0	219.6	222.1	224.7	227.2	229.8	234.9	240.0	245.1	250.2	255.3	4.4
4.5	208.9	211.5	214.1	216.7	219.4	222.0	224.6	227.2	229.8	223.4	235.0	240.2	245.5	250.7	255.9	261.1	4.5
4.6	213.6	216.2	218.9	221.6	224.2	226.9	229.6	232.2	234.9	237.6	240.2	245.6	250.9	256.3	261.6	266.9	4.6
4.7	218.2	220.9	223.6	226.4	229.1	231.8	234.6	237.3	240.0	242.7	245.5	250.9	256.4	261.8	267.3	272.7	4.7
4.8	222.8	225.6	228.4	231.2	234.0	236.8	239.5	242.3	245.1	247.9	250.7	256.3	261.8	267.4	273.0	278.5	4.8
4.9	227.5	230.3	233.2	236.0	238.9	241.7	244.5	247.4	250.2	253.1	255.9	261.6	267.3	273.0	278.7	284.3	4.9
5.0	232.1	235.0	237.9	240.8	243.7	246.6	249.5	252.4	255.3	258.2	261.1	266.9	272.7	278.5	284.3	290.2	5.0
5.1	236.8	239.7	242.7	245.6	248.6	251.6	254.5	257.5	260.4	263.4	266.4	272.3	278.2	284.1	290.0	296.0	5.1
5.2	241.4	244.4	247.4	250.5	253.5	256.5	259.5	262.5	265.5	268.6	271.6	277.6	283.7	289.7	295.7	301.8	5.2
5.3	246.0	249.1	252.2	255.3	258.4	261.4	264.5	267.6	270.7	273.7	276.8	283.0	289.1	295.3	301.4	307.6	5.3
5.4	250.7	253.8	257.0	260.1	263.2	266.4	269.5	272.6	275.8	278.9	282.0	288.3	294.6	300.8	307.1	313.4	5.4
5.5	255.3	258.5	261.7	264.9	268.1	271.3	274.5	277.7	280.9	284.1	287.3	293.6	300.0	306.4	312.8	319.2	5.5
5.6	260.0	263.2	266.5	269.7	273.0	276.2	279.5	282.7	286.0	289.2	292.5	299.0	305.5	312.0	318.5	325.0	5.6
5.7	264.6	267.9	271.2	274.5	277.8	281.2	284.5	287.8	291.1	294.4	297.7	304.3	310.9	317.5	324.2	330.8	5.7
5.8	269.3	272.6	276.0	279.4	282.7	286.1	289.5	292.8	296.2	299.6	302.9	309.7	316.4	323.1	329.8	336.6	5.8
5.9	273.9	277.3	280.8	284.2	287.6	291.0	294.4	297.9	301.3	304.7	308.1	315.0	321.8	328.7	335.5	342.4	5.9
6.0	278.5	282.0	285.5	289.0	292.5	296.0	299.4	302.9	306.4	309.9	313.4	320.3	327.3	334.3	341.2	348.2	6.0

Petroleum: relation between volume and mass[a] Density (kg/l) at 15°C (59°F)

Density (kg/l) at 15°C	°API	UK tons per kilolitre (m^3)	lb per UK gal	US gal	barrel	UK gal per UK ton	US barrels per US ton	tonne	UK ton	US barrels per day to US tons per year	tonnes per year	UK tons per year	Density (kg/l) at 15°C
0.50		0.492	5.01	4.17	175	447	11.41	12.58	12.78	32.0	29.0	28.6	0.50
0.52		0.512	5.21	4.34	182	430	10.97	12.10	12.29	33.3	30.2	29.7	0.52
0.54		0.531	5.41	4.51	189	414	10.57	11.65	11.83	34.5	31.3	30.8	0.54
0.56		0.551	5.61	4.67	196	399	10.19	11.23	11.41	35.8	32.5	32.0	0.56
0.58		0.571	5.81	4.84	203	385	9.84	10.84	11.02	37.1	33.7	33.1	0.58
0.60		0.591	6.01	5.01	210	372	9.51	10.48	10.65	38.4	34.8	34.3	0.60
0.61		0.600	6.11	5.09	214	366	9.35	10.31	10.48	39.0	35.4	34.8	0.61
0.62	96.5	0.610	6.21	5.17	217	360	9.20	10.14	10.31	39.7	36.0	35.4	0.62
0.63	92.9	0.620	6.31	5.26	221	355	9.06	9.98	10.14	40.3	36.6	36.0	0.63
0.64	89.4	0.630	6.41	5.34	224	349	8.92	9.83	9.99	40.9	37.1	36.6	0.64
0.65	86.0	0.640	6.51	5.42	228	344	8.78	9.68	9.83	41.6	37.7	37.1	0.65
0.66	82.7	0.650	6.61	5.51	231	339	8.65	9.53	9.68	42.2	38.3	37.7	0.66
0.67	79.5	0.659	6.72	5.59	235	334	8.52	9.39	9.54	42.9	38.9	38.3	0.67
0.68	76.4	0.669	6.82	5.67	238	329	8.39	9.25	9.40	43.5	39.5	38.8	0.68
0.69	73.4	0.679	6.92	5.76	242	324	8.27	9.12	9.26	44.1	40.0	39.4	0.69
0.70	70.4	0.689	7.02	5.84	245	319	8.15	8.99	9.13	44.8	40.6	40.0	0.70
0.71	67.6	0.699	7.12	5.93	249	315	8.04	8.86	9.00	45.4	41.2	40.6	0.71
0.72	64.8	0.709	7.22	6.01	252	310	7.93	8.74	8.88	46.1	41.8	41.1	0.72
0.73	62.1	0.718	7.32	6.09	256	306	7.82	8.62	8.75	46.7	42.4	41.7	0.73
0.74	59.5	0.728	7.42	6.18	259	302	7.71	8.50	8.64	47.3	42.9	42.3	0.74
0.75	57.0	0.738	7.52	6.26	263	298	7.61	8.39	8.52	48.0	43.5	42.8	0.75
0.76	54.5	0.748	7.62	6.34	266	294	7.51	8.28	8.41	48.6	44.1	43.4	0.76
0.77	52.1	0.758	7.72	6.43	270	290	7.41	8.17	8.30	49.3	44.7	44.0	0.77
0.78	49.7	0.768	7.82	6.51	273	287	7.32	8.06	8.19	49.9	45.3	44.5	0.78
0.79	47.4	0.778	7.92	6.59	277	283	7.22	7.96	8.09	50.5	45.8	45.1	0.79
0.80	45.2	0.787	8.02	6.68	280	279	7.13	7.86	7.99	51.2	46.4	45.7	0.80
0.81	43.0	0.797	8.12	6.76	284	276	7.04	7.77	7.89	51.8	47.0	46.3	0.81
0.82	40.9	0.807	8.22	6.84	287	273	6.96	7.67	7.79	52.5	47.6	46.8	0.82
0.83	38.8	0.817	8.32	6.93	291	269	6.87	7.58	7.70	53.1	48.2	47.4	0.83
0.84	36.8	0.827	8.42	7.01	294	266	6.79	7.49	7.61	53.7	48.7	48.0	0.84
0.85	34.8	0.837	8.52	7.09	298	263	6.71	7.40	7.52	54.4	49.3	48.5	0.85
0.86	32.9	0.846	8.62	7.18	301	260	6.63	7.31	7.43	55.0	49.9	49.1	0.86
0.87	31.0	0.856	8.72	7.26	305	257	6.56	7.23	7.35	55.7	50.5	49.7	0.87
0.88	29.1	0.866	8.82	7.34	308	254	6.48	7.15	7.26	56.3	51.1	50.3	0.88
0.89	27.3	0.876	8.92	7.43	312	251	6.41	7.07	7.18	56.9	51.6	50.8	0.89
0.90	25.6	0.886	9.02	7.51	315	248	6.34	6.99	7.10	57.6	52.2	51.4	0.90
0.91	23.8	0.896	9.12	7.59	319	246	6.27	6.91	7.02	58.2	52.8	52.0	0.91
0.92	22.1	0.905	9.22	7.68	322	243	6.20	6.84	6.95	58.9	53.4	52.5	0.92
0.93	20.5	0.915	9.32	7.76	326	240	6.14	6.76	6.87	59.5	54.0	53.1	0.93
0.94	18.9	0.925	9.42	7.84	329	238	6.07	6.69	6.80	60.1	54.5	53.7	0.94
0.95	17.3	0.935	9.52	7.93	333	235	6.01	6.62	6.73	60.8	55.1	54.3	0.95
0.96	15.7	0.945	9.62	8.01	336	233	5.94	6.55	6.66	61.4	55.7	54.8	0.96
0.97	14.2	0.955	9.72	8.10	340	230	5.88	6.48	6.59	62.0	56.3	55.4	0.97
0.98	12.7	0.965	9.82	8.18	343	228	5.82	6.42	6.52	62.7	56.9	56.0	0.98
0.99	11.3	0.974	9.92	8.26	347	226	5.76	6.35	6.46	63.3	57.5	56.5	0.99
1.00	9.9	0.984	10.02	8.35	351	223	5.71	6.29	6.39	64.0	58.0	57.1	1.00
1.01	8.5	0.994	10.12	8.43	354	221	5.65	6.23	6.33	64.6	58.6	57.7	1.01
1.02	7.1	1.004	10.22	8.51	358	219	5.59	6.17	6.27	65.2	59.2	58.3	1.02
1.03	5.7	1.014	10.32	8.60	361	217	5.54	6.11	6.20	65.9	59.8	58.8	1.03
1.04	4.4	1.024	10.42	8.68	365	215	5.49	6.05	6.14	66.5	60.4	59.4	1.04
1.05	3.1	1.033	10.52	8.76	368	213	5.43	5.99	6.09	67.2	60.9	60.0	1.05
1.06	1.8	1.043	10.62	8.85	372	211	5.38	5.93	6.03	67.8	61.5	60.5	1.06
1.07	0.6	1.053	10.72	8.93	375	209	5.33	5.88	5.97	68.4	62.1	61.1	1.07
1.08		1.063	10.82	9.01	379	207	5.28	5.82	5.92	69.1	62.7	61.7	1.08
1.09		1.073	10.92	9.10	382	205	5.23	5.77	5.86	69.7	63.3	62.3	1.09
1.10		1.083	11.02	9.18	386	203	5.19	5.72	5.81	70.4	63.8	62.8	1.10

[a]Information adapted from *Petroleum Measurement Tables* of the American Society for Testing Materials (ASTM) and the Institute of Petroleum (IP).

Engineering

For other measures see Engineering, pages 80–84.

Kilowatts to UK horsepower 1 kW = 1.341 02 UK hp

kW → ↓	0	1	2	3	4	5	6	7	8	9	← kW ↓
	UK hp	UK hp	UK hp	UK hp	UK hp	UK hp	UK hp	UK hp	UK hp	UK hp	
0	0.000	1.341	2.682	4.023	5.364	6.705	8.046	9.387	10.728	12.069	0
10	13.410	14.751	16.092	17.433	18.774	20.115	21.456	22.797	24.138	25.479	10
20	26.820	28.161	29.502	30.844	32.185	33.526	34.867	36.208	37.549	38.890	20
30	40.231	41.572	42.913	44.254	45.595	46.936	48.277	49.618	50.959	52.300	30
40	53.641	54.982	56.323	57.664	59.005	60.346	61.687	63.028	64.369	65.710	40
50	67.051	68.392	69.733	71.074	72.415	73.756	75.097	76.438	77.779	79.120	50
60	80.461	81.802	83.143	84.484	85.825	87.166	88.507	89.848	91.190	92.531	60
70	93.872	95.213	96.554	97.895	99.236	100.577	101.918	103.259	104.600	105.941	70
80	107.282	108.623	109.964	111.305	112.646	113.987	115.328	116.669	118.010	119.351	80
90	120.692	122.033	123.374	124.715	126.056	127.397	128.738	130.079	131.420	132.761	90
100	134.102										100

UK horsepower to kilowatts 1 UK hp = 0.745 700 kW

UK hp → ↓	0	1	2	3	4	5	6	7	8	9	← UK hp ↓
	kW	kW	kW	kW	kW	kW	kW	kW	kW	kW	
0	0.000	0.746	1.491	2.237	2.983	3.728	4.474	5.220	5.966	6.711	0
10	7.457	8.203	8.948	9.694	10.440	11.185	11.931	12.677	13.423	14.168	10
20	14.914	15.660	16.405	17.151	17.897	18.642	19.388	20.134	20.880	21.625	20
30	22.371	23.117	23.862	24.608	25.354	26.099	26.845	27.591	28.337	29.082	30
40	29.828	30.574	31.319	32.065	32.811	33.556	34.302	35.048	35.794	36.539	40
50	37.285	38.031	38.776	39.522	40.268	41.013	41.759	42.505	43.251	43.996	50
60	44.742	45.488	46.233	46.979	47.725	48.470	49.216	49.962	50.708	51.453	60
70	52.199	52.945	53.690	54.436	55.182	55.927	56.673	57.419	58.165	58.910	70
80	59.656	60.402	61.147	61.893	62.639	63.384	64.130	64.876	65.622	66.367	80
90	67.113	67.859	68.604	69.350	70.096	70.841	71.587	72.333	73.079	73.824	90
100	74.570										100

Kilowatts to metric horsepower 1 kW = 1.359 62 ch or PS

kW → ↓	0	1	2	3	4	5	6	7	8	9	← kW ↓
	ch or PS	ch or PS	ch or PS	ch or PS	ch or PS	ch or PS	ch or PS	ch or PS	ch or PS	ch or PS	
0	0.000	1.360	2.719	4.079	5.438	6.798	8.158	9.517	10.877	12.237	0
10	13.596	14.956	16.315	17.675	19.035	20.394	21.754	23.114	24.473	25.833	10
20	27.192	28.552	29.912	31.271	32.631	33.991	35.350	36.710	38.069	39.429	20
30	40.789	42.148	43.508	44.868	46.227	47.587	48.946	50.306	51.666	53.025	30
40	54.385	55.744	57.104	58.464	59.823	61.183	62.543	63.902	65.262	66.621	40
50	67.981	69.341	70.700	72.060	73.420	74.779	76.139	77.498	78.858	80.218	50
60	81.577	82.937	84.297	85.656	87.106	88.375	89.735	91.095	92.454	93.814	60
70	95.174	96.533	97.893	99.252	100.612	101.972	103.331	104.691	106.050	107.410	70
80	108.770	110.129	111.489	112.849	114.208	115.568	116.927	118.287	119.647	121.006	80
90	122.366	123.726	125.085	126.445	127.804	129.164	130.524	131.883	133.243	134.603	90
100	135.962										100

Metric horsepower to kilowatts 1 ch or PS = 0.735 499 kW

ch or PS → ↓	0	1	2	3	4	5	6	7	8	9	← ch or PS ↓
	kW	kW	kW	kW	kW	kW	kW	kW	kW	kW	
0	0.000	0.735	1.471	2.206	2.942	3.677	4.413	5.148	5.884	6.619	0
10	7.355	8.090	8.826	9.561	10.297	11.032	11.768	12.503	13.239	13.974	10
20	14.710	15.445	16.181	16.916	17.652	18.387	19.123	19.858	20.594	21.329	20
30	22.065	22.800	23.536	24.271	25.007	25.742	26.478	27.213	27.949	28.684	30
40	29.420	30.155	30.891	31.626	32.362	33.097	33.833	34.568	35.304	36.039	40
50	36.775	37.510	38.246	38.981	39.717	40.452	41.188	41.923	42.659	43.394	50
60	44.130	44.865	45.601	46.336	47.072	47.807	48.543	49.278	50.014	50.749	60
70	51.485	52.220	52.956	53.691	54.427	55.162	55.898	56.633	57.369	58.104	70
80	58.840	59.575	60.311	61.046	61.782	62.517	63.253	63.988	64.724	65.459	80
90	66.195	66.930	67.666	68.401	69.137	69.872	70.608	71.343	72.079	72.814	90
100	73.550										100

Finance

For other measures see Finance, pages 85–90.

Use of the table. This table shows the value of one unit of currency invested at a given rate of interest for a given period of time. For example, if interest rates are 6% per annum and £1 or $1 (for instance) is to be received in ten years' time, the intersection of the 6% column and the ten-year row indicates that the net present value of this £1 or $1 is £0.564 5. In other words, £0.564 5 invested at a compound rate of 6% per annum will have grown to £1 or $1 after 10 years.

Net present value of one unit of currency (all figures are after the decimal point)

%	Years 1	2	3	4	5	6	7	8	9	10	11	12
1	990 1	980 3	970 6	961 0	951 5	942 0	932 7	923 5	914 3	905 3	896 3	887 4
2	980 4	961 2	942 3	923 8	905 7	888 0	870 6	853 5	836 8	820 3	804 3	788 5
3	970 9	942 6	915 1	888 5	862 6	837 5	813 1	789 4	766 4	744 1	722 4	701 4
4	961 5	924 6	889 0	854 8	821 9	790 3	759 9	730 7	702 6	675 6	649 6	624 6
5	952 4	907 0	863 8	822 7	783 5	746 2	710 7	676 8	644 6	613 9	584 7	556 8
6	943 4	890 0	839 6	792 1	747 3	705 0	665 1	627 4	591 9	558 4	526 8	497 0
7	934 6	873 4	816 3	762 9	713 0	666 3	622 7	582 3	543 9	508 3	475 1	444 0
8	925 9	857 3	793 8	735 0	680 6	630 2	583 5	540 3	500 2	463 2	428 9	397 1
9	917 4	841 7	772 2	708 4	649 9	596 3	547 0	501 9	460 4	422 4	387 5	355 5
10	909 1	826 4	751 3	683 0	620 9	564 5	513 2	466 5	424 1	385 5	350 5	318 6
11	900 9	811 6	731 2	658 7	593 5	534 6	481 7	433 9	390 9	352 2	317 3	285 8
12	892 9	797 2	711 8	635 5	567 4	506 6	452 3	403 9	360 6	322 0	287 5	256 7
13	885 0	783 1	693 1	613 3	542 8	480 3	425 1	376 2	332 9	294 6	260 7	230 7
14	877 2	769 5	675 0	592 1	519 4	455 6	399 6	350 6	307 5	269 7	236 6	207 6
15	869 5	756 1	657 5	571 8	497 1	432 3	375 9	326 9	284 3	247 2	214 9	186 9
16	862 1	743 2	640 7	552 3	476 1	410 4	353 8	305 0	263 0	226 7	195 4	168 5
17	854 7	730 5	624 4	533 7	456 1	389 8	333 2	284 8	243 4	208 0	177 8	152 0
18	847 5	718 2	608 6	515 8	437 1	370 4	313 9	266 0	225 5	191 1	161 9	137 2
19	840 3	706 2	593 4	498 7	419 0	352 1	295 9	245 7	209 0	175 6	147 6	124 0
20	833 3	694 4	578 7	482 3	401 9	334 9	279 1	232 6	193 8	161 5	134 6	112 2
21	826 4	683 0	564 5	466 5	385 5	318 6	263 3	217 6	179 9	148 6	122 8	101 5
22	819 7	671 9	550 7	451 4	370 0	303 3	248 6	203 8	167 0	136 9	112 2	092 0
23	813 0	661 0	537 4	436 9	355 2	288 8	234 8	190 9	155 2	126 2	102 6	083 4
24	806 5	650 4	524 5	423 0	341 1	275 1	221 8	178 9	144 3	116 4	093 8	075 7
25	800 0	640 0	512 0	409 6	327 7	262 1	209 7	167 8	134 2	107 4	085 9	068 7
26	793 7	629 9	499 9	396 8	314 9	249 9	198 3	157 4	124 9	099 2	078 7	062 5
27	787 4	620 0	488 2	384 4	302 7	238 3	187 7	147 8	116 4	091 6	072 1	056 8
28	781 3	610 4	476 8	372 5	291 0	227 4	177 6	138 8	108 4	084 7	066 2	051 7
29	775 2	600 9	465 8	361 1	279 9	217 0	168 2	130 4	101 1	078 4	060 7	047 1
30	769 2	591 7	455 2	350 1	269 3	207 2	159 4	122 6	098 3	072 5	055 8	042 9

%	Years 13	14	15	16	17	18	19	20	21	22	23	24
1	878 7	870 0	861 3	852 8	844 4	836 0	827 7	819 5	811 4	803 4	795 4	787 6
2	773 0	757 9	743 0	728 4	714 2	700 2	686 4	673 0	659 8	646 8	634 2	621 7
3	681 0	661 1	641 9	623 2	605 0	587 4	570 3	553 7	537 5	521 9	506 7	491 9
4	600 6	577 5	555 3	533 9	513 4	493 6	474 6	456 4	438 8	422 0	405 7	398 1
5	530 3	505 1	481 0	458 1	436 3	415 5	395 7	376 9	358 9	341 8	325 6	310 1
6	468 8	442 3	417 3	393 6	371 4	350 3	330 5	311 8	294 2	277 5	261 8	247 0
7	415 0	387 8	362 4	338 7	316 0	295 9	276 5	258 4	241 5	225 7	210 9	197 1
8	367 7	340 5	315 2	291 9	270 3	250 2	231 7	214 5	198 7	183 9	170 3	157 7
9	326 2	299 2	274 5	251 9	231 1	212 0	194 5	178 4	163 7	150 2	137 8	126 4
10	289 7	263 3	239 4	217 6	197 8	179 9	163 5	148 6	135 1	122 8	111 7	101 5
11	257 5	232 0	209 0	188 3	169 6	152 8	137 7	124 0	111 7	100 7	090 7	081 7
12	229 2	204 6	182 7	163 1	145 6	130 0	116 1	103 7	092 6	082 6	073 8	065 9
13	204 2	180 7	159 9	141 5	125 2	110 8	098 1	086 8	076 8	068 0	060 1	053 2
14	182 1	159 7	140 1	122 9	107 8	094 6	082 9	072 8	063 8	056 0	049 1	043 1
15	162 5	141 3	122 9	106 9	092 9	080 8	070 3	061 1	053 1	046 2	040 2	034 9
16	145 2	125 2	107 9	093 0	080 2	069 1	059 6	051 4	044 3	038 2	032 9	028 4
17	129 9	111 0	094 9	081 1	069 3	059 2	050 6	043 3	037 0	031 6	027 0	023 1
18	116 3	098 5	083 5	070 8	060 0	050 8	043 1	036 5	030 9	026 2	022 2	018 8
19	104 0	087 6	073 6	061 8	052 0	043 7	036 7	030 8	025 9	021 8	018 3	015 4
20	093 5	077 9	064 9	054 1	045 1	037 6	031 3	026 1	021 7	018 1	015 1	012 6
21	083 9	069 3	057 3	047 4	039 1	032 3	026 7	022 1	018 3	015 1	012 5	010 3
22	075 4	061 8	050 7	041 5	034 0	027 9	022 9	018 7	015 4	012 6	010 3	008 5
23	067 8	055 1	044 8	036 4	029 6	024 1	019 6	015 9	012 9	010 5	008 6	007 0
24	061 0	049 2	039 7	032 0	025 8	020 8	016 8	013 5	010 9	008 8	007 1	005 7
25	055 0	044 0	035 2	028 1	022 5	018 0	014 4	011 5	009 2	007 4	005 9	004 7
26	049 6	039 3	031 2	024 8	019 7	015 6	012 4	009 8	007 8	006 2	004 3	003 9
27	044 7	035 2	027 7	021 8	017 2	013 5	010 7	008 4	006 6	005 2	004 1	003 2
28	040 4	031 6	024 7	019 3	015 0	011 8	009 2	007 2	005 6	004 4	003 4	002 7
29	036 5	028 3	021 9	017 0	013 2	010 2	007 9	006 1	004 8	003 7	002 9	002 2
30	033 1	025 4	019 5	015 0	011 6	008 9	006 8	005 3	004 0	003 1	002 4	001 8

se of the tables. See page 86 for an explanation of how the table on this page and on pages 204 and 205 work.

lortgage repayments with capital instalment variable, fixed total sum repayable annually

ased on a loan of £10 000 or $10 000)

	Rate of interest											
	7.5%				10%				12.5%			
	Payments			Capital balance owing (end-year)	Payments			Capital balance owing (end-year)	Payments			Capital balance owing (end-year)
	Total	Capital	Interest		Total	Capital	Interest		Total	Capital	Interest	
0-year nortgage												
'ears to pay												
0	980.92	230.92	750.00	9769.08	1174.60	174.60	1000.00	9825.40	1380.96	130.96	1250.00	9869.04
9	980.92	248.24	732.68	9520.84	1174.60	192.06	982.54	9633.35	1380.96	147.33	1233.63	9721.72
8	980.92	266.86	714.06	9253.98	1174.60	211.26	963.33	9422.09	1380.96	165.74	1215.21	9555.97
7	980.92	286.87	694.05	8967.10	1174.60	232.39	942.21	9189.70	1380.96	186.46	1194.50	9369.51
6	980.92	308.39	672.53	8658.72	1174.60	255.63	918.97	8934.07	1380.96	209.77	1171.19	9159.74
5	980.92	331.52	649.40	8327.20	1174.60	281.19	893.41	8652.88	1380.96	235.99	1144.97	8923.75
4	980.92	356.38	624.54	7970.81	1174.60	309.31	865.29	8343.58	1380.96	265.49	1115.47	8658.27
3	980.92	383.11	597.81	7587.70	1174.60	340.24	834.36	8003.34	1380.96	298.67	1082.28	8359.59
2	980.92	411.84	569.08	7175.86	1174.60	374.26	800.33	7629.07	1380.96	336.01	1044.95	8023.58
1	980.92	442.73	538.19	6733.13	1174.60	411.69	762.91	7217.39	1380.96	378.01	1002.95	7645.57
0	980.92	475.94	504.98	6257.19	1174.60	452.86	721.74	6764.53	1380.96	425.26	955.70	7220.31
9	980.92	511.63	469.29	5745.56	1174.60	498.14	676.45	6266.38	1380.96	478.42	902.54	6741.90
8	980.92	550.01	430.92	5195.55	1174.60	547.96	626.64	5718.43	1380.96	538.22	842.74	6203.68
7	980.92	591.26	389.67	4604.30	1174.60	602.75	571.84	5115.67	1380.96	605.50	775.46	5598.18
6	980.92	635.60	345.32	3968.70	1174.60	663.03	511.57	4452.64	1380.96	681.19	699.77	4916.99
5	980.92	683.27	297.65	3285.43	1174.60	729.33	445.26	3723.31	1380.96	766.33	614.62	4150.66
4	980.92	734.51	246.41	2550.91	1174.60	802.27	372.33	2921.05	1380.96	862.12	518.83	3288.53
3	980.92	789.60	191.32	1761.31	1174.60	882.49	292.10	2038.56	1380.96	969.89	411.07	2318.64
2	980.92	848.82	132.10	912.49	1174.60	970.74	203.86	1067.81	1380.96	1091.13	289.83	1227.52
1	980.92	912.49	68.44	0.00	1174.60	1067.81	106.78	0.00	1380.96	1227.52	153.44	0.00
otal paid	19618.44	10000.00	9618.44		23491.92	10000.00	13491.92		27619.15	10000.00	17619.15	
lonthly rate	81.74	41.67	40.08		97.88	41.67	56.22		115.08	41.67	73.41	
5-year nortgage												
'ears to pay												
5	897.11	147.11	750.00	9852.89	1101.68	101.68	1000.00	9898.32	1319.43	69.43	1250.00	9930.57
4	897.11	158.14	738.97	9694.75	1101.68	111.85	989.83	9786.47	1319.43	78.11	1241.32	9852.45
3	897.11	170.00	727.11	9524.75	1101.68	123.03	978.65	9663.44	1319.43	87.88	1231.56	9764.57
2	897.11	182.75	714.36	9342.00	1101.68	135.34	966.34	9528.10	1319.43	98.86	1220.57	9665.71
1	897.11	196.46	700.65	9145.55	1101.68	148.87	952.81	9379.23	1319.43	111.22	1208.21	9554.49
0	897.11	211.19	685.92	8934.36	1101.68	163.76	937.92	9215.47	1319.43	125.12	1194.31	9429.37
9	897.11	227.03	670.08	8707.33	1101.68	180.13	921.55	9035.34	1319.43	140.76	1178.67	9288.60
8	897.11	244.06	653.05	8463.27	1101.68	198.15	903.53	8837.19	1319.43	158.36	1161.08	9130.25
7	897.11	262.36	634.75	8200.91	1101.68	217.96	883.72	8619.23	1319.43	178.15	1141.28	8952.09
6	897.11	282.04	615.07	7918.87	1101.68	239.76	861.92	8379.47	1319.43	200.42	1119.01	8751.67
5	897.11	303.19	593.92	7615.68	1101.68	263.73	837.95	8115.74	1319.43	225.48	1093.96	8526.19
4	897.11	325.93	571.18	7289.75	1101.68	290.11	811.57	7825.63	1319.43	253.66	1065.77	8272.53
3	897.11	350.38	546.73	6939.37	1101.68	319.12	782.56	7506.51	1319.43	285.37	1034.07	7987.16
2	897.11	376.65	520.45	6562.72	1101.68	351.03	750.65	7155.48	1319.43	321.04	998.40	7666.13
1	897.11	404.90	492.20	6157.81	1101.68	386.13	715.55	6769.35	1319.43	361.17	958.27	7304.96
0	897.11	435.27	461.84	5722.54	1101.68	424.75	676.94	6344.61	1319.43	406.31	913.12	6898.64
9	897.11	467.92	429.19	5254.63	1101.68	467.22	634.46	5877.39	1319.43	457.10	862.33	6441.54
8	897.11	503.01	394.10	4751.62	1101.68	513.94	587.74	5363.44	1319.43	514.24	805.19	5927.30
7	897.11	540.74	356.37	4210.88	1101.68	565.34	536.34	4798.11	1319.43	578.52	740.91	5348.77
6	897.11	581.29	315.82	3629.59	1101.68	621.87	479.81	4176.24	1319.43	650.84	668.60	4697.94
5	897.11	624.89	272.22	3004.70	1101.68	684.06	417.62	3492.18	1319.43	732.19	587.24	3965.74
4	897.11	671.75	225.35	2332.95	1101.68	752.46	349.22	2739.72	1319.43	823.72	495.72	3142.03
3	897.11	722.14	174.97	1610.81	1101.68	827.71	273.97	1912.01	1319.43	926.68	392.75	2215.35
2	897.11	776.30	120.81	834.52	1101.68	910.48	191.20	1001.53	1319.43	1042.52	276.92	1172.83
1	897.11	834.52	62.59	0.00	1101.68	1001.53	100.15	0.00	1319.43	1172.83	146.60	0.00
otal paid	22427.67	10000.00	12427.67		27542.02	10000.00	17542.02		32985.86	10000.00	22985.86	
lonthly rate	74.76	33.33	41.43		91.81	33.33	58.47		109.95	33.33	76.62	

Mortgage repayments with capital instalment variable, fixed total sum repayable annually
(based on a loan of £10 000 or $10 000)

	Rate of interest 15% Payments				17.5% Payments				20% Payments			
	Total	Capital	Interest	Capital balance owing (end-year)	Total	Capital	Interest	Capital balance owing (end-year)	Total	Capital	Interest	Capit balan owin (end- year)
20-year mortgage												
Years to pay												
20	1597.61	97.61	1500.00	9902.39	1822.43	72.43	1750.00	9927.57	2053.57	53.57	2000.00	9946.
19	1597.61	112.26	1485.36	9790.13	1822.43	85.10	1737.33	9842.47	2053.57	64.28	1989.29	9882.
18	1597.61	129.10	1468.52	9661.03	1822.43	99.99	1722.43	9742.48	2053.57	77.13	1976.43	9805.
17	1597.61	148.46	1449.15	9512.57	1822.43	117.49	1704.93	9624.99	2053.57	92.56	1961.00	9712.
16	1597.61	170.73	1426.89	9341.84	1822.43	138.05	1684.37	9486.94	2053.57	111.07	1942.49	9601.
15	1597.61	196.34	1401.28	9145.51	1822.43	162.21	1660.21	9324.73	2053.57	133.29	1920.28	9468.
14	1597.61	225.79	1371.83	8919.72	1822.43	190.60	1631.83	9134.13	2053.57	159.95	1893.62	9308.
13	1597.61	259.66	1337.96	8660.06	1822.43	223.95	1598.47	8910.17	2053.57	191.93	1861.63	9116.
12	1597.61	298.61	1299.01	8361.46	1822.43	263.15	1559.28	8647.03	2053.57	230.32	1823.24	8885.
11	1597.61	343.40	1254.22	8018.06	1822.43	309.20	1513.23	8337.83	2053.57	276.39	1777.18	8609.
10	1597.61	394.91	1202.71	7623.15	1822.43	363.30	1459.12	7974.53	2053.57	331.66	1721.90	8277.
9	1597.61	454.14	1143.47	7169.01	1822.43	426.88	1395.54	7547.65	2053.57	397.99	1655.57	7879.
8	1597.61	522.26	1075.35	6646.75	1822.43	501.59	1320.84	7046.06	2053.57	477.59	1575.97	7402.
7	1597.61	600.60	997.01	6046.15	1822.43	589.37	1233.06	6456.69	2053.57	573.11	1480.45	6829.
6	1597.61	690.69	906.92	5355.45	1822.43	692.50	1129.92	5764.19	2053.57	687.73	1365.83	6141.
5	1597.61	794.30	803.32	4561.16	1822.43	813.69	1008.73	4950.49	2053.57	825.28	1228.28	5316.
4	1597.61	913.44	684.17	3647.71	1822.43	956.09	866.34	3994.41	2053.57	990.34	1063.23	4325.
3	1597.61	1050.46	547.16	2597.26	1822.43	1123.40	699.02	2871.00	2053.57	1188.41	865.16	3137.
2	1597.61	1208.03	389.59	1389.23	1822.43	1320.00	502.43	1551.00	2053.57	1426.09	627.48	1711.
1	1597.61	1389.23	208.38	0.00	1822.43	1551.00	271.43	0.00	2053.57	1711.30	342.26	0.
Total paid	31952.29	10000.00	21952.29		36448.51	10000.00	26448.51		41071.31	10000.00	31071.31	
Monthly rate	133.13	41.67	91.47		151.87	41.67	110.20		171.13	41.67	129.46	
25-year mortgage												
Years to pay												
25	1546.99	46.99	1500.00	9953.01	1781.61	31.61	1750.00	9968.39	2021.19	21.19	2000.00	9978.
24	1546.99	54.04	1492.95	9898.96	1781.61	37.15	1744.47	9931.24	2021.19	25.42	1995.76	9953.
23	1546.99	62.15	1484.84	9836.81	1781.61	43.65	1737.97	9887.60	2021.19	30.51	1990.68	9922.
22	1546.99	71.47	1475.52	9765.34	1781.61	51.28	1730.33	9836.31	2021.19	36.61	1984.58	9886.
21	1546.99	82.19	1464.80	9683.15	1781.61	60.26	1721.35	9776.05	2021.19	43.93	1977.25	9842.
20	1546.99	94.52	1452.47	9588.63	1781.61	70.80	1710.81	9705.25	2021.19	52.72	1968.47	9789.
19	1546.99	108.70	1438.29	9479.93	1781.61	83.19	1698.42	9622.06	2021.19	63.26	1957.92	9726.
18	1546.99	125.01	1421.99	9354.92	1781.61	97.75	1683.86	9524.30	2021.19	75.92	1945.27	9650.
17	1546.99	143.76	1403.24	9211.17	1781.61	114.86	1666.75	9409.44	2021.19	91.10	1930.09	9559.
16	1546.99	165.32	1381.67	9045.85	1781.61	134.96	1646.65	9274.48	2021.19	109.32	1911.87	9450.
15	1546.99	190.12	1356.88	8855.73	1781.61	158.58	1623.03	9115.90	2021.19	131.19	1890.00	9318.
14	1546.99	218.63	1328.36	8637.09	1781.61	186.33	1595.28	8929.57	2021.19	157.42	1863.76	9161.
13	1546.99	251.43	1295.56	8385.67	1781.61	218.94	1562.68	8710.63	2021.19	188.91	1832.28	8972.
12	1546.99	289.14	1257.85	8096.52	1781.61	257.25	1524.36	8453.38	2021.19	226.69	1794.50	8745.
11	1546.99	332.52	1214.48	7764.01	1781.61	302.27	1479.34	8151.11	2021.19	272.03	1749.16	8473.
10	1546.99	382.39	1164.60	7381.61	1781.61	355.17	1426.44	7795.94	2021.19	326.43	1694.75	8147.
9	1546.99	439.75	1107.24	6941.86	1781.61	417.32	1364.29	7378.62	2021.19	391.72	1629.47	7755.
8	1546.99	505.72	1041.28	6436.14	1781.61	490.35	1291.26	6888.26	2021.19	470.06	1551.12	7285.
7	1546.99	581.57	965.42	5854.57	1781.61	576.17	1205.45	6312.10	2021.19	564.08	1457.11	6721.
6	1546.99	668.81	878.19	5185.76	1781.61	677.00	1104.62	5635.10	2021.19	676.89	1344.30	6044.
5	1546.99	769.13	777.86	4416.63	1781.61	795.47	986.14	4839.63	2021.19	812.27	1208.92	5232.
4	1546.99	884.50	662.50	3532.14	1781.61	934.68	846.94	3904.95	2021.19	974.72	1046.46	4257.
3	1546.99	1017.17	529.82	2514.96	1781.61	1098.25	683.37	2806.71	2021.19	1169.67	851.52	3087.
2	1546.99	1169.75	377.24	1345.21	1781.61	1290.44	491.17	1516.27	2021.19	1403.60	617.59	1684.
1	1546.99	1345.21	201.78	0.00	1781.61	1516.27	265.35	0.00	2021.19	1684.32	336.86	0.
Total paid	38674.85	10000.00	28674.85		44540.33	10000.00	34540.33		50529.68	10000.00	40529.68	
Monthly rate	128.92	33.33	95.58		148.47	33.33	115.13		168.43	33.33	135.10	

Mortgage repayments with capital instalment fixed, variable total sum repayable annually
based on a loan of £10 000 or $10 000)

	Rate of interest 10% Payments Total	Capital	Interest	Capital balance owing (end-year)	15% Payments Total	Capital	Interest	Capital balance owing (end-year)	20% Payments Total	Capital	Interest	Capital balance owing (end-year)
0-year mortgage Years to pay												
0	1500.00	500.00	1000.00	9500.00	2000.00	500.00	1500.00	9500.00	2500.00	500.00	2000.00	9500.00
9	1450.00	500.00	950.00	9000.00	1925.00	500.00	1425.00	9000.00	2400.00	500.00	1900.00	9000.00
8	1400.00	500.00	900.00	8500.00	1850.00	500.00	1350.00	8500.00	2300.00	500.00	1800.00	8500.00
7	1350.00	500.00	850.00	8000.00	1775.00	500.00	1275.00	8000.00	2200.00	500.00	1700.00	8000.00
6	1300.00	500.00	800.00	7500.00	1700.00	500.00	1200.00	7500.00	2100.00	500.00	1600.00	7500.00
5	1250.00	500.00	750.00	7000.00	1625.00	500.00	1125.00	7000.00	2000.00	500.00	1500.00	7000.00
4	1200.00	500.00	700.00	6500.00	1550.00	500.00	1050.00	6500.00	1900.00	500.00	1400.00	6500.00
3	1150.00	500.00	650.00	6000.00	1475.00	500.00	975.00	6000.00	1800.00	500.00	1300.00	6000.00
2	1100.00	500.00	600.00	5500.00	1400.00	500.00	900.00	5500.00	1700.00	500.00	1200.00	5500.00
1	1050.00	500.00	550.00	5000.00	1325.00	500.00	825.00	5000.00	1 600.00	500.00	1100.00	5000.00
0	1000.00	500.00	500.00	4500.00	1250.00	500.00	750.00	4500.00	1500.00	500.00	1000.00	4500.00
9	950.00	500.00	450.00	4000.00	1175.00	500.00	675.00	4000.00	1400.00	500.00	900.00	4000.00
8	900.00	500.00	400.00	3500.00	1100.00	500.00	600.00	3500.00	1300.00	500.00	800.00	3500.00
7	850.00	500.00	350.00	3000.00	1025.00	500.00	525.00	3000.00	1200.00	500.00	700.00	3000.00
6	800.00	500.00	300.00	2500.00	950.00	500.00	450.00	2500.00	1100.00	500.00	600.00	2500.00
5	750.00	500.00	250.00	2000.00	875.00	500.00	375.00	2000.00	1000.00	500.00	500.00	2000.00
4	700.00	500.00	200.00	1500.00	800.00	500.00	300.00	1500.00	900.00	500.00	400.00	1500.00
3	650.00	500.00	150.00	1000.00	725.00	500.00	225.00	1000.00	800.00	500.00	300.00	1000.00
2	600.00	500.00	100.00	500.00	650.00	500.00	150.00	500.00	700.00	500.00	200.00	500.00
1	550.00	500.00	50.00	0.00	575.00	500.00	75.00	0.00	600.00	500.00	100.00	0.00
Total paid	20500.00	10000.00	10500.00		25750.00	10000.00	15750.00		31000.00	10000.00	21000.00	
Monthly rate	85.42	41.67	43.75		107.29	41.67	65.62		129.17	41.67	87.50	
5-year mortgage Years to pay												
5	1400.00	400.00	1000.00	9600.00	1900.00	400.00	1500.00	9600.00	2400.00	400.00	2000.00	9600.00
4	1360.00	400.00	960.00	9200.00	1840.00	400.00	1440.00	9200.00	2320.00	400.00	1920.00	9200.00
3	1320.00	400.00	920.00	8800.00	1780.00	400.00	1380.00	8800.00	2240.00	400.00	1840.00	8800.00
2	1280.00	400.00	880.00	8400.00	1720.00	400.00	1320.00	8400.00	2160.00	400.00	1760.00	8400.00
1	1240.00	400.00	840.00	8000.00	1660.00	400.00	1260.00	8000.00	2080.00	400.00	1680.00	8000.00
0	1200.00	400.00	800.00	7600.00	1600.00	400.00	1200.00	7600.00	2000.00	400.00	1600.00	7600.00
9	1160.00	400.00	760.00	7200.00	1540.00	400.00	1140.00	7200.00	1920.00	400.00	1520.00	7200.00
8	1120.00	400.00	720.00	6800.00	1480.00	400.00	1080.00	6800.00	1840.00	400.00	1440.00	6800.00
7	1080.00	400.00	680.00	6400.00	1420.00	400.00	1020.00	6400.00	1760.00	400.00	1360.00	6400.00
6	1040.00	400.00	640.00	6000.00	1360.00	400.00	960.00	6000.00	1680.00	400.00	1280.00	6000.00
5	1000.00	400.00	600.00	5600.00	1300.00	400.00	900.00	5600.00	1600.00	400.00	1200.00	5600.00
4	960.00	400.00	560.00	5200.00	1240.00	400.00	840.00	5200.00	1520.00	400.00	1120.00	5200.00
3	920.00	400.00	520.00	4800.00	1180.00	400.00	780.00	4800.00	1440.00	400.00	1040.00	4800.00
2	880.00	400.00	480.00	4400.00	1120.00	400.00	720.00	4400.00	1360.00	400.00	960.00	4400.00
1	840.00	400.00	440.00	4000.00	1060.00	400.00	660.00	4000.00	1280.00	400.00	880.00	4000.00
0	800.00	400.00	400.00	3600.00	1000.00	400.00	600.00	3600.00	1200.00	400.00	800.00	3600.00
9	760.00	400.00	360.00	3200.00	940.00	400.00	540.00	3200.00	1120.00	400.00	720.00	3200.00
8	720.00	400.00	320.00	2800.00	880.00	400.00	480.00	2800.00	1040.00	400.00	640.00	2800.00
7	680.00	400.00	280.00	2400.00	820.00	400.00	420.00	2400.00	960.00	400.00	560.00	2400.00
6	640.00	400.00	240.00	2000.00	760.00	400.00	360.00	2000.00	880.00	400.00	480.00	2000.00
5	600.00	400.00	200.00	1600.00	700.00	400.00	300.00	1600.00	800.00	400.00	400.00	1600.00
4	560.00	400.00	160.00	1200.00	640.00	400.00	240.00	1200.00	720.00	400.00	320.00	1200.00
3	520.00	400.00	120.00	800.00	580.00	400.00	180.00	800.00	640.00	400.00	240.00	800.00
2	480.00	400.00	80.00	400.00	520.00	400.00	120.00	400.00	560.00	400.00	160.00	400.00
1	440.00	400.00	40.00	0.00	460.00	400.00	60.00	0.00	480.00	400.00	80.00	0.00
Total paid	23000.00	10000.00	13000.00		29500.00	10000.00	19500.00		36000.00	10000.00	26000.00	
Monthly rate	76.67	33.33	43.33		98.33	33.33	65.00		120.00	33.33	86.67	

Use of the tables. The monthly rate, made up by the number at each side of a line and the fraction or decimal unit at the head of a column, is equivalent to the annual percentage rate shown in the position where line and column meet. For example, the APR for a monthly rate of $2\frac{1}{4}$% is 30.6%

Actual annual percentage rate of interest per year (APR) corresponding to the rate per month indicated

Monthly rates with fractions

	0	$\frac{1}{8}$	$\frac{1}{4}$	$\frac{3}{8}$	$\frac{1}{2}$	$\frac{5}{8}$	$\frac{3}{4}$	$\frac{7}{8}$
0	0.0	1.5	3.0	4.6	6.2	7.8	9.4	11.0
1	12.7	14.4	16.1	17.8	19.6	21.3	23.1	25.0
2	26.8	28.7	30.6	32.5	34.5	36.5	38.5	40.5
3	42.6	44.7	46.8	48.9	51.1	53.3	55.5	57.8
4	60.1	62.4	64.8	67.2	69.6	72.0	74.5	77.0
5	79.6	82.2	84.8	87.4	90.1	92.8	95.6	98.4
6	101.2	104.1	107.0	109.9	112.9	115.9	119.0	122.1
7	125.2	128.4	131.6	134.9	138.2	141.5	144.9	148.3
8	151.8	155.3	158.9	162.5	166.2	169.9	173.6	177.4
9	181.3	185.2	189.1	193.1	197.1	201.2	205.4	209.6
10	213.8	218.1	222.5	226.9	231.4	235.9	240.5	245.1
11	249.8	254.6	259.4	264.3	269.2	274.2	279.3	284.4
12	289.6	294.8	300.2	305.5	311.0	316.5	322.1	327.7
13	333.5	339.2	345.1	351.0	357.0	363.1	369.3	375.5
14	381.8	388.2	394.6	401.2	407.8	414.5	421.2	428.1
15	435.0	442.0	449.2	456.3	463.6	471.0	478.4	486.0
16	493.6	501.3	509.1	517.0	525.0	533.1	541.3	549.6
17	558.0	566.5	575.1	583.8	592.6	601.4	610.4	619.5
18	628.8	638.1	647.5	657.0	666.7	676.5	686.3	696.3
19	706.4	716.6	727.0	737.5	748.0	758.7	769.6	780.5
20	791.6	802.8	814.2	825.6	837.2	849.0	860.8	872.8
21	885.0	897.3	909.7	922.2	934.9	947.8	960.8	973.9
22	987.2	1000.7	1014.3	1028.0	1041.9	1056.0	1070.2	1084.6
23	1099.1	1113.8	1128.7	1143.7	1158.9	1174.3	1189.9	1205.6
24	1221.5	1237.6	1253.8	1270.2	1286.9	1303.7	1320.6	1337.8
25	1355.2	1372.8	1390.5	1408.5	1426.6	1444.9	1463.5	1482.2

Monthly rates with decimals

	0.0	0.1	0.2	0.3	0.4	0.5	0.6	0.7	0.8	0.9
0	0.0	1.2	2.4	3.7	4.9	6.2	7.4	8.7	10.0	11.4
1	12.7	14.0	15.4	16.8	18.2	19.6	21.0	22.4	23.9	25.3
2	26.8	28.3	29.8	31.4	32.9	34.5	36.1	37.7	39.3	40.9
3	42.6	44.2	45.9	47.6	49.4	51.1	52.9	54.6	56.4	58.3
4	60.1	62.0	63.8	65.7	67.7	69.6	71.5	73.5	75.5	77.5
5	79.6	81.6	83.7	85.8	88.0	90.1	92.3	94.5	96.7	99.0
6	101.2	103.5	105.8	108.2	110.5	112.9	115.3	117.8	120.2	122.7
7	125.2	127.8	130.3	132.9	135.5	138.2	140.9	143.6	146.3	149.0
8	151.8	154.6	157.5	160.3	163.2	166.2	169.1	172.1	175.1	178.2
9	181.3	184.4	187.5	190.7	193.9	197.1	200.4	203.7	207.1	210.4
10	213.8	217.3	220.8	224.3	227.8	231.4	235.0	238.7	242.4	246.1
11	249.8	253.6	257.5	261.4	265.3	269.2	273.2	277.3	281.3	285.4
12	289.6	293.8	298.0	302.3	306.6	311.0	315.4	319.8	324.3	328.9
13	333.5	338.1	342.7	347.5	352.2	357.0	361.9	366.8	371.7	376.7
14	381.8	386.9	392.0	397.2	402.5	407.8	413.1	418.5	424.0	429.5
15	435.0	440.6	446.3	452.0	457.8	463.6	469.5	475.4	481.4	487.5
16	493.6	499.8	506.0	512.3	518.6	525.0	531.5	538.0	544.6	551.3
17	558.0	564.8	571.6	578.5	585.5	592.6	599.7	606.8	614.1	621.4
18	628.8	636.2	643.7	651.3	659.0	666.7	674.5	682.4	690.3	698.3
19	706.4	714.6	722.8	731.2	739.6	748.0	756.6	765.2	773.9	782.7
20	791.6	800.6	809.6	818.7	827.9	837.2	846.6	856.1	865.6	875.2
21	885.0	894.8	904.7	914.7	924.8	934.9	945.2	955.6	966.0	976.6
22	987.2	998.0	1008.8	1019.7	1030.8	1041.9	1053.1	1064.5	1075.9	1087.5
23	1099.1	1110.9	1122.7	1134.7	1146.8	1158.9	1171.2	1183.6	1196.1	1208.7
24	1221.5	1234.3	1247.3	1260.4	1273.6	1286.9	1300.3	1313.8	1327.5	1341.3
25	1355.2	1369.2	1383.4	1397.7	1412.1	1426.6	1441.3	1456.0	1471.0	1486.0

se of the table. The table shows the annual percentage rate of interest actually paid when 100 units are repaid with the amount of units shown the column at each side of a line after the number of months shown at the top of a column. For example, the APR when 100 units is repaid with)5 units after 2 months is 34.0%.

nnual percentage rate (APR) corresponding to the amount repaid per 100 units borrowed after the umber of months shown

months / mount paid	1	2	3	4	5	6	7	8	9	10	11	12 months / amount repaid	
0	0.0	0.0	0.0	0.0	0.0	0.0	0.0	0.0	0.0	0.0	0.0	0.0	100
1	12.7	6.2	4.1	3.0	2.4	2.0	1.7	1.5	1.3	1.2	1.1	1.0	101
2	26.8	12.6	8.2	6.1	4.9	4.0	3.5	3.0	2.7	2.4	2.2	2.0	102
3	42.6	19.4	12.6	9.3	7.4	6.1	5.2	4.5	4.0	3.6	3.3	3.0	103
4	60.1	26.5	17.0	12.5	9.9	8.2	7.0	6.1	5.4	4.8	4.4	4.0	104
5	79.6	34.0	21.6	15.8	12.4	10.2	8.7	7.6	6.7	6.0	5.5	5.0	105
6	101.2	41.9	26.2	19.1	15.0	12.4	10.5	9.1	8.1	7.2	6.6	6.0	106
7	125.2	50.1	31.1	22.5	17.6	14.5	12.3	10.7	9.4	8.5	7.7	7.0	107
8	151.8	58.7	36.0	26.0	20.3	16.6	14.1	12.2	10.8	9.7	8.8	8.0	108
9	181.3	67.7	41.2	29.5	23.0	18.8	15.9	13.8	12.2	10.9	9.9	9.0	109
0	213.8	77.2	46.4	33.1	25.7	21.0	17.7	15.4	13.6	12.1	11.0	10.0	110
1	249.8	87.0	51.8	36.8	28.5	23.2	19.6	16.9	14.9	13.3	12.1	11.0	111
2	289.6	97.4	57.4	40.5	31.3	25.4	21.4	18.5	16.3	14.6	13.2	12.0	112
3	333.5	108.2	63.0	44.3	34.1	27.7	23.3	20.1	17.7	15.8	14.3	13.0	113
4	381.8	119.5	68.9	48.2	37.0	30.0	25.2	21.7	19.1	17.0	15.4	14.0	114
5	435.0	131.3	74.9	52.1	39.9	32.2	27.1	23.3	20.5	18.3	16.5	15.0	115
6	493.6	143.6	81.1	56.1	42.8	34.6	29.0	24.9	21.9	19.5	17.6	16.0	116
7	558.0	156.5	87.4	60.2	45.8	36.9	30.9	26.6	23.3	20.7	18.7	17.0	117
8	628.8	170.0	93.9	64.3	48.8	39.2	32.8	28.2	24.7	22.0	19.8	18.0	118
9	706.4	184.0	100.5	68.5	51.8	41.6	34.7	29.8	26.1	23.2	20.9	19.0	119
20	791.6	198.6	107.4	72.8	54.9	44.0	36.7	31.5	27.5	24.5	22.0	20.0	120
21	885.0	213.8	114.4	77.2	58.0	46.4	38.6	33.1	28.9	25.7	23.1	21.0	121
22	987.2	229.7	121.5	81.6	61.2	48.8	40.6	34.8	30.4	26.9	24.2	22.0	122
23	1099.1	246.3	128.9	86.1	64.4	51.3	42.6	36.4	31.8	28.2	25.3	23.0	123
24	1221.5	263.5	136.4	90.7	67.6	53.8	44.6	38.1	33.2	29.5	26.4	24.0	124
25	1355.2	281.5	144.1	95.3	70.8	56.2	46.6	39.8	34.7	30.7	27.6	25.0	125
26	1501.2	300.2	152.0	100.0	74.1	58.8	48.6	41.4	36.1	32.0	28.7	26.0	126
27	1660.5	319.6	160.1	104.8	77.5	61.3	50.6	43.1	37.5	33.2	29.8	27.0	127
28	1834.3	339.8	168.4	109.7	80.8	63.8	52.7	44.8	39.0	34.5	30.9	28.0	128
29	2023.6	360.8	176.9	114.7	84.3	66.4	54.7	46.5	40.4	35.7	32.0	29.0	129
30	2229.8	382.7	185.6	119.7	87.7	69.0	56.8	48.2	41.9	37.0	33.1	30.0	130
31	2454.2	405.4	194.5	124.8	91.2	71.6	58.9	49.9	43.3	38.3	34.3	31.0	131
32	2698.3	429.0	203.6	130.0	94.7	74.2	61.0	51.7	44.8	39.5	35.4	32.0	132
33	2963.5	453.5	212.9	135.3	98.3	76.9	63.0	53.4	46.3	40.8	36.5	33.0	133
34	3251.6	478.9	222.4	140.6	101.9	79.6	65.2	55.1	47.7	42.1	37.6	34.0	134
35	3564.4	505.3	232.2	146.0	105.5	82.2	67.3	56.9	49.2	43.4	38.7	35.0	135
36	3903.7	532.8	242.1	151.5	109.2	85.0	69.4	58.6	50.7	44.6	39.9	36.0	136
37	4271.7	561.2	252.3	157.1	112.9	87.7	71.5	60.4	52.2	45.9	41.0	37.0	137
38	4670.3	590.7	262.7	162.8	116.6	90.4	73.7	62.1	53.6	47.2	42.1	38.0	138
39	5102.1	621.3	273.3	168.6	120.4	93.2	75.9	63.9	55.1	48.5	43.2	39.0	139
40	5569.4	653.0	284.2	174.4	124.2	96.0	78.0	65.7	56.6	49.7	44.3	40.0	140
41	6074.9	685.8	295.3	180.3	128.1	98.8	80.2	67.4	58.1	51.0	45.5	41.0	141
42	6621.4	719.8	306.6	186.3	132.0	101.6	82.4	69.2	59.6	52.3	46.6	42.0	142
43	7211.9	755.1	318.2	192.4	135.9	104.5	84.6	71.0	61.1	53.6	47.7	43.0	143
44	7849.7	791.6	330.0	198.6	139.9	107.4	86.8	72.8	62.6	54.9	48.9	44.0	144
45	8538.1	829.4	342.1	204.9	143.9	110.2	89.1	74.6	64.1	56.2	50.0	45.0	145
50	12874.6	1039.1	406.2	237.5	164.6	125.0	100.4	83.7	71.7	62.7	55.6	50.0	150
55	19130.0	1286.7	477.2	272.4	186.3	140.2	112.0	93.0	79.4	69.2	61.3	55.0	155
50	28047.5	1577.7	555.4	309.6	208.9	156.0	123.8	102.4	87.1	75.8	67.0	60.0	160
55	40620.0	1917.9	641.2	349.2	232.6	172.2	136.0	111.9	95.0	82.4	72.7	65.0	165
70	58162.2	2313.8	735.2	391.3	257.3	189.0	148.3	121.7	102.9	89.0	78.4	70.0	170
75	82400.5	2772.3	837.9	435.9	283.1	206.2	161.0	131.5	110.9	95.7	84.1	75.0	175
80	115583.1	3301.2	949.8	483.2	309.9	224.0	173.9	141.5	119.0	102.5	89.9	80.0	180
90	221231.5	4604.6	1203.2	585.9	366.7	261.0	200.5	161.9	135.3	116.0	101.4	90.0	190
00	409500.0	6300.0	1500.0	700.0	427.8	300.0	228.1	182.8	152.0	129.7	113.0	100.0	200

$$F = 1 \times \left[1 + \frac{r}{100}\right]^n$$

Use of the table. The table shows the annual compound rate per cent of interest or growth (r in the formula) which, accumulating over the period shown at the head of a column (n), makes 1 unit increase (or decrease) to the amount shown in the column at each side of a line (F). For example, a increase from 1 to 1.10 (a 10% increase), if achieved over 5 years, will have resulted from an annual compound interest or growth rate of 1.92%.

Interest rate or growth rate producing an accumulated amount from 1 unit compounded annually

F \ n	months 3	months 6	months 9	years 1	years 2	years 3	years 4	years 5	years 6	years 7	years 8	years 9	years 10	years 11	years 12	years 13
0.90	−34.39	−19.00	−13.11	−10.00	−5.13	−3.45	−2.60	−2.09	−1.74	−1.49	−1.31	−1.16	−1.05	−0.95	−0.87	−0.81
0.91	−31.43	−17.19	−11.82	−9.00	−4.61	−3.09	−2.33	−1.87	−1.56	−1.34	−1.17	−1.04	−0.94	−0.85	−0.78	−0.72
0.92	−28.36	−15.36	−10.52	−8.00	−4.08	−2.74	−2.06	−1.65	−1.38	−1.18	−1.04	−0.92	−0.83	−0.76	−0.69	−0.64
0.93	−25.19	−13.51	−9.22	−7.00	−3.56	−2.39	−1.80	−1.44	−1.20	−1.03	−0.90	−0.80	−0.72	−0.66	−0.60	−0.56
0.94	−21.93	−11.64	−7.92	−6.00	−3.05	−2.04	−1.53	−1.23	−1.03	−0.88	−0.77	−0.69	−0.62	−0.56	−0.51	−0.47
0.95	−18.55	−9.75	−6.61	−5.00	−2.53	−1.70	−1.27	−1.02	−0.85	−0.73	−0.64	−0.57	−0.51	−0.47	−0.43	−0.39
0.96	−15.07	−7.84	−5.30	−4.00	−2.02	−1.35	−1.02	−0.81	−0.68	−0.58	−0.51	−0.45	−0.41	−0.37	−0.34	−0.31
0.97	−11.47	−5.91	−3.98	−3.00	−1.51	−1.01	−0.76	−0.61	−0.51	−0.43	−0.38	−0.34	−0.30	−0.28	−0.25	−0.23
0.98	−7.76	−3.96	−2.66	−2.00	−1.01	−0.67	−0.50	−0.40	−0.34	−0.29	−0.25	−0.22	−0.20	−0.18	−0.17	−0.16
0.99	−3.94	−1.99	−1.33	−1.00	−0.50	−0.33	−0.25	−0.20	−0.17	−0.14	−0.13	−0.11	−0.10	−0.09	−0.08	−0.08
1.00	0.00	0.00	0.00	0.00	0.00	0.00	0.00	0.00	0.00	0.00	0.00	0.00	0.00	0.00	0.00	0.00
1.01	4.06	2.01	1.34	1.00	0.50	0.33	0.25	0.20	0.17	0.14	0.12	0.11	0.10	0.09	0.08	0.08
1.02	8.24	4.04	2.68	2.00	1.00	0.66	0.50	0.40	0.33	0.28	0.25	0.22	0.20	0.18	0.17	0.15
1.03	12.55	6.09	4.02	3.00	1.49	0.99	0.74	0.59	0.49	0.42	0.37	0.33	0.30	0.27	0.25	0.23
1.04	16.99	8.16	5.37	4.00	1.98	1.32	0.99	0.79	0.66	0.56	0.49	0.44	0.39	0.36	0.33	0.30
1.05	21.55	10.25	6.72	5.00	2.47	1.64	1.23	0.98	0.82	0.70	0.61	0.54	0.49	0.44	0.41	0.38
1.06	26.25	12.36	8.08	6.00	2.96	1.96	1.47	1.17	0.98	0.84	0.73	0.65	0.58	0.53	0.49	0.45
1.07	31.08	14.49	9.44	7.00	3.44	2.28	1.71	1.36	1.13	0.97	0.85	0.75	0.68	0.62	0.57	0.52
1.08	36.05	16.64	10.81	8.00	3.92	2.60	1.94	1.55	1.29	1.11	0.97	0.86	0.77	0.70	0.64	0.59
1.09	41.16	18.81	12.18	9.00	4.40	2.91	2.18	1.74	1.45	1.24	1.08	0.96	0.87	0.79	0.72	0.67
1.10	46.41	21.00	13.55	10.00	4.88	3.23	2.41	1.92	1.60	1.37	1.20	1.06	0.96	0.87	0.80	0.74
1.11	51.81	23.21	14.93	11.00	5.36	3.54	2.64	2.11	1.75	1.50	1.31	1.17	1.05	0.95	0.87	0.81
1.12	57.35	25.44	16.31	12.00	5.83	3.85	2.87	2.29	1.91	1.63	1.43	1.27	1.14	1.04	0.95	0.88
1.13	63.05	27.69	17.70	13.00	6.30	4.16	3.10	2.47	2.06	1.76	1.54	1.37	1.23	1.12	1.02	0.94
1.14	68.90	29.96	19.09	14.00	6.77	4.46	3.33	2.66	2.21	1.89	1.65	1.47	1.32	1.20	1.10	1.01
1.15	74.90	32.25	20.48	15.00	7.24	4.77	3.56	2.83	2.36	2.02	1.76	1.57	1.41	1.28	1.17	1.08
1.16	81.06	34.56	21.88	16.00	7.70	5.07	3.78	3.01	2.50	2.14	1.87	1.66	1.50	1.36	1.24	1.15
1.17	87.39	36.89	23.29	17.00	8.17	5.37	4.00	3.19	2.65	2.27	1.98	1.76	1.58	1.44	1.32	1.22
1.18	93.88	39.24	24.69	18.00	8.63	5.67	4.22	3.37	2.80	2.39	2.09	1.86	1.67	1.52	1.39	1.28
1.19	100.53	41.61	26.10	19.00	9.09	5.97	4.44	3.54	2.94	2.52	2.20	1.95	1.75	1.59	1.46	1.35
1.20	107.36	44.00	27.52	20.00	9.54	6.27	4.66	3.71	3.09	2.64	2.31	2.05	1.84	1.67	1.53	1.41
1.21	114.36	46.41	28.94	21.00	10.00	6.56	4.88	3.89	3.23	2.76	2.41	2.14	1.92	1.75	1.60	1.48
1.22	121.53	48.84	30.36	22.00	10.45	6.85	5.10	4.06	3.37	2.88	2.52	2.23	2.01	1.82	1.67	1.54
1.23	128.89	51.29	31.79	23.00	10.91	7.14	5.31	4.23	3.51	3.00	2.62	2.33	2.09	1.90	1.74	1.61
1.24	136.42	53.76	33.22	24.00	11.36	7.43	5.53	4.40	3.65	3.12	2.73	2.42	2.17	1.97	1.81	1.67
1.25	144.14	56.25	34.65	25.00	11.80	7.72	5.74	4.56	3.79	3.24	2.83	2.51	2.26	2.05	1.88	1.73
1.26	152.05	58.76	36.09	26.00	12.25	8.01	5.95	4.73	3.93	3.36	2.93	2.60	2.34	2.12	1.94	1.79
1.27	160.14	61.29	37.53	27.00	12.69	8.29	6.16	4.90	4.06	3.47	3.03	2.69	2.42	2.20	2.01	1.86
1.28	168.44	63.84	38.98	28.00	13.14	8.58	6.37	5.06	4.20	3.59	3.13	2.78	2.50	2.27	2.08	1.92
1.29	176.92	66.41	40.43	29.00	13.58	8.86	6.57	5.22	4.34	3.70	3.23	2.87	2.58	2.34	2.14	1.98
1.30	185.61	69.00	41.88	30.00	14.02	9.14	6.78	5.39	4.47	3.82	3.33	2.96	2.66	2.41	2.21	2.04
1.31	194.50	71.61	43.34	31.00	14.46	9.42	6.98	5.55	4.60	3.93	3.43	3.05	2.74	2.49	2.28	2.10
1.32	203.60	74.24	44.80	32.00	14.89	9.70	7.19	5.71	4.74	4.05	3.53	3.13	2.82	2.56	2.34	2.16
1.33	212.90	76.89	46.26	33.00	15.33	9.97	7.39	5.87	4.87	4.16	3.63	3.22	2.89	2.63	2.40	2.22
1.34	222.42	79.56	47.73	34.00	15.76	10.25	7.59	6.03	5.00	4.27	3.73	3.31	2.97	2.70	2.47	2.28
1.35	232.15	82.25	49.20	35.00	16.19	10.52	7.79	6.19	5.13	4.38	3.82	3.39	3.05	2.77	2.53	2.34
1.36	242.10	84.96	50.68	36.00	16.62	10.79	7.99	6.34	5.26	4.49	3.92	3.48	3.12	2.83	2.60	2.39
1.37	252.28	87.69	52.16	37.00	17.05	11.06	8.19	6.50	5.39	4.60	4.01	3.56	3.20	2.90	2.66	2.45
1.38	262.67	90.44	53.64	38.00	17.47	11.33	8.39	6.65	5.51	4.71	4.11	3.64	3.27	2.97	2.72	2.51
1.39	273.30	93.21	55.13	39.00	17.90	11.60	8.58	6.81	5.64	4.82	4.20	3.73	3.35	3.04	2.78	2.57
1.40	284.16	96.00	56.62	40.00	18.32	11.87	8.78	6.96	5.77	4.92	4.30	3.81	3.42	3.11	2.84	2.62
1.41	295.25	98.81	58.11	41.00	18.74	12.13	8.97	7.11	5.89	5.03	4.39	3.89	3.50	3.17	2.90	2.68
1.42	306.59	101.64	59.61	42.00	19.16	12.40	9.16	7.26	6.02	5.14	4.48	3.97	3.57	3.24	2.97	2.73
1.43	318.16	104.49	61.11	43.00	19.58	12.66	9.35	7.42	6.14	5.24	4.57	4.05	3.64	3.31	3.03	2.79
1.44	329.98	107.36	62.61	44.00	20.00	12.92	9.54	7.57	6.27	5.35	4.66	4.13	3.71	3.37	3.09	2.84

$$= 1 \times \left[1 + \frac{r}{100}\right]^n$$

se of the table. An increase from 1 to 1.50 (a 50% increase), if achieved over 5 years, will have resulted from an annual compound interest or owth rate of 8.45%.

nterest rate or growth rate producing an accumulated amount from 1 unit compounded annually

n	months 3	months 6	months 9	years 1	years 2	years 3	years 4	years 5	years 6	years 7	years 8	years 9	years 10	years 11	years 12	years 13	n / F
45	342.05	110.25	64.12	45.00	20.42	13.19	9.73	7.71	6.39	5.45	4.75	4.21	3.79	3.44	3.14	2.90	1.45
46	354.37	113.16	65.63	46.00	20.83	13.44	9.92	7.86	6.51	5.56	4.84	4.29	3.86	3.50	3.20	2.95	1.46
47	366.95	116.09	67.14	47.00	21.24	13.70	10.11	8.01	6.63	5.66	4.93	4.37	3.93	3.56	3.26	3.01	1.47
48	379.79	119.04	68.66	48.00	21.66	13.96	10.30	8.16	6.75	5.76	5.02	4.45	4.00	3.63	3.32	3.06	1.48
49	392.88	122.01	70.18	49.00	22.07	14.22	10.48	8.30	6.87	5.86	5.11	4.53	4.07	3.69	3.38	3.12	1.49
50	406.25	125.00	71.71	50.00	22.47	14.47	10.67	8.45	6.99	5.96	5.20	4.61	4.14	3.75	3.44	3.17	1.50
51	419.89	128.01	73.24	51.00	22.88	14.73	10.85	8.59	7.11	6.06	5.29	4.69	4.21	3.82	3.49	3.22	1.51
52	433.79	131.04	74.77	52.00	23.29	14.98	11.04	8.73	7.23	6.16	5.37	4.76	4.28	3.88	3.55	3.27	1.52
53	447.98	134.09	76.30	53.00	23.69	15.23	11.22	8.88	7.35	6.26	5.46	4.84	4.34	3.94	3.61	3.33	1.53
54	462.45	137.16	77.84	54.00	24.10	15.48	11.40	9.02	7.46	6.36	5.55	4.91	4.41	4.00	3.66	3.38	1.54
55	477.20	140.25	79.38	55.00	24.50	15.73	11.58	9.16	7.58	6.46	5.63	4.99	4.48	4.06	3.72	3.43	1.55
56	492.24	143.36	80.93	56.00	24.90	15.98	11.76	9.30	7.69	6.56	5.72	5.07	4.55	4.13	3.78	3.48	1.56
57	507.57	146.49	82.47	57.00	25.30	16.23	11.94	9.44	7.81	6.66	5.80	5.14	4.61	4.19	3.83	3.53	1.57
58	523.20	149.64	84.02	58.00	25.70	16.47	12.12	9.58	7.92	6.75	5.88	5.21	4.68	4.25	3.89	3.58	1.58
59	539.13	152.81	85.58	59.00	26.10	16.72	12.29	9.72	8.04	6.85	5.97	5.29	4.75	4.31	3.94	3.63	1.59
60	555.36	156.00	87.14	60.00	26.49	16.96	12.47	9.86	8.15	6.94	6.05	5.36	4.81	4.37	3.99	3.68	1.60
61	571.90	159.21	88.70	61.00	26.89	17.20	12.64	9.99	8.26	7.04	6.13	5.43	4.88	4.42	4.05	3.73	1.61
62	588.75	162.44	90.26	62.00	27.28	17.45	12.82	10.13	8.37	7.13	6.22	5.51	4.94	4.48	4.10	3.78	1.62
63	605.91	165.69	91.83	63.00	27.67	17.69	12.99	10.26	8.48	7.23	6.30	5.58	5.01	4.54	4.16	3.83	1.63
64	623.39	168.96	93.40	64.00	28.06	17.93	13.16	10.40	8.59	7.32	6.38	5.65	5.07	4.60	4.21	3.88	1.64
65	641.20	172.25	94.97	65.00	28.45	18.17	13.34	10.53	8.70	7.42	6.46	5.72	5.14	4.66	4.26	3.93	1.65
66	659.33	175.56	96.55	66.00	28.84	18.40	13.51	10.67	8.81	7.51	6.54	5.79	5.20	4.72	4.31	3.98	1.66
67	677.80	178.89	98.13	67.00	29.23	18.64	13.68	10.80	8.92	7.60	6.62	5.86	5.26	4.77	4.37	4.02	1.67
68	696.59	182.24	99.72	68.00	29.61	18.88	13.85	10.93	9.03	7.69	6.70	5.93	5.32	4.83	4.42	4.07	1.68
69	715.73	185.61	101.30	69.00	30.00	19.11	14.02	11.07	9.14	7.78	6.78	6.00	5.39	4.89	4.47	4.12	1.69
70	735.21	189.00	102.89	70.00	30.38	19.35	14.19	11.20	9.25	7.88	6.86	6.07	5.45	4.94	4.52	4.17	1.70
71	755.04	192.41	104.49	71.00	30.77	19.58	14.35	11.33	9.35	7.97	6.94	6.14	5.51	5.00	4.57	4.21	1.71
72	775.21	195.84	106.08	72.00	31.15	19.81	14.52	11.46	9.46	8.06	7.01	6.21	5.57	5.05	4.62	4.26	1.72
73	795.75	199.29	107.68	73.00	31.53	20.05	14.69	11.59	9.57	8.15	7.09	6.28	5.63	5.11	4.67	4.31	1.73
74	816.64	202.76	109.28	74.00	31.91	20.28	14.85	11.71	9.67	8.23	7.17	6.35	5.70	5.16	4.72	4.35	1.74
75	837.89	206.25	110.89	75.00	32.29	20.51	15.02	11.84	9.78	8.32	7.25	6.42	5.76	5.22	4.77	4.40	1.75
76	859.51	209.76	112.50	76.00	32.66	20.74	15.18	11.97	9.88	8.41	7.32	6.48	5.82	5.27	4.82	4.44	1.76
77	881.51	213.29	114.11	77.00	33.04	20.96	15.34	12.10	9.98	8.50	7.40	6.55	5.88	5.33	4.87	4.49	1.77
78	903.88	216.84	115.72	78.00	33.42	21.19	15.51	12.22	10.09	8.59	7.47	6.62	5.94	5.38	4.92	4.54	1.78
79	926.63	220.41	117.34	79.00	33.79	21.42	15.67	12.35	10.19	8.67	7.55	6.68	5.99	5.44	4.97	4.58	1.79
80	949.76	224.00	118.96	80.00	34.16	21.64	15.83	12.47	10.29	8.76	7.62	6.75	6.05	5.49	5.02	4.63	1.80
81	973.28	227.61	120.58	81.00	34.54	21.87	15.99	12.60	10.39	8.85	7.70	6.81	6.11	5.54	5.07	4.67	1.81
82	997.20	231.24	122.21	82.00	34.91	22.09	16.15	12.72	10.50	8.93	7.77	6.88	6.17	5.59	5.12	4.71	1.82
83	1021.51	234.89	123.84	83.00	35.28	22.32	16.31	12.85	10.60	9.02	7.85	6.95	6.23	5.65	5.16	4.76	1.83
84	1046.23	238.56	125.47	84.00	35.65	22.54	16.47	12.97	10.70	9.10	7.92	7.01	6.29	5.70	5.21	4.80	1.84
85	1071.35	242.25	127.11	85.00	36.01	22.76	16.63	13.09	10.80	9.19	7.99	7.07	6.35	5.75	5.26	4.85	1.85
86	1096.88	245.96	128.74	86.00	36.38	22.98	16.78	13.21	10.90	9.27	8.07	7.14	6.40	5.80	5.31	4.89	1.86
87	1122.83	249.69	130.39	87.00	36.75	23.20	16.94	13.34	11.00	9.35	8.14	7.20	6.46	5.86	5.35	4.93	1.87
88	1149.20	253.44	132.03	88.00	37.11	23.42	17.10	13.46	11.09	9.44	8.21	7.27	6.52	5.91	5.40	4.98	1.88
89	1175.99	257.21	133.68	89.00	37.48	23.64	17.25	13.58	11.19	9.52	8.28	7.33	6.57	5.96	5.45	5.02	1.89
90	1203.21	261.00	135.33	90.00	37.84	23.86	17.41	13.70	11.29	9.60	8.35	7.39	6.63	6.01	5.49	5.06	1.90
91	1230.86	264.81	136.98	91.00	38.20	24.07	17.56	13.82	11.39	9.69	8.42	7.45	6.68	6.06	5.54	5.10	1.91
92	1258.95	268.64	138.64	92.00	38.56	24.29	17.71	13.94	11.49	9.77	8.50	7.52	6.74	6.11	5.59	5.15	1.92
93	1287.49	272.49	140.29	93.00	38.92	24.50	17.87	14.05	11.58	9.85	8.57	7.58	6.80	6.16	5.63	5.19	1.93
94	1316.47	276.36	141.96	94.00	39.28	24.72	18.02	14.17	11.68	9.93	8.64	7.64	6.85	6.21	5.68	5.23	1.94
95	1345.90	280.25	143.62	95.00	39.64	24.93	18.17	14.29	11.77	10.01	8.71	7.70	6.91	6.26	5.72	5.27	1.95
96	1375.79	284.16	145.29	96.00	40.00	25.15	18.32	14.41	11.87	10.09	8.78	7.76	6.96	6.31	5.77	5.31	1.96
97	1406.14	288.09	146.96	97.00	40.36	25.36	18.47	14.52	11.96	10.17	8.84	7.82	7.02	6.36	5.81	5.35	1.97
98	1436.95	292.04	148.63	98.00	40.71	25.57	18.62	14.64	12.06	10.25	8.91	7.89	7.07	6.41	5.86	5.40	1.98
99	1468.24	296.01	150.31	99.00	41.07	25.78	18.77	14.75	12.15	10.33	8.98	7.95	7.12	6.46	5.90	5.44	1.99

$$F = 1 \times \left[1 + \frac{r}{100}\right]^n$$

Use of the table. An increase from 1 to 2.10 (a 110% increase), if achieved over 5 years, will have resulted from an annual compound interest or growth rate of 16.00%.

Interest rate or growth rate producing an accumulated amount from 1 unit compounded annually

F \ n	months 3	months 6	months 9	years 1	years 2	years 3	years 4	years 5	years 6	years 7	years 8	years 9	years 10	years 11	years 12	years 13
2.00	1500.00	300.00	151.98	100.00	41.42	25.99	18.92	14.87	12.25	10.41	9.05	8.01	7.18	6.50	5.95	5.48
2.01	1532.24	304.01	153.67	101.00	41.77	26.20	19.07	14.98	12.34	10.49	9.12	8.07	7.23	6.55	5.99	5.52
2.02	1564.97	308.04	155.35	102.00	42.13	26.41	19.22	15.10	12.43	10.57	9.19	8.13	7.28	6.60	6.03	5.56
2.03	1598.18	312.09	157.04	103.00	42.48	26.62	19.36	15.21	12.53	10.64	9.25	8.18	7.34	6.65	6.08	5.60
2.04	1631.89	316.16	158.73	104.00	42.83	26.83	19.51	15.33	12.62	10.72	9.32	8.24	7.39	6.70	6.12	5.64
2.05	1666.10	320.25	160.42	105.00	43.18	27.03	19.66	15.44	12.71	10.80	9.39	8.30	7.44	6.74	6.16	5.68
2.06	1700.81	324.36	162.11	106.00	43.53	27.24	19.80	15.55	12.80	10.88	9.45	8.36	7.49	6.79	6.21	5.72
2.07	1736.04	328.49	163.81	107.00	43.87	27.45	19.95	15.66	12.89	10.95	9.52	8.42	7.55	6.84	6.25	5.76
2.08	1771.77	332.64	165.51	108.00	44.22	27.65	20.09	15.77	12.98	11.03	9.59	8.48	7.60	6.88	6.29	5.80
2.09	1808.03	336.81	167.22	109.00	44.57	27.85	20.24	15.89	13.07	11.11	9.65	8.54	7.65	6.93	6.34	5.83
2.10	1844.81	341.00	168.92	110.00	44.91	28.06	20.38	16.00	13.16	11.18	9.72	8.59	7.70	6.98	6.38	5.87
2.11	1882.12	345.21	170.63	111.00	45.26	28.26	20.52	16.11	13.25	11.26	9.78	8.65	7.75	7.02	6.42	5.91
2.12	1919.96	349.44	172.34	112.00	45.60	28.46	20.67	16.22	13.34	11.33	9.85	8.71	7.80	7.07	6.46	5.95
2.13	1958.35	353.69	174.06	113.00	45.95	28.66	20.81	16.33	13.43	11.41	9.91	8.76	7.85	7.12	6.50	5.99
2.14	1997.27	357.96	175.77	114.00	46.29	28.87	20.95	16.43	13.52	11.48	9.98	8.82	7.90	7.16	6.55	6.03
2.15	2036.75	362.25	177.49	115.00	46.63	29.07	21.09	16.54	13.61	11.56	10.04	8.88	7.96	7.21	6.59	6.07
2.16	2076.78	366.56	179.21	116.00	46.97	29.27	21.23	16.65	13.70	11.63	10.10	8.93	8.01	7.25	6.63	6.10
2.17	2117.37	370.89	180.94	117.00	47.31	29.47	21.37	16.76	13.78	11.70	10.17	8.99	8.06	7.30	6.67	6.14
2.18	2158.53	375.24	182.67	118.00	47.65	29.66	21.51	16.87	13.87	11.78	10.23	9.05	8.10	7.34	6.71	6.18
2.19	2200.26	379.61	184.40	119.00	47.99	29.86	21.65	16.97	13.96	11.85	10.29	9.10	8.15	7.39	6.75	6.22
2.20	2242.56	384.00	186.13	120.00	48.32	30.06	21.79	17.08	14.04	11.92	10.36	9.16	8.20	7.43	6.79	6.25
2.21	2285.44	388.41	187.87	121.00	48.66	30.26	21.93	17.19	14.13	12.00	10.42	9.21	8.25	7.48	6.83	6.29
2.22	2328.91	392.84	189.60	122.00	49.00	30.45	22.06	17.29	14.22	12.07	10.48	9.27	8.30	7.52	6.87	6.33
2.23	2372.97	397.29	191.34	123.00	49.33	30.65	22.20	17.40	14.30	12.14	10.54	9.32	8.35	7.56	6.91	6.36
2.24	2417.63	401.76	193.09	124.00	49.67	30.84	22.34	17.50	14.39	12.21	10.61	9.37	8.40	7.61	6.95	6.40
2.25	2462.89	406.25	194.83	125.00	50.00	31.04	22.47	17.61	14.47	12.28	10.67	9.43	8.45	7.65	6.99	6.44
2.26	2508.76	410.76	196.58	126.00	50.33	31.23	22.61	17.71	14.56	12.35	10.73	9.48	8.50	7.69	7.03	6.47
2.27	2555.24	415.29	198.33	127.00	50.67	31.42	22.75	17.82	14.64	12.42	10.79	9.54	8.54	7.74	7.07	6.51
2.28	2602.34	419.84	200.09	128.00	51.00	31.62	22.88	17.92	14.72	12.50	10.85	9.59	8.59	7.78	7.11	6.55
2.29	2650.06	424.41	201.84	129.00	51.33	31.81	23.02	18.02	14.81	12.57	10.91	9.64	8.64	7.82	7.15	6.58
2.30	2698.41	429.00	203.60	130.00	51.66	32.00	23.15	18.13	14.89	12.64	10.97	9.70	8.69	7.87	7.19	6.62
2.31	2747.40	433.61	205.36	131.00	51.99	32.19	23.28	18.23	14.97	12.71	11.03	9.75	8.73	7.91	7.23	6.65
2.32	2797.02	438.24	207.13	132.00	52.32	32.38	23.42	18.33	15.06	12.77	11.09	9.80	8.78	7.95	7.26	6.69
2.33	2847.30	442.89	208.89	133.00	52.64	32.57	23.55	18.43	15.14	12.84	11.15	9.85	8.83	7.99	7.30	6.72
2.34	2898.22	447.56	210.66	134.00	52.97	32.76	23.68	18.53	15.22	12.91	11.21	9.91	8.87	8.04	7.34	6.76
2.35	2949.80	452.25	212.43	135.00	53.30	32.95	23.81	18.64	15.30	12.98	11.27	9.96	8.92	8.08	7.38	6.79
2.36	3002.04	456.96	214.21	136.00	53.62	33.14	23.94	18.74	15.39	13.05	11.33	10.01	8.97	8.12	7.42	6.83
2.37	3054.96	461.69	215.98	137.00	53.95	33.33	24.08	18.84	15.47	13.12	11.39	10.06	9.01	8.16	7.46	6.86
2.38	3108.54	466.44	217.76	138.00	54.27	33.51	24.21	18.94	15.55	13.19	11.45	10.11	9.06	8.20	7.49	6.90
2.39	3162.81	471.21	219.54	139.00	54.60	33.70	24.34	19.04	15.63	13.25	11.51	10.17	9.10	8.24	7.53	6.93
2.40	3217.76	476.00	221.33	140.00	54.92	33.89	24.47	19.14	15.71	13.32	11.56	10.22	9.15	8.28	7.57	6.97
2.41	3273.40	480.81	223.11	141.00	55.24	34.07	24.60	19.23	15.79	13.39	11.62	10.27	9.19	8.33	7.61	7.00
2.42	3329.74	485.64	224.90	142.00	55.56	34.26	24.73	19.33	15.87	13.46	11.68	10.32	9.24	8.37	7.64	7.03
2.43	3386.78	490.49	226.69	143.00	55.88	34.44	24.85	19.43	15.95	13.52	11.74	10.37	9.29	8.41	7.68	7.07
2.44	3444.54	495.36	228.49	144.00	56.20	34.63	24.98	19.53	16.03	13.59	11.80	10.42	9.33	8.45	7.72	7.10
2.45	3503.00	500.25	230.28	145.00	56.52	34.81	25.11	19.63	16.11	13.66	11.85	10.47	9.37	8.49	7.75	7.14
2.46	3562.19	505.16	232.08	146.00	56.84	34.99	25.24	19.73	16.19	13.72	11.91	10.52	9.42	8.53	7.79	7.17
2.47	3622.10	510.09	233.88	147.00	57.16	35.18	25.36	19.82	16.27	13.79	11.97	10.57	9.46	8.57	7.83	7.20
2.48	3682.74	515.04	235.69	148.00	57.48	35.36	25.49	19.92	16.34	13.85	12.02	10.62	9.51	8.61	7.86	7.24
2.49	3744.12	520.01	237.49	149.00	57.80	35.54	25.62	20.02	16.42	13.92	12.08	10.67	9.55	8.65	7.90	7.27
2.50	3806.25	525.00	239.30	150.00	58.11	35.72	25.74	20.11	16.50	13.99	12.14	10.72	9.60	8.69	7.93	7.30
2.51	3869.13	530.01	241.11	151.00	58.43	35.90	25.87	20.21	16.58	14.05	12.19	10.77	9.64	8.73	7.97	7.34
2.52	3932.76	535.04	242.93	152.00	58.75	36.08	25.99	20.30	16.65	14.12	12.25	10.82	9.68	8.77	8.01	7.37
2.53	3997.15	540.09	244.74	153.00	59.06	36.26	26.12	20.40	16.73	14.18	12.30	10.86	9.73	8.80	8.04	7.40
2.54	4062.31	545.16	246.56	154.00	59.37	36.44	26.24	20.49	16.81	14.24	12.36	10.91	9.77	8.84	8.08	7.43

$$F = 1 \times \left[1 + \frac{r}{100}\right]^n$$

Use of the table. An increase from 1 to 2.60 (a 160% increase), if achieved over 5 years, will have resulted from an annual compound interest or growth rate of 21.06%.

Interest rate or growth rate producing an accumulated amount from 1 unit compounded annually

F \ n	months 3	months 6	months 9	years 1	years 2	years 3	years 4	years 5	years 6	years 7	years 8	years 9	years 10	years 11	years 12	years 13	n / F
2.55	4128.25	550.25	248.38	155.00	59.69	36.62	26.37	20.59	16.88	14.31	12.41	10.96	9.81	8.88	8.11	7.47	2.55
2.56	4194.97	555.36	250.20	156.00	60.00	36.80	26.49	20.68	16.96	14.37	12.47	11.01	9.86	8.92	8.15	7.50	2.56
2.57	4262.47	560.49	252.03	157.00	60.31	36.98	26.61	20.78	17.04	14.44	12.52	11.06	9.90	8.96	8.18	7.53	2.57
2.58	4330.77	565.64	253.86	158.00	60.62	37.15	26.74	20.87	17.11	14.50	12.58	11.11	9.94	9.00	8.22	7.56	2.58
2.59	4399.86	570.81	255.69	159.00	60.93	37.33	26.86	20.97	17.19	14.56	12.63	11.15	9.98	9.04	8.25	7.60	2.59
2.60	4469.76	576.00	257.52	160.00	61.25	37.51	26.98	21.06	17.26	14.63	12.69	11.20	10.03	9.07	8.29	7.63	2.60
2.61	4540.47	581.21	259.35	161.00	61.55	37.68	27.10	21.15	17.34	14.69	12.74	11.25	10.07	9.11	8.32	7.66	2.61
2.62	4612.00	586.44	261.19	162.00	61.86	37.86	27.23	21.24	17.41	14.75	12.79	11.30	10.11	9.15	8.36	7.69	2.62
2.63	4684.35	591.69	263.03	163.00	62.17	38.03	27.35	21.34	17.49	14.81	12.85	11.34	10.15	9.19	8.39	7.72	2.63
2.64	4757.53	596.96	264.87	164.00	62.48	38.21	27.47	21.43	17.56	14.88	12.90	11.39	10.19	9.23	8.43	7.75	2.64
2.65	4831.55	602.25	266.71	165.00	62.79	38.38	27.59	21.52	17.64	14.94	12.96	11.44	10.24	9.26	8.46	7.78	2.65
2.66	4906.41	607.56	268.56	166.00	63.10	38.56	27.71	21.61	17.71	15.00	13.01	11.48	10.28	9.30	8.49	7.82	2.66
2.67	4982.12	612.89	270.14	167.00	63.40	38.73	27.83	21.70	17.78	15.06	13.06	11.53	10.32	9.34	8.53	7.85	2.67
2.68	5058.69	618.24	272.26	168.00	63.71	38.90	27.95	21.79	17.86	15.12	13.11	11.58	10.36	9.38	8.56	7.88	2.68
2.69	5136.11	623.61	274.11	169.00	64.01	39.08	28.07	21.89	17.93	15.18	13.17	11.62	10.40	9.41	8.60	7.91	2.69
2.70	5214.41	629.00	275.97	170.00	64.32	39.25	28.19	21.98	18.00	15.25	13.22	11.67	10.44	9.45	8.63	7.94	2.70
2.71	5293.58	634.41	277.83	171.00	64.62	39.42	28.30	22.07	18.08	15.31	13.27	11.71	10.48	9.49	8.66	7.97	2.71
2.72	5373.63	639.84	279.69	172.00	64.92	39.59	28.42	22.16	18.15	15.37	13.32	11.76	10.52	9.52	8.70	8.00	2.72
2.73	5454.57	645.29	281.55	173.00	65.23	39.76	28.54	22.25	18.22	15.43	13.38	11.81	10.56	9.56	8.73	8.03	2.73
2.74	5536.41	650.76	283.41	174.00	65.53	39.93	28.66	22.33	18.29	15.49	13.43	11.85	10.61	9.60	8.76	8.06	2.74
2.75	5619.14	656.25	285.28	175.00	65.83	40.10	28.78	22.42	18.36	15.55	13.48	11.90	10.65	9.63	8.80	8.09	2.75
2.76	5702.78	661.76	287.15	176.00	66.13	40.27	28.89	22.51	18.44	15.61	13.53	11.94	10.69	9.67	8.83	8.12	2.76
2.77	5787.34	667.29	289.02	177.00	66.43	40.44	29.01	22.60	18.51	15.67	13.58	11.99	10.73	9.70	8.86	8.15	2.77
2.78	5872.82	672.84	290.89	178.00	66.73	40.61	29.13	22.69	18.58	15.73	13.63	12.03	10.77	9.74	8.89	8.18	2.78
2.79	5959.22	678.41	292.77	179.00	67.03	40.78	29.24	22.78	18.65	15.79	13.68	12.08	10.81	9.78	8.93	8.21	2.79
2.80	6046.56	684.00	294.65	180.00	67.33	40.95	29.36	22.87	18.72	15.85	13.74	12.12	10.84	9.81	8.96	8.24	2.80
2.85	6497.50	712.25	304.07	185.00	68.82	41.78	29.93	23.30	19.07	16.14	13.99	12.34	11.04	9.99	9.12	8.39	2.85
2.90	6972.81	741.00	313.55	190.00	70.29	42.60	30.50	23.73	19.42	16.43	14.24	12.56	11.23	10.16	9.28	8.53	2.90
2.95	7473.35	770.25	323.09	195.00	71.76	43.42	31.06	24.16	19.76	16.71	14.48	12.77	11.42	10.33	9.43	8.68	2.95
3.00	8000.00	800.00	332.67	200.00	73.21	44.22	31.61	24.57	20.09	16.99	14.72	12.98	11.61	10.50	9.59	8.82	3.00
3.05	8553.65	830.25	342.32	205.00	74.64	45.02	32.15	24.99	20.42	17.27	14.96	13.19	11.80	10.67	9.74	8.96	3.05
3.10	9135.21	861.00	352.01	210.00	76.07	45.81	32.69	25.39	20.75	17.54	15.19	13.40	11.98	10.83	9.89	9.09	3.10
3.15	9745.60	892.25	361.76	215.00	77.48	46.59	33.22	25.79	21.07	17.81	15.42	13.60	12.16	10.99	10.03	9.23	3.15
3.20	10385.76	924.00	371.56	220.00	78.89	47.36	33.75	26.19	21.39	18.08	15.65	13.80	12.33	11.15	10.18	9.36	3.20
3.25	11056.64	956.25	381.41	225.00	80.28	48.12	34.27	26.58	21.71	18.34	15.87	13.99	12.51	11.31	10.32	9.49	3.25
3.30	11759.21	989.00	391.31	230.00	81.66	48.88	34.78	26.97	22.02	18.60	16.10	14.19	12.68	11.46	10.46	9.62	3.30
3.35	12494.45	1022.25	401.26	235.00	83.03	49.63	35.29	27.35	22.32	18.85	16.31	14.38	12.85	11.62	10.60	9.75	3.35
3.40	13263.36	1056.00	411.26	240.00	84.39	50.37	35.79	27.73	22.63	19.10	16.53	14.57	13.02	11.77	10.74	9.87	3.40
3.45	14066.95	1090.25	421.31	245.00	85.74	51.10	36.29	28.10	22.92	19.35	16.74	14.75	13.18	11.92	10.87	9.99	3.45
3.50	14906.25	1125.00	431.40	250.00	87.08	51.83	36.78	28.47	23.22	19.60	16.95	14.93	13.35	12.06	11.00	10.12	3.50
3.60	16696.16	1196.00	451.74	260.00	89.74	53.26	37.74	29.20	23.80	20.08	17.36	15.30	13.67	12.35	11.26	10.36	3.60
3.70	18641.61	1269.00	472.27	270.00	92.35	54.67	38.69	29.91	24.37	20.55	17.77	15.65	13.98	12.63	11.52	10.59	3.70
3.80	20751.36	1344.00	492.99	280.00	94.94	56.05	39.62	30.60	24.92	21.01	18.16	15.99	14.28	12.90	11.77	10.82	3.80
3.90	23034.41	1421.00	513.88	290.00	97.48	57.41	40.53	31.28	25.46	21.46	18.54	16.33	14.58	13.17	12.01	11.04	3.90
4.00	25500.00	1500.00	534.96	300.00	100.00	58.74	41.42	31.95	25.99	21.90	18.92	16.65	14.87	13.43	12.25	11.25	4.00
4.10	28157.61	1581.00	556.21	310.00	102.48	60.05	42.30	32.60	26.51	22.33	19.29	16.97	15.15	13.69	12.48	11.46	4.10
4.20	31016.96	1664.00	577.64	320.00	104.94	61.34	43.16	33.24	27.02	22.75	19.65	17.29	15.43	13.94	12.70	11.67	4.20
4.30	34088.01	1749.00	599.24	330.00	107.36	62.61	44.00	33.87	27.52	23.17	20.00	17.59	15.70	14.18	12.92	11.87	4.30
4.40	37380.96	1836.00	621.00	340.00	109.76	63.86	44.83	34.49	28.01	23.57	20.35	17.89	15.97	14.42	13.14	12.07	4.40
4.50	40906.25	1925.00	642.93	350.00	112.13	65.10	45.65	35.10	28.49	23.97	20.68	18.19	16.23	14.65	13.35	12.27	4.50
4.60	44674.56	2016.00	665.03	360.00	114.48	66.31	46.45	35.69	28.96	24.36	21.02	18.48	16.49	14.88	13.56	12.46	4.60
4.70	48696.81	2109.00	687.28	370.00	116.79	67.51	47.24	36.28	29.42	24.74	21.34	18.76	16.74	15.11	13.76	12.64	4.70
4.80	52984.16	2204.00	709.70	380.00	119.09	68.69	48.02	36.85	29.88	25.12	21.66	19.04	16.98	15.33	13.96	12.82	4.80
4.90	57548.01	2301.00	732.26	390.00	121.36	69.85	48.78	37.42	30.33	25.49	21.98	19.31	17.22	15.54	14.16	13.00	4.90
5.00	62400.00	2400.00	754.99	400.00	123.61	71.00	49.53	37.97	30.77	25.85	22.28	19.58	17.46	15.76	14.35	13.18	5.00

$$F = 1 \times \left[1 + \frac{r}{100}\right]^n$$

Use of the table. An increase from 1 to 1.10 (a 10% increase), if achieved over 5 years, will have resulted from an annual compound interest or growth rate of 0.64%.

Interest rate or growth rate producing an accumulated amount from 1 unit compounded annually

F \ n	years 14	years 15	years 16	years 17	years 18	years 19	years 20	years 21	years 22	years 23	years 24	years 25	years 30	years 35	years 40	years 45	years 50
0.90	−0.75	−0.70	−0.66	−0.62	−0.58	−0.55	−0.53	−0.50	−0.48	−0.46	−0.44	−0.42	−0.35	−0.30	−0.26	−0.23	−0.21
0.91	−0.67	−0.63	−0.59	−0.55	−0.52	−0.50	−0.47	−0.45	−0.43	−0.41	−0.39	−0.38	−0.31	−0.27	−0.24	−0.21	−0.19
0.92	−0.59	−0.55	−0.52	−0.49	−0.46	−0.44	−0.42	−0.40	−0.38	−0.36	−0.35	−0.33	−0.28	−0.24	−0.21	−0.19	−0.17
0.93	−0.52	−0.48	−0.45	−0.43	−0.40	−0.38	−0.36	−0.34	−0.33	−0.32	−0.30	−0.29	−0.24	−0.21	−0.18	−0.16	−0.15
0.94	−0.44	−0.41	−0.39	−0.36	−0.34	−0.33	−0.31	−0.29	−0.28	−0.27	−0.26	−0.25	−0.21	−0.18	−0.15	−0.14	−0.12
0.95	−0.37	−0.34	−0.32	−0.30	−0.28	−0.27	−0.26	−0.24	−0.23	−0.22	−0.21	−0.20	−0.17	−0.15	−0.13	−0.11	−0.10
0.96	−0.29	−0.27	−0.25	−0.24	−0.23	−0.21	−0.20	−0.19	−0.19	−0.18	−0.17	−0.16	−0.14	−0.12	−0.10	−0.09	−0.08
0.97	−0.22	−0.20	−0.19	−0.18	−0.17	−0.16	−0.15	−0.14	−0.14	−0.13	−0.13	−0.12	−0.10	−0.09	−0.08	−0.07	−0.06
0.98	−0.14	−0.13	−0.13	−0.12	−0.11	−0.11	−0.10	−0.10	−0.09	−0.09	−0.08	−0.08	−0.07	−0.06	−0.05	−0.04	−0.04
0.99	−0.07	−0.07	−0.06	−0.06	−0.06	−0.05	−0.05	−0.05	−0.05	−0.04	−0.04	−0.04	−0.03	−0.03	−0.03	−0.02	−0.02
1.00	0.00	0.00	0.00	0.00	0.00	0.00	0.00	0.00	0.00	0.00	0.00	0.00	0.00	0.00	0.00	0.00	0.00
1.01	0.07	0.07	0.06	0.06	0.06	0.05	0.05	0.05	0.05	0.04	0.04	0.04	0.03	0.03	0.02	0.02	0.02
1.02	0.14	0.13	0.12	0.12	0.11	0.10	0.10	0.09	0.09	0.09	0.08	0.08	0.07	0.06	0.05	0.04	0.04
1.03	0.21	0.20	0.18	0.17	0.16	0.16	0.15	0.14	0.13	0.13	0.12	0.12	0.10	0.08	0.07	0.07	0.06
1.04	0.28	0.26	0.25	0.23	0.22	0.21	0.20	0.19	0.18	0.17	0.16	0.16	0.13	0.11	0.10	0.09	0.08
1.05	0.35	0.33	0.31	0.29	0.27	0.26	0.24	0.23	0.22	0.21	0.20	0.20	0.16	0.14	0.12	0.11	0.10
1.06	0.42	0.39	0.36	0.34	0.32	0.31	0.29	0.28	0.27	0.25	0.24	0.23	0.19	0.17	0.15	0.13	0.12
1.07	0.48	0.45	0.42	0.40	0.38	0.36	0.34	0.32	0.31	0.29	0.28	0.27	0.23	0.19	0.17	0.15	0.14
1.08	0.55	0.51	0.48	0.45	0.43	0.41	0.39	0.37	0.35	0.34	0.32	0.31	0.26	0.22	0.19	0.17	0.15
1.09	0.62	0.58	0.54	0.51	0.48	0.45	0.43	0.41	0.39	0.38	0.36	0.35	0.29	0.25	0.22	0.19	0.17
1.10	0.68	0.64	0.60	0.56	0.53	0.50	0.48	0.45	0.43	0.42	0.40	0.38	0.32	0.27	0.24	0.21	0.19
1.11	0.75	0.70	0.65	0.62	0.58	0.55	0.52	0.50	0.48	0.45	0.44	0.42	0.35	0.30	0.26	0.23	0.21
1.12	0.81	0.76	0.71	0.67	0.63	0.60	0.57	0.54	0.52	0.49	0.47	0.45	0.38	0.32	0.28	0.25	0.23
1.13	0.88	0.82	0.77	0.72	0.68	0.65	0.61	0.58	0.56	0.53	0.51	0.49	0.41	0.35	0.31	0.27	0.24
1.14	0.94	0.88	0.82	0.77	0.73	0.69	0.66	0.63	0.60	0.57	0.55	0.53	0.44	0.38	0.33	0.29	0.26
1.15	1.00	0.94	0.88	0.83	0.78	0.74	0.70	0.67	0.64	0.61	0.58	0.56	0.47	0.40	0.35	0.31	0.28
1.16	1.07	0.99	0.93	0.88	0.83	0.78	0.74	0.71	0.68	0.65	0.62	0.60	0.50	0.42	0.37	0.33	0.30
1.17	1.13	1.05	0.99	0.93	0.88	0.83	0.79	0.75	0.72	0.68	0.66	0.63	0.52	0.45	0.39	0.35	0.31
1.18	1.19	1.11	1.04	0.98	0.92	0.87	0.83	0.79	0.76	0.72	0.69	0.66	0.55	0.47	0.41	0.37	0.33
1.19	1.25	1.17	1.09	1.03	0.97	0.92	0.87	0.83	0.79	0.76	0.73	0.70	0.58	0.50	0.44	0.39	0.35
1.20	1.31	1.22	1.15	1.08	1.02	0.96	0.92	0.87	0.83	0.80	0.76	0.73	0.61	0.52	0.46	0.41	0.37
1.21	1.37	1.28	1.20	1.13	1.06	1.01	0.96	0.91	0.87	0.83	0.80	0.77	0.64	0.55	0.48	0.42	0.38
1.22	1.43	1.33	1.25	1.18	1.11	1.05	1.00	0.95	0.91	0.87	0.83	0.80	0.67	0.57	0.50	0.44	0.40
1.23	1.49	1.39	1.30	1.23	1.16	1.10	1.04	0.99	0.95	0.90	0.87	0.83	0.69	0.59	0.52	0.46	0.41
1.24	1.55	1.44	1.35	1.27	1.20	1.14	1.08	1.03	0.98	0.94	0.90	0.86	0.72	0.62	0.54	0.48	0.43
1.25	1.61	1.50	1.40	1.32	1.25	1.18	1.12	1.07	1.02	0.97	0.93	0.90	0.75	0.64	0.56	0.50	0.45
1.26	1.66	1.55	1.45	1.37	1.29	1.22	1.16	1.11	1.06	1.01	0.97	0.93	0.77	0.66	0.58	0.51	0.46
1.27	1.72	1.61	1.51	1.42	1.34	1.27	1.20	1.14	1.09	1.04	1.00	0.96	0.80	0.69	0.60	0.53	0.48
1.28	1.78	1.66	1.55	1.46	1.38	1.31	1.24	1.18	1.13	1.08	1.03	0.99	0.83	0.71	0.62	0.55	0.49
1.29	1.84	1.71	1.60	1.51	1.42	1.35	1.28	1.22	1.16	1.11	1.07	1.02	0.85	0.73	0.64	0.57	0.51
1.30	1.89	1.76	1.65	1.56	1.47	1.39	1.32	1.26	1.20	1.15	1.10	1.05	0.88	0.75	0.66	0.58	0.53
1.31	1.95	1.82	1.70	1.60	1.51	1.43	1.36	1.29	1.23	1.18	1.13	1.09	0.90	0.77	0.68	0.60	0.54
1.32	2.00	1.87	1.75	1.65	1.55	1.47	1.40	1.33	1.27	1.21	1.16	1.12	0.93	0.80	0.70	0.62	0.56
1.33	2.06	1.92	1.80	1.69	1.60	1.51	1.44	1.37	1.30	1.25	1.20	1.15	0.96	0.82	0.72	0.64	0.57
1.34	2.11	1.97	1.85	1.74	1.64	1.55	1.47	1.40	1.34	1.28	1.23	1.18	0.98	0.84	0.73	0.65	0.59
1.35	2.17	2.02	1.89	1.78	1.68	1.59	1.51	1.44	1.37	1.31	1.26	1.21	1.01	0.86	0.75	0.67	0.60
1.36	2.22	2.07	1.94	1.83	1.72	1.63	1.55	1.47	1.41	1.35	1.29	1.24	1.03	0.88	0.77	0.69	0.62
1.37	2.27	2.12	1.99	1.87	1.76	1.67	1.59	1.51	1.44	1.38	1.32	1.27	1.05	0.90	0.79	0.70	0.63
1.38	2.33	2.17	2.03	1.91	1.81	1.71	1.62	1.55	1.47	1.41	1.35	1.30	1.08	0.92	0.81	0.72	0.65
1.39	2.38	2.22	2.08	1.96	1.85	1.75	1.66	1.58	1.51	1.44	1.38	1.33	1.10	0.95	0.83	0.73	0.66
1.40	2.43	2.27	2.13	2.00	1.89	1.79	1.70	1.62	1.54	1.47	1.41	1.35	1.13	0.97	0.84	0.75	0.68
1.41	2.48	2.32	2.17	2.04	1.93	1.82	1.73	1.65	1.57	1.51	1.44	1.38	1.15	0.99	0.86	0.77	0.69
1.42	2.54	2.37	2.22	2.08	1.97	1.86	1.77	1.68	1.61	1.54	1.47	1.41	1.18	1.01	0.88	0.78	0.70
1.43	2.59	2.41	2.26	2.13	2.01	1.90	1.80	1.72	1.64	1.57	1.50	1.44	1.20	1.03	0.90	0.80	0.72
1.44	2.64	2.46	2.31	2.17	2.05	1.94	1.84	1.75	1.67	1.60	1.53	1.47	1.22	1.05	0.92	0.81	0.73

$$F = 1 \times \left[1 + \frac{r}{100}\right]^n$$

se of the table. An increase from 1 to 1.50 (a 50% increase), if achieved over 15 years, will have resulted from an annual compound interest or rowth rate of 2.74%.

nterest rate or growth rate producing an accumulated amount from 1 unit compounded annually

n / *F*	years 14	years 15	years 16	years 17	years 18	years 19	years 20	years 21	years 22	years 23	years 24	years 25	years 30	years 35	years 40	years 45	years 50	*n* / *F*
1.45	2.69	2.51	2.35	2.21	2.09	1.97	1.88	1.79	1.70	1.63	1.56	1.50	1.25	1.07	0.93	0.83	0.75	1.45
1.46	2.74	2.56	2.39	2.25	2.12	2.01	1.91	1.82	1.74	1.66	1.59	1.53	1.27	1.09	0.95	0.84	0.76	1.46
1.47	2.79	2.60	2.44	2.29	2.16	2.05	1.94	1.85	1.77	1.69	1.62	1.55	1.29	1.11	0.97	0.86	0.77	1.47
1.48	2.84	2.65	2.48	2.33	2.20	2.08	1.98	1.88	1.80	1.72	1.65	1.58	1.32	1.13	0.98	0.88	0.79	1.48
1.49	2.89	2.69	2.52	2.37	2.24	2.12	2.01	1.92	1.83	1.75	1.68	1.61	1.34	1.15	1.00	0.89	0.80	1.49
1.50	2.94	2.74	2.57	2.41	2.28	2.16	2.05	1.95	1.86	1.78	1.70	1.64	1.36	1.17	1.02	0.91	0.81	1.50
1.51	2.99	2.79	2.61	2.45	2.32	2.19	2.08	1.98	1.89	1.81	1.73	1.66	1.38	1.18	1.04	0.92	0.83	1.51
1.52	3.04	2.83	2.65	2.49	2.35	2.23	2.12	2.01	1.92	1.84	1.76	1.69	1.41	1.20	1.05	0.93	0.84	1.52
1.53	3.08	2.88	2.69	2.53	2.39	2.26	2.15	2.05	1.95	1.87	1.79	1.72	1.43	1.22	1.07	0.95	0.85	1.53
1.54	3.13	2.92	2.74	2.57	2.43	2.30	2.18	2.08	1.98	1.90	1.82	1.74	1.45	1.24	1.09	0.96	0.87	1.54
1.55	3.18	2.96	2.78	2.61	2.46	2.33	2.22	2.11	2.01	1.92	1.84	1.77	1.47	1.26	1.10	0.98	0.88	1.55
1.56	3.23	3.01	2.82	2.65	2.50	2.37	2.25	2.14	2.04	1.95	1.87	1.79	1.49	1.28	1.12	0.99	0.89	1.56
1.57	3.27	3.05	2.86	2.69	2.54	2.40	2.28	2.17	2.07	1.98	1.90	1.82	1.51	1.30	1.13	1.01	0.91	1.57
1.58	3.32	3.10	2.90	2.73	2.57	2.44	2.31	2.20	2.10	2.01	1.92	1.85	1.54	1.32	1.15	1.02	0.92	1.58
1.59	3.37	3.14	2.94	2.77	2.61	2.47	2.35	2.23	2.13	2.04	1.95	1.87	1.56	1.33	1.17	1.04	0.93	1.59
1.60	3.41	3.18	2.98	2.80	2.65	2.50	2.38	2.26	2.16	2.06	1.98	1.90	1.58	1.35	1.18	1.05	0.94	1.60
1.61	3.46	3.23	3.02	2.84	2.68	2.54	2.41	2.29	2.19	2.09	2.00	1.92	1.60	1.37	1.20	1.06	0.96	1.61
1.62	3.51	3.27	3.06	2.88	2.72	2.57	2.44	2.32	2.22	2.12	2.03	1.95	1.62	1.39	1.21	1.08	0.97	1.62
1.63	3.55	3.31	3.10	2.92	2.75	2.60	2.47	2.35	2.25	2.15	2.06	1.97	1.64	1.41	1.23	1.09	0.98	1.63
1.64	3.60	3.35	3.14	2.95	2.79	2.64	2.50	2.38	2.27	2.17	2.08	2.00	1.66	1.42	1.24	1.11	0.99	1.64
1.65	3.64	3.39	3.18	2.99	2.82	2.67	2.54	2.41	2.30	2.20	2.11	2.02	1.68	1.44	1.26	1.12	1.01	1.65
1.66	3.69	3.44	3.22	3.03	2.86	2.70	2.57	2.44	2.33	2.23	2.13	2.05	1.70	1.46	1.28	1.13	1.02	1.66
1.67	3.73	3.48	3.26	3.06	2.89	2.74	2.60	2.47	2.36	2.25	2.16	2.07	1.72	1.48	1.29	1.15	1.03	1.67
1.68	3.78	3.52	3.30	3.10	2.92	2.77	2.63	2.50	2.39	2.28	2.19	2.10	1.74	1.49	1.31	1.16	1.04	1.68
1.69	3.82	3.56	3.33	3.13	2.96	2.80	2.66	2.53	2.41	2.31	2.21	2.12	1.76	1.51	1.32	1.17	1.05	1.69
1.70	3.86	3.60	3.37	3.17	2.99	2.83	2.69	2.56	2.44	2.33	2.24	2.15	1.78	1.53	1.34	1.19	1.07	1.70
1.71	3.91	3.64	3.41	3.21	3.03	2.86	2.72	2.59	2.47	2.36	2.26	2.17	1.80	1.54	1.35	1.20	1.08	1.71
1.72	3.95	3.68	3.45	3.24	3.06	2.90	2.75	2.62	2.50	2.39	2.29	2.19	1.82	1.56	1.37	1.21	1.09	1.72
1.73	3.99	3.72	3.49	3.28	3.09	2.93	2.78	2.64	2.52	2.41	2.31	2.22	1.84	1.58	1.38	1.23	1.10	1.73
1.74	4.04	3.76	3.52	3.31	3.12	2.96	2.81	2.67	2.55	2.44	2.33	2.24	1.86	1.60	1.39	1.24	1.11	1.74
1.75	4.08	3.80	3.56	3.35	3.16	2.99	2.84	2.70	2.58	2.46	2.36	2.26	1.88	1.61	1.41	1.25	1.13	1.75
1.76	4.12	3.84	3.60	3.38	3.19	3.02	2.87	2.73	2.60	2.49	2.38	2.29	1.90	1.63	1.42	1.26	1.14	1.76
1.77	4.16	3.88	3.63	3.42	3.22	3.05	2.90	2.76	2.63	2.51	2.41	2.31	1.92	1.64	1.44	1.28	1.15	1.77
1.78	4.20	3.92	3.67	3.45	3.26	3.08	2.93	2.78	2.66	2.54	2.43	2.33	1.94	1.66	1.45	1.29	1.16	1.78
1.79	4.25	3.96	3.71	3.48	3.29	3.11	2.95	2.81	2.68	2.56	2.46	2.36	1.96	1.68	1.47	1.30	1.17	1.79
1.80	4.29	4.00	3.74	3.52	3.32	3.14	2.98	2.84	2.71	2.59	2.48	2.38	1.98	1.69	1.48	1.31	1.18	1.80
1.81	4.33	4.03	3.78	3.55	3.35	3.17	3.01	2.87	2.73	2.61	2.50	2.40	2.00	1.71	1.49	1.33	1.19	1.81
1.82	4.37	4.07	3.81	3.59	3.38	3.20	3.04	2.89	2.76	2.64	2.53	2.42	2.02	1.73	1.51	1.34	1.20	1.82
1.83	4.41	4.11	3.85	3.62	3.41	3.23	3.07	2.92	2.78	2.66	2.55	2.45	2.03	1.74	1.52	1.35	1.22	1.83
1.84	4.45	4.15	3.88	3.65	3.45	3.26	3.10	2.95	2.81	2.69	2.57	2.47	2.05	1.76	1.54	1.36	1.23	1.84
1.85	4.49	4.19	3.92	3.69	3.48	3.29	3.12	2.97	2.84	2.71	2.60	2.49	2.07	1.77	1.55	1.38	1.24	1.85
1.86	4.53	4.22	3.95	3.72	3.51	3.32	3.15	3.00	2.86	2.73	2.62	2.51	2.09	1.79	1.56	1.39	1.25	1.86
1.87	4.57	4.26	3.99	3.75	3.54	3.35	3.18	3.03	2.89	2.76	2.64	2.54	2.11	1.80	1.58	1.40	1.26	1.87
1.88	4.61	4.30	4.02	3.78	3.57	3.38	3.21	3.05	2.91	2.78	2.67	2.56	2.13	1.82	1.59	1.41	1.27	1.88
1.89	4.65	4.34	4.06	3.82	3.60	3.41	3.23	3.08	2.94	2.81	2.69	2.58	2.14	1.84	1.60	1.42	1.28	1.89
1.90	4.69	4.37	4.09	3.85	3.63	3.44	3.26	3.10	2.96	2.83	2.71	2.60	2.16	1.85	1.62	1.44	1.29	1.90
1.91	4.73	4.41	4.13	3.88	3.66	3.46	3.29	3.13	2.99	2.85	2.73	2.62	2.18	1.87	1.63	1.45	1.30	1.91
1.92	4.77	4.44	4.16	3.91	3.69	3.49	3.32	3.16	3.01	2.88	2.76	2.64	2.20	1.88	1.64	1.46	1.31	1.92
1.93	4.81	4.48	4.20	3.94	3.72	3.52	3.34	3.18	3.03	2.90	2.78	2.66	2.22	1.90	1.66	1.47	1.32	1.93
1.94	4.85	4.52	4.23	3.98	3.75	3.55	3.37	3.21	3.06	2.92	2.80	2.69	2.23	1.91	1.67	1.48	1.33	1.94
1.95	4.89	4.55	4.26	4.01	3.78	3.58	3.40	3.23	3.08	2.95	2.82	2.71	2.25	1.93	1.68	1.50	1.34	1.95
1.96	4.92	4.59	4.30	4.04	3.81	3.61	3.42	3.26	3.11	2.97	2.84	2.73	2.27	1.94	1.70	1.51	1.35	1.96
1.97	4.96	4.62	4.33	4.07	3.84	3.63	3.45	3.28	3.13	2.99	2.87	2.75	2.29	1.96	1.71	1.52	1.37	1.97
1.98	5.00	4.66	4.36	4.10	3.87	3.66	3.47	3.31	3.15	3.01	2.89	2.77	2.30	1.97	1.72	1.53	1.38	1.98
1.99	5.04	4.69	4.39	4.13	3.90	3.69	3.50	3.33	3.18	3.04	2.91	2.79	2.32	1.99	1.74	1.54	1.39	1.99

$$F = 1 \times \left[1 + \frac{r}{100}\right]^n$$

Use of the table. An increase from 1 to 2.10 (a 110% increase), if achieved over 15 years, will have resulted from an annual compound interest or growth rate of 5.07%.

Interest rate or growth rate producing an accumulated amount from 1 unit compounded annually

F \ n	years 14	years 15	years 16	years 17	years 18	years 19	years 20	years 21	years 22	years 23	years 24	years 25	years 30	years 35	years 40	years 45	years 50
2.00	5.08	4.73	4.43	4.16	3.93	3.72	3.53	3.36	3.20	3.06	2.93	2.81	2.34	2.00	1.75	1.55	1.40
2.01	5.11	4.76	4.46	4.19	3.95	3.74	3.55	3.38	3.22	3.08	2.95	2.83	2.35	2.01	1.76	1.56	1.41
2.02	5.15	4.80	4.49	4.22	3.98	3.77	3.58	3.40	3.25	3.10	2.97	2.85	2.37	2.03	1.77	1.57	1.42
2.03	5.19	4.83	4.52	4.25	4.01	3.80	3.60	3.43	3.27	3.13	2.99	2.87	2.39	2.04	1.79	1.59	1.43
2.04	5.22	4.87	4.56	4.28	4.04	3.82	3.63	3.45	3.29	3.15	3.02	2.89	2.40	2.06	1.80	1.60	1.44
2.05	5.26	4.90	4.59	4.31	4.07	3.85	3.65	3.48	3.32	3.17	3.04	2.91	2.42	2.07	1.81	1.61	1.45
2.06	5.30	4.94	4.62	4.34	4.10	3.88	3.68	3.50	3.34	3.19	3.06	2.93	2.44	2.09	1.82	1.62	1.46
2.07	5.33	4.97	4.65	4.37	4.12	3.90	3.70	3.53	3.36	3.21	3.08	2.95	2.45	2.10	1.84	1.63	1.47
2.08	5.37	5.00	4.68	4.40	4.15	3.93	3.73	3.55	3.38	3.24	3.10	2.97	2.47	2.11	1.85	1.64	1.48
2.09	5.41	5.04	4.72	4.43	4.18	3.96	3.75	3.57	3.41	3.26	3.12	2.99	2.49	2.13	1.86	1.65	1.49
2.10	5.44	5.07	4.75	4.46	4.21	3.98	3.78	3.60	3.43	3.28	3.14	3.01	2.50	2.14	1.87	1.66	1.49
2.11	5.48	5.10	4.78	4.49	4.24	4.01	3.80	3.62	3.45	3.30	3.16	3.03	2.52	2.16	1.88	1.67	1.50
2.12	5.51	5.14	4.81	4.52	4.26	4.03	3.83	3.64	3.47	3.32	3.18	3.05	2.54	2.17	1.90	1.68	1.51
2.13	5.55	5.17	4.84	4.55	4.29	4.06	3.85	3.67	3.50	3.34	3.20	3.07	2.55	2.18	1.91	1.69	1.52
2.14	5.58	5.20	4.87	4.58	4.32	4.09	3.88	3.69	3.52	3.36	3.22	3.09	2.57	2.20	1.92	1.71	1.53
2.15	5.62	5.24	4.90	4.61	4.34	4.11	3.90	3.71	3.54	3.38	3.24	3.11	2.58	2.21	1.93	1.72	1.54
2.16	5.65	5.27	4.93	4.63	4.37	4.14	3.93	3.74	3.56	3.40	3.26	3.13	2.60	2.22	1.94	1.73	1.55
2.17	5.69	5.30	4.96	4.66	4.40	4.16	3.95	3.76	3.58	3.43	3.28	3.15	2.62	2.24	1.96	1.74	1.56
2.18	5.72	5.33	4.99	4.69	4.42	4.19	3.97	3.78	3.61	3.45	3.30	3.17	2.63	2.25	1.97	1.75	1.57
2.19	5.76	5.36	5.02	4.72	4.45	4.21	4.00	3.80	3.63	3.47	3.32	3.19	2.65	2.26	1.98	1.76	1.58
2.20	5.79	5.40	5.05	4.75	4.48	4.24	4.02	3.83	3.65	3.49	3.34	3.20	2.66	2.28	1.99	1.77	1.59
2.21	5.83	5.43	5.08	4.78	4.50	4.26	4.04	3.85	3.67	3.51	3.36	3.22	2.68	2.29	2.00	1.78	1.60
2.22	5.86	5.46	5.11	4.80	4.53	4.29	4.07	3.87	3.69	3.53	3 38	3.24	2.69	2.30	2.01	1.79	1.61
2.23	5.90	5.49	5.14	4.83	4.56	4.31	4.09	3.89	3.71	3.55	3.40	3.26	2.71	2.32	2.03	1.80	1.62
2.24	5.93	5.52	5.17	4.86	4.58	4.34	4.11	3.92	3.73	3.57	3.42	3.28	2.72	2.33	2.04	1.81	1.63
2.25	5.96	5.56	5.20	4.89	4.61	4.36	4.14	3.94	3.75	3.59	3.44	3.30	2.74	2.34	2.05	1.82	1.64
2.26	6.00	5.59	5.23	4.91	4.63	4.38	4.16	3.96	3.78	3.61	3.46	3.32	2.76	2.36	2.06	1.83	1.64
2.27	6.03	5.62	5.26	4.94	4.66	4.41	4.18	3.98	3.80	3.63	3.47	3.33	2.77	2.37	2.07	1.84	1.65
2.28	6.06	5.65	5.29	4.97	4.69	4.43	4.21	4.00	3.82	3.65	3.49	3.35	2.79	2.38	2.08	1.85	1.66
2.29	6.10	5.68	5.31	4.99	4.71	4.46	4.23	4.02	3.84	3.67	3.51	3.37	2.80	2.40	2.09	1.86	1.67
2.30	6.13	5.71	5.34	5.02	4.74	4.48	4.25	4.05	3.86	3.69	3.53	3.39	2.82	2.41	2.10	1.87	1.68
2.35	6.29	5.86	5.49	5.15	4.86	4.60	4.36	4.15	3.96	3.78	3.62	3.48	2.89	2.47	2.16	1.92	1.72
2.40	6.45	6.01	5.62	5.28	4.98	4.72	4.47	4.26	4.06	3.88	3.72	3.56	2.96	2.53	2.21	1.96	1.77
2.45	6.61	6.16	5.76	5.41	5.10	4.83	4.58	4.36	4.16	3.97	3.80	3.65	3.03	2.59	2.27	2.01	1.81
2.50	6.76	6.30	5.89	5.54	5.22	4.94	4.69	4.46	4.25	4.06	3.89	3.73	3.10	2.65	2.32	2.06	1.85
2.60	7.06	6.58	6.15	5.78	5.45	5.16	4.89	4.66	4.44	4.24	4.06	3.90	3.24	2.77	2.42	2.15	1.93
2.70	7.35	6.85	6.40	6.02	5.67	5.37	5.09	4.84	4.62	4.41	4.23	4.05	3.37	2.88	2.51	2.23	2.01
2.80	7.63	7.11	6.65	6.24	5.89	5.57	5.28	5.03	4.79	4.58	4.38	4.20	3.49	2.99	2.61	2.31	2.08
2.90	7.90	7.36	6.88	6.46	6.09	5.76	5.47	5.20	4.96	4.74	4.54	4.35	3.61	3.09	2.70	2.39	2.15
3.00	8.16	7.60	7.11	6.68	6.29	5.95	5.65	5.37	5.12	4.89	4.68	4.49	3.73	3.19	2.78	2.47	2.22
3.10	8.42	7.83	7.33	6.88	6.49	6.14	5.82	5.54	5.28	5.04	4.83	4.63	3.84	3.29	2.87	2.55	2.29
3.20	8.66	8.06	7.54	7.08	6.68	6.31	5.99	5.70	5.43	5.19	4.97	4.76	3.95	3.38	2.95	2.62	2.35
3.30	8.90	8.28	7.75	7.28	6.86	6.49	6.15	5.85	5.58	5.33	5.10	4.89	4.06	3.47	3.03	2.69	2.42
3.40	9.13	8.50	7.95	7.46	7.04	6.65	6.31	6.00	5.72	5.46	5.23	5.02	4.16	3.56	3.11	2.76	2.48
3.50	9.36	8.71	8.14	7.65	7.21	6.82	6.46	6.15	5.86	5.60	5.36	5.14	4.26	3.64	3.18	2.82	2.54
3.60	9.58	8.91	8.34	7.83	7.38	6.97	6.61	6.29	6.00	5.73	5.48	5.26	4.36	3.73	3.25	2.89	2.59
3.70	9.80	9.11	8.52	8.00	7.54	7.13	6.76	6.43	6.13	5.85	5.60	5.37	4.46	3.81	3.32	2.95	2.65
3.80	10.01	9.31	8.70	8.17	7.70	7.28	6.90	6.56	6.26	5.98	5.72	5.49	4.55	3.89	3.39	3.01	2.71
3.90	10.21	9.50	8.88	8.33	7.85	7.43	7.04	6.70	6.38	6.10	5.83	5.59	4.64	3.97	3.46	3.07	2.76
4.00	10.41	9.68	9.05	8.50	8.01	7.57	7.18	6.82	6.50	6.21	5.95	5.70	4.73	4.04	3.53	3.13	2.81
4.10	10.60	9.86	9.22	8.65	8.15	7.71	7.31	6.95	6.62	6.33	6.06	5.81	4.82	4.11	3.59	3.19	2.86
4.20	10.79	10.04	9.38	8.81	8.30	7.85	7.44	7.07	6.74	6.44	6.16	5.91	4.90	4.19	3.65	3.24	2.91
4.30	10.98	10.21	9.54	8.96	8.44	7.98	7.57	7.19	6.85	6.55	6.27	6.01	4.98	4.26	3.71	3.29	2.96
4.40	11.16	10.38	9.70	9.11	8.58	8.11	7.69	7.31	6.97	6.65	6.37	6.11	5.06	4.32	3.77	3.35	3.01
4.50	11.34	10.55	9.86	9.25	8.72	8.24	7.81	7.42	7.08	6.76	6.47	6.20	5.14	4.39	3.83	3.40	3.05

$= 1 \times \left[1 + \frac{r}{100}\right]^n$

se of the table. An increase from 1 to 5.10 (a 410% increase), if achieved over 15 years, will have resulted from an annual compound interest or owth rate of 11.47%.

nterest rate or growth rate producing an accumulated amount from 1 unit compounded annually

n	years 14	years 15	years 16	years 17	years 18	years 19	years 20	years 21	years 22	years 23	years 24	years 25	years 30	years 35	years 40	years 45	years 50	n F
4.60	11.52	10.71	10.01	9.39	8.85	8.36	7.93	7.54	7.18	6.86	6.57	6.29	5.22	4.46	3.89	3.45	3.10	4.60
4.70	11.69	10.87	10.16	9.53	8.98	8.49	8.05	7.65	7.29	6.96	6.66	6.39	5.29	4.52	3.94	3.50	3.14	4.70
4.80	11.86	11.02	10.30	9.67	9.11	8.61	8.16	7.76	7.39	7.06	6.75	6.48	5.37	4.58	4.00	3.55	3.19	4.80
4.90	12.02	11.18	10.44	9.80	9.23	8.72	8.27	7.86	7.49	7.15	6.85	6.56	5.44	4.65	4.05	3.59	3.23	4.90
5.00	12.18	11.33	10.58	9.93	9.35	8.84	8.38	7.97	7.59	7.25	6.94	6.65	5.51	4.71	4.11	3.64	3.27	5.00
5.10	12.34	11.47	10.72	10.06	9.47	8.95	8.49	8.07	7.69	7.34	7.02	6.73	5.58	4.77	4.16	3.69	3.31	5.10
5.20	12.50	11.62	10.85	10.18	9.59	9.06	8.59	8.17	7.78	7.43	7.11	6.82	5.65	4.82	4.21	3.73	3.35	5.20
5.30	12.65	11.76	10.99	10.31	9.71	9.17	8.70	8.27	7.88	7.52	7.20	6.90	5.72	4.88	4.26	3.78	3.39	5.30
5.40	12.80	11.90	11.12	10.43	9.82	9.28	8.80	8.36	7.97	7.61	7.28	6.98	5.78	4.94	4.31	3.82	3.43	5.40
5.50	12.95	12.04	11.24	10.55	9.93	9.39	8.90	8.46	8.06	7.69	7.36	7.06	5.85	4.99	4.35	3.86	3.47	5.50
5.60	13.09	12.17	11.37	10.67	10.04	9.49	9.00	8.55	8.15	7.78	7.44	7.13	5.91	5.05	4.40	3.90	3.51	5.60
5.70	13.24	12.30	11.49	10.78	10.15	9.59	9.09	8.64	8.23	7.86	7.52	7.21	5.97	5.10	4.45	3.94	3.54	5.70
5.80	13.38	12.43	11.61	10.89	10.26	9.69	9.19	8.73	8.32	7.94	7.60	7.28	6.03	5.15	4.49	3.98	3.58	5.80
5.90	13.52	12.56	11.73	11.01	10.36	9.79	9.28	8.82	8.40	8.02	7.68	7.36	6.10	5.20	4.54	4.02	3.61	5.90
6.00	13.65	12.69	11.85	11.12	10.47	9.89	9.37	8.91	8.49	8.10	7.75	7.43	6.15	5.25	4.58	4.06	3.65	6.00
6.10	13.79	12.81	11.97	11.22	10.57	9.98	9.46	8.99	8.57	8.18	7.83	7.50	6.21	5.30	4.62	4.10	3.68	6.10
6.20	13.92	12.93	12.08	11.33	10.67	10.08	9.55	9.08	8.65	8.26	7.90	7.57	6.27	5.35	4.67	4.14	3.72	6.20
6.30	14.05	13.05	12.19	11.43	10.77	10.17	9.64	9.16	8.73	8.33	7.97	7.64	6.33	5.40	4.71	4.17	3.75	6.30
6.40	14.18	13.17	12.30	11.54	10.86	10.26	9.73	9.24	8.80	8.41	8.04	7.71	6.38	5.45	4.75	4.21	3.78	6.40
6.50	14.31	13.29	12.41	11.64	10.96	10.35	9.81	9.32	8.88	8.48	8.11	7.77	6.44	5.49	4.79	4.25	3.81	6.50
6.60	14.43	13.41	12.52	11.74	11.05	10.44	9.89	9.40	8.96	8.55	8.18	7.84	6.49	5.54	4.83	4.28	3.85	6.60
6.70	14.55	13.52	12.62	11.84	11.15	10.53	9.98	9.48	9.03	8.62	8.25	7.91	6.55	5.58	4.87	4.32	3.88	6.70
6.80	14.67	13.63	12.73	11.94	11.24	10.62	10.06	9.56	9.10	8.69	8.31	7.97	6.60	5.63	4.91	4.35	3.91	6.80
6.90	14.79	13.74	12.83	12.03	11.33	10.70	10.14	9.63	9.18	8.76	8.38	8.03	6.65	5.67	4.95	4.39	3.94	6.90
7.00	14.91	13.85	12.93	12.13	11.42	10.78	10.22	9.71	9.25	8.83	8.45	8.09	6.70	5.72	4.99	4.42	3.97	7.00
7.10	15.03	13.96	13.03	12.22	11.50	10.87	10.30	9.78	9.32	8.90	8.51	8.16	6.75	5.76	5.02	4.45	4.00	7.10
7.20	15.14	14.07	13.13	12.31	11.59	10.95	10.37	9.86	9.39	8.96	8.57	8.22	6.80	5.80	5.06	4.48	4.03	7.20
7.30	15.26	14.17	13.23	12.40	11.68	11.03	10.45	9.93	9.46	9.03	8.64	8.28	6.85	5.84	5.10	4.52	4.06	7.30
7.40	15.37	14.27	13.33	12.49	11.76	11.11	10.53	10.00	9.52	9.09	8.70	8.34	6.90	5.89	5.13	4.55	4.08	7.40
7.50	15.48	14.38	13.42	12.58	11.84	11.19	10.60	10.07	9.59	9.16	8.76	8.39	6.95	5.93	5.17	4.58	4.11	7.50
7.60	15.59	14.48	13.51	12.67	11.93	11.27	10.67	10.14	9.66	9.22	8.82	8.45	6.99	5.97	5.20	4.61	4.14	7.60
7.70	15.70	14.58	13.61	12.76	12.01	11.34	10.75	10.21	9.72	9.28	8.88	8.51	7.04	6.01	5.24	4.64	4.17	7.70
7.80	15.80	14.68	13.70	12.84	12.09	11.42	10.82	10.28	9.79	9.34	8.94	8.56	7.09	6.04	5.27	4.67	4.19	7.80
7.90	15.91	14.77	13.79	12.93	12.17	11.49	10.89	10.34	9.85	9.40	8.99	8.62	7.13	6.08	5.30	4.70	4.22	7.90
8.00	16.01	14.87	13.88	13.01	12.25	11.57	10.96	10.41	9.91	9.46	9.05	8.67	7.18	6.12	5.34	4.73	4.25	8.00
8.10	16.12	14.97	13.97	13.09	12.32	11.64	11.03	10.47	9.98	9.52	9.11	8.73	7.22	6.16	5.37	4.76	4.27	8.10
8.20	16.22	15.06	14.05	13.18	12.40	11.71	11.09	10.54	10.04	9.58	9.16	8.78	7.27	6.20	5.40	4.79	4.30	8.20
8.30	16.32	15.15	14.14	13.26	12.48	11.78	11.16	10.60	10.10	9.64	9.22	8.83	7.31	6.23	5.43	4.82	4.32	8.30
8.40	16.42	15.24	14.23	13.34	12.55	11.85	11.23	10.67	10.16	9.69	9.27	8.89	7.35	6.27	5.46	4.84	4.35	8.40
8.50	16.52	15.34	14.31	13.42	12.62	11.92	11.29	10.73	10.22	9.75	9.33	8.94	7.39	6.31	5.50	4.87	4.37	8.50
8.60	16.61	15.43	14.39	13.49	12.70	11.99	11.36	10.79	10.28	9.81	9.38	8.99	7.44	6.34	5.53	4.90	4.40	8.60
8.70	16.71	15.51	14.48	13.57	12.77	12.06	11.42	10.85	10.33	9.86	9.43	9.04	7.48	6.38	5.56	4.92	4.42	8.70
8.80	16.81	15.60	14.56	13.65	12.84	12.13	11.49	10.91	10.39	9.92	9.48	9.09	7.52	6.41	5.59	4.95	4.45	8.80
8.90	16.90	15.69	14.64	13.72	12.91	12.19	11.55	10.97	10.45	9.97	9.54	9.14	7.56	6.45	5.62	4.98	4.47	8.90
9.00	16.99	15.78	14.72	13.80	12.98	12.26	11.61	11.03	10.50	10.02	9.59	9.19	7.60	6.48	5.65	5.00	4.49	9.00
9.10	17.09	15.86	14.80	13.87	13.05	12.32	11.67	11.09	10.56	10.08	9.64	9.23	7.64	6.51	5.68	5.03	4.52	9.10
9.20	17.18	15.95	14.88	13.94	13.12	12.39	11.74	11.15	10.61	10.13	9.69	9.28	7.68	6.55	5.70	5.06	4.54	9.20
9.30	17.27	16.03	14.96	14.02	13.19	12.45	11.80	11.20	10.67	10.18	9.74	9.33	7.72	6.58	5.73	5.08	4.56	9.30
9.40	17.36	16.11	15.03	14.09	13.26	12.52	11.86	11.26	10.72	10.23	9.79	9.38	7.76	6.61	5.76	5.11	4.58	9.40
9.50	17.45	16.19	15.11	14.16	13.32	12.58	11.91	11.32	10.78	10.28	9.83	9.42	7.79	6.64	5.79	5.13	4.61	9.50
9.60	17.53	16.27	15.18	14.23	13.39	12.64	11.97	11.37	10.83	10.33	9.88	9.47	7.83	6.68	5.82	5.15	4.63	9.60
9.70	17.62	16.35	15.26	14.30	13.45	12.70	12.03	11.43	10.88	10.38	9.93	9.51	7.87	6.71	5.84	5.18	4.65	9.70
9.80	17.71	16.43	15.33	14.37	13.52	12.76	12.09	11.48	10.93	10.43	9.98	9.56	7.90	6.74	5.87	5.20	4.67	9.80
9.90	17.79	16.51	15.41	14.44	13.58	12.82	12.15	11.54	10.98	10.48	10.02	9.60	7.94	6.77	5.90	5.23	4.69	9.90
10.00	17.88	16.59	15.48	14.50	13.65	12.88	12.20	11.59	11.03	10.53	10.07	9.65	7.98	6.80	5.93	5.25	4.71	10.00

$$F = 1 \times \left[1 + \frac{r}{100}\right]^n$$

Use of the table. The table shows the amount (*F* in the formula) accumulated from 1 unit growing at the annual compound interest rate shown at the head of a column (*r*) over the period shown in the column at each side of a line (*n*). For example, where the annual compound interest rate earned is 0.50%, 1 unit accumulates after 5 years to 1.0253.

Interest rates: accumulated amount of 1 unit

n Years \ *r*	% rate 0.25	% rate 0.50	% rate 0.75	% rate 1.00	% rate 1.25	% rate 1.50	% rate 1.75	% rate 2.00	% rate 2.25	% rate 2.50
1	1.0025	1.0050	1.0075	1.0100	1.0125	1.0150	1.0175	1.0200	1.0225	1.0250
2	1.0050	1.0100	1.0151	1.0201	1.0252	1.0302	1.0353	1.0404	1.0455	1.0506
3	1.0075	1.0151	1.0227	1.0303	1.0380	1.0457	1.0534	1.0612	1.0690	1.0769
4	1.0100	1.0202	1.0303	1.0406	1.0509	1.0614	1.0719	1.0824	1.0931	1.1038
5	1.0126	1.0253	1.0381	1.0510	1.0641	1.0773	1.0906	1.1041	1.1177	1.1314
6	1.0151	1.0304	1.0459	1.0615	1.0774	1.0934	1.1097	1.1262	1.1428	1.1597
7	1.0176	1.0355	1.0537	1.0721	1.0909	1.1098	1.1291	1.1487	1.1685	1.1887
8	1.0202	1.0407	1.0616	1.0829	1.1045	1.1265	1.1489	1.1717	1.1948	1.2184
9	1.0227	1.0459	1.0696	1.0937	1.1183	1.1434	1.1690	1.1951	1.2217	1.2489
10	1.0253	1.0511	1.0776	1.1046	1.1323	1.1605	1.1894	1.2190	1.2492	1.2801
11	1.0278	1.0564	1.0857	1.1157	1.1464	1.1779	1.2103	1.2434	1.2773	1.3121
12	1.0304	1.0617	1.0938	1.1268	1.1608	1.1956	1.2314	1.2682	1.3060	1.3449
13	1.0330	1.0670	1.1020	1.1381	1.1753	1.2136	1.2530	1.2936	1.3354	1.3785
14	1.0356	1.0723	1.1103	1.1495	1.1900	1.2318	1.2749	1.3195	1.3655	1.4130
15	1.0382	1.0777	1.1186	1.1610	1.2048	1.2502	1.2972	1.3459	1.3962	1.4483
16	1.0408	1.0831	1.1270	1.1726	1.2199	1.2690	1.3199	1.3728	1.4276	1.4845
17	1.0434	1.0885	1.1354	1.1843	1.2351	1.2880	1.3430	1.4002	1.4597	1.5216
18	1.0460	1.0939	1.1440	1.1961	1.2506	1.3073	1.3665	1.4282	1.4926	1.5597
19	1.0486	1.0994	1.1525	1.2081	1.2662	1.3270	1.3904	1.4568	1.5262	1.5987
20	1.0512	1.1049	1.1612	1.2202	1.2820	1.3469	1.4148	1.4859	1.5605	1.6386
21	1.0538	1.1104	1.1699	1.2324	1.2981	1.3671	1.4395	1.5157	1.5956	1.6796
22	1.0565	1.1160	1.1787	1.2447	1.3143	1.3876	1.4647	1.5460	1.6315	1.7216
23	1.0591	1.1216	1.1875	1.2572	1.3307	1.4084	1.4904	1.5769	1.6682	1.7646
24	1.0618	1.1272	1.1964	1.2697	1.3474	1.4295	1.5164	1.6084	1.7058	1.8087
25	1.0644	1.1328	1.2054	1.2824	1.3642	1.4509	1.5430	1.6406	1.7441	1.8539
26	1.0671	1.1385	1.2144	1.2953	1.3812	1.4727	1.5700	1.6734	1.7834	1.9003
27	1.0697	1.1442	1.2235	1.3082	1.3985	1.4948	1.5975	1.7069	1.8235	1.9478
28	1.0724	1.1499	1.2327	1.3213	1.4160	1.5172	1.6254	1.7410	1.8645	1.9965
29	1.0751	1.1556	1.2420	1.3345	1.4337	1.5400	1.6539	1.7758	1.9065	2.0464
30	1.0778	1.1614	1.2513	1.3478	1.4516	1.5631	1.6828	1.8114	1.9494	2.0976
31	1.0805	1.1672	1.2607	1.3613	1.4698	1.5865	1.7122	1.8476	1.9933	2.1500
32	1.0832	1.1730	1.2701	1.3749	1.4881	1.6103	1.7422	1.8845	2.0381	2.2038
33	1.0859	1.1789	1.2796	1.3887	1.5067	1.6345	1.7727	1.9222	2.0840	2.2589
34	1.0886	1.1848	1.2892	1.4026	1.5256	1.6590	1.8037	1.9607	2.1308	2.3153
35	1.0913	1.1907	1.2989	1.4166	1.5446	1.6839	1.8353	1.9999	2.1788	2.3732
36	1.0941	1.1967	1.3086	1.4308	1.5639	1.7091	1.8674	2.0399	2.2278	2.4325
37	1.0968	1.2027	1.3185	1.4451	1.5835	1.7348	1.9001	2.0807	2.2779	2.4933
38	1.0995	1.2087	1.3283	1.4595	1.6033	1.7608	1.9333	2.1223	2.3292	2.5557
39	1.1023	1.2147	1.3383	1.4741	1.6233	1.7872	1.9672	2.1647	2.3816	2.6196
40	1.1050	1.2208	1.3483	1.4889	1.6436	1.8140	2.0016	2.2080	2.4352	2.6851
41	1.1078	1.2269	1.3585	1.5038	1.6642	1.8412	2.0366	2.2522	2.4900	2.7522
42	1.1106	1.2330	1.3686	1.5188	1.6850	1.8688	2.0723	2.2972	2.5460	2.8210
43	1.1133	1.2392	1.3789	1.5340	1.7060	1.8969	2.1085	2.3432	2.6033	2.8915
44	1.1161	1.2454	1.3893	1.5493	1.7274	1.9253	2.1454	2.3901	2.6619	2.9638
45	1.1189	1.2516	1.3997	1.5648	1.7489	1.9542	2.1830	2.4379	2.7218	3.0379
46	1.1217	1.2579	1.4102	1.5805	1.7708	1.9835	2.2212	2.4866	2.7830	3.1139
47	1.1245	1.2642	1.4207	1.5963	1.7929	2.0133	2.2600	2.5363	2.8456	3.1917
48	1.1273	1.2705	1.4314	1.6122	1.8154	2.0435	2.2996	2.5871	2.9096	3.2715
49	1.1301	1.2768	1.4421	1.6283	1.8380	2.0741	2.3398	2.6388	2.9751	3.3533
50	1.1330	1.2832	1.4530	1.6446	1.8610	2.1052	2.3808	2.6916	3.0420	3.4371
51	1.1358	1.2896	1.4639	1.6611	1.8843	2.1368	2.4225	2.7454	3.1105	3.5230
52	1.1386	1.2961	1.4748	1.6777	1.9078	2.1689	2.4648	2.8003	3.1805	3.6111
53	1.1415	1.3026	1.4859	1.6945	1.9317	2.2014	2.5080	2.8563	3.2520	3.7014
54	1.1443	1.3091	1.4970	1.7114	1.9558	2.2344	2.5519	2.9135	3.3252	3.7939
55	1.1472	1.3156	1.5083	1.7285	1.9803	2.2679	2.5965	2.9717	3.4000	3.8888

$= 1 \times \left[1 + \frac{r}{100}\right]^n$

se of the table. Where the annual compound interest rate earned is 3.5%, 1 unit accumulates after 5 years to 1.1877.

nterest rates: accumulated amount of 1 unit

n Years \ r	% rate 3.0	% rate 3.5	% rate 4.0	% rate 4.5	% rate 5.0	% rate 5.5	% rate 6.0	% rate 6.5	% rate 7.0	% rate 7.5
1	1.0300	1.0350	1.0400	1.0450	1.0500	1.0550	1.0600	1.0650	1.0700	1.0750
2	1.0609	1.0712	1.0816	1.0920	1.1025	1.1130	1.1236	1.1342	1.1449	1.1556
3	1.0927	1.1087	1.1249	1.1412	1.1576	1.1742	1.1910	1.2079	1.2250	1.2423
4	1.1255	1.1475	1.1699	1.1925	1.2155	1.2388	1.2625	1.2865	1.3108	1.3355
5	1.1593	1.1877	1.2167	1.2462	1.2763	1.3070	1.3382	1.3701	1.4026	1.4356
6	1.1941	1.2293	1.2653	1.3023	1.3401	1.3788	1.4185	1.4591	1.5007	1.5433
7	1.2299	1.2723	1.3159	1.3609	1.4071	1.4547	1.5036	1.5540	1.6058	1.6590
8	1.2668	1.3168	1.3686	1.4221	1.4775	1.5347	1.5938	1.6550	1.7182	1.7835
9	1.3048	1.3629	1.4233	1.4861	1.5513	1.6191	1.6895	1.7626	1.8385	1.9172
10	1.3439	1.4106	1.4802	1.5530	1.6289	1.7081	1.7908	1.8771	1.9672	2.0610
11	1.3842	1.4600	1.5395	1.6229	1.7103	1.8021	1.8983	1.9992	2.1049	2.2156
12	1.4258	1.5111	1.6010	1.6959	1.7959	1.9012	2.0122	2.1291	2.2522	2.3818
13	1.4685	1.5640	1.6651	1.7722	1.8856	2.0058	2.1329	2.2675	2.4098	2.5604
14	1.5126	1.6187	1.7317	1.8519	1.9799	2.1161	2.2609	2.4149	2.5785	2.7524
15	1.5580	1.6753	1.8009	1.9353	2.0789	2.2325	2.3966	2.5718	2.7590	2.9589
16	1.6047	1.7340	1.8730	2.0224	2.1829	2.3553	2.5404	2.7390	2.9522	3.1808
17	1.6528	1.7947	1.9479	2.1134	2.2920	2.4848	2.6928	2.9170	3.1588	3.4194
18	1.7024	1.8575	2.0258	2.2085	2.4066	2.6215	2.8543	3.1067	3.3799	3.6758
19	1.7535	1.9225	2.1068	2.3079	2.5270	2.7656	3.0256	3.3086	3.6165	3.9515
20	1.8061	1.9898	2.1911	2.4117	2.6533	2.9178	3.2071	3.5236	3.8697	4.2479
21	1.8603	2.0594	2.2788	2.5202	2.7860	3.0782	3.3996	3.7527	4.1406	4.5664
22	1.9161	2.1315	2.3699	2.6337	2.9253	3.2475	3.6035	3.9966	4.4304	4.9089
23	1.9736	2.2061	2.4647	2.7522	3.0715	3.4262	3.8197	4.2564	4.7405	5.2771
24	2.0328	2.2833	2.5633	2.8760	3.2251	3.6146	4.0489	4.5331	5.0724	5.6729
25	2.0938	2.3632	2.6658	3.0054	3.3864	3.8134	4.2919	4.8277	5.4274	6.0983
26	2.1566	2.4460	2.7725	3.1407	3.5557	4.0231	4.5494	5.1415	5.8074	6.5557
27	2.2213	2.5316	2.8834	3.2820	3.7335	4.2444	4.8223	5.4757	6.2139	7.0474
28	2.2879	2.6202	2.9987	3.4297	3.9201	4.4778	5.1117	5.8316	6.6488	7.5759
29	2.3566	2.7119	3.1187	3.5840	4.1161	4.7241	5.4184	6.2107	7.1143	8.1441
30	2.4273	2.8068	3.2434	3.7453	4.3219	4.9840	5.7435	6.6144	7.6123	8.7550
31	2.5001	2.9050	3.3731	3.9139	4.5380	5.2581	6.0881	7.0443	8.1451	9.4116
32	2.5751	3.0067	3.5081	4.0900	4.7649	5.5473	6.4534	7.5022	8.7153	10.1174
33	2.6523	3.1119	3.6484	4.2740	5.0032	5.8524	6.8406	7.9898	9.3253	10.8763
34	2.7319	3.2209	3.7943	4.4664	5.2533	6.1742	7.2510	8.5092	9.9781	11.6920
35	2.8139	3.3336	3.9461	4.6673	5.5160	6.5138	7.6861	9.0623	10.6766	12.5689
36	2.8983	3.4503	4.1039	4.8774	5.7918	6.8721	8.1473	9.6513	11.4239	13.5115
37	2.9852	3.5710	4.2681	5.0969	6.0814	7.2501	8.6361	10.2786	12.2236	14.5249
38	3.0748	3.6960	4.4388	5.3262	6.3855	7.6488	9.1543	10.9467	13.0793	15.6143
39	3.1670	3.8254	4.6164	5.5659	6.7048	8.0695	9.7035	11.6583	13.9948	16.7853
40	3.2620	3.9593	4.8010	5.8164	7.0400	8.5133	10.2857	12.4161	14.9745	18.0442
41	3.3599	4.0978	4.9931	6.0781	7.3920	8.9815	10.9029	13.2231	16.0227	19.3976
42	3.4607	4.2413	5.1928	6.3516	7.7616	9.4755	11.5570	14.0826	17.1443	20.8524
43	3.5645	4.3897	5.4005	6.6374	8.1497	9.9967	12.2505	14.9980	18.3444	22.4163
44	3.6715	4.5433	5.6165	6.9361	8.5572	10.5465	12.9855	15.9729	19.6285	24.0975
45	3.7816	4.7024	5.8412	7.2482	8.9850	11.1266	13.7646	17.0111	21.0025	25.9048
46	3.8950	4.8669	6.0748	7.5744	9.4343	11.7385	14.5905	18.1168	22.4726	27.8477
47	4.0119	5.0373	6.3178	7.9153	9.9060	12.3841	15.4659	19.2944	24.0457	29.9363
48	4.1323	5.2136	6.5705	8.2715	10.4013	13.0653	16.3939	20.5485	25.7289	32.1815
49	4.2562	5.3961	6.8333	8.6437	10.9213	13.7838	17.3775	21.8842	27.5299	34.5951
50	4.3839	5.5849	7.1067	9.0326	11.4674	14.5420	18.4202	23.3067	29.4570	37.1897
51	4.5154	5.7804	7.3910	9.4391	12.0408	15.3418	19.5254	24.8216	31.5190	39.9790
52	4.6509	5.9827	7.6866	9.8639	12.6428	16.1856	20.6969	26.4350	33.7253	42.9774
53	4.7904	6.1921	7.9941	10.3077	13.2749	17.0758	21.9387	28.1533	36.0861	46.2007
54	4.9341	6.4088	8.3138	10.7716	13.9387	18.0149	23.2550	29.9833	38.6122	49.6658
55	5.0821	6.6331	8.6464	11.2563	14.6356	19.0058	24.6503	31.9322	41.3150	53.3907

$$F = 1 \times \left[1 + \frac{r}{100}\right]^n$$

Use of the table. Where the annual compound interest rate earned is 8.5%, 1 unit accumulates after 5 years to 1.504.

Interest rates: accumulated amount of 1 unit

n \ r (Years)	% rate 8.0	% rate 8.5	% rate 9.0	% rate 9.5	% rate 10.0	% rate 11.0	% rate 12.0	% rate 13.0	% rate 14.0	% rate 15.0
1	1.080	1.085	1.090	1.095	1.100	1.110	1.120	1.130	1.140	1.150
2	1.166	1.177	1.188	1.199	1.210	1.232	1.254	1.277	1.300	1.323
3	1.260	1.277	1.295	1.313	1.331	1.368	1.405	1.443	1.482	1.521
4	1.360	1.386	1.412	1.438	1.464	1.518	1.574	1.630	1.689	1.749
5	1.469	1.504	1.539	1.574	1.611	1.685	1.762	1.842	1.925	2.011
6	1.587	1.631	1.677	1.724	1.772	1.870	1.974	2.082	2.195	2.313
7	1.714	1.770	1.828	1.888	1.949	2.076	2.211	2.353	2.502	2.660
8	1.851	1.921	1.993	2.067	2.144	2.305	2.476	2.658	2.853	3.059
9	1.999	2.084	2.172	2.263	2.358	2.558	2.773	3.004	3.252	3.518
10	2.159	2.261	2.367	2.478	2.594	2.839	3.106	3.395	3.707	4.046
11	2.332	2.453	2.580	2.714	2.853	3.152	3.479	3.836	4.226	4.652
12	2.518	2.662	2.813	2.971	3.138	3.498	3.896	4.335	4.818	5.350
13	2.720	2.888	3.066	3.254	3.452	3.883	4.363	4.898	5.492	6.153
14	2.937	3.133	3.342	3.563	3.797	4.310	4.887	5.535	6.261	7.076
15	3.172	3.400	3.642	3.901	4.177	4.785	5.474	6.254	7.138	8.137
16	3.426	3.689	3.970	4.272	4.595	5.311	6.130	7.067	8.137	9.358
17	3.700	4.002	4.328	4.678	5.054	5.895	6.866	7.986	9.276	10.761
18	3.996	4.342	4.717	5.122	5.560	6.544	7.690	9.024	10.575	12.375
19	4.316	4.712	5.142	5.609	6.116	7.263	8.613	10.197	12.056	14.232
20	4.661	5.112	5.604	6.142	6.727	8.062	9.646	11.523	13.743	16.367
21	5.034	5.547	6.109	6.725	7.400	8.949	10.804	13.021	15.668	18.822
22	5.437	6.018	6.659	7.364	8.140	9.934	12.100	14.714	17.861	21.645
23	5.871	6.530	7.258	8.064	8.954	11.026	13.552	16.627	20.362	24.891
24	6.341	7.085	7.911	8.830	9.850	12.239	15.179	18.788	23.212	28.625
25	6.848	7.687	8.623	9.668	10.835	13.585	17.000	21.231	26.462	32.919
26	7.396	8.340	9.399	10.587	1.918	15.080	19.040	23.991	30.167	37.857
27	7.988	9.049	10.245	11.593	13.110	16.739	21.325	27.109	34.390	43.535
28	8.627	9.818	11.167	12.694	14.421	18.580	23.884	30.633	39.204	50.066
29	9.317	10.653	12.172	13.900	15.863	20.624	26.750	34.616	44.693	57.575
30	10.063	11.558	13.268	15.220	17.449	22.892	29.960	39.116	50.950	66.212
31	10.868	12.541	14.462	16.666	19.194	25.410	33.555	44.201	58.083	76.144
32	11.737	13.607	15.763	18.250	21.114	28.206	37.582	49.947	66.215	87.565
33	12.676	14.763	17.182	19.983	23.225	31.308	42.092	56.440	75.485	100.700
34	13.690	16.018	18.728	21.882	25.548	34.752	47.143	63.777	86.053	115.805
35	14.785	17.380	20.414	23.960	28.102	38.575	52.800	72.069	98.100	133.176
36	15.968	18.857	22.251	26.237	30.913	42.818	59.136	81.437	111.834	153.152
37	17.246	20.460	24.254	28.729	34.004	47.528	66.232	92.024	127.491	176.125
38	18.625	22.199	26.437	31.458	37.404	52.756	74.180	103.987	145.340	202.543
39	20.115	24.086	28.816	34.447	41.145	58.559	83.081	117.506	165.687	232.925
40	21.725	26.133	31.409	37.719	45.259	65.001	93.051	132.782	188.884	267.864
41	23.462	28.354	34.236	41.303	49.785	72.151	104.217	150.043	215.327	308.043
42	25.339	30.764	37.318	45.227	54.764	80.088	116.723	169.549	245.473	354.250
43	27.367	33.379	40.676	49.523	60.240	88.897	130.730	191.590	279.839	407.387
44	29.556	36.217	44.337	54.228	66.264	98.676	146.418	216.497	319.017	468.495
45	31.920	39.295	48.327	59.379	72.890	109.530	163.988	244.641	363.679	538.769
46	34.474	42.635	52.677	65.020	80.180	121.579	183.666	276.445	414.594	619.585
47	37.232	46.259	57.418	71.197	88.197	134.952	205.706	312.383	472.637	712.522
48	40.211	50.191	62.585	77.961	97.017	149.797	230.391	352.992	538.807	819.401
49	43.427	54.457	68.218	85.367	106.719	166.275	258.038	398.881	614.239	942.311
50	46.902	59.086	74.358	93.477	117.391	184.565	289.002	450.736	700.233	1083.657
51	50.654	64.109	81.050	102.358	129.130	204.867	323.682	509.332	798.266	1246.206
52	54.706	69.558	88.344	112.082	142.043	227.402	362.524	575.545	910.023	1433.137
53	59.083	75.470	96.295	122.729	156.247	252.417	406.027	650.366	1037.426	1648.108
54	63.809	81.885	104.962	134.389	171.872	280.182	454.751	734.913	1182.666	1895.324
55	68.914	88.846	114.408	147.156	189.059	311.002	509.321	830.452	1348.239	2179.622

$= 1 \times \left[1 + \frac{r}{100}\right]^n$

se of the table. Where the annual compound interest rate earned is 17%, 1 unit accumulates after 5 years to 2.192.

nterest rates: accumulated amount of 1 unit

n (Years) \ r	% rate 16	% rate 17	% rate 18	% rate 19	% rate 20	% rate 21	% rate 22	% rate 23	% rate 24	% rate 25
1	1.160	1.170	1.180	1.190	1.200	1.210	1.220	1.230	1.240	1.250
2	1.346	1.369	1.392	1.416	1.440	1.464	1.488	1.513	1.538	1.562
3	1.561	1.602	1.643	1.685	1.728	1.772	1.816	1.861	1.907	1.953
4	1.811	1.874	1.939	2.005	2.074	2.144	2.215	2.289	2.364	2.441
5	2.100	2.192	2.288	2.386	2.488	2.594	2.703	2.815	2.932	3.052
6	2.436	2.565	2.700	2.840	2.986	3.138	3.297	3.463	3.635	3.815
7	2.826	3.001	3.185	3.379	3.583	3.797	4.023	4.259	4.508	4.768
8	3.278	3.511	3.759	4.021	4.300	4.595	4.908	5.239	5.590	5.960
9	3.803	4.108	4.435	4.785	5.160	5.560	5.987	6.444	6.931	7.451
10	4.411	4.807	5.234	5.695	6.192	6.727	7.305	7.926	8.594	9.313
11	5.117	5.624	6.176	6.777	7.430	8.140	8.912	9.749	10.657	11.642
12	5.936	6.580	7.288	8.064	8.916	9.850	10.872	11.991	13.215	14.552
13	6.886	7.699	8.599	9.596	10.699	11.918	13.264	14.749	16.386	18.190
14	7.988	9.007	10.147	11.420	12.839	14.421	16.182	18.141	20.319	22.737
15	9.266	10.539	11.974	13.590	15.407	17.449	19.742	22.314	25.196	28.422
16	10.748	12.330	14.129	16.172	18.488	21.114	24.086	27.446	31.243	35.527
17	12.468	14.426	16.672	19.244	22.186	25.548	29.384	33.759	38.741	44.409
18	14.463	16.879	19.673	22.901	26.623	30.913	35.849	41.523	48.039	55.511
19	16.777	19.748	23.214	27.252	31.948	37.404	43.736	51.074	59.568	69.389
20	19.461	23.106	27.393	32.429	38.338	45.259	53.358	62.821	73.864	86.736
21	22.574	27.034	32.324	38.591	46.005	54.764	65.096	77.269	91.592	108.420
22	26.186	31.629	38.142	45.923	55.206	66.264	79.418	95.041	113.574	135.525
23	30.376	37.006	45.008	54.649	66.247	80.180	96.889	116.901	140.831	169.407
24	35.236	43.297	53.109	65.032	79.497	97.017	118.205	143.788	174.631	211.758
25	40.874	50.658	62.669	77.388	95.396	117.391	144.210	176.859	216.542	264.698
26	47.414	59.270	73.949	92.092	114.475	142.043	175.936	217.537	268.512	330.872
27	55.000	69.345	87.260	109.589	137.371	171.872	214.642	267.570	332.955	413.590
28	63.800	81.134	102.967	130.411	164.845	207.965	261.864	329.112	412.864	516.988
29	74.009	94.927	121.501	155.189	197.814	251.638	319.474	404.807	511.952	646.235
30	85.850	111.065	143.371	184.675	237.376	304.482	389.758	497.913	634.820	807.794
31	99.586	129.946	169.177	219.764	284.852	368.423	475.505	612.433	787.177	1009.742
32	115.520	152.036	199.629	261.519	341.822	445.792	580.116	753.292	976.099	1262.177
33	134.003	177.883	235.563	311.207	410.186	539.408	707.741	926.550	1210.363	1577.722
34	155.443	208.123	277.964	370.337	492.224	652.683	863.444	1139.656	1500.850	1972.152
35	180.314	243.503	327.997	440.701	590.668	789.747	1053.402	1401.777	1861.054	2465.190
36	209.164	284.899	387.037	524.434	708.802	955.594	1285.150	1724.186	2307.707	3081.488
37	242.631	333.332	456.703	624.076	850.562	1156.269	1567.883	2120.748	2861.557	3851.860
38	281.452	389.998	538.910	742.651	1020.675	1399.085	1912.818	2608.520	3548.330	4814.825
39	326.484	456.298	635.914	883.754	1224.810	1692.893	2333.638	3208.480	4399.930	6018.531
40	378.721	533.869	750.378	1051.668	1469.772	2048.400	2847.038	3946.430	5455.913	7523.164
41	439.317	624.626	885.446	1251.484	1763.726	2478.564	3473.386	4854.109	6765.332	9403.955
42	509.607	730.813	1044.827	1489.266	2116.471	2999.063	4237.531	5970.555	8389.011	11754.944
43	591.144	855.051	1232.896	1772.227	2539.765	3628.866	5169.788	7343.782	10402.374	14693.679
44	685.727	1000.410	1454.817	2108.950	3047.718	4390.928	6307.141	9032.852	12898.944	18367.099
45	795.444	1170.479	1716.684	2509.651	3657.262	5313.023	7694.712	11110.408	15994.690	22958.874
46	922.715	1369.461	2025.687	2986.484	4388.714	6428.757	9387.549	13665.802	19833.416	28698.593
47	1070.349	1602.269	2390.311	3553.916	5266.457	7778.796	11452.810	16808.937	24593.436	35873.241
48	1241.605	1874.655	2820.567	4229.160	6319.749	9412.344	13972.428	20674.992	30495.860	44841.551
49	1440.262	2193.346	3328.269	5032.701	7583.698	11388.936	17046.362	25430.240	37814.867	56051.939
50	1670.704	2566.215	3927.357	5988.914	9100.438	13780.612	20796.561	31279.195	46890.435	70064.923
51	1938.016	3002.472	4634.281	7126.808	10920.526	16674.541	25371.805	38473.410	58144.139	87581.154
52	2248.099	3512.892	5468.452	8480.901	13104.631	20176.195	30953.602	47322.295	72098.732	109476.443
53	2607.795	4110.084	6452.773	10092.272	15725.557	24413.195	37763.395	58206.422	89402.428	136845.553
54	3025.042	4808.798	7614.272	12009.804	18870.669	29539.966	46071.341	71593.899	110859.011	171056.941
55	3509.049	5626.294	8984.841	14291.667	22644.802	35743.359	56207.036	88060.496	137465.173	213821.177

$$x = \frac{\frac{r}{100}}{1 - \left[1 + \frac{r}{100}\right]^{-n}}$$

Use of the table. The table shows the equal annual payment (x in the formula) required to pay off a loan of 1 unit were the annual compound interest rate paid is shown at the head of a column (r) and the number of years for which payment is made is shown in the column at each side of a line (n). For example, where the annual compound interest rate paid is 0.5%, 1 unit is paid off after 5 years by an equal annual payment of 0.2030.

Interest rates: equal annual payment to pay off a loan of 1 unit (mortgage repayments)

n Years \ r	% rate 0.25	% rate 0.50	% rate 0.75	% rate 1.00	% rate 1.25	% rate 1.50	% rate 1.75	% rate 2.00	% rate 2.25	% rate 2.50
1	1.0025	1.0050	1.0075	1.0100	1.0125	1.0150	1.0175	1.0200	1.0225	1.0250
2	0.5019	0.5038	0.5056	0.5075	0.5094	0.5113	0.5132	0.5150	0.5169	0.5188
3	0.3350	0.3367	0.3383	0.3400	0.3417	0.3434	0.3451	0.3468	0.3484	0.3501
4	0.2516	0.2531	0.2547	0.2563	0.2579	0.2594	0.2610	0.2626	0.2642	0.2658
5	0.2015	0.2030	0.2045	0.2060	0.2076	0.2091	0.2106	0.2122	0.2137	0.2152
6	0.1681	0.1696	0.1711	0.1725	0.1740	0.1755	0.1770	0.1785	0.1800	0.1815
7	0.1443	0.1457	0.1472	0.1486	0.1501	0.1516	0.1530	0.1545	0.1560	0.1575
8	0.1264	0.1278	0.1293	0.1307	0.1321	0.1336	0.1350	0.1365	0.1380	0.1395
9	0.1125	0.1139	0.1153	0.1167	0.1182	0.1196	0.1211	0.1225	0.1240	0.1255
10	0.1014	0.1028	0.1042	0.1056	0.1070	0.1084	0.1099	0.1113	0.1128	0.1143
11	0.0923	0.0937	0.0951	0.0965	0.0979	0.0993	0.1007	0.1022	0.1036	0.1051
12	0.0847	0.0861	0.0875	0.0888	0.0903	0.0917	0.0931	0.0946	0.0960	0.0975
13	0.0783	0.0796	0.0810	0.0824	0.0838	0.0852	0.0867	0.0881	0.0896	0.0910
14	0.0728	0.0741	0.0755	0.0769	0.0783	0.0797	0.0812	0.0826	0.0841	0.0855
15	0.0680	0.0694	0.0707	0.0721	0.0735	0.0749	0.0764	0.0778	0.0793	0.0808
16	0.0638	0.0652	0.0666	0.0679	0.0693	0.0708	0.0722	0.0737	0.0751	0.0766
17	0.0602	0.0615	0.0629	0.0643	0.0657	0.0671	0.0685	0.0700	0.0714	0.0729
18	0.0569	0.0582	0.0596	0.0610	0.0624	0.0638	0.0652	0.0667	0.0682	0.0697
19	0.0540	0.0553	0.0567	0.0581	0.0595	0.0609	0.0623	0.0638	0.0653	0.0668
20	0.0513	0.0527	0.0540	0.0554	0.0568	0.0582	0.0597	0.0612	0.0626	0.0641
21	0.0489	0.0503	0.0516	0.0530	0.0544	0.0559	0.0573	0.0588	0.0603	0.0618
22	0.0468	0.0481	0.0495	0.0509	0.0523	0.0537	0.0552	0.0566	0.0581	0.0596
23	0.0448	0.0461	0.0475	0.0489	0.0503	0.0517	0.0532	0.0547	0.0562	0.0577
24	0.0430	0.0443	0.0457	0.0471	0.0485	0.0499	0.0514	0.0529	0.0544	0.0559
25	0.0413	0.0427	0.0440	0.0454	0.0468	0.0483	0.0497	0.0512	0.0527	0.0543
26	0.0398	0.0411	0.0425	0.0439	0.0453	0.0467	0.0482	0.0497	0.0512	0.0528
27	0.0383	0.0397	0.0411	0.0424	0.0439	0.0453	0.0468	0.0483	0.0498	0.0514
28	0.0370	0.0384	0.0397	0.0411	0.0425	0.0440	0.0455	0.0470	0.0485	0.0501
29	0.0358	0.0371	0.0385	0.0399	0.0413	0.0428	0.0443	0.0458	0.0473	0.0489
30	0.0346	0.0360	0.0373	0.0387	0.0402	0.0416	0.0431	0.0446	0.0462	0.0478
31	0.0336	0.0349	0.0363	0.0377	0.0391	0.0406	0.0421	0.0436	0.0452	0.0467
32	0.0326	0.0339	0.0353	0.0367	0.0381	0.0396	0.0411	0.0426	0.0442	0.0458
33	0.0316	0.0329	0.0343	0.0357	0.0372	0.0386	0.0401	0.0417	0.0433	0.0449
34	0.0307	0.0321	0.0334	0.0348	0.0363	0.0378	0.0393	0.0408	0.0424	0.0440
35	0.0299	0.0312	0.0326	0.0340	0.0355	0.0369	0.0385	0.0400	0.0416	0.0432
36	0.0291	0.0304	0.0318	0.0332	0.0347	0.0362	0.0377	0.0392	0.0408	0.0425
37	0.0283	0.0297	0.0311	0.0325	0.0339	0.0354	0.0369	0.0385	0.0401	0.0417
38	0.0276	0.0290	0.0303	0.0318	0.0332	0.0347	0.0362	0.0378	0.0394	0.0411
39	0.0269	0.0283	0.0297	0.0311	0.0326	0.0341	0.0356	0.0372	0.0388	0.0404
40	0.0263	0.0276	0.0290	0.0305	0.0319	0.0334	0.0350	0.0366	0.0382	0.0398
41	0.0257	0.0270	0.0284	0.0299	0.0313	0.0328	0.0344	0.0360	0.0376	0.0393
42	0.0251	0.0265	0.0278	0.0293	0.0307	0.0323	0.0338	0.0354	0.0371	0.0387
43	0.0246	0.0259	0.0273	0.0287	0.0302	0.0317	0.0333	0.0349	0.0365	0.0382
44	0.0240	0.0254	0.0268	0.0282	0.0297	0.0312	0.0328	0.0344	0.0360	0.0377
45	0.0235	0.0249	0.0263	0.0277	0.0292	0.0307	0.0323	0.0339	0.0356	0.0373
46	0.0230	0.0244	0.0258	0.0272	0.0287	0.0303	0.0318	0.0335	0.0351	0.0368
47	0.0226	0.0239	0.0253	0.0268	0.0283	0.0298	0.0314	0.0330	0.0347	0.0364
48	0.0221	0.0235	0.0249	0.0263	0.0278	0.0294	0.0310	0.0326	0.0343	0.0360
49	0.0217	0.0231	0.0245	0.0259	0.0274	0.0290	0.0306	0.0322	0.0339	0.0356
50	0.0213	0.0227	0.0241	0.0255	0.0270	0.0286	0.0302	0.0318	0.0335	0.0353
51	0.0209	0.0223	0.0237	0.0251	0.0266	0.0282	0.0298	0.0315	0.0332	0.0349
52	0.0205	0.0219	0.0233	0.0248	0.0263	0.0278	0.0294	0.0311	0.0328	0.0346
53	0.0202	0.0215	0.0229	0.0244	0.0259	0.0275	0.0291	0.0308	0.0325	0.0343
54	0.0198	0.0212	0.0226	0.0241	0.0256	0.0272	0.0288	0.0305	0.0322	0.0339
55	0.0195	0.0208	0.0223	0.0237	0.0253	0.0268	0.0285	0.0301	0.0319	0.0337

$$x = \frac{\frac{r}{100}}{1 - \left[1 + \frac{r}{100}\right]^{-n}}$$

se of the table. Where the annual compound interest rate paid is 3.5%, 1 unit is paid off after 5 years by an equal annual payment of 0.2215.

nterest rates: equal annual payment to pay off a loan of 1 unit (mortgage repayments)

n \ r	% rate 3.0	% rate 3.5	% rate 4.0	% rate 4.5	% rate 5.0	% rate 5.5	% rate 6.0	% rate 6.5	% rate 7.0	% rate 7.5	r \ n
Years											Years
1	1.0300	1.0350	1.0400	1.0450	1.0500	1.0550	1.0600	1.0650	1.0700	1.0750	1
2	0.5226	0.5264	0.5302	0.5340	0.5378	0.5416	0.5454	0.5493	0.5531	0.5569	2
3	0.3535	0.3569	0.3603	0.3638	0.3672	0.3707	0.3741	0.3776	0.3811	0.3845	3
4	0.2690	0.2723	0.2755	0.2787	0.2820	0.2853	0.2886	0.2919	0.2952	0.2986	4
5	0.2184	0.2215	0.2246	0.2278	0.2310	0.2342	0.2374	0.2406	0.2439	0.2472	5
6	0.1846	0.1877	0.1908	0.1939	0.1970	0.2002	0.2034	0.2066	0.2098	0.2130	6
7	0.1605	0.1635	0.1666	0.1697	0.1728	0.1760	0.1791	0.1823	0.1856	0.1888	7
8	0.1425	0.1455	0.1485	0.1516	0.1547	0.1579	0.1610	0.1642	0.1675	0.1707	8
9	0.1284	0.1314	0.1345	0.1376	0.1407	0.1438	0.1470	0.1502	0.1535	0.1568	9
10	0.1172	0.1202	0.1233	0.1264	0.1295	0.1327	0.1359	0.1391	0.1424	0.1457	10
11	0.1081	0.1111	0.1141	0.1172	0.1204	0.1236	0.1268	0.1301	0.1334	0.1367	11
12	0.1005	0.1035	0.1066	0.1097	0.1128	0.1160	0.1193	0.1226	0.1259	0.1293	12
13	0.0940	0.0971	0.1001	0.1033	0.1065	0.1097	0.1130	0.1163	0.1197	0.1231	13
14	0.0885	0.0916	0.0947	0.0978	0.1010	0.1043	0.1076	0.1109	0.1143	0.1178	14
15	0.0838	0.0868	0.0899	0.0931	0.0963	0.0996	0.1030	0.1064	0.1098	0.1133	15
16	0.0796	0.0827	0.0858	0.0890	0.0923	0.0956	0.0990	0.1024	0.1059	0.1094	16
17	0.0760	0.0790	0.0822	0.0854	0.0887	0.0920	0.0954	0.0989	0.1024	0.1060	17
18	0.0727	0.0758	0.0790	0.0822	0.0855	0.0889	0.0924	0.0959	0.0994	0.1030	18
19	0.0698	0.0729	0.0761	0.0794	0.0827	0.0862	0.0896	0.0932	0.0968	0.1004	19
20	0.0672	0.0704	0.0736	0.0769	0.0802	0.0837	0.0872	0.0908	0.0944	0.0981	20
21	0.0649	0.0680	0.0713	0.0746	0.0780	0.0815	0.0850	0.0886	0.0923	0.0960	21
22	0.0627	0.0659	0.0692	0.0725	0.0760	0.0795	0.0830	0.0867	0.0904	0.0942	22
23	0.0608	0.0640	0.0673	0.0707	0.0741	0.0777	0.0813	0.0850	0.0887	0.0925	23
24	0.0590	0.0623	0.0656	0.0690	0.0725	0.0760	0.0797	0.0834	0.0872	0.0911	24
25	0.0574	0.0607	0.0640	0.0674	0.0710	0.0745	0.0782	0.0820	0.0858	0.0897	25
26	0.0559	0.0592	0.0626	0.0660	0.0696	0.0732	0.0769	0.0807	0.0846	0.0885	26
27	0.0546	0.0579	0.0612	0.0647	0.0683	0.0720	0.0757	0.0795	0.0834	0.0874	27
28	0.0533	0.0566	0.0600	0.0635	0.0671	0.0708	0.0746	0.0785	0.0824	0.0864	28
29	0.0521	0.0554	0.0589	0.0624	0.0660	0.0698	0.0736	0.0775	0.0814	0.0855	29
30	0.0510	0.0544	0.0578	0.0614	0.0651	0.0688	0.0726	0.0766	0.0806	0.0847	30
31	0.0500	0.0534	0.0569	0.0604	0.0641	0.0679	0.0718	0.0758	0.0798	0.0839	31
32	0.0490	0.0524	0.0559	0.0596	0.0633	0.0671	0.0710	0.0750	0.0791	0.0832	32
33	0.0482	0.0516	0.0551	0.0587	0.0625	0.0663	0.0703	0.0743	0.0784	0.0826	33
34	0.0473	0.0508	0.0543	0.0580	0.0618	0.0656	0.0696	0.0737	0.0778	0.0820	34
35	0.0465	0.0500	0.0536	0.0573	0.0611	0.0650	0.0690	0.0731	0.0772	0.0815	35
36	0.0458	0.0493	0.0529	0.0566	0.0604	0.0644	0.0684	0.0725	0.0767	0.0810	36
37	0.0451	0.0486	0.0522	0.0560	0.0598	0.0638	0.0679	0.0720	0.0762	0.0805	37
38	0.0445	0.0480	0.0516	0.0554	0.0593	0.0633	0.0674	0.0715	0.0758	0.0801	38
39	0.0438	0.0474	0.0511	0.0549	0.0588	0.0628	0.0669	0.0711	0.0754	0.0798	39
40	0.0433	0.0468	0.0505	0.0543	0.0583	0.0623	0.0665	0.0707	0.0750	0.0794	40
41	0.0427	0.0463	0.0500	0.0539	0.0578	0.0619	0.0661	0.0703	0.0747	0.0791	41
42	0.0422	0.0458	0.0495	0.0534	0.0574	0.0615	0.0657	0.0700	0.0743	0.0788	42
43	0.0417	0.0453	0.0491	0.0530	0.0570	0.0611	0.0653	0.0696	0.0740	0.0785	43
44	0.0412	0.0449	0.0487	0.0526	0.0566	0.0608	0.0650	0.0693	0.0738	0.0782	44
45	0.0408	0.0445	0.0483	0.0522	0.0563	0.0604	0.0647	0.0691	0.0735	0.0780	45
46	0.0404	0.0441	0.0479	0.0518	0.0559	0.0601	0.0644	0.0688	0.0733	0.0778	46
47	0.0400	0.0437	0.0475	0.0515	0.0556	0.0598	0.0641	0.0686	0.0730	0.0776	47
48	0.0396	0.0433	0.0472	0.0512	0.0553	0.0596	0.0639	0.0683	0.0728	0.0774	48
49	0.0392	0.0430	0.0469	0.0509	0.0550	0.0593	0.0637	0.0681	0.0726	0.0772	49
50	0.0389	0.0426	0.0466	0.0506	0.0548	0.0591	0.0634	0.0679	0.0725	0.0771	50
51	0.0385	0.0423	0.0463	0.0503	0.0545	0.0588	0.0632	0.0677	0.0723	0.0769	51
52	0.0382	0.0420	0.0460	0.0501	0.0543	0.0586	0.0630	0.0676	0.0721	0.0768	52
53	0.0379	0.0417	0.0457	0.0498	0.0541	0.0584	0.0629	0.0674	0.0720	0.0767	53
54	0.0376	0.0415	0.0455	0.0496	0.0539	0.0582	0.0627	0.0672	0.0719	0.0765	54
55	0.0373	0.0412	0.0452	0.0494	0.0537	0.0581	0.0625	0.0671	0.0717	0.0764	55

$$x = \frac{\frac{r}{100}}{1 - \left[1 + \frac{r}{100}\right]}$$

Use of the table. Where the annual compound interest rate paid is 8.5%, 1 unit paid off after 5 years by an equal annual payment of 0.25377.

Interest rates: equal annual payment to pay off a loan of 1 unit (mortgage repayments)

n (Years) \ r	% rate 8.0	% rate 8.5	% rate 9.0	% rate 9.5	% rate 10.0	% rate 11.0	% rate 12.0	% rate 13.0	% rate 14.0	% rate 15.0
1	1.08000	1.08500	1.09000	1.09500	1.10000	1.11000	1.12000	1.13000	1.14000	1.15000
2	0.56077	0.56462	0.56847	0.57233	0.57619	0.58393	0.59170	0.59948	0.60729	0.61512
3	0.38803	0.39154	0.39505	0.39858	0.40211	0.40921	0.41635	0.42352	0.43073	0.43798
4	0.30192	0.30529	0.30867	0.31206	0.31547	0.32233	0.32923	0.33619	0.34320	0.35027
5	0.25046	0.25377	0.25709	0.26044	0.26380	0.27057	0.27741	0.28431	0.29128	0.29832
6	0.21632	0.21961	0.22292	0.22625	0.22961	0.23638	0.24323	0.25015	0.25716	0.26424
7	0.19207	0.19537	0.19869	0.20204	0.20541	0.21222	0.21912	0.22611	0.23319	0.24036
8	0.17401	0.17733	0.18067	0.18405	0.18744	0.19432	0.20130	0.20839	0.21557	0.22285
9	0.16008	0.16342	0.16680	0.17020	0.17364	0.18060	0.18768	0.19487	0.20217	0.20957
10	0.14903	0.15241	0.15582	0.15927	0.16275	0.16980	0.17698	0.18429	0.19171	0.19925
11	0.14008	0.14349	0.14695	0.15044	0.15396	0.16112	0.16842	0.17584	0.18339	0.19107
12	0.13270	0.13615	0.13965	0.14319	0.14676	0.15403	0.16144	0.16899	0.17667	0.18448
13	0.12652	0.13002	0.13357	0.13715	0.14078	0.14815	0.15568	0.16335	0.17116	0.17911
14	0.12130	0.12484	0.12843	0.13207	0.13575	0.14323	0.15087	0.15867	0.16661	0.17469
15	0.11683	0.12042	0.12406	0.12774	0.13147	0.13907	0.14682	0.15474	0.16281	0.17102
16	0.11298	0.11661	0.12030	0.12403	0.12782	0.13552	0.14339	0.15143	0.15962	0.16795
17	0.10963	0.11331	0.11705	0.12083	0.12466	0.13247	0.14046	0.14861	0.15692	0.16537
18	0.10670	0.11043	0.11421	0.11805	0.12193	0.12984	0.13794	0.14620	0.15462	0.16319
19	0.10413	0.10790	0.11173	0.11561	0.11955	0.12756	0.13576	0.14413	0.15266	0.16134
20	0.10185	0.10567	0.10955	0.11348	0.11746	0.12558	0.13388	0.14235	0.15099	0.15976
21	0.09983	0.10370	0.10762	0.11159	0.11562	0.12384	0.13224	0.14081	0.14954	0.15842
22	0.09803	0.10194	0.10590	0.10993	0.11401	0.12231	0.13081	0.13948	0.14830	0.15727
23	0.09642	0.10037	0.10438	0.10845	0.11257	0.12097	0.12956	0.13832	0.14723	0.15628
24	0.09498	0.09897	0.10302	0.10713	0.11130	0.11979	0.12846	0.13731	0.14630	0.15543
25	0.09368	0.09771	0.10181	0.10596	0.11017	0.11874	0.12750	0.13643	0.14550	0.15470
26	0.09251	0.09658	0.10072	0.10491	0.10916	0.11781	0.12665	0.13565	0.14480	0.15407
27	0.09145	0.09556	0.09973	0.10397	0.10826	0.11699	0.12590	0.13498	0.14419	0.15353
28	0.09049	0.09464	0.09885	0.10312	0.10745	0.11626	0.12524	0.13439	0.14366	0.15306
29	0.08962	0.09381	0.09806	0.10236	0.10673	0.11561	0.12466	0.13387	0.14320	0.15265
30	0.08883	0.09305	0.09734	0.10168	0.10608	0.11502	0.12414	0.13341	0.14280	0.15230
31	0.08811	0.09237	0.09669	0.10106	0.10550	0.11451	0.12369	0.13301	0.14245	0.15200
32	0.08745	0.09174	0.09610	0.10051	0.10497	0.11404	0.12328	0.13266	0.14215	0.15173
33	0.08685	0.09118	0.09556	0.10000	0.10450	0.11363	0.12292	0.13234	0.14188	0.15150
34	0.08630	0.09066	0.09508	0.09955	0.10407	0.11326	0.12260	0.13207	0.14165	0.15131
35	0.08580	0.09019	0.09464	0.09914	0.10369	0.11293	0.12232	0.13183	0.14144	0.15113
36	0.08534	0.08976	0.09424	0.09876	0.10334	0.11263	0.12206	0.13162	0.14126	0.15099
37	0.08492	0.08937	0.09387	0.09843	0.10303	0.11236	0.12184	0.13143	0.14111	0.15086
38	0.08454	0.08901	0.09354	0.09812	0.10275	0.11213	0.12164	0.13126	0.14097	0.15074
39	0.08419	0.08868	0.09324	0.09784	0.10249	0.11191	0.12146	0.13112	0.14085	0.15065
40	0.08386	0.08838	0.09296	0.09759	0.10226	0.11172	0.12130	0.13099	0.14075	0.15056
41	0.08356	0.08811	0.09271	0.09736	0.10205	0.11155	0.12116	0.13087	0.14065	0.15049
42	0.08329	0.08786	0.09248	0.09715	0.10186	0.11139	0.12104	0.13077	0.14057	0.15042
43	0.08303	0.08763	0.09227	0.09696	0.10169	0.11125	0.12092	0.13068	0.14050	0.15037
44	0.08280	0.08741	0.09208	0.09678	0.10153	0.11113	0.12083	0.13060	0.14044	0.15032
45	0.08259	0.08722	0.09190	0.09663	0.10139	0.11101	0.12074	0.13053	0.14039	0.15028
46	0.08239	0.08704	0.09174	0.09648	0.10126	0.11091	0.12066	0.13047	0.14034	0.15024
47	0.08221	0.08688	0.09160	0.09635	0.10115	0.11082	0.12059	0.13042	0.14030	0.15021
48	0.08204	0.08673	0.09146	0.09623	0.10104	0.11074	0.12052	0.13037	0.14026	0.15018
49	0.08189	0.08659	0.09134	0.09613	0.10095	0.11067	0.12047	0.13033	0.14023	0.15016
50	0.08174	0.08646	0.09123	0.09603	0.10086	0.11060	0.12042	0.13029	0.14020	0.15014
51	0.08161	0.08635	0.09112	0.09594	0.10078	0.11054	0.12037	0.13026	0.14018	0.15012
52	0.08149	0.08624	0.09103	0.09586	0.10071	0.11049	0.12033	0.13023	0.14015	0.15010
53	0.08138	0.08614	0.09094	0.09578	0.10064	0.11044	0.12030	0.13020	0.14014	0.15009
54	0.08127	0.08605	0.09087	0.09571	0.10059	0.11039	0.12026	0.13018	0.14012	0.15008
55	0.08118	0.08597	0.09079	0.09565	0.10053	0.11035	0.12024	0.13016	0.14010	0.15007

$$x = \frac{\frac{r}{100}}{1 - \left[1 + \frac{r}{100}\right]^{-n}}$$

Use of the table. Where the annual compound interest rate paid is 17%, 1 unit paid off after 5 years by an equal annual payment of 0.312564.

Interest rates: equal annual payment to pay off a loan of 1 unit (mortgage repayments)

n \ r	% rate 16	% rate 17	% rate 18	% rate 19	% rate 20	% rate 21	% rate 22	% rate 23	% rate 24	% rate 25	r / n
Years											Years
1	1.160000	1.170000	1.180000	1.190000	1.200000	1.210000	1.220000	1.230000	1.240000	1.250000	1
2	0.622963	0.630829	0.638716	0.646621	0.654545	0.662489	0.670450	0.678430	0.686429	0.694444	2
3	0.445258	0.452574	0.459924	0.467308	0.474725	0.482175	0.489658	0.497173	0.504718	0.512295	3
4	0.357375	0.364533	0.371739	0.378991	0.386289	0.393632	0.401020	0.408451	0.415926	0.423442	4
5	0.305409	0.312564	0.319778	0.327050	0.334380	0.341765	0.349206	0.356700	0.364248	0.371847	5
6	0.271390	0.278615	0.285910	0.293274	0.300706	0.308203	0.315764	0.323389	0.331074	0.338819	6
7	0.247613	0.254947	0.262362	0.269855	0.277424	0.285067	0.292782	0.300568	0.308422	0.316342	7
8	0.230224	0.237690	0.245244	0.252885	0.260609	0.268415	0.276299	0.284259	0.292293	0.300399	8
9	0.217082	0.224691	0.232395	0.240192	0.248079	0.256053	0.264111	0.272249	0.280465	0.288756	9
10	0.206901	0.214657	0.222515	0.230471	0.238523	0.246665	0.254895	0.263208	0.271602	0.280073	10
11	0.198861	0.206765	0.214776	0.222891	0.231104	0.239411	0.247807	0.256289	0.264852	0.273493	11
12	0.192415	0.200466	0.208628	0.216896	0.225265	0.233730	0.242285	0.250926	0.259648	0.268448	12
13	0.187184	0.195378	0.203686	0.212102	0.220620	0.229234	0.237939	0.246728	0.255598	0.264543	13
14	0.182898	0.191230	0.199678	0.208235	0.216893	0.225647	0.234491	0.243418	0.252423	0.261501	14
15	0.179358	0.187822	0.196403	0.205092	0.213882	0.222766	0.231738	0.240791	0.249919	0.259117	15
16	0.176414	0.185004	0.193710	0.202523	0.211436	0.220441	0.229530	0.238697	0.247936	0.257241	16
17	0.173952	0.182662	0.191485	0.200414	0.209440	0.218555	0.227751	0.237021	0.246359	0.255759	17
18	0.171885	0.180706	0.189639	0.198676	0.207805	0.217020	0.226313	0.235676	0.245102	0.254586	18
19	0.170142	0.179067	0.188103	0.197238	0.206462	0.215769	0.225148	0.234593	0.244098	0.253656	19
20	0.168667	0.177690	0.186820	0.196045	0.205357	0.214745	0.224202	0.233720	0.243294	0.252916	20
21	0.167416	0.176530	0.185746	0.195054	0.204444	0.213906	0.223432	0.233016	0.242649	0.252327	21
22	0.166353	0.175550	0.184846	0.194229	0.203690	0.213218	0.222805	0.232446	0.242132	0.251858	22
23	0.165447	0.174721	0.184090	0.193542	0.203065	0.212652	0.222294	0.231984	0.241716	0.251485	23
24	0.164673	0.174019	0.183454	0.192967	0.202548	0.212187	0.221877	0.231611	0.241382	0.251186	24
25	0.164013	0.173423	0.182919	0.192487	0.202119	0.211804	0.221536	0.231308	0.241113	0.250948	25
26	0.163447	0.172917	0.182467	0.192086	0.201762	0.211489	0.221258	0.231062	0.240897	0.250758	26
27	0.162963	0.172487	0.182087	0.191750	0.201467	0.211229	0.221030	0.230863	0.240723	0.250606	27
28	0.162548	0.172121	0.181765	0.191468	0.201221	0.211015	0.220843	0.230701	0.240583	0.250485	28
29	0.162192	0.171810	0.181494	0.191232	0.201016	0.210838	0.220691	0.230570	0.240470	0.250387	29
30	0.161886	0.171545	0.181264	0.191034	0.200846	0.210692	0.220566	0.230463	0.240379	0.250310	30
31	0.161623	0.171318	0.181070	0.190869	0.200705	0.210572	0.220464	0.230376	0.240305	0.250248	31
32	0.161397	0.171126	0.180906	0.190729	0.200587	0.210472	0.220380	0.230306	0.240246	0.250198	32
33	0.161203	0.170961	0.180767	0.190612	0.200489	0.210390	0.220311	0.230249	0.240198	0.250159	33
34	0.161036	0.170821	0.180650	0.190514	0.200407	0.210322	0.220255	0.230202	0.240160	0.250127	34
35	0.160892	0.170701	0.180550	0.190432	0.200339	0.210266	0.220209	0.230164	0.240129	0.250101	35
36	0.160769	0.170599	0.180466	0.190363	0.200283	0.210220	0.220171	0.230133	0.240104	0.250081	36
37	0.160662	0.170512	0.180395	0.190305	0.200235	0.210182	0.220140	0.230109	0.240084	0.250065	37
38	0.160571	0.170437	0.180335	0.190256	0.200196	0.210150	0.220115	0.230088	0.240068	0.250052	38
39	0.160492	0.170373	0.180284	0.190215	0.200163	0.210124	0.220094	0.230072	0.240055	0.250042	39
40	0.160424	0.170319	0.180240	0.190181	0.200136	0.210103	0.220077	0.230058	0.240044	0.250033	40
41	0.160365	0.170273	0.180204	0.190152	0.200113	0.210085	0.220063	0.230047	0.240035	0.250027	41
42	0.160315	0.170233	0.180172	0.190128	0.200095	0.210070	0.220052	0.230039	0.240029	0.250021	42
43	0.160271	0.170199	0.180146	0.190107	0.200079	0.210058	0.220043	0.230031	0.240023	0.250017	43
44	0.160234	0.170170	0.180124	0.190090	0.200066	0.210048	0.220035	0.230025	0.240019	0.250014	44
45	0.160201	0.170145	0.180105	0.190076	0.200055	0.210040	0.220029	0.230021	0.240015	0.250011	45
46	0.160174	0.170124	0.180089	0.190064	0.200046	0.210033	0.220023	0.230017	0.240012	0.250009	46
47	0.160150	0.170106	0.180075	0.190053	0.200038	0.210027	0.220019	0.230014	0.240010	0.250007	47
48	0.160129	0.170091	0.180064	0.190045	0.200032	0.210022	0.220016	0.230011	0.240008	0.250006	48
49	0.160111	0.170078	0.180054	0.190038	0.200026	0.210018	0.220013	0.230009	0.240006	0.250004	49
50	0.160096	0.170066	0.180046	0.190032	0.200022	0.210015	0.220011	0.230007	0.240005	0.250004	50
51	0.160083	0.170057	0.180039	0.190027	0.200018	0.210013	0.220009	0.230006	0.240004	0.250003	51
52	0.160071	0.170048	0.180033	0.190022	0.200015	0.210010	0.220007	0.230005	0.240003	0.250002	52
53	0.160061	0.170041	0.180028	0.190019	0.200013	0.210009	0.220006	0.230004	0.240003	0.250002	53
54	0.160053	0.170035	0.180024	0.190016	0.200011	0.210007	0.220005	0.230003	0.240002	0.250001	54
55	0.160046	0.170030	0.180020	0.190013	0.200009	0.210006	0.220004	0.230003	0.240002	0.250001	55

Food and drink

For other measures see Food and drink, pages 91–96.

Measurement of alcoholic strength by density

Density in air at 20°C kg/m³	Alcoholic strength (% ethanol) by volume at 20°C (% vol)	by mass (% mas)
997.15	0.00	0.00
997.1	0.03	0.03
997	0.10	0.08
996	0.76	0.60
995	1.44	1.14
994	2.13	1.69
993	2.83	2.24
992	3.54	2.81
991	4.26	3.39
990	5.00	3.98
989	5.75	4.59
988	6.52	5.20
987	7.30	5.83
986	8.09	6.47
985	8.90	7.12
984	9.72	7.78
983	10.55	8.46
982	11.40	9.15
981	12.26	9.85
980	13.14	10.57
979	14.03	11.30
978.5	14.47	11.66
978	14.93	12.03
977.5	15.38	12.40
977	15.84	12.78
976.5	16.29	13.15
976	16.75	13.53
975.5	17.21	13.91
975	17.68	14.29
974.5	18.14	14.68
974	18.61	15.06
973.5	19.07	15.45
973	19.54	15.83
972.5	20.00	16.22
972	20.47	16.60
971.5	20.93	16.99
971	21.40	17.37
970.5	21.86	17.76
970	22.32	18.14
969.5	22.78	18.52
969	23.24	18.90
968.5	23.69	19.28
968	24.14	19.66
967.5	24.59	20.04
967	25.04	20.41
966.5	25.48	20.79
966	25.92	21.16
965.5	26.36	21.52
965	26.79	21.89
964.5	27.22	22.25
964	27.65	22.61
963.5	28.07	22.97
963	28.49	23.32
962.5	28.90	23.67
962	29.31	24.02
961.5	29.72	24.37
961	30.12	24.71
960.5	30.52	25.05
960	30.92	25.39
959.5	31.31	25.73

Density in air at 20°C kg/m³	Alcoholic strength (% ethanol) by volume at 20°C (% vol)	by mass (% mas)
959	31.70	26.06
958.5	32.08	26.39
958	32.46	26.71
957.5	32.84	27.04
957	33.21	27.36
956.5	33.58	27.68
956	33.95	27.99
955.5	34.31	28.31
955	34.67	28.62
954.5	35.02	28.93
954	35.37	29.23
953.5	35.72	29.54
953	36.07	29.84
952.5	36.14	30.14
952	36.75	30.43
951.5	37.09	30.73
951	37.42	31.02
950.5	37.75	31.31
950	38.08	31.60
949.5	38.40	31.89
949	38.73	32.17
948	39.36	32.74
947	39.99	33.29
946	40.61	33.84
945	41.22	34.39
944	41.82	34.93
943	42.41	35.46
942	43.00	35.99
941	43.58	36.51
940	44.15	37.02
939	44.71	37.54
938	45.27	38.05
937	45.82	38.55
936	46.37	39.05
935	46.91	39.55
934	47.44	40.04
933	47.97	40.53
932	48.49	41.02
931	49.01	41.50
930	49.53	41.99
929	50.04	42.46
928	50.55	42.94
927	51.05	43.42
926	51.55	43.89
925	52.05	44.36
924	52.54	44.83
923	53.03	45.29
922	53.51	45.76
921	54.00	46.22
920	54.48	46.68
919	54.95	47.14
918	55.43	47.60
917	55.90	48.05
916	56.37	48.51
915	56.83	48.96
914	57.29	49.42
913	57.76	49.87
912	58.21	50.32
911	58.67	50.77
910	59.12	51.22

Density in air at 20°C kg/m³	Alcoholic strength (% ethanol) by volume at 20°C (% vol)	by mass (% mas)
909	59.57	51.66
908	60.02	52.11
907	60.47	52.56
906	60.91	53.00
905	61.36	53.45
904	61.80	53.89
903	62.24	54.33
902	62.67	54.77
901	63.11	55.21
900	63.54	55.65
899	63.97	56.09
898	64.40	56.53
897	64.82	56.97
896	65.25	57.41
895	65.67	57.84
894	66.09	58.28
893	66.51	58.71
892	66.93	59.15
891	67.34	59.58
890	67.76	60.01
889	68.17	60.45
888	68.58	60.88
887	68.99	61.31
886	69.39	61.74
885	69.80	62.17
884	70.20	62.60
883	70.60	63.03
882	71.00	63.45
881	71.40	63.88
880	71.79	64.31
879	72.19	64.74
878	72.58	65.16
877	72.97	65.59
876	73.36	66.01
875	73.74	66.43
874	74.13	66.86
873	74.51	67.28
872	74.89	67.70
871	75.28	68.13
870	75.65	68.55
869	76.03	68.97
868	76.41	69.39
867	76.78	69.81
866	77.15	70.23
865	77.52	70.65
864	77.89	71.06
863	78.26	71.48
862	78.62	71.90
861	78.99	72.32
860	79.35	72.73
859	79.71	73.15
858	80.07	73.56
857	80.43	73.98
856	80.78	74.39
855	81.14	74.80
854	81.49	75.22
853	81.84	75.63
852	82.19	76.04
851	82.54	76.45
850	82.89	76.86

Density in air at 20°C kg/m³	Alcoholic strength (% ethanol) by volume at 20°C (% vol)	by mass (% mas)
849	83.23	77.27
848	83.57	77.68
847	83.91	78.09
846	84.25	78.50
845	84.59	78.91
844	84.93	79.32
843	85.26	79.72
842	85.59	80.13
841	85.92	80.53
840	86.25	80.93
839	86.58	81.34
838	86.90	81.74
837	87.22	82.14
836	87.54	82.54
835	87.86	82.94
834	88.18	83.34
833	88.49	83.74
832	88.81	84.13
831	89.12	84.53
830	89.42	84.92
829	89.73	85.31
828	90.03	85.71
827	90.33	86.10
826	90.63	86.49
825	90.93	86.87
824	91.22	87.26
823	91.51	87.65
822	91.80	88.03
821	92.09	88.41
820	92.37	88.79
819	92.66	89.17
818	92.94	89.55
817	93.21	89.93
816	93.49	90.30
815	93.76	90.68
814	94.03	91.05
813	94.29	91.42
812	94.56	91.79
811	94.82	92.15
810	95.08	92.52
809	95.33	92.88
808	95.59	93.24
807	95.84	93.60
806	96.08	93.96
805	96.33	94.32
804	96.57	94.67
803	96.81	95.02
802	97.05	95.37
801	97.28	95.72
800	97.51	96.07
799	97.74	96.41
798	97.96	96.75
797	98.18	97.09
796	98.40	97.43
795	98.61	97.77
794	98.83	98.10
793	99.04	98.43
792	99.24	98.76
791	99.44	99.09
790	99.64	99.41
788.16	100.00	100.00

Comparing different systems of measurement of alcoholic strength

UK (Sikes) (obsolete) % proof spirit	Density in air at 20°C kg/m^3	OIML Alcoholic strength (% ethanol) by volume at 20°C (% vol)	OIML Alcoholic strength (% ethanol) by mass (% mas)	USA % US proof spirit at 15.56°C	Gay-Lussac % vol at 15°C (% by vol)	UK (Sikes) (obsolete) % proof spirit	Density in air at 20°C kg/m^3	OIML Alcoholic strength (% ethanol) by volume at 20°C (% vol)	OIML Alcoholic strength (% ethanol) by mass (% mas)	USA % US proof spirit at 15.56°C	Gay-Lussac % vol at 15°C (% by vol)
0	997.1	0.0	0.0	0.0	0.0	60	955.5	34.3	28.3	68.5	34.3
1	996.3	0.6	0.5	1.1	0.6	61	954.7	34.9	28.8	69.6	34.9
2	995.5	1.1	0.9	2.3	1.1*	62	953.8	35.5	29.3	70.7	35.4
3	994.6	1.7	1.4	3.4	1.7	63	953.1	36.0	29.8	71.9	36.0
4	993.8	2.3	1.8	4.6	2.3	64	952.2	36.6	30.3	73.0	36.6
5	992.9	2.9	2.3	5.7	2.9	65	951.3	37.2	30.8	74.2	37.1
6	992.2	3.4	2.7	6.8	3.4	66	950.4	37.8	31.4	75.3	37.7
7	991.3	4.0	3.2	8.0	4.0	67	949.6	38.3	31.8	76.4	38.3
8	990.5	4.6	3.7	9.1	4.6	68	948.8	38.9	32.3	77.6	38.9
9	989.8	5.2	4.1	10.3	5.2	69	947.8	39.5	32.8	78.7	39.4
10	988.9	5.8	4.6	11.4	5.7	70	947.0	40.0	33.3	79.9	40.0
11	988.3	6.3	5.0	12.5	6.3	71	946.0	40.6	33.8	81.0	40.6
12	987.5	6.9	5.5	13.7	6.9	72	945.1	41.2	34.3	82.1	41.1
13	986.7	7.5	6.0	14.8	7.4	73	944.0	41.8	34.9	83.3	41.7
14	986.1	8.1	6.4	16.0	8.0	74	943.2	42.3	35.4	84.4	42.3
15	985.4	8.6	6.9	17.1	8.6	75	942.2	42.9	35.9	85.6	42.9
16	984.6	9.2	7.4	18.3	9.2	76	941.1	43.5	36.4	86.7	43.4
17	983.9	9.8	7.8	19.4	9.7	77	940.2	44.0	36.9	87.8	44.0
18	983.3	10.3	8.3	20.5	10.3	78	939.2	44.6	37.4	89.0	44.6
19	982.6	10.9	8.7	21.7	10.9	79	938.1	45.2	38.0	90.1	45.1
20	982.0	11.4	9.2	22.8	11.5	80	937.1	45.8	38.5	91.3	45.7
21	981.3	12.0	9.7	24.0	12.0	81	936.1	46.3	39.0	92.4	46.3
22	980.6	12.6	10.1	25.1	12.6	82	935.0	46.9	39.5	93.6	46.8
23	979.9	13.2	10.6	26.2	13.2	83	933.9	47.5	40.1	94.7	47.4
24	979.4	13.7	11.1	27.4	13.7*	84	932.9	48.0	40.6	95.8	48.0
25	978.7	14.3	11.5	28.5	14.3	85	931.8	48.6	41.1	97.0	48.5
26	978.0	14.9	12.0	29.7	14.9	86	930.8	49.1	41.6	98.1	49.1
27	977.4	15.5	12.5	30.8	15.5	87	929.7	49.7	42.1	99.3	49.7
28	976.8	16.0	12.9	31.9	16.0	88	928.5	50.3	42.7	100.4	50.2*
29	976.2	16.6	13.4	33.1	16.6	89	927.5	50.8	43.2	101.5	50.8
30	975.5	17.2	13.9	34.2	17.2	90	926.3	51.4	43.7	102.7	51.4
31	975.0	17.7	14.3	35.4	17.8	91	925.2	52.0	44.3	103.8	52.0
32	974.3	18.3	14.8	36.5	18.3	92	924.1	52.5	44.8	105.0	52.5
33	973.7	18.9	15.3	37.6	18.9	93	922.8	53.1	45.4	106.1	53.1
34	973.1	19.4	15.7	38.8	19.5	94	921.6	53.7	45.9	107.2	53.7
35	972.4	20.1	16.3	39.9	20.1	95	920.3	54.3	46.5	108.4	54.2*
36	971.8	20.6	16.8	41.1	20.6	96	919.2	54.8	47.0	109.5	54.8
37	971.2	21.2	17.2	42.2	21.2	97	918.0	55.4	47.6	110.7	55.4
38	970.6	21.8	17.7	43.4	21.7*	98	916.7	56.0	48.2	111.8	56.0
39	970.0	22.3	18.1	44.5	22.3	99	915.6	56.5	48.6	112.9	56.5
40	969.4	22.9	18.6	45.6	22.9	100	914.4	57.1	49.2	114.1	57.1
41	968.7	23.5	19.1	46.8	23.5	101	913.1	57.7	49.8	115.2	57.7
42	968.1	24.1	19.6	47.9	24.0	102	912.0	58.2	50.3	116.4	58.2
43	967.5	24.6	20.0	49.1	24.6	103	910.7	58.8	50.9	117.5	58.8
44	966.8	25.2	20.6	50.2	25.2	104	909.4	59.4	51.5	118.7	59.4
45	966.1	25.8	21.1	51.3	25.7*	105	908.1	60.0	52.1	119.8	60.0
46	965.6	26.3	21.5	52.5	26.3	110	901.8	62.8	54.9	125.5	62.8
47	964.9	26.9	22.0	53.6	26.9	115	894.9	65.7	57.9	131.2	65.6
48	964.2	27.5	22.5	54.8	27.5	120	888.2	68.5	60.8	136.9	68.5
49	963.6	28.0	22.9	55.9	28.0	125	881.0	71.4	63.9	142.6	71.3
50	962.9	28.6	23.4	57.0	28.6	130	873.8	74.2	66.9	148.3	74.2
51	962.1	29.2	23.9	58.2	29.1	135	866.2	77.1	70.1	154.0	77.0
52	961.5	29.7	24.4	59.3	29.7	140	858.5	79.9	73.3	159.7	79.9
53	960.8	30.3	24.9	60.5	30.3	145	850.5	82.7	76.7	165.4	82.7
54	960.0	30.9	25.4	61.6	30.9	150	842.3	85.5	80.0	171.1	85.6
55	959.2	31.5	25.9	62.7	31.5	155	833.3	88.4	83.6	176.8	88.4
56	958.6	32.0	26.3	63.9	32.0	160	824.1	91.2	87.2	182.5	91.3
57	957.8	32.6	26.8	65.0	32.6	165	813.8	94.1	91.1	188.2	94.1
58	957.0	33.2	27.4	66.2	33.2	170	802.6	96.9	95.2	194.0	96.9
59	956.3	33.7	27.8	67.3	33.7	175.3	788.2	100.0	100.0	200.0	100.0

Health

For other measures see Health, pages 97–103.

Millimetres of mercury to kilopascals   1 mm Hg = 0.133 322 kPa

mm Hg → ↓	0	1	2	3	4	5	6	7	8	9	← mm Hg ↓
	kPa	kPa	kPa	kPa	kPa	kPa	kPa	kPa	kPa	kPa	
0	0.000	0.133	0.267	0.400	0.533	0.667	0.800	0.933	1.067	1.200	0
10	1.33	1.47	1.60	1.73	1.87	2.00	2.13	2.27	2.40	2.53	10
20	2.67	2.80	2.93	3.07	3.20	3.33	3.47	3.60	3.73	3.87	20
30	4.00	4.13	4.27	4.40	4.53	4.67	4.80	4.93	5.07	5.20	30
40	5.33	5.47	5.60	5.73	5.87	6.00	6.13	6.27	6.40	6.53	40
50	6.67	6.80	6.93	7.07	7.20	7.33	7.47	7.60	7.73	7.87	50
60	8.00	8.13	8.27	8.40	8.53	8.67	8.80	8.93	9.07	9.20	60
70	9.33	9.47	9.60	9.73	9.87	10.00	10.13	10.27	10.40	10.53	70
80	10.7	10.8	10.9	11.1	11.2	11.3	11.5	11.6	11.7	11.9	80
90	12.0	12.1	12.3	12.4	12.5	12.7	12.8	12.9	13.1	13.2	90
100	13.3	13.5	13.6	13.7	13.9	14.0	14.1	14.3	14.4	14.5	100
110	14.7	14.8	14.9	15.1	15.2	15.3	15.5	15.6	15.7	15.9	110
120	16.0	16.1	16.3	16.4	16.5	16.7	16.8	16.9	17.1	17.2	120
130	17.3	17.5	17.6	17.7	17.9	18.0	18.1	18.3	18.4	18.5	130
140	18.7	18.8	18.9	19.1	19.2	19.3	19.5	19.6	19.7	19.9	140
150	20.0	20.1	20.3	20.4	20.5	20.7	20.8	20.9	21.1	21.2	150
160	21.3	21.5	21.6	21.7	21.9	22.0	22.1	22.3	22.4	22.5	160
170	22.7	22.8	22.9	23.1	23.2	23.3	23.5	23.6	23.7	23.9	170
180	24.0	24.1	24.3	24.4	24.5	24.7	24.8	24.9	25.1	25.2	180
190	25.3	25.5	25.6	25.7	25.9	26.0	26.1	26.3	26.4	26.5	190
200	26.7	26.8	26.9	27.1	27.2	27.3	27.5	27.6	27.7	27.9	200
210	28.0	28.1	28.3	28.4	28.5	28.7	28.8	28.9	29.1	29.2	210
220	29.3	29.5	29.6	29.7	29.9	30.0	30.1	30.3	30.4	30.5	220
230	30.7	30.8	30.9	31.1	31.2	31.3	31.5	31.6	31.7	31.9	230
240	32.0	32.1	32.3	32.4	32.5	32.7	32.8	32.9	33.1	33.2	240
250	33.3	33.5	33.6	33.7	33.9	34.0	34.1	34.3	34.4	34.5	250
260	34.7	34.8	34.9	35.1	35.2	35.3	35.5	35.6	35.7	35.9	260
270	36.0	36.1	36.3	36.4	36.5	36.7	36.8	36.9	37.1	37.2	270
280	37.3	37.5	37.6	37.7	37.9	38.0	38.1	38.3	38.4	38.5	280
290	38.7	38.8	38.9	39.1	39.2	39.3	39.5	39.6	39.7	39.9	290
300	40.0	40.1	40.3	40.4	40.5	40.7	40.8	40.9	41.1	41.2	300

Kilopascals to millimetres of mercury   1 kPa = 7.500 616 mm Hg

kPa → ↓	0	1	2	3	4	5	6	7	8	9	← kPa ↓
	mm Hg	mm Hg	mm Hg	mm Hg	mm Hg	mm Hg	mm Hg	mm Hg	mm Hg	mm Hg	
0	0.0	7.5	15.0	22.5	30.0	37.5	45.0	52.5	60.0	67.5	0
10	75.0	82.5	90.0	97.5	105.0	112.5	120.0	127.5	135.0	142.5	10
20	150	158	165	173	180	188	195	203	210	218	20
30	225	233	240	248	255	263	270	278	285	293	30
40	300	308	315	323	330	338	345	353	360	368	40

Centimetres of water to kilopascals   1 cm H_2O = 0.098 066 5 kPa

cm H_2O → ↓	0	1	2	3	4	5	6	7	8	9	← cm H_2O ↓
	kPa	kPa	kPa	kPa	kPa	kPa	kPa	kPa	kPa	kPa	
0	0.000	0.098	0.196	0.294	0.392	0.490	0.588	0.686	0.785	0.883	0
10	0.981	1.079	1.177	1.275	1.373	1.471	1.569	1.667	1.765	1.863	10
20	1.96	2.06	2.16	2.26	2.35	2.45	2.55	2.65	2.75	2.84	20
30	2.94	3.04	3.14	3.24	3.33	3.43	3.53	3.63	3.73	3.82	30
40	3.92	4.02	4.12	4.22	4.31	4.41	4.51	4.61	4.71	4.81	40
50	4.90	5.00	5.10	5.20	5.30	5.39	5.49	5.59	5.69	5.79	50

Iron and steel

For other measures see Iron and steel, pages 104–106.

Steel products: multipliers for different levels of density (kg/m³)

kg/m³		kg/m³		kg/m³		kg/m³		kg/m³		kg/m³		kg/m³		kg/m³	
7500	0.955	7650	0.975	7800	0.994	7950	1.013	8100	1.032	8250	1.051	8400	1.070	8550	1.089
7510	0.957	7660	0.976	7810	0.995	7960	1.014	8110	1.033	8260	1.052	8410	1.071	8560	1.090
7520	0.958	7670	0.977	7820	0.996	7970	1.015	8120	1.034	8270	1.054	8420	1.073	8570	1.092
7530	0.959	7680	0.978	7830	0.997	7980	1.017	8130	1.036	8280	1.055	8430	1.074	8580	1.093
7540	0.961	7690	0.980	7840	0.999	7990	1.018	8140	1.037	8290	1.056	8440	1.075	8590	1.094
7550	0.962	7700	0.981	7850	1.000	8000	1.019	8150	1.038	8300	1.057	8450	1.076	8600	1.096
7560	0.963	7710	0.982	7860	1.001	8010	1.020	8160	1.039	8310	1.059	8460	1.078	8610	1.097
7570	0.964	7720	0.983	7870	1.003	8020	1.022	8170	1.041	8320	1.060	8470	1.079	8620	1.098
7580	0.966	7730	0.985	7880	1.004	8030	1.023	8180	1.042	8330	1.061	8480	1.080	8630	1.099
7590	0.967	7740	0.986	7890	1.005	8040	1.024	8190	1.043	8340	1.062	8490	1.082	8640	1.101
7600	0.968	7750	0.987	7900	1.006	8050	1.025	8200	1.045	8350	1.064	8500	1.083	8650	1.102
7610	0.969	7760	0.989	7910	1.008	8060	1.027	8210	1.046	8360	1.065	8510	1.084	8660	1.103
7620	0.971	7770	0.990	7920	1.009	8070	1.028	8220	1.047	8370	1.066	8520	1.085	8670	1.104
7630	0.972	7780	0.991	7930	1.010	8080	1.029	8230	1.048	8380	1.068	8530	1.087	8680	1.106
7640	0.973	7790	0.992	7940	1.011	8090	1.031	8240	1.050	8390	1.069	8540	1.088	8690	1.107

Weight (mass) of steel: wire with standard density of 7 850 kg/m³ (kg per 100 m length)

Diameter → in mm ↓	0.00	0.01	0.02	0.03	0.04	0.05	0.06	0.07	0.08	0.09	← Diameter in mm ↓
	kg/100m	kg/100m	kg/100m	kg/100m	kg/100m	kg/100m	kg/100m	kg/100m	kg/100m	kg/100m	
0.0	0.0000000	0.0000617	0.0002466	0.0005549	0.0009865	0.0015413	0.0022195	0.0030210	0.0039458	0.0049940	0.0
0.1	0.0061654	0.0074601	0.0088781	0.0104195	0.0120841	0.0138721	0.0157834	0.0178179	0.0199758	0.0222570	0.1
0.2	0.0246615	0.0271893	0.0298404	0.0326148	0.0355126	0.0385336	0.0416779	0.0449456	0.0483365	0.0518508	0.2
0.3	0.0554884	0.0592493	0.0631334	0.0671409	0.0712717	0.0755259	0.0799033	0.0844040	0.0890280	0.0937754	0.3
0.4	0.0986460	0.1036400	0.1087572	0.1139978	0.1193617	0.1248489	0.1304593	0.1361931	0.1420503	0.1480307	0.4
0.5	0.1541344	0.1603614	0.1667118	0.1731854	0.1797824	0.1865026	0.1933462	0.2003131	0.2074032	0.2146167	0.5
0.6	0.2219535	0.2294136	0.2369970	0.2447038	0.2525338	0.2604871	0.2685638	0.2767637	0.2850870	0.2935335	0.6
0.7	0.3021034	0.3107966	0.3196131	0.3285529	0.3376160	0.3468024	0.3561121	0.3655451	0.3751015	0.3847811	0.7
0.8	0.3945840	0.4045103	0.4145599	0.4247327	0.4350289	0.4454484	0.4559912	0.4666573	0.4774467	0.4883594	0.8
0.9	0.4993954	0.5105548	0.5218374	0.5332433	0.5447726	0.5564251	0.5682010	0.5801002	0.5921227	0.6042685	0.9
1.0	0.6165376	0.6289300	0.6414457	0.6540847	0.6668470	0.6797327	0.6927416	0.7058739	0.7191294	0.7325083	1.0
1.1	0.7460104	0.7596359	0.7733847	0.7872568	0.8012522	0.8153709	0.8296129	0.8439783	0.8584669	0.8730788	1.1
1.2	0.8878141	0.9026726	0.9176545	0.9327597	0.9479881	0.9633399	0.9788150	0.9944134	1.0101351	1.0259802	1.2
1.3	1.0419485	1.0580401	1.0742550	1.0905933	1.1070548	1.1236397	1.1403479	1.1571793	1.1741341	1.1912122	1.3
1.4	1.2084136	1.2257383	1.2431863	1.2607577	1.2784523	1.2962702	1.3142115	1.3322760	1.3504639	1.3687750	1.4
1.5	1.3872095	1.4057673	1.4244484	1.4432528	1.4621805	1.4812315	1.5004058	1.5197034	1.5391244	1.5586686	1.5
1.6	1.5783361	1.5981270	1.6180412	1.6380786	1.6582394	1.6785235	1.6989309	1.7194616	1.7401156	1.7608929	1.6
1.7	1.7817935	1.8028175	1.8239647	1.8452353	1.8666291	1.8881463	1.9097867	1.9315505	1.9534376	1.9754480	1.7
1.8	1.9975817	2.0198387	2.0422190	2.0647226	2.0873496	2.1100998	2.1329733	2.1559702	2.1790903	2.2023338	1.8
1.9	2.2257006	2.2491907	2.2728041	2.2965408	2.3204008	2.3443841	2.3684907	2.3927206	2.4170738	2.4415504	1.9

Diameter → in mm ↓	0.0	0.1	0.2	0.3	0.4	0.5	0.6	0.7	0.8	0.9	← Diameter in mm ↓
	kg/100m	kg/100m	kg/100m	kg/100m	kg/100m	kg/100m	kg/100m	kg/100m	kg/100m	kg/100m	
2	2.4662	2.7189	2.9840	3.2615	3.5513	3.8534	4.1678	4.4946	4.8337	5.1851	2
3	5.5488	5.9249	6.3133	6.7141	7.1272	7.5526	7.9903	8.4404	8.9028	9.3775	3
4	9.8646	10.3640	10.8757	11.3998	11.9362	12.4849	13.0459	13.6193	14.2050	14.8031	4
5	15.4134	16.0361	16.6712	17.3185	17.9782	18.6503	19.3346	20.0313	20.7403	21.4617	5
6	22.1954	22.9414	23.6997	24.4704	25.2534	26.0487	26.8564	27.6764	28.5087	29.3534	6
7	30.2103	31.0797	31.9613	32.8553	33.7616	34.6802	35.6112	36.5545	37.5101	38.4781	7
8	39.4584	40.4510	41.4560	42.4733	43.5029	44.5448	45.5991	46.6657	47.7447	48.8359	8
9	49.9395	51.0555	52.1837	53.3243	54.4773	55.6425	56.8201	58.0100	59.2123	60.4268	9
10	61.6538	62.8930	64.1446	65.4085	66.6847	67.9733	69.2742	70.5874	71.9129	73.2508	10
11	74.6010	75.9636	77.3385	78.7257	80.1252	81.5371	82.9613	84.3978	85.8467	87.3079	11
12	88.7814	90.2673	91.7655	93.2760	94.7988	96.3340	97.8815	99.4413	101.0135	102.5980	12
13	104.1948	105.8040	107.4255	109.0593	110.7055	112.3640	114.0348	115.7179	117.4134	119.1212	13
14	120.8414	122.5738	124.3186	126.0758	127.8452	129.6270	131.4211	133.2276	135.0464	136.8775	14
15	138.7210	140.5767	142.4448	144.3253	146.2180	148.1231	150.0406	151.9703	153.9124	155.8669	15
16	157.8336	159.8127	161.8041	163.8079	165.8239	167.8524	169.8931	171.9462	174.0116	176.0893	16

Weight (mass) of steel: sheet and strip with standard density of 7 850 kg/m³ (kg per m length)

Thickness → in mm / Width in mm ↓	0.2 kg/m	0.3 kg/m	0.4 kg/m	0.5 kg/m	0.6 kg/m	0.7 kg/m	0.8 kg/m	0.9 kg/m	1.0 kg/m	2.0 kg/m	3.0 kg/m	← Thickness in mm / Width in mm ↓
20	0.03140	0.04710	0.06280	0.07850	0.09420	0.10990	0.12560	0.14130	0.15700	0.31400	0.47100	20
25	0.03925	0.05888	0.07850	0.09812	0.11775	0.13737	0.15700	0.17662	0.19625	0.39250	0.58875	25
30	0.04710	0.07065	0.09420	0.11775	0.14130	0.16485	0.18840	0.21195	0.23550	0.47100	0.70650	30
35	0.05495	0.08243	0.10990	0.13737	0.16485	0.19232	0.21980	0.24727	0.27475	0.54950	0.82425	35
40	0.06280	0.09420	0.12560	0.15700	0.18840	0.21980	0.25120	0.28260	0.31400	0.62800	0.94200	40
45	0.07065	0.10597	0.14130	0.17662	0.21195	0.24727	0.28260	0.31792	0.35325	0.70650	1.05975	45
50	0.07850	0.11775	0.15700	0.19625	0.23550	0.27475	0.31400	0.35325	0.39250	0.78500	1.17750	50
55	0.08635	0.12953	0.17270	0.21587	0.25905	0.30222	0.34540	0.38857	0.43175	0.86350	1.29525	55
60	0.09420	0.14130	0.18840	0.23550	0.28260	0.32970	0.37680	0.42390	0.47100	0.94200	1.41300	60
70	0.10990	0.16485	0.21980	0.27475	0.32970	0.38465	0.43960	0.49455	0.54950	1.09900	1.64850	70
80	0.12560	0.18840	0.25120	0.31400	0.37680	0.43960	0.50240	0.56520	0.62800	1.25600	1.88400	80
90	0.14130	0.21195	0.28260	0.35325	0.42390	0.49455	0.56520	0.63585	0.70650	1.41300	2.11950	90
100	0.15700	0.23550	0.31400	0.39250	0.47100	0.54950	0.62800	0.70650	0.78500	1.57000	2.35500	100
150	0.23550	0.35325	0.47100	0.58875	0.70650	0.82425	0.94200	1.05975	1.17750	2.35500	3.53250	150
200	0.31400	0.47100	0.62800	0.78500	0.94200	1.09900	1.25600	1.41300	1.57000	3.14000	4.71000	200
250	0.39250	0.58875	0.78500	0.98125	1.17750	1.37375	1.57000	1.76625	1.96250	3.92500	5.88750	250
500	0.78500	1.17750	1.57000	1.96250	2.35500	2.74750	3.14000	3.53250	3.92500	7.85000	11.77500	500
750	1.17750	1.76625	2.35500	2.94375	3.53250	4.12125	4.71000	5.29875	5.88750	11.77500	17.66250	750
1000	1.57000	2.35500	3.14000	3.92500	4.71000	5.49500	6.28000	7.06500	7.85000	15.70000	23.55000	1000
1250	1.96250*	2.94375	3.92500*	4.90625	5.88750	6.86875	7.85000	8.83125	9.81250	19.62500	29.43750	1250
1500	2.35500*	3.53250*	4.71000	5.88750	7.06500	8.24250	9.42000	10.59750	11.77500	23.55000	35.32500	1500
1750	2.74750*	4.12125*	5.49500	6.86875	8.24250	9.61625	10.99000	12.36375	13.73750	27.47500	41.21250	1750
2000	3.14000*	4.71000*	6.28000*	7.85000*	9.42000*	10.99000*	12.56000*	14.13000*	15.70000*	31.40000*	47.10000*	2000
2250	3.53250*	5.29875*	7.06500*	8.83125*	10.59750*	12.36375*	14.13000*	15.89625*	17.66250*	35.32500*	52.98750*	2250
2500	3.92500*	5.88750*	7.85000*	9.81250*	11.77500*	13.73750*	15.70000*	17.66250*	19.62500*	39.25000*	58.87500*	2500

Thickness → in mm / Width in mm ↓	4 kg/m	6 kg/m	8 kg/m	10 kg/m	12 kg/m	14 kg/m	16 kg/m	18 kg/m	20 kg/m	25 kg/m	30 kg/m	← Thickness in mm / Width in mm ↓
20	0.6280	0.9420	1.2560	1.5700	1.8840	2.1980	2.5120	2.8260	3.1400	3.9250	4.7100	20
25	0.7850	1.1775	1.5700	1.9625	2.3550	2.7475	3.1400	3.5325	3.9250	4.9062	5.8875	25
30	0.9420	1.4130	1.8840	2.3550	2.8260	3.2970	3.7680	4.2390	4.7100	5.8875	7.0650	30
35	1.0990	1.6485	2.1980	2.7475	3.2970	3.8465	4.3960	4.9455	5.4950	6.8687	8.2425	35
40	1.2560	1.8840	2.5120	3.1400	3.7680	4.3960	5.0240	5.6520	6.2800	7.8500	9.4200	40
45	1.4130	2.1195	2.8260	3.5325	4.2390	4.9455	5.6520	6.3585	7.0650	8.8312	10.5975	45
50	1.5700	2.3550	3.1400	3.9250	4.7100	5.4950	6.2800	7.0650	7.8500	9.8125	11.7750	50
55	1.7270	2.5905	3.4540	4.3175	5.1810	6.0445	6.9080	7.7715	8.6350	10.7938	12.9525	55
60	1.8840	2.8260	3.7680	4.7100	5.6520	6.5940	7.5360	8.4780	9.4200	11.7750	14.1300	60
70	2.1980	3.2970	4.3960	5.4950	6.5940	7.6930	8.7920	9.8910	10.9900	13.7375	16.4850	70
80	2.5120	3.7680	5.0240	6.2800	7.5360	8.7920	10.0480	11.3040	12.5600	15.7000	18.8400	80
90	2.8260	4.2390	5.6520	7.0650	8.4780	9.8910	11.3040	12.7170	14.1300	17.6625	21.1950	90
100	3.1400	4.7100	6.2800	7.8500	9.4200	10.9900	12.5600	14.1300	15.7000	19.6250	23.5500	100
150	4.7100	7.0650	9.4200	11.7750	14.1300	16.4850	18.8400	21.1950	23.5500	29.4375	35.3250	150
200	6.2800	9.4200	12.5600	15.7000	18.8400	21.9800	25.1200	28.2600	31.4000	39.2500	47.1000	200
250	7.8500	11.7750	15.7000	19.6250	23.5500	27.4750	31.4000	35.3250	39.2500	49.0625	58.8750	250
500	15.7000	23.5500	31.4000	39.2500	47.1000	54.9500	62.8000	70.6500	78.5000	98.1250	117.7500	500
750	23.5500	35.3250	47.1000	58.8750	70.6500	82.4250	94.2000	105.9750	117.7500	147.1875	176.6250	750
1000	31.4000	47.1000	62.8000	78.5000	94.2000	109.9000	125.6000	141.3000	157.0000	196.2500	235.5000	1000
1250	39.2500	58.8750	78.5000	98.1250	117.7500	137.3750	157.0000	176.6250	196.2500	245.3125	294.3750	1250
1500	47.1000	70.6500	94.2000	117.7500	141.3000	164.8500	188.4000	211.9500	235.5000	294.3750	353.2500	1500
1750	54.9500	82.4250	109.9000	137.3750	164.8500	192.3250	219.8000	247.2750	274.7500	343.4375	412.1250	1750
2000	62.8000*	94.2000	125.6000	157.0000	188.4000	219.8000	251.2000	282.6000	314.0000	392.5000	471.0000	2000
2250	70.6500*	105.9750	141.3000	176.6250	211.9500	247.2750	282.6000	317.9250	353.2500	441.5625	529.8750	2250
2500	78.5000*	117.7500	157.0000	196.2500	235.5000	274.7500	314.0000	353.2500	392.5000	490.6250	588.7500	2500

Note. For meaning of asterisk on this page and page 229, see Iron and steel, page 106.

Weight (mass) of steel: plate, sheet and strip with standard density of 7 850 kg/m^3 (kg per m length)

Thickness → in mm / Width in mm ↓	35	40	45	50	55	60	65	70	75	80	85	← Thickness in mm / Width in mm ↓
	kg/m	kg/m	kg/m	kg/m	kg/m	kg/m	kg/m	kg/m	kg/m	kg/m	kg/m	
300	82.425	94.200	105.975	117.750	129.525	141.300	153.075	164.850	176.625	188.400	200.175	300
350	96.163	109.900	123.637	137.375	151.112	164.850	178.587	192.325	206.062	219.800	233.538	350
400	109.900	125.600	141.300	157.000	172.700	188.400	204.100	219.800	235.500	251.200	266.900	400
450	123.637	141.300	158.962	176.625	194.288	211.950	229.612	247.275	264.937	282.600	300.263	450
500	137.375	157.000	176.625	196.250	215.875	235.500	255.125	274.750	294.375	314.000	333.625	500
550	151.112	172.700	194.288	215.875	237.462	259.050	280.638	302.225	323.812	345.400	366.987	550
600	164.850	188.400	211.950	235.500	259.050	282.600	306.150	329.700	353.250	376.800	400.350	600
700	192.325	219.800	247.275	274.750	302.225	329.700	357.175	384.650	412.125	439.600	467.075	700
800	219.800	251.200	282.600	314.000	345.400	376.800	408.200	439.600	471.000	502.400	533.800	800
900	247.275	282.600	317.925	353.250	388.575	423.900	459.225	494.550	529.875	565.200	600.525	900
1000	274.750	314.000	353.250	392.500	431.750	471.000	510.250	549.500	588.750	628.000	667.250	1000
1250	343.437	392.500	441.562	490.625	539.687	588.750	637.812	686.875	735.937	785.000	834.062	1250
1500	412.125	471.000	529.875	588.750	647.625	706.500	765.375	824.250	883.125	942.000	1000.875	1500
1750	480.812	549.500	618.187	686.875	755.562	824.250	892.937	961.625	1030.312	1099.000	1167.687	1750
2000	549.500	628.000	706.500	785.000	863.500	942.000	1020.500	1099.000	1177.500	1256.000	1334.500	2000
2250	618.187	706.500	794.812	883.125	971.437	1059.750	1148.062	1236.375	1324.687	1413.000	1501.312	2250
2500	686.875	785.000	883.125	981.250	1079.375	1177.500	1275.625	1373.750	1471.875	1570.000	1668.125	2500
2750	755.562	863.500	971.437	1079.375	1187.312	1295.250	1403.187	1511.125	1619.062	1727.000	1834.937	2750
3000	824.250	942.000	1059.750	1177.500	1295.250	1413.000	1530.750	1648.500	1766.250	1884.000	2001.750	3000
3250	892.937	1020.500	1148.062	1275.625	1403.187	1530.750	1658.312	1785.875	1913.437	2041.000	2168.562	3250
3500	961.625	1099.000	1236.375	1373.750	1511.125	1648.500	1785.875	1923.250	2060.625	2198.000	2335.375	3500
3750	1030.312	1177.500	1324.687	1471.875	1619.062	1766.250	1913.437	2060.625	2207.812	2355.000	2502.187	3750
4000	1099.000*	1256.000*	1413.000*	1570.000*	1727.000*	1884.000*	2041.000*	2198.000*	2355.000*	2512.000*	2669.000*	4000
4500	1236.375*	1413.000*	1589.625*	1766.250*	1942.875*	2119.500*	2296.125*	2472.750*	2649.375*	2826.000*	3002.625*	4500
5000	1373.750*	1570.000*	1766.250*	1962.500*	2158.750*	2355.000*	2551.250*	2747.500*	2943.750*	3140.000*	3336.250*	5000

Thickness → in mm / Width in mm ↓	90	95	100	105	110	115	120	125	130	135	140	150	← Thickness in mm / Width in mm ↓
	kg/m	kg/m	kg/m	kg/m	kg/m	kg/m	kg/m	kg/m	kg/m	kg/m	kg/m	kg/m	
300	211.95	223.73	235.50	247.27	259.05	270.83	282.60	294.37	306.15	317.92	329.70	353.25	300
350	247.27	261.01	274.75	288.49	302.22	315.96	329.70	343.44	357.17	370.91	384.65	412.12	350
400	282.60	298.30	314.00	329.70	345.40	361.10	376.80	392.50	408.20	423.90	439.60	471.00	400
450	317.92	335.59	353.25	370.91	388.58	406.24	423.90	441.56	459.22	476.89	494.55	529.87	450
500	353.25	372.87	392.50	412.12	431.75	451.37	471.00	490.62	510.25	529.87	549.50	588.75	500
550	388.58	410.16	431.75	453.34	474.92	496.51	518.10	539.69	561.28	582.86	604.45	647.62	550
600	423.90	447.45	471.00	494.55	518.10	541.65	565.20	588.75	612.30	635.85	659.40	706.50	600
700	494.55	522.03	549.50	576.97	604.45	631.93	659.40	686.87	714.35	741.82	769.30	824.25	700
800	565.20	596.60	628.00	659.40	690.80	722.20	753.60	785.00	816.40	847.80	879.20	942.00	800
900	635.85	671.18	706.50	741.82	777.15	812.47	847.80	883.12	918.45	953.78	989.10	1059.75	900
1000	706.50	745.75	785.00	824.25	863.50	902.75	942.00	981.25	1020.50	1059.75	1099.00	1177.50	1000
1250	883.12	932.19	981.25	1030.31	1079.37	1128.44	1177.50	1226.56	1275.62	1324.69	1373.75	1471.87	1250
1500	1059.75	1118.62	1177.50	1236.37	1295.25	1354.12	1413.00	1471.87	1530.75	1589.62	1648.50	1766.25	1500
1750	1236.37	1305.06	1373.75	1442.44	1511.12	1579.81	1648.50	1717.19	1785.87	1854.56	1923.25	2060.62	1750
2000	1413.00	1491.50	1570.00	1648.50	1727.00	1805.50	1884.00	1962.50	2041.00	2119.50	2198.00	2355.00	2000
2250	1589.62	1677.94	1766.25	1854.56	1942.87	2031.19	2119.50	2207.81	2296.12	2384.44	2472.75	2649.37	2250
2500	1766.25	1864.37	1962.50	2060.62	2158.75	2256.87	2355.00	2453.12	2551.25	2649.37	2747.50	2943.75	2500
2750	1942.87	2050.81	2158.75	2266.69	2374.62	2482.56	2590.50	2698.44	2806.37	2914.31	3022.25	3238.12	2750
3000	2119.50	2237.25	2355.00	2472.75	2590.50	2708.25	2826.00	2943.75	3061.50	3179.25	3297.00	3532.50	3000
3250	2296.12	2423.69	2551.25	2678.81	2806.37	2933.94	3061.50	3189.06	3316.62	3444.19	3571.75	3826.87	3250
3500	2472.75	2610.12	2747.50	2884.87	3022.25	3159.62	3297.00	3434.37	3571.75	3709.12	3846.50	4121.25	3500
3750	2649.37	2796.56	2943.75	3090.94	3238.12	3385.31	3532.50	3679.69	3826.87	3974.06	4121.25	4415.62	3750
4000	2826.00*	2983.00*	3140.00*	3297.00*	3454.00*	3611.00*	3768.00*	3925.00*	4082.00*	4239.00*	4396.00*	4710.00*	4000
4500	3179.25*	3355.87*	3532.50*	3709.12*	3885.75*	4062.37*	4239.00*	4415.62*	4592.25*	4768.87*	4945.50*	5298.75*	4500
5000	3532.50*	3728.75*	3925.00*	4121.25*	4317.50*	4513.75*	4710.00*	4906.25*	5102.50*	5298.75*	5495.00*	5887.50*	5000

Textiles

For other measures see Textiles, pages 144–147.

Tex to other count systems

Tex	Cotton (UK) spun silk	Denier	Linen dry spun, hemp, jute, woollen: Aberdeen	Metric	Typp	Woollen: American cut, linen, wet or dry spun	American run	Dewsbury, cotton, bump yarn	Galashiels	Hawick	West of England	Yorkshire	Worsted	Tex
1	590.5	9	0.03	1000.0	496.1	1654.0	310.0	31003	2480	2687	1550	1938	885.8	1
2	295.3	18	0.06	500.0	248.0	827.0	155.0	15502	1240	1343	775	969	442.9	2
3	196.8	27	0.09	333.3	165.4	551.3	103.3	10334	827	896	517	646	295.3	3
4	147.6	36	0.12	250.0	124.0	413.5	77.5	7751	620	672	388	485	221.5	4
5	118.1	45	0.15	200.0	99.2	330.8	62.0	6201	496	537	310	388	177.2	5
6	98.4	54	0.17	166.7	82.7	275.7	51.7	5167	413	448	258	323	147.6	6
7	84.4	63	0.20	142.9	70.9	236.3	44.3	4429	354	384	221	277	126.5	7
8	73.8	72	0.23	125.0	62.0	206.8	38.8	3875	310	336	194	242	110.7	8
9	65.6	81	0.26	111.1	55.1	183.8	34.4	3445	276	299	172	215	98.4	9
10	59.1	90	0.29	100.0	49.6	165.4	31.0	3100	248	269	155	194	88.6	10
11	53.7	99	0.32	90.9	45.1	150.4	28.2	2818	225	244	141	176	80.5	11
12	49.2	108	0.35	83.3	41.3	137.8	25.8	2584	207	224	129	162	73.8	12
13	45.4	117	0.38	76.9	38.2	127.2	23.8	2385	191	207	119	149	68.1	13
14	42.2	126	0.41	71.4	35.4	118.1	22.1	2215	177	192	111	138	63.3	14
15	39.4	135	0.44	66.7	33.1	110.3	20.7	2067	165	179	103	129	59.1	15
16	36.9	144	0.46	62.5	31.0	103.4	19.4	1938	155	168	97	121	55.4	16
18	32.8	162	0.52	55.6	27.6	91.9	17.2	1722	138	149	86	108	49.2	18
20	29.5	180	0.58	50.0	24.8	82.7	15.5	1550	124	134	78	97	44.3	20
22	26.8	198	0.64	45.5	22.6	75.2	14.1	1409	113	122	70	88	40.3	22
24	24.6	216	0.70	41.7	20.7	68.9	12.9	1292	103	112	65	81	36.9	24
26	22.7	234	0.75	38.5	19.1	63.6	11.9	1192	95	103	60	75	34.1	26
28	21.1	252	0.81	35.7	17.7	59.1	11.1	1107	89	96	55	69	31.6	28
30	19.7	270	0.87	33.3	16.5	55.1	10.3	1033	83	90	52	65	29.5	30
32	18.5	288	0.93	31.3	15.5	51.7	9.7	969	78	84	48	61	27.7	32
34	17.4	306	0.99	29.4	14.6	48.6	9.1	912	73	79	46	57	26.1	34
36	16.4	324	1.04	27.8	13.8	45.9	8.6	861	69	75	43	54	24.6	36
38	15.5	342	1.10	26.3	13.1	43.5	8.2	816	65	71	41	51	23.3	38
40	14.8	360	1.16	25.0	12.4	41.4	7.8	775	62	67	39	48	22.1	40
42	14.1	378	1.22	23.8	11.8	39.4	7.4	738	59	64	37	46	21.1	42
44	13.4	396	1.28	22.7	11.3	37.6	7.0	705	56	61	35	44	20.1	44
46	12.8	414	1.34	21.7	10.8	36.0	6.7	674	54	58	34	42	19.3	46
48	12.3	432	1.39	20.8	10.3	34.5	6.5	646	52	56	32	40	18.5	48
50	11.8	450	1.45	20.0	9.9	33.1	6.2	620	50	54	31	39	17.7	50
52	11.4	468	1.51	19.2	9.5	31.8	6.0	596	48	52	30	37	17.0	52
54	10.9	486	1.57	18.5	9.2	30.6	5.7	574	46	50	29	36	16.4	54
56	10.5	504	1.63	17.9	8.9	29.5	5.5	554	44	48	28	35	15.8	56
60	9.8	540	1.74	16.7	8.3	27.6	5.2	517	41	45	26	32	14.8	60
64	9.2	576	1.86	15.6	7.8	25.8	4.8	484	39	42	24	30	13.8	64
68	8.7	612	1.97	14.7	7.3	24.3	4.6	456	36	40	23	29	13.0	68
72	8.2	648	2.09	13.9	6.9	23.0	4.3	431	34	37	22	27	12.3	72
76	7.8	684	2.21	13.2	6.5	21.8	4.1	408	33	35	20	26	11.7	76
80	7.4	720	2.32	12.5	6.2	20.7	3.9	388	31	34	19	24	11.1	80
84	7.0	756	2.44	11.9	5.9	19.7	3.7	369	30	32	18	23	10.5	84
88	6.7	792	2.55	11.4	5.6	18.8	3.5	352	28	31	18	22	10.1	88
92	6.4	828	2.67	10.9	5.4	18.0	3.4	337	27	29	17	21	9.6	92
100	5.9	900	2.90	10.0	5.0	16.5	3.1	310	25	27	16	19	8.9	100
200	3.0	1800	5.81	5.0	2.5	8.3	1.6	155	12	13	8	10	4.4	200
300	2.0	2700	8.71	3.3	1.7	5.5	1.0	103	8	9	5	6	3.0	300
400	1.5	3600	11.61	2.5	1.2	4.1	0.8	78	6	7	4	5	2.2	400
500	1.2	4500	14.51	2.0	1.0	3.3	0.6	62	5	5	3	4	1.8	500
600	1.0	5401	17.42	1.7	0.8	2.8	0.5	52	4	4	3	3	1.5	600
700	0.8	6301	20.32	1.4	0.7	2.4	0.4	44	4	4	2	3	1.3	700
800	0.7	7201	23.22	1.3	0.6	2.1	0.4	39	3	3	2	2	1.1	800
900	0.7	8101	26.12	1.1	0.6	1.8	0.3	34	3	3	2	2	1.0	900
1000	0.6	9001	29.03	1.0	0.5	1.7	0.3	31	2	3	2	2	0.9	1000

Transport

For other measures see Transport, pages 148–153.

Miles per UK gallon to SI litres per 100 kilometres (miles per UK gal = 282.481/l per 100 km)

Miles/UK gal → ↓	0.0	0.1	0.2	0.3	0.4	0.5	0.6	0.7	0.8	0.9	← Miles/UK gal ↓
	l/100 km	l/100 km	l/100 km	l/100 km	l/100 km	l/100 km	l/100 km	l/100 km	l/100 km	l/100 km	
1	282.5	256.8	235.4	217.3	201.8	188.3	176.6	166.2	156.9	148.7	1
2	141.2	134.5	128.4	122.8	117.7	113.0	108.6	104.6	100.9	97.4	2
3	94.2	91.1	88.3	85.6	83.1	80.7	78.5	76.3	74.3	72.4	3
4	70.6	68.9	67.3	65.7	64.2	62.8	61.4	60.1	58.9	57.6	4
5	56.5	55.4	54.3	53.3	52.3	51.4	50.4	49.6	48.7	47.9	5
6	47.1	46.3	45.6	44.8	44.1	43.5	42.8	42.2	41.5	40.9	6
7	40.4	39.8	39.2	38.7	38.2	37.7	37.2	36.7	36.2	35.8	7
8	35.3	34.9	34.4	34.0	33.6	33.2	32.8	32.5	32.1	31.7	8
9	31.4	31.0	30.7	30.4	30.1	29.7	29.4	29.1	28.8	28.5	9
10	28.2	28.0	27.7	27.4	27.2	26.9	26.6	26.4	26.2	25.9	10
11	25.7	25.4	25.2	25.0	24.8	24.6	24.4	24.1	23.9	23.7	11
12	23.5	23.3	23.2	23.0	22.8	22.6	22.4	22.2	22.1	21.9	12
13	21.7	21.6	21.4	21.2	21.1	20.9	20.8	20.6	20.5	20.3	13
14	20.2	20.0	19.9	19.8	19.6	19.5	19.3	19.2	19.1	19.0	14
15	18.8	18.7	18.6	18.5	18.3	18.2	18.1	18.0	17.9	17.8	15
16	17.7	17.5	17.4	17.3	17.2	17.1	17.0	16.9	16.8	16.7	16
17	16.6	16.5	16.4	16.3	16.2	16.1	16.1	16.0	15.9	15.8	17
18	15.7	15.6	15.5	15.4	15.4	15.3	15.2	15.1	15.0	14.9	18
19	14.9	14.8	14.7	14.6	14.6	14.5	14.4	14.3	14.3	14.2	19
20	14.1	14.1	14.0	13.9	13.8	13.8	13.7	13.6	13.6	13.5	20
21	13.5	13.4	13.3	13.3	13.2	13.1	13.1	13.0	13.0	12.9	21
22	12.8	12.8	12.7	12.7	12.6	12.6	12.5	12.4	12.4	12.3	22
23	12.3	12.2	12.2	12.1	12.1	12.0	12.0	11.9	11.9	11.8	23
24	11.8	11.7	11.7	11.6	11.6	11.5	11.5	11.4	11.4	11.3	24
25	11.3	11.3	11.2	11.2	11.1	11.1	11.0	11.0	10.9	10.9	25
26	10.9	10.8	10.8	10.7	10.7	10.7	10.6	10.6	10.5	10.5	26
27	10.5	10.4	10.4	10.3	10.3	10.3	10.2	10.2	10.2	10.1	27
28	10.1	10.1	10.0	10.0	9.9	9.9	9.9	9.8	9.8	9.8	28
29	9.7	9.7	9.7	9.6	9.6	9.6	9.5	9.5	9.5	9.4	29
30	9.4	9.4	9.4	9.3	9.3	9.3	9.2	9.2	9.2	9.1	30
31	9.1	9.1	9.1	9.0	9.0	9.0	8.9	8.9	8.9	8.9	31
32	8.8	8.8	8.8	8.7	8.7	8.7	8.7	8.6	8.6	8.6	32
33	8.6	8.5	8.5	8.5	8.5	8.4	8.4	8.4	8.4	8.3	33
34	8.3	8.3	8.3	8.2	8.2	8.2	8.2	8.1	8.1	8.1	34
35	8.1	8.0	8.0	8.0	8.0	8.0	7.9	7.9	7.9	7.9	35
36	7.8	7.8	7.8	7.8	7.8	7.7	7.7	7.7	7.7	7.7	36
37	7.6	7.6	7.6	7.6	7.6	7.5	7.5	7.5	7.5	7.5	37
38	7.4	7.4	7.4	7.4	7.4	7.3	7.3	7.3	7.3	7.3	38
39	7.2	7.2	7.2	7.2	7.2	7.2	7.1	7.1	7.1	7.1	39
40	7.1	7.0	7.0	7.0	7.0	7.0	7.0	6.9	6.9	6.9	40
41	6.9	6.9	6.9	6.8	6.8	6.8	6.8	6.8	6.8	6.7	41
42	6.7	6.7	6.7	6.7	6.7	6.6	6.6	6.6	6.6	6.6	42
43	6.6	6.6	6.5	6.5	6.5	6.5	6.5	6.5	6.4	6.4	43
44	6.4	6.4	6.4	6.4	6.4	6.3	6.3	6.3	6.3	6.3	44
45	6.3	6.3	6.2	6.2	6.2	6.2	6.2	6.2	6.2	6.2	45
46	6.1	6.1	6.1	6.1	6.1	6.1	6.1	6.0	6.0	6.0	46
47	6.0	6.0	6.0	6.0	6.0	5.9	5.9	5.9	5.9	5.9	47
48	5.9	5.9	5.9	5.8	5.8	5.8	5.8	5.8	5.8	5.8	48
49	5.8	5.8	5.7	5.7	5.7	5.7	5.7	5.7	5.7	5.7	49
50	5.6	5.6	5.6	5.6	5.6	5.6	5.6	5.6	5.6	5.5	50
51	5.5	5.5	5.5	5.5	5.5	5.5	5.5	5.5	5.5	5.4	51
52	5.4	5.4	5.4	5.4	5.4	5.4	5.4	5.4	5.4	5.3	52
53	5.3	5.3	5.3	5.3	5.3	5.3	5.3	5.3	5.3	5.2	53
54	5.2	5.2	5.2	5.2	5.2	5.2	5.2	5.2	5.2	5.1	54
55	5.1	5.1	5.1	5.1	5.1	5.1	5.1	5.1	5.1	5.1	55

Miles per US gallon to SI litres per 100 kilometres (miles per US gal = 235.215/l per 100 km)

Miles/US gal → ↓	0.0	0.1	0.2	0.3	0.4	0.5	0.6	0.7	0.8	0.9	← Miles/US gal ↓
	l/100 km	l/100 km	l/100 km	l/100 km	l/100 km	l/100 km	l/100km	l/100km	l/100km	l/100km	
1	235.2	213.8	196.0	180.9	168.0	156.8	147.0	138.4	130.7	123.8	1
2	117.6	112.0	106.9	102.3	98.0	94.1	90.5	87.1	84.0	81.1	2
3	78.4	75.9	73.5	71.3	69.2	67.2	65.3	63.6	61.9	60.3	3
4	58.8	57.4	56.0	54.7	53.5	52.3	51.1	50.0	49.0	48.0	4
5	47.0	46.1	45.2	44.4	43.6	42.8	42.0	41.3	40.6	39.9	5
6	39.2	38.6	37.9	37.3	36.8	36.2	35.6	35.1	34.6	34.1	6
7	33.6	33.1	32.7	32.2	31.8	31.4	30.9	30.5	30.2	29.8	7
8	29.4	29.0	28.7	28.3	28.0	27.7	27.4	27.0	26.7	26.4	8
9	26.1	25.8	25.6	25.3	25.0	24.8	24.5	24.2	24.0	23.8	9
10	23.5	23.3	23.1	22.8	22.6	22.4	22.2	22.0	21.8	21.6	10
11	21.4	21.2	21.0	20.8	20.6	20.5	20.3	20.1	19.9	19.8	11
12	19.6	19.4	19.3	19.1	19.0	18.8	18.7	18.5	18.4	18.2	12
13	18.1	18.0	17.8	17.7	17.6	17.4	17.3	17.2	17.0	16.9	13
14	16.8	16.7	16.6	16.4	16.3	16.2	16.1	16.0	15.9	15.8	14
15	15.7	15.6	15.5	15.4	15.3	15.2	15.1	15.0	14.9	14.8	15
16	14.7	14.6	14.5	14.4	14.3	14.3	14.2	14.1	14.0	13.9	16
17	13.8	13.8	13.7	13.6	13.5	13.4	13.4	13.3	13.2	13.1	17
18	13.1	13.0	12.9	12.9	12.8	12.7	12.6	12.6	12.5	12.4	18
19	12.4	12.3	12.3	12.2	12.1	12.1	12.0	11.9	11.9	11.8	19
20	11.8	11.7	11.6	11.6	11.5	11.5	11.4	11.4	11.3	11.3	20
21	11.2	11.1	11.1	11.0	11.0	10.9	10.9	10.8	10.8	10.7	21
22	10.7	10.6	10.6	10.5	10.5	10.5	10.4	10.4	10.3	10.3	22
23	10.2	10.2	10.1	10.1	10.1	10.0	10.0	9.9	9.9	9.8	23
24	9.8	9.8	9.7	9.7	9.6	9.6	9.6	9.5	9.5	9.4	24
25	9.4	9.4	9.3	9.3	9.3	9.2	9.2	9.2	9.1	9.1	25
26	9.0	9.0	9.0	8.9	8.9	8.9	8.8	8.8	8.8	8.7	26
27	8.7	8.7	8.6	8.6	8.6	8.6	8.5	8.5	8.5	8.4	27
28	8.4	8.4	8.3	8.3	8.3	8.3	8.2	8.2	8.2	8.1	28
29	8.1	8.1	8.1	8.0	8.0	8.0	7.9	7.9	7.9	7.9	29
30	7.8	7.8	7.8	7.8	7.7	7.7	7.7	7.7	7.6	7.6	30
31	7.6	7.6	7.5	7.5	7.5	7.5	7.4	7.4	7.4	7.4	31
32	7.4	7.3	7.3	7.3	7.3	7.2	7.2	7.2	7.2	7.1	32
33	7.1	7.1	7.1	7.1	7.0	7.0	7.0	7.0	7.0	6.9	33
34	6.9	6.9	6.9	6.9	6.8	6.8	6.8	6.8	6.8	6.7	34
35	6.7	6.7	6.7	6.7	6.6	6.6	6.6	6.6	6.6	6.6	35
36	6.5	6.5	6.5	6.5	6.5	6.4	6.4	6.4	6.4	6.4	36
37	6.4	6.3	6.3	6.3	6.3	6.3	6.3	6.2	6.2	6.2	37
38	6.2	6.2	6.2	6.1	6.1	6.1	6.1	6.1	6.1	6.0	38
39	6.0	6.0	6.0	6.0	6.0	6.0	5.9	5.9	5.9	5.9	39
40	5.9	5.9	5.9	5.8	5.8	5.8	5.8	5.8	5.8	5.8	40
41	5.7	5.7	5.7	5.7	5.7	5.7	5.7	5.6	5.6	5.6	41
42	5.6	5.6	5.6	5.6	5.5	5.5	5.5	5.5	5.5	5.5	42
43	5.5	5.5	5.4	5.4	5.4	5.4	5.4	5.4	5.4	5.4	43
44	5.3	5.3	5.3	5.3	5.3	5.3	5.3	5.3	5.3	5.2	44
45	5.2	5.2	5.2	5.2	5.2	5.2	5.2	5.1	5.1	5.1	45
46	5.1	5.1	5.1	5.1	5.1	5.1	5.0	5.0	5.0	5.0	46
47	5.0	5.0	5.0	5.0	5.0	5.0	4.9	4.9	4.9	4.9	47
48	4.9	4.9	4.9	4.9	4.9	4.8	4.8	4.8	4.8	4.8	48
49	4.8	4.8	4.8	4.8	4.8	4.8	4.7	4.7	4.7	4.7	49
50	4.7	4.7	4.7	4.7	4.7	4.7	4.6	4.6	4.6	4.6	50
51	4.6	4.6	4.6	4.6	4.6	4.6	4.6	4.5	4.5	4.5	51
52	4.5	4.5	4.5	4.5	4.5	4.5	4.5	4.5	4.5	4.4	52
53	4.4	4.4	4.4	4.4	4.4	4.4	4.4	4.4	4.4	4.4	53
54	4.4	4.3	4.3	4.3	4.3	4.3	4.3	4.3	4.3	4.3	54
55	4.3	4.3	4.3	4.3	4.2	4.2	4.2	4.2	4.2	4.2	55

PART IV

APPENDICES

Common abbreviations and symbols

Some of the symbols shown here are not among those recommended under the International System of Units.

See also table on pages 47–48 for symbols of elements and page 145 for symbols of textile measuring systems.

a	atto (as prefix) or are
A	ampere
Å	ångström
a/c	account
ac	acre
AC	appellation contrôlée
ACT	advance corporation tax
ASA	American Standards Association
@	at
at	technical atmosphere
AT	atomic time
atm	standard atmosphere
AU	astronomical unit
av. / avdp / avoir	avoirdupois
bbl	barrel
b/d	barrels per day
bd ft	board foot
bhp	brake horsepower
bi	biot
bn	billion
bpd	barrels per day
BPI	bits per inch
BST	British summer time
Btu	British thermal unit
bu	bushel
c	centi (as prefix) or carat
C	coulomb, Celsius or centigrade
cal	calorie
Cal	calorie (dieticians')
cc	cubic centimetre
cd	candela or cord
cf	cubic foot
c & f	cost and freight
cg	centigram
ch	chain or metric horsepower
ch^2	square chain
Chu	centigrade heat unit
Ci	curie
c & i	cost and insurance
cif	cost, insurance and freight
cl	centilitre
cm	centimetre
cm^2	square centimetre
cm^3	cubic centimetre
CM	metric carat
coa	cash on arrival
cod	cash on delivery
cP	centipoise
CPU	central processing unit
cSt	centistokes
ct	metric carat
cwo	cash with order
cwt	hundredweight
d	deci (as prefix) or day
da	deca or deka
dB	decibel
DCE	domestic credit expansion
DCF	discounted cash flow
DIN	Deutsche Industrie Normen
dk	deka or deca
dl	decilitre
dm	decimetre
dm^3	cubic decimetre
DOS	disk operating system
dr	dram
drm	drachm
dwt	pennyweight
dw / DWT	deadweight tonnage
E	Engler
E & OE	errors and omissions excepted
EMU	electromagnetic unit
est.	estimated
ESU	electrostatic unit
ET	ephemeris time
eV	electron volt
f	femto (as prefix)
F	farad or Fahrenheit
fa	free alongside
faa	free of all average
faq	fair average quality
fas	free alongside ship
fbm	foot board measure
FEU	forty-foot equivalent unit
ffa	free from alongside
fg	frigorie
fga	foreign general average
fib	free into bunkers
fifo	first in, first out
fio	free in and out
fios	free in and out stowed
fiot	free in and out trimmed
fl drm	fluid drachm
fl oz	fluid ounce
fob	free on board
foq	free on quay
for	free on rail
fos	free on steamer
fot	free on trucks
ft	foot
ft^2	square foot
ft^3	cubic foot
fur	furlong
g	gram
G	giga (as prefix)
γ	microgram
g_n	standard gravity value
gal	gallon
Gal	galileo
GHz	gigahertz
gm	gram
gn	grain
gr	grain
grt / GRT	gross registered tonnage
gsm	grams per square metre
GW	gigawatt
h	hecto (as prefix) or hour
H	henry
ha	hectare
HF	high frequency
hl	hectolitre
hp	horsepower
hw	high water
Hz	hertz
ihp	indicated horsepower
in	inch
ips	inches per second
iu	international unit
J	joule
k	kilo (as prefix)
K	kelvin
kb, Kb	kilobyte
kcal	kilocalorie
kg	kilogram
kgf	kilogram-force
kHz	kilohertz
kilo	kilogram
kJ	kilojoule
kl	kilolitre
km	kilometre
km^2	square kilometre
kn	international knot
kp	kilopond
kPa	kilopascals
ksi	kips per square inch
kWh	kilowatt hour
l or L	litre
lat.	latitude
lb	pound
lbf	pound-force
lf	low frequency
Lifo	last in, first out
lk	link
lm	lumen
ln	logarithm to base e
LNG	liquefied natural gas
loa	length overall
long.	longitude
LPG	liquefied petroleum gas
lw	low water
lwl	length on waterline
ly	light year
m	milli (as prefix) or metre
M	mega (as prefix) or money stock

μ	micro (as prefix) or micron
m^2	square metre
m^3	cubic metre
mb, mbar	millibar
Mb	megabyte
md	maund
MF	medium frequency
mg	milligram
MHz	megahertz
mi	mile
min	minute or minim
MIPS	millions of instructions per second
ml	millilitre
mm	millimetre
μm	micrometre
mm^2	square millimetre
mm^3	cubic millimetre
mn	million
MODEM	modulator/demodulator
m_n^3	normal cubic metre
mph	miles per hour
mrd	milliard
MW	megawatt
my	myria (as prefix)
n	nano (as prefix)
N	newton
na	not available
ndw, NDW	net deadweight
nex	not elsewhere shown or specified
net	netto (lowest)
nm	nanometre
Nm^3	normal cubic metre
n mile	international nautical mile
nom.	nominal
nop	not otherwise provided
nos	not otherwise shown
npv	no par value
nrt, NRT	net registered tonnage
Ω	ohm
op	overproof
oz	ounce, avoirdupois
ozf	ounce-force
oz tr	ounce, troy
p	pico (as prefix)
P	poise
Pa	pascal
pc	parsec
pdl	poundal
P/E	price/earnings ratio
pH	potential hydrogen
pk	peck
pm	picometre
ppm	parts per million
psi	pounds per square inch
pt	pint
ptg std	petrograd standard
pz	pièze
q	quintal
qn	quotation
qr	quarter
qt	quart
R	Rankine or röntgen
rad	radian
RAM	random access memory
rd	running days
RD	refer to drawer or relative density
Red	Redwood
rp	return of post
ROM	read only memory
rpm	revolutions per minute
s	second
S	siemens
SAE	Society of Automotive Engineers
Scf	standard cubic foot
SDR	special drawing right
sec	second
sg	specific gravity
SI	International System of Units
sk	sack
smd	standard man-day
sn	sthène
sr	steradian
st	stone
St	stokes
std	standard
stp	standard temperature and pressure
SUS	Saybolt universal second
t	tonne or metric ton
T	tera (as prefix) or tesla
tce	tonnes of coal equivalent
TEU	twenty-foot equivalent unit
TPI	tons per inch immersion
tr	troy
TR	tons registered
u	unified atomic mass unit
UA	unit of account
up	underproof
UT	universal time
UTC	coordinated universal time
V	volt
VHF	very high frequency
W	watt
Wb	weber
wpa	with particular average
xc	ex coupon
xc	ex dividend
yd	yard
yd^2	square
yd^3	cubic yard

Rough conversions

his table provides rough conversions from some metric (SI) neasures to UK (Imperial) and US measures. Metric units not enerally recommended as SI units or for use with SI are narked with an asterisk (eg, Calorie*).

For more accurate conversions see pages 160–163.

.ength

Vidth of thumb = 25 millimetres = 1 inch
.5 centimetres = 1 inch
centimetres = 2 inches

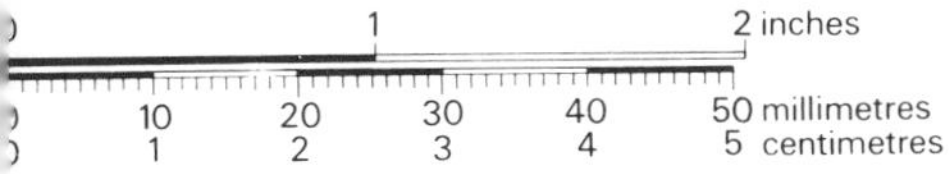

30 centimetres = 0.3 metre	= 1 foot
metre	= 3.25 feet
metre	= 39 inches
0 metres	= 11 yards
kilometre	= ⅝ mile
kilometres	= 5 miles
nautical miles (international)	= 8 miles

Area

.5 square centimetres	= 1 square inch
13 square centimetres	= 2 square inches
1 square metre	= 10.75 square feet
4 square metres	= 43 square feet
5 square metres	= 6 square yards
1 hectare	= 2.5 acres
2 hectares	= 5 acres
1 square kilometre	= 250 acres
8 square kilometres	= 3 square miles

Volume and capacity

5 millilitres	= 1 teaspoonful
28 millilitres	= 1 UK fluid ounce
25 US liquid ounces	= 26 UK fluid ounces
49 cubic centimetres / 49 millilitres	= 3 cubic inches
1 litre	= 1.75 UK pints
4 litres	= 7 UK pints
8 litres	= 7 UK quarts
6 US liquid pints	= 5 UK pints
9 litres	= 19 US liquid pints
4.5 litres	= 1 UK gallon
9 litres	= 2 UK gallons
6 US gallons	= 5 UK gallons
3.75 litres	= 1 US gallon
15 litres	= 4 US gallons
85 cubic decimetres / 85 litres	= 3 cubic feet
1 cubic metre	= 35 cubic feet
3 cubic metres	= 4 cubic yards
32 US bushels	= 31 UK bushels
1 cubic metre	= 27.5 UK bushels
1 cubic metre	= 28.3 US bushels
4 hectolitres	= 11 UK bushels
5 hectolitres	= 14 US bushels
1.25 US bushels (struck)	= 1 US bushel (heaped)
3.25 US bushels	= 1 US dry barrel
2.75 US bushels	= 1 US cranberry barrel
42 US gallons = 35 UK gallons	= 1 barrel (petroleum)
50 tonnes per year	= 1 barrel per day

Yield

2 quintals* per hectare	= 3 UK or US bushels per acre
9 hectolitres per hectare	= 10 UK or US bushels per acre
1.25 quintals* per hectare	= 1 UK hundredweight per acre
2.5 tonnes per hectare	= 1 UK ton per acre
10 kilograms per hectare	= 9 pounds per acre

Weight (mass)

65 milligrams	= 1 grain
1 gram	= 15.5 grains
10 ounces troy	= 11 ounces
28 grams	= 1 ounce
31 grams	= 1 ounce troy
454 grams	= 1 pound
1 kilogram	= 35 ounces
1 kilogram	= 2.25 pounds
70 kilograms	= 11 stone
5 quintals*	= 11 US hundredweights
1 quintal*	= 2 UK hundredweights
1 tonne	= 2 205 pounds
10 tonnes	= 11 US tons
63 tonnes	= 62 UK tons
112 US (short) tons	= 100 UK (long) tons

Velocity (speed)

3 feet per second	= 2 miles per hour
4 metres per second	= 9 miles per hour
5 metres per second	= 18 kilometres per hour
10 feet per second	= 11 kilometres per hour
48 kilometres per hour	= 30 miles per hour
80 kilometres per hour	= 50 miles per hour
113 kilometres per hour	= 70 miles per hour

Fuel consumption

14 litres per kilometre	= 5 UK gallons per mile
7 kilometres per litre	= 20 miles per UK gallon
14 litres per 100 kilometres	= 20 miles per UK gallon
6 miles per UK gallon	= 5 miles per US gallon

Acceleration

Standard gravity = 10 metres per second squared
= 32 feet per second squared

Density and concentration

25 grams per litre	= 4 ounces per UK gallon
15 grams per litre	= 2 ounces per US gallon
16 kilograms per cubic metre	= 1 pound per cubic foot
1 kilogram per litre / density of 1	= 62.5 pounds per cubic foot

Force

1 newton = 7.25 poundals
4.5 newtons = 1 pound-force
40 newtons = 9 pounds-force
10 newtons = 1 kilogram-force

Pressure and stress

48 pascals (newtons per square metre)	= 1 pound-force per square foot
7 kilopascals (kilonewtons per square metre)	= 1 pound-force per square inch
1 standard atmosphere 14.5 pounds-force per square inch	= 1 bar
7 kilograms-force per square centimetre	= 100 pounds-force per square inch

Energy

19 kilojoules = 18 British thermal units
1 kilocalorie* = 4 British thermal units
4 kilojoules = 1 kilocalorie* (Calorie*)

Power

3 kilowatts = 4 UK horsepower
73 metric horsepower* = 72 UK horsepower

Local units of measurement

All countries of the world use mainly the metric system or are changing to it, with the present exceptions of Brunei and Myanmar. However, many countries use local units of measurement as well. The following table lists alphabetically those units, other than metric or imperial, used or formerly used in countries other than the UK. Many of these are obsolete or obsolescent, but are of historical interest. Where measures are ancient or medieval, or applicable to particular towns or regions, this is indicated in brackets in the country column. The units listed here relate to length, weight, area,

Unit	Country	Metric equivalent
A		
abbas	Iran	187.5 mg
abbassi	Iran	375 g
abraa	Morocco	0.18 ha
abucco	Myanmar	204 g
acetabulum	Italy (ancient Roman)	67 ml
acheintaya	Myanmar	163.29 kg
acre	Bangladesh	0.405 ha
actus	Italy (ancient Roman)	1 258 m^2
adarme	Argentina	1.79 g
adarme	Mexico	1.79 g
adarme	Peru	1.79 g
adarme	Spain	1.79 g
adowly	India	1.866 kg
aftari	Morocco	900 m^2
ahm	Sweden	1.57 hl
ako	Hungary	0.543 hl
album	Denmark	57.461 m^2
aldan^2	Mongolia	2.56 m^2
aldan	Mongolia	1.6 m
alen	Denmark	0.628 m
alen^2	Denmark	0.394 m^2
alen	Sweden	0.594 m
Aleppo cantar	Cyprus	228.611 kg
alma	Turkey	5.24 l
almud	Belize	5.683 l
almud	Brazil	31.95 l
almud (cereals)	Chile	8.08 l
almud	Ecuador	12.88 kg
almud (dry)	Mexico	7.568 l
almud	Venezuela	9–50 kg
almud	Venezuela	400–25 600 m^2
almude (dry)	Paraguay	24 l
almude (liquid)	Portugal	16.54 l
alqueire (dry)	Cape Verde	41.593 l
alqueire	Brazil	36.37 l
alqueire (dry)	Portugal	13.841 l
alqueire (liquid)	Portugal	8.27 l
alqueiro	Brazil (Rio de Janiero)	4.86 ha
alqueiro	Brazil (São Paulo)	2.43 ha
alqueres	Cape Verde	1.859 ha
ambar	Turkey	0.435 m^3
amma	Greece (ancient)	19.5 m
amma	Israel (ancient Hebrew)	47 cm
amphora	Greece (ancient)	21 l
amphora	Italy (ancient Roman)	25.8 l
ancre (liquid)	Germany	34.35 l
ancre	Netherlands	38.8 l
anker	South Africa	34.1 l
ankre	Denmark	38.645 l
anna (precious metals)	Bangladesh	729 mg
anna	Pakistan	16.862 m^2
annuk	Cambodia	0.002 mm
anóman (dry)	Sri Lanka	2.04 hl
archine	Soviet Union[a]	71.12 cm
ardab	Egypt	1.98 hl
ardeb	Saudi Arabia	1.98 hl
ardeb (dry)	Sudan	1.98 hl
area	Venezuela	555 m^2
arkana	Greece (ancient)	30.8 m
arpent	Canada	58.47 m
arpent	Canada	0.342 ha
arpent	France (medieval)	0.511 ha
arpent	Mauritius	0.422 ha
arpent	Seychelles	0.422 ha
arpent	Switzerland	0.36 ha
arratel	Portugal	468.75 g
arratel	Portugal (old system)	459 g
arrátel	Macao	459 g
arroba	Argentina	11.5 kg
arroba	Belize	11.34 kg
arroba	Bolivia	11.5 kg
arroba (dry)	Bolivia	30.46 l
arroba	Brazil	14.69 kg
arroba	Chile	11.5 kg
arroba (centre)	Chile	40 l
arroba (north)	Chile	35.5 l
arroba	Colombia	12.5 kg
arroba	Costa Rica	11.5 kg
arroba	Cuba	11.5 kg
arroba (liquid)	Cuba	16.13 l
arroba	Dominican Republic	11.34 kg
arroba	Ecuador	11.5 kg
arroba	El Salvador	11.5 kg
arroba	Guatemala	11.5 kg
arroba	Honduras	11.5 kg
arroba	Honduras	16.6 l
arroba	Macao	14.688 kg
arroba	Mexico	11.5 kg
arroba	Nicaragua	11.5 kg
arroba	Paraguay	11.5 kg
arroba	Peru	11.5 kg
arroba (wine)	Peru	16.13 l
arroba	Philippines	11.5 kg
arroba	Portugal	15 kg
arroba	Portugal (old system)	14.688 kg
arroba	Spain	11.5 kg
arroba (liquid)	Spain	16.13 l
arroba	Uruguay	10 kg
arroba	Uruguay (old system)	11.5 kg
arroba	Venezuela	11.5 kg
arroba (liquid)	Venezuela	16.13 l
arshin	Turkey	1 m
arshin (çarsi)	Turkey	68 cm
arshin (mimar)	Turkey	75.8 cm
arshin^2 (mimar)	Turkey	0.575 m^2
artaba (dry)	Iran	65.9 l
assbaa	Iraq (medieval Arab)	1.97 cm
atado	Costa Rica	1.035 kg
aune	Belgium	1.2 m
aune	France (medieval)	1.188 m
aune	Haiti	1.191 m
aune (textiles)	Haiti	1.4 m
aune	Jersey	1.22 m
aune	Mauritius	1.191 m
aune	Seychelles	1.191 m
aune	Switzerland	1.2 m
azumbre	Colombia	2.02 l
azumbre	Panama	2.02 l
azumbre (liquid)	Spain	2.02 l
B		
ba'a	Oman	1.44 m

volume and capacity. Units used for other commodities and for other purposes will be found in the relevant sections.

Unit	Country	Metric equivalent
baa	Saudi Arabia	13.97 cm
bag (dry)	Myanmar	1.227 hl
bag	Sierra Leone	80 l
bahar	Iran	3.25 cm
bahár	Oman	0.808 t
baht	Thailand	15 g
bahu	Indonesia	0.71 ha
bak (opium)	Laos	3.75 g
balde	Ecuador	10 l
bale	Indonesia	180 kg
bale (fibres)	Philippines	126.5 kg
balli	South Africa	46 l
ban	Thailand	10 hl
barile	Italy	58.34 l
barmil (beer, wine, spirits)	Malta	43.188 l
barrel	Belize	125.02 l
barrel (limes)	Dominica	1.182 hl
barrel (herring)	Germany	100 kg
barrica (dry)	Cape Verde	1.248 hl
barril (liquid)	Argentina	76 l
barril (liquid)	Mexico	76 l
barril (liquid)	Paraguay	96.93 l
barril (liquid)	Venezuela	70–100 l
barrique (wine)	France (medieval)	2.262 hl
barrique	Haiti	2.25 hl
barrique	Mauritius	2.272 hl
barrique (liquid)	Portugal	215 l
barrique	Seychelles	1.636 hl
bat (liquid)	Israel (ancient Hebrew)	38 l
bát (cereals)	Vietnam	50 cl
bath	Laos	15 g
batman	Turkey (old system)	7.698 kg
batman	Turkey	10 kg
beczka	Poland	100 l
beczka (liquid)	Poland	136.54 l
behar	Saudi Arabia	199.3 kg
bei ke`	China	100 g
bei mi	China	100 m
bei sheng (dan)	China	1 hl
beit-se'a	Israel (ancient Hebrew)	740 m^2
beit-zemed	Israel (ancient Hebrew)	0.22 ha
beka	Israel (ancient Hebrew)	6.3 g
benequen	Belize	17.048 l
berkovec	Soviet Union[a]	163.8 kg
besana	Cuba	2 588.77 m^2
beswa	Afghanistan	97.68 m^2
beswasa	Afghanistan	4.884 m^2
bhara	Brunei	181.4 kg
bhara	Malaysia	181.4 kg
bhara	Singapore	181.4 kg
bhari (precious metals)	Bangladesh	11.664 g
bia (opium)	Laos	37.5 g
big hogga	Iraq (Mosul)	2.053 kg
big mal	Korea, South	18.039 l
bigha	Bangladesh	0.135 ha
bigha	India	0.134 ha
bigha	Nepal (plain)	0.677 ha
bigha	Pakistan	0.202 ha
bin	Taiwan	3.306 m^2
bing-fand kung ch'ih	Taiwan	1 m^2

Unit	Country	Metric equivalent
bitta	Nepal	22.86 cm
boccale	Italy	1.823 l
bocka (liquid)	Soviet Union[a]	4.92 hl
bocoy	Cuba	6.624 hl
boisseau (dry)	Belgium	15 l
boisseau	France (medieval)	13.008 l
bongkal (precious metals)	Malaysia	53.913 g
bongkal (precious metals)	Singapore	53.913 g
boot (wine)	Netherlands	5.3 hl
bota (liquid)	Spain	4.838 hl
botella	Costa Rica	67 cl
botella	Cuba	72.5 cl
botella	El Salvador	75 cl
botella	Guatemala	65 cl
botella	Honduras	69.12 cl
botella	Nicaragua	66.6 cl
botella	Panama	75.7 cl
botija	Ecuador	5.75 kg
botijuela	Venezuela	5 kg
botte	Italy	9.33 hl
bottle	Sri Lanka	75.7 cl
bouteille	Mauritius	80 cl
bouteille	Seychelles	68 cl
boutylka (vodka)	Soviet Union[a]	61.5 cl
boutylka (wine)	Soviet Union[a]	76.9 cl
braca	Brazil	2.2 m
braça	Cape Verde	2.2 m
braça^2	Cape Verde	4.84 m^2
braça	Macao	2.2 m
braça	Portugal	2.2 m
brasse	France (medieval)	1.624 m
brasse	Seychelles	1.949 m
braza	Argentina	1.733 m
braza	Chile	1.672 m
braza	Colombia	1.672 m
braza	Costa Rica	1.672 m
braza	Spain	1.672 m
brazada	El Salvador	1.672 m
briquette	Indonesia	0.5 kg
bu	Japan (kujira shaku)	3.03 mm
bu	Japan	3.78 mm
bugday	Turkey	50.1 mg
bulto	Venezuela	18–80 kg
bunder	Netherlands	1 ha
busa	Saudi Arabia	2.54 cm
busa	Sudan	2.54 cm
bushel	Sierra Leone	40 l
bushel	Sri Lanka	36.369 l
byee (liquid)	Myanmar	0.505 l
C		
caba (liquid)	Somalia	453 ml
cabaho	Ethiopia	6 l
caballeria	Canada	43.7 ha
caballería	Costa Rica	45.254 ha
caballería	Cuba	13.42 ha
caballería	Dominican Republic	75.46 ha
caballeria	Ecuador	11.29 ha
caballería	El Salvador	44.965 ha
caballería	Guatemala	44.72 ha

nit	Country	Metric equivalent
aballeria	Honduras	45.028 ha
abellería	Mexico	42.795 ha
abellería	Nicaragua	45.158 ha
abda	Iraq (medieval Arab)	7.9 cm
abot	Jersey	19.75 l
abulla	Venezuela	20 kg
abulla	Venezuela	80 m
adastral yoke	Hungary	0.575 ha
affiso	Italy (Sicily)	21.2 l
affiso	Malta	20.46 l
aga	El Salvador	92 kg
ahiz (dry)	Spain	6.66 hl
aja	Nicaragua	16 kg
aja	Venezuela	18–63 kg
ajon (dry)	Venezuela	25–55 l
ajuela	Costa Rica	17 l
ajuela	Guatemala	16.6 l
ajuela	Nicaragua	16.6 l
alc	Greece (ancient)	101 mg
aliber	USA	0.254 mm
alow	Poland	2.4 cm
amionada	El Salvador	3 m^3
amionada	El Salvador	2.722 t
ân	Vietnam	604.5 g
ana	Netherlands Antilles	0.75 kg
anada (liquid)	Cape Verde	1.4 l
anada (liquid)	Portugal	1.38 l
anasto (dry)	Venezuela	28–140 l
andy	India	0.746 t
andy (copra)	Sri Lanka	254.012 kg
andy (general)	Sri Lanka	226.8 kg
aneca	Cuba	21.751 l
antar	Cyprus	55.883 kg
antar	Malta	79.379 kg
antar	Tunisia	50.38 kg
antero	Ecuador	441 m^2
ap (cereals)	Vietnam	20 cl
ape foot	Botswana	0.315 m
ape foot	South Africa	0.315 m
ape inch	South Africa	2.624 cm
ape rood	South Africa	3.778 m
ape rood[2]	South Africa	14.276 m^2
apicha (dry & liquid)	Iran	2.63 l
arga	Colombia	125 kg
arga	Costa Rica	161 kg
arga	Mexico	138.074 kg
arga (dry)	Mexico	1.816 hl
arga	Nicaragua	92 kg
arga	Venezuela	22–345 kg
arga	Venezuela	1 ha
arga de papa	Costa Rica	828 kg
argo	Belize	90.72 kg
argo	Belize	68.19 l
aró	Dominican Republic	1.293 ha
arreau de terre	Haiti	1.293 ha
arretada	El Salvador	1 m^3
arretada	El Salvador	0.907 t
ase (bananas)	Fiji	32.7 kg
ase (bananas)	Samoa	25.401 kg
ase (taro)	Samoa	32.659 kg
asel	Cape Verde	2 178 m^2

Unit	Country	Metric equivalent
cash	Seychelles	2.235 hl
cassaba	Iraq (medieval Arab)	3.8 m
cassaba[2]	Iraq (medieval Arab)	14.4 m^2
cast (dry)	Soviet Union[a]	109.3 ml
castellano	Spain	4.793 g
cate	Macao	604.79 g
catty	Indonesia	617.613 g
catty	Philippines	632.5 g
catty	Thailand	600 g
cavan	Philippines	75 l
cavan (milled rice)	Philippines	56 kg
cavan (paddy rice)	Philippines	44 kg
cawnie	India	0.535 ha
çekirdek	Turkey	401 mg
celemin	Colombia	4.625 l
celemin	Panama	4.625 l
celemín (dry)	Spain	4.625 l
centner	Denmark	50 kg
centner	Norway	49.81 kg
centner	Sweden	42.515 kg
centuria	Italy (ancient Roman)	50.33 ha
ceston (dry)	Venezuela	70 l
chabba	Iraq (medieval Arab)	3.3 mm
chamam	Cambodia	25 cm
chang	Thailand	1.2 kg
chapah	Malaysia	0.816 kg
charac	Iran	26 cm
charak	Afghanistan	1.777 kg
charka (liquid)	Soviet Union[a]	123 ml
charruba (gold, silver, silk)	Libya	191.7 mg
chattak	Pakistan	58.319 g
chawal	Pakistan	15.187 mg
check	Malaysia	37.465 cm
chee	Malaysia	3.78 g
chek	Hong Kong	0.371 m
chela (dry)	Somalia	1.359 l
chemica (dry & liquid)	Iran	1.32 l
cheong	Macao	12.69 m^2
chetverik (dry)	Soviet Union[a]	26.24 l
chetvert (dry)	Soviet Union[a]	2.099 hl
cheung	Hong Kong	3.715 m
cheung	Malaysia	3.746 m
cheung	Singapore	3.746 m
chhatak	Bangladesh	58.319 g
chhek	Singapore	37.465 cm
chhun	Singapore	3.747 cm
chi	Cambodia	3.75 g
chi	Korea, South	3.03 cm
chia or ko	Taiwan	0.97 ha
ch'ien	China	3.78 g
chien	Singapore	3.445 g
chih	China (treaty system)	35.814 cm
chih	China	0.333 m
chinbul (cereals)	Lebanon	150 kg
ch'ing	China	0.674 ha
ching	China	11.241 m^2
chittack	India	58.319 g
cho	Japan	0.992 ha
chô	Japan	109.09 m
chok	Korea, South	0.303 m

Unit	Country	Metric equivalent
chok[2]	Korea, South	0.092 m^2
chong	Cambodia	30 kg
chopine	France (medieval)	47 cl
chopine	Mauritius	40 cl
chopine	Seychelles	34 cl
choryos	Egypt (Alexandria)	9 cm
choryos	Egypt (ancient)	7.49 cm
chuchok	Brunei	378 mg
chum	Malaysia	3.747 cm
chung	Korea, South	109.09 m
chungbo	Korea, South	0.992 ha
chüo	China	168.62 m^2
chupa	Macao	1.031 l
chupa	Philippines	0.375 l
chupak	Brunei	1.137 l
chupak (liquid)	Malaysia	1.137 l
chupak	Singapore	1.137 l
clima	Italy (ancient Roman)	315 m^2
cochliarion	Greece (ancient)	4.9 ml
collothum (dry & liquid)	Iran	8.23 l
condorim	Macao	3.76 mm
condorim	Macao	377.99 mg
congius	Italy (ancient Roman)	3.23 l
corde	Mauritius	2.742 m^3
corde	Seychelles	4.47 m^3
cordel	Cuba	20.352 m
cordel[2]	Cuba	414.204 m^2
coss	Pakistan	1.829 km
courd	Morocco	450 m^2
côvado	Macao (old Chinese)	0.376 m
côvado	Macao	0.127 m^2
côvado	Macao (old Portuguese)	66 cm
côvado	Portugal	66 cm
crosh	Bangladesh	3.218 km
cuadra	Argentina	130 m
cuadra	Chile	125.39 m
cuadra[2]	Chile	1.572 ha
cuadra	Colombia	80 m
cuadra	Ecuador	84 m
cuadra[2]	Ecuador	0.706 ha
cuadra	El Salvador	70.258 m^2
cuadra	Paraguay	86.66 m
cuadra	Spain	125.4 m
cuadra	Uruguay	85.9 m
cuadra[2]	Uruguay	0.738 ha
cuadro	Venezuela	60 kg
cuadro	Venezuela (east)	0.64–1 ha
cuadro	Venezuela (west)	0.64–1.8 ha
cuarta (liquid)	Argentina	0.594 l
cuarta	Colombia	20 cm
cuarta	Costa Rica	21 cm
cuarta	Guatemala	21 cm
cuarta	Nicaragua	21 cm
cuarta	Nicaragua	16.666 cl
cuarta (liquid)	Paraguay	75.73 cl
cuarter (liquid)	Argentina	114 l
cuarterón (dry)	Mexico	25 l
cuartilla (dry)	Argentina	34.3 l
cuartilla	Ecuador	23 kg
cuartilla	Venezuela	100–2 500 m^2
cuartilla	Venezuela	2–10 kg

Unit	Country	Metric equivalent
cuartillo	Costa Rica	4.25 l
cuartillo	Cuba	0.86 l
cuartillo	Guatemala	1.16 l
cuartillo (dry)	Mexico	1.892 l
cuartillo (liquid)	Mexico	0.456 l
cuartillo (oil)	Mexico	0.506 l
cuartillo (dry)	Spain	1.156 l
cuartillo (liquid)	Spain	0.504 l
cuarto	Ecuador	21 cm
cubit	Egypt (ancient)	44.9 cm
cubit of land	Egypt (Alexandria)	27.5 m^2
cubito	Somalia	55.88 cm
cubitus	Italy (ancient Roman)	44.34 cm
cuenta	Venezuela	10–50 kg
cuerda	Paraguay	69.88 m
cuerda	Philippines	0.393 ha
cuerda	Puerto Rico	0.393 ha
culleus	Italy (ancient Roman)	5.17 hl
Cunningham acre	Ireland	0.523 ha
cup	Sierra Leone	33.3 cl
custom quintal	Czechoslovakia	50 kg
cyathus	Italy (ancient Roman)	45 ml
Cyprus litre	Cyprus	3.182 l
Cyprus litre	Cyprus	2.286 kg
D		
dai	Korea, South	1.804 l
daktylos	Greece (ancient)	1.92 cm
damleng	Cambodia	37.5 g
dan	China	100 kg
dan	Mongolia	65 l
danar	Iran	187.5 g
danda	India	1.829 m
danda	Pakistan	1.829 m
darat	Somalia	0.8 ha
dareb	Somalia	0.25 ha
daribah	Egypt	15.84 hl
dau	Hong Kong	10 l
dau (cereals)	Vietnam	1 l
dau chung	Hong Kong	674.5 m^2
daula	Ethiopia	0.88 hl
dawulla	Ethiopia	100 kg
debbie (paraffin)	Zambia	18.184 l
deben	Egypt (ancient)	94 g
decempeda	Italy (ancient Roman)	2.956 m
demi-aune	Switzerland	60 cm
demi-livre	Seychelles	244.75 g
denaro	Italy	1.18 g
denier	France (medieval)	1.275 g
denk	Turkey	0.802 g
denum	Lebanon	919.302 m^2
depa	Malaysia	1.829 m
depa[2]	Malaysia	3.345 m^2
depa	Singapore	1.829 m
depa[2]	Singapore	3.345 m^2
deraga (Al-mamoun)	Iraq (medieval Arab)	53.3 cm
deraga akhdam	Iraq (medieval Arab)	63 cm
deraga cabda	Iraq (medieval Arab)	47.4 cm
derham	Lebanon	3.205 g
derime	Ethiopia	2.59 g
dessetine	Soviet Union[a]	1.093 ha

it	Country	Metric equivalent
an (precious metals)	Bangladesh	30.4 mg
an	India	36.4 mg
ara	Bahrain	48.26 cm
ara	Oman	45.7 cm
arni	Nepal	2.333 kg
iraa	Iraq (Aleppo)	68.5 cm
iraa	Iraq (Baghdad)	74.5 cm
iraa	Iraq (Mosul)	70 cm
ur	Nepal (plain)	16.929 m^2
drachm	Egypt (Alexandria)	7.78 g
drachm	Greece (ancient)	9.72 g
git	Iraq (ancient Sumerian)	3.3 cm
gitus	Italy (ancient Roman)	1.85 cm
ra	Saudi Arabia	45.7 cm
ra	Yemen	45.7 cm
raa (building)	Egypt	75 cm
raa (textiles)	Egypt	58 cm
raa mémari	Egypt	0.563 m^2
rham	Iraq (Istanbul)	3.205 g
rham	Jordan	3.205 g
rham	Libya	3.205 g
rham (gold, silver, silk)	Libya	3.067 g
rham	Sudan	3.12 g
rham	Syria (Aleppo & Homs)	3.205 g
rham	Syria (Damascus)	3.205 g
rhem	Egypt	3.12 g
rhem	Iran	9.375 g
rhem	Iraq (medieval Arab)	3.12 g
ung	Indonesia	1.419 ha
oli	Soviet Union[a]	44.435 mg
on	Korea, South	3.75 g
ong	Vietnam	3.778 g
onum	Cyprus	1 337.8 m^2
önüm	Libya	919 m^2
önüm	Syria (Aleppo & Homs)	919.3 m^2
önüm	Turkey	25 ha
önüm	Turkey	919.3 m^2
oppelzentner	Germany	100 kg
ouble fanega	Uruguay	2.745 hl
ra Arbi (textiles)	Libya	49 cm
ra (building)	Jordan	75.8 cm
ra (textiles)	Jordan	68 cm
ra	Syria (Aleppo & Homs)	68 cm
ra	Syria (Damascus)	70 cm
ra	Yemen	67 cm
ra maghmari	Syria	75.8 cm
ra maghmari[2]	Syria	0.575 m^2
raa milki (land)	Libya	50 cm
rachm	Egypt (Alexandria)	3.9 g
rachma	Greece (ancient)	4.86 g
rachma	Greece	14.175 g
rachma	Italy (ancient Roman)	3.36 g
rachma	Netherlands	3.9 g
rachma	Turkey	10 g
rachma	Turkey (old system)	3.207 g
rachme	Switzerland	3.9 g
rah (textiles)	Lebanon	68 cm
rah (agriculture & construction)	Lebanon	75.8 cm
rah	Morocco	55.9 cm

Unit	Country	Metric equivalent
dram	Cyprus	3.175 g
dram	Greece	115.3 mg
ducat	Austria (Vienna)	3.491 g
duim	Netherlands (Rhineland)	2.618 cm
duim	Netherlands	1 cm
duim	Netherlands (Amsterdam)	2.574 cm
duim	Soviet Union[a]	2.54 cm
dun	China	1 t
dung	Iran	781 mg
dunum	Jordan	0.1 ha
dunum	Yugoslavia	1 000 m^2
dzhin	Mongolia	600 g
E		
efa (dry)	Israel (ancient Hebrew)	38 l
eimer	Germany	68.7 l
el	Indonesia	0.688 m
el	Surinam	0.688 m
ela	Brunei	0.914 m
ela	Malaysia	0.914 m
ela	Singapore	0.914 m
ell	Netherlands (Amsterdam)	0.688 m
ell	Netherlands	1 m
ell	Seychelles	1.219 m
emine (dry)	Switzerland	1.5 l
endazeh	Turkey	65 cm
engjateigur	Iceland	0.319 ha
ertragsfestmeter	Austria	1 m^3
estadio	Portugal	257.3 m
estado	Spain	3.344 m
estado	Spain	11.182 m^2
evlek	Cyprus	334.5 m^2
evlek	Turkey	0.144 m^2
ezba	Israel (ancient Hebrew)	1.94 cm
F		
fad øl	Denmark	9.275 hl
faddan	Iraq	5 ha
faddan	Yemen	0.405 ha
famn	Finland	4 m^3
fan sheng (he')	China	10 cl
fan gong lǐ	China	1 km^2
fan	Hong Kong	0.378 g
fan	Hong Kong	3.715 mm
fan	Macao	76.14 m^2
fanega (dry)	Argentina	1.372 hl
fanega	Bolivia	92 kg
fanega	Chile	0.97 hl
fanega	Colombia	0.56 hl
fanega	Costa Rica	92 kg
fanega (coffee)	Costa Rica	0.34 hl
fanega (other)	Costa Rica	0.41 hl
fanega (dry)	Cuba	0.56 hl
fanega	Dominican Republic	0.56 hl
fanega	Ecuador	92 kg
fanega	El Salvador	199–331 kg
fanega	Guatemala	0.56 hl
fanega	Honduras	11.028 hl
fanega	Mexico	3.566 ha
fanega (dry)	Mexico	0.908 hl
fanega	Morocco	0.56 hl
fanega	Nicaragua	161 kg

Unit	Country	Metric equivalent
fanega (dry)	Paraguay	2.88 hl
fanega	Peru	0.56 hl
fanega (dry)	Portugal	0.55hl
fanega (dry)	Spain	0.56 hl
fanega (cocoa beans)	Trinidad & Tobago	49.9 kg
fanega	Uruguay	1.373 hl
fanega	Uruguay	100 kg
fanega	Venezuela	46–400 kg
fanega (dry)	Venezuela	1.17 hl
fanegada	Colombia	0.64 ha
fanegada	Peru	0.64 ha
fanegada	Spain	0.64 ha
fanegada	Venezuela	0.45–4 ha
farasalah	Oman	40.4 kg
fardo de tabaco	Costa Rica	57.6 kg
farsakh	Oman	4.8 km
farsang	Iran	6.24 km
fatar	Oman	18 cm
favn	Denmark	1.882 m
favn	Norway	2.4 m^3
favn	Norway	1.882 m
favn	Sweden	1.782 m
favn brænde	Denmark	2.226 m^3
feddân	Egypt	0.42 ha
feddan	Iraq (medieval Arab)	0.575 ha
feddan	Saudi Arabia	0.42 ha
feddan	Sudan	0.42 ha
feddan	Syria (Aleppo)	0.23–0.34 ha
fen	China	0.5 g
fen	China	66.667 m^2
fen	China (treaty system)	377.99 mg
fen ke`	China	100 mg
fen mi	China	10 cm
fern	Singapore	0.344 g
ferrah (cereals)	Oman	11.3 kg
fershi kadim	Turkey	5.685 km
feuillette (wine)	France (medieval)	1.131 hl
fitil	Turkey	12.5 mg
fitr	Saudi Arabia	15.24 cm
fjerdingkar	Denmark	172.382 m^2
fjerdingkar	Denmark	4.348 l
fod	Denmark	31.385 cm
fod^3	Denmark	30.916 dm^3
foglietta	Italy	456 ml
folha (liquid)	Cape Verde	1.05 l
food^2 (hide processing)	Luxembourg	0.305 m^2
foot	Iraq (medieval Arab)	31.6 cm
fot	Finland	0.297 m
fot	Norway	0.314 m
fot	Sweden	0.297 m
fot^3	Sweden	26.172 l
frasco (liquid)	Argentina	2.375 l
frasco (liquid)	Cape Verde	2.45 l
frasco	Cuba	2.175 l
frasco (liquid)	Mexico	2.366 l
frasco (liquid)	Paraguay	3.029 l
frasila	Tanzania	16.33 kg
frasila	Yemen	12.7 kg
frasla	Somalia	16.128 kg
frasla	Yemen	11.22 kg
frasoulla	Ethiopia	17 kg

Unit	Country	Metric equivale
fuang	Laos	1.875 g
fuang	Thailand	1.875 g
fuant	Saudi Arabia	1.769 kg
fuder	Germany	8.244 hl
fun	China (treaty system)	3.581 mm
fun	China	3.333 mm
fun	Japan	375 mg
funt (new)	Poland	500 g
funt (old)	Poland	405.5 g
funt	Soviet Union[a]	409.5 g
fuss	Germany	31.39 cm
fuss	Soviet Union[a]	35.6 cm
fusz	Austria	31.k608 cm
G		
gadula	Libya	12.25 m^2
galao (liquid)	Cape Verde	3.7 l
galon (liquid)	Argentina	38 l
galon	Bolivia	3.36 l
galón	Chile	4.54 l
galón	Dominican Republic	3.24 l
galón	El Salvador	3.75 l
galón	Honduras	3.456 l
gan	Iraq (ancient Sumerian)	2.7 ha
gana (textiles)	Libya	1.6 m
gandom	Iran	48.83 mg
gang	Vietnam	0.04 m^2
ganta	Macao	10.31 l
ganta	Philippines	3 l
gantang	Brunei	4.546 l
gantang (paddy)	Brunei	2.419 kg
gantang (rice)	Brunei	3.629 kg
gantang	Indonesia	8.577 l
gantang	Malaysia	2.419 kg
gantang (liquid)	Malaysia	4.546 l
gantang	Singapore	4.546 l
gantang	South Africa	9.201 l
gar	Iraq (ancient Sumerian)	11.9 m
garava	Syria	14.5 l
garmida	Israel (ancient Hebrew)	0.3 m^2
garnetz (dry)	Soviet Union[a]	3.28 l
garniec	Poland	4 l
garniec (liquid)	Poland	3.793 l
garra (beer, wine, spirits)	Malta	10.797 l
garrafa	Brazil	666 ml
garrafa (liquid)	Cape Verde	0.7 l
garrafón	Cuba	18.126 l
garwoke	Myanmar	20.483 km
gasha	Ethiopia	40 ha
gatsar	Mongolia	576 m
gaulette	Mauritius	3.248 m
gaulette	Seychelles	3.248 m
gaz	Bangladesh	0.914 m
gaz	India	0.914 m
gaz	Pakistan	0.914 m
gazi sha	Afghanistan	1.067 m
gazi jerib	Afghanistan	73.66 cm
gazi jerib^2	Afghanistan	0.543 m^2
gazi memar	Afghanistan	82.28 cm
gera	Israel (ancient Hebrew)	633 mg
gereh gazi sha	Afghanistan	6.668 cm

nit	Country	Metric equivalent
e	Vietnam	0.16 m^2
umaon	Pakistan	0.405 ha
an sheng	China	1 kl
án	China	5 g
n	Iraq (ancient Sumerian)	4.82 l
n	Iraq (ancient Sumerian)	0.25 m^2
ra	Bangladesh	5.715 cm
rah	Pakistan	5.715 cm
reh	Iran	6.5 cm
rib	Turkey	1 ha
rib	Turkey (old system)	0.207 ha
la	Tanzania	163.3 kg
zla (dry)	Somalia	1.631 hl
zla	Somalia	161.28 kg
	Japan	0.331 m^2
	Japan	18.039 cl
dük	Turkey	25.2 l
old mane	Israel (ancient Hebrew)	633 g
ong li	China	1 km
ong li'	China	1 m^2
ong mu	China	1 a
ong qing	China	1 ha
ouffa	Morocco	0.5 ha
adus	Italy (ancient Roman)	0.739 m
ain	Bahrain	64.8 mg
ain	France (medieval)	53.115 mg
ain	Mauritius	53.115 mg
ain	Seychelles	53.115 mg
ain	Soviet Union[a]	62.2 mg
ain	Switzerland	65.104 mg
amma	Greece (ancient)	1.62 g
ano	Argentina	0.05 g
ano	Chile	64.8 mg
ano	Italy	49.05 mg
ano	Spain	49.9 mg
rao	Macao	49 mg
rao	Portugal	4.58 mm
reat mina	Iraq (ancient Sumerian)	0.962 kg
rein	Netherlands	0.064 g
ros	France (medieval)	3.824 g
ros	Mauritius	3.824 g
ros	Seychelles	3.824 g
ubiar	Mongolia	9.216 ha
udge	Saudi Arabia	63.5 cm
untha	Pakistan	101.17 m^2
ur	Iraq (ancient Sumerian)	2.89 hl
urraf (liquid)	Libya	2.307 l
uz	Nepal	0.914 m
aat	Nepal	45.72 cm
abba shair	Egypt	5.22 mm
abba (gold)	Sudan	100 mg
abbe	Turkey	0.783 mg
abl (land)	Libya	35 m
ak	Turkey	33.7 l
albstück	Netherlands	6 hl
alibin	Romania	70.1 cm
and (horses)	USA	10.16 cm
andaza or pik (textiles)	Libya	68 cm
andbreadth	Iraq (ancient Sumerian)	9.9 cm

Unit	Country	Metric equivalent
hang	China	50 g
hao	China	0.667 m^2
hao	China	5 mg
hao	China (treaty system)	3.78 mg
hao	China	33.333 μm
hao	China (treaty system)	35.814 μm
hao ke	China	1 mg
hao mi	China	1 mm
hao sheng (cuo)	China	1 ml
hào	Vietnam	0.04 mm
hào	Vietnam	3.778 mg
hap	Cambodia	60 kg
hap	Macao	103.1 ml
hat	Cambodia	50 cm
hath	Bangladesh	0.457 m
hath	Pakistan	0.457 m
hebbeh	Iraq (medieval Arab)	65 mg
hekat	Egypt (ancient)	4.8 l
hema	Greece (ancient)	0.77 m
hembl	Sudan	312 kg
hemikotylion	Greece (ancient)	146 ml
hemina	Italy (ancient Roman)	269 ml
hemipodion	Greece (ancient)	15.4 cm
heml	Egypt	249.6 kg
heml	Iraq (medieval Arab)	249.6 kg
hemla	Sudan	74.88 kg
henu	Egypt (ancient)	300 ml
heredium	Italy (ancient Roman)	0.503 ha
hesta	Malaysia	45.72 cm
hesta	Singapore	45.72 cm
hin	Egypt (Alexandria)	5.83 l
hin (dry & liquid)	Israel (ancient Hebrew)	6.3 l
hindaza	Saudi Arabia	68.6 cm
hippicon	Greece (ancient)	739 m
hiro	Japan	1.515 m
hoc	Vietnam	16 m^3
hôc (cereals)	Vietnam	60 l
hogga	Iraq (Baghdad)	4.167 kg
hogga	Iraq (Istanbul)	1.283 kg
hogshead	Singapore	2.864 hl
hoi	Laos	120 g
homer (dry)	Israel (ancient Hebrew)	3.8 hl
hoon	Malaysia	378 mg
hop	Hong Kong	10 cl
hop	Korea, South	18.039 cl
hop	Korea, South	0.331 m^2
hot	Vietnam	0.4 μm
hôt	Vietnam	0.038 mg
houn	Laos	375 mg
hout	Netherlands	1 421.3 m^2
hu	China	51.773 l
hu	China	37.8 μg
hu mi	China	10 μm
huacal (dry)	Venezuela	28–70 l
huitième	Seychelles	61.188 g
hun	Cambodia	0.375 g
hundredweight	Canada	45.359 kg
Hungarian yoke	Hungary	0.432 ha
hvat	Yugoslavia	1.896 m
hvat^2	Yugoslavia	3.597 m^2
hyaku-me	Japan	375 g

Unit	Country	Metric equivalent
I		
imagu	Mongolia	3.2 cm
Ionian litre	Greece	454 g
ippyong	Korea, South	6.011 m^3
Irish acre	Ireland	0.656 ha
J		
jabia	Libya	1 225 m^2
jae (timber)	Korea, South	3.339 dm^3
jak	Korea, South	18.039 ml
jak	Korea, South	0.033 m^2
jarda	Cape Verde	0.88 m
jareeb	Pakistan	20.117 m
jareeb^2	Pakistan	404.69 m^2
jarib	India	54.864 m
jarra (liquid)	Libya	14.13 l
jarra (liquid)	Mexico	8.213 l
Java paal	Indonesia	1.507 km
jemba	Malaysia	13.378 m^2
jemba	Singapore	13.378 m^2
jengkal	Malaysia	22.86 cm
jengkal	Singapore	22.86 cm
jerib	Afghanistan	0.195 ha
jerib	Iran	0.108 ha
jin	China (metric)	1 kg
jin	China	0.5 kg
jin	China (treaty system)	0.605 kg
jō	Japan	3.03 m
jo	Japan (kujira shaku)	3.78 m
joch	Austria	0.576 ha
jugerum	Italy (ancient Roman)	0.252 ha
jumfru	Sweden	40.9 ml
jungbo	Korea, North	0.992 ha
K		
kâ	Laos	937.5 mg
kabiet	Laos	4.167 mm
kada	Yemen	40 l
kada (barley, foreign)	Yemen	27 kg
kada (barley, local)	Yemen	23.3 kg
kada (beans)	Yemen	33.2 kg
kada (maize)	Yemen	29.2 kg
kada (sorghum, red)	Yemen	26.9 kg
kada (sorghum, yellow)	Yemen	31 kg
kada (wheat)	Yemen	32.2 kg
kadah	Egypt	2.06 l
kadne	Lebanon	0.23–0.34 ha
kaila	Tanzania	2.722 kg
kaing	Philippines	19–21 kg
kalong	Laos	20 l
kam	Laos	10 cm
kambeh	Iraq (medieval Arab)	48.75 mg
kan	Hong Kong	0.605 kg
kan	Korea, South	1.818 m
kan	Netherlands	1 l
kanal	Pakistan	505.86 m^2
kanchha	Bangladesh	14.58 g
kandi	Yemen	304.8 kg
kandy	Myanmar	8.165 t
kanee	Pakistan	1618.7 m^2
kanne (liquid)	Germany	1.718 l

Unit	Country	Metric equivalent
kanne	South Africa	1.488 l
kanne	Sweden	2.615 l
kannland	Sweden	44.08 m^2
kantar	Greece	56.32 kg
kantar	Jordan (Nabulsi)	288.46 kg
kantar	Jordan (Shami)	256.41 kg
kantar	Lebanon	256.397 kg
kantar	Libya (Cyrenaica)	64.1 kg
kantar	Libya (Tripolitania)	51.28 kg
kantar	Morocco (old system)	51.26 kg
kantar	Morocco	100 kg
kantar	Saudi Arabia	51.35 kg
kantar	Sudan	44.928 kg
kantar	Syria (Aleppo & Homs)	320.5 kg
kantar	Syria (Damascus)	256.5 kg
kantar	Turkey	100 kg
kantar	Turkey	56.45 kg
kantje (herring)	Germany	74 kg
kappe (new)	Finland	5 l
kappe (old)	Finland	4.58 l
kappland	Sweden	154.29 m^2
karam	Pakistan	1.676 m
karam^2	Pakistan	2.81 m^2
kard	Morocco	10 l
kartocc (beer, wine, spirits)	Malta	1.136 l
kartocc (oil, milk)	Malta	1.279 l
kartos	Cyprus	5.092 l
kasbu	Iraq (ancient Sumerian)	21.3 km
kassaba	Egypt	3.55 m
kassabé	Syria	23.814 m^2
katang	Cambodia	7.5 l
katastarsko jutro	Yugoslavia	0.576 ha
katha	Bangladesh	67.4 m^2
kathouah	Iraq (medieval Arab)	1.9 m
kati	Brunei	605 g
kati	Malaysia	605 g
kati (precious metals)	Malaysia	647 g
kati	Myanmar	544 g
kati	Singapore	605 g
kati (precious metals)	Singapore	647 g
kattha	Nepal (plain)	338.57 m^2
kavan	Cambodia	0.152 m^3
kawtha	Myanmar	5.121 km
ke	China	1 g
kedet	Egypt (ancient)	9.4 g
keila	Libya	0.32 ha
keila (dry)	Sudan	16.5 l
keila	Yemen	36 l
kejla	Malta	18.735 m^2
kela	Saudi Arabia	3.221 kg
ken	Japan	1.818 m
kend (new)	Ethiopia	50 cm
kend (old)	Ethiopia	50.8 cm
kental	Turkey	17.96 kg
kettle	Sierra Leone	9.99 l
keun	Korea, South	600 g
kfiz	Tunisia	5.819 hl
khana	Laos	5 l
khandi (cereals)	Oman	227 kg
khar	Egypt (ancient)	0.96 hl
kharrouba	Morocco	40 l

Unit	Country	Metric equivalent
kharvar	Iran	300 kg
kharwar	Afghanistan	565.28 kg
khashkha	Pakistan	1.898 mg
khat	Turkey	1 cm
khedem	Morocco	0.1 ha
khet	Egypt (ancient)	52.4 m
khluon chay	Cambodia	0.217 mm
khord	Afghanistan	110.406 g
khos aldan	Mongolia	3.2 m
khou	Mongolia	3.75 mg
khubi	Mongolia	57.6 m
khup	Laos	20 cm
khup	Thailand	25 cm
khwe (dry)	Myanmar	20.457 l
khwẹt (dry)	Myanmar	1.279 l
kibaba	Tanzania	1 l
kikkar	Iraq (medieval Arab)	56.16 kg
kilá	Egypt	16.5 l
kilé	Cyprus	36.369 l
kilé (dry)	Libya	36 l
kileh	Turkey	101 l
kileh	Turkey	37 l
kilo	Greece	37.7 l
kin	Japan	600 g
kintar	Iraq (Baghdad)	274.3 kg
kirat	Egypt	175.035 m^2
kirat	Iraq (medieval Arab)	195 mg
kirat	Lebanon	2.833 cm
kirat (agriculture & construction)	Lebanon	3.158 cm
kirat	Sudan	195 mg
kitmir	Turkey	3.13 mg
kiya	Oman	168.3 g
klafter	Austria	1.896 m
klafter^3	Austria	6.281 m^3
ko	China	103.547 ml
kob	Laos	2.5 l
köddi	Saudi Arabia	4.95 l
koilon	Greece	33.2 l
koku	Japan	1.804 hl
koku	Japan	0.278 m^3
koltuk	Turkey	1.48 m^2
konak	Turkey	30 km
kondylos	Greece (ancient)	3.85 cm
konge	Greece (ancient)	3.51 l
kor (liquid)	Israel (ancient Hebrew)	3.8 hl
kordofan mukhamas	Sudan	0.727 ha
korn-tönde	Norway	1.39 hl
korn-topmaal	Norway	1.6 hl
korrel	Netherlands	100 mg
kosh	Nepal	3.219 km
koss	India	1.829 km
kotyle	Greece (ancient)	292 ml
kouza	Cyprus	10.229 l
koyan	Brunei	2.419 t
koyan	Malaysia	2.419 t
koyan (dry & liquid)	Malaysia	36.369 hl
koyan	Singapore	36.369 hl
koyan	Singapore	2.419 t
koyan	Thailand	1.2 t
koyang	Indonesia	1.668 t
krâp sran	Cambodia	2.604 mm
krat	Turkey	200 mg
krina	Bulgaria	20 l
kul tonde	Denmark	1.7 hl
kula	Morocco	24.047 l
kulba	Afghanistan	7.814 ha
kung	China	2.006 m
kung chang	Taiwan	10 m
kung ch'ien	Taiwan	10 g
kung ch'ih	Taiwan	1 m
kung chin	Taiwan	1 kg
kung ch'ing	Taiwan	1 ha
kung chu	Taiwan	100 mg
kung fun	Taiwan	1 cm
kung haeng	Taiwan	10 kg
kung hao	Taiwan	10 mg
kung hao	Taiwan	10 cl
kung k'o	Taiwan	1 g
kung li	Taiwan	1 km
kung li'	Taiwan	1 mm
kung liang	Taiwan	100 g
kung mou	Taiwan	1 a
kung ping	Taiwan	1 kl
kung sheng	Taiwan	1 l
kung so	Taiwan	1 cl
kung szu	Taiwan	1 mg
kung tan	Taiwan	1 hl
kung tan	Taiwan	100 kg
kung tou	Taiwan	10 l
kung ts'o	Taiwan	1 ml
kung t'sun	Taiwan	10 cm
kung tun	Taiwan	1 t
kung yin	Taiwan	100 m
kunna	Ethiopia	5 kg
kunna	Ethiopia	4.4 l
kupang	Brunei	37.8 mg
kutu	Turkey	4.6 l
kvint	Denmark	5 g
kwai (liquid)	Myanmar	4.041 l
kwan	Japan	3.75 kg
kwan	Korea, South	3.75 kg
kwarta (beer, wine, spirits)	Malta	5.398 l
kwarta (oil, milk)	Malta	5.114 l
kwarti	Poland	1 l
kwarti (liquid)	Poland	0.948 l
kwien	Thailand	20 hl
kyathos	Greece (ancient)	49 ml
L		
labor	Canada	716.8 m^2
lackilo	Laos	1 km
lai	Vietnam	0.064 m^3
lamany (liquid)	Myanmar	63 ml
lame (dry)	Myanmar	320 ml
lan	Myanmar	1.829 m
lan	Mongolia	37.5 g
lan (land)	Portugal	5.5 km
lan (sea)	Portugal	6.11 km
lana	Soviet Union[a]	34.13 g
lanac	Yugoslavia	0.719 ha
lança	Cape Verde	4.4 m

Unit	Country	Metric equivalent
lança[2]	Cape Verde	19.36 m^2
lane	Laos	1.2 t
lang (dry)	Malaysia	56.826 cl
lang	Vietnam	37.783 g
large artaba	Egypt (Alexandria)	46.7 l
large kantar	Sudan	141.523 kg
large kus	Iraq (ancient Sumerian)	99 cm
last (dry)	Germany	39.57 hl
last	Netherlands	2 t
last	Netherlands	30 hl
lastre (dry)	Argentina	2.058 m^3
lata	Costa Rica	453.1 g
lata (dry)	Venezuela	7–17 l
lath	India	2.743 m
latro	Czechoslovakia	1.917 m
lé	Vietnam	1.6 m^3
lé (cereals)	Vietnam	10 cl
lea	Singapore	34.447 mg
legana (dry)	Iran	39.5 l
legua	Argentina	5.2 km
legua	Chile	4.514 km
legua	Colombia	5 km
legua	Cuba	4.24 km
legua	Ecuador	5 km
legua	El Salvador	4 km
legua	Guatemala	5.573 km
legua	Honduras	4.175 km
legua	Mexico	4.19 km
legua	Paraguay	4.333 km
legua	Peru	5.56 km
legua	Spain	5.573 km
legua	Uruguay	5.154 km
legua	Venezuela	5.56 km
legua	Venezuela	1 600–2 500 ha
lei	Hong Kong	0.557 km
lelong	Malaysia	222.97 m^2
lelong	Singapore	222.97 m^2
letekh (dry)	Israel (ancient Hebrew)	1.9 hl
leung	Hong Kong	37.799 g
li	Cambodia	37.5 mg
li	China	0.5 km
li	China (treaty system)	0.645 km
li	China	37.799 mg
li	Korea, South	3.927 km
li	Laos	37.5 mg
li	Macao	0.376 mm
li	Macao	37.799 mg
li	Mongolia	0.32 mm
li	Mongolia	37.5 mg
li'	China	0.333 mm
li'	China (treaty system)	0.358 mm
li'	China	50 mg
li'	China	6.667 m^2
liang	China	37.799 g
libra	Argentina	460 g
libra	Bolivia	460 g
libra	Brazil	459 g
libra	Cape Verde	459 g
libra	Chile	460 g
libra	Colombia	500 g
libra	Costa Rica	460 g
libra	Cuba	460 g

Unit	Country	Metric equivalent
libra	Dominican Republic	453.6 g
libra	Ecuador	460 g
libra	El Salvador	460 g
libra	Guatemala	460 g
libra	Honduras	460 g
libra	Italy (ancient Roman)	323 g
libra	Malta	453.6 g
libra	Mexico	460 g
libra	Nicaragua	460 g
libra	Paraguay	459 g
libra	Peru	460 g
libra	Philippines	460 g
libra	Puerto Rica	461 g
libra	Spain	460 g
libra	Venezuela	461 g
libra	Uruguay	460 g
lichar	Greece (ancient)	19.2 cm
lieue	Mauritius	4 km
lieue	Switzerland	4.8 km
lieue[2]	Switzerland	23.04 km^2
lieue de poste	France (medieval)	3.898 km
light mina	Iraq (ancient Sumerian)	481 g
light shekel	Iraq (ancient Sumerian)	5.34 g
ligne	France (medieval)	2.256 mm
ligne	Haiti	2.256 mm
ligne	Mauritius	2.256 mm
ligne	Seychelles	2.256 mm
ligne	Switzerland	3 mm
ligula	Italy (ancient Roman)	11.2 ml
li' ke	China	10 mg
li' mi	China	1 cm
linea	Chile	1.93 mm
linea	Honduras	1.93 mm
linea	Mexico	1.93 mm
linea	Paraguay	2.006 mm
linea	Spain	1.93 mm
linhada	Cape Verde	22 m
linia	Sudan	3.175 mm
linie	Denmark	2.18 mm
liniya	Soviet Union[a]	2.54 mm
liño	Paraguay	75.1 m^2
li' sheng (shao)	China	1 cl
lispond	Norway	8 kg
lispund	Denmark	8 kg
litre	Indonesia	0.8 kg
litro	Venezuela	2.5 kg
litron	France (medieval)	0.813 l
livre	Belgium	1 kg
livre	France (medieval)	489.51 kg
livre	Mauritius	0.5 kg
livre	Mauritius (old French)	0.49 kg
livre	Seychelles	0.49 kg
livre	Switzerland	0.5 kg
livre de Charlemagne	France (medieval)	0.367 kg
livre de pharmacie	Switzerland	0.375 kg
livre français	Haiti	0.489 kg
load	Cyprus	163.659 l
load (cocoa)	Gambia	27.2 kg
load (cocoa, new)	Ghana	30 kg
load (cocoa, old)	Ghana	27.2 kg
load (cocoa)	Nigeria	27.2 kg
load (cocoa)	Sierra Leone	27.2 kg

Unit	Country	Metric equivalent
lod	Denmark (medieval)	14.706 g
log	Egypt (ancient)	48.6 cl
log (dry)	Israel (ancient Hebrew)	53 cl
log (liquid)	Israel (ancient Hebrew)	53 cl
loket	Czechoslovakia (Moravia)	0.594 m
loket	Czechoslovakia (Silesia)	0.579 m
loket	Czechoslovakia (Prague)	0.593 m
lokiec	Poland	0.576 m
lolti	Soviet Union[a]	12.8 g
lood	Indonesia	15.44 g
lood	Netherlands	10 kg
lood	Netherlands (Amsterdam)	15.4 g
lot	Germany (old system)	14.62 g
lot	Germany	10 g
loth	Austria	270.1 g
loth	Norway	15.6 g
loth	Switzerland	15.6 g
ludra	Turkey	0.564 kg
ly	Vietnam	0.4 mm
ly	Vietnam	37.78 mg
M		
ma	Hong Kong	0.892 m
maatje	Netherlands	10 cl
mace	Malaysia	6.048 g
madeja	Venezuela	5–15 kg
maess (dry & liquid)	Germany	0.859 l
mahud	Saudi Arabia	0.925 kg
makhammus	Sudan	0.323 ha
malter (dry)	Germany	6.595 hl
malwa (dry)	Sudan	4.125 l
man	Iran	3 kg
mana	Nepal	56.83 cl
manazana	Guatemala	0.7 ha
mancuerna	Honduras	1.438 kg
mancuerna	Venezuela	2–15 kg
man-i-shah	Iran	6 kg
mann	Iraq (Baghdad)	25 kg
mann (coffee)	Iraq (Basra)	64.15 kg
mann (hillana)	Iraq (Basra)	76.98 kg
mano (corn)	Honduras	1.134 kg
manzana	Belize	0.835 ha
manzana	Costa Rica	0.699 ha
manzana	El Salvador	0.703 ha
manzana	Honduras	0.679 ha
manzana	Nicaragua	0.706 ha
mara	Venezuela	50–200 kg
marasseh	Lebanon	50 m^2
marc	Austria	280.6 g
marc	France (medieval)	244.8 g
marc	Germany	233.8 g
marco	Bolivia	230 g
marco	Portugal	230 g
marco	Spain	230 g
marhala	Iraq (medieval Arab)	45.5 km
Maria Theresa thaler	Oman	28.05 g
mark	Denmark (medieval)	235.294 g
mark	Netherlands	247 g
mark	Norway	249 g
mark	Sweden	212.6 g
marla	Pakistan	25.293 m^2
marok	Hungary	6.676 km
marta (cereals)	Libya	20.75 l
mas	Brunei	3.78 g
masha (precious metals)	Bangladesh	0.972 g
masha	India	1.166 g
masha	Pakistan	0.972 g
mat	Myanmar	4.082 g
matomana	Nepal (mountains)	0.795 m^2
matomuri	Nepal (mountains)	127.18 m^2
matopathi	Nepal (mountains)	6.359 m^2
mau	Vietnam	0.36 ha
mau (soil)	Vietnam	0.144 ha
maund	Afghanistan	35.33 kg
maund	Bahrain	25.4 kg
maund	India	37.32 kg
maund	Kuwait	25.4 kg
maund	Nepal	37.32 kg
maund	Pakistan	37.32 kg
maund	Saudi Arabia	37.32 kg
maund	Tanzania	1.338 kg
maund	Yemen	37.32 kg
mayam (precious metals)	Malaysia	3.37 g
mayam (precious metals)	Singapore	3.37 g
maz	Macao	3.78 g
maz	Macao	761.4 m^2
mázsa	Hungary	100 kg
measure	Sri Lanka	1.137 l
measure (dry)	Sri Lanka	1.06 l
mecate	Belize	5.22 a
mecate	Costa Rica	20.06 m
mecate	Guatemala	20.06 m
mecate	Nicaragua	20.16 m
med (wheat)	Lebanon	18–20 kg
media	Ecuador	46 kg
medida	Honduras	2.872 l
medida	Venezuela	625 m^2
medimnos	Greece (ancient)	39 l
medio	El Salvador	8.3–13.8 kg
medio	Honduras	45.95 l
medio	Venezuela	0.5 ha
meias-canada (liquid)	Portugal	0.689 l
meile	Hungary	8.354 km
Mekyas cubit	Egypt (Alexandria)	54 cm
mengel	Netherlands	1.212 l
menor (liquid)	Iran	12.55 l
mercal	India	12.29 l
merice	Czechoslovakia	70.5 l
messe	Ethiopia	1.5 l
mesurette	France (medieval)	50.814 ml
meterzentner	Austria	100 kg
metical	Tunisia	3.936 g
metkal (gold, silver, silk)	Libya	4.601 g
metretes	Greece (ancient)	29.2 l
metric dunam	Israel	1 000 m^2
metze	Austria	61.5 l
metze (dry)	Germany	3.435 l
mi	China	1 m
mid (oil)	Jordan	18 l

Unit	Country	Metric equivalent
miê'ng	Vietnam	36 m^2
miê'ng (soil)	Vietnam	14.4 m^3
mil	Denmark	7.532 km
mil	Norway	11.295 km
mil	Sweden	10.689 km
mil	Turkey	1 km
mil	Venezuela	400 kg
mile	Austria	7.586 km
mile	Bangladesh	1.609 km
mile passum	Italy (ancient Roman)	1.478 km
milha	Portugal	2.058 km
milla	Ecuador	1.4 km
milla	Nicaragua	1.848 km
mille	Belgium (medieval)	2.015 km
minah	Egypt (Alexandria)	778 g
minah	Iraq (medieval Arab)	899 g
mine	France (medieval)	78.05 l
minot	Canada	38.91 hl
minot	France (medieval)	39.025 l
mira	Czechoslovakia	0.192 ha
mishara	Iraq	0.25 ha
miskal	Iran	4.688 g
miskal	Turkey	4.811 g
misqal	Afghanistan	4.6 g
misura (dry)	Libya	19.8 l
mitkal	Iraq (medieval Arab)	4.68 g
mkono	Tanzania	45.72 cm
mna	Greece (ancient)	486 g
mō	Japan	0.03 mm
mō	Japan	3.75 mg
mo	Korea, South	0.03 mm
mocha	Ethiopia	31.1 g
modd	Malta	1.798 ha
modd (cereals)	Malta	2.909 hl
modius	Italy (ancient Roman)	8.61 l
moio (dry)	Cape Verde	24.956 hl
momme	Japan	3.75 g
mon	Bangladesh	37.324 kg
moo	Myanmar	2.041 g
moraba	Pakistan	10.117 ha
morgen	Botswana	0.857 ha
morgen	Germany	0.255 ha
morgen	Netherlands	0.853 ha
morgen	South Africa	0.857 ha
mou	China	0.067 ha
mow	Hong Kong	0.084 ha
mu	China	6.667 a
mud	Netherlands	1 hl
mudd	Morocco	46.7 l
mudd	Syria (Chakba)	26 l
mudd	Syria (Soueida)	27.5 l
mudu (dry)	Nigeria	1.13 kg
muid	France (medieval)	18.732 hl
muid	Seychelles	2.682 hl
muid	South Africa	1.091 hl
muid (liquid)	Switzerland	1.5 hl
mune	Laos	12 kg
muscat maund	Oman	4.04 kg
musus kibaba	Tanzania	0.5 l
mutsje	Netherlands	15.2 cl
myo	Korea, South	99.174 m^2

Unit	Country	Metric equivalent
N		
nafer	Yemen	0.625 l
nakhad	Afghanistan	191.8 mg
nakir	Turkey	6.26 mg
néal	Cambodia	600 g
négyszögöl	Hungary	3.597 m^2
neter	Ethiopia	450 g
ngamu	Myanmar	8.165 g
ngan	Thailand	400 m^2
ngane	Laos	400 m^2
ngu	Vietnam	2 m
nijo	Japan	15 g
niou	Laos	1.666 cm
niu	Thailand	2.083 cm
node	Antigua	11.4 cm
nofs (beer, wine, spirits)	Malta	56.8 cl
nofs (oil, milk)	Malta	63.9 cl
nokhod	Iran	195 mg
O		
ô (soil)	Vietnam	0.064 m^3
obol	Greece (ancient)	0.81 g
obolus	Italy (ancient Roman)	0.56 g
ochava	Mexico	3.596 g
octava (liquid)	Argentina	0.148 l
octavillo (liquid)	Spain	0.252 l
ohm (liquid)	Germany	1.374 hl
oitava	Brazil	3.59 mg
oitava	Macao	3.59 g
oitavo (dry)	Portugal	1.73 l
oka	Greece	1.28 kg
oke	Bulgaria	1.28 kg
oke	Bulgaria	1.28 l
oke	Cyprus	1.27 g
oke	Cyprus	1.27 l
oke	Egypt	1.25 kg
oke	Iraq (medieval Arab)	1.25 kg
oke	Lebanon	1.28 kg
oke	Libya	1.28 kg
oke	Saudi Arabia	1.25 kg
oke	Syria (Damascus)	1.28 kg
oke	Turkey (old system)	1.28 kg
oke	Turkey	1 kg
oke	Turkey	72.7 cl
oke thapa	Myanmar	64.008 m
okia	Somalia	28 g
okia	Sudan	37.44 g
okia	Syria (Aleppo & Homs)	320.5 g
okia	Syria (Damascus)	213.7 g
okiya	Iraq (Basra)	3.208 kg
okiya	Iraq (Baghdad)	1.042 kg
okiya	Iraq (Istanbul)	320.5 g
okiya	Iraq (Mosul)	128.3 g
okka	Jordan	1.282 kg
okiya	Lebanon	213.7 g
okka	Yemen	0.85 kg
okshoofd	Netherlands	2.328 hl
olc	Iraq	100 m^2
ölçek	Turkey (Anatolian system)	50.5 l
ölçek	Turkey (Istanbul)	18.5 l
omer (dry)	Israel (ancient Hebrew)	3.8 l

Unit	Country	Metric equivalent
ona	Dominican Republic	1.188 m
onça	Cape Verde	1 161.6 m^2
onça	Macao	28.69 g
onça	Portugal (old system)	28.69 g
onça	Portugal	29.3 g
once	France (medieval)	30.594 g
once	Mauritius	30.594 g
once	Seychelles	30.594 g
once	Switzerland	31.25 g
ons	Indonesia	30.9 g
ons	Netherlands	100 g
ons	Netherlands (Amsterdam)	30.9 g
ons	Surinam	100 g
onza	Argentina	28.75 g
onza	Chile	28.75 g
onza	Colombia	31.25 g
onza	Cuba	28.75 g
onza	Dominican Republic	28.35 g
onza	El Salvador	28.75 g
onza	Guatemala	28.75 g
onza	Honduras	28.75 g
onza	Honduras	2.88 cl
onza	Mexico	28.75 g
onza	Nicaragua	28.75 g
onza	Paraguay	28.688 g
onza	Peru	28.75 g
onza	Spain	28.75 g
oquia	Jordan (Nabulsi)	240.38 g
oquia	Jordan (Shami)	213.67 g
orguia	Greece (ancient)	1.848 m
orlong	Malaysia	0.535 ha
orlong	Singapore	0.535 ha
ort	Denmark	500 mg
ort	Denmark (medieval)	919 mg
ort (liquid)	Germany	215 ml
ort	Sweden	4.252 g
ottingkar	Denmark	2.174 l
oukeia	Morocco	125 g
ounce	Norway	31.1 g
ourob	Iran	13 cm
oxhoft (liquid)	Germany	2.061 hl
oxybaphon	Greece (ancient)	73 ml
P		
pa	India	233.28 g
paca	Venezuela	50 kg
pace	USA	76.2 cm
packen	Soviet Union[a]	0.491 t
pægle	Denmark	241.53 ml
pai	Myanmar	1.021 g
palaiste	Greece (ancient)	7.7 cm
palgat	Myanmar	2.54 cm
pali (cereals)	Oman	280 g
palito	Venezuela	9–18 kg
palm	Netherlands	10 cm
palma	Italy (ancient Roman)	7.39 cm
palmipes	Italy (ancient Roman)	36.95 cm
palmo	Brazil	22 cm
palmo (textiles)	Libya	25 cm
palmo	Macao	22 cm
palmo	Portugal	22 cm
palmo	Spain	20.9 cm

Unit	Country	Metric equivalent
panchang	Malaysia	3.058 m^3
panchar	Indonesia	2.839 ha
pao	Nepal	194.4 g
pao	Pakistan	233.28 g
paquete	Venezuela	1.2–2 kg
para	Malaysia	40.823 kg
para (liquid)	Malaysia	45.46 l
para	Singapore	45.46 l
parah (dry & liquid)	Sri Lanka	25.5 l
parasang	Greece (ancient)	5.544 km
parasang	Iraq (medieval Arab)	5.69 km
parcela	Puerto Rica	982.6 m^2
Paris foot	Canada	0.325 m
parmak	Turkey	10 cm
passeree	India	4.665 kg
passo (land)	Libya	1 m
passus	Italy (ancient Roman)	1.478 m
pathi	Nepal	4.546 l
pau	Brunei	284 ml
pau (liquid)	Malaysia	284 ml
pau	Singapore	284 ml
pé	Cape Verde	0.305 m
pé	Macao	0.33 m
pé	Portugal	0.33 m
pechus	Greece (ancient)	46.2 cm
pecheus (masonry)	Greece	1.5 m
pedra	Cape Verde	1.377 kg
peninkulma	Finland	10 km
penjuru	Malaysia	1 337.8 m^2
penjuru	Singapore	0.134 ha
perch	Canada	34.189 m^2
perch	Canada	5.847 m
perch or pole	Ireland	6.401 m
perch^2	Ireland	40.97 m^2
perche	France (medieval)	7.146 m
perche	France (medieval)	51.072 m^2
perche	Jersey	6.7 m
perche^2	Jersey	44.97 m^2
perche	Mauritius	6.497 m
perche^2	Mauritius	42.208 m^2
perche	Seychelles	6.497 m
perche	Switzerland	3 m
perche^2	Switzerland	9 m^2
pes	Italy (ancient Roman)	29.56 cm
pes^2	Italy (ancient Roman)	0.087 m^2
pfund	Austria (old system)	561 g
pfund	Austria	500 g
pfund	Denmark (medieval)	470.588 g
pfund	Germany	500 g
pfund	Germany (old system)	467.7 g
phaï mû	Laos	1.25 l
phâ'n	Vietnam	0.24 m^2
phân	Vietnam	4 mm
phân	Vietnam	377.8 mg
pharoagh	Turkey	10 km
phlan	Cambodia	0.1 m^3
phuong (cereals)	Vietnam	30 l
phyéam	Cambodia	2 m
pic	Cyprus	0.61 m
pic (masonry)	Greece	0.75 m
pic^2	Greece	0.563 m^2

Unit	Country	Metric equivalent
pico	Macao	60.479 kg
picol	Indonesia	61.761 kg
picul	Japan	60 kg
picul	Laos	60 kg
picul	Philippines	63.25 kg
picul	Thailand	60 kg
pié	Argentina	28.9 cm
pie	Bolivia	28.9 cm
pie	Cuba	28.267 cm
pie	El Salvador	27.86 cm
pie	Guatemala	27.86 cm
pie	Honduras	27.833 cm
pie	Mexico	27.933 cm
pie	Paraguay	28.9 cm
pie	Spain	27.86 cm
pied	Belgium (medieval)	33.58 cm
pied	Belgium	30 cm
pied	France (medieval)	0.325 m
pied	Haiti	0.325 m
pied	Mauritius	0.325 m
pied^3	Mauritius	0.034 m^3
pied	Seychelles	0.325 m
pied	Switzerland	0.3 m
pie de madera	Cuba	2.36 l
pied de perche	Jersey	279 mm
pied de perche^2	Jersey	780.6 cm^2
pijp	Netherlands	4.123 hl
pijp (wine)	Netherlands	5.4 hl
pik Andoulsi	Tunisia	64.9 cm
pik Arbi	Tunisia	49.3 cm
pik Turki	Tunisia	64.5 cm
pikul	Brunei	60.479 kg
pikul	Malaysia	60.479 kg
pikul	Singapore	60.479 kg
pinar	Iran	93.75 g
pinta	Chile	0.56 l
pinta (beer, wine, spirits)	Malta	0.142 l
pinte	France (medieval)	0.931 l
pinte (reputed)	Mauritius	0.379 l
pinte (colonial)	Mauritius	0.931 l
pinte	Seychelles	0.931 l
pintji	Netherlands Antilles	0.375 kg
pipa (liquid)	Argentina	4.56 hl
pipa	Cuba	4.769 hl
pipa	Dominican Republic	5.728 hl
pipa (liquid)	Paraguay	5.816 hl
pipa (liquid)	Portugal	4.30 hl
pipe	Singapore	5.728 hl
pipe (liquid)	Soviet Union[a]	4.428 hl
pipe (liquid)	Spain	4.355 hl
pishi	Tanzania	4 l
plaza	Venezuela	10–20 m^2
plethron	Greece (ancient)	30.8 m
point	Denmark	0.182 mm
point	France (medieval)	0.188 mm
polegada	Macao	2.75 cm
polegada	Portugal	2.75 cm
pond	Indonesia	494.1 g
pond	Netherlands (Amsterdam)	494.1 g
pond	Netherlands	500 g
pond	Surinam	500 g
pong (opium)	Laos	375 g
pong chay	Cambodia	0.018 mm
ponto	Macao	3.76 cm
ponto	Macao	12.69 cm^2
pood	Soviet Union[a]	16.38 kg
posson	France (medieval)	0.116 l
pot (dry)	Belgium	1.5 l
pot (liquid)	Belgium	0.5 l
pot	Denmark	0.965 l
pot	France (medieval)	1.863 l
pot	Jersey	1.975 l
pot	Norway	0.965 l
pot (liquid)	Switzerland	1.5 l
pouce	Belgium (medieval)	3.358 cm
pouce	Belgium	3 cm
pouce	France (medieval)	2.707 cm
pouce	Haiti	2.707 cm
pouce	Mauritius	2.707 cm
pouce	Seychelles	2.707 cm
pouce	Switzerland	3 cm
pous	Greece (ancient)	30.8 cm
pow	Afghanistan	441.625 g
powa	Bangladesh	233.28 g
pu	China	1.791 m
pu	Macao	3.173 m^2
puddee	India	1.536 l
pulgada	Argentina	2.41 cm
pulgada	Bolivia	2.41 cm
pulgada	Colombia	2.5 cm
pulgada	Cuba	2.36 cm
pulgada	El Salvador	2.32 cm
pulgada	Guatemala	2.32 cm
pulgada	Honduras	2.32 cm
pulgada	Mexico	2.32 cm
pulgada	Nicaragua	2.67 cm
pulgada	Paraguay	2.41 cm
pulgada	Spain	2.32 cm
pulgada maderera	Chile	23.597 dm^3
pulzier	Malta	21.83 mm
pun	Korea, South	3.03 mm
pun	Mongolia	375 mg
pun	Mongolia	3.2 mm
pund	Denmark	500 g
pund	Norway	498.1 g
punk	India	9.11 mg
punto	Honduras	0.161 mm
punto	Venezuela	600 kg
pushuri	Bangladesh	4.666 kg
pygme	Greece (ancient)	34.6 cm
pygon	Greece (ancient)	38.5 cm
pyi	Myanmar	2.126 kg
pyi (dry)	Myanmar	2.557 l
pyong	Korea, South	3.306 m^2
pyong (timber)	Korea, South	2.004 m^3
pyong	Korea, North	3.306 m^2
Q		
qadaa	Sudan	2.204 ha
qadah (dry)	Sudan	2.063 l
qadah	Yemen	90.72 kg
qadam	Sudan	0.305 m
qama	Yemen	1.65 m

Unit	Country	Metric equivalent
qantâr	Egypt	44.928 kg
qantar	Iraq (medieval Arab)	44.928 kg
qasa	Yemen	1.134 kg
qasba	Malta	2.095 m
qassabeh	Lebanon	23.814 m^2
qav (dry & liquid)	Israel (ancient Hebrew)	2.1 l
qilli (olive oil)	Lebanon	33.345 kg
qing	China	6.667 ha
qirat	Egypt	0.87 mm
quadrans	Italy (ancient Roman)	80.6 g
quart (reputed)	Mauritius	75.77 cl
quarta	Cape Verde	0.465 ha
quarta (dry)	Cape Verde	10.398 l
quartarella	Italy	36.8 l
quartarius	Italy (ancient Roman)	135 ml
quarteau	France (medieval)	4.683 hl
quarteron (dry)	Switzerland	15 l
quartia	Belize	2.841 l
quartilho (liquid)	Portugal	0.345 l
quarto	Italy	0.736 hl
quarto (dry)	Portugal	3.46 l
quartuccio	Italy	114 ml
quê (cereals)	Vietnam	0.02 ml
quenten	Norway	3.89 g
quilate	Colombia	20 mg
quintal	Argentina	46 kg
quintal	Belize	45.36 kg
quintal	Bolivia	46 kg
quintal	Brazil	58.75 kg
quintal	Chile	46 kg
quintal	Colombia	50 kg
quintal	Costa Rica	46 kg
quintal	Cuba	46 kg
quintal	Dominican Republic	45.36 kg
quintal	El Salvador	46 kg
quintal	France (medieval)	48.95 kg
quintal	Guatemala	46 kg
quintal	Honduras	46 kg
quintal	Macao	58.75 kg
quintal	Mexico	46 kg
quintal	Nicaragua	46 kg
quintal	Paraguay	46 kg
quintal	Peru	46 kg
quintal	Philippines	46 kg
quintal	Portugal	60 kg
quintal	Portugal	58.75 kg
quintal	Spain	46 kg
quintal	Switzerland	50 kg
quintal	Uruguay	46 kg
quintal	Venezuela	46 kg
R		
rabâa	Morocco	250 g
racione (dry)	Spain	0.289 l
rafa	Bahrain	254.01 kg
rageil	Sudan	1.676 m
rai	Laos	0.16 ha
rai	Thailand	0.16 ha
rajabah	Oman	3 cm
rati (precious metals)	Bangladesh	121.5 mg
ratili	Tanzania	453.6 g

Unit	Country	Metric equivalent
ratl	Bahrain	454 g
ratl	Libya	512.8 g
ratl	Yemen	453.6 g
raummeter	Austria	1 m^3
real (precious metals)	Indonesia	27.045 g
rebée	Syria	4.75 l
red (corn)	Honduras	45.359 kg
ref	Sweden	29.692 m
relong	Malaysia	0.287 ha
relong	Singapore	0.287 ha
rey	Iran	12 kg
Rhineland acre	Netherlands	0.426 ha
Rhineland acre	Surinam	0.426 ha
Rhynland acre	Guyana	0.426 ha
ri	Japan	3.927 km
ri	Korea, North	392.727 m
ri	Korea, South	0.303 mm
rin	Japan	0.303 mm
rin	Japan	37.5 mg
robo kibaba	Tanzania	0.25 l
rode	Denmark	3.77 m
roe	Netherlands (Rhineland)	3.77 m
roe	Netherlands	10 m
roe^2	Netherlands	100 m^2
roede	Indonesia	3.767 m
roede^2	Indonesia	14.193 m^2
roede	Netherlands	14.213 m^2
ropani	Nepal (mountains)	508.72 m^2
roquille	France (medieval)	29.1 ml
rotal	Morocco (old system)	513 g
rotal	Morocco	500 g
rotl	Ethiopia	311 g
rotl	Israel (north)	2.4 kg
rotl	Israel (south)	2.88 kg
rotl	Jordan (Shami)	2.564 kg
rotl	Saudi Arabia	462.5 g
rotl	Sudan	449 g
rotle (liquid)	Yemen	778 g
rotle (meat)	Yemen	672 g
rotle (sugar)	Yemen	560 g
rotolo	Malta	794 g
rottel	Iran	468.75 g
rottel	Tunisia	503.8 g
rottle	Egypt	449 g
rottle	Iraq (medieval Arab)	449 g
rottol	Syria (Aleppo & Homs)	3.205 kg
rottol	Syria (Damascus)	2.565 kg
rottol	Turkey	2.565 kg
rottol	Turkey	1.6 l
rottolo	Lebanon	2.565 kg
rottolo	Somalia	449 g
roupi	Cyprus	7.62 cm
rova	Israel (ancient Hebrew)	3.2 g
royal cubit	Egypt (ancient)	52.4 cm
royal cubit^2	Egypt (ancient)	0.275 m^2
royal cubit^3	Egypt (ancient)	0.144 m^3
royal stremma	Greece	1 000 m^2
roza	Cuba	0.746 ha
rub	Egypt	8.25 l
ruba	Bahrain	1.814 kg
ruba	Saudi Arabia	9.344 kg

Unit	Country	Metric equivalent
ruba (dry)	Sudan	8.25 l
rubbiatella	Italy	1.472 hl
rubbio	Italy	2.944 hl
rute	Germany	3.766 m
ruttee	India	146 mg
ruttee	Pakistan	121.5 mg
ryutsubo	Japan	6.01 m^3
S		
sa'	Tunisia	3.031 l
saa (oil)	Jordan	6 l
saa	Libya	0.96 ha
saa (dry)	Libya	1.188 hl
saagh	Syria	9.73 l
sabbitha (dry)	Iran	7.24 l
sac (coffee)	Haiti	60 kg
sac (dry)	Switzerland	1.5 hl
sac (coffee)	Zaire	60 kg
sack (cement)	Indonesia	40 or 50 kg
saco (coffee)	Colombia	62.5 kg
saco (coffee)	Costa Rica	69 kg
saco (coffee)	Cuba	90 kg
saco (sugar)	Cuba	115.023 kg
saco	Dominican Republic	75 kg
saco	Honduras	69 kg
saco	Nicaragua	69 kg
saco (coffee)	Peru	69 kg
saco	Venezuela	20–60 kg
sacred amma	Israel (ancient Hebrew)	54 cm
sacred mane	Israel (ancient Hebrew)	760 g
sacred shekel	Israel (ancient Hebrew)	25.3 g
saddirham	Iran	1.5 kg
saga (precious metals)	Malaysia	280.8 mg
saga (precious metals)	Singapore	280.8 mg
sahm	Egypt	7.293 m^2
sai	Japan	27.826 dm^3
sajon	Soviet Union[a]	2.134 m
$sajon^2$	Soviet Union[a]	4.552 m^2
sale (dry)	Myanmar	639 ml
salm	Malta	222.3 kg
saltus	Italy (ancient Roman)	2.013 km^2
salung	Laos	3.75 g
salung	Thailand	3.75 g
sandong	Myanmar	55.88 cm
sao (cereals)	Vietnam	2 ml
sào	Vietnam	360 m^2
sào (soil)	Vietnam	144 m^3
sar	Iraq (ancient Sumerian)	15 m^2
sat	Egypt (Alexandria)	11.7 l
sat	Thailand	20 l
sayut (dry)	Myanmar	5.114 l
scheffel (dry)	Germany	54.96 l
schepel	Netherlands	10 l
schibr	Egypt (medieval)	22.5 cm
schoenus	Italy (ancient Roman)	5.912 km
schoinos	Greece (ancient)	11.09 km
schoppen (liquid)	Germany	429 ml
schtoff (liquid)	Soviet Union[a]	1.23 l
scruple	Switzerland	1.302 g
scrupulus	Italy (ancient Roman)	8.74 m^2
scrupulus	Italy (ancient Roman)	1.12 g
se	Iraq (ancient Sumerian)	45 mg
sê	Japan	99.174 m^2
se'a (dry)	Israel (ancient Hebrew)	12.7 l
seak	Macao	103.1 l
section	Canada	2.59 km^2
seer (Kabul)	Afghanistan	7.066 kg
seer	Bangladesh	0.933 kg
seer	India	0.933 kg
seer	Iran	75 g
seer	Nepal	0.933 kg
seer	Pakistan	0.933 kg
seer (liquid)	Sri Lanka	1.06 l
seer	Yemen	0.933 kg
seh	Hong Kong	1 hl
seidel (beer)	Austria	0.354 l
seik (dry)	Myanmar	2.02 l
seik (liquid)	Myanmar	10.229 l
semodius	Italy (ancient Roman)	4.3 l
semuncia	Italy (ancient Roman)	13.4 g
sen	Cambodia	40 m
sen	Thailand	40 m
sène	Laos	120 kg
sénh	Laos	40 m
senzer	Ethiopia	22.86 cm
sep	Egypt (ancient)	0.94 kg
set	Egypt (ancient)	0.275 ha
setier	France (medieval)	1.561 hl
setier (liquid)	Switzerland	37.5 l
sett	Antigua	22.9 cm
sextario (dry)	Iran	0.329 l
sextarius	Italy (ancient Roman)	0.538 l
shaku	Japan	0.303 m
shaku	Japan	0.033 m^2
shaku	Japan (kujira shaku)	0.378 m
shaku	Japan	18.039 ml
she	Iraq (ancient Sumerian)	14 cm^2
shekel	Egypt (Alexandria)	15.6 g
shekel	Iraq (ancient Sumerian)	8.02 g
shekel	Israel (ancient Hebrew)	12.7 g
sheng	China (old system)	1.035 l
sheng (sheng)	China	1 l
shibr	Oman	24 cm
shibr	Saudi Arabia	17.78 cm
shi' ke`	China	10 g
shi' mi	China	10 m
shin	Mongolia	65 cl
shippond	Norway	159.4 kg
ships-last	Sweden	2.45 t
ships-pund	Sweden	170 kg
shi' sheng (dou)	China	10 l
sho	China	10.355 ml
shō	Japan	1.804 l
shushack	Belize	22.73 l
shusi	Iraq (ancient Sumerian)	1.65 cm
si mi	China	0.1 mm
sicilicus	Italy (ancient Roman)	6.72 g
side of a besana	Cuba	50.88 m
side of a beswasa	Afghanistan	2.21 m
side of a jerib	Afghanistan	44.2 m
siegh	Malta	187.354 m^2
siki	Bangladesh	2.916 g
sila	Iraq (ancient Sumerian)	0.963 l
síldar mál	Iceland	1.5 hl

Unit	Country	Metric equivalent
síldar tunna	Iceland	1.18–1.2 hl
siliqua	Italy (ancient Roman)	187 mg
sing	Hong Kong	1 l
sinik	Turkey	9.2 l
sitarion	Greece (ancient)	68 mg
sitio de ganado mayor	Mexico	17.556 km^2
sjomila	Iceland	1.855 km
skal-pund	Sweden	425.15 g
skæpper	Denmark	17.39 l
skæpper	Denmark	689.528 m^2
skjeppe	Norway	17.37 l
small Hungarian yoke	Hungary	0.36 ha
small hogga	Iraq (Mosul)	1.54 kg
small kus	Iraq (ancient Sumerian)	49.4 cm
small mal	Korea, South	9.02 l
small mann	Iraq (Mosul)	12.317 kg
sok	Laos	40 cm
sok	Thailand	50 cm
solar	Costa Rica	873.62 m^2
solar	Ecuador	1 764 m^2
sossus	Iraq (ancient Sumerian)	1.65 mm
spanland	Sweden	0.247 ha
spint	Netherlands	5 l
spithame	Greece (ancient)	23.1 cm
square	Sri Lanka	83.613 m^2
square	USA	9.29 m^2
square Paris foot	Canada	0.106 m^2
ssu	China (treaty system)	0.378 mg
ssu	China	0.5 mg
stab	Germany	66.69 cm
stadion	Greece (ancient)	185 m
stadium	Italy (ancient Roman)	185 m
stajo	Italy	24.53 l
stangiew	Poland	200 l
stangiew (liquid)	Poland	273.08 l
starello	Italy	18.4 l
stöng	Sweden	2.969 m
stoop	Netherlands (Amsterdam)	2.425 l
stoop	Netherlands	6 l
stopa	Poland	28.8 cm
streep	Netherlands	1 mm
stremma	Greece (ancient)	949 m^2
strich	Germany	1.046 mm
Sudan diraa	Sudan	0.58 m
suerte	Uruguay	1 992 ha
suk	Korea, South	1.804 hl
suku (precious metals)	Indonesia	6.761 g
sulga	Mongolia	6.5 l
sultchek	Turkey	1 l
sun	Japan	3.03 cm
sun	Japan (kujira shaku)	3.78 cm
sus	Somalia	1.475 kg
T		
ta	Vietnam	60.453 kg
tabla (dry)	Somalia	20.385 l
tablé (cereals)	Lebanon	15 kg
tablón	Venezuela	0.6–1 ha
tac	Vietnam	2.4 m^2
tac	Vietnam	4 cm
tael (gold)	Hong Kong	37.5 g
tael	Japan	37.5 g

Unit	Country	Metric equivalent
tael	Macao	37.8 g
tael	Philippines	39.531 g
tael	Singapore	34.447 g
tahil	Brunei	37.8 g
tahil	Malaysia	37.8 g
tahil	Singapore	37.8 g
tai or catty	Taiwan	600 g
taim	India	45.72 cm
taim²	India	0.209 m^2
taing	Myanmar	3.912 km
talangva	Laos	4 m^2
talanton	Greece (ancient)	29 kg
talent	Egypt (Alexandria)	46.7 kg
talent	Iraq (ancient Sumerian)	29 kg
talent	Israel (ancient Hebrew)	38 kg
talentum	Italy (ancient Roman)	25.8 kg
tali (precious metals)	Indonesia	3.381g
tam	Hong Kong	60.479 kg
tamlung	Thailand	60 g
tamna	Morocco	225 m^2
tamuga	Costa Rica	2.07 kg
tan	China (treaty system)	60.479 kg
tan	China	50 kg
tan	China	1.035 hl
tan	Japan	991.74 m^2
tan	Korea, South	991.74 m^2
tanica (liquid)	Somalia	18 l
tank	India	12.96 g
tao	Cambodia	15 l
tar	Myanmar	3.2 m
tarea	Dominican Republic	628.8 m^2
tarea	El Salvador	280–875 m^2
tarea	Venezuela	50–833 m^2
tarialte	Morocco	0.36 ha
tau	China	10.355 l
taung	Myanmar	45.72 cm
taza	Cuba	236 ml
tcharak	Iran	0.75 kg
tcheki	Turkey	225.8 kg
tefah	Israel (ancient Hebrew)	7.8 cm
teman (dry)	Libya	26.8 l
teminye	Syria	2.41 l
teneka	Iraq	18.184 l
teningsfet	Iceland	0.031 m^3
tercia	Costa Rica	28 cm
tercia	Nicaragua	28 cm
tercio	Ecuador	36.8 kg
tercio	Mexico	73.639 kg
tercio	Venezuela	40 kg
terz (beer, wine, spirits)	Malta	284 ml
terz (oil, milk)	Malta	32 cl
tetradrachm	Greece (ancient)	19.4 g
thail (precious metals)	Indonesia	54.09 g
thail (opium)	Indonesia	38.601 g
thamardi tin	Myanmar	40.915 l
thamin	Yemen	2.381 kg
than	Vietnam	4 m^2
than (soil)	Vietnam	1.6 m^3
thanan	Thailand	1 l
thang	Cambodia	30 l
thang	Laos	200 l

Unit	Country	Metric equivalent
thùng (cereals)	Vietnam	2 l
theb	Egypt (Alexandria)	2.2 cm
theb	Egypt (ancient)	1.87 cm
thneap	Cambodia	2.083 cm
thoum	Yemen	50 l
thruong	Vietnam	4 m
thng (cereals)	Vietnam	20 l
thuoc	Vietnam	24 m^2
thuoc	Vietnam	0.4 m
thuoc (cereals)	Vietnam	2 cl
ti	Vietnam	4 µm
ti	Vietnam	0.378 mg
tia	Yemen	1.166 g
tical	Myanmar	16.33 g
tierçon	Mauritius	1.91 hl
timbang (opium)	Indonesia	386.01 mg
tinaja	Philippines	48 l
tiya (dry)	Nigeria	2.27 kg
tjære tonde	Denmark	1.159 hl
tji (opium)	Indonesia	3.86 g
to	Japan	18.039 l
toát (cereals)	Vietnam	0.2 ml
toesa	Macao	1.98 m
toise	Belgium (medieval)	2.015 m
toise	France (medieval)	1.949 m
toise	Mauritius	1.949 m
toise	Seychelles	1.949 m
toise	Switzerland	1.8 m
tokhoi	Mongolia	32 cm
tola	Bahrain	11.664 g
tola	Bangladesh	11.664 g
tola	India	11.664 g
tola	Pakistan	11.664 g
tola	Yemen	11.664 g
tomande	Saudi Arabia	84.9 kg
tomín	Spain	599.1 mg
tomini	Morocco	6.985 cm
tomini	Morocco	5.83 l
tomma (new)	Iceland	2.54 cm
tomma (old)	Iceland	2.61 cm
tomme	Denmark	2.61 cm
tomna	Malta	0.112 ha
tomnas (cereals)	Malta	18.184 l
ton	Canada	0.907 t
tonde korn	Denmark	1.391 hl
tonde land	Denmark	0.552 ha
tonde ol	Denmark	1.314 hl
tonde sild	Denmark	1.082 hl
tonelada	Argentina	0.92 t
tonelada (dry)	Argentina	1.029 m^3
tonelada	Bolivia	0.92 t
tonelada	Brazil	0.793 t
tonelada	Colombia	1 t
tonelada	Costa Rica	0.92 t
tonelada	Cuba	0.92 t
tonelada	Guatemala	0.92 t
tonelada	Nicaragua	0.92 t
tonelada	Paraguay	0.92 t
tonelada	Peru	0.92 t
tonelada	Portugal	0.793 t
tonelada (liquid)	Portugal	860 l
tonelada, corto	Spain	0.92 t
tonelada, grande	Spain	1 t
tonelada corta	El Salvador	0.92 t
tonna	Hungary	1 t
tonne	Sweden	1.674 hl
tonneau (wine)	France (medieval)	9.048 hl
tonos	Greece	1.5 t
top	Somalia	3.91 m
topo	Peru (general)	0.349 ha
topo	Peru (Cuzco)	0.272 ha
topo	Peru (Puno)	0.461 ha
toque	Seychelles	22 l
tovar	Bulgaria	128.2 kg
town lot	Sierra Leone	348.39 m^2
trait	Switzerland	0.3 mm
t'ser	Egypt (Alexandria)	36 cm
tsin	Hong Kong	3.78 g
tsin	Mongolia	3.75 g
tsubo	Japan	3.306 m^2
ts'un	China (treaty system)	3.581 cm
ts'un	China	3.333 cm
tsün	Hong Kong	37.148 mm
tu	China	161.2 km
túc (cereals)	Vietnam	0.003 ml
tughar	Iraq (Baghdad)	2 t
tughar	Iraq (Basra)	2.053 t
tughar	Iraq (Mosul)	0.267 t
tuht	Turkey	160.4 g
tum	Finland	2.47 cm
tum	Sweden	2.969 cm
tumoli (cereals)	Malta	72.737 hl
tun (liquid)	Malaysia	11.456 hl
tun	Singapore	11.456 hl
tunnland	Sweden	0.494 ha
U		
ud	Sudan	2.32 m
ueba (cereals)	Libya	2.905 hl
ukia	Libya	32.05 g
ukia (gold, silver, silk)	Libya	30.672 g
una	Iran	12.21 mg
uncia	Italy (ancient Roman)	2.46 cm
uncia	Italy (ancient Roman)	26.9 g
unglie	Pakistan	1.905 cm
ungul	India	1.905 cm
unser	Denmark (medieval)	29.412 g
untzia	Bulgaria	30 g
unzen	Germany	29.23 g
uqija	Malta	26.46 g
ure	Mongolia	921.6 m^2
urna	Italy (ancient Roman)	12.9 l
US standard box	Philippines	57–63 kg
ush	Iraq (ancient Sumerian)	711 m
uzan	Tunisia	31.487 g
V		
va	Laos	2 m
vadem	Netherlands	1.829 m
vagon	Hungary	10 t
vagon	Yugoslavia	10 t
vara	Argentina	0.866 m
vara	Bolivia	0.866 m
vara	Brazil	1.111 m

nit	Country	Metric equivalent
ara	Canada	0.847 m
ara^2	Canada	0.717 m^2
ara	Cape Verde	1.21 m^2
ara	Chile	0.836 m
ara	Colombia	0.8 m
ara^2	Colombia	0.64 m^2
ara	Costa Rica	0.836 m
ara^2	Costa Rica	0.699 m^2
ara	Cuba	0.848 m
ara^2	Cuba	0.719 m^2
ara	Dominican Republic	0.836 m
ara	Ecuador	0.84 m
ara	El Salvador	0.836 m
ara^2	El Salvador	0.7 m^2
ara	Guatemala	0.836 m
ara^2	Guatemala	0.7 m^2
ara	Honduras	0.835 m
ara^2	Honduras	0.697 m^2
ara	Macao	1.10 m
ara	Mexico	0.838 m
ara	Nicaragua	0.84 m
ara^2	Nicaragua	0.706 m^2
ara	Paraguay	0.867 cm
ara^2	Paraguay	0.751 m^2
ara	Peru	0.838 m
ara	Philippines	0.848 m
ara	Portugal	1.10 m
ara	São Tomé & Principe	4.84 m
ara	Spain	0.836 m
ara	Uruguay	0.859 m
ara	USA (Texas)	0.847 m
ara	Venezuela	0.838 m
ara	Venezuela	0.86 m^2
ara	Venezuela	250 g
archok	Soviet Union[a]	4.445 cm
edro	Bulgaria	10 l
edro (liquid)	Soviet Union[a]	12.299 l
elte	France (medieval)	7.451 l
elte (wine)	France (medieval)	7.54 l
elte	Mauritius	7.451 l
elte	Seychelles	7.451 l
enetian litre	Greece	480 g
erst	Soviet Union[a]	1.067 km
	Vietnam	40 nm
	Vietnam	0.004 mg
iertel	Denmark	7.729 l
iertel (dry)	Germany	13.74 l
iss	Myanmar	1.633 kg
oet	Netherlands (Amsterdam)	28.313 cm
oet	Netherlands (Rhineland)	31.417 cm
a	Thailand	2 m
a^2	Thailand	4 m^2
agia dahabia (gold)	Sudan	32 g

Unit	Country	Metric equivalent
wang (precious metals)	Indonesia	1.127 g
war	Yemen	0.914 m
wari	Tanzania	0.914 m
wazna	Iraq (Baghdad)	100 kg
wazna	Iraq (Basra)	102.64 kg
wazna	Iraq (Mosul)	13.343 kg
wazna	Saudi Arabia	1.588 kg
wei mi	China	1 µm
wiba	Tunisia	36.369 l
wichtje	Netherlands	1 g
winspel (dry)	Germany	13.19 hl
wise	Netherlands	10 hl
wizna	Malta	3.969 kg
woket	Ethiopia	25.9 g
wukiyeh	Iraq (medieval Arab)	37.4 g
X		
xang	Laos	1.2 kg
xeste	Greece (ancient)	584 ml
xiber	Malta	26.19 cm
Y		
yang	Korea, South	37.5 g
yarda	Colombia	90 cm
yen	Vietnam	6.045 kg
ying	China	33.333 m
ying	China (treaty system)	35.814 m
yoch	Cambodia	16 km
yote	Thailand	16 km
yugada	Peru	32.3 ha
yusdroman	Iraq (medieval Arab)	374 g
yuzanar	Myanmar	75.834 km
ywegale	Myanmar	255 mg
ywegyi	Myanmar	0.51 g
Z		
zalay (liquid)	Myanmar	126 ml
zar	Iran	1.04 m
zar^2	Iran	1.082 m^2
zarf	Turkey	2.3 l
zayoot (liquid)	Myanmar	1.01 l
zentner	Austria	50 kg
zentner	Germany	50 kg
zeret	Israel (ancient Hebrew)	23 cm
zevre	Turkey	2.09 mg
zhang	China	3.333 m
zhang	China (treaty system)	3.581 m
zögöl	Hungary	1.896 m
zoll	Austria	2.634 cm
zoll	Germany	26.15 mm
zolotnik	Soviet Union[a]	4.266 g

[a]Former name.

Historical measurements of the UK

AD 410–1215

On the end of occupation, Roman measures merged with those of the Angles, Saxons, Danes and Normans who occupied parts of Britain and brought their own measures with them.

The Saxon yard was established as a unit of length, and eventually fixed as a standard in iron in the 12th century. The grain was in use from the 8th century, and there were 18–24 grains to the silver penny, varying by region and with time; generally there 240 pennies to 1 pound.

In 1215 the Magna Carta established that there should be a single set of measures throughout the Kingdom; the London quarter was mentioned among other units.

AD 1215–1351

During this period the main medieval system of measurements was codified by statute.

1266 (approximate; statute date uncertain). The London system was defined by statute.

32 wheat corns	= 1 English penny (a sterling or d)
20 pennies	= 1 ounce
12 ounces	= 1 pound[a]
8 pounds	= 1 gallon of wine
8 gallons of wine	= 1 London bushel
8 London bushels	= 1 London quarter[b]

[a]Equal to 7 680 wheat grains; later also called the Tower or moneyer's pound.
[b]As mentioned in the Magna Carta.

1303 (approximate; statute date uncertain). The 1266 London system was confirmed, and distinction made between a "lesser" and a "greater" pound (a range of special units was also defined).

12 pence	= 1 shilling
20 pence	= 1 ounce
12 ounces	= 1 "lesser" pound (= 20 shillings = 240 pence)[a]
15 ounces	= 1 "greater" pound (= 25 shillings = 300 pence)[b]
12½ pounds	= 1 London stone

[a]Equal to 5 400 (barley) grains; later to be replaced by the Troy pound.
[b]Commercial or mercantile pound, equal to 6 750 grains; later modified to have 7 000 grains, and contain 16 ounces, to become the avoirdupois pound.

1324 (approximate; statute date uncertain). Length and area units were codified.

3 barleycorns (round and dry)	= 1 inch
12 inches	= 1 foot
3 feet	= 1 yard (or ulnam)
5½ yards	= 1 perch
40 perches by 4 perches	= 1 acre (= 4 840 square yards)

1340 (14 Edward III). Established, for wool:

14 pounds (lb)	= 1 stone
26 stones	= 1 sack (= 364 pounds)

1351 (25 Edward III). Established as a general system (for which the term "averdepois" was used in 1353).

14 pounds	= 1 stone
2 stones	= 1 quarter (= 28 pounds)
4 stones	= 1 half-hundredweight (= 56 pounds)
6½ stones	= 1 quarter-sack (= 91 pounds)
2 half-hundredweights	= 1 hundredweight (= 112 pounds)
26 stones	= 1 sack (= 364 pounds)

AD 1351–1824

The basic medieval system, as already established, was varied by some extensions and redefinitions; some main changes were as follows.

1430 (9 Henry VI). For cheese:

7 pounds (li)	= 1 clove
32 cloves	= 1 wey (= 224 pounds)

1496 (12 Henry VII). The Troy system became legal and the main system to use.

1526 (18 Henry VIII). The Troy system replaced the Tower system for weighing silver and gold.

1532 (24 Henry VIII). All meat was to be sold by Haberdepayes (averdupois) weight, replacing other "mercantile" weights.

1558 (1 Elizabeth I). A set of standards was established for averdepois weight, retaining also the Troy weights (these being referred to as the two ancient weights).

1587 (30 Elizabeth I). The 1558 weights were redefined and clarified; the two pounds were confirmed for use, and the modern avoirdupois pound was established.

7 000 grains	= 1 pound (av)
112 pounds	= 1 hundredweight
2 240 pounds	= 1 ton

The furlong was increased from 625 feet to 660 feet; since the relationship of 8 furlongs to the mile was retained, the mile was increased from 5 000 feet to 5 280 feet.

1706 (5 Anne). The wine gallon was defined as a cylinder with 7 inches diameter and 6 inches height, or a content of 231 cubic inches.

1824 (5 George IV). The imperial system was legally established.

SUMMARY

Length[a]

		UK imperial equivalent	Metric equivalent
	1 line	$\frac{1}{12}$ in	0.212 cm
4 lines	= 1 barleycorn	⅓ in	0.847 cm
9 lines	= 1 nail[b]	¾ in	1.905 cm
3 barleycorns	= 1 inch[c]	1 in	2.54 cm
2¼ inches	= 1 nail-of-a-yard[d]	2¼ in	5.715 cm
4 inches	= 1 hand[e]	4 in	10.16 cm
4½ inches	= 1 finger	4½ in	11.43 cm
9 inches	= 1 span	9 in	22.86 cm

		UK imperial equivalent	Metric equivalent
inches	= 1 foot	1 ft	30.48 cm
⅓ inches	= 1 long foot[f]	1.1 ft	33.528 cm
feet	= 1 cubit	18 in	45.72 cm
feet	= 1 yard[g]	36 in	91.44 cm
long feet	= 1 yard and hand[h]	40 in	101.60 cm
nails-of-a-yard	= 1 ell[i]	45 in	114.30 cm
feet	= 1 pace	5 ft	152.40 cm
5 paces	= 1 furlong[j]	625 ft	190.50 m
furlongs	= 1 mile[j]	5 000 ft	1 524.00 m
urveyor's (Gunter's) system (from about 1620)			
	1 link	7.92 in	20.117 cm
links	= 1 rod, perch or pole[k]	16½ ft	502.92 cm
00 links	= 1 chain[l]	22 yd	20.117 m
chains	= 1 old rode[m]	220 yd	201.168 m

he basic system was in general laid down in statute in the last half of e 13th century and early 14th century. As for other old measures, the ctual sizes varied according to time and region. The old foot varied om 0.97 to 1.10 of the imperial foot, other units varying accordingly; ea values varied markedly. [b]Approximate width of thumb-nail bout equal to the Roman digit). [c]Approximate width of thumb. ⅙ yard (cloth unit), analogous to the nail as $\frac{1}{16}$ foot. [e]As defined 535 (27 Henry VIII); also used as equal to 3 inches. [f]As introduced y Belgic tribes; abolished 1439. Originally based on a Roman long foot, nd remained as a Rhineland unit, and until recently as the Cape foot of outh Africa. [g]Or gird or gyrd. [h]As introduced by Belgic tribes; bolished 1439. [i]Or ulna or aulne; English unit of "a yard and a uarter yard". [j]Before 1588; the furlong was increased during the eign of Queen Elizabeth 1 to 660 ft (= 40 rods), the mile (old London nile of 5 000 ft) then becoming the statute mile of 5 280 ft. Surveyor's measure only; in the 16th century, 1 rod = 1 rood = 16 feet; lso 1 rode = 660 ft. [l]The breadth for the main definition of an acre. The length for the main definition of an acre.

rea[a]

		UK imperial equivalent	Metric equivalent
	1 sq rod or perch	30¼ yd^2	25.293 m^2
60 sq rod	= 1 acre[b]	4 840 yd^2	4 046.869 m^2
0 acres	= 1 sq old rode	48 400 yd^2	40 468.692 m^2
0 acres	= 1 yard[c]	20 acres	8.094 ha^2
yards	= 1 hide[d]	80 acres	32.375 ha^2
hides	= 1 knight's fee[e]	640 acres	
		= 1 square mile	2.590 km^2

As for Length above. [b]Area basically 4 rods or perches wide by 40 ods or perches long. [c]Or yard-land or virgate; varied from 14 to 30 cres. [d]Or hyde; household size area of a farm; varied from 60 to 20 acres. [e]Varied from 300 to 960 acres (0.5–1.5 square miles); the umber of hides per knight's fee varied from 5 to 8, depending on the uality of the land.

Capacity[a]

		UK imperial equivalent	Metric equivalent
Wine measures[a]			
231 cubic inches	= 1 wine gallon	0.83 gal	3.773 l
31½ wine gallons	= 1 wine barrel[b]	26.2 gal	119.108 l
2 wine barrels (63 wine gallons)	= 1 hogshead	52.5 gal	238.670 l
2 hogsheads (126 wine gallons)	= 1 pipe[c]	104.9 gal	476.886 l
2 pipes (252 wine gallons)	= 1 tun[d]	209.8 gal	953.772 l
Ale measures			
282 cubic inches	= 1 ale gallon	1.02 gal	4.637 l
4 gallons	= 1 pin	4.07 gal	18.503 l
6 gallons	= 1 six	6.10 gal	27.731 l
2 pins (8 ale gallons)	= 1 firkin	8.13 gal	36.960 l
2 sixes (12 ale gallons)	= 1 anker	12.2 gal	55.462 l
2 firkins (16 ale gallons)	= 1 kilderkin[f]	16.3 gal	74.101 l
2 kilderkins (32 ale gallons)	= 1 barrel[g]	32.5 gal	147.748 l
2 barrels (64 ale gallons)	= 1 puncheon	65.1 gal	295.951 l
3 barrels (96 ale gallons)	= 1 butt	97.6 gal	443.699 l
Corn measures[h]			
272¼ cubic inches	= 1 corn gallon	0.98 gal	4.455 l
8 corn gallons	= 1 corn bushel	7.85 gal	35.687 l
8 corn bushels (64 corn gallons)	= 1 quarter	63 gal	286.404 l

[a]Values for Queen Anne's wine gallon (1706); the value for Edward III's gallon of the mid-1300s was 8 pounds of wine which would have been about 216 in^3 (0.78 imperial gallon). [b]Or half-hogshead or quarter-cask. [c]Or cask. [d]Or 12 score and 12 wine gallons. [e]As established by Henry VIII in 1531. [f]Or rundlet. [g]Beer barrel is 36 gallons. [h]As defined end-15th century (Winchester corn gallon); about 1300 AD the corn gallon = 8 pounds of wheat = about 270 in^3 (0.9 imperial gallon). The old London corn gallon was 268.8 in^3, and London bushel 2 150.42 in^3 (cylinder 18½ in diameter and 8 in deep).

Weight

		UK imperial equivalent	Metric equivalent
London system (Tower or moneyer's; about 1303)[a]			
32 wheat corns[b]	= 1 English penny[c]	22½ gr	1.458 g
12 pence	= 1 shilling	270 gr	17.496 g
20 pence	= 1 ounce	450 gr	29.159 g
6 ounces	= 1 half-pound	2 700 gr	174.957 g
8 ounces	= 1 mark[d]	3 600 gr	233.276 g
12 ounces	= 1 "lesser" pound[e]	5 400 g = 0.94 lb tr	349.914 g
15 ounces	= 1 "greater" pound[f]	6 750 gr = 0.96 lb	437.393 g
16 ounces = 2 marks	= 1 dimark[dg]	7 200 gr = 1.03 lb	466.552 g
8 pounds (greater)	= 1 gallon of wine	7.8 lb	3.538 kg
12½ pounds (greater)	= 1 London stone	12.1 lb	5.488 kg
8 gallons of wine	= 1 London bushel	62 lb	28.123 kg
8 London bushels	= 1 London quarter	496 lb	224.982 kg

		UK imperial equivalent	Metric equivalent
Averdepois system (1351)[h]			
14 pounds	= 1 stone	13½ lb	6.123 kg
2 stones (28 pounds)	= 1 quarter	27 lb	12.247 kg
4 stones (56 pounds)	= 1 half-hundredweight	54 lb	24.494 kg
6½ stones (91 pounds)	= 1 quarter-sack	87¾ lb	39.803 kg
8 stones (112 pounds)	= 1 hundredweight	108 lb	48.988 kg
26 stones (364 pounds)	= 1 sack	352 lb	159.211 kg
Troy system (1526)[i]			
	1 silver penny	12 gr	0.778 g
2 pennies	= 1 pennyweight	24 gr	1.556 g
20 pennyweights	= 1 ounce	480 gr	31.103 g
12 ounces	= 1 pound	5 760 gr (= 1 troy pound)	373.242 g
15 ounces	= 1 mercantile pound[j]	7 200 gr	466.552 g

[a]As mentioned in the Magna Carta (1215), and codified at about the end of the 13th century. [b]Average of grains of wheat taken from the middle of the ear, and well dried. [c]In early medieval times, the silver penny varied from 18 to 24½ grains (barley grains which weigh about one-third more than wheat grains). [d]Not part of the main London system. [e]London, Tower or moneyer's pound; later to be replaced by the Troy pound. [f]Commercial, mercantile or merchant's pound; later to be replaced by the avoirdupois pound of 7 000 grains, with 16 ounces. [g]The "double mark" of Cologne and Hamburg, or merchant's pound of the Hanseatic League. [h]Shown here based on the "greater" pound of 6 750 grains; there were different commercial pounds in use, ranging up to 7 200 grains. [i]At the date at which the Troy system replaced the Tower (London) system as the legal standard for money. [j]Equal to 16 Tower ounces.

Apothecaries' system (officially discontinued 1971)

		Metric equivalent
20 grains	= 1 scruple	1.296 g
24 grains	= 1 pennyweight (dwt)	1.555 g
60 grains	= 1 drachm (drm)	3.888 g
480 grains	= 1 ounce (oz apoth)	31.103 g
5 760 grains	= 1 pound	373.242 g

OTHER OLD UNITS

Miscellaneous

	UK imperial equivalent	Metric equivalent
Barony of land (40 hides)	3 200 acres	1 294.994 ha
Boll	140 pounds	63.504 kg
Bolt of canvas	42 yards	38.405 m
Bovate	10–18 acres	4.047–7.284 ha
Cask (cider)	110 gallons	500.07 l
Chopin (or Choppin)	½ pint	0.284 l
Faggot: wood	3 feet long, 2 feet around	91.44 cm, 60.96 cm
steel	120 pounds	54.431 kg
Goad	4½ feet	137.16 cm
Line: buttons	1/40 inch	0.063 5 cm
watches	1/12 inch	0.211 6 cm
Perit	1/9 600 grain	0.000 007 g
Pig (ballast)	56 pounds	25.401 kg
Point, silversmith's	1/4 000 inch	0.000 635 cm
Tub (butter)	84 pounds	38.102 kg
Yard of ale	1–3 pints	0.568–1.705 l

Cereals

Barrel	barley	= 224 lb	= 101.605 kg
	oats	= 196 lb	= 88.904 kg
	wheat	= 280 lb	= 127.006 kg
Bushel	barley	= 50 lb	= 22.680 kg
	maize	= 56 lb	= 25.401 kg
	oats	= 39 lb	= 17.690 kg
	rye	= 56 lb	= 25.401 kg
	wheat	= 60 lb	= 27.216 kg
Firlot	barley	= 73 lb	= 33.112 kg
	oats	= 57 lb	= 25.855 kg
	wheat	= 60 lb	= 27.216 kg
Hobbet	barley	= 147 lb	= 66.678 kg
	wheat	= 168 lb	= 76.204 kg
Kemple	straw	= 440 lb	= 199.581 kg
Load	hay & straw	= 26 trusses	
Quarter[a]	barley	= 448 lb	= 203.209 kg
	malt	= 336 lb	= 152.407 kg
Truss	hay[b]	= 56 lb	= 25.401 kg
	hay[c]	= 60 lb	= 27.216 kg
	straw	= 36 lb	= 16.329 kg
Windle	wheat	= 220 lb	= 99.790 kg

[a]Malting industry. [b]Old (Sep 1st–Jun 1st). [c]New (Jun 2nd–Aug 31st).

Old dry measures

2 pints	= 1 quart	2 bushels	= 1 strike
2 quarts	= 1 pottle	4 bushels	= 1 coomb (or coom)
2 pottles	= 1 gallon	8 bushels	= 1 quarter
2 gallons	= 1 peck	4 quarters	= 1 chaldron
4 pecks	= 1 bushel	5 quarters	= 1 load (or wey or weigh)
8 gallons	= 1 bushel	2 loads	= 1 last

Old wheat flour measures

Gallon	= 7 lb	= 3.175 kg	
Peck	= 14 lb	= 6.350 kg	
Bushel	= 56 lb	= 25.401 kg	
Boll or bag	= 140 lb	= 63.503 kg	
Load or pack	= 240 lb	= 108.862 kg	
Sack	= 280 lb	= 127.006 kg	

Fruit

Apples	barrel	= 120 lb	= 54.431 kg
	bushel or case	= 40 lb	= 18.144 kg
Cherries	sieve	= 48 lb	= 21.772 kg
Pears	bushel	= 48 lb	= 21.772 kg
Plums	sieve	= 56 lb	= 25.401 kg

egetables

eans	barrel	= 280 lb	= 127.006 kg
	bushel box	= 30 lb	= 13.608 kg
abbages	half bag	= 36–40 lb	= 16.3–18.1 kg
	mat	= 56–60 lb	= 25.4–27.2 kg
arrots	half bag	= 56 lb	= 25.401 kg
nions	case	= 120 lb	= 54.431 kg
eas	half bag	= 40 lb	= 18.144 kg
	bushel box	= 30–36 lb	= 13.6–16.3 kg
otatoes	bag	= 112 lb	= 50.802 kg
	barrel	= 200 lb	= 90.718 kg
	bushel	= 60 lb	= 27.216 kg
	cubic foot	= about 42 lb	= about 19 kg
	sack (metric)	= 55.116 lb	= 25 kg

ilk products

utter

oll	= 24 oz	= 0.680 kg
rkin	= 56 lb	= 25.401 kg
ub	= 84 lb	= 38.102 kg
arrel	= 224 lb	= 101.605 kg

heese

love	= 8 lb	= 3.629 kg
tone	= 16 lb	= 7.257 kg
tone (Scotland)	= 24 lb	= 10.886 kg
uffolk wey	= 32 cloves	= 116.120 kg
ssex wey	= 42 cloves	= 152.407 kg

eat

eef	firkin	= 100 lb	= 45.359 kg
	barrel	= 200 lb	= 90.718 kg
	tierce	= 304 lb	= 137.892 kg
ork	firkin	= 100 lb	= 45.359 kg
	tierce	= 320 lb	= 145.15 kg
igs	1 score deadweight	= 20 lb	= 9.072 kg

mithfield stone = 8 lb = 3.63 kg. This measure was the pproximate dressed carcass weight yielded by a live weight of imperial stone of 14 pounds, ie, a yield of about 57%.

Natural fibres: from animals

Hides and skins

10 skins = 1 dicker
20 dickers = 1 last

Wool

Clove	= 7 lb	= 3.175 kg
Stone	= 14 lb	= 6.350 kg
Stone (Scotland)	= 24 lb	= 10.886 kg
Score	= 20 lb	= 9.072 kg
Tod	= 28 lb	= 12.701 kg
Wey	= 182 lb	= 82.554 kg
Pack	= 240 lb	= 108.862 kg
Sack = 2 weys	= 364 lb	= 165.108 kg
Last = 12 sacks	= 4 368 lb	= 1 981.291 kg

Textiles

Cotton yarn

$1\frac{1}{2}$ yards = 1 thread
120 yards = 1 skein or lea
840 yards = 1 hank
1 spyndle = 18 hanks
= 15 120 yards

Linen yarn

300 yards = 1 lea (or cut)
2 leas = 1 hear (or heer)
6 hears = 1 hasp (or hank)
4 hasps = 1 spyndle
48 leas = 1 spyndle
= 14 400 yards

Spun silk yarn

840 yards = 1 hank

Woollen yarn

256 yards = skein
300 yards = 1 cut
320 yards = 1 snap
45 skeins = 1 spyndle
= 11 520 yards

Worsted yarn

80 yards = 1 wrap
560 yards = 1 hank

Fabric

$2\frac{1}{4}$ inches = 1 nail
4 nails = 1 quarter
= 1 span
= 9 inches
4 quarters = 1 yard
$1\frac{1}{4}$ yards = 45 inches
= 1 ell

See also Agriculture, fishing and forestry, pages 27–41.

Index

A

B

D

E

F

G

T